Weekending in New England

Weekending in New England

22 COMPLETE GETAWAYS TO PURSUE YOUR PASSIONS

Betsy Wittemann

THE COUNTRYMAN PRESS ◆ WOODSTOCK, VERMONT

A Note to the Reader: The prices quoted for lodging, restaurants, and activities were current when this guide went to press in fall 2002. But they are inherently subject to change and are offered here only as a relative guide; please check before traveling.

Copyright © 2003 by Betsy Wittemann
First Edition

Library of Congress Cataloging-in-Publication Data:
Wittemann, Betsy.
Weekending in New England : 22 complete getaways to pursue your passions / Betsy Wittemann.—1st ed.
p.   cm.
Includes index.
ISBN 0-88150-522-6
1. New England—Tours. I. Title.
F2.3 .W578 2003
917.404'44—dc21
2002035270

Book design by Joanna Bodenweber
Text composition by Melinda Belter
Cover photo © Pat and Chuck Blackley
Interior photos by Betsy Wittemann unless otherwise indicated
Maps by Paul Woodward, © 2003 The Countryman Press

Published by The Countryman Press, P.O. Box 748, Woodstock, Vermont 05091
Distributed by W. W. Norton & Company, Inc., 500 Fifth Avenue, New York, NY 10110

Printed in the United States of America
10 9 8 7 6 5 4 3 2 1

For Ross, my sidekick

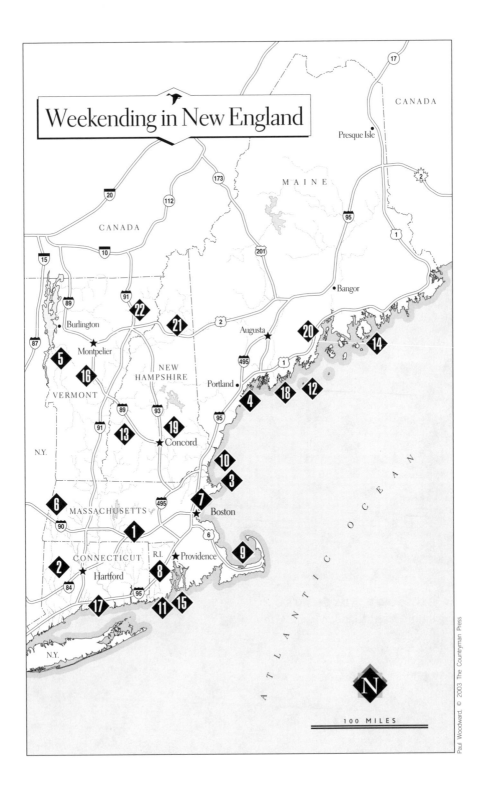

Weekending in New England

CANADA

Presque Isle

MAINE

CANADA

Burlington

Montpelier

VERMONT

NEW HAMPSHIRE

Bangor

Augusta

Portland

Concord

MASSACHUSETTS

Boston

CONNECTICUT

Hartford

R.I. Providence

N.Y.

N.Y.

ATLANTIC OCEAN

N

100 MILES

Contents

Introduction

Here's to the weekend! Our intense schedules require frequent breaks, chances to "get away from it all." A short trip of 2 to 4 days can do much to help us recharge our batteries, clear our heads, and return to our everyday lives with a new, fresh outlook.

New England is made for weekending. Distances are relatively short and diversions, many. You can drive everywhere. There's so much to discover. Within the compact six-state area are rugged mountains, rolling hills, open ocean and picturesque harbors, exciting cities and charming towns. There are lakes, rivers, and plenty of islands to explore.

But what kind of weekend do you want? Are you a beach bum or an antiques aficionado? Love to hike or love to read? History buff or island idler? Off-season adventurer?

Weekending in New England responds to these impulses and more. Each of 22 weekend destinations appeals to a major interest. There are weekends for beach lovers and weekends for history hounds. Weekends for antiquers and others for city slickers. A boating weekend and one in a classic New England college town are included.

Interested in Shaker beliefs and objects? There's a Shaker weekend just for you. Art enthusiasts? Visit America's oldest art colony.

Want to luxuriate in regal splendor and eat high on the hog? "Ritzy retreat" weekends—two of them—are calling to you.

Just pick a destination and this book does the rest. You'll find options for lodging, dining, and exploring.

A word about research methods. I visit in person (usually with husband, sometimes with friends). I check out the inns and the B&Bs, staying in as many as time and budget will allow. I talk to restaurant owners and chefs and eat in as many places as possible. I explore the way any weekender would—and take notes while I'm doing it. The result is a carefully researched volume intended to help you in your planning.

Of course, things change. New places open and others turn over. I appreciate hearing from you if you have new destinations to suggest—or comments to make. Meanwhile, happy weekending!

1 ▸ Brimfield/Sturbridge, Massachusetts (and nearby Connecticut)

The Brimfield Outdoor Antique Show—actually several shows under one name—is the most famous open-air flea market in the country. The hamlet of Brimfield, Massachusetts (population 3,000), becomes a site of mad activity among antiques and collectibles dealers, collectors, browsers, and the merely curious for three 1-week stretches annually. This may not sound like much, but it is. For a full mile along usually quiet Route 20 in a not-very-well-known town, grassy fields become temporary homes to thousands of tents where dealers sell wares that range from delicate European textiles to early American furniture to Mickey Mouse watches. If you can't find it in Brimfield, they say, you can't find it, period.

For those who can't or don't want to visit during one of the Brimfield show weeks, there still is much to draw the antiques lover or collector to the area. While termed "the black hole of Massachusetts" by one local acutely aware of the draw of the Berkshires to the west and Boston to the east, the south-central part of the state has particular appeal to those who love to hunt for treasure.

The Brimfield show is the biggest treasure hunt of all.

The event originated when Gordon Reid, a local auctioneer, signed up 67 dealers in 1959 for an outdoor antiques show on the grass in front of his Brimfield home. In those days Brimfield was hardly known, but enough people managed to find Reid's first show that the event continued. The show grew over the years to the mega-attraction it is today. Reid's two daughters, Judy Mathieu and Jill Lukesh, carry on the tradition with J&J Productions, the oldest of the 20 or so individual Brimfield shows. Mathieu lives in the house where she and her sister grew up. They use the same field their dad did.

These days an estimated 5,000 dealers crowd about 20 fields in all. All are along Route 20 about 5 miles west of Sturbridge. They sell everything from turquoise-painted cement garden fountains and elegant estate jewelry to old tools, depression glass, Empire furniture, and Elvis memorabilia. Some 20,000 visitors come to look and buy. Accommodations are filled for miles around—often 6 months to a year ahead.

There's no official organization to the show or, for that matter, of the show. All the individual proprietors rent out spaces—usually in front of their own homes —at anywhere from a couple of hundred dollars to $800 a spot. Every field has hundreds of dealers, most of them sheltered from the heat, the cold, the rain— and the relentless sun—by scallop-edged yellow, white, or striped tents.

In the old days dealers camped out in the fields close to their merchandise. Some still do, although more are likely to stay in hotels or motels from Springfield to Boston.

A BRIMFIELD PRIMER

Here's what you need to know about the Brimfield shows.

♦ Book accommodations well in advance—as far ahead as 6 months to a year—if you are coming from a distance and want to spend more than a single day. Most serious shoppers spend part of 2 or 3 days at the outdoor shows.

♦ Bring a variety of comfortable clothing including rain parkas and umbrellas—and footwear to handle dusty or muddy fields. Dress in layers. Mornings (especially in May and September) can be incredibly cool and midday, uncomfortably warm.

♦ Carry water. There are refreshment stands here and there, but lines can be long, and you can find yourself inconveniently far from one.

♦ Expect to use portable toilets. That's it for rest rooms.

♦ Have cash with you. Bring a checkbook, too. And have your ATM card available in case "the perfect thing" appears and you absolutely have to have it. Dealers prefer cash. Credit cards are often not taken.

♦ Bring or buy a wheeled shopping cart or a little red wagon or other wheeled vehicle if you think you'll be seriously shopping. A backpack is fine for smaller items.

♦ Drive a station wagon or van if furniture is in your future.

♦ Know that items can be shipped. UPS has a booth, and private entrepreneurs also set up.

♦ Do not expect to find items easily. Relax, grab a cup of coffee, and meander around the various fields at a comfortable pace. Dealers are not placed according to specialty. Indeed, the fun of Brimfield is in seeing turn-of-the-20th-century clocks next to Shirley Temple memorabilia. Surprise is part of the excitement.

♦ Pets are not allowed in most areas.

♦ Parking costs $3-6. It's worth it to pay more and park close. The lots fill fast. Cars are towed from illegal spaces.

♦ If you are with others, agree on a central place to meet. It's easy to lose your way; one booth looks so much like others.

♦ The best map of the show is that found inside the handy little *Quaboag Hills Region Visitor's Guide.* You can pick one up at the show. Lorna Lanza's *Brimfield Antique Guide* available free at the show is also a helpful resource.

Brimfield looks like a carnival and feels like one. The food is carnival food. Fried dough. Soft ice cream. Hot dogs and hamburgers. Sausage, pepper, and onion grinders.

Those who attend are known as "fleas." Diehard Brimfielders get up as early as 4 AM to make the 5 or 6 AM opening of some of the shows. Kindhearted innkeepers put out coffeepots on timers or pack bag breakfasts. A few get up very early and cook. Different shows open at various times; some are open for the entire week, others for just a day or two. If a show (a field) is to open at noon, there's heck to pay if a dealer opens his tent flaps a moment before the official bell, whistle, or horn is sounded. (That can result in an eviction, or a refusal to allow another booking.)

The hordes rush in as soon as a particular field opens. Most shows are free; a few charge $5. Showgoers drag carts, red wagons, and other wheeled containers behind them. They wear backpacks to stuff small items into. Some are on bikes. All wear comfortable walking shoes, and most have hats to shield them from the sun. Dealers stocking shops and looking for particular items often work in twos or threes with walkie-talkies, spreading out to check the goods.

Even with the advent of on-line Internet shopping at sites like eBay, Brimfield continues strong. "People come here to buy for eBay," said one dealer. Others say people who are serious collectors have to "touch and see the piece." Then there's the fact that there's simply nothing like Brimfield. It's a wild, never-to-be-forgotten scene.

Brimfield shows are held the second week of May, of July, and of September from Tuesday through Sunday (unless the Jewish New Year interferes, in which case the September show is held a week later). The May show is the largest, the July show the smallest (and likeliest to be uncomfortably hot in those treeless expanses). Hours are 6 AM to 5 or 6 PM, generally speaking; each field has its own rules.

Other Nearby Lures

After, before, or during Brimfield, antiques buffs can go into Sturbridge—just 5 miles east—to check out individual antiques shops or, common these days, multi-dealer buildings. Most of the nearby country and mill towns in this part of central Massachusetts have an antiques shop or two, as well. On the way to a Brimfield show, you'll see garage and tag sales along the side of the road.

On the Monday before the shows, the **Sturbridge Vintage Fashion & Textile Show** is held in the Sturbridge Host Hotel & Conference Center on Route 20, Sturbridge. This 1-day show—described by the producer as "the biggest table show of its type"—draws people from far and wide to buy and sell vintage fabrics and accoutrements (buttons, for example), dresses, hats, and shoes. Designers come to get ideas for fabrics. (Fabric patterns before 1940 are not copyrighted.) Some 150 dealers are involved. Linda Zukas (207-439-2334) is the show manager. Hours are 9:30–5. Admission is $20 between 9:30 and 11, $5 thereafter.

More antiques are found nearby in northeastern Connecticut. Just a quick 25-minute drive south of Brimfield and Sturbridge is the former mill town of **Putnam**, now turned into an antiques center with more than 20 shops and over 300 dealers. Other antiques shops can be found in adjacent towns. (See *Nearby Connecticut* toward the end of this chapter.)

Antiques enthusiasts can stay in vintage bed & breakfast inns, dine in old-fashioned taverns and inns, and visit sites such as **Old Sturbridge Village,** a working museum that re-creates life from the late 1700s through the 1830s.

Getting There

Brimfield is located at the intersection of I-84 and the Massachusetts Turnpike (I-90) in south-central Massachusetts. Sturbridge is just to the east. Hartford is 45 miles away; Boston, 60 miles; Providence, Rhode Island, 90 miles; and Albany, New York, 100 miles.

If you are traveling west on the Massachusetts Turnpike, take Exit 8 in Palmer, Massachusetts, and look for Route 20, which runs east and west. If you are traveling east on the Pike, take Exit 9 in Sturbridge.

For More Information

♦ **Sturbridge's Information Center** is located at 380 Main Street, Route 20, in a small white house in what is known as the "cup handle"—a circular turn by which you enter Old Sturbridge Village. There is plenty of parking. If you have not made lodging reservations ahead of time, the staff will attempt to help, but they probably can't do much during Brimfield show weeks.

♦ **Sturbridge Area Tourist Association and Tri-Community Chamber of Commerce** (508-347-7594; 1-800-628-8379; www.sturbridge.org), 380 Main Street, Sturbridge, MA 01566.

♦ **Quaboag Valley Chamber of Commerce** (413-283-2418; www.quaboag.com), 3 Converse Street, Palmer, MA 01069-0269. Covers Brimfield.

For the Brimfield shows, www.brimfieldshow.com.

■ SEEING AND DOING ◄

Antiques Shops

A brochure, *The Sturbridge Area Antique Trail,* lists nearly 20 antiques dealers or multidealer shops in south-central Massachusetts and northeastern Connecticut. Hours can be tricky in individual shops, but multidealer shops tend to be open on a more regular schedule, often 10–5 at least Wednesday through Sunday.

♦ **The Black Crow** (508-769-5404), 572 Main Street, Sturbridge, opened in 2001 with primitives, Americana, and estate finds. Owner David Straight was an auctioneer who then went on to clearing out estates. He and his wife, Rebecca, operate the well-arranged little shop in the brick Blackington building.

♦ **Stonemill Antique Center** (413-967-5820), 44 East Main Street, Ware, Massachusetts, in the historic brick millyard is a particularly attractive shop. Donna and Joe Lotuff own one big old brick building, a former textile mill, and their adult kids operate the Berkshire Blanket Co. (cotton blankets and Polarfleece) next door.

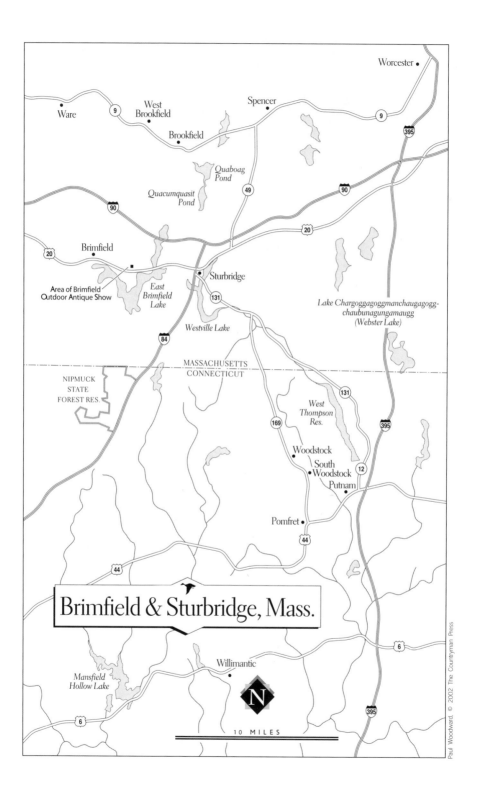

Worcester

Ware
9
West
Brookfield
Spencer
9
395
Brookfield

Quaboag
Pond
Quacumquasit
Pond
49
90
90
20

20
Brimfield

Sturbridge
Area of Brimfield
Outdoor Antique Show
East
Brimfield
Lake
131

Lake Chargoggagoggmanchaugagogg-
chaubunagungamaugg
(Webster Lake)

Westville Lake
84

MASSACHUSETTS
CONNECTICUT

NIPMUCK
STATE
FOREST RES.

131
West
Thompson
Res.
395
169

Woodstock
South
Woodstock
12
Putnam

Pomfret
44

44

Brimfield & Sturbridge, Mass.

6

Willimantic

Mansfield
Hollow Lake

N

395
6

10 MILES

Browsing at Brimfield

♦ **Showcase Antique Center** (508-347-5183), Route 20, Sturbridge, is a multidealer shop with the emphasis on china and pottery displayed in glass cases. Next door is an outlet store for **Crabtree & Evelyn** cosmetics and fragrances. And nearby is **Country Curtains,** a shop with Colonial-style window treatments.

♦ **Sturbridge Antiques Shops** (508-347-2744), Route 20, Sturbridge, advertises 75 dealers selling antiques and collectibles. The **Antique Center of Sturbridge** (508-347-5150), 426 Main Street, Sturbridge, has items from several dealers.

♦ **Faxon's Antique Center** (508-867-2515), Route 148, Brookfield, is an 80-dealer shop selling antiques and collectibles.

Looking for old *Life* magazines or other vintage periodicals? Want to get a free book with your coffee? Take I-84 a few miles south to Union, Connecticut, and get off at Exit 74. There, at 1257 Buckley Highway, you'll find **Traveler Book Cellar and Traveler Collectibles** along with **Traveler Restaurant** (860-684-2324); open daily 9–6. You can take a free book whenever you stop for a cup of coffee or a sandwich or even a meal (roast turkey is a specialty). On Wednesday you can take three. The Book Cellar downstairs specializes in old and out-of-print books. The Collectibles Shop—across the parking lot—has furniture, tableware, and all sorts of funky stuff.

Other Shopping

♦ **The Seraph** (508-347-2241), 420 Main Street, Sturbridge. Alexandra Pifer and her husband, Michael, live in a 17th-century saltbox in Connecticut. Their shop specializes in "17th- and 18th-century rooms." This resource for homeowners interested in re-creating the environment of colonial American homes has been drawing shoppers from far and wide for 20 years and continues to expand its lines. Just walking in here makes you feel as if you've stumbled into another century. Mike Pifer makes the chandeliers and lighting fixtures. Everything from early-American-style textiles to painted floorcloths to paints in colors like earth, straw, and maize is available. Reproduction William and Mary and Pilgrim furnishings can be found. Many styles of wing chairs and "settles" are available. Lanterns abound. This is a one-of-a-kind shop.

Other interesting shops in Sturbridge: **Wild Bird Crossing** (508-347-BIRD), a particularly nice bird and nature shop on Cedar Street; **The Handmaiden** (508-347-7757), 538 Main Street, Route 20, with unusual gifts, wreaths, ribbon, candles, and garden items all vying for attention in two large rooms; and **Susan's Secret Garden** (508-347-9303), 531 Main Street (Route 20), Sturbridge, a place to buy teacups and teapots, bridal gifts, flowery wreaths. **Hebert Candies** (508-347-3051), 1 River Road, is a retail shop for candies made in Shrewsbury, Massachusetts. They are particularly proud of their white chocolate.

The gift shop at **Old Sturbridge Village** is chock-full and includes items made by craftspeople at the village such as tinware, sconces, and so forth.

Jams and jellies are produced by the monks at the **Trappist Monastery** (508-885-8700) on Route 31 in nearby Spencer, Massachusetts.

♦ **Old Sturbridge Village** (508-347-3362; fax 508-347-0249; www.osv.org), 1 Old Sturbridge Village Road, Sturbridge, MA 01566. The prime tourist destination in the area, with some 425,000 visitors annually, is this, the largest outdoor history museum in the Northeast. First opened in 1946, the village—which purports to be a rural New England community of the 1830s—has grown and flourished. Costumed interpreters staff many of more than 40 buildings on the 200-acre site, most of them authentic 17th- and 18th-century structures brought from towns throughout New England.

"Farmers" plant fields and oxen pull wagons on village roads. Craftspeople make shoes and sconces. A water-powered mill area shows the beginnings of the industrial revolution. Old Sturbridge Village concentrates on that time when everyday life was being transformed by revolutions in commerce and manufacturing, the westward migration and growth of cities, and improvements in farming and transportation. The museum has gained an international reputation for its innovations in research and education. And there's always something new to see. In 2001 the village opened the Tavern (see *Eating and Drinking*), a built-from-scratch dining center with seating for more than 300 patrons. Its purpose is to interpret the foods, fun and games, and community life of rural New England. Hearth cooking demonstrations are but one of the appealing activities. Foods include historical treats like Green Corn Pudding, Chicken on a String, and Washington Cake.

The village also began crafts activities, offered for a modest additional fee, in 2001. Relatively new, as well, is the Samson's Children's Museum, which provides hands-on learning opportunities for children aged 3 to 7. There are a play kitchen with pretend hearth, costumes to dress up in, and a one-room school with benches and slates. On weekends Fitch House, portraying the home of a printer and his family, allows visitors to "help" as interpreters go about their morning chores such as cooking and folding laundry.

Old Sturbridge Village traces its beginnings to a collection of early New England artifacts collected by two brothers, industrialists Albert B. and J. Cheney Wells of nearby Southbridge. The Wells family later decided to display the collection within a working village.

Many special events are held throughout the year. The three most popular days are Washington's Birthday (observed on Presidents' Day), with games, toasts to George, and dancing; the Fourth of July, with picnics on the green, an informal parade, the firing of muskets, and speeches; and Thanksgiving, with dinner prepared in the individual houses and served to staffers, and when—if snow is on the ground—sleigh rides might be offered.

Admission is for 2 consecutive days; all activities in the village, unless otherwise noted, are free with admission. Open March 31 through October, 9–5; the rest of the year, 9–4; closed on weekdays January to mid-February. Adults $20, seniors $18, youths (6–15) $10. Many buildings are handicapped accessible, and a good printed guide details access for persons of varying disabilities.

♦ **Hyland Orchard and Brewery** (508-347-7500), 199 Arnold Road, Sturbridge. Apples, beer, and ice cream? Well yes, and people love to visit this hillside area where you can, in fall, pick your own apples and take hayrides and tractor rides. Llamas are for viewing, and there's a children's play area and picnic site. Ice cream is sold in warm weather. Amber ale is the most popular of the brews. The place is open weekends in spring and fall, but weekdays as well in summer. Call for hours, because they are somewhat fluid. Guided tours of the brewery are offered Saturday afternoon.

♦ **Stageloft Repertory Theater** (508-347-9005), 450 Main Street, Sturbridge. This professional community-based theater offers American musicals and comedies and classics in an air-conditioned, handicapped-accessible building. The summer season begins in late June and runs through September.

♦ **Keep Homestead Museum** (413-267-4137; www.keephomesteadmuseum.org), 35 Ely Road, Monson. If you'd like to see this museum, you have to be poised and ready: Its "open to the public" hours never coincide with the Brimfield antiques shows. Yet it has one of the largest button collections in the country, and its mosaic button assortment is described by a spokesperson as "fabulous." The house is open regularly 1–3 PM on the first Sunday of the month, and there is no admission charge. Should you miss this narrow window of opportunity, call and try to set up a private viewing. As a house museum, the furniture and belongings of one family are interesting in addition to the buttons. But if you fail to get in, there's something else to draw you to the site: 75 acres of land with many marked, groomed trails. So take a walk. Monson is about 10 miles west of Brimfield.

WHERE TO STAY

Accommodations are found primarily in Sturbridge, and spottily in towns nearby. For the Brimfield antiques show weeks, rooms are snapped up long in advance; some people stay as far away as Boston, Providence, and Hartford.

IN BRIMFIELD

♦ **Elias Carter House** (413-245-3267; fax 413-245-7619), on the common, Brimfield, MA 01010. Carolyn Haley describes her B&B as being "on the edge of the action." And so it is, at the eastern corner of the common in Brimfield, at the Sturbridge end of town. The large gray 18th-century house offers three comfortably furnished guest rooms, all with private bath, on the second floor. Two of the rooms are especially large and have a single bed along with a queen or double. A more modern first-floor "conservatory" with lots of windows and a ceiling of western pine is where guests have breakfast and hang out. It has an upright piano. Carolyn makes a full breakfast even during show weeks—a real plus. Free parking for guests behind the house is another. A refrigerator and microwave in the second-floor hall are for guests' use. No children under 12. Doubles during show weeks, $125; other times, $80.

♦ **Nathan Goodale House** (413-245-9228), 11 Warren Road, Brimfield, MA 01010. Location! This B&B is so close to the action that you can walk out the back door and across the lawn to the start of the Brimfield show. Three charmingly decorated guest rooms on the second floor of this white Italianate house with green shutters share two baths (one on the first floor). Large prints of works by Norman Rockwell, including *The Four Freedoms,* on loan from a friend decorate many walls. Quilts on beds and other homey touches are marks of innkeeper Kay Koprowski, who also gets up early on show days to make a full breakfast. Stuffed French toast with strawberry sauce is one signature item. Doubles, $150 during show weeks; $80 at other times.

IN STURBRIDGE

♦ **Publick House** (508-347-3313; 1-800-PUBLICK; fax 508-347-5073; www. publickhouse.com), on the common, Route 131, P.O. Box 187, Sturbridge, MA 01566-0187. A total of 126 rooms are found in four different buildings and styles of accommodation. There's an attempt to put country touches everywhere, although the Country Lodge is more like a motel. The 17 rooms in the main inn, dating from 1771, are delightfully quirky, some with beamed ceilings, canopy beds, and comfortable wing chairs. All are decorated in country-inn fashion, and some are on the small side, so ask. All have private bath, a TV in an armoire, and telephone. The halls are narrow and floors uneven in places. Coffee and muffins are set out early in the morning. Next door is the **Chamberlain House,** with four two-room suites. These larger, more modern rooms offer easy access to the inn, which is close by. Beds are queen sized; there are sliding doors to balconies.

Up the hill is **Country Lodge.** In five identical brick-and-clapboard buildings, the rooms, with two double beds and simple white colonial spreads, are more basic. Antiques dealers (and serious collectors) love them because they can back their vans up to the door. All have private bath, balcony, TV, and telephone. And the Publick House pool is here on the hill—actually more convenient to Country Lodge guests than to inn guests. If you have kids, this is where you'd want to be.

Finally, the **Ebenezer Crafts Inn,** an eight-room Federalist farmhouse, offers the most elegant and private accommodations of all. Located about a mile and a half from the Publick House, on a street of handsome homes, the inn has its own pool, available only to guests staying here. Breakfast is served in a pretty dining room.

There is an "away-from-it-all" feeling, with rooms individually and tastefully decorated in period style. A sunroom with wicker furniture and a TV is a place for guests to gather. A wood-burning fireplace warms the breakfast room on cool mornings. Guest rooms are found on the second and third floors, and all have private bath. Fishnet canopy beds, flowered wallpaper, and wing chairs are found in many. A third-floor suite is good for families. Doubles at the Country Lodge are $79–121; townhouse suites are $109–155. Otherwise doubles range $99–160, suites $140–175. Breakfast is standard only at the Crafts Inn, although several package plans are available at the other sites. Call to ask.

♦ **Old Sturbridge Village Lodges and Oliver Wight House** (508-347-3327; fax 508-347-3018; www.osv.org), Route 20, Sturbridge, MA 01566. These accommodations, at the entrance to Old Sturbridge Village, are also owned by the village. Seven buildings are grouped around a common area with 59 accommodations in all. One of these, the Oliver Wight House, dates to 1789 and has 10 guest rooms decorated in period fashion. Perhaps the most interesting detail in the house is the front-hall mural believed to have been painted by the itinerant colonial artist Rufus Porter. Rooms in the Wight House each have one queen bed covered with a white George Washington bedspread and other period furnishings. Eight of 10 rooms have canopy beds, for instance. This is the only two-story building in the complex.

The other six buildings are single story, and cars can conveniently park right by their unit. Each has an entrance from outside. One building allows smoking; another (the yellow building) is designated for families. Rooms have two doubles or two queen-sized beds, wall-to-wall carpeting, private bath, TV, and phone.

A heated pool and swing set for children are located in the common area outdoors. The place is quiet. Doubles, $85–105.

♦ **The Thomas Henry Hearthstone Inn** (508-347-2224; 1-888-781-7775; www.hearthstonestur.com), Route 20, P.O. Box 31, Sturbridge, MA 01566. This two-building complex in the center of town was built new and opened in 2000 by the Petrofsky family from Prince Edward Island, Canada. A full-service restaurant and 12 guest rooms are located in the inn. Across the parking lot is the building where the **Village Chair and Table Co.** is located. Here members of the family, especially sons of Tom and Priscilla Ann Petrofsky, make Windsor-style chairs by hand. Eight of the inn's rooms are termed "whirlpool suites" and are large rooms. The Governor's Grand Suite also has a wood-burning fireplace. Furnishings are period-style. Guests enjoy a continental breakfast in the cathedral-ceilinged dining room in the morning. Doubles, $129; whirlpool suites, $169. Grand Governor and Presidential Suites, $249 and $279.

♦ **Sturbridge Coach Motor Lodge** (508-347-7327; fax 508-347-2954), 408 Main Street, Route 20, Sturbridge, MA 01566. Set on a quiet hillside overlooking busy Route 20, this motor lodge offers 54 rooms in a two-floor motel to the rear of the property. Each has one queen or two double beds, a shower-tub combination bathroom, coffeemaker, air-conditioning, and television. An outdoor pool is attractive, and a continental breakfast of muffins, pastries, juices, and coffee is served in the morning in the office/lobby across the parking lot. Wood furniture, floral bedspreads, and a separate sink area in each room give the place a little character. Doubles, $65–95; $110 during Brimfield show week.

Unloading goods at the Knight Store at Old Sturbridge Village

♦ **Econo Lodge Sturbridge** (508-347-2324; 1-800-446-6900), 682 Main Street, Route 20, Sturbridge. This national chain motel is on the Brimfield side of town and well located for both the shows and the town of Sturbridge. It's a basic two-story motel with 48 rooms and an outdoor pool in front. Rooms have two double, one king-sized, or one queen-sized bed. Doubles, $79; during Brimfield weeks, $120.

Other accommodations in Sturbridge include **Holiday Inn Express** (508-347-5141), a **Days Inn** (508-347-3391), and a **Rodeway Inn** (508-347-9673).

ELSEWHERE IN MASSACHUSETTS

♦ **The Red Maple Inn** (508-885-9205; fax 508-885-9255), 217 Main Street, Route 9, Spencer, MA 01562. Tiny white lights in each window announce a welcome at this bed & breakfast inn, run with style by Joe and Wendy Beauvais. It's located a few miles northeast of Sturbridge and gets you out of the traffic and confusion during busy weeks. Spencer is one of the small mill towns in this part of Massachusetts. The building dates to 1765. Joe says they wanted their six guest rooms to be "comfortable," and while there are antiques and authentic period pieces, you'll also find a large king-bedded room with two unpainted Adirondack chairs at the foot, waiting for cocktail hour or for you to settle in with a book. This is the Master Suite, which also has a trundle bed that can convert to two twins. A television set with VCR is a plus. Braided rugs on wide floorboards, quilts on beds, and a homey feeling characterize the inn. Guests eat breakfast at small tables in a breakfast room with wood-burning fireplace. Banana-stuffed French toast with raspberry sauce is a popular entrée. The rooms are air-conditioned. Doubles, $99–149.

♦ **The Wildwood Inn** (413-967-7798; 1-800-860-8098; www.wildwoodinn.net), 121 Church Street, Ware, MA 01082. A wide porch with white railing and turned posts is a welcoming introduction to this nine-room inn in a residential neighborhood in the former mill town of Ware. A porch swing, comfortable chairs, and a quiet street draw guests to the porch in good weather. Innkeeper Fraidell "Fredi" Fenster also keeps up the gardens on the extensive property and encourages guests to stroll around the large, deep yard. Although this is an 1891 Queen Anne Victorian, the first-floor parlors are filled with early American items like a spinning wheel, early cradles, and quilts. In the bookcase is a huge collection of *National Geographic* magazines. The Flower Garden Quilt Room, while not large, is cozy with a double spool bed and a handmade quilt on the bed. All the beds are topped with handmade quilts, and rooms are named for the quilts. Seven rooms have private baths. There is also a two-room suite sharing a bath on the third floor. All are air-conditioned.

A hot breakfast is served daily at 8. Specialties include noodle pudding, potato frittata, and Chipmunk Pie—an apple-and-walnut concoction that is "like a coffee cake," says the innkeeper. During Brimfield she'll leave out independent breakfast fixings for "those people who wear miners' helmets and get up at 4:30 AM." This consists of cereals, muffins, coffee, tea, and juices. Doubles, $65–105. Add $5 to the highest rate for Brimfield weeks.

EATING AND DRINKING

♦ **Salem Cross Inn** (508-867-8337; 508-867-2345; www.salemcrossinn.com), Route 9, West Brookfield. For a true early American experience—including baked goods from a 1699 beehive oven and meat prepared over an open hearth using a circa-1700 roasting jack—you may want to drive a few miles northwest of the Sturbridge area to West Brookfield. Route 19 north out of Brimfield offers a particularly pleasant country drive. At the inn, with 600 acres of land, you'll see herds of Herefords and Black Angus cattle. The main inn building, originally constructed by a grandson of Peregrine White, the first child born on the *Mayflower,* has been restored and is a national historic landmark. In addition to daily dining, many special events are offered, including—in summer—a couple of Drover's Roasts modeled on 1700s trailside feasts. Hand-rubbed prime ribs of beef are roasted for hours over a huge fieldstone pit. Fritters and chowder are made in cast-iron cauldrons over open fires. Hayrides are offered. These are daylong events, offered at a fixed price of $50.

In winter Fireplace Feasts take place in the lower-level dining room, with cooking taking place in a huge fieldstone fireplace. These are offered many weekend evenings, but check on dates. The annual bake-off to determine the best apple pie in New England is held here using the beehive oven.

The inn serves lunch and dinner. At lunchtime New England Chowder of the Sea is always on the menu, along with a soup of the day. Other starters are onion soup, shrimp cocktail, and garden salad. Sandwiches might be grilled chicken or an oven-roasted turkey pita, in the $7–9 range. In the evening entrées are priced $15–27. House specialties include calf's liver and bacon, fried or broiled scallops, baked stuffed fillet of sole, and sautéed pork tenderloin with a sauce of spices, wine, and Romano cheese. Fireplace-roasted prime rib at $20 is on the Saturday-night menu. Desserts include Indian pudding, apple pie, cheesecake, and pecan pie. Open Tuesday through Friday 11:30–9, Saturday 5–9, Sunday noon–8. Closed Monday.

◆ **Publick House** (508-347-3313; 1-800-PUBLICK), Route 131, Sturbridge. The 18th-century Tap Room is in the original part of the inn at this popular hostelry. It's all dark wood-paneled walls and wide-board floors with subdued lighting from electric candles in hurricane lamps. Several other dining rooms are pressed into service as needed to serve breakfast, lunch, and dinner daily. Although the menu is the same, the original Tap Room, with its huge brick fireplace, is special; you might want to ask for it. Downstairs, Ebenezer's Tavern, the only eating space where smoking is allowed, offers beer on tap and lighter fare, a comfortable ambience, and a blackboard menu.

"Every day is Thanksgiving at the Publick House" reads the menu, and a turkey dinner with all the fixings is offered daily for $24 in the Tap Room. In addition the place is hugely popular on actual Thanksgiving Day, when seatings from noon to 8 are packed; the price rises to $40 and includes taxes, gratuities, and desserts. Although the inn is currently owned by a restaurant conglomerate, the innkeeper, Albert Cournoyer, has been on staff for more than 30 years and does much to maintain the integrity of the place. Many people stop for breakfast. A traditional New England favorite, hot apple pie and cheddar cheese, is available at $3.95. The Farmhand's Special at $7.95 is hot mulled cider, red flannel hash with two eggs, home-fried potatoes, and the deep-dish apple pie with cheddar cheese. At lunchtime you'll find sandwiches and salads in the $6–9 range. Dinner entrées include prime rib and broiled scrod in the $20–29 range. Sticky buns from the on-premises Bake Shop (where you can also buy Joe Frogger molasses cookies and fresh-baked pies) are found in the bread basket.

Tap Room hours are: breakfast 7:30–10:30, lunch noon–4, and dinner 4–9. On Sunday, dinner is served noon–8:30. Ebenezer's Tavern opens at 11:30 Monday through Friday and serves until 10 PM; on Saturday hours are 4–10; and on Sunday, noon–9.

◆ **Tavern at Old Sturbridge Village** (508-347-0395; fax 508-347-3099; www.osv. org), at the entrance to the Village. The new Tavern at Old Sturbridge Village is a huge white-clapboard building with small-paned windows. It houses dining rooms where lunch and dinner are served, a ballroom—usually used for special events— a bake shop, and the large Gift Shop for the Village. Making a reservation, even for lunch, is a good idea in high season. We arrived on a July Saturday at 2:30 PM and were told there would be a half-hour wait for a table! There are two main dining rooms, one with wide-plank floors and bare tables, the other carpeted with tablecloths on tables, seating about 150 in all. Waitstaff are in period costume. The menu is the same in both rooms. The village logo appears next to items that are specialties of the house. At lunchtime, these include clam chowder (made with clams, bacon, potatoes, and cream), pounded cheese (a spicy cheddar served with relish and crackers), and tavern-smoked salmon with baby spinach, goat cheese, and spicy brown mustard vinaigrette (all starters at $4–6). Chicken potpie is a specialty-of-the-house entrée at lunchtime. Other choices ($7–9) include roast turkey sandwich, macaroni and cheese, mincemeat pie, and a half-pound burger.

In the evening special starters include seafood pie or a sausage, meat, and cheese plate. You can get a Caesar or watercress salad. Dinner entrées ($14–25) include baked scrod with a broth of oysters, smoked bacon, and tomatoes, served with crisp potato sticks; prime rib with mashed potatoes; salmon baked in pastry; and rack of lamb. Special events are held in the tavern on certain evenings—hearth cooking demonstrations on Wednesday, a tavern evening with literary characters on Thursday, and meeting with costumed village staff on Friday. On Saturday evening, dinner music is provided in a variety of styles. Lunch daily 11:30–3:30, dinner 5 to 8 or 9. Light fare is served 3:30–5. In the off-season, the tavern follows the village schedule.

♦ **Cedar Street Restaurant** (508-347-5800), 12 Cedar Street, Sturbridge. The intimacy of two dining rooms in a small house is appealing, and this restaurant proudly lists its four-star ratings from area newspapers. Locals flock here for dinner, so reservations are in order. Chef David Vadenais, a graduate of the Culinary Institute of America, offers exceptional selections in vegetarian, fish, and meat categories. Starters could be a baked wild mushroom, chèvre, and arugula strudel; smoked salmon and potato pancake Napoleon with chive crème fraîche; or sautéed lemon and rosemary marinated quail. A salad might be made from fennel and orange with sweet-and-sour dressing over mixed greens, or a warm spinach salad with sautéed veal sweetbreads. Entrées, priced $22–24, can be roasted salmon fillet with cumin, mint, and potato crust prepared with white beans, chickpeas, lentils, and roasted eggplants, or a mixed game plate with rabbit, venison, and duck breast with celery root puree, wild rice pilaf, and fried leeks. Do you have room for dessert? How about green apple and golden raisin crumble tartlet with cranberry sorbet or hazelnut linzertorte with crème anglaise? Dinner from 5 Monday through Saturday.

♦ **The Whistling Swan and Ugly Duckling** (508-347-2321), 502 Main Street, Route 20, Sturbridge. Carl and Rita Lofgren have provided top-flight dining in Sturbridge for years. The fancy restaurant, the Swan, is on the ground floor of this big white building in the center of town. White tablecloths, Chippendale chairs, and a formal setting are found here. Upstairs, the Duckling has lighter fare and a happening bar. Here, you sit around on sofas, in wing chairs, at mismatched tables, or at a long bar toward the rear where meals may be taken. The Swan's dinner menu includes blue cheese and herb crusted rack of lamb; veal scallops with wild mushrooms and sage; and braised lamb shank with tomatoes and white beans over penne. Entrées are $18–28. Upstairs, you can get sandwiches in the evening like lobster club and a grilled Reuben as well as entrées such as chicken potpie, Swedish meatballs, and sausage and spinach lasagna in the $9–18 range. The rack of lamb at $26 appears on both menus. At the Swan lunch is served Tuesday through Sunday 11:30–2, dinner 5:30–9. Dinner is served all day Sunday 11:30–8. Reservations are a good idea. The Duckling is open daily 11:30–10, and it's first come, first served.

♦ **Rovezzi's** (508-347-0100; fax 508-347-1799), behind the Sturbridge Country Inn, 530 Main Street, Sturbridge. "It's supposed to look like Tuscany," says chef-owner Christopher Rovezzi, whose father had a restaurant by the same name for years in Worcester. And it does, with terra-cotta-colored walls and a faux grape arbor winding around some of the overhead wood beams. Tablecloths are white; the room is modest in size and invites a convivial feeling. The Vitello Valdostana—medallions of veal topped with roasted mushrooms, Fontina cheese, and a demiglaze at $18.95 —is a crowd pleaser. Pollo Gorgonzola at $15.95 is a boneless chicken breast stuffed with fresh spinach, roasted red peppers, aged provolone, and mushrooms and finished with a Gorgonzola cream sauce. Medallions of salmon are served with fresh oregano and mint. Pastas include cheese tortellini tossed with fresh shrimp and sautéed mushrooms in pesto. Open Tuesday through Sunday for dinner at 5. Reservations are a good idea.

♦ **Snows Restaurant** (413-967-7024), 136 Pleasant Street, Ware. This unassuming little seafood restaurant—named for the pond across the street—is only open Thursday through Sunday and also closes from mid-December to early January. But whenever it's open, it's packed. Joe and Heather Novitsky and their kids run the place, which has three small dining rooms inside with captain's chairs and tables, and picnic tables on the outdoor deck right on the road looking toward the distant pond. Deep-fried clams, scallops, shrimp, and even lobster chunks are listed as side orders on the all-day menu. Clam and seafood chowder are available, and you can get lobster stew, a tossed salad, and Buffalo chicken wings as starters. Also on the menu are baked haddock and scallop dinners ($10–14 range) and Maine lobster in butter at $11 last we knew. For dessert, hot apple pie goes for $2, strawberry shortcake for $2.25, and cheesecake with strawberries for $3.25. Open Thursday through Sunday 11–9.

NEARBY CONNECTICUT

Less than half an hour south of Brimfield and Sturbridge is the northeast corner of Connecticut, the so-called Quiet Corner. It recently has become a center for antiques dealers and lovers. **Putnam,** an old mill town on the Quinebaug River, many of whose downtown storefronts were empty or not doing well, was almost single-handedly revived by Jerry Cohen in the early 1990s. He opened the first multidealer antiques shop in the old Bugbee's department store, a four-story building in the center of downtown. Cohen and his wife, native New Yorkers, had just returned to the Northeast from California where he had an antiques business.

Cohen now has 250 dealers in his **Antiques Marketplace** (860-928-0442) at the corner of Main and Front Streets in Putnam. Other dealers were drawn to the town; now about 20 shops compete for attention.

Some are single-dealer shops like **Brighton Antiques** (860-928-419), specializing in fine china. Fancy furniture and lamps can be found at **Palace Antiques** (860-963-1124). And then there's **G. A. Renshaw Architecturals** (860-928-3743), with 30,000 square feet of architectural details and large items like statues, fountains, and bars. It has been featured on national TV and in major newspapers.

Don't miss **Mrs. Bridges' Pantry** at 136 Main Street. Here two transplanted Englishwomen, Diana Jackson of Denham and her partner Veronica Harris from Hempstead, offer a typical English tearoom and much more. They sell all sorts of teapots and teacups and English goodies (like Black's chocolates) as well as an assortment of antiques, some English, some not. You can have tea at a lace-covered table inside or at a little table out on the street.

The real beauty of Putnam is that "it is a generalist-type town," says one antiques purveyor. For sure it is a fun place to prowl. Nearby are gorgeous country towns like Pomfret, home to private schools; Woodstock, for shopping, dining, and overnighting; and bucolic Brooklyn. Route 169, which wends its way south from Massachusetts, has been declared a national scenic highway and is a lovely winding road.

Nearby antiques shops include **Antiques and Uniques** (860-928-6020) on Route 171 in Woodstock, with an emphasis on old clocks and clock repair; **Scranton's Shops** (860-928-3738) on Route 169, South Woodstock, with seven rooms full of antiques, collectibles, crafts, and gifts; and **Pomfret Antique World** (860-928-5006) on Route 101, Pomfret, another multidealer shop.

Sight-Seeing

♦ **Roseland Cottage, Bowen House** (860-928-4074), 556 Route 169, Woodstock, CT 06281. Known locally as "the pink house" for its stunning salmon exterior, this onetime summerhouse was the setting for parties with famous people, including numerous presidents. The 1846 Gothic Revival structure has original furnishings, an interesting old bowling alley, and a boxwood parterre garden. It's a national historic landmark and maintained by the Society for the Preservation of New England Antiquities. Open June through October 15, Wednesday through Sunday 11–5. Adults $4, seniors $3.50, children $2.

♦ **Windham Textile & History Museum** (860-456-2178), 157 Union/Main Street, Willimantic, CT 06226. Willimantic was also a mill city—known primarily as a producer of thread—and this museum is located in an 1877 building that served as the mill's store, library, and warehouse. The museum has permanent and changing exhibits. Visitors experience life in a mill worker's home and a mill owner's mansion and tour a re-creation of a 19th-century textile mill. Open Friday through Sunday 1–5. Adults $4, students and seniors $2.

WHERE TO STAY

You can easily get out of crowded Brimfield and Sturbridge and stay in more peaceful northeast Connecticut, making forays into Massachusetts in less than half an hour. Many people do that. Route 131 is an easy route from Sturbridge to Putnam.

♦ **Celebrations! Inn** (860-928-5492; 1-877-928-5492; fax: 860-928-3306; www. CelebrationsInn.com), 330 Pomfret Street, Route 44, Pomfret, CT 06259-1512. Jean and Bill Barton have decorated their dark brown 1885 Queen Anne Victorian in luxurious yet comfortable style. Five accommodations include two two-room suites. The Far East Suite has an antique white iron queen bed with bonnet canopy, a gas fireplace with remote control, and a separate sitting room with trundle bed. All rooms have private bath. *Romantic* is the word for the Sweet Celebrations Room, wallpapered in navy with salmon design and featuring a king sleigh bed and fireplace flanked by two comfortable blue chairs. An oversized shower and double pedestal sinks are found in the good-sized bathroom. The Bartons set out coffee, tea, and muffins for early risers, then serve a full breakfast between 8 and 9. Triple-ginger-baked pears is a popular fruit course; pepperoni breakfast pie with eggs might be the main dish. The parlor has a fireplace and TV. There's also a library for quiet reading and an expansive porch outside for sitting and enjoying the gardens. Special packages include the "Antiquing Getaway" during Brimfield show weeks. The innkeepers are especially helpful in guiding you around the area. Doubles, $105–140.

♦ **Elias Child House** (860-974-9836; 1-877-974-9836; www.eliaschildhouse.com), 50 Perrin Road, Woodstock, CT 06281. Every guest room has a working fireplace at this early-18th-century home, now a welcoming bed & breakfast inn. Hearth cooking demonstrations and meals prepared in the huge fireplace in the keeping room are occasionally provided by veteran innkeepers Mary Beth and Tony Felice. This is their second innkeeping venture, and they really have it down. The house dates from the early 1700s. The keeping room is a place to put your feet up, have a cup of tea or a glass of wine, and chill out. All told the house has nine fireplaces, and Mary Beth likes to use them. A screened porch filled with dark wicker pieces even has the remains of the original old outhouse—tastefully transformed, of course. Outdoors, there are 47 acres with trails for walking or, in winter, cross-country skiing.

Guests have use of a parlor with wide floorboards, decorated in blue and green. Modern amenities include a TV and VCR. All rooms have private bath. On the second floor is Polly's Room, with a queen bed and pieces of brown summer wicker furniture. The suite—Aimee's Room—has a queen and a single bed, a sitting room, and a step-up bath. There's a walk-through area filled with antique dolls. Finally, the Sunshine Room faces east with a beautiful view and has a half bath attached; you have to go downstairs for the shower.

Breakfast is served around one large table in a handsome dining room with another huge fireplace, lighted on chilly mornings. Mary Beth leaves a breakfast menu at each door, and guests fill it out the night before. Doubles, $100–125.

♦ **B&B at Taylor's Corner** (860-974-0490; 1-888-503-9057; www.neguide.com/taylors), 880 Route 171, Woodstock, CT 06281-2930. Peggy and Doug Tracy welcome you into their home as if you are an old friend. The large brown-clapboard house dates from 1795. Out in back is a fenced pasture with a mother and a daughter cow, shaggy Scottish Highlanders. All three guest rooms at this B&B are on the second floor and have private bath and working fireplace, with fire logs provided. Peggy and Doug are also into hearth cooking and plan Fireside Weekends when a hearth-cooked dinner on Saturday is part of the package. The largest guest room is the Lemuel Allen Room with five windows, a fancy walnut high-backed queen bed, comfortable wing-backed chairs, and morning light. The Tracy Room has twin beds; an oak commode and Boston rocker are among the interesting furnishings. Everyone enjoys breakfast at a big table set with Hitchcock chairs in the first-floor dining room. A specialty of the house is Pannukakku, Finnish pancakes that are baked in the oven and are "like a custard" according to Peggy. Full breakfasts are the rule on weekends; continental breakfast is served during the week. Baked muffins are always available. Doubles, $90–140.

♦ **The Harvest** (860-928-0008; fax 860-928-6511; www.harvestrestaurant.com), 37 Putnam Road, Route 44, Pomfret. Peter Cooper has developed an exceptional following for his restaurant. It's a large place, with several dining rooms and add-ons, although the heart of the building is a historic home, circa 1765. The Harvest Room has a color scheme of red and green, and there's a great little alcove for an intimate dinner. The bar area is large and open; those sitting at tables there can order dinner or something lighter. A pianist plays on Friday evening, a jazz ensemble on Saturday. Many special events are scheduled and reservations are advised; this is one popular place.

At lunchtime you might have a grilled sushi tuna salad (the medallions of tuna are served medium rare atop mesclun and other greens), a classic Caesar salad, or a Tuscan portobello sandwich with Boursin cheese, tomato, grilled onion, and eggplant. At dinner starters include grilled sea scallops served with pineapple salsa, escargots served in a broiled garlic-buttered portobello mushroom cap, or seafood cakes ($10–12). Baked blue cheese onion soup is a specialty of the house. Entrées might be seafood bouillabaisse, grill-roasted chicken seasoned with herbs, seared breast of duckling with an orange sauce, or a châteaubriand for one (a refreshing twist). Entrées range $16–25. Sunday brunch is popular and priced at $13.95. A buffet of baked goods, fruit, desserts, and coffee is set out and entrées—like citrus herb chicken, seafood crêpe, or potato pancakes served with grilled ham and vegetables—ordered individually. Men are requested, not required, to wear jackets in the evening. Lunch Tuesday through Friday 11:30–2, dinner Monday through Saturday 5:30 to 8:30 or 9; Sunday brunch is served 11–2, and dinner, 3–8. Reservations please.

♦ **The Courthouse Bar & Grille** (860-963-0074; fax 860-963-9524), 121 Main Street, Putnam. "A guy who sets out to make a name for himself as a lawyer usually gets to hear plenty of other names directed at him along the way." That was a "Lawyer Thought of the Day" on the menu at this popular eatery located in the heart of Putnam's downtown antiques district. Owners are James and Sheila Frost. He grew up in Putnam, and both worked in restaurants before opening their own. They chose the name easily, because the Putnam Courthouse was upstairs in the building. The courthouse/lawyer theme sparks the menu. The room you enter has high-backed oak booths on one side and a long bar with three TVs on the other. Hard Core Crisp Apple Cider is listed among the bottled beers. A second dining room has well-spaced tables.

Appetizers are Opening Statements. You'll find Big House Burgers. And sandwiches are listed as "Not Just Bread and Water." The Pilgrim—real roast turkey served with cranberry sauce, lettuce, and American cheese on grilled wheat bread—is a favorite. Others include French dip, a grilled Reuben, and jailhouse chicken (grilled breast topped with "Chain Gang Chili," cheddar cheese, and scallions). Most are $6–7. Entrées on the all-day menu are priced $10–17 and include fettuccine Alfredo, shrimp scampi, prime rib in two sizes (a misdemeanor cut and a felony cut), and barbecued baby back ribs/chicken combo. There's a good selection of seafood, including a clam strip platter, baked scallops, and a lobster casserole. Open Monday through Thursday 11 AM–midnight, Friday and Saturday 11 AM–1 AM, and Sunday noon–10 PM.

◆ **The Vine Bistro** (860-928-1660), 85 Main Street, Putnam. Lisa Cassettari, whose family had a produce store in nearby Danielson—so she more or less grew up in the business—presides over this pretty storefront spot. Banquette seating along the walls in soft green with puffy pillows strewn about, and tables and chairs in light wood make for a sophisticated atmosphere. Local art is displayed—and is for sale—on the walls. Starters include eggplant rollatini, thinly sliced eggplant rolled with ricotta cheese, mozzarella, Parmesan, sun-dried tomatoes, and marinara sauce; Maryland crabcakes finished with a butter cream sauce; and a soup of the day. Caesar salads or baby greens tossed with raspberry vinaigrette, raisins, crumbled Gorgonzola, and pine nuts are among the salad choices. Entrées at dinner might be pastas like vodka rigatoni, pasta with fresh basil cream, or pasta tossed with chicken, artichoke hearts, black olives, mushrooms, tomatoes, white wine, and garlic. Other possibilities include veal Marsala, grilled boneless duck breast, and roast rack of lamb (entrées are priced $11–25). Specials are also offered. Among the wines are those from the locally regarded Sharpe Hill Vineyard. Try Seraph Red, hearty and smooth. The restaurant has a full liquor license. Hours are 11–4 for lunch Tuesday through Sunday; 5–9 for dinner Tuesday through Saturday; and 5–7 Sunday. Closed Monday.

Other casual dining spots include the **Vanilla Bean Café** at the intersection of Routes 44, 169, and 97 in Pomfret, with patio dining, soups, chilis, salads, sandwiches, and light dinner specials, as well as lots of musical events. This is where vanilla Coke was introduced nationally. **Calabash Coffee Company,** 18 Providence Road, Brooklyn, where they roast their own coffee, is a place to get breakfast, lunch, and snacks. How about an apple sandwich with grilled cheddar cheese, sliced apples, and onions on cinnamon bread?

Wayne Pratt
Antiques
346
OPEN

2   Litchfield County, Connecticut

Connecticut's northwest corner—Litchfield County, but especially the villages of Woodbury and Litchfield—is a rich hunting ground for lovers of antiquity. Vintage houses line the roads. High-quality antiques dealers abound.

Leslie White, an Englishman and antiques specialist, decided some 40 years ago to establish his business in Woodbury. At the time Route 7, which snakes its way northward farther west in Connecticut, was considered "antiques row."

But White said he could see that changes were in the offing. He moved his shop to a riverside site in an old mill just outside Woodbury.

Woodbury is one of the state's oldest inland towns, dating from the mid–17th century, and a handsome place. It wasn't the age and beauty of the town alone that drew him, said White. More than anything, it was the location. Just 1½ hours from New York City, 2½ hours from Boston, and an hour from Hartford, Woodbury would be able to draw from those urban areas.

White established Mill House Antiques, now a multibuilding complex overlooking the Nonewaug River west of the town center. After White came others. Today Woodbury—with extravagant 17th- and 18th-century homes lining its beautiful and wide Main Street—is the antiques capital of Connecticut. More than 40 dealers, most of them selling high-quality items, have clustered here, which makes it convenient to spend all day or weekend browsing.

There is also a Saturday-morning flea market from spring until fall on Main Street (Route 6). Here you'll find everything from comic books to depression glass to Barbie dolls. Afterward—or even beforehand—you can hit Phillips Diner just down the road for a homemade doughnut and a cup of java.

Woodbury is at the southern end of a loop through Connecticut's Litchfield County that is particularly rich in antiques emporia. From Route 6 in Woodbury pick up Route 63 north to another antiques center—the town of Litchfield. From there head west on Route 202 through the section known as Bantam and then continue north on Route 45 into New Preston. You can backtrack for a mile or two to Route 47 through Washington Depot and back into Woodbury. All along your way you'll find places to stop and hunt for that perfect little something.

An elegant antiques shop on Woodbury's Main Street   ◆

The roads are winding and amazingly rural. The shops are tony, the dining fine. There are good vineyards and great vistas. Picturesque stone walls and white-fenced horse pastures swing into view. Why do you think all those New York celebrities live here? (Author William Styron and actresses Susan St. James and Meryl Streep among them.)

To augment your search for old *things*, there are some fine old *places* to visit. In Woodbury itself the historic Glebe House counts itself the birthplace of Episcopalianism in America and is the only site in this country of a Gertrude Jekyll garden designed by the famous English horticulturist. In Litchfield are the nation's first law school (now a museum) and one of the finest historical society museums in New England. In Litchfield, too, are craftspeople of the highest order, including basket makers and potters. They sell beautiful wares you may allow to age into your very own antiques someday.

Everywhere you look are excellent examples of Colonial and Federal architecture, particularly in the center of the town of Litchfield. Some old houses have been turned into inns or B&Bs, so that you can actually stay in a vintage building, probably among antique furnishings.

Getting There

This area is approximately 100 miles from New York City, and 115 to 150 miles from Boston. It is most easily reached by car. The nearest major airport is **Bradley International Airport,** Windsor Locks, Connecticut, close to Interstate 91. You can rent a car at the airport and drive west.

By car from Boston or Hartford: Take the Mass Turnpike (I-91) west to the Sturbridge exit to I-84 west via Hartford to Exit 39 (Farmington). Pick up Route 4 west to Route 118 to Route 202 into Litchfield.

From New Jersey or New York: Take the Tappan Zee Bridge, Exit 8, to either Route 287 east or the Saw Mill River Parkway to I-684 north to I-84 east via Danbury. Then pick up Route 8 north to Exit 42 (Route 118 west to Route 202 into Litchfield).

For More Information

Contact the **Litchfield Hills Visitors Bureau** (860-567-4506; fax 860-567-5214; www.litchfieldhills.com), P.O. Box 968, Litchfield, CT 06759-0968.

SEEING AND DOING

Antiques

IN WOODBURY

The greatest concentration of high-quality antiques shops is found in Woodbury. A printed directory, *Woodbury: Antiques Capital of Connecticut,* is helpful. Most shops are located on Route 6 (Main Street). A sampling of some of the largest or

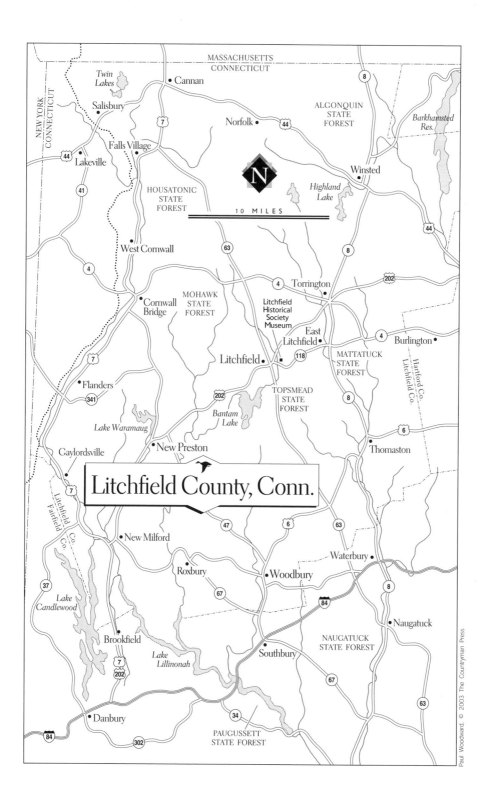

most important shops follows. While dealers are open most days in-season, it's best to call ahead to be sure. Many in Woodbury are closed on Tuesday.

♦ **Monique Shay Antiques and Design** (203-263-3186), 920 Main Street South. One of Woodbury's oldest established dealers. Located in a large red barn that goes on and on. Specializing in authentic Canadian painted cupboards, armoires, tables, and accessories. Six showrooms.

♦ **Country Loft Antiques** (203-266-4500), 557 Main Street South. Almost a complete interior design center. An assortment of fine French and European 17th-, 18th-, and 19th-century antiques, pottery, art, and wine-related objects (you can peek down into a completely designed wine cellar from an upper floor). Also French fabrics and linens.

♦ **Wayne Pratt Antiques** (203-263-5676), 346 Main Street South. Early American furniture, especially shaped pieces (chests with serpentine fronts, for example) in original condition. Some unusual mermaid items, such as andirons. Fine-quality reproductions on the upper level.

♦ **Eleish–Van Breems Antiques** (203-263-7030), 487 Main Street South. Emphasis on 18th- and 19th-century Scandinavian and Northern European antiques, Swedish reproductions, and decorative accessories shown in a historic 1760 house.

♦ **G. Sergeant Antiques** (203-266-4177), 88 Main Street North. Distinctive 17th-, 18th-, and 19th-century English, Continental, and American furnishings from fine estates.

♦ **Hamrah's Oriental Rug Company** (203-266-4343), 115 Main Street North. A family tradition since 1895, now run by Claire Hamrah Falk. The reputation of this rug company is unrivaled. An amazing collection of Persian and European rugs and tapestries in fine condition. Washing and restoration services.

♦ **Mill House Antiques** (203-263-3446), 1068 Main Street North. This was the first. There's a large stock of 18th- and 19th-century English and French formal and country furniture along with custom-made dining tables and chairs.

♦ **David Dunton** (203-263-5355), Route 132 off Route 47, second house on left. High-quality American and Federal furniture and accessories. Paintings.

IN LITCHFIELD

♦ **Jeffrey Tillou Antiques** (860-567-9693), 39 West Street, on the green. Specializing in fine American furniture and paintings from the 18th and 19th centuries. Fireplace accessories, folk art, glass, porcelain, 19th-century weather vanes. Tillou is a second-generation antiques dealer who expanded his shop substantially in 2002.

♦ **Bradford House Antiques** (860-567-0951), 33 West Street, on the green. The area's leading dealer in silver, specializing in American coin and sterling silver—also English and Continental pieces. Large jewelry collection, paintings, and smalls.

♦ **Tyler Antiques and Appraisals** (860-567-0755), 495B Bantam Road (Route 202). Seventeenth- to 19th-century Continental furniture and decorative arts.

♦ **Tullyvale Antiques and Interiors** (860-567-4425), 499 Bantam Road (Route 202). English and Continental antiques, some American. Imported European handmade furnishings.

Jeffrey Tillou Antiques

♦ **Black Swan Antiques** (860-567-4429), Route 202, 710 Bantam Road. English and European country furniture. Quite a few Dutch pieces, because one of the owners is Dutch.

♦ **Canterbury Antiques** (860-567-8130), 710 Bantam Road (Route 202). English country furniture, lots of blue ware, majolica, tea sets.

IN WASHINGTON DEPOT

♦ **Tulip Tree Collection** (860-868-2802), Route 47, 38 Bee Brook Road. Antique and reproduction antique furniture, much from Canada. Also upholstery, lamps, rugs, tableware. A wonderful array.

Historic Sites and Museums

♦ **Glebe House Museum and Gertrude Jekyll Garden** (203-263-2855), Hollow Road, Woodbury. A *glebe* is the farmland enjoyed by a rural clergyman as part of his benefice. If his dwelling were on the glebe, it was called a glebe house—as in this case. Here's where a group of Anglican clergy met secretly to make a momentous decision: to take part in the American Revolution while upholding their English religious heritage. As a result, this house claims to be the birthplace of the Episcopal Church in America. Elected the first bishop in the New World was the Reverend Dr. Samuel Seabury. The house was built about 1750 and is an unusual

Country Loft Antiques

combination of gambrel and saltbox. The Reverend John Rutgers Marshall, his wife, and their nine children originally lived here. The building was restored in 1923 under the direction of Henry Watson Kent, pioneer in early American decorative arts at the Metropolitan Museum of Art in New York. It became a museum in 1925, at which time the famed English horticultural designer Gertrude Jekyll (pronounced *JEE-kl*) was commissioned to plant an "old-fashioned" garden. The Glebe House garden includes 600 feet of classic English-style mixed border and foundation plantings, a stone terrace, and an intimate rose allée. The garden plans were lost and rediscovered in the 1970s, with the project taken up in earnest in the 1990s. Open April to October, Wednesday through Sunday 1–4; in November, weekends only. Adults $5, children $2. Garden only, $2. An annual garden tour is usually conducted in June.

♦ **Litchfield Historical Society Museum** (860-567-4501), corner of Routes 63 and 118, center of Litchfield. Located in an early-20th-century beaux-arts brick-and-stone building originally designed as a library, this museum celebrates the history of the village of Litchfield. The rich collection focuses particularly on Litchfield's "Golden Age" — 1780 to 1840 — when it was an active, growing urban village and an intellectual center of Federalist New England. Not only was the nation's first law school, the Tapping Reeve Law School, located in Litchfield, but the Litchfield Female Academy was sited here, as well. Founded by Sarah Pierce, the latter school had more than 3,000 students before it closed around the same time that the law school did. The museum's textile collection is rich.

There are also examples of fine early silver and china and unusual papier-mâché furniture that was made in the village. There's a fine museum shop that sells, among other items, handmade baskets and the early American pottery of Guy Wolff of nearby Woodville. Open late April through mid-November, Tuesday through Saturday 11–5, Sunday 1–5. Admission, adults $5 (includes admission to both the museum and the Tapping Reeve House), seniors and students $3. Kids under 12 are free.

♦ **Tapping Reeve House and Law School** (860-567-4501), 82 South Street (Route 63), Litchfield. In 1774 a young lawyer named Tapping Reeve—who lived with his wife in Litchfield—began teaching law to his first student, Aaron Burr. Over the next 60 years hundreds of our nation's future leaders studied at Tapping Reeve's pioneering institution, known as the Litchfield Law School. More than 1,100 students attended the school before it closed in 1833. The list includes two vice presidents, 101 U.S. congressmen, 28 U.S. senators, and three justices of the U.S. Supreme Court. The museum focuses on the journeys of real law students through role-playing and interpretive exhibits. An introductory video, *Coming to Litchfield*, sets the scene. Open late April through mid-November, Tuesday through Saturday 11–5, Sunday 1–5. Admission is $5 for adults (which admits you to the Litchfield Historical Society Museum as well) and $3 for seniors and students. Kids under 12 are free.

♦ **Institute for American Indian Studies** (860-868-0518; www.instituteforaistudies. org), 38 Curtis Road, Washington. A replicated Algonquin village and simulated archaeological sites make this an interesting place. There is a medicine wheel garden outdoors. The museum reflects the cultures and history of many different Native American tribes. An exciting discovery was made here in 1977 when a group of mostly amateur archaeologists came across a fluted "clovis-type" spear point typical of those used by hunters who followed the glaciers north at the end of the last ice age. That was about 10,000 years ago. This became the first such Paleo-Indian site discovered in Connecticut. There's a gift shop on site. Open weekdays and Saturday 10–5, Sunday noon–5; closed Monday and Tuesday from January through March. Adults $4, children $2.

Drives

This is glorious country, and just about every road you take yields lovely views. It is particularly pleasant to drive around **Lake Waramaug** on the shore road. A state park at the western end is fine for picnicking, swimming, and launching a canoe. Route 47 south from Washington Depot into Woodbury also offers particularly pretty vistas.

Walks

In **Washington** a 3¼-mile foot trail known as the Shepaug Greenway is a place to loosen up your limbs. Pets on leashes are permitted. Pick up a map at the Hickory Stick Bookshop.

Shopping

Shopping—not only for antiques—is great in the entire area. The village of **Litchfield** has several stores of note. These are located on West Street, to one side of the green. At **Kitchen Works** you will find an excellent selection of ceramics (quite a lot from Portugal) and a full array of kitchen utensils. **Barnidge & McEnroe** has books and gifts including some lovely china, candles, and cosmetics toward the back of the store. **Hayseed** has glorious women's clothes, and **J. Derwin Clothiers** offers conservative and pricey men's and women's duds. Upstairs in this complex of shops is **Tina's Baskets.** Tina was out when I tried to stop, but her baskets looked fantastic.

In **Washington Depot** are more good shops, including **Hickory Stick Bookshop** and **The Pantry** for a quick bite (sandwiches, salads, and wondrous desserts) along with kitchen utensils and tableware. There are also a couple of women's clothing shops. The center of **New Preston** (Route 45 north of 202) has more. One of our favorites is **J. Seitz,** with marvelous clothing, furniture, home decorator items, cards, just about everything to entice you. There are a few more antiques shops in this area, as well. Just past the Hopkins Inn is **Hopkins Vineyard** with an excellent shop selling wines and wine-related items.

In **Woodbury,** besides antiques shops, you will find a wonderful children's toy store, **Geppetto's.** You can purchase excellent **Bridgewater Chocolates** at **Carole Peck's Good News Café** in Woodbury.

WHERE TO STAY

Lodging isn't as easy to find as you'd think. The inns around Lake Waramaug in New Preston are an excellent choice. If you can afford it, try the Mayflower Inn in Washington, possibly the most elegant small hotel in the state. Woodbury has disappointingly few good lodging options—but in nearby Southbury are a major hotel and a fine B&B.

IN LITCHFIELD

♦ **The Litchfield Inn** (860-567-4503; 1-800-499-3444; fax 860-567-5358; www. litchfieldinnct.com), Route 202, P.O. Box 798, Litchfield, CT 06759. This 32-room, two-story inn is of recent vintage but was built and furnished to look old. A large parlor off the entryway with pegged floors and fireplace sets the tone. Eight themed rooms include one decorated to evoke Sherlock Holmes, another known as "The Irish Room," and one devoted to Victoriana. Standard rooms have two queen beds, coffeemaker, hair dryer, TV, phone, and bathroom with a tub-shower combination. Deluxe rooms are a bit larger, usually L-shaped, and offer a VCR and refrigerator in addition to other amenities. All have wall-to-wall carpeting and reproduction furniture. Doubles, $130–225, with continental breakfast. The inn's restaurant, **Le Bistro East,** is well regarded and offers lunch and dinner.

♦ **Lilac Hedges** (860-567-8839; fax 860-567-4895), 40 East Litchfield Road, P.O. Box 446, Litchfield, CT 06759. Two large, luxurious suites are offered by Diantha and John Bowling in this house on a side road just off Route 118 east of town. Their home, a former dairy barn, has two self-sufficient apartments for rent. Both have refrigerators stocked for breakfast and snacks; guests are then "on their own," says Diantha. The Library Suite on the ground floor offers a book-lined sitting room with original wood floors, a twin-bedded guest room, a private bath, and a kitchenette—but no stove. Upstairs on the second and third floors is a huge space—about 1,500 square feet. On the second floor is a spacious living room with original chestnut beams, ceiling with skylights, and a full kitchen with dishwasher. Up the stairs is the bedroom with queen bed and the adjacent private bath. The bedroom overlooks a tranquil horse pasture. This is a nice out-of-the-way country spot. Doubles, $150 and $175 with 2-night minimum.

IN NEW PRESTON

♦ **The Birches Inn** (860-868-1735; 1-888-590-7945; fax 860-868-1815; www.the-birchesinn.com), 233 West Shore Road, New Preston, CT 06777. Located on beautiful Lake Waramaug and with its own dock, canoes, and Sunfish for guests to use, the Birches Inn is run with style by innkeeper Nancy Conant. The inn is comprised of the main building on a hillside with five guest rooms, the Birch House out back with four rooms with their own balconies, and the Lake House at water's edge. The Lake House has two queen-bedded rooms and a two-room, king-bedded suite, all with decks and front-on lake views. The buildings have stained wood clapboard siding with dark green trim. Completely renovated in 1999, the inn's guest rooms are beautifully appointed. They are furnished with a mix of antiques and more modern pieces. All have comfortable private bathroom, television, air-conditioning, and phone. Our lakeview room in the main inn had a king bed, two comfortable reading chairs, and a picture-window view of the lake where we watched a thunderstorm gather force as if part of a sound and light show. A couple of rooms in the main inn have decks to the rear. A comfortable common living room with fireplace on the first floor is a good place to read or relax, and a sunny breakfast room has great water views. Here a full breakfast is served—including breads, cereals, yogurts, fruits, and a hot entrée (tomato, basil, and feta omelet when we stayed). Dinner is offered in a well-rated dining room (see *Where to Eat*). Doubles, with breakfast, $185–350.

♦ **The Hopkins Inn** (860-868-7295; www.thehopkinsinn.com), 22 Hopkins Road, New Preston, CT 06777. Franz Schober of Austria, a chef, and his wife have been in charge here for more than 20 years. The inn is best known for its dining (see *Where to Eat*), but its 11 guest rooms on the second and third floors are old-fashioned, pristine, and a bargain. Nine have private bath; two share. Five of the rooms have lake views. There is a small, private beach; it's not sandy, but there is direct lake access down the hill and through a small section of woods. Rooms have twin, queen, and king beds, all with plain white spreads. Some rooms are on the small side. Room 15 has a great lake view and an old-fashioned tub and shower in the adjoining bathroom. The rooms are air-conditioned. Doubles, $80 and $90. Breakfast is available at an extra cost.

♦ **The Boulders** (860- 868-0541; 1-800-55-BOULDERS; www.bouldersinn.com), East Shore Road, New Preston, CT 06777. New owners Martin O'Brien and

Steven Goldstone took over this exceptional inn in spring 2002, and the shakedown cruise was still under way when I stopped. Located just across the road from Lake Waramaug and with wonderful views of the lake from its large-windowed dining room, the inn has a reputation for both fine dining and accommodations. Renovations were going full tilt in the Carriage House, which was being converted into three luxury rooms and suites. The Guest House, a short distance up the hill toward the rear of the inn, has rooms with fireplace, lake-view deck, full bath, refrigerator, and coffeemaker. In the main inn, a gracious building that was once a country home, are six more antiques-furnished bedrooms, four with views of the lake, which is surrounded by hills. Refreshments—including delectable pastries and lemonade on the warm day I visited—are set out in the charming wood-paneled parlor in the afternoon. A full breakfast is included in the rates. Doubles, $260–895 (for the two-bedroom luxury suite in the Carriage House). A dining room with a well-credentialed chef (see *Where to Eat*) is popular.

IN WASHINGTON

♦ **The Mayflower Inn** (860-868-9466; fax 860-868-1497; www.mayflowerinn.com), Route 47, Washington, CT 06793. This is Connecticut's most exquisite country inn. A total of 25 rooms are located in three classic clapboard-sided buildings that look as settled in the landscape as if they've been here forever. A large pillared porch along the side of the main inn and an outdoor terrace add to the appeal in good weather. There are fabulous flower gardens and an outdoor heated pool. A Shakespeare garden and an American poets garden host occasional readings. Trails wend through the 28-acre pleasantly hilly landscape. Although an inn named the Mayflower has been on the site for many, many years, these buildings were recast and opened anew in 1992 by owners Adriana and Robert Mnuchin. The Mnuchins collected art and antiques extensively prior to opening their inn and share the pieces in spacious guest rooms and especially appealing common rooms. My favorite is the dark and cozy library in the main building— wood paneled and warmed with a wood-burning fireplace. Here's the ultimate place to curl up with a book and relax. The dining room at the Mayflower is top-notch. You'll find a small fitness center, sauna, steam room, and spa on the lower level of the main inn. A list of area antiques shops—with descriptions of their specialties—is available to guests. Guest rooms are luxuri-

The Mayflower Inn in Washington

ous with king or queen bed (often an antique four-poster), beautiful linens, and comfortable chairs. Many have gas fireplace. Two-night stays are required, 3 nights on holiday weekends. Doubles, EP, $400–650; suites, $700–1,300.

IN WOODBURY

♦ **The Cornucopia at Oldfield** (203-267-6707; 1-888-760-7947; fax 203-267-6703), 782 Main Street North, Southbury, CT 06488. "Our house is open to our guests," says welcoming innkeeper Dave Andros who—with his wife, Sue—opens his vintage early-19th-century home as a B&B. The house is impeccably and charmingly decorated. Common rooms on the main floor include a Victorian-era parlor and a large fireplaced keeping room. A candlelit breakfast is served to guests at one large table in the dining room—a specialty of the house being baked apple and pecan pancake. Three guest rooms have private bath, CD player, ceiling fan, and air-conditioning. An outdoor swimming pool is charmingly landscaped and very private behind concealing shrubbery. The Admiral Aston Bedchamber, the largest and most luxurious guest room, has a working fireplace for which fire logs are provided, a private balcony with view of the pool and gardens, and a bathroom with whirlpool tub. A queen-sized wicker bed and a chaise lounge are both found in the room. The John Moseley bedroom has a high-backed double Victorian bed and a bathroom with clawfoot tub. The Rebecca Moseley guest room comes with a half bath in the room and a full bathroom down the hall. Dave loves to help people get around the area and direct them to good restaurants and sites of interest. The location is just over the line south from Woodbury on Route 6. Doubles, $140–200.

♦ **Dolce Heritage Inn** (203-264-8200; 1-800-932-3466; www.dolce.com), 522 Heritage Road, Southbury, CT 06488. This 163-room hotel has almost a California feeling to it with its open floor plan, tall stone fireplaces, and barn-wood walls. Countering this sensation are the oversized wing chairs and traditional sofas found in small groupings throughout the common areas. A very large lounge with pool tables is a place to go for a drink or to meet friends. The dining room is an Eight Mile Brook steakhouse. Guest rooms are located in two major wings; floor-to-ceiling glass walls in corridors look out on a nine-hole golf course and an outdoor pool. There are also an indoor pool and racquetball courts. Guest rooms have one king or queen bed or two double beds. Green-and-red floral bedspreads add a touch of color, and furnishings are traditional. All rooms have a TV with Internet connection, coffeemaker, and hair dryer. Doubles, EP, $99–150. Some package plans are available.

♦ **Longwood Country Inn** (203-266-0800; www.longwoodcountryinn.com), 1204 Main Street South, Woodbury, CT 06798. Husband and wife Gary Nurnberger and Pat Ubaldi are the innkeepers at this B&B-*cum*-restaurant, located in what was once a country home whose original section dates from 1789. The couple renovated to make four guest rooms, all with private bath, which they opened in 2000. Three rooms on the second floor have twin beds, a queen four-poster, or—in the so-called bridal suite—a king-sized four-poster bed. This third-floor suite—part of the original house—has an unusual open bathroom area with sink and tub on a platform and a European-style handheld shower. A king bed draped in a toile fabric and a gas fireplace are found in this suite. All rooms have TV. The dining room—in which a full breakfast is served to inn guests—is quite formal with shield-back chairs and white linen tablecloths. This windowed room looks over the grounds; lunch and dinner are served Tuesday through Saturday. Doubles, $115–250 (for the suite).

♦ **Curtis House** (203-263-2101), Main Street (Route 6), Woodbury, CT 06798. "Connecticut's oldest inn" is the claim to fame at this white ark of a place in the center of town. Best known for its old-fashioned main-floor dining rooms, the inn also has 18 guest rooms, 14 in the main inn and 4 in a nearby carriage house. In the main inn, 8 have private bath; 6 rooms on the third floor share. Narrow, creaking staircases lead up to the rooms where canopy beds and in-room sinks are the rule. Two beds in a room may not be the same height. The carriage house rooms are very basic, furnished in wicker. They have private bath with stall shower. Doubles with private bath, $80–135; with shared bath, $56.

WHERE TO EAT

This corner of Connecticut has some marvelous restaurants.

IN LITCHFIELD

♦ **West Street Grill** (860-567-3885), 43 West Street, on the green, Litchfield. James O'Shea and Charles Kafferman have created a winning formula here. This is deservedly one of the most popular restaurants in the entire area. Lemon-yellow walls with red below the wainscoting are hung with large mirrors and changing art-work. Black booths, tables, and chairs and gorgeous flower arrangements add to the feeling of sophistication. The setting and the cuisine attract celebrities such as Diane Sawyer, William Styron, and Sarah Jessica Parker and Matthew Broderick, I'm told. Lunch could be a grilled chicken, watercress, and poached pear salad with crumbled Gorgonzola, spicy pecans, and a citrus Dijon dressing, or a sandwich like fresh dill and lemon tuna salad on a focaccia roll with house-made slaw and crisp corn tortilla noodles. Luncheon entrées ($11–15) might be Thai-style crab and potato cake or Irish beef stew made with Pinot Noir and roasted root vegetables. For dinner, try an appetizer ($10–12) like smoked rainbow trout tartare served with golden corn cakes and quail eggs or a chilled seafood salad with squid, shrimp, mussels, shaved fennel, and olives in a fresh lemon and olive oil dressing. When I stopped, dinner entrées ($20–34) included confit of duck leg and breast with whipped potato, spring vegetables, cranberry compote, and mission fig sauce, as well as cashew-crusted baked halibut with fresh coconut rice fritters and golden pineapple mango salsa. Additions to the menu appear daily. Full liquor license with extensive wine list. Lunch daily 11:30–3; dinner from 5:30 nightly. Reservations, please.

♦ **The Village Restaurant** (860-567-8307), 25 West Street, Litchfield. Two couples, Greg and Denise Raap and David and Thea Vigeant, are co-owners of this lively lit-tle storefront restaurant with two rooms—a pub on one side and tables on the other. David Vigeant is also in the kitchen. Locals enjoy this spot—it's a bit more relaxed than West Street, and a bit less expensive, as well. Prime rib is on the menu Friday and Saturday nights. Other dinner entrées ($15–22) are veal Piccata or

Marsala served with rice; steaks; seafood; and chicken. The pub menu—served on both sides of the restaurant—offers burgers, Caesar salad, barbecued ribs, and fish-and-chips ($8–12 range). At lunchtime the popular chopped salad ($8) has chicken, eggs, bacon, black olives, roasted red peppers, cucumbers, tomatoes, carrots, and Swiss cheese. Lunch 11:30–3; dinner from 5 every day except Tuesday.

♦ **Zini's** (860-567-1613), Route 202, Bantam. Located just west of Litchfield on busy Route 202 is this small yellow building where wonderful Italian food is prepared. Owner and chef Zini Adili is actually Albanian, but he trained with Italian chefs. His kitchen is one of the cleanest and best organized imaginable. From here come fine entrées, all the breads served in the restaurant, and desserts. The restaurant has one main room with stone interior walls, a gas fireplace, and tables with small shaded lamps. Dinner entrées include chicken Piccata, veal Marsala, pollo Barase (chicken breast with roasted red peppers, artichoke hearts, and asparagus in a wine sauce over capellini), and pesce alla vodka (grilled shrimp and scallops over onions, mushrooms, and zucchini in a light tomato vodka cream sauce, tossed with penne). Entrées are priced $13–19; there is a full bar. Open nightly for dinner from 5.

♦ **Wood's Pit BBQ and Mexican Café** (860-567-9869), 123 Bantam Lake Road (Route 209), Bantam. "Real Bar-B-Que Takes Time" is the warning on the menu of this very popular spot. Owner-chef Paul Haas spent time in Arizona and also in the South before perfecting the recipes he serves at this little roadside spot. The bar side is packed with the local gentry at lunch and dinner; a second dining room is more sedate. The food's the same. Margaritas are among the specialty drinks, and there's a good selection of brews including Hammer and Nail Brown Ale on draft. "Starter Ruppers" include Saddle Bags (crispy bundles of barbecued pork served with jalapeño sauce and smoked sausage with garlic cheese crisp). You will find pork and beef ribs, chicken, shredded or sliced brisket, and pulled pork served with two sides like baked beans, slaw, and potato salad. The sampler for two ($31) is a half rack of ribs, two beef back ribs, a quarter chicken, pulled pork, coleslaw, ranch baked beans, potato salad, and jalapeño corn bread. Now, there's a meal. Mexican specialties and barbecued sandwich baskets are also on the menu. Lunch daily 11:30–4, dinner from then until 9 or 10.

IN NEW PRESTON

♦ **Oliva** (860-868-1787), Route 45 and East Shore Road, New Preston. Weekenders with homes in fancy Litchfield County are known to grab a bottle of wine before leaving for their getaways on Friday evening—and to stop for dinner at Oliva en route. This extremely popular Italian café in the village of New Preston is a local favorite, as well. It's a good idea to make a reservation. Ensconced in the lower level of a big white house overlooking the road, Oliva's main dining space indoors is cozy but cramped. Mismatched painted wood tables and a brick fireplace with little white lights set the mood here. An outdoor terrace with variously sized tables under a striped awning is a necessary addition. Clear plastic side drapes keep things from becoming too cold or windy, and there's a space heater. Chef-owner Riad Aamar offers up delectable dishes on an ambitious menu that changes daily.

Chewy, crusty Italian bread comes to the table with olive oil, and your waiter or waitress is quick to open your wine and pour it into low glasses reminiscent of Mediterranean dining. A plate of mixed olives, appropriately enough, appears next. The soup of the night (pureed roasted pepper when we stopped) is one starter. We shared baby greens with garlic, Reggiano cheese, lemon, and olive oil and found the mix marvelously subtle. Entrées ($13–25) included sweet potato gnocchi alla Romana and veal stew with sage, porcini mushrooms, and white wine. I chose linguine with garlic, shrimp, leek, Gorgonzola, and tomato and cleaned my plate. My husband had a Lebanese dish (a rare departure from the Italian emphasis) described as "lamb meatloaf." It was baked kafta with onions, parsley, potato, cumin, and tomato over mashed vegetables and was delicious. There are also pizzas with intriguing toppings. Lunch served Saturday and Sunday noon–2; dinner Wednesday through Sunday 5:30–9:30. BYOB.

♦ **Le Bon Coin** (860-868-7763), Route 202, New Preston. *Le bon coin* means "a good place" or "a good spot," and since 1983 it has been just that. William Janega, chef-owner, established a classic French restaurant in this little white Cape Cod house west of Litchfield after working in French kitchens for 16 years. Seating just more than 40 diners in two small dining rooms—the one to the left of the front door is known as the bar because it's also where drinks are prepared—the restaurant thrives because of its predictably good fare. Classic French dishes like pâté de maison or escargots to start, sweetbreads, rack of lamb, and duckling as entrées, and crêpes Suzettes (pour deux) as desserts are augmented by specials.

Especially popular during fall and winter are the wild game dishes—pheasant, wild turkey, guinea hen, and wild boar among them. Customers also come for the Dover sole, prepared with mushrooms and artichokes, that is almost always on the dinner menu. Other entrées ($19–24) could be filet mignon with a cognac pepper sauce, veal scallops in a tomato basil salsa, and free-range chicken with wild mushrooms. At lunchtime omelets and salads are added to the menu. For dessert, try crème caramel, chocolate mousse, or poached pear with raspberry puree. Close your eyes and you can almost believe you're in a small restaurant in the French countryside. Lunch Monday, Thursday, Friday, and Saturday noon–2; dinner Monday, Thursday, and Friday 6–9, Saturday until 10; Sunday dinner is 5–9. The restaurant is closed Tuesday and Wednesday.

♦ **Doc's Trattoria & Pizzeria** (860-868-9415), 62 Flirtation Avenue (Route 45), New Preston. This small restaurant close to Lake Waramaug is run by Roberto Pizzo, who grew up in the restaurant business. White tablecloths, votive candles, fresh flowers, and bare wood floors set the stage for a romantic dinner. Bring your own bottle of wine and settle in for a dinner of farfalle alla Bolognese, fettuccine al pomodoro, or grilled beefsteak marinated in garlic and herbs. Seafood, chicken, and veal dishes are also offered. Pizza is on the menu as well, in both individual and large sizes. Entrées are priced $11–19. This is a very popular little place, so reservations may be in order. No credit cards. Lunch Tuesday through Sunday noon–3, dinner 5–10. Closed Monday.

♦ **The Hopkins Inn** (860-868-7295), 22 Hopkins Road, New Preston. The wonderful large terrace overlooking the lake—crowned with a huge chestnut tree—is an idyllic place to dine. The lake is below and ringed with hills—you might almost think you're in Switzerland or Austria. The mood is enhanced by the waitresses in Austrian dirndls, reminiscent of the homeland of chef-owner Franz Schober. If you're here in winter, there are two comfortable indoor dining rooms, one with a large wood-burning fireplace. Tables are covered with simple homespun cloths and surrounded by locally made Hitchcock chairs from Riverton, Connecticut. Appetizers include marinated herring, eggs à la russe, and shrimp cocktail. Entrées could be *backhendl* with lingonberries (a chicken dish from Austria that the inn is known for), Wiener schnitzel, or salmon with herb butter ($19–25). Green salad, a starch, and a vegetable are included with most entrées. The dessert menu is extensive and includes Grand Marnier soufflé glacé, frozen éclair, strawberries Romanof, and meringue glacé. Open for lunch and dinner Tuesday through Saturday and dinner only, noon–8, on Sunday. Closed Monday.

♦ **The Boulders** (860-868-0541), East Shore Road, New Preston. The dining room with huge glass windows overlooks the lake and is a charming space. In good weather a few tables are set outdoors on the terraces below for open-air dining. A new chef, Jean Claude, who had spent time at New York's Tavern on the Green and the Rainbow Room, was just taking over when I stopped. Starters could be an onion tarte made with caramelized onion and Gruyère cheese; saffron-steamed mussels; or lobster and crabmeat spring roll with apricot chili dipping sauce ($7.50–10). Entrée choices ($15–28) might include rack of lamb with country-roasted tomatoes and oven-baked potatoes; grilled pork chop with sweet potato pancetta hash and a cashew cranberry chutney; or veal Scaloppine with a lemon caper sauce, Lyonnaise potato, and fresh asparagus. Dinner is served nightly year-round from 5:30. Lunch is available mid-May to November, daily noon–3.

♦ **The Birches** (860-868-1735), 233 West Shore Road, New Preston. The Birches has a large dining room with widely spaced tables and as such lacks the coziness I prefer. Meals are, however, served outdoors in good weather, and this gives a nice view of the lake. The cuisine is well rated, and for those staying at the inn, nothing could be more convenient than to walk downstairs to dinner. Appetizers ($10 range) could be a barbecued chicken; wild rice and goat cheese tartlette; house mesquite-smoked salmon-wrapped scallop; or Zinfandel-braised short rib tortellini with smoked shallots and Saga blue cheese. Soups are inventive; consider a charred yellow tomato gazpacho served with chive whipped cream and white truffle oil. Entrées ($18–28) could be poached smoked lobster and braised veal leg served with sweet peas and a spring herbed risotto, salmon grilled in fresh corn husks and served with apple and roasted parsnip hash, or grilled fillet of beef with Maytag blue cheese and roasted Vidalia onions. A three-course menu can be had for $45; four courses, $55. Dinner is served Wednesday through Monday 5:30–9.

IN WASHINGTON

♦ **The Mayflower Inn** (860-868-9466), Route 47. The dining room at the Mayflower is both sedate and smashing. Elegant fabrics drape the opening. Well-spaced tables have comfortable Chippendale chairs. A coffered ceiling painted white is a crowning touch to the room, which is done in soft peach tones. Fresh flowers are always arranged beautifully. Breakfast, lunch, and dinner are served. Eggs Benedict with spinach and hollandaise sauce, cinnamon apple waffles, or old-fashioned Irish oats with brown sugar are all possible ways to start the day. Lunch can be a four-cheese frittata; char-broiled burger; pan-seared salmon with melted leeks, Pernod, and lentils; or crisp fish-and-chips ($11–16). In the evening, starters may include lobster bisque, Boston bibb salad with blue cheese, shallots, and a truffle vinaigrette, or warm ricotta crêpes with crisp eggplant and shaved basil ($8–15). Entrées ($18–30) might be a halibut fillet roasted with sweet corn, summer tomatoes, and Maine lobster stew; a braised lamb shank with baby vegetables, herbs, and rosemary sauce; or confit of duck leg with seared breast and fruit compote. Executive chef Thomas Moran is in charge. Breakfast daily 7:30–10:30, lunch noon–2, dinner 6–8:30.

♦ **G. W. Tavern** (860-868-6633), 20 Bee Brook Road. This deep red colonial tavern named for—who else?—George Washington is a great place for lunch or a casual dinner. It's the sort of place at which the father of our country might have hitched up his horse and then enjoyed some victuals. Owner Robert Margolis has accumulated several items that reference the first president—including a bust of George that peers down on the crowd in the rear, yellow room with high ceiling. Here are also two early-American-style chandeliers that swing from the rafters, pictures of Washington, and other touches of colonial Americana. In the pub room in front are high-backed booths and a huge stone fireplace. During the summer a large flagstone terrace under a striped awning is the place to be. It looks down over the Shepaug River meandering far below.

The G. W. Burger and the veggie burger are on the menu for lunch, dinner, and Sunday brunch and are very popular. They are served on bulky rolls and come with a choice of melted cheeses. Other lunch entrées could be a fruit and cheese plate; a crock of chili with fresh corn chips; classic cobb salad; or hickory-smoked pork ribs with barbecue sauce, fries, and slaw (entrées $8–14).

In the evening you'll find some comfort foods like meat loaf with roasted garlic mashed potatoes and carrots, or a chicken potpie with biscuit topping. Other entrées might include roast duck with sour cherry sauce; oven-roasted cod steak with white beans, tomato, and rosemary; or peppercorn filet mignon with brandied cream sauce ($12–24). Sunday brunch offers a mix of lunch and breakfast items including buttermilk pancakes, quiches, and omelets.

Finish up with cherry pie, a house favorite; a vanilla custard pudding with caramel at the bottom; or chocolate layer cake. Lunch Monday through Saturday 11:30–2:30, Sunday brunch 11:30–3; dinner from 5:30 Monday through Saturday, from 5 on Sunday. Between lunch and dinner a pub menu is available.

♦ **The Pantry** (860-868-0258), Titus Square. This kitchen-store-*cum*-café is a wonderful place to have continental breakfast, lunch, or afternoon tea at café tables surrounded by hand-painted pottery, linens, and kitchenware items. Baking is excellent; you can get scrumptious scones, muffins, pies, and cakes. The sandwiches and salads are also terrific. Here's a great place to pick up take-out foods for a picnic. Open Tuesday through Saturday 10–6.

♦ **Carole Peck's Good News Café** (203-266-4663), 694 Main Street South. This is the hippest, most happening restaurant in town and for several miles around. Two dining rooms—one with screaming yellow walls and the other with red walls—seem to be always busy, and sometimes people are craning their necks in search of celebrities. Many regulars prefer to sit in the bar, in the center of the restaurant, with its 1950s vintage café tables and chairs and a few booths. Changing artwork on the walls in all rooms sets a contemporary mood. The food is acclaimed. An ambitious lunch menu offers several soups including the Good News First Edition Soup—always a vegetarian offering—and possibly lobster soup with lobster chunks. Other starters can be pecan-crusted fresh oysters with cherry tomatillo salsa; warm portobello mushroom toast and goat cheese; or country pâté with herb toast and prune and raisin marmalade ($7–12). Many inspired salads (how about shrimp on orange slices with jicama, watercress, romaine, chickpeas, and feta in a sesame tahini dressing?) compete for attention with entrées like grilled semibone-less quails with lentils and escarole in a tomato and green olive tapenade ($12–16 range). At dinner, entrées ($19–29) might be fried sea scallops accompanied by lump crab and squid with celery, snow peas, and sweet potato puree; gemelli pasta with asparagus, spiced pecans, Gorgonzola, capers, sage, and balsamic "drizzle"; or spice-rubbed double-cut venison chop with onions, celery root puree, and green beans in hazelnut butter. And, oh, the desserts. A flight of three puddings—butter-scotch, white chocolate, and dark chocolate—come each with its own topping. You might have warm chocolate chunk banana cake with walnut brittle and brown butter caramel sauce or a coconut layer cake with mango and raspberry sauce. Bridgewater Chocolates, handmade in Connecticut, are sold at the counter up front, as are some desserts and breads. Open weekdays (except Tuesday) 11:30–10, Sunday noon–10.

♦ **John's Café** (203-263-0188), 693 Main Street South. Chef-owner Bill Okesson gets fine marks for his cozy little French café, ensconced in a small brown house and set back from busy Route 6. White tablecloths, a tile floor, and dark wood lad-derback chairs offer a French bistro atmosphere. A new main-floor bar area was being added when last we stopped. Lunch offers burgers, sandwiches (including grilled vegetables on Tuscan-style bread), grilled pizzas, and a few entrées ($7–9) like fish-and-chips and house-made fettuccine with white clam sauce. For dinner you can start with crab and salmon cakes with celery rémoulade or a seasonal mesclun salad with apples, walnuts, Gorgonzola, and lemon olive oil vinaigrette. Entrées might be grilled pork chop with scalloped potatoes, sautéed spinach, and sweet Gorgonzola onions; pan-roasted duck with French lentils, green beans, and a sherry vinaigrette; or roast chicken with garlic mashed potatoes, vegetables, and dried cherry chutney. Specials, including wine specials, appear nightly, as well. Excellent wines are available by the glass. Lunch Monday through Saturday 11:30–2:30, dinner 5:30–9. Closed Sunday.

♦ **Carmen Anthony Fishhouse** (203-266-0011), 757 Main Street South. This bright blue-green building with rust-colored trim specializes in fresh seafood—empha-sized by the lobster tank and the huge sculpture of a mermaid in the center of the main dining room. Diners sit at dark wood library-style chairs at white-clothed tables or at large perimeter booths in blue-green vinyl. The same menu is served in the bar, a large space with adjacent dining area. This was the second in a Connecticut chain of four restaurants. At lunchtime you can get burgers and lobster rolls, plus salads and the like. Dinner starters include a jumbo shrimp cocktail, potato-encrusted crabcake with rémoulade sauce, baked clams casino, or littleneck clams on the half shell. New England clam chowder and seafood bisque are offered. Entrées range from Italian-style, such as sea bass Calabrese served with rotini pasta, to several kinds of fish (tuna, red snapper, swordfish, sea bass, salmon, scrod, or fillet of sole) served grilled with a starch and a vegetable. The fish can be poached, broiled, or "blackened" if desired. A few steaks and other meats are available for landlubbers. Entrées are priced $20–40 (the latter for 2 pounds of Alaskan king crab legs served with drawn butter). Lunch is served Monday through Friday 11:30–4, Saturday noon–4. Dinner is available from 5 nightly except all day, noon–9, on Sunday.

♦ **Mrs. White's Tea Room** (203-263-6022), 308 Sherman Hill Road (Route 64). Thomas Winters, who was formerly in the kitchen at The Boulders Inn, took over this little restaurant in spring 2002 and immediately set to making changes and creating a real hit. He continued with "veddy" English-style selections for late breakfast, lunch, or afternoon tea, but was adding dinners on Thursday, Friday, and Saturday with what he described as "cutting-edge" menus. Breakfasts include a "Sampler"—an assortment of scones, teacakes, and date-nut bread, served with lemon curd tartlet—and French toast with raspberry cream cheese. Tea comes in small (for one) or large (for two) pots. At lunchtime, sandwiches include bacon and watercress; English egg salad; and classic chicken salad with grapes ($6–9). Lady Emily's Spinach Salad is made with red and green apples, walnut halves, and applewood-smoked bacon, tossed in a raspberry vinaigrette. High tea ($16.95 per person) calls for a 24-hour advance reservations and includes a personal pot of tea, scones, tea sandwiches, carrot salad, tea pastries, and fresh fruit. Open Tuesday through Saturday 9–3, Sunday 9–2; Thursday through Saturday 5–8 for dinner. Closed Monday.

♦ **Sandwich Construction Company** (203-263-4444), 670 Main Street South. A seriously long list of sandwiches, delicious homemade soups, breakfast items, scrumptious pastries, and desserts combined with a casual atmosphere have made this little restaurant in a shopping center very popular. You get in line (there usually is one) to order, continue to the cash register area to pay and maybe grab a handful of peanuts in the shell, and then wait for your food to be delivered to a table indoors or out. Breads are baked on the premises. Some hot entrées, like macaroni and cheese or lasagna, are also available. Sandwiches are priced in the $6 range. Open Monday through Saturday 7–4.

3 Rockport and Gloucester, Massachusetts

The sea is everywhere in Rockport and its next-door neighbor, Gloucester. Low-growing shrubbery allows the light to spread gloriously across the rocky promontory. Artists discovered this more than 150 years ago; since then Rockport and Gloucester have been art colonies of note.

Cape Ann, the peninsula on which the two towns are located, is 32 miles north of Boston—which can, on a clear day, be seen easily from Gloucester. It juts out into the Atlantic Ocean, defiant, rockbound, and rugged. Large boulders, deposited by retreating glaciers thousands of years ago, are everywhere. You find them at the water's edge but also tossed about on lawns and incorporated into domestic landscaping.

The two towns are at the very tip of the land named for Queen Anne of Denmark. It was English explorer John Smith who charted the eastern coast of the United States in 1614 and presented his map to then Prince Charles of England. The prince approved the name *New England* for the entire region and called the headland Cape Anne for his mother.

Writers, too, have been enamored of the spot. They include Ralph Waldo Emerson, Robert Louis Stevenson, T. S. Eliot, Louisa May Alcott, and Rudyard Kipling. Emerson's name lives on as that of a good-sized inn in the Pigeon Cove section of Rockport, just north of the village.

Writers are still drawn to Cape Ann, the most famous recently being Sebastian Junger, author of the best-selling *The Perfect Storm*, the true story of the sinking of a Gloucester fishing vessel in a wild offshore tempest in 1991. It was later made into a movie, much of it filmed in Gloucester.

But Gloucester and Rockport are especially well known for their art colonies. Rocky Neck, a long, narrow spit of land sticking out into the water in East Gloucester, claims to be the oldest working art colony in the country and is a national landmark. It was a Rocky Neck sculptor, Leonard Craske, who in 1920 fashioned the famous bronze statue of *The Man at the Wheel* that overlooks Gloucester harbor and symbolizes the hardy fishermen who have gone to sea from what was once America's busiest commercial fishing port.

Art galleries line Rockport's Main Street

The fishermen and their brightly painted boats, the tumbling seas, the charming lanes and picturesque homes, all were recorded by the artists of Cape Ann. They were painters of the caliber of Winslow Homer, Childe Hassam, John Singer Sargent, and Maurice Prendergast. Edward Hopper painted his first watercolors in Gloucester and spent two consecutive summers painting there.

The first of the famous artists was Fitz Hugh Lane, a fine marine painter who was born in Gloucester and painted in the early to mid–19th century. The best collection of his seascapes is to be found in the Cape Ann Historical Museum, a must-see spot in downtown Gloucester. Lane's little granite house sits on a hill over-looking the waterfront, the grounds of which serve as a public park with benches and views of the working harbor.

Winslow Homer came to Gloucester in 1870, renting space from the lighthouse keeper on Ten Pound Island, just offshore in Gloucester Harbor. His famous work A Fair Wind, or Breezing Up — painted in Gloucester — is in the National Gallery in Washington.

Aldro T. Hibbard gets the credit for creating the Rockport art colony. He moved to town in 1920 and began the Rockport Summer School of Drawing and Painting. The school evolved into a club and eventually sponsored the first exhibit of the work of professional artists in Rockport. In time the growing art community turned fishing shacks and old barns into studios and homes.

Rockport, looking like an English seaside village, and Gloucester, a rough, tough workingmen's community where sons of Italian and Portuguese immigrants still wrest their living from the sea (albeit fewer all the time), offer a striking contrast on the island they share. And it is an island. For once you cross the bridge on Route 128 over the Annisquam River, you are surrounded by water.

Each town has its own thriving art association. The Rockport Art Association, with more than 1,000 members (a quarter of them "exhibiting members"), dates from 1921; the North Shore Arts Association on Reeds Wharf in East Gloucester, from 1922.

As you drive or stroll around Cape Ann, it is common to see an artist with an easel set up, or a group of art students huddled near an instructor. One favorite place to paint is at Eastern Point Lighthouse at the far end of the exclusive Eastern Point area in Gloucester. The deep pinkish red fishing "shack" so prominent in Rockport Harbor has been so often the subject of artists' work that it has become known as "Motif #1." When destroyed in a winter storm in the late 1970s, townspeople hastily rebuilt it.

The works of local artists are displayed proudly in many of the inns and restaurants of Cape Ann. And while there are many other things to draw you to Rockport and Gloucester — from whale-watch trips to fish-and-chips — it is the artistic side of the cape that is the focus of this chapter.

Getting There

Cape Ann is reached by driving I-95 north of Boston and then branching off onto Route 128 north to the end. If you're coming from Maine or New Hampshire, simply take I-95 south and look for the Route 128 cutoff. You will pass exits for Salem and Marblehead off Route 128 on your way out to Rockport and Gloucester.

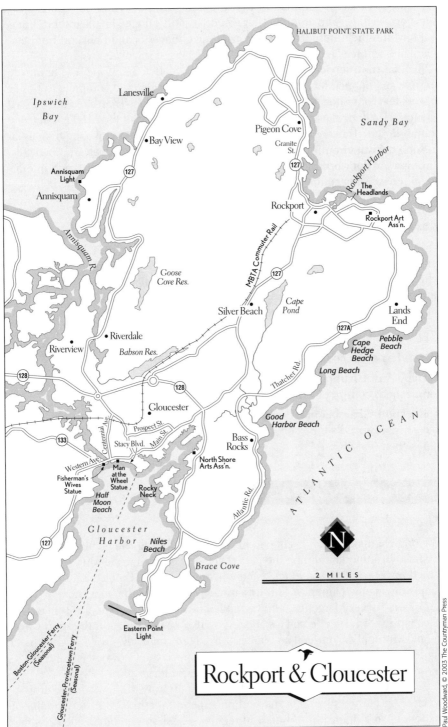

HALIBUT POINT STATE PARK

Ipswich Bay

Lanesville

Bay View

Pigeon Cove

Sandy Bay

Granite St.

127

Annisquam Light

Annisquam

127

Rockport Harbor

The Headlands

Rockport

Rockport Art Ass'n.

Annisquam R.

MBTA Commuter Rail

Goose Cove Res.

127

Silver Beach

Cape Pond

Lands End

127A

Riverview

Riverdale

Babson Res.

Cape Hedge Beach

Pebble Beach

128

Long Beach

128

Thatcher Rd.

Gloucester

Good Harbor Beach

Prospect St.

Main St.

Bass Rocks

Centennial Ave.

Stacy Blvd.

133

North Shore Arts Ass'n.

Western Ave.

Man at the Wheel Statue

Fisherman's Wives Statue

Half Moon Beach

Rocky Neck

Atlantic Rd.

A T L A N T I C

O C E A N

127

Gloucester Harbor

Niles Beach

N

Brace Cove

2 MILES

Boston-Gloucester Ferry (Seasonal)

Gloucester–Provincetown Ferry (Seasonal)

Eastern Point Light

Rockport & Gloucester

Paul Woodward, © 2003 The Countryman Press

Once there, Routes 127 and 127A—the latter hugging the ocean from Gloucester to Rockport—will get you around. After you drive across the high, albeit short, bridge that traverses the Annisquam River, separating Gloucester and Rockport from the mainland, you feel as if you're in another world.

Regular **train service** between Boston's North Station and Cape Ann has made it possible and popular for Gloucester and Rockport residents to commute to Boston to work and for visitors to take the train there from Boston. Train stops are in West Gloucester, Gloucester, and Rockport. For information, call the MBTA (Metropolitan Boston Transit Authority) at (617) 222-3200. Those who take the train as far as Rockport can easily walk to a B&B in town from the train depot.

Logan Airport in Boston is the closest major airport, with national and international service. It's about a 40-minute drive from Cape Ann.

Getting Around

It's nice to have a car but not absolutely necessary. The Cape Ann Transportation Authority (CATA) operates buses around Cape Ann. For information or a complete schedule, call (978) 283-7916. In summer a sprightly trolley takes visitors around Rockport, stopping at several inns and beaches and at Bearskin Neck, a picturesque shopping area.

For More Information

♦ **Cape Ann Chamber of Commerce** (978-283-1601; 1-800-321-0133; www.cape annvacations.com), 33 Commercial Street, Gloucester, MA 01930.

♦ **Rockport Chamber of Commerce** (978-546-6575; 1-888-726-3922; www. rockportusa.com), P.O. Box 67, Rockport, MA 01966. The office is at 22 Broadway and is open year-round.

SEEING AND DOING

The Art Scene

The original mainstays of livelihood in Rockport—fishing and granite quarrying—became less important during the period between the two world wars. By then something else had begun to replace them: art and artists. People painting, and people buying the paintings. This was also becoming true in Gloucester.

Gilbert Tucker Margeson, a Nova Scotian by birth, opened the first studio in Rockport in 1873. He also had a stationery store on Main Street in Rockport where he sold art supplies. A friend and fellow artist, Harrison Cady, once bought a painting Margeson had done late in life, saying he wanted the Cady descendants to know "what a man could do when he was 87 years old."

Today Rockport and Gloucester offer the opportunity to view working artists up close. In summer painters and sculptors spend time in their gallery/studios or are found working nearby. Some lead regular workshops, and many demonstrate techniques at the Rockport Art Association—which has regular Tuesday- and Thursday-evening demonstrations in July and August—or through the North Shore Arts Association. There are regularly scheduled art classes year-round sponsored by the RAA. Both towns' artists join forces for "Open Studio" days a couple of times a season.

Rockport

About 40 galleries open seasonally, most of them on Main Street or nearby Bearskin Neck. There are also galleries located off Route 127 and 127A—most of them well marked. Rockport artists pride themselves on the fact that the artist–gallery owner is usually available to chat with customers during some part of the week. The Main Street galleries include those of Donald and Christine Mosher, Ivan Kamalic, and John Caggiano. Ohrvel Carlson has a gallery on Broadway. Several artists are represented in Fine Arts of Rockport on Main Street. Bob Lerch, a talented photographer, has a gallery on Bearskin Neck. The Mercury Gallery at 20 Main Street represents many fine artists.

Public Art

There are several public buildings where you can view art by Cape Ann artists in Rockport. The post office on Broadway and the Rockport National Bank on Main Street both have large expressive paintings of waterfront scenes by native son W.

Motif #1 in Rockport Harbor

Lester Stevens, who was a member of the National Academy. A charming bronze sculpture, *Baby and Frog* by Richard Recchia, is just outside the Rockport Art Association at 12 Main Street. Paintings by Aldro Hibbard, Emile Gruppe, Stanley Woodward, and Anthony Thieme, all well-known Cape Ann artists, are among those on view in the Rockport Town Hall on Broadway and in the public library on School Street. The Sandy Bay Historical Society on King Street also has many works by local artists.

Motif #1, the red fishing shack in Rockport Harbor that so many have painted, can be seen from between the buildings on Mount Pleasant Street, from T Wharf, or from the wharves off Bearskin Neck.

Gloucester

Rocky Neck in East Gloucester (off East Main Street) is where some 30 artists live and work, including Robert Gruppe, third-generation artist; John Nesta, Ward Mann, and Judith Steele Goetemann. In 1999, for the first time ever, the publication *ART NOW* produced a special edition of *Gallery Guide to Rockport and Gloucester.* Rocky Neck is a wonderful place to prowl and has several restaurants where you can stop for a bite. A harbor full of boats is engaging to watch; you can sit on the open-air decks of three restaurants and do so.

The **Fishermen's Wives** statue on Stacy Boulevard in Gloucester

Public Art

Probably the most famous piece of art in Gloucester is the man-at-the-wheel statue by Leonard Craske that overlooks Gloucester Harbor from Stacy Boulevard. Installed in 1923, on the 300th anniversary of the seaport, the statue is now enhanced by tablets containing more than 5,000 names of fishermen lost at sea from Gloucester vessels. In 2001 a second statue, this one known as the *Fishermen's Wives Memorial*, was dedicated. Designed by Morgan Faulds Pike, this bronze sculpture shows a mother with a baby in her arms and a young boy at her knees. She is peering out to sea as if in search of a missing fisherman spouse. It's located off the Boulevard on the other side of the Blynman Bridge, the drawbridge that spans the Annisquam River.

The Art Associations

♦ **Rockport Art Association** (978-546-6604), 12 Main Street, Rockport. Founded in 1921 in the studio of the late Aldro T. Hibbard, the RAA occupies three large buildings on Main Street. The high-ceilinged main gallery to the rear of the complex is where major exhibitions regularly are mounted. This is also the location for demonstrations—demos—by Cape Ann artists on Tuesday and Thursday evenings in July and August. These are free to members; otherwise, adults pay $4 and children, $2. They are worth every penny. You sit for about 2 hours as a painting is brought to life, an artist explaining his or her techniques along the way. Open Monday through Saturday 10–5, Sunday noon–5. Closed in January and on winter Mondays. The exhibitions are free for viewing—you may make a donation.

♦ **North Shore Arts Association** (978-283-1857), 197R East Main Street (Pirates Lane), Gloucester. Wonderfully situated on the water's edge, overlooking the inner harbor and Smith's Cove, the big red wood building that houses the arts association is a great place to visit. Two major juried artist members' exhibitions are presented each season, with several rotating smaller exhibits. In 2002 a fascinating show, *Legacy,* showed the works of families of artists who worked—and some still work—on Cape Ann, including the Gruppes, Curtises, Beals, and Hudsons. Late May to late October, Monday through Saturday 10–5, Sunday noon–5. It's usually easy to park here, and you might even bring a picnic to lunch nearby. Free.

Theater

♦ **Gloucester Stage Company** (978-281-4099; box office 978-281-4433), The Gorton Theatre, 267 East Main Street, Gloucester. Israel Horovitz is founder and longtime artistic director for this summer theater company. Approximately six shows per season are offered. Showtimes are Wednesday through Saturday at 8 PM and Sunday at 5 PM. Tickets, $25 each. Rush seats.

♦ **North Shore Music Theatre** (978-232-7200; www.nsmt.org), 62 Dunham Road, Beverly. Folks from Cape Ann drive down Route 128 to Beverly for these Broadway musicals presented in the round. Performances are Tuesday through Saturday evenings at 8 except the second Tuesday at 7; Wednesday, Saturday, and Sunday matinees at 2 PM. $20–56.

Museums and Historic Houses

♦ **Cape Ann Historical Museum** (978-283-0455), 27 Pleasant Street, Gloucester. This is one of the best small museums in New England. Its art collection alone is stunning. An entire main-floor gallery is devoted to the marine paintings of native son Fitz Hugh Lane. These are gorgeous. Other galleries display work by Maurice Prendergast, Milton Avery, John Sloane, Nell Blaine, and others—artists who worked on Cape Ann. There is a new sculpture garden with works by sculptors who labored in the area. The museum's Fisheries and Maritime Collections are especially rich. There are photographs of the life at sea, scale models of famous vessels sailing out of Gloucester, and the actual ships used by some famous Gloucester sailors—including Howard Blackburn, who sailed solo across the Atlantic Ocean more than once. Furniture and decorative arts from Gloucester homes also find a place in this wonderful museum. Tuesday through Saturday 10–5. Closed February. Adults $5, retirees $4.50, students $3.50.

♦ **Sandy Bay Historical Society and Museum** (978-546-9533), 40 King Street, Rockport. Local artworks are among the pieces displayed in the **Sewall Scripture House,** a beautiful granite-block structure. Levi Sewall built the house in 1832 with granite from his own quarry. Exhibits include a Victorian parlor, marine room, a keeping room, quarrying tools, and a children's room. There are also paintings by well-known Rockport artists including Aldro Hibbard, Wayne Morrell, George Harvey, Alfred Wiggin, and Harrison Cady. Local Rockport scenes and important historical enterprises, such as granite workers, are among the subjects. Open mid-June to mid-September, Thursday through Saturday 2–5 PM; year-round, Monday 9 AM–1 PM. Adults $3, children $2.

♦ **Beauport** (978-283-0800; www.spnea.org), 75 Eastern Point Boulevard, Gloucester. The home of the late interior designer Henry Davis Sleeper of Boston is an exceptional house museum operated by the Society for the Preservation of New England Antiquities (SPNEA). Located on Eastern Point in Gloucester, with sweeping views of Gloucester Harbor, it was named for the expression used by French explorer Samuel de Champlain when he first saw the same harbor—*beau port* or "beautiful harbor." Sleeper used the house as a summer home and tinkered endlessly with it. The guide for our 2-hour tour helped us understand that Beauport was as much Sleeper's beloved hobby as it was his living "catalog," a place to show off the kinds of things he could do as an interior decorator. Each of the 26 rooms visited is in a different style or color scheme, and there are many whimsical touches. The owner was fascinated by old architectural materials and often purchased other houses or parts of them to incorporate into rooms at Beauport. Although the house is quite dark in some areas—and some rooms are very small—he was also a champion of the bay window and of skylights. The pine kitchen is famous, a studied reproduction of an early American keeping room that showcases Sleeper's redware collection. For the student of architecture, of antiques, of color, of fabrics, of pottery, this is a place that ought to be visited. Open May through September 15, Monday through Friday; tours hourly 10–4. September 15 through October 15, open daily, with tours hourly 10–4. Adults $6, seniors $5.50, children and students $3.

♦ **The Sargent House Museum** (978-281-2432), 49 Middle Street, Gloucester. The art enthusiast will be intrigued by the drawings and paintings done by the great New England artist John Singer Sargent on the second floor of this elegant Georgian mansion. The house sits high above Gloucester's Main Street and overlooks the harbor. The views must have been grand when the structure was built in 1782 for Judith Sargent Murray, a philosopher, writer, and women's rights activist. She was also a distant relative of the famous painter. Her husband, the Reverend John Murray, was the founder of Universalism in America. The museum has a fine small collection of early American furnishings and textiles, China trade porcelain, oil portraits, and personal items. The house's architectural details, particularly elaborate dentil molding, an incredible serpentine newel post, and graceful balusters, are of particular interest. Before leaving, pick up a flyer with the heading WELCOME TO THE HISTORIC DISTRICT and take your own walking tour of the neighborhood. Open Memorial Day through Columbus Day, Friday through Monday noon–4. Adults $5, seniors $4, free to children under 12.

Tours

♦ **Footprints Walking Tours** (978-546-7730; www.footprintsofrockport.com), Bearskin Neck, North Road, Rockport. Vicki Hogan and assistants conduct 60-minute historic walking tours of Rockport. The tours, offered daily in-season, are of the Bearskin Neck area, Rockport Harbor, and to the Headlands, a public park from which a panoramic view of harbor and ocean is seen. Vicki likes to get into the background of the town, which separated from Gloucester in 1840. The Hannah Jumper House, a white house that backs up to the harbor, is the place to hear about Hannah's brigade of 60 Rockport women who set out on July 8, 1856, to rid the town of liquor. Unhappy because their fishermen-husbands were away at sea most of the time and then in the taverns when "at home," they took hatchets and broke open kegs and barrels, allowing the liquor to run into the streets. A local magistrate upheld their actions, and Rockport is still a dry town. Tours at 11, 1, and 3 for adults, $8; kids' tours at 10 and 2, $5. Evening lantern tours on customized schedules. Reservations are requested.

♦ **Moby Duck Tours** (978-281-DUCK), Harbor Loop, Rogers Street, Gloucester. Weekends Memorial Day through September; daily mid-June through Labor Day. Tours on the hour 10–4. These amphibious vehicles take riders on a 1-hour tour of Gloucester. The "ducks" bounce through the streets and then enter the waters of Gloucester Harbor at the Boulevard. Tours are narrated. Adults $14, seniors $12, children, $8. No credit cards.

♦ **Harbor Tours, Inc.** (978-283-1979), Harbor Loop, Gloucester. Harbor tour and lobstering trip, 1 hour long, leaves at 1 PM daily. A lighthouse tour, which is a circumnavigation of Cape Ann, takes 2½ hours and leaves at 2:30 PM daily in-season. Reservations are advised. Harbor tour, $10 adults, $5 children; lighthouse tour, $20 adults, $10 children.

♦ **Tour Cape Ann** (877-552-TOUR; www.tourcapeann.com), 14 Parker Street, Gloucester. Narrated tours of 90 minutes each (Gloucester or Rockport) are offered from April to November. They are scheduled between 10 and 4. Air-conditioned cars or vans pick up passengers at any B&B, inn, hotel, motel, or private residence in Gloucester or Rockport. Adults $15, seniors $13, children $6. Customized tours are also available.

Beaches

The waters off Cape Ann are brisk, and swimming is usually not comfortable until July at least. September can be spectacular. In **Rockport,** Front Beach right in town is a little gem; a short walk beyond it is Back Beach; both have access to toilet facilities. Cape Hedge Beach at the end of South Street is stony in high tide but wonderful when the water is a bit lower; Pebble Beach nearby off Penzance Road is also stony. Old Garden Beach is close to town (reached off Old Garden Road). Nearby there is a shoreline path, Old Garden Path, accessible from several points and wonderful for walking. Parking stickers are required and are only available to residents.

In **Gloucester** my favorite is sandy Good Harbor Beach on Route 127A. The parking lot fills up fast, and nonresident parking fees can be pricey—$20 on weekends, $15 weekdays. There are changing facilities and a snack stand. If you can park near the footbridge on Bass Avenue and walk in, you're lucky. Wingaersheek Beach on Atlantic Street is a bit of a drive and tends to be shallow—but families love it. Parking fees are the same as at Good Harbor. Niles Beach on Eastern Point Road is smaller and has parking for residents only. Overnight camping is strictly prohibited on all Cape Ann beaches.

Golf

The **Cape Ann Golf Course** in nearby Essex offers nine holes and is open to the public. The **Rockport Golf Club** on Country Club Road is semiprivate, with non-members allowed to play weekdays.

Whale-Watches

Gloucester and Rockport are famous starting points for whale-watches. Most are half-day trips. **Cape Ann Whale Watch** (1-800-877-5110) leaves from Rose's Wharf, Gloucester. **Seven Seas Whale Watch** (978-283-1776; 1-888-283-1776) goes out from Seven Seas Wharf on Rogers Street (Route 127), Gloucester. **Captain Bill's Whale Watch** (978-283-6995; 1-800-33-WHALE) departs from Harbor Loop in Gloucester. **The Yankee Fleet** (1-800-942-5464) leaves from 75 Essex Avenue (Route 133), Gloucester. Reservations are a good idea.

Sea Kayaking

◆ **North Shore Outdoor Center** (978-546-5050; www.northshorekayak.com), Tuna Wharf, Bearskin Neck, Rockport. This is a major kayaking center. Guided tours are offered, boats rented and sold, and equipment available. An overnight camping trip to nearby Thacher Island with its twin lights is one of the trips offered. Kayaks rent for $15–25 for a half day; $25–40 for a full day.

Lobstering Trips

◆ **Rockport Lobstering Trips and Island Cruises** (978-546-3642), T Wharf, Rockport. Morning trips at 9:30 and 11 are about 90 minutes long and show how lobsters are caught. Adults $10, children $6. Afternoon trips at 1:30 and 3 take an hour and cruise around Thacher Island with its twin lighthouses. The cost is $8 for adults, $5 for children.

Movies

◆ **The Little Art Cinema** on School Street, Rockport, on the second floor of the Spiran Lodge building, is the best little movie theater. Only one film is offered, usually two viewings, on weekend nights, and everybody goes. The films are fairly current. If you don't like the movie, wait until next weekend. Closed in winter.

Parks, Drives, and Walks

◆ **Halibut Point State Park** on Gott Avenue, off Route 127, Rockport, is open 8–8 daily, Memorial Day through Labor Day. A parking fee is charged. This is a beautiful site with an easy walk out on flat rocks to the edge of the ocean—perfect for picnics. You can also walk around the old Babson Farm Quarry—a quarry that operated until 1929. It's a beautiful, serene area. No swimming.

♦ **The Headlands** off Atlantic Avenue, Rockport, is very near the center of the village, but a world apart. On the busiest summer day you can walk out Atlantic Avenue, past attractive harborfront homes, to this wonderful open, flat-rock area for a panoramic view of town, harbor, and ocean. There are granite benches for sitting. Artists like to work here.

♦ **Eden Road** and **Marmion Way,** both south of the village off 127A, are the best roads for viewing the ocean as you ride along. Eden Road has a long, rocky section that leads down to the water. If you can find a place to park your car—or if you're on a bike—you may want to clamber over the rocks or have a picnic here.

The **Bass Rocks** section of Gloucester along Atlantic Road offers vistas of crashing ocean. People love to walk the rocks here, and artists sometimes are seen painting the wild sea.

Eastern Point Lighthouse is reached via Eastern Point Avenue. You drive past mansions to get there—just tell the guard at the entrance in summer that you are going out to the lighthouse. Here you can walk on a short path to the huge flat breakwater, and you can fish from the breakwater or walk all the way out. It's cool and windy and grand.

Annual Events

The **Rockport Art Association Auction** is held on a Saturday in early May and is the association's major fund-raiser. People come from around the country to bid on original works of art by deceased Cape Ann artists. It's a lively session. For information, call the art association at (978) 546-6604.

♦ **Rockport Chamber Music Festival** takes place on Thursday through Sunday for three weekends at the Rockport Art Association, Rockport. High-level talent appears for these concerts, many of them sellouts. Arrive early to find a parking place. Most concerts start at 8 PM, with a 5 PM concert on Sunday. Call (978) 546-7391.

Concerts at the Rockport Bandstand take place every Sunday in July and August at 7:30 PM. The bandstand is located off Beach Street. Folks spread out blankets and bring folding chairs. It's a fun local event, one that has been held for many years.

The **Blessing of the Fleet** in Gloucester occurs during the St. Peter's Fiesta on the last weekend in June. This festival is a 3-day extravaganza with everything from a parade of sail to arts and crafts booths to a greasy pole contest. The bishop does bless the fleet on Sunday afternoon. Much of the activity centers on the Boulevard. Local artists did chalk paintings on the sidewalks and streets in 2002.

Annual Christmas Pageant. This is an amazing outdoor pageant that takes place just as the streets get dark on the Saturday before Christmas. The biblical story of the Nativity is acted out, with players walking up Main Street and then gathering at a crèche on the lawn of the First Congregational Church, where a carol sing is held. It's a lovely event, more than 50 years old.

New Year's Rockport Eve on December 31 is a low-key, delightful evening held 6–midnight. After purchasing a button, you can go to a different venue on each hour—to hear musicians, see theatrical events, and so on. Parents bring their kids. It's really fun.

Shopping

After visiting the art galleries on Main Street in **Rockport,** check out **Tuck's** for fudge and candies; **The Madras Shop** for casual clothes for all members of the family; and **Toad Hall,** a fine independent bookstore in an old granite bank building, whose proceeds go to environmental causes. Women's fashions are found at **Willoughby's, Sand Castles,** and **The Enchanted Lady.** The **John Tarr Store** is the place to get menswear including foul-weather gear, preppy pants and sweaters, shoes, and sandals. **Hannah Wingate** and **Woodbine** have the best antiques. **N. Cassel** in Dock Square has the most tasteful gifts imaginable, including candles, soaps, glasses—all sorts of wonderful items. **La Provence,** also in Dock Square, has lovely items from France. **Books from Yesterday** on Main Street in the big red building is a wonderful used-book shop; owner Jeanne Speizer will search for books for you.

In **Gloucester** we're partial to the **Stone Leaf** gift store on Main Street. **The Glass Sail Boat** has clothing and giftware. **The Bookstore** at 61 Main Street is a good one and usually carries the lovely hardcover book *Artists of Cape Ann.* **Bananas** on Main Street is a wild place with vintage clothing, jewelry, and funky items of various sorts. There's a branch on Rocky Neck in East Gloucester along with some other interesting little shops that seem to come and go. But not Bananas; it's here to stay.

WHERE TO STAY

Most of the accommodations—and nearly all the small B&Bs—are found in Rockport. Gloucester has some good motels with great water views. The prices tend to be low in Rockport compared to other parts of coastal New England. Many places are open seasonally. If you're staying in Rockport—and may eat out in a nearby restaurant—you may want to pack a bottle of wine. Rockport is a dry town, but restaurants are glad to have you bring your own.

IN ROCKPORT

♦ **Rocky Shores Inn & Cottages** (978-546-2823; 1-800-348-4003; www.rockportusa. com/rockyshores), 65 Eden Road, Rockport, MA 01966. Perhaps because my family and I stayed here on our first-ever visit to Rockport in the mid-1970s, I have always been partial to this inn. Owned and operated for 20-plus years by Renate and Gunter Kostke, the complex consists of a gracious main inn with nine rooms, nine two-bedroom cottages with full kitchen facilities, and two ocean-view housekeeping cottages with three bedrooms each. All are painted deep brown with white trim. Thacher Island with its twin lights sits directly offshore in front of the inn. From the wide front porch you can watch the changing ocean moods and—at night—the steady flash of the lighthouse beams. Rooms across the front of the main inn—spacious and airy—have great views. They have wall-to-wall carpeting and a TV. There is one first-floor room. The immaculately kept knotty-pine-walled cottages out back are good for families. These two-bedroom units have one room with double bed and one with twins, plus a living room/kitchen across the front. In order to get a view, you have to walk out to the front of the inn. Two larger cottages out front have three bedrooms, picture windows, and good-sized living rooms. A buffet breakfast for inn guests is served in an ocean-view dining room with small separate tables. Hard-boiled eggs are always served. Cottages are rented by the week only in the high season, but may be available on weekends in spring or fall. This area is great for walking; two small beaches are not far. Open mid-May to end of October. Doubles in the inn, $95–152.

♦ **Eden Pines Inn** (978-546-2505; www.edenpinesinn.com), 48 Eden Road, Rockport, MA 01966. New owners—in 2002—of this smashing oceanfront B&B are Bob Kern of Madison, New Jersey, and his son and daughter-in-law, Michael and Nicole Kern. Nicky—as Nicole is known—is the innkeeper, assisted by a capable staff. She, her husband, two young children, and a black Lab make this their home. Six guest rooms all have a balcony or outdoor deck overlooking the ocean, with the waves splashing on rocks below. Five rooms on the second floor and one on the third all have private bath. Many are in a summery yellow-and-blue color scheme; crocheted white spreads are often found on the beds. The third-floor room is especially large with a king-sized bed, a tub plus separate stall shower in the bathroom, and pale blue wall-to-wall carpeting. Guests love to sunbathe on their balconies. Sunbathing or fishing from the rocks is also encouraged. The house was built in 1900 as a summer home and was run for more than 30 years by the Sullivans, who gave it a great sense of style. The common living room has pine paneling and a wood-burning stone fireplace. A wraparound sunporch furnished in wicker has ocean views. Here is where guests have a continental-plus breakfast. There's a refrigerator for guest use. Original works of art adorn the walls. Open May through October. Doubles, $195–205.

♦ **Seacrest Manor** (978-546-2211; www.seacrestmanor.com), 99 Marmion Way, Rockport, MA 01966. Dwight B. MacCormack Jr. and the late Leighton T. Saville opened this wonderful small inn in 1972 and soon gained a reputation for having one of the best B&Bs in town. "Decidedly small. Intentionally quiet" is the inn's motto. Dwight continues as innkeeper, making the breakfasts for which the inn has long been famous—a fresh mixed fruit cup, freshly squeezed orange juice, hot spiced Irish oatmeal, eggs and bacon or sausage, and a specialty item—perhaps banana pancakes! There are six rooms with private bath, and two small rooms that share a bath—usually rented together and located at a very private end of the second-floor hall. All rooms have a television, and a daily newspaper is delivered each morning. Two rooms are on the main floor; the rest are on the second floor. A large wood deck off the second floor—with distant views of the ocean and the twin lighthouses—is divided in three. Two rooms each have their own section; the third part is shared by other guests. There are sitting areas in the gorgeous gardens. Wonderful paintings adorn the walls, especially those of the sunken living room with bow window where guests gather to read, relax, and chat. Open mid-April to November 1 and on weekends only in November. Doubles with private bath, $150 and $170; doubles with shared bath, $98.

♦ **The Captain's House** (978-546-3825), 69 Marmion Way, Rockport, MA 01966. "We've got the best rocks in Rockport," quipped George Dangerfield, who with his wife, Carole, runs this five-room B&B right on the ocean. Indeed, terraces have been created among the rocks where chaises are set out. Our group of three women enjoyed predinner wine there, with the surging surf just beyond. All rooms have private bath and are on the second floor. Forget about televisions—you'll have to count on reading, relaxing, and enjoying the smashing view for entertainment. (There is a TV on the breakfast porch for group use.) A large living room—with fireplaces at both ends—is done in soft hues and has a beamed ceiling. Directly off the open oceanside porch, it also has excellent water views. The Dangerfields are knowledgeable about Rockport and Gloucester and can steer you toward good dining and sight-seeing. The guest rooms are furnished mostly with reproduction furniture and have double, queen, or twin beds. A corner room with nonworking fireplace and smashing views of the ocean also has two cozy window seats. Another room has its own separate sunporch. A continental breakfast is set out on the enclosed breakfast porch. Doubles, $100–150. Open February to mid-December.

♦ **The Seafarer Inn** (978-546-6248; 1-800-394-9394; www.seafarer-inn.com), 50 Marmion Way, Rockport, MA 01966. Dolores and Stephen Vagi, formerly of Chicago where he taught at DePaul University, took over this B&B in 2001. Stephen is an MIT graduate who wanted to come east again after retirement. The Seafarer offers many rooms with partial or full ocean views. All seven guest rooms have a queen-sized bed, small refrigerator, and TV. The Captain's Quarters on the second floor is a spacious room with Oriental-style rug and an old-fashioned bathtub with hand shower. On the third floor both large rooms with ocean views have a small kitchenette. A continental-plus breakfast includes home-baked breads, coffee cake, and fruit spreads. Guests can take trays to the outside porch or into the adjoining living room. Open year-round. Doubles, $110–275.

♦ **Addison Choate Inn** (978-546-7543; 1-800-245-7543; www.addisonchoate.com), 49 Broadway, Rockport, MA 01966. Cynthia Francis, a Gloucester native and former restaurateur, and Ed Cambron, who used to give tours of Cape Ann, are the new innkeepers at this wonderfully located village inn. Now a soft peach color with cream trim and black shutters, the Addison Choate is a late Greek Revival house set sidewise on a lot close to the center of town. The main-floor common rooms are especially inviting, including a fireplaced dining area, formal parlor, and small TV room with two cozy nooks, one with a telephone. There are six guest rooms in the main house, one a suite with its own entrance. All have private bath and queen beds or two twins that can be put together to form a king. They are tastefully furnished in an early American style. A main-floor room with wide-pine floorboards has dark blue wallpaper, a crocheted canopy queen bed, and two wing chairs covered in a subtle plaid. A quilt is placed at the foot of each bed. Breakfast is extravagant and may include a veggie omelet with cheese, scones, home-baked coffee cake or Irish soda bread, homemade granola, fruits, and beverages. Doubles, $110–175.

♦ **The Sally Webster Inn** (978- 546-9251; 1-877-546-9251; www.sallywebster.com), 34 Mount Pleasant Street, Rockport, MA 01966. This gray-clapboard house with deep red shutters is a comfortable B&B close to the village shopping district, yet far enough to be out of the fray on busy summer weekends. John and Kathy Fitzgerald, who had vacationed in Rockport for years, fulfilled a dream when they became innkeepers. The house dates from 1832 and has original wide-plank pine floors, six fireplaces, herringbone brick terraces, and colonial flower and herb gardens. On cool evenings a fire burns in the parlor. Seven guest rooms—all with private bath—have a queen- or king-sized bed. The first-floor room, Sally's Room, has twin beds that can be joined as a king, lace curtains at the windows, an electric fireplace set into the fireplace opening, and a bathroom with pedestal sink and stall shower. On the third floor is a jaunty room in red, white, and blue with a ceiling painted like sky and clouds. In a crisp blue-and-white breakfast room, a continental breakfast of fresh fruit, muffins, juices, and hot beverages is served. Closed January. Doubles, $85–115.

♦ **Lantana House** (978-546-3535; 1-800-291-3535; www.shore.net/~lantana), 22 Broadway, Rockport, MA 01966. This house—gray with purple shutters—has a great village location. And its large front porch overlooking the busy street, Broadway, is a fine place to sit and watch the passing scene. In a retail space just below the house, the chamber of commerce has its office—what could be more convenient? Innkeepers Vicky and Steve VanDerwerken have labored hard to decorate and renovate the inn, putting in many new bathrooms. Rooms have a crisp look with all-white George Washington–style bedspreads on queen and twin beds. There are five air-conditioned rooms, all with private bath and small television. Room 3 on the second floor has wicker furniture and a real summery feeling. Breakfast is served in the dark green main-floor parlor, where guests pick up juice, fresh-baked breads and muffins, and hot beverages either to eat in the room or take out onto the porch. There is also a side terrace with tables and chairs. Once you've parked your car, you can walk everywhere. Doubles, $85–95. Open year-round.

♦ **The Inn on Cove Hill** (978-546-2701; 1-888-546-2701), 37 Mount Pleasant Street, Rockport, MA 01966. Betsy Eck claims she had no intention of becoming an innkeeper—but when she walked into this vintage B&B in Rockport, "I loved the house immediately and felt like I was home." That afternoon she made an offer on the property. She took to renovating the house with a vengeance—adding a new cedar-shake roof and 48 new weathertight windows, solidifying the foundation, and removing vinyl siding to reveal original clapboards. Now a sign on the house, originally built in 1771 and added onto in 1830, reads CALEB NORWOOD JR. for the original owner. There are eight guest rooms, six with private bath. Two small guest rooms on the third floor—often rented by two friends traveling together—share a bath. All rooms have air-conditioning and television. Room 4 is especially pretty with a four-poster queen-sized bed with quilt at the foot, tiny blue-and-white-print wallpaper, and a clawfoot tub in bathroom with a shower. The deck off the third floor has a to-die-for view of Rockport Harbor. There is also a small second-floor deck. Stairs from the first to the second and third floors are narrow and steep, but it's an old house. Two rooms are on the first floor, one with private entrance. Betsy serves an expanded continental breakfast on bone china in the dining room and outdoors. It includes muffins, bagels, fruit, and yogurt. Open year-round. Doubles, $95–140.

♦ **Tuck Inn** (978-546-7260; 1-800-789-7260; www.thetuckinn.com), 17 High Street, Rockport, MA 01966. Despite the corny name, this little 10-room inn on a side street of town is a find. In addition to its well-kept guest rooms, it has an in-ground pool—a real plus. Liz and Scott Wood have been caring innkeepers here for a dozen years. The continental-plus breakfast set out in the dining room is enough to keep you going for a good while and includes many baked items. Two rooms accommodate families of up to four. Decorating is homey and comfortable, and all rooms have private bath. An additional efficiency unit can accommodate four. Doubles, $79–139. Open year-round.

♦ **Yankee Clipper Inn** (978-546-3407; 1-800-545-3699; fax 978-546-9730; www. yankeeclipperinn.com), 127 Granite Street, Rockport, MA 01966. Location! Two oceanfront buildings, a breakfast room with an unequaled view of the sea, a heated saltwater swimming pool, and a grassy lawn and beautiful gardens comprise the Yankee Clipper. For years the Ellis family ran the inn—including a separate building across the street that is now an independently operated bed & breakfast—until Cathy and Randy Marks bought it in 2001. Jack and Jackie Kennedy stayed here when he was campaigning for president. John Lennon and Yoko Ono were also guests at one time. Now there are 16 rooms with private bath—8 in each building. Guests check in at an oceanfront 1929 art deco mansion. An ample breakfast is set out buffet-style at one end of a large common room and enjoyed in a glassed-in dining area with killer ocean views. Rooms on the second and third floors of the main inn are furnished with a mixture of antiques and traditional pieces. The Red Jacket is a second-floor suite with a queen and a single bed plus a wicker-filled porch with views of the sea. Sea Witch has an adjoining room with wicker pullout sofa. In the more contemporary Quarterdeck building, rooms on four levels all have sea views. New marble bathrooms with whirlpool tubs have been installed in some rooms. Closed January and February. Doubles, $141–349.

♦ **Carlson's Bed and Breakfast** (978-546-2770), 43 Broadway, Rockport, MA 01966. Do you want to stay in the home of an artist? You can. Carol Carlson, whose husband, S. Ohrvel Carlson, is a highly regarded artist with a gallery in the house, offers a guest room with private bath and separate entrance. Guests enter from the back of the house, walk up a flight of stairs, and enjoy a room with canopy double bed. Well-behaved pets are welcome. Carol, who is an artist in her own right, makes a big breakfast—from bacon and eggs to pancakes. The house is well located in the village. Open year-round. Double, $80–90.

IN GLOUCESTER

♦ **Cape Ann Motor Inn** (978-281-2900; 1-800-464-VIEW), 33 Rockport Road, Gloucester, MA 01930. This three-story motor inn directly on the white sands of Long Beach is a great choice for the beach bum. The 31 rooms on three floors all have ocean views, and half have kitchenette. The so-called Honeymoon Suite has a working fireplace. Rooms have a double bed and a pullout sofa. Coffee, juice, and muffins are served in the fireplaced lobby in the morning. Under the ownership of Brad Pierce for 30 years, the motel is open year-round. This is a kid-friendly place. Doubles, $130; kitchenettes, $145.

♦ **Bass Rocks Ocean Inn** (978-283-7600; 1-800-528-1234), 107 Atlantic Road, Gloucester, MA 01930. This white-pillared, redbrick motor inn is connected to an 1899 oceanfront mansion where breakfast is taken. There's also a billiard and game room. Outdoors, there's a heated pool. And across the street is the ocean. Here it crashes up on huge boulders known as Bass Rocks—favored by anyone who likes to watch the changing sea. Now under the umbrella of the Best Western chain, the motel has 48 rooms on two levels. Each air-conditioned and heated room has two doubles or one king bed, a coffeemaker, refrigerator, television, and VCR with complimentary videos. Each also has a balcony or small patio with chairs. Artwork from the John Nesta gallery on Rocky Neck is displayed in the public rooms. The buffet breakfast includes blueberry muffins, breads, fruits, cereal, oatmeal, and a choice of juices and hot beverages. Books may be borrowed from the stocked shelves in the billiard room. Bicycles are available to borrow. Open late April through October. Doubles, $125–245.

♦ **Atlantis Motor Inn** (978-283-0014; 1-800-732-6313; www.atlantismotorinn.com), 125 Atlantic Road, Gloucester, MA 01930. This 40-room motel offers a terrific view of Bass Rocks from each balconied room—or, on the ground level, room with patio. The higher rooms have the best views. All have two double beds, air-conditioning, and rather contemporary furnishings. You can rent a refrigerator if you'd like. Breakfast is available at the adjoining Atlantis Café, where a full menu of breakfast items is offered. Good Harbor Beach, a wonderful sandy strand, is within walking distance. Walking or biking along the oceanfront is a prime activity in this neighborhood. Open from late April through late October. Doubles, $90–160.

♦ **Charles Hovey House** (978-281-7732; fax 978-281-7745; www.hoveyhouse.com), 4 Hovey Street, Gloucester, MA 01930. Views of Gloucester Harbor, Ten Pound Island (and its lighthouse), and Eastern Point Light are fabulous from the front porch of this pale peach mansion built as the first summerhouse in Gloucester in 1845. Jane and Rob Nickse took over the house from a private family in the late 1990s and now offer three guest rooms with private bath as well as a spot for weddings and special events. (In such cases several more bedrooms can be rented to one party.) The house's 12-foot ceilings and magnificent crown moldings attest to its fine workmanship. Guests enjoy the use of a pretty living room with couches and chairs slipcovered in white, and with a large bowl of seashells on the coffee table. If the weather is good, however, they are inclined to settle in on the large porch and just inhale that view. Jane keeps her gardens in lovely shape. A large mahogany dining room table is a place to gather for a continental-plus breakfast of Portuguese and Italian breads, something hot from the oven, and perhaps yogurt and fruit. The mural of the Gloucester salt marsh around this room is terrific. The two front second-floor guest bedrooms are corner rooms with cross-ventilation and interesting decor. Jane's collection of antique fans is on display. Two rooms have working fireplace. One has a bathroom that is up one flight. Air conditioners are available on request. Doubles, $135–290.

WHERE TO EAT

Most of Rockport's restaurants are seasonal, as are those on Rocky Neck in East Gloucester. Rockport is also a dry town, has been since the mid–19th century. Bring your own wine if you'd like to; the restaurants are happy to open it for you. Both towns have a range of dining places—from elegant to casual. Fish is, of course, king.

♦ **My Place By the Sea** (978-546-9667), 68 Bearskin Neck Road. This is the most romantic restaurant in town. Located at the very end of Bearskin Neck, with the ocean splashing on rocks below, the restaurant has two levels of outdoor dining with panoramic water views. There's an awning-covered terrace on one side with wrought-iron tables and chairs. The main room indoors, with soft pastel fabric-covered lights and pale mismatched chairs at tables with light-colored cloths, is also charming. Chef Kathy Milbury presents wonderfully creative cuisine; her partner, Barbara Stavropoulos, does the decorating and manages the front of the house. Having rented for years, the two women acquired their special spot in 2002. At lunch, the grilled chicken raspberry salad with mandarin oranges and spiced pecans is a stopper. Other possibilities ($7–12): freshly shucked lobster salad on a French baguette; a bowl of vegetarian chili; poached mussels; and Caesar salad with grilled chicken and portobello mushroom. The recipe for the Portuguese Fishermen's Stew on the dinner menu was requested by *Gourmet* magazine. Other favorites include appetizers like lobster wontons in spicy cucumber relish, or a grilled baby pear salad with Maytag blue cheese and candied walnuts. Dinner entrées stress seafood; the "My Place Swordfish" in a tangy béarnaise sauce with pecan butter and parsleyed potatoes is terrific. Finish up with warmed apple crunch and cinnamon ice cream drizzled with caramel sauce or "Best Ever" chocolate cake served with espresso ice cream, hot fudge sauce, and crushed chocolate-covered espresso beans. Open from mid-April through October. Lunch 11:30–3, dinner 5–9. Closed Tuesdays before Memorial Day and after Labor Day. Dinner reservations may be made after noon on the same day.

♦ **LoGrasso's After Hours** (978-546-7977), 13 Railroad Avenue. What is an Italian deli by day turns into an Italian bistro for dinner with red-and-white-checked tablecloths, a bustling atmosphere, and a convivial feel. Locals love it here, and one reason is that it's open for dinner on weekends year-round. Owners just throw a cloth over the deli case and soften the lighting. The food is excellent. Appetizers ($6–7) could be pan-seared sea scallops with basil sauce, or grilled boneless chicken with artichoke hearts and sweet red peppers in a Dijon sauce. Several salads are available—the tossed garden salad with a choice of homemade dressings is just $3. Entrées include sautéed scallops Puttanesca with artichoke hearts, pitted Italian olives, tomatoes, and herbs over linguine; homemade gnocchi sautéed with tomato, basil, and garlic; roast duck served with a Parmesan wild rice risotto; and steak braciole topped with pan-fried eggplant and tomato sauce. Entrées are $10–17; there's no corkage fee for the wine. Open for dinner from 5:30 Wednesday through Saturday in summer, Thursday through Saturday in winter. Reservations are important.

♦ **The Grand Café, Emerson's Inn by the Sea** (978-546-9500), 1 Cathedral Avenue, Rockport, MA 01966. The main dining room of this big white inn in the Pigeon Cove section of Rockport—north of the village—is well rated. Located off the main lobby, it's a somewhat formal room with dark red leatherlike chairs, white-clothed tables, and small shaded lamps on each table. Off the room is the veranda with distant views out to the water; meals are served there in summer. The Grand Café has an interesting policy of "lending" a bottle of wine to you if you have forgotten; your only requirement is to replace it—red with red, white with white.

They even have the phone number of a store that will deliver for you. Starters on the dinner menu include crispy sweet-and-sour calamari with fresh scallions, toasted sesame seeds, and Thai chili paste or a mélange of European mushrooms and Stilton cheese in puff pastry ($7–12). Entrées might be pan-seared, oven-roasted filet mignon stuffed with caramelized red onion and garlic chutney; roasted breast of chicken with Parma ham, spinach, and Fontina cheese; or pomegranate-glazed rack of New Zealand lamb ($19–29). Open for dinner nightly in-season and on Friday and Saturday nights in winter, when special evenings—like murder mystery dinners—are often offered. The inn has 36 rooms on three floors, half with ocean views, and a heated outdoor swimming pool.

♦ **The Fish Shack** (978-546-6667), 12 Dock Square. Located for years above Roy Moore's Lobster Co. (and fish store) on Bearskin Neck, the Fish Shack moved in 2002 to a more central location—and larger space—just off Dock Square. The new digs aren't quite as atmospheric as the old place (with all the fishing gear hanging from the ceilings and the view down onto Motif #1), but the views of the old port and Sandy Bay from here are still good. Most people sit in booths, with the window row being favored, of course. The connection with the fish store is still intact, and fish here is fresh, fresh, fresh. An all-day menu is available. You can get hamburgers, PB&J, or grilled cheese sandwiches; a clam roll with fries; clam or haddock chowder; and appetizers like scallops wrapped in bacon. For entrées, we're partial to the grilled salmon with dill butter (served with a tossed salad and a baked potato or fresh vegetable); grilled swordfish; haddock Provençal; or shrimp scampi over pasta (entrées $9–15). Lobsters (at market price) come in about six different ways, including twin lobsters with french fries—served to one person. If you are still hungry, you can finish up with a piece of chocolate truffle cake, pumpkin swirl cheesecake, or apple crisp tart, perhaps. Locals love the place, as do visitors, so you may have a wait for a table. Open from March through December, 11–9.

♦ **Portside Chowder House** (978-546-7045), 7 Tuna Wharf. Located just off Bearskin Neck, with fabulous views of Rockport Harbor and a selection of sandwiches, soups, and fried fish, this place gets the crowds. It's open year-round for lunch, with extended hours in summer. The food is adequate. You can get chowders: clam, corn, and Italian clam stew. Among the entrées, the salmon or swordfish with salad (at $12.50) was a good-sized portion and tasty. Lobster and crab rolls, fried fish sandwiches, and clam rolls are all available. The lines out the door sometimes mean a substantial wait. Between Memorial Day and Labor Day, open 11–8:30; in winter, open 11 to 2 or 3 for lunch.

♦ **The Greenery** (978-546-9593), 15 Dock Square. From the back room of this restaurant where there's table service you get a good view of the harbor and of Motif No. 1. But many visitors simply stay up front, off the busy square, where they can enjoy the good salad bar or order fresh sandwiches and pastries, grab a cappuccino or a cup of soup. This is one of those places that seem to have something for everyone. Among the popular sandwiches are fresh crab and avocado, turkey and avocado, the veggie burger or char-broiled hamburger, and the native crab roll. The muffins and breakfast pastries are great. Breakfast in the back room offers a full menu, as do lunch and dinner. Open daily in-season about 10–9. In winter hours are 10 to 5 or 6. Closed for about 3 weeks in March usually.

♦ **Flav's Red Skiff** (978-546-7647), 15 Mount Pleasant Street. The best breakfast in Rockport is available at this very popular little spot in the village. GREAT FOOD, GRUMPY COOKS read the T-shirts worn by waitresses. There is so little space to wait inside that customers are often ganged up on the sidewalk outside. Service is efficient but not rushed. Order the anadama bread French toast, the eggs Florentine (like Benedict, only over fresh spinach), the omelets such as tomato, basil, and cheese, the homemade pecan rolls. I like the way they cut the half grapefruit; it's so easy to eat. And the oatmeal with brown sugar and raisins is excellent. Copies of the *Boston Globe* are usually available so you can read a section. Flav's stays open through lunch, when excellent sandwiches, soups, and salads are available. Open daily about 6–2 year-round.

♦ **The Folly Cove Lobster Pool** (978-546-7808), 329 Granite Street (Route 127). Here's your basic lobster-in-the-rough place, with red picnic tables strewn across the lawn outside and wonderful views of the waters of Ipswich Bay. Of course you can eat inside, too, on an inclement day or when the picnic tables are taken (go early to get one). You can get a lobster, crab, or clam roll, fried seafood plates with coleslaw and french fries, and homemade desserts (blueberry cobbler once when we stopped). Bring along beer or wine if you want; soft drinks are available here. Open mid-May to October, daily 11:30–8:30.

♦ **Helmut's Strudel** on Bearskin Neck is a great place to stop for delectable pastries and coffee; a tiny deck out back allows you to enjoy them with a harbor view.

IN GLOUCESTER

♦ **Passports** (978-281-3680), 110 Main Street. Two side-by-side storefront dining rooms at the west end of Main Street in the shopping district are popular for lunch and dinner. Wonderful, creative cuisine emanates from the chef-owner Eric Lorden's kitchen. "International cuisine" is advertised, and there are always good choices. On a lunch menu you might find Jamaican fish cakes garnished with banana chutney or chicken satay as a starter. A Tuscan five-bean soup and a sea stew were offered one day. There are sandwiches, too, from a veggie roll-up to a Porto Burger (the mushroom marinated with soy and ginger first): $6–10. Seafood fettuccine (with the seafood changing according to the catch) is a popular dinner entrée. Others might be lobster ravioli, pork chops marinated with pink peppercorns and fresh citrus and served with a raspberry rhubarb compote, or Sister's Haddock, a popular dish in which haddock fillets are crusted with hazelnut and then panroasted. Entrées are $12–18. Open Monday through Saturday 11:30–10, Sunday from 5 for dinner only.

♦ **The Franklin** (978-283-7888), 118 Main Street. This somewhat dark little restaurant with booths on each side and a row of tables between is open for dinner only. It is the sister restaurant to one of the same name in Boston. Locals definitely gravitate here. In addition to a house mixed green salad, it's possible to order iceberg lettuce with smoked bacon, buttermilk dressing, and beets. Other starters include seared soy-marinated chicken liver with horseradish and fennel; warm napa cabbage salad with blue cheese and smoked bacon; and seared local scallops with celery root puree ($7–9). The most popular entrées ($15–18) are the lavender and honey basted salmon served with roast sweet potato, and roast turkey meat loaf with spiced fig gravy and chive mashed potatoes. You can also get prime sirloin *au poivre* and oven-braised osso buco. Open 4:30–midnight.

♦ **The Rudder** (978-283-7967), 73 Rocky Neck Avenue. The atmosphere at the Rudder—and the food—makes this the most popular restaurant on Rocky Neck. Located in a building that was once a fish-packing establishment with a sail loft above, it's dark and narrow with little white lights twinkling amid greenery on the ceiling and all sorts of little baubles and funky items about. We do hope the several references to the *Titanic* on the walls are just in fun. A gas fireplace in the corner can be welcome on a chilly June day. Heavy slat-backed library-style chairs are at tables indoors and on the protected part of a deck; beyond that there's a small open deck right over the waters of the inner harbor—the best place on a hot night. Lunch is available on Saturday and Sunday only and includes burgers, lobster roll, boiled lobster with fries and slaw, crabcakes, and oysters on the half shell for dipping. Dinner offers a raw bar, salads such as the classic Caesar or a grilled pear salad, and appetizers such as homemade ravioli, tuna tartare, and herbed artichoke dip with crostini. Entrées ($17–26) might be oven-baked scrod, the Rudder Steak grilled and served with red onion relish and roasted garlic mashed potatoes, or Caribbean pork tenderloin with red wine demiglaze. Prime rib is available Thursday, Friday, and Saturday nights. Open from mid-May through Halloween. Between mid-June and Labor Day, dinner is served nightly. On Saturday and Sunday the Rudder is open noon–midnight. There's a pub menu offered between lunch and dinner.

♦ **The Studio** (978-283-4123), 51 Rocky Neck Avenue, East Gloucester. Frank Ahearn's restaurant on Rocky Neck really was the location for an art school in the 1930s and 1940s. The art theme is carried throughout—from the white artist's palette tables in the lounge to fine works by Gloucester artists on the walls. Many are by Robert Gruppe, a major talent. There's a huge open deck overlooking Smith Cove where you can watch the water activity. Food is just okay, but the fish is fresh and it's delightful to sit of a Friday or Saturday evening and listen to the piano player in the bar. Entrées are in the $16–22 range, and grilled fish includes salmon, halibut, mahimahi, and the catch of the day. You can also get sandwiches and salads at lunch. Open 11–10 Memorial Day to October. The piano bar continues until midnight.

♦ **Halibut Point** (978-281-1900), 289 Main Street. This narrow brick restaurant—once the site of Howard Blackburn's famous tavern—is hands-down the favorite place for chowder on all of Cape Ann. Also known for its char-grilled burgers and fish and its convivial atmosphere—try to get in here on a Friday or Saturday night—the place has an adjacent outdoor patio that helps with summer crowds. Dennis Flavin has owned this popular spot for 20 years. Open daily 11:30–11.

♦ **Sailor Stan's** (978-281-4470), Rocky Neck, East Gloucester. This is a good little place for breakfast or lunch. Located at the V where the road splits and becomes one-way as you enter the neck, Sailor Stan's is in a little white house with a tiny deck out front. Breakfast includes eggs and veggie Benedict, many omelets including Portuguese with linguica (Portuguese sausage) and onion, breakfast sandwiches, pancakes, and French toast. At lunch you can get fish or clam chowder, chili, half sandwiches with chili or chowder, and hamburgers, linguica roll, and the usual sandwiches. Open April through December, daily except Monday 7 AM–1:30 PM. Weekends only in March. Closed January and February.

♦ **McT's** on the water in Gloucester is often mentioned for its lobsters. **The Boulevard Oceanview** on Stacy Boulevard opposite the harbor is a no-nonsense Portuguese restaurant—with a lot of American-style dishes. **Caffe Sicilia** on Main Street is the place to get good Italian pastries and a cup of cappuccino served in a real cup with a saucer.

4 Portland, Maine

The interaction between its islands and the city of Portland—to which all of them but independent Long Island belong politically—is just one of the things that make the appellation *city by the sea* so valid. The sea has been Portland's lifeblood for years, and it is the closeness of the water, its smell, its look, and the activity around it that also make the city a major attraction for visitors.

But this waterfront is much more than just a tourist destination. It's a working port from which fishing boats, freighters, lobstermen, and commercial passenger boats—the overnight boat to Nova Scotia, for instance—operate. The harbor is one of the deepest and best protected on the East Coast.

The islands of Casco Bay are such a part of Portland that some year-round residents commute as easily into the city as do Staten Islanders into Manhattan. From Peaks Island, so close that on a clear day it almost looks like a part of the city, it is but a 20-minute ride across.

Famous and favorite son is poet Henry Wadsworth Longfellow, whose boyhood home in Portland is open to the public as a house museum. When he was a child, he could view the waterfront from his third-floor bedroom. He wrote of his home city: "I remember the gray wharves and the ships, And the sea tides tossing free; And the beauty and mystery of the ships, And the magic of the sea."

Portland's best-known artist has to be Winslow Homer, famed for his seascapes. He lived for years and painted in a waterfront studio at Prouts Neck, an exclusive seaside community a few miles south of Portland. The Portland Museum of Art has a good selection of Homer's works.

Down by the waterfront is Portland's most exciting neighborhood, the Old Port. Here, buildings that were once warehouses for merchants now hold restaurants, one-of-a-kind shops, and art and crafts galleries. The narrow streets are eminently walkable, and once you've rid yourself of your car—hardly a necessity in this part of town—you may well find yourself entertained for hours.

Although Portland is not a large city, with an in-town population of less than 65,000, it is incredibly vibrant. Activity in the Old Port continues until late at night.

Portland Head Light, Maine's first lighthouse

Other neighborhoods are thriving as well, particularly an identifiable Downtown Arts District anchored by the fine Portland Museum of Art and galleries nearby. Congress Street, one of the major east–west thoroughfares, has experienced a resurgence of late. The opening of the wonderful Portland Public Market—with stalls for purveyors of fine foods from around the state and home to one of the top restaurants in the city—has given a major boost to its part of town.

Located on a 3½-mile peninsula stretching into the sea, Portland has both a Western Promenade and an Eastern Promenade. The west end of town with its tree-lined streets is home to beautiful brick mansions and residences, some of them turned into high-style bed & breakfast inns. The Eastern Promenade, a lovely drive with a public park overlooking the water, is a favorite place for bridal parties to stop and take photos, and for people to park and simply enjoy the beauty and activity of Casco Bay. There are also public boat launches here that are busy all summer long.

On a clear day and from a high enough vantage point—perhaps the Portland Observatory on Munjoy Hill—you can see the ocean to the east and the mountains of New Hampshire, even Mount Washington, to the west. South of Portland is Cape Elizabeth with the famous Portland Head Light, Maine's first lighthouse and one of the nation's most picturesque. It was commissioned by George Washington in 1791.

The city's symbol is the phoenix, an apt choice after its devastation on four different occasions by fire. It finally was rebuilt in the mid-1800s of brick, the mellow red stone and architecturally graceful designs of its buildings giving it almost the feel of a European city. Bustling outdoor cafés, busy streets, and a real working class enhance that image.

People move to Portland and stay. Natives don't go far—or they come back. The city seems filled with inventive entrepreneurs who have opened unusually fine restaurants, creatively decorated inns, and nifty retail shops and galleries. Portland is just great place to spend a weekend, any time of year.

Getting There

Take I-95 north and follow signs to I-295 and the ferry. Portland is about 2 hours north of Boston. U.S. Route 1 also goes through the city as it wanders along the coast.

The **Portland International Jetport** (207-774-7301) is just 3 miles from downtown Portland and is served by many major airlines, including American, Delta, and United. **Vermont Transit Lines/Greyhound** (207-772-6587) links Portland with Boston and coastal areas with frequent bus service.

From Yarmouth, Nova Scotia, to Portland, **Prince of Fundy Cruises** (207-775-5616) operates the *Scotia Prince* with auto and passenger service in-season.

Getting Around

Metro buses operate within the city and to nearby outlying areas. There are lots of places to park your car in Portland. Meters are 25 cents per half hour, but most limit you to 2 hours.

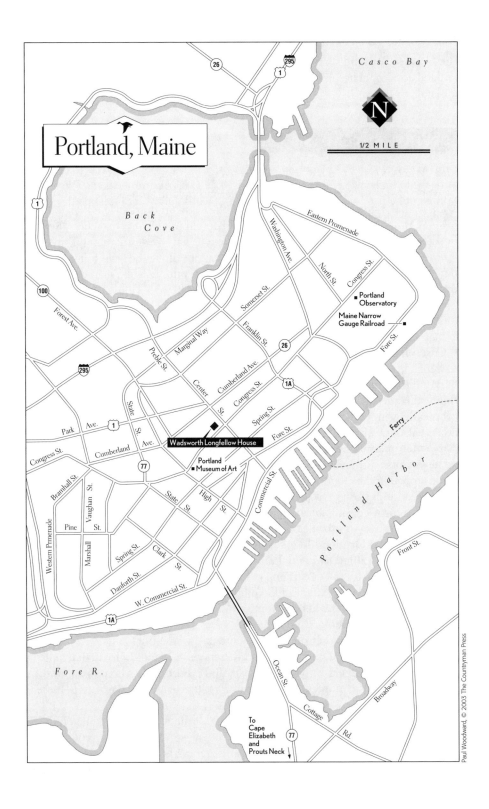

Portland, Maine

Casco Bay

N

1/2 MILE

Back Cove

Eastern Promenade

Washington Ave.

North St.

Congress St.

Portland Observatory

Maine Narrow Gauge Railroad

Somerset St.

Franklin St.

Fore St.

Marginal Way

Preble St.

Center St.

Cumberland Ave.

Congress St.

Spring St.

Fore St.

State St.

Park Ave.

Congress St.

Cumberland Ave.

Wadsworth Longfellow House

Portland Museum of Art

Bramhall St.

Vaughan St.

State St.

High St.

Commercial St.

Portland Harbor

Ferry

Front St.

Pine St.

Marshall St.

Spring St.

Clark St.

Danforth St.

W. Commercial St.

Western Promenade

Fore R.

Ocean St.

Broadway

Cottage Rd

To Cape Elizabeth and Prouts Neck

Forest Ave.

For More Information

The **Greater Portland Convention & Visitors Bureau** (207-772-5800; www.visit-portland.com) operates its central information service at 305 Commercial Street, Portland.

SEEING AND DOING

The Waterfront and the Islands

Everyone, it seems, wants to be near the water in Portland. You can get pretty close as you walk the streets and shop the stores of the Old Port district. The Portland Regency Hotel, an upscale hostelry located in an old brick armory, anchors the district at its east end. Narrow streets like Exchange, Wharf (pedestrians only), and Fore Street wind through. Commercial Street runs directly along the waterfront, and some of the restaurants here (Flatbread, RiRa's Irish pub, DiMillo's famous floating restaurant) have waterside decks or views. Gilbert's Chowder House on Commercial is said to have the best clam chowder in town.

Of course the most satisfying way to be near the water is to be out on it. You can do that, too.

♦ **Casco Bay Lines** (207-774-7871; www.cascobaylines.com), Casco Bay Ferry Terminal, 56 Commercial Street, Portland. Founded in 1845, this business claims to have the oldest continuing service of one kind at least—the famous mailboat, which runs several times a day to inhabited islands of Casco Bay. The enterprise technically went bankrupt in 1980, and the current line is run by the quasi-municipal Casco Bay Island Transit District. The ferry terminal, which feels like a large metropolitan bus or train depot with slat-backed benches and people reading newspapers as they wait with their luggage, is a busy place. It operates the major service to the islands.

The islands of Casco Bay, although not so far offshore, seem rough and remote. Each has its own personality and loyal followers.

Passenger service is provided to Chebeague Island, Cliff Island, Diamond Cove (a resort on Great Diamond Island with a restaurant, Diamond's Edge, nearby), Great Diamond, Little Diamond, Long Island, and Peaks Island. Although there are many more ferries to Peaks Island (where most commuters live and where some day-trippers head) than to many of the other islands. Some ferries go to all populated islands and let you off wherever you want. Fares range from $6 for Peaks to $9.25 to Cliff (half price for seniors and children). All tickets are round-trip, collected in Portland. I guess they figure you have to come back sometime.

You can stay overnight on Peaks Island, Chebeague Island, Long Island, and Great Diamond. Lodging is sparse, however, and most people who remain on the islands are residents (summer or year-round). Visitors can enjoy day trips to these rocky places.

The mailboat trip to Cliff Island is the longest of the regularly scheduled ferry trips—except for the Bailey Island Cruise (see below)—it takes about 3 hours. Usually the trip is narrated. However, the early-evening boat at 5:45 is not a narrated trip and is the one we took. Because it was on a Friday evening, we found it fascinating just to overhear the other passengers—most of them locals—as they discussed doings on the islands. The ferry service operates as a lifeline to these islands, and therefore a great deal of stuff is being shipped to and fro—furniture, food, lumber, bikes, baby strollers, on and on.

Also, on a hot day—and Portland can get hot in the summer like anyplace else—we found this the quickest way to cool off.

The **Bailey Island Cruise** is a 5¾ hour cruise once daily. The boat leaves Portland at 10 AM, arriving at Bailey Island at 11:45 AM and leaving the island at 2 to return to Portland at 3:45 PM. There's enough time for lunch on the island; you can buy it there or tote your own. The cost is $15.50 adult, $14 senior, $7 child. While on Bailey, you can hop aboard the boat again for a 1¾-hour island nature cruise. This costs an additional $9.50 adult, $8 senior, or $4 child. The Bailey Island Cruise boat operates between late June and Labor Day.

◆ **Bay View Cruises** (207-761-0496), Fisherman's Wharf, 184 Commercial Street, Portland. The *Bay View Lady* is a 66-foot boat that makes weekend cruises in May and June and daily runs from late June through September. These include a Casco Bay/Portland Headlight/ Seal Watch cruise at 10:30 AM, returning at noon; and two other cruises at 1:15 and 3:15 PM that concentrate on seals and the harbor or islands. There is also a sunset seal-watch cruise at 6:30 PM. The cost is $10 per person, $9 for seniors, and $7 for children. If you want to have a lobster bake on board, you need only give a short advance notice to the crew and it can be provided.

◆ **Coast Watch & Guiding Light Navigation Co., Inc.** (207-774-6498), 170 Commercial Street, Portland. This company runs cruises out to Eagle Island and the home of Admiral Robert E. Peary, the first explorer to reach the North Pole. It's a fascinating home to visit. Tours leave daily in-season at 10 AM, give you about an hour and a half on the island, and return by 2 PM. The cost is $18 adults, $15 seniors, $10.50 kids, and it includes admission to the residence. You can make reservations ahead— and it's not a bad idea. Other tours are run to Portland Head Light or for seal-watching; there's a sunset cruise, too.

Street musician at the Old Port

◆ **Olde Port Mariner Fleet** (207-775-0727; 1-800-437-3270 from out of state), Custom House Wharf, Commercial Street, Portland. Whale-watches are offered daily in July and August and weekends in June and September, leaving at 10 AM and returning at 4 PM. The company also offers several sight-seeing cruises through the harbor and upper islands.

♦ **Lucky Catch Lobstering** (207-233-2026), 170 Commercial Street, Portland. You are guided through the daily routines of a Maine lobsterman while enjoying close-up views of historic lighthouses, forts, and seal rocks. Several 80- to 90-minute cruises are offered daily in-season. Adults $15, children $10.

♦ **Scotia Prince Cruises** (207-775-5616), 468 Commercial Street, Portland. This 11-hour trip to Yarmouth, Nova Scotia, can be an overnight outing—and often is. The "Overnight Sensation" package includes stateroom, buffet breakfast on the way over, dinner on return, and an opportunity to gamble (slot machines, gaming tables), to see on-board shows, or just to cruise along. Prices for two people start at $179 for an economy cabin without private head, and go up. Reservations are important. If you want to take a car to Nova Scotia and stay for a few days, you can do that, too. Two people taking a car one-way pay $265. It saves you 1,500 miles of driving round-trip, they say.

Beaches

The best beaches are south of the city and include **Crescent Beach State Park**, 8 miles south via Route 77 on Cape Elizabeth, with a mile-long sandy strand, changing facilities, picnic tables, and snack bar. **Scarborough Beach State Park** on Black Point Road (Route 207) at Prouts Neck, is a 243-acre park with beach, only a small portion of which is open to the public. Parking is limited. Changing rooms, rest rooms, and picnic facilities are included. There is a small, stony beach at **Fort Williams State Park** on Cape Elizabeth where Portland Head Light is located, but we saw only a couple of kids in the water on a very hot day.

Lighthouses

♦ **Portland Head Light** (207-799-2661; www.portlandheadlight.com), Fort Williams State Park, Shore Road, off Route 77, Cape Elizabeth. This beautiful lighthouse—white with green trim and classic red roof—was the first in the state of Maine. It was commissioned to be built by George Washington in 1791 and stands atop a pile of rocks, with the sea crashing below. The former keeper's house has been turned into a museum, open June through October, daily 10–4; and November, December, April, and May, weekends only 10–4. Exhibits focus on the history of the light and of Fort Williams, a military site that was a part of the coastal defense system. This is a very nice spot, with picnic tables, trails, and great views of the water.

♦ **Spring Point Ledge Lighthouse** at the end of a breakwater is close by the **Portland Harbor Museum** (207-799-6337; www.PortlandHarborMuseum.org), Fort Road, off Route 77, South Portland. This maritime museum and gift shop is located in the former cannon repair building of historic Fort Preble at the base of the breakwater leading to the light. Spectacular views of Casco Bay and Portland Harbor. Changing exhibitions are mounted. This is on the campus of the Southern

Maine Technical College. Open April, May, October, and November, Saturday and Sunday 1–4; June, Friday through Sunday; July through September, daily. Adults $3, children $1.

A Train Ride Along the Water

♦ **Maine Narrow Gauge Railroad Company & Museum** (207-828-0814), 58 Fore Street, Portland. This museum is open year-round, and we actually took a train ride on a snowy Saturday in late February. The little narrow-gauge railroad line uses mostly cars once owned by the Edaville Railway from Plymouth, Massachusetts. It's a little hard to find the spot, amid a complex of industrial brick buildings, but dedicated volunteers are on hand in the gift shop, at the small museum, and to drive the train. Inside the building are a couple of pretty nifty parlor cars that you can walk through. A short video presents the history of Maine's 2-foot-wide railroads. The 3-mile round-trip excursion runs along the bay. At Christmastime it's decorated with thousands of holiday lights. Adults $6, children $3.50.

Museums and Historic Sites

♦ **Wadsworth-Longfellow House** (207-879-0427), 487 Congress Street, Portland. June through October, Tuesday through Sunday 10–4. Adults $6, children $2 for the house and gallery next door, all part of the **Center for Maine History.** Poet Henry Wadsworth Longfellow's boyhood home is a Portland treasure. It has been under renovation—and was in the process when I visited—but ought to be finished when you do. Built in 1785 by Henry's grandfather, this was the first brick dwelling in town—and weren't they smart, considering subsequent fires! The house retains most of its original furnishings and has been a museum for a century. It is being restored to the period of 1850, when Henry's beloved sister, Ann Longfellow Pierce, a young widow, came to live here. Henry lived in the house from the age of 7 months. When he was 14, he went off to Bowdoin College to study and he was, at the age of 18, in the same graduating class with Nathaniel Hawthorne. He then toured for 3 years in Europe before returning to Bowdoin to teach. All the time this home was his touchstone, and he was very devoted to his mother. He returned annually for a visit from his later home in Cambridge, Massachusetts, with wife and children. "The Rainy Day," one of his poems, was written in the rear dining room. A pretty garden is out back.

♦ **Portland Museum of Art** (207-775-6148), 7 Congress Square, Portland. Edward Hopper's *Pemaquid Light* and many paintings by Winslow Homer, Rockwell Kent, and Andrew Wyeth—all of whom worked much in Maine—are among the rich collections at this terrific art museum. There is a nice selection of works by European impressionists, and changing exhibits here are on a high level. There's a good museum shop and a café as well. This is Maine's largest art museum. Open year-round Tuesday, Wednesday, Saturday, and Sunday 10–5; Thursday and Friday, 10–9; Monday, 10–5, Memorial Day through Columbus Day only. Adults $6, seniors and students $5, children $1. Free Friday 5–9.

♦ **Portland Observatory** (207-774-5561), 138 Congress Street, Portland.This newly restored signal light tower is one of a few once located at significant coastal points as watchtowers and is the last to remain from the 19th century. Baltimore and San Francisco, for example, also had them. It is located on Portland's highest elevation, atop Munjoy Point. Built in 1807, the structure is an octagonal, 86-foot-high wood-shingled building, painted a deep orangey red, as it would have been in the year 1900. If you're up to it—we weren't, on the very hot day we stopped—you can climb the 102 steps to the top to scan the horizon. On a clear day you can see 20 miles out to sea, we were told. Sunset tours are offered every Thursday by reservation. The tower is owned by the city of Portland. A few displays are located in the base. Open daily late May to early October, 10–5. Closed July 4. Adults $3, children $2.

♦ **The Tate House** (207-774-6177), 1270 Westbrook Street, Portland. This is the only remaining pre-Revolutionary home in Portland open to the public. It's a Georgian-style town house with unusual architectural details and period herb gardens. The house was built by Captain George Tate in 1755. Tate was mast agent for the English company that provided masts to the Royal Navy of King George II. An unusual clerestory roof, extensive use of window glass, and an elaborate front door indicate the family's lofty status in the community. Open June 15 through September 30, Tuesday through Saturday 10–4, Sunday 1–4. Adults $5, seniors $4, children $1.

♦ **Osher Map Library and Smith Center for Cartographic Education** (207-780-4850), University of Southern Maine, 314 Forest Avenue, Portland. This is a fascinating place, the only separately established rare-map library in northern New England. The cartographic collections include nautical charts, atlases, geographies, and original maps spanning the years from 1475 to the present. They were formed from two major gifts, from Dr. Harold and Mrs. Peggy Osher and from the late Lawrence M. C. and Eleanor Houston Smith. The combined collection has some 30,000 maps. The strength is in the discovery, exploration, and mapping of North America. Exhibits are mounted—a charming one on road maps when we visited. Serious researchers have access to the collections. The 20th international conference on the history of cartography was to be held here during summer 2003. Open Saturday 9–1; Tuesday, Wednesday, and Thursday 12:30–4:30; Wednesday and Thursday, 6:30–8:30 PM. Free.

Winslow Homer

The **studio of artist Winslow Homer** at Prouts Neck, south of Portland, is not particularly easy to find, and even more difficult to visit by car, since it's located next to what's now a private home in an exclusive summer colony with no public parking. The simple word STUDIO outside the dark green house, and another word, ENTRANCE, just outside the room itself, are the only clues. The door is left open 10–4 daily during the summer. The studio is reached off Route 207, Black Point Road. The best way to get to the fascinating place, especially if you are a Homer fan, is to take the 1¾-mile **Cliff Walk** along the water on the Prouts Neck peninsula.

Perhaps you can ask to park in one of the lots of the Black Point Inn near the start. Once there, you realize how close to the ocean Homer lived. It is said he would take many walks, observing the action of waves. Copies of his some of his paintings are mounted on the walls of the room. An interesting 45-minute video tells about the painter, but there's no guide and the entire experience is very low-key. You can sign a guest book and pick up a postcard. There is a can for donations.

Culture

Portland has a slew of cultural and arts organizations. They include the **Portland Ballet Company** (207-772-9671), **Portland Opera Repertory Theatre** (207-879-7678), **Portland Stage Company** (207-774-0465), and **Portland Symphony Orchestra** (207-842-0800). Call to check on schedules when you plan to be in town.

Shopping

This is a great city for shopping. Head directly for the Old Port district, particularly Exchange Street, where there are wonderful boutiques and gift shops. They include crafts shops **Abacus, Gallery Seven,** and **Edgecomb Potters;** stylish women's clothing at **Serendipity** (the best sweaters ever!) and **Amaryllis;** good kids' frocks at **The Golden Giraffe;** and a great selection of reading matter at **Books, Etc.** (Nice touch: They'll wrap your package for a donation to literacy volunteers.) Around the corner on Middle is one of our favorite boutiques, **Carrots & Co.,** with an old green VW bug, a convertible, in the window. Sorry, that's not for sale, but you'll find all sorts of fun items, from cocktail napkins, to clothes for mother and for baby, to neat little gift books.

In the same area **West Port Antiques** on Milk Street has great pieces, especially crockery. **Miranda's Vineyard** sells beer, wine, and flowers. **Maxwell's Pottery** has nice pottery from Italy and from Maine.

♦ **Cunningham Books,** on State Street at Longfellow Square where a huge statue of the poet sits—toward the west end of town—has more than 50,000 rare and used books.

♦ **Chris Heilman's hot glass studio** on Federal Street at India claims to be Maine's only glassblowing studio and gallery. Some of the artist's work is in the Portland Museum of Art. **Scott Potter's** decoupage work is showcased in a store on High Street.

This is just the beginning. You can spend a whole day shopping in Portland.

A Special Excursion

♦ **Poland Spring Preservation Park** (207-998-6452), Route 26, Poland Spring, Maine. Open mid-May to mid-September, Tuesday through Thursday 7–4, Friday 7–11 AM, Saturday and Sunday 7–5. September to May, Wednesday and Thursday 7–3; Friday, Saturday, and Sunday 9–9. Closed major holidays. Free. Historic buildings on the grounds of the Poland Spring Resort and golf course, and a new museum in the old bottling plant for Poland Spring water, make this an interesting and highly recommended stop. Located 26 miles north of Portland, the site is about a 45-minute drive from the city. The ride through the countryside and right past the Sabbathday Lake Shaker community (see the "Shaker Weekend" chapter for more information on it) is quiet and pretty.

The **Maine State Building** from the Columbian Exposition at the Chicago World's Fair of 1893 was dismantled and brought to this site in the late 1890s by the Rickers, owners of the Poland Spring House resort. The only state building to be saved, it was used as a library and place of relaxation for guests at the huge Victorian hotel, the first in the country with an adjoining golf course. That resort building burned in 1975, and a more modern, two-story hotel was built in its place. Now on the National Register of Historic Places, the Maine State Building is used to display historic photos and crockery related to the old landmark resort. Across the road is the **All Souls Chapel,** a beautiful stone building built as an interdenominational place of worship in 1912. There are nine stained-glass windows, a paneled oak ceiling, a mosaic tile floor, and a marble-and-gilt pulpit. It's home to a summer concert series.

Down the road is the old bottling plant building with café. An exhibit was in the process of being developed when we visited.

The atmosphere was pretty basic, but the restaurant next to the golf course here served me the best lobster roll I had in Maine—at a bargain price, too, of $8.75.

WHERE TO STAY

Portland hotels and inns tend to be filled on weekends in summer and increasingly in spring and fall, so it's wise to plan ahead. The options we prefer are the downtown hotels, the small inns and B&Bs (most located in the city's west end), and a couple of oceanside resorts south of the city.

DOWNTOWN

♦ **Portland Regency Hotel** (207-774-4200; 1-800-727-3436; fax 207-775-2150; www.theregency.com), 20 Milk Street, Portland, ME 04101. The 95 well-appointed guest rooms and public rooms of the Regency have been carved out of the 19th-century brick State of Maine Armory. The location is terrific; just walk out the door and you are close to the waterfront and also next to the Old Port district for shopping and lots of great restaurants. Valet parking is available. The hotel has a fitness room with Jacuzzi, a full-service restaurant serving three meals a day, and a feeling of elegance. This property is under the same ownership as the prestigious Black Point Inn at Prouts Neck. Furnishings in rooms are traditional, with dark mahogany beds and tables. Many have space for a dining table and chairs. Through the halls you see nautical charts on walls or prints of sailing ships. The Armory restaurant is located on the lower level. Doubles, $149–289. Special packages are sometimes offered off-season.

♦ **Portland Harbor Hotel** (207-775-9090; 1-888-798-9090; fax 207-775-9990; www.theportlandharborhotel.com), 468 Fore Street, Portland, ME 04101. New in July 2002, this four-story, 100-room facility describes itself as a "boutique" hotel. It certainly is welcome in Portland, where rooms can be devilishly difficult to get in summer. Rooms—with queen or king beds—are said to be furnished traditionally, most in blues and yellows. There are several different styles, from a standard room with a queen bed to a one-bedroom suite with king bed and additional pullout sofa. Deluxe rooms have a separate glass shower in addition to a tub, and six rooms have a whirlpool tub. An interior garden courtyard is viewable from the lobby and the lobby restaurant, **Eve's Garden,** and bar. A parking garage is a real plus. Three meals a day are served. There's an exercise room. The management group is Hart Hotels of Buffalo, New York. Doubles, $179–329 (for suites).

♦ **Holiday Inn By the Bay** (207-775-2311; 1-800-345-5050), 88 Spring Street, Portland, ME 04101. The 239 rooms in this well-located hotel with parking next door have two double beds or a king-sized bed. Those with views of the bay are a bit higher priced and the most sought after. There are an indoor pool and fitness center, a spacious L-shaped lounge, and a comfortable restaurant on premises. The high-rise building may seem a little startling in mellow old redbrick Portland, but this is one of the more comfortable places to stay in the city. Doubles, $141–161 in high season.

♦ **Eastland Park Hotel** (207-775-5411; fax 207-775-2872), 157 High Street, Portland, ME 04101. This 12-story landmark hotel in the center of the city calls itself "the grande dame of Portland hotels," but how often does a Holiday Inn get a better rating than a supposedly refurbished old charmer? Well, our weekend at the Eastland was fraught with so many glitches that we think it still needs to get its act together. Some rooms have been completely refurbished, as was ours on one of two concierge floors. We felt it was a bit small for the price, but amenities were there. The problems had to do with service—such as complimentary continental breakfast being offered for concierge floors and the breakfast room being locked up on a Saturday morning in August with an excuse from the front desk that someone "forgot" to open up. They scrambled around to offer us something in the lobby, but it was haphazard. Our complimentary drinks at the Top of the East, the hotel's 12th-floor lounge with reputed great view, also never happened because the room was closed due to "mechanical difficulties." We later heard that the air-conditioning was not working. The front desk was swamped, and phones rang interminably. The restaurant, Decoupage, with wonderful artwork by local artist Scott Potter, was said to be good, but we didn't risk it. The lobby is pretty—all marble and columned—and a pianist played there on Saturday night while people had drinks at a lobby lounge. This hotel has great potential and a good location. Doubles, $139–209.

Bed & Breakfast Inns

♦ **Pomegranate Inn** (207-772-1006; 1-800-356-0408; fax 207-773-4426; www. pomegranateinn.com), 49 Neal Street, Portland, ME 04102. Isabel Smiles's former life as an interior designer in Greenwich, Connecticut, was a great background for the incredible decorating job she has done at this B&B. The circa-1884 Italianate house in the posh west end of town has eight stunning guest rooms, no two alike, with original artwork hung—and sometimes painted—on the walls. All rooms are furnished with antiques and unusual pieces of furniture and have well-appointed private bath. Telephone and television are in all rooms, and five have gas fireplace.

The guest rooms are also air-conditioned. The first-floor parlor and breakfast room is filled with gorgeous artwork and sculpture, much of it contemporary. A full breakfast is served at one long table or at one of two smaller ones in the high-ceilinged parlor. The entrée might be poached eggs with salmon and capers. Doubles, $95–225.

♦ **West End Inn** (207-772-1377; 1-800-639-1779), 146 Pine Street, Portland, ME 04102. Around the corner from the Pomegranate Inn, in the same residential section of Portland's west end, is this charmer. When Rosa Maria and Nicholas Higgins took over a couple of years ago, Rosa redid the place with real panache. The high-ceilinged walls of the common room are a solid deep golden yellow with white trim, and the front hall with staircase is a vibrant red. The dining room has been moved to the front of the house, with a large white communal table and two smaller ones where breakfast is served. Six rooms all have air-conditioning and cable TV. All have private bath, most with a tub-shower combination, two with a shower only. There are a queen-bedded room on the first floor, three rooms on the second floor, and two on the third floor. Beds are king and queen sized, and one room has two twin beds. In winter guests like to sit near the fireplace in the parlor, where Rosa serves tea in the afternoon. The first-floor bedroom is serene with a blue trellis-design wallpaper, blue solid comforter, and white shutters on the windows. Breakfast might be lemon pancakes with raspberry sauce or a sausage strata. Doubles $99–199.

♦ **The Danforth** (207-879-8755; 1-800-991-6557; fax 207-879-8754; www.danforth-maine.com), 163 Danforth Street, Portland, ME 04102. Barbara Hathaway, innkeeper, did a smashing job when she converted this landmark 1821 mansion into a bed & breakfast inn. The nine deluxe guest rooms all have private bath, wood-burning fireplace, television, telephone, comfortable seating, and antique furnishings. The common rooms on the main floor are elegant and large. A wood-paneled billiard room is in the lower level. A hearty continental breakfast is served buffet-style in the morning—or you can ask that breakfast be delivered to your room. Off-street parking is available. There is a fitness club affiliation, with complimentary day passes available for guests. Doubles, $115–285.

♦ **The Percy Inn** (207-871-7638; 1-888-417-3729; fax 207-775-2599; www.percyinn.com), 15 Pine Street, Portland, ME 04102. Dale Northrup, a professional travel writer, saw enough hotels and inns in his 20-year career that he knew what he wanted to offer in his hometown of Portland. He said he waited for years to find the right spot, and this 1830 Federal-style brick row house close to Longfellow Square caught his eye. The location is terrific, and Dale offers eight rooms and suites, all named for poets—including favorite son Henry Wadsworth Longfellow. The Percy Room is named for Percy Bysshe Shelley, but the Percy Inn itself is named for Dale's father, Percy Northrup, who helped him with the rehabbing. All rooms have television, VCR, and refrigerator complimentarily stocked with soft drinks; phone, CD player, and weather radio; air-conditioning; queen-sized bed; and private bath. It's a bit of a steep climb up the staircase of the main inn to the second and third floors, but the rooms are great. A second-floor breakfast room (open for snacks all day) is where Dale serves a continental breakfast including fruits, muffins, boiled eggs, breads, cereal, and yogurt. Doubles, $89–250.

Inn at St. John (207-773-6481; 1-800-636-9127; www.innatstjohn.com), 939 Congress Street, Portland, ME 04102. This inn—with 37 rooms on four floors—has the feel of a small European hotel and, say desk clerks, is popular with overseas visitors. Single travelers can rejoice at actually finding small single rooms—like room 3A on the second floor. This room has but a single bed in the center, an in-room sink, a paisley comforter, and muted floral wallpaper. It shares a bath but, like all rooms, had a local *Portland Press Herald* newspaper lying on the bed and a few snacks and water on a table when we peeked in. There are TVs in all rooms. Room 101 off the lobby is the top of the mark—a large room with two double beds and its own private, good-sized bathroom (the most expensive ever at $164.70, double). Baths are designated to be used by certain rooms; often three share one small bath with stall shower. A buffet continental breakfast is served off the lobby in the morning and is complimentary. The hotel is directly across the street from the bus station. There's parking out back. It's a bit of a hike from downtown Portland—and not through all the best neighborhoods—but once you're here, the inn has some good things to offer. The owner is Paul Hood. Doubles, $69.70-164.70.

BY THE SEA

♦ **Inn by the Sea** (207-799-3134; fax 207-799-4779; www.innbythesea.com), 40 Bowery Beach Road, Cape Elizabeth, ME 04107. This inn has a great location. The ocean is viewable from the rear gardens and many rooms of the inns, and you can take a path directly from the property to sandy Crescent Beach nearby. All 25 accommodations are suites with fully stocked kitchenette; the ground-floor garden suites are designated "pet-friendly" for dog lovers. These one-level suites have a queen-bedded bedroom, a well-appointed bath, a living room adjoining the kitchen, and a patio opening directly onto the inn grounds. A swimming pool, tennis court, shuffleboard court, and beautiful gardens (with garden tours led daily by the head groundskeeper at 10 AM) make this a popular choice for couples and families. Owner Maureen McQuade is constantly upgrading and taking stock. Loft suites have two levels with bed and bath on the upper level, and living/dining area, kitchen, and oceanview balcony on the first level. The six-suite Beach House offers freestanding woodstoves in the units. Cottage suites have two bedrooms and are used for extended stays primarily. Doubles, $149–549; the latter price is for the Presidential Suite, with two bedrooms and two baths, a gas fireplace, and a wraparound porch with ocean view. The on-site **Audubon dining room** (207-767-0888) serves three meals a day in a tranquil setting and is very highly regarded. It's a short ride into Portland.

♦ **Black Point Inn** (207-883-2500; 1-800-258-0003; fax 207-883-9976), Prouts Neck, Scarborough, ME 04074. This 80-room hotel dates from 1878. Located about 20 minutes south of Portland in the exclusive Prouts Neck area, the inn has the feeling of long-ago summer vacations. Since being taken over by the owner of the Portland

Regency in the late 1990s, however, the place has been opened year-round, and upgrading is taking place. This is a destination resort. Guests have use of a beautiful outdoor pool overlooking the ocean, 17 tennis courts belonging to the private Prouts Neck Country Club next door (bring your whites!), golfing privileges, and an indoor pool and fitness center. There are beaches on both sides (little Sand Dollar Beach or larger Scarborough State Beach) and wonderfully appointed rooms. High tea is served in the pretty music room, one of several large public rooms. In summer guests love to sit in chairs on the open porch, looking at the ocean. There is also a wicker-filled enclosed sunroom that might beckon on rainy days. The pleasantly old-fashioned dining room serves three meals a day (and room rates include breakfast and dinner). Lunch is also served poolside in summer. Families are catered to, and children actually eat in a separate dining room. Kayaks can be rented here. Cottages have fireplaced common rooms (just ask a bellman to light yours if it's cold and damp), and most have an outside deck. If you arrive at the Portland airport—just 8 miles north of here—and need to be picked up, the inn will send its vintage English taxicab. Package plans are offered off-season. Doubles, MAP, $250–520. A B&B plan is available in winter. (You can walk from here to the Winslow Homer studio.)

WHERE TO EAT

Portland is a restaurant city. There are so many—with new ones coming in all the time—that it's impossible to detail them all. Here are some of our favorite places.

◆ **Fore Street** (207-775-271), 288 Fore Street, Portland. Sam Hayward, former acclaimed chef of the Harraseeket Inn in Freeport, has been at the helm here for a few years now, and he doesn't seem to lose his edge. It's tough to get a reservation at this restaurant located in a high-ceilinged old brick warehouse, but sometimes— if you're lucky—you can walk right in and get a stool at the pleasant and dark marble bar where you can also eat dinner. That's what we did one Friday night after returning from a boat ride to the Casco Bay islands. The rich smell of the applewood smoking fills this place and tantalizes you. My fish and shellfish stew (at $15.95 one of the least expensive entrées on the menu) was a hearty, aromatic mixture, just filled with mussels, kingfish, tuna, halibut, and salmon. Wood-roasted and simmered local haddock fillet came with mashed potatoes and julienned vegetables on my husband's plate, also delicious. We had plenty to eat without appetizers but could have started with the Fore Street salad (garden arugula, tomatoes, Reggiano cheese, balsamic vinaigrette), chilled local oysters, applewood-grilled Vermont quail in a mushroom salad, or a tomato tart ($8–13). Other entrées include the applewood-grilled tuna loin, hanger steak, duckling, Maine lamb, and turnspit-roasted pork loin, half chicken, or rabbit. All come with starch and vegetables. Entrées, $16–28. Call a couple of weeks ahead for weekend reservations.

◆ **Saltwater Grille** (207-799-5400), 231 Front Street, South Portland. Give me a good view of a working waterfront any day. But when you call for reservations, ask how to get to this great new spot located next door to the Sunset Marina in South Portland. A big deck out front is a preferred dining spot on nice days, but even from indoors the two-level dining space allows for water views from just about every table. This is yet a new venture for the Loring brothers (Mark and Joe), who own other restaurants in town. (Mark Loring owns Walter's on Exchange Street in the city.) This is such a great location that it's sure to be popular year-round (a floor-to-ceiling stone see-through fireplace that can be viewed in dining room and bar will entice winter diners). Wood floors are polished to a high sheen, and wicker chairs with rounded arms are set at tables with painted pale green wood tops. Although service was said to be still uneven at this place when we ate lunch here, we had no problems—and after all, this was just the second month. Portions are generous— one of us had the wild mushroom and chicken sauté with bowtie pasta, and the other the special lemon herb chicken salad on greens, both excellent. Lunch entrées are in the $8–12 range. At night, starters include shrimp cocktail, steamed mussels, and crispy lobster ravioli ($7–9). For entrées, try fisherman's stew in a creamy saffron broth over linguine, potato-encrusted local haddock, or lobster several different ways ($17–20). Lunch daily 11–3; dinner nightly 5–9:30.

♦ **Street & Company** (207-775-0887), 33 Wharf Street, Portland. This seafood restaurant is très popular. It's simple and sincere and what you get is fresh, fresh, fresh fish. The menu is short and to the point. Four appetizers—mussels Provençal, salad, calamari, or clams ($7–8) are offered. Entrées include grilled or blackened tuna, salmon, or halibut; or broiled sole, salmon, or scallops. Some are served right in the pan. There's also grilled lobster on linguine with butter and garlic. Most entrées $15–18. Lobster diavolo for two is $36. Open nightly for dinner.

♦ **Cinque Terra** (207-347-6154), Wharf Street, Portland. New in 2001, this restaurant describes its cuisine as "Ligourian" for that part of Italy. The chef is Jeff Landry, who is also an organic farmer. The high-ceilinged warehouse where the restaurant is located has a mezzanine level in addition to the regular ground-floor dining space. A few tables are set outside on a terrace. Inside, white-clothed tables are set with wood chairs on bare wood floors. The bare brick walls of the warehouse add to the ambience. Fresh flowers in pots were on tables when we looked in. Open for dinner only at the start, Cinque Terra's menu was decidedly Italian, and the wine list was all Italian, too. Appetizers were beef carpaccio with arugula and shaved Parmigiano Reggiano cheese; baked asparagus; and grilled vegetables with goat cheese ($6–10). Spaghetti with clams, garlic parsley, and white wine, or a whole Maine lobster with taglioni and white wine sauce are among the pastas (with two portion sizes, small and large). Three risotti are offered, including risotto alla Milanese and another with local crabmeat ($12–18). Lamb chops with rosemary garlic and red wine, grilled tuna steak with red onions and Chianti vinaigrette, and Tuscan-grilled steak were among the entrées (also offered in two sizes, with larger portions priced $15–22). You could finish with warm rich chocolate cake or panna cotta, an Italian-style custard. Dinner nightly from 6; from 5 on Fridays and Saturday.

♦ **Bibo's Madd Apple Café** (207-774-9698), 23 Forest Avenue, Portland. This wonderfully funky little space is located right next door to the **Portland Stage Company** and so draws theatergoers. In summer it's slower, and if you're having trouble getting into restaurants in the Old Port area, here is one to consider. It's located out closer to the Portland Museum of Art. A mural of an Italian city landscape—once part of a set at the stage company—adorns one wall. Bright Indian cotton tablecloths and multicolored walls on different levels (orange, pink, yellow) set the scene. My steamed salmon with julienned vegetables and slices of steamed sweet potato was delivered in an Asian basket and was wonderful on a hot night. The other choice was tuna Provençal—black pepper-encrusted tuna served with a tomato sauce, tossed gnocchi, and seared spinach. Other entrées included shrimp and scallops served over white truffle whipped potatoes, and seared marinated hanger steak over a roasted potato salad ($15–20). Desserts might be a homemade ginger ale float with lemongrass ice cream, or chocolate macadamia pâté. Open for lunch Wednesday through Friday 11:30–2; dinner Wednesday through Saturday from 5:30, Sunday from 4; and brunch Sunday 11–2:30.

♦ **Walter's Café** (207-871-9258), 15 Exchange Street, Portland. This is a popular storefront bistro in the heart of the shopping area of the Old Port. Haddock and mussel chowder is popular in this two-level dining spot, open for lunch and dinner. You can sit in the window to dine and keep your eye on the street action. A barbecued pork sandwich or lobster pasta salad might be your choice at lunchtime ($7–10). At dinner lobster-crab cakes or cracklin' calamari (offered at all the Loring restaurants, it seems) can be appetizers. Entrées might be Montego grilled salmon with island spices; Asian duck with crisp vegetables stir-fried; or crisp crusted haddock ($17–22). Lunch, Monday through Saturday 11–3; dinner nightly from 5 to 9 or 10.

♦ **Perfetto** (207-828-0001), 28 Exchange Street, Portland. Another restaurant in the heart of the Old Port shopping district is this sophisticated little spot serving northern Italian specialties. Once again, there are old brick walls and high ceilings in this former warehouse strip. The dining room has high-backed banquettes with wood tables and ladderback chairs. On the bar side are galvanized steel chairs and black tables; meals are served here when the place is full. At lunch you can have Caesar panzanella salad, grilled portobello sandwich, or penne perfetto (grilled chicken, sweet onions, lemon, peas, and Parmesan cream). For dinner, popular meals are the pine nut salmon served with pancetta orzo; an herbed pork loin with clams and smoked tomato lobster broth; and linguine Milano-style with Kalamata olives, tomatoes, and feta cheese in a white wine and butter sauce. Entrées, $13–20. Open for lunch Monday through Saturday 11:30–3; for dinner daily from 5.

♦ **Flatbread Company** (207-772-8777), 72 Commercial Street, Portland. Fire and water are paired together here. An innovative rounded stone oven glows with a hot fire in the center of the large restaurant space, whereas outside the big windows is a deck overlooking the harbor. Cool waterside in summer; cozy fireside in winter. "The very best pizza we can imagine" is the motto on the menu, and this is a pizza restaurant—substitute the word *flatbread* for pizza. The simple menu offers one salad of the day ($1.75) and several pizzas made with 100 percent organically grown wheat milled into white flour, and the wheat germ restored. Toppings are also natural—maybe cheese and herb, homemade sausage, and sun-dried tomatoes with caramelized onions and organic mushrooms. There are also flatbreads with wood-fired cauldron tomato sauce and other toppings, but usually three or four to choose from. A whole pizza is said to serve two, and the cost is in the $10–14 range. Homemade brownies topped with vanilla ice cream, their own chocolate sauce, and whipped cream are $5 each for dessert. Open daily 11:30 to 9:30 or 10:30. This is right across the water from the wharf where the Casco Bay Line ferries dock—in case you have to catch a boat.

Portland Public Market

♦ **RiRa Irish Pub** (207-761-4446), 72 Commercial Street, Portland. Are you wondering what the name means? According to the menu, a *RiRa* is "a place or state where exuberance and revelry prevail, where music and merriment compete and the conversation flows smooth as the Guinness ebbs in the glass."

The main floor, a rather dark pub, is open all day. Upstairs in the dining room, lunch and dinner are served. The dinner menu definitely makes you think you've crossed "the pond" for a meal. You'll find fish-and-chips, Irish lamb stew, bangers and mash, and corned beef and cabbage, all in the pub. Upstairs, things get a little more sophisticated, although the Irish lamb stew remains. Here you might also have grilled boneless pork loin, whole roasted rainbow trout stuffed with salmon and fennel, and white navy bean and vegetable casserole. Entrées, $11–18. Lunch 11–2; dinner from 5 daily.

♦ **Sebago Brewing Company** (207-775-2337), 164 Middle Street, Portland. Here's one of the microbrew pubs for which the Portland area is famous. Northern Light, Lake Trout Stout, and Bass Ackwards were three of the local brews on the menu when we stopped. A few outdoor tables under blue-and-yellow umbrellas overlook the street; otherwise, it's a typically wood-and-brass interior with a long bar, natch. The all-day menu is fairly ambitious with potato nachos, baked Brie, seafood-stuffed mushrooms, and boneless chicken tenders to munch. You can also order a char-grilled 12-ounce sirloin steak with brandy sauce, teriyaki chicken, pan-seared scallops, or shrimp and scallop scampi. Slow-cooked chili is warming in winter. Entrées, $10–15. Open daily 11–11 for food, until 1 AM for the bar.

♦ **Gilbert's Chowder House** (207-871-5636), 92 Commercial Street, Portland. This is the lowest of low-key—Formica tables with mustard and ketchup dispensers—but it is said to have the best chowders in town. They come in clam, corn, fish, seafood, and seafood chili versions in small, medium, and large. Or you can have them in a bread bowl. Prices range from $4 for the smallest to $7.25 for the bread bowl of seafood chili. Hot dogs, hamburgers, fried clam rolls, lobster, and crabmeat rolls are also on the menu. Entrées include fried or broiled scallops, fried clam strips, a clam cake plate, fried oysters, and Gilbert's seafood platter (the priciest at $23.95). Most other entrées are in the $8–10 range at lunchtime and in the $10–14 range at dinner. These are served with french fries or rice pilaf and coleslaw. Open daily 11–4 for lunch and 4–9 for dinner.

♦ **Portland Public Market** (207-228-2000; www.portlandmarket.com), corner Cumberland and Preble, Portland. You can eat here, too, at any one of several stalls with seating, or buy food to eat as you walk. The fancy restaurant, Commissary, closed in spring 2002, but another restaurant was expected to take over the handsome space. The market is home to purveyors of all kinds of wonderful products including baked goods, wines, upscale pastas, bread, cheese, smoked meats, take-out sushi, soups, and sandwiches. Tables and chairs are strategically located so you can sit down to have a cup of coffee and a scone, say, or soup and a sandwich. This is a wonderful place to prowl. Open Monday through Saturday 9–7, Sunday 10–5.

Chef Matthew Kenney's fabulous restaurant, **Commissary,** at the Portland Public Market left for downtown and was expected to reopen on Wharf Street in the Old Port. As of late summer 2002, it had not yet opened.

5 Middlebury, Vermont

Middlebury, Vermont, is the quintessential New England college town. What makes it so is Vermont's preeminent institution of higher learning, Middlebury College, whose 2,200 undergraduates—and several hundred more summer language students—fill the place year-round with a vibrant presence.

The college was founded in 1800, the town only a few years earlier. The two are yoked for better or worse—mostly for better—in an idyllic setting in the Champlain Valley region of the Green Mountain State. To the west are the Adirondack Mountains; to the east, Vermont's own Green Mountains. Lake Champlain is less than an hour away. Just 35 miles to the north is Burlington—Vermont's largest city and home to the fine state University of Vermont.

Middlebury, with a year-round population of 8,500—exclusive of college students—is the largest town in Addison County, a bucolic midstate region that is home to large dairy farms and apple orchards. Town roads become country roads as soon as they exit the populated area. The views are stunning: classic red barns, white farmhouses, silos, cows, horses. Vermont's edict against billboards is appreciated here in a special way, for there are long, open stretches where you can see the farms and the forests instead of advertisements for the nearest motel.

There aren't many motels, anyway. Old center-of-town inns like the Middlebury Inn and the Brandon Inn are supplemented by cozy bed & breakfast inns that range from rustic to ritzy. The lodging situation is such that when Middlebury College hosts graduation or a parent weekend, rooms are filled all over the area.

Middlebury's limestone hilltop campus is one of the most unified and attractive in all New England. The profile of Old Chapel, an administrative and classroom building, is used as a symbol of the school.

Middlebury takes pride in its past but does not glory in it. Instead, the school looks to the future and seems to be on a roll of expansion. A $200 million capital fund-raising campaign recently helped to build huge Bicentennial Hall, a science center and library, along with other buildings. Brand-new athletic facilities, a new arts center, dormitories that look something like ski lodges, and a huge new wing on the library are part of the package. The school's student population is slowly being expanded so that within a few years it will be add another 150 to 200 undergraduates.

Middlebury is a member of the high-caliber small liberal-arts colleges informally known as the "Little Ivy League." The all–New England group includes Amherst, Wesleyan, Williams, Colby, Bates, Bowdoin, and Tufts. The schools compete against one another in a sports league.

Those who weekend in the Middlebury area can avail themselves of many college activities—as long as the school is not on vacation. The arts center, with its fine Museum of Art, schedules music, dance, and theatrical performances regularly. Athletic contests—from football games in fall to ice hockey in winter (the Middlebury team is particularly good)—are fun to attend. An 18-hole golf course on campus is open to the public from April to November. In winter cross-country skiing is available on the Bread Loaf campus in nearby Ripton on Route 125, while the Middlebury Snow Bowl in neighboring Hancock offers low-key downhill skiing at affordable prices.

A visit to the campus can include a meal at The Grille in the campus center, a stop to see the Robert Frost and Henry David Thoreau collections in Starr Library, shopping at the college bookstore, or simply a walk among beautiful buildings.

The town of Middlebury has more to offer. A fine regional museum, the Henry Sheldon Museum, is of interest. The Vermont Folklife Center seeks to capture the essence of state life through recording oral histories of longtime residents and producing books. Shopping is varied. One of the state's fine crafts centers—with handmade items by Vermonters—is in Middlebury. Excellent independent bookstores are fun to browse. Handcrafted pewter, sports gear, Austrian woolens, and many gift items are found in shops in Middlebury and nearby towns. Antiques and collectibles can be tracked down throughout the region.

Not far from Middlebury are several other charming small villages. The poet Robert Frost spent 23 summers in nearby Ripton when he taught on the Bread Loaf campus of Middlebury College.

The inn that was pictured in *The Bob Newhart Show* credits for years, the Waybury Inn, stands in East Middlebury and is a highly regarded lodging and dining establishment, one of several in the area.

Church steeples and country inns, dairy farms and apple orchards, covered bridges and beautiful mountains—all are found in this picturesque region of Vermont.

We can't imagine a prospective college student coming to Middlebury on a bright autumn day and being able to resist the place. Weekenders can enjoy vicariously the area in which such lucky students get to spend 4 years.

Getting There

By car: Route 7, a major north–south route, cuts directly through Middlebury. A particularly scenic way to approach the town from the south is to take Route 89 from I-91, getting off at Bethel. Take Route 107 to Route 100 to Route 125. This takes you through the Middlebury Gap and into town. En route you pass the Bread Loaf campus of Middlebury College, Middlebury Snow Bowl, and the Robert Frost National Recreation Trail. It is a very pretty drive.

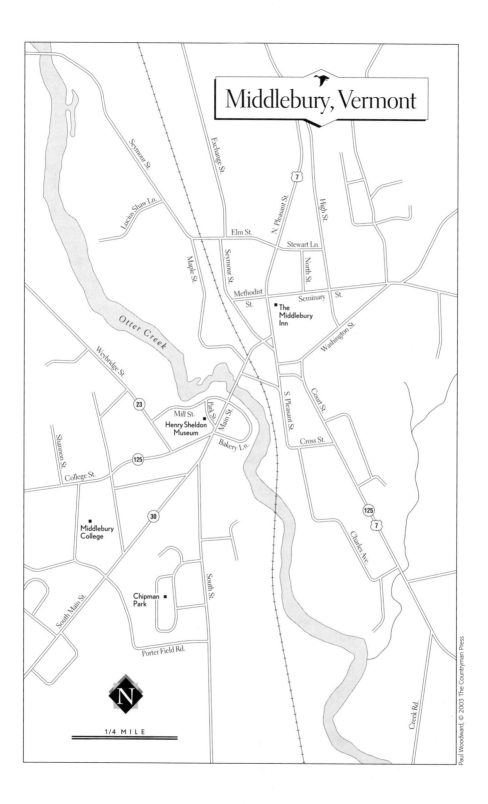

Middlebury, Vermont

Otter Creek

Seymour St.

Exchange St.

Lucius Shaw Ln.

Maple St.

Seymour St.

Elm St.

N. Pleasant St.

High St.

7

Stewart Ln.

North St.

Methodist St.

Seminary St.

■ The Middlebury Inn

Washington St.

Weybridge St.

23

Mill St.

Park St.

Main St.

Henry Sheldon Museum

Bakery Ln.

S. Pleasant St.

Court St.

Cross St.

125

Shannon St.

College St.

30

■ Middlebury College

125

7

Charles Ave.

South Main St.

Chipman Park ■

South St.

Porter Field Rd.

Creek Rd.

N

1/4 MILE

Paul Woodward, © 2003 The Countryman Press

From New York, take the New York Thruway (Interstate 87) north through Albany, picking up Route 149 to Fort Ann, New York, where the route becomes Route 4. Continue on Route 4 to Route 30 and travel north until you reach Route 7 in the center of town.

By bus: Vermont Transit (802-864-6811; 1-800-552-8737) stops in Brandon, Vergennes, and Middlebury. If coming from New York, you change buses from Greyhound to Vermont Transit in Albany and continue to Middlebury. From Boston, you take Vermont Transit and change in Rutland for Middlebury.

By air: The closest commercial airport is **Burlington International Airport.** Rental cars and ground transportation are available. Take Route 7 south to Middlebury.

For More Information

♦ **Addison County Chamber of Commerce** (802-388-7951; 1-800-733-8376; www.midvermont.com), 2 Court Street, Middlebury VT 05753.

♦ The **Middlebury College** main number is (802) 443-5000.

SEEING AND DOING

Touring the Campus

Middlebury College's campus is located just beyond the center of town and can be reached via either Route 30 (South Main Street) or Route 125 (College Street). On Route 30 you'll find the Center for the Arts and the Myhre Golf Course, field houses, the football stadium, and athletic facilities. From Route 125 you can more easily reach Bicentennial Hall. Either route can be used to access the center of campus with classrooms, libraries, and the student center.

♦ **Museum of Art** (802-443-5007), Center for the Arts, Route 30, Middlebury. A wonderful variety of works from ancient cultures—as befits a college art museum— is combined here with a selection of contemporary items. There are also changing

The Middlebury College campus

The McCullough Campus Center at Middlebury College

exhibitions, many of them from other museums around the country. Check out the terra-cotta Chinese camel dating from the Tang dynasty, A.D. 618–906. Open Tuesday through Friday 10–5, Saturday and Sunday noon–5, except for college holidays, the week between Christmas and New Year's Day, and 2 weeks at the end of August. Free.

◆ **Center for the Arts** (box office 802-443-6433), Route 30, Middlebury. Completed in 1992, the Center for the Arts is an impressive, sprawling, multilevel building that houses theater, dance, film and video, and music departments and mounts an impressive array of performances year-round. Guest performers are brought to campus. Many films are scheduled. The music library has media carrels for public use equipped to play compact discs, LPs, and cassettes. Check out the schedule for the weekend you plan to be in town.

◆ **Ralph Myhre Golf Course** (802-443-5125), 317 Golf Course Road, off Route 30. This par-71, 18-hole golf course is open to the public from April to November.

◆ **Athletics.** Football, ice hockey (both men's and women's teams at Middlebury are recent national champions of Division III schools), soccer, lacrosse, swimming, baseball, basketball, and field hockey can be enjoyed as spectator sports if you happen to be visiting when a game is on. A huge sculpture of a panther (yes, the teams are known as the Panthers) overlooks the athletic fields from Route 30. Call the athletic department at (802) 443-5250 to discover what's on when you're in town.

◆ **McCullough Campus Center.** Here's the place to get a cup of coffee or a light lunch or supper at **The Grille.** You can also get beer if you are 21 or older; if so, you're served a "beer bracelet" to wear on your arm denoting your legality. Pizzas, hamburgers, sandwiches, and salads are featured.

◆ **Old Stone Row.** Old Chapel and the two buildings on either side (Painter Hall is the oldest college building in use in Vermont, built in 1815) constitute what is known as Old Stone Row. The three buildings are on the National Register of Historic Places.

♦ **Starr Library.** The main campus library has the Abernathy Room with the Robert Frost memorabilia as well as some items from Henry David Thoreau. Thoreau did not have a particular connection with Middlebury College, but an alumnus was able to purchase some important items at auction and donate them.

♦ **College bookstore.** Want to take home a Middlebury sweatshirt, a book written by a faculty member (novels by Julia Alvarez were being featured when we stopped in), or a teddy bear dressed in a dark blue Middlebury sweater? The college colors are blue and white. MIDD is on the stickers you can buy to put on your car. Find them at the official campus bookstore in Proctor Hall. It's next to the tennis courts. You can probably pick up a copy of the college's weekly newspaper, *The Middlebury Campus.* Through it you get a sense of the goings-on and mood of the college.

♦ **Bread Loaf Campus,** Route 125, Ripton. In 1915 Colonel Joseph Battell, class of 1860, bequeathed more than 30,000 acres of land—including the Inn at Bread Loaf—to the college. After unsuccessfully trying to run the inn for a few years, college officials decided to use the facility for its summer School of English. Later, poet Robert Frost, who taught at the School of English, founded the nationally famed summer Bread Loaf Writers' Conference. The golden yellow buildings on the Bread Loaf campus are classic wood structures with a lot of charm. **Rikert Ski Touring Center** (802-388-2759), Bread Loaf campus, Route 125, Ripton. Here you'll find 26 miles of groomed trails and a ski shop with rentals and refreshments in winter.

♦ **Middlebury College Snow Bowl** (802-388-4356), Route 125, southeast of town, just beyond the Bread Loaf Campus in Ripton. Three chairlifts—two doubles and a triple—service this downhill skiing area owned and operated by the college. Snowboarders are welcome on all 14 trails. The vertical drop is 1,200 feet. Lines are usually short and all-day lift tickets much more affordable than at many larger areas in the state. An adult all-day weekend ticket is $32; students pay $25. Ski rentals are available, and lessons are offered. Plaques with the names of collegiate ski champions are mounted in the low-key lodge.

What to See in Town

Middlebury is a great little town to prowl about. The center (Main Street) is quite walkable, and there are plenty of places to park.

From the Addison County Chamber of Commerce on Court Street, pick up the pamphlet *A Self-Guided Walking Tour* of Middlebury. Middlebury is known for several firsts. The state's marble industry was born here. Middlebury is home to the first chartered village museum (Sheldon Museum), the first state symphony, and the first community-founded college. John Deere, whose invention was the "plow that broke the plains," was born in Middlebury. More than 100 points of interest are described on the walking tour, including the house that was lived in by Gamaliel Painter, one of the founders of Middlebury College. Otter Creek is a significant river with waterfalls running through the center of town; there's a **pedestrian bridge** to walk over it. From the bridge you get a great view of the falls.

♦ **Henry Sheldon Museum of Vermont History** (802-388-2117), 1 Park Street, Middlebury. Located in the 1829 **Judd-Harris House,** this museum was chartered in 1882. Henry Sheldon, a lifelong bachelor, moved here as a boarder in the 1850s. He served as town clerk, owner of a music store, and church organist, among other occupations. Spurred by the country's centennial, he began collecting artifacts and written material documenting everyday life in Addison County. Regional Vermont furniture, paintings, household objects, and tools are here. Open Monday through Friday 10–5, as well as Saturday May to October, and Sunday 11–4 in December, when the house is decorated for the holidays. Adults $4, seniors $3.50, kids 6–18 $2.

♦ **Vermont Folklife Center** (802-388-4964), 2 Court Street, Middlebury. This serious—and rather new—museum was founded in 1984 and seeks to capture in voice, in story, and in photo or picture the history of Vermont people. Oral histories of Vermonters are preserved on tape; books are produced that tell of the state's history through its people's lives. There is always an exhibit to view. Open May through December, Tuesday through Saturday 11–4; winter months, Saturday 11–4. Free. A small gift shop features work by Vermont artisans.

♦ **UVM Morgan Horse Farm** (802-388-2011), 74 Battell Drive, Weybridge. From Middlebury center, take Route 125 west to Route 23 north, go ¾ mile, and follow the signs. Located just 2.5 miles north of Middlebury, open May to October, daily 9–4 with tours on the hour. A 15-minute video can be seen before the tour. The Morgan horse dates back to the late 1790s when the first Morgan was born from unproven parentage. This one stallion became the founder of an entire breed of horse because of his genetic ability to pass on his characteristics to his offspring. Colonel Joseph Battell began breeding Morgans on his farm in the 1870s and had an intense interest in preserving and promoting the breed. He deeded his farm to the United States in 1907, and in 1951 the U.S. government handed over the reins to the University of Vermont. Visitors see the stables and paddocks. Adults $4, teens $3, children $1.

♦ **The Pulp Mill Covered Bridge,** spanning Otter Creek near the Morgan Horse Farm, is the oldest in the state (built between 1808 and 1820). It's also the last two-lane span still in use. The bridge was restored in the 1980s.

♦ **Otter Creek Brewing** (802-388-0727), 85 Exchange Street, across the railroad tracks from the Marble Works, Middlebury. Open Monday through Saturday 10–6. Tours at 1, 3, and 5. Ales and other beers can be sampled in the Tasting Room. The visitors center has a gift shop.

Shopping

Middlebury is an appealing town to shop in, with one-of-a-kind stores—mostly located on Main Street in the center of town or the streets immediately adjacent. The **Frog Hollow** section down by Otter Creek has the **Vermont Craft Center,** one of three in the state that promotes and sells wares made by Vermont artists and artisans. Down in this small area also are **The Candy Jar** where you can get a quick chocolate fix; **Middlebury Mountaineer** with gear and apparel for outdoors types; and **Jennifer Ellsworth Landmarks,** an unusual and enticing store for purchasing historical landmark glass ornaments. She has a New England collection, a Vermont towns collection, and ornaments from cities of the world (like Big Ben from London or the Ferris wheel at Navy Pier from Chicago).

Dada on Main Street is a store filled with unusual and interesting housewares and gourmet foods. **Holy Cow!** is Woody Jackson's store, with cow-themed mugs, T-shirts, prints, cards, and many other things. Jackson's cow-and-barn Vermont landscape art was the inspiration for the Ben & Jerry's ice cream cartons. **The Vermont Book Shop** on Main is a high-ceilinged emporium with a well-rounded selection of books and music. Robert Frost used to spend time here. Just a couple of doors away is **Otter Creek Used Books,** a good place to poke around. There's a **Ben Franklin Store**—a throwback to the days of the old five-and-dime stores—with lots of patterns and fabric for home sewers as well as a slew of other things.

Also in Middlebury are **Danforth Pewterers** in the Marble Works area and **Geiger,** a shop selling Austrian woolens and other Austrian fashion items. The large gift shop at the **Middlebury Inn** is kind of fun to poke through—everything from refrigerator magnets to inspirational signs. **The Alpine Shop**—across from the town green—sells outdoor gear, and sells and rents downhill and cross-country skis. You can rent a bike from **The Bike Center** on Main Street.

Outdoors

Middlebury and environs appeal to outdoor types. Here are some—just some— of the ways you may want to spend a day, or a portion of a day, outdoors.

Day hiking. Pick up the pamphlet *Day Hikes on the Middlebury & Rochester Ranger Districts of the Green Mountain National Forest* from the USDA Forest Service office (802-388-4362) on Route 7 south of Middlebury—or from the chamber of commerce. This lists 24 hikes ranging from easy to difficult and includes information on Vermont's Long Trail, which cuts through the area.

The **Trail Around Middlebury (TAM)** is a 14-mile footpath encircling the town. You can get a free map showing the trail from the Addison County Chamber of Commerce (802-388-7951).

Swimming. Lake Dunmore—accessible from **Branbury State Park** on Route 53 south of Middlebury—is a good spot for swimming, with a sandy beach.

Biking. If you like to bike, there is no better place than the gentle, rolling terrain of Addison County.

Country Inns Along the Trail. The **Churchill House Inn** in Brandon (see *Where to Stay*) offers bike tours with other inns as stops along the way. The inn has a fleet of bikes for rent.

Cross-country skiing. In addition to the Rikert Ski Touring Center at the Bread Loaf campus of Middlebury College, **Blueberry Hill Inn** (802-247-6735) in Goshen has 50 km of tracked and groomed trails on elevations of 1,400 to 3,100 feet. Some of the trails are challenging, but there's a flat area for novices. The ski center has retail and rental equipment, waxing, and a repair shop.

Robert Frost National Recreational Trail (formerly the Interpretive Trail) is an easy 1-mile trail accessed from Route 125 near Ripton. You begin by walking across Beaver Pond on a bridge and then head into the woods and across open fields. At several spots on the trail you can read from portions of Frost poems. From one spot you can see Bread Loaf mountain (it really looks like its name). The trail is especially nice in autumn and the poem "In Hardwood Groves," particularly apt at

The Robert Frost Interpretive Trail near Ripton

that time of year. There are benches for resting along the way. The **Wayside Picnic Area** across the road is a good place to stop. Toilet facilities are located both here and at the recreational trail.

♦ **Spirit in Nature Trail** (802-388-7244; www.spiritinnature.com). Located off the Goshen Road, south of Route 125 (take the road that has a sign for Blueberry Hill Inn). Early in 1998 a group of local naturalists and environmentalists representing various faiths came up with the idea of Spirit in Nature. A Middlebury College student cleared the first path. Ten different paths—each ½ to 4 miles long—include sayings along the way from a particular faith tradition. All paths eventually lead to the sacred circle, a large 60-foot circle with rustic benches surrounded by towering white pines. Among the faiths represented are Bahai, Hindu, Jewish, Friends, Christian, Buddhist, Muslim, and Unitarian-Universalist; there's also an Interfaith Path. It's very peaceful here. Open year-round, dawn to dusk. Donation.

Other Nearby Attractions

The towns. Small towns and villages near Middlebury are charming and fun to explore. Those we especially like are Vergennes, Bristol, and Brandon. Brandon has the largest Fourth of July parade in Vermont. Vergennes and Bristol both have charming downtown areas and good shopping.

♦ **Lake Champlain Maritime Museum** (802-475-2022), 4472 Basin Harbor Road, Vergennes. Open May to mid-October, daily 10–5. A dozen exhibit areas—including a replica of the gunboat *Philadelphia II*—are available at this growing museum. It focuses on the stories and people of Lake Champlain with hands-on exhibits and other learning adventures for all ages. Blacksmiths and boatbuilders work on site. You can learn about shipwrecks on the lake. While here, take a quick detour through the grounds of the Basin Harbor Club just across the way—it's one of the most low-key, yet exclusive places to stay in the area. It's open summers only.

♦ **Warren Kimble Studio and Shop,** Route 73, Brandon. This Americana artist—flag-decorated pillows, a lighthouse line of coasters, trays, and glasses, hooked rugs, and more—works in a big red barn in Brandon and has an extensive gift shop next door. It's fun to look around.

WHERE TO STAY

IN MIDDLEBURY

♦ **Swift House Inn** (802-388-9925; fax 802-388-9927; www.swifthouseinn.com), 25 Stewart Lane (at the intersection with Route 7), Middlebury, VT 05753. This exceptional inn, owned and run by the Nelson family, has 21 rooms in three buildings: the 1814 main house, the nearby Carriage House, and the Victorian Gatehouse across the street. This was once the home of former Vermont governor John W. Stewart and his daughter, Jessica Stewart Swift. Set back from Route 7 and with a huge front lawn, the inn is elegantly decorated, and many rooms have wood-burning fireplaces. The Governor's Room in the main inn, with fireplace, has a king bed and a blue-and-white decorating scheme. An intricately carved fireplace graces the Swift Room, wallpapered in a soft peach floral and with a queen canopy bed. There's a private balcony with a good view of the beautiful grounds.

The Carriage House, where rooms are named for Morgan horses in a nod to the nearby state Morgan Horse Farm, has six large rooms with wall-to-wall carpeting, reproduction mahogany furniture, and coffeemakers for that first morning cup. The pretty Gladstone Room has an iris-print bedspread and matching Roman shades; its bathroom has a double whirlpool tub. A huge Cupola Suite at the top of the Carriage House is the ultimate in luxury, with two large sitting areas, a full kitchen, a double whirlpool tub, and a two-person shower in the bath. Five rooms in the Victorian Gatehouse across the way are a bit smaller and apt to be noisier because the house is directly on Route 7. But they are equally charming, all with private bath and with queen, twin, or king bed.

Everyone breakfasts in the gorgeous main-house dining room, eating at separate tables, seated in Chippendale chairs. An expanded continental breakfast includes home-baked breads and coffee cakes; guests may add quiche, smoked salmon, or the like for an additional charge. Doubles, $90–235. The suite is $600 per night.

♦ **The Middlebury Inn** (802-388-4961; 1-800-842-4666; fax 802-388-4563; www.middleburyinn.com), on the green, Middlebury, VT 05753. This large brick center-of-town inn has been a place of hospitality for 170 years. Parents of Middlebury students regularly fill the place for parent-student weekends, graduation, and other special events, and prospective students and their folks can be spotted year-round. The Emanuel family, owners for 25 years, have done a lot of updating, but expect the rooms—especially in the main inn—also to reflect their age. (Bathrooms can be quite small, for example, carved from old closets.) Our room was high ceilinged, long, and narrow, with twin beds and a TV in an armoire, plus phone, air-conditioning, and two easy chairs. On the third floor, it meant climbing two flights of stairs or calling on someone from the front desk to deal with the old hand-operated Otis elevator. The motel-like building out back has more updated rooms and easy car-to-room access. The Porter House mansion next door, part of the inn, has nine guest rooms decorated in the Victorian style.

All guests have breakfast in the big old dining room, with a plant-filled bay window looking out over the town. Guests of the inn get the continental portion of the buffet-style repast; $4 extra gets you eggs, pancakes, and breakfast meats from the warming table. Afternoon tea is complimentary, served in the Morgan Tavern, a pub with equestrian touches. Special weekend package plans including "Thanksgiving Inn Vermont" are offered. The big main lobby is a busy place, and the gift shop sprawls. The restaurant is open for three meals per day. Doubles, $88–185; suites, $195–365. Add $38 per person for MAP.

♦ **The Inn on the Green** (802-388-7512; 1-888-244-7512), 19 South Pleasant Street, Middlebury, VT 05753. An 1803 mansard-roofed building—on the National Register of Historic Places—has been converted to a tasteful bed & breakfast inn by Vermonters Steve and Mickey Paddock. Seven accommodations (two suites, five rooms) in the main house are named for nearby counties and are appealingly decorated. All have private bathroom, queen bed, TV, air-conditioning, and individual thermostat. Breakfast in bed—delivered on trays to individual rooms—is a nice touch. Next door, a new carriage house has four more rooms with queen bed. Walls are deep jewel tones. Lemon yellow in the main-floor hallway is striking. The green New Haven Room has a view of the town. Original doors from the house form a ceiling grid for the Lincoln Room. Doubles, $98–225.

NEARBY

♦ **Waybury Inn** (802-388-4015; 1-800-348-1810; fax 802-388-1248; www.wayburyinn. com), Route 125, East Middlebury, VT 05753. The Waybury Inn seems instantly familiar. That's because the exterior of this appealing spot was seen for years on the Bob Newhart television show. It served as the model for his "Stratford Inn." The green-gold pillared inn has 15 guest rooms, gracious public rooms, a well-regarded restaurant, and a cozy downstairs pub. You don't have to leave! Middlebury Gap on

The Waybury Inn in East Middlebury

the second floor has a king four-poster bed with blue-and-white ticking comforter, blue walls, comfortable wing chairs, and wall-to-wall carpeting. The Robert Frost Room has a four-poster king-sized bed and a file box where those who've stayed can write about their stay—some with great flair. The inn claims 200 years of hospitality, from the time a simple boardinghouse stood on the site. Other rooms have floral carpets, sleigh beds, wainscoting, and individual touches—but no TVs. If you must, there's one in a main-floor parlor. Doubles include a full breakfast, served in the dining room and ordered from a menu. You might have eggs Benedict or stuffed French toast. Double, $95–185.

♦ **The Chipman Inn** (802-388-2390; 1-800-890-2390; www.chipmaninn.com), Route 125, Ripton, VT 05766. If you're looking for an informal, low-key Vermont inn, this could be your place. Husband and wife Bill Pierce and Joyce Henderson have been catering to guests for years in the town that Robert Frost also called home for many summers. A fireplaced pub with sofas and comfortable chairs on the main floor is a place to hang out. Eight guest rooms are named for colors. Four are in the main house and four in the wing. The latter are reached by a back staircase with a primitive mural painted on the walls. The inn participates in the program Country Inns Along the Trail for hikers and bikers. Many rooms have more than one bed—perhaps a double and a single or twins and a double, good for families or groups (but no children under 12). Bill's famous baked eggs with sage and cheese—featured in *Gourmet* magazine—might appear at breakfast. Guests sit at long tables with ladder-back chairs and enjoy a group experience. The inn closes from mid-November to the end of December and for the month of April. Doubles, $125–135.

♦ **Blueberry Hill Inn** (802-247-6735; 1-800-448-0707; fax 802-247-3983; www.blueberryhillinn.com), Goshen, VT 05733. This is a destination inn, offering a one-of-a-kind experience. It's located high off a well-trod dirt road that winds its way from Ripton to Goshen. Although not far from Middlebury—and a popular choice of Middlebury parents and students—it's more the sort of inn where you'd go to spend a long weekend doing nothing but mountain biking, swimming, cross-country skiing, or reading. No TVs or telephones are in guest rooms, by design. Fine food is a major part of the picture. Longtime innkeeper Tony Clark, a Welshman who grew up in France, brings high epicurean standards to the dining room, where a full breakfast and dinner are included in the rates. Guests dine in a fireplaced room at long tables where interaction is part of the fun. Guests can bring their own wine and enjoy a cocktail hour with great hors d'oeuvres as a prelude to dinner. Big bowls of fruit and the inn's famed chocolate chip cookies are always available for snacks. Tony's wife, Shari Brown, is a gardener whose green thumb is everywhere evident—especially in the "greenhouse area" along the brick walk between the 1813 main house and a newer wing out back with four guest rooms. Altogether there are 12 accommodations, including a cottage for two. The new rooms in back are called the "blue rooms"—named for varieties of blueberries. They have queen beds. Guests enjoy 120 acres of private land around the inn, including a swimmable pond and 60 km of cross-country ski trails. Rentals and lessons are offered. A good place to swim is Lake Dunmore in nearby Branbury State Park. The public can come to Blueberry Hill Inn for dinner at $45 per person. Doubles, including full breakfast and dinner, $230–300. Kids 4–12 pay half price. B&B rates are available.

♦ **Churchill House Inn** (802-247-3078; 1-877-248-7444; fax 802-247-0113), 3128 Forest Dale Road (Route 73 east), Brandon, VT 05733. Linda and Richard Daybell offer nine comfortable rooms on the first, second, and third floors of this big old white inn out in the country. All have private bath. Beds are queens, doubles, and twins. While rates include breakfast, there is often a dinner option as well because there aren't many restaurants close by. A hiking trail system—accessible directly from the inn—leads to Silver Lake, the cascading falls of Mount Moosalamoo, and the summit of the mountain. The Long Trail is nearby. Bikers and hikers love this place. The inn offers beer and wine. A big porch, a library, a parlor, and an in-ground pool are all favorite guest hangouts. Guest rooms are simply and pleasantly furnished; one has deep salmon walls and a bed with handmade quilt. Most bathrooms have a tub-shower combination. The feeling is country casual. Closed for the month of April. Doubles, B&B, $125–155. Add $25 per person for a four-course dinner. On the menu when we stopped were cream of wild mushroom soup, pear and walnut salad, cedar-planked salmon with pecan crust, and key lime cheesecake.

♦ **The Lilac Inn** (802-247-5463; 1-800-221-0720; www.lilacinn.com), 53 Park Street, Brandon, VT 05733. There really are some unusual yellow lilacs on the property, so the hue of this elegant and sprawling village inn is not inappropriate, says Doug Sawyer, innkeeper. He and his wife, Shelly, oversee one of the most luxurious B&Bs in all Vermont—with everything from a cozy pub, to fine dining, to a fireplaced ballroom where special events (especially weddings) are often held. The house, with a five-arched front facade, was built by a local man, Albert Farr, who established himself as a financier in the Mideast. Constructed as a summer cottage in 1909, the Greek Revival mansion is located on one of the prettiest—and widest—streets in the area, lined with many other gorgeous homes. Much of the inn is devoted to public space so that guests have plenty of room to stroll and enjoy the house and grounds. Outside are a large courtyard, gazebo, and shaded yard. Nine guest rooms are exquisitely outfitted. All have air-conditioning, TV, private bath, and—in three cases—wood-burning fireplace. Room 1, known as the Bridal Suite (a bride doll collection is part of the decor), is huge, with king-sized bed, a Jacuzzi-style tub, and comfortable chairs and sofas. Room 8 is the Warren Kimble room with a huge American flag on one wall—named for the artist who creates so much Americana and who works in Brandon. There's even an old iron cage elevator in the mansion. A full breakfast is served in a handsome dining room done in green and white. Dinners are also offered—to the public as well as guests. Doubles, with breakfast, $135–300.

♦ **The Brandon Inn** (802-247-5766; 1-800-639-8685; fax 802-247-5768; www. historicbrandoninn.com), Brandon, VT 05733. This center-of-town brick inn has a real old-fashioned feeling about it. Built in 1786 and listed on the National Historic Register, the inn has 37 guest rooms that are comfortable but not flashy. There are no TVs, for example, although there are phones. And a decanter of sherry adds a welcoming touch. Bed sizes include twins, doubles, and queens (sometimes two), and bathrooms have clawfoot tubs in some cases. Sizes of bathrooms vary from small to quite large. Rooms are on the second, third, and fourth floors. The common rooms on the first floor are large and offer many seating areas, plus fireplaces. A large dining room is used for guest breakfasts and special events. Doubles, $120–150.

♦ **Strong House Inn** (802-877-3337; fax 802-877-2599; www.stronghouseinn.com), 94 West Main Street, Vergennes, VT 05491. A big pale yellow house with dark green trim offers country-elegant accommodations in the midst of dairy country northwest of Middlebury. It isn't far from Lake Champlain. The town of Vergennes, just down the road, is a fun place to prowl, with one of the finest restaurants in the region, Christophe's (see *Where to Eat*). Hugh and Mary Bargiel, former Floridians, offer 13 rooms in all, 6 of them in the newly constructed Rabbit Ridge country house out back. The room called Adirondack has a king bed, twig-style furniture, a garden patio, and floor-to-ceiling stone fireplace. A double Jacuzzi tub and separate shower are found in the luxurious bathroom. You might never want to leave your digs, except the common areas in the main inn are so inviting. A newly built great room attached to the 1834 house, with a full bar, is a place to spend much of a wintry day. The library, with wing chairs upholstered in a horsey fabric, is also a sophisticated space. All guest rooms have TV, private bath, and predominantly king and queen beds. Those in Rabbit Ridge also have hair dryer, heat light, and balcony or patio. There's even a massage room with a masseuse available by appointment. A full breakfast might include omelets, a cheese and egg strata, or blueberry buttermilk pancakes. Vermont quilting weekends are a specialty here offered in winter and spring. Doubles, $115–275.

WHERE TO EAT

IN MIDDLEBURY

♦ **Tully & Marie's** (802-388-4182), 7 Bakery Lane, Middlebury. The former Woody's down by Otter Creek has been transformed by the husband-and-wife duo Laurie Tully Reed and Carolyn Marie Reed. A bit more innovative than many Middlebury eateries, "T&M's" offers an eclectic menu featuring Italian, southern, and international fare. Pad Thai—made with tofu, chicken, or shrimp—is such a favorite that it almost never leaves the menu. Other entrées at dinner include vegetarian risotto, bourbon shrimp, grilled and roasted honey-mustard rack of lamb, and New York strip steak served with mashed potato and roasted vegetables ($13–20). A warm spinach salad with pancetta and eggs is so popular, it's on both lunch and dinner menus. Other lunch possibilities include a crabcake sandwich, black bean burger, and hickory-smoked turkey sandwich. There's an outside deck for good-weather dining. Open daily for lunch (11:30–3); light fare (3–5); and dinner (5–10). Sunday brunch.

♦ **Fire & Ice** (802-388-7166; 1-800-367-7166), 26 Seymour Street, Middlebury. This is a hard-to-believe spot, describing itself as a "museum dinnerhouse." Two Middlebury College graduates opened it in 1974, and the place expanded recently. Fire & Ice is a warren of normal-sized dining rooms, each with a different theme (the library, the sunporch), all leading off a central make-your-own salad area. Shrimp on the salad bar are famed, as is the restaurant's own carrot cake, tiny cubes of which are available for a quick sugar fix on your way out. The name comes from a Robert Frost poem. Among the memorabilia scattered about are half a dozen World War I wooden airplane propellers, model boats and ships, antique wood skis, snowshoes and tennis rackets, on and on. A 1921 Hackercraft motorboat with wood

The Dog Team Tavern, one of Middlebury's most famous restaurants

trim is definitely the star, displayed close to the salad bar. The menu is fairly standard, focusing on seafood and steaks. Prime rib is a specialty, coming in several sizes. A cashew and vegetable stir-fry and pasta primavera help solve the vegetarian question. Entrées are $15–24. Reservations are a must on weekend nights. Dinner daily from 11:30 AM, except from 5 PM Monday and from 1 PM Sunday. A lunch menu is offered Tuesday through Saturday 11:30–4.

♦ **Dog Team Tavern** (802-388-7651), Dog Team Road off Route 7, 4 miles north of Middlebury (watch for signs). A huge pile of Middlebury College yearbooks (called *Kaleidoscope*) invites perusal in the bustling lobby of this 75-year-old restaurant. It's a legend in town and is as popular locally as with visitors. The name comes from the founder's interests. Sir Wilfred Grenfell, who opened it in the 1930s, was a medical missionary who established hospitals and schools in Labrador and near the Arctic Circle. Inside, antique implements—and many old black stoves—add to the rustic, New England feeling. It's a tradition for many to have Thanksgiving dinner here; there are several seatings throughout the day. Simple wood tables have blue woven place mats. The menu features fish, chicken, and beef—although you can also get Vermont baked ham, roast pork with gravy, and, often, roast duck. Entrées range $14–25 and come with salads and large helpings of home-style vegetables. Open Monday through Saturday 5–9, Sunday noon–9.

♦ **Mr. Up's** (802-388-6724), Bakery Lane, Middlebury. This is a favorite of Middlebury College students. It has just the right pub atmosphere, with brick walls, stained glass, and wood booths. A deck serves in mild weather, overlooking Otter Creek. An extensive salad bar and breadboard are popular—French onion soup is always available. Then you can get chicken wings, baby back pork ribs, hamburgers, pizza, sandwiches. And beer. What more could a college kid want? There are even a few dinners—pasta, strip steak, catch of the day ($10–14). Open 11:30 AM–midnight daily.

◆ **Middlebury Inn** (802-388-4961), on the green, Middlebury. The big old dining room here recently was serving a dinner known as The Carvery. Five meat choices (including turkey, beef, and ham) were carved on the buffet line upon request. You picked up your vegetables and starches and salad fixings. It was all being offered at one price: $16.95.

◆ **The Storm Café** (802-388-1063), 3 Mill Street, Middlebury. Great dinners are found at this creative eatery on the banks of Otter Creek in the Frog Hollow section. Karen and John Goettelmann are the husband-wife team in charge. The dining room is painted bright yellow. In good weather the preferred seating is the wide deck overlooking the river. Mushroom bisque was extraordinary. A winter salad is a mix of wild greens tossed with pears, caramelized onions, bacon, walnuts, and Gorgonzola cheese in a sherry Dijon vinaigrette. Entrées ($13–22) could be grilled New York sirloin over wild mushrooms and caramelized onions, or paella, a very popular dish. Karen is the dessert chef, and her white chocolate banana cream pie in Oreo cookie crust is famed. Dinner 5–9, Tuesday through Saturday.

◆ **The Grille** at the McCullough Student Center on the Middlebury College campus has burgers, sandwiches, salads, and pizzas.

NEARBY

◆ **Christophe's on the Green** (802-877-3413), 5 Green Street, Vergennes. Christophe's is a classy little French restaurant that people will go out of their way to get to. It's housed in the old hotel opposite the green in the center of town. Intimate dining rooms have smallish tables; no parties of more than eight are accommodated. Appetizers ($10) might be white asparagus and morels with a chive sabayon; grilled rabbit and fennel boudin with lima bean printanière; or mussels with a red pepper apple compote. Entrées ($25) could be roasted salmon with a shitake and truffle crust; braised veal breast with sautéed pearl onions and a white truffle potato puree; or soft-shell crabs meunière with zucchini strips and cherry tomatoes. Desserts ($9) could be espresso crème caramel or chocolate brioche and bombe with mint ice cream. Open for dinner from late spring through mid-December, Tuesday through Saturday 5:30–9.

◆ **Mary's at Baldwin Creek** (802-453-2432), Route 116N and Route 17, east of Bristol. Doug Mack, chef-owner, bought the restaurant nearly 20 years ago, but the original owner's name lives on. Mack moved the storefront restaurant from the center of Bristol to this sprawling white farmhouse complex where dinner is served in four atmospheric dining rooms, all but one of them fireplaced. Mary's is known for fine cuisine. It's also a pretty drive to get here. Forty-clove chicken (that's garlic cloves), spicy orange scallops, and potato-crusted trout might be on the dinner entrée list ($19–24), which changes seasonally. Starters include a famous cream of garlic soup, smoked brook trout, and New England crabcakes. All dinners are served with salads, breads, and seasonal vegetables. Local farms are used as suppliers. The annual Wine and Game dinner in late November is legendary. The feeling at Mary's is intimate yet relaxed. Open for dinner from 5 nightly. A few B&B guest rooms are offered upstairs.

♦ **Waybury Inn** (802-388-4015), Route 125, East Middlebury. The Waybury Inn's dining rooms are well respected. The main room has ladderback chairs at tables with cream-colored cloths and green-shaded small lamps. Walls are red, making for a cozy atmosphere. There is also a porch area adjacent with bentwood chairs. Starters ($6–8) could be a mushroom puff, grilled tuna Niçoise, or an asparagus crêpe. Several soups and salads including French onion soup are also offered. Entrées ($15–24) could be the black and tan roast duck, a house specialty, marinated with soy, sherry, and honey and served in an orange sesame sauce; rack of lamb with a rosemary brown sauce; or grilled salmon with a fruit salsa. In the downstairs pub more casual fare is offered. You can get shepherd's pie, a venison burger, a chicken sandwich served with olive tapenade, or a bourbon pub steak ($8–12). Sunday brunch items ($7–10) might be steak and eggs, buttermilk griddlecakes served with apple-smoked ham, or steak and eggs. Dinner 5–9 nightly; from 4 in the pub; Sunday brunch 11–2.

♦ **Lilac Inn** (802-247-5463), Park Street, Brandon. The dining room at the Lilac Inn is open to the public for dinner. Dress up and have a big night out. Starters might be a blue claw crab and artichoke tortolloni, duck confit over corn and celery root flan, or quail broth with rabbit sausage ($5–7). Entrée choices ($17–24) could be fig mango pork short ribs with braised red cabbage and slow-roasted yams; boneless hen finished with port wine and natural pan jus and served with hubbard squash spaetzle; or wood-grilled rainbow trout. Open for dinner Wednesday through Friday in summer; Thursday through Saturday in winter.

♦ **Sully's Place** (802-247-3223), 18–20 Center Street, Brandon. This is about the only place to get a modest bite in Brandon, and it's popular locally. The storefront restaurant does seem to have a taxidermist on staff, what with the little woodland creatures stuffed and on view. If you can get past that, you might be happy to find a place where you can still order a peanut butter and jelly sandwich for lunch, or get a good egg salad sandwich. Burgers, hot dogs, French dip, and grilled cheese are available. Dinner includes chopped sirloin, chicken parmigiana, broiled or fried sea scallops, haddock amandine, and spaghetti with meatballs, sausage, plain sauce, or butter. The entrées are priced $7–16.50. Roast prime rib is available on Friday and Saturday nights. Open daily 11–9; Sunday brunch is served 9–3.

 6 Music and More: The Southern Berkshires, Massachusetts

There's something different—and special—about a summer dose of culture. The straw-hat circuit of theater, the grand summer festivals of music and dance, outdoor concerts, picnics on the lawn. Browsing, sandal-clad, in art museums and galleries, and maybe even watching a sculptor at work. It all seems so lighthearted and easily digestible.

You can enjoy a full slate of cultural experiences in a single summer weekend in the Berkshires in western Massachusetts. Touting the area as "America's Premier Cultural Resort," the Berkshires claim Tanglewood, the summer home of the Boston Symphony Orchestra; Jacob's Pillow, the premier summer dance festival in America; and the Berkshire Theatre Festival, a summer theater founded in 1928 in Stockbridge. There are evenings of baroque music, an opera company, summer jazz, music clubs, a Shakespearean theater company, art museums and galleries, on and on. Certainly in New England—and possibly the country—there is no greater concentration of cultural offerings in a resort setting.

All these riches are found within a relatively small area in the southwestern corner of Massachusetts—just east of New York State and north of Connecticut. The geographic center of this cultural scene is the towns of Lenox and Stockbridge, where traffic backups on Route 7 can make New York visitors (of whom there are many) feel right at home. Nearby towns of Lee, Great Barrington, South Egremont, Sheffield, and Becket—plus tiny villages scattered among the hills—offer their own delights.

The first summer residents to appreciate the virtues of these cool and verdant hills in large numbers came in the late 1880s and early 1900s. Wealthy urbanites, they built some 75 extravagant vacation houses around Lenox and Stockbridge. They were people who hobnobbed with the Newport crowd, but chose the mountains—rather than the sea—to retreat to. Among them were the writer Edith Wharton, whose beautiful estate in Lenox is being returned to its former glory; the illustrious New York lawyer Joseph Choate, whose home in Stockbridge, called Naumkeag, is a magnificent place to see; and Daniel Chester French, sculptor of the *Seated Lincoln* in Washington's Lincoln Memorial. His gracious home, Chesterwood (with his studio), in Stockbridge is a fascinating place to visit.

The depression of the 1920s had no lasting effect upon the allure of the Berkshires. In the late 1920s the theater in Stockbridge that was to become the Berkshire Theatre Festival was founded. In 1932 Ted Shawn created Jacob's Pillow. And in 1937 the Boston Symphony Orchestra made Lenox its summer home. From that time to this, the Berkshires have attracted more and more cultural organizations and festivals, and the "season"—once strictly July and August—is being extended gradually. The theater group Shakespeare & Company now starts up in late spring and continues through October, for example.

Foliage is glorious in the Berkshires, and winter sports like skiing attract a band of devotees. But there's nothing like a visit in summer to sate the cultural palate. Who can resist an afternoon picnic on the Tanglewood lawn in the company of Bach or Beethoven? An evening spent in the rough wood Ted Shawn theater at Jacob's Pillow or the Stanford White–designed building that houses the Berkshire Theatre Festival? How can one not enjoy a morning touring mansions or art museums or galleries, or just sleeping late and rousing oneself for a sumptuous brunch? The Berkshires are, simply, the place to be.

Lodgings are luxurious and restaurants, refined. Prices are high—close to those of New York or Boston—but no one seems to quibble. The pleasures are simply worth the cost. And so, here's to a summer weekend in the Berkshires.

For More Information

♦ **The Berkshire Visitors Bureau** (413-443-9186; 1-800-237-5747; fax 413-443-1970; www.berkshires.org), Berkshire Common, Plaza Level, Pittsfield, MA 01201.

♦ **Lenox Chamber of Commerce** (413-637-3646; fax 413-637-0041; www.lenox.org), 5 Walker Street, P.O. Box 646, Lenox, MA 01240.

♦ **Stockbridge Chamber of Commerce** (413-298-5200; fax 413-298-4321; www. stockbridgechamber.org), 6 Elm Street, P.O. Box 224, Stockbridge, MA 01262.

♦ **Southern Berkshire Chamber of Commerce** (413-528-1510; fax 413-528-6062; www.greatbarrington.org), 40 Railroad Street, Suite 1A, P.O. Box 810, Great Barrington, MA 01230.

Getting There

By air. The major nearby airports are Albany Airport in Albany, New York, 45 miles; Bradley International Airport, Windsor Locks, Connecticut, 70 miles; Logan International Airport, Boston, Massachusetts, 135 miles.

By bus: From Boston, **Peter Pan/Trailways** (1-800-343-9999) serves Lee and Lenox daily. You can make connections to Stockbridge. From New York, **Bonanza bus lines** (1-800-556-3815) serves Sheffield, Great Barrington, Stockbridge, Lee, and Lenox 7 days a week.

By car: From Boston, take the Mass Pike (Route 20) to Lee (2 hours). From New York City, most people take the Henry Hudson Parkway or Major Deegan

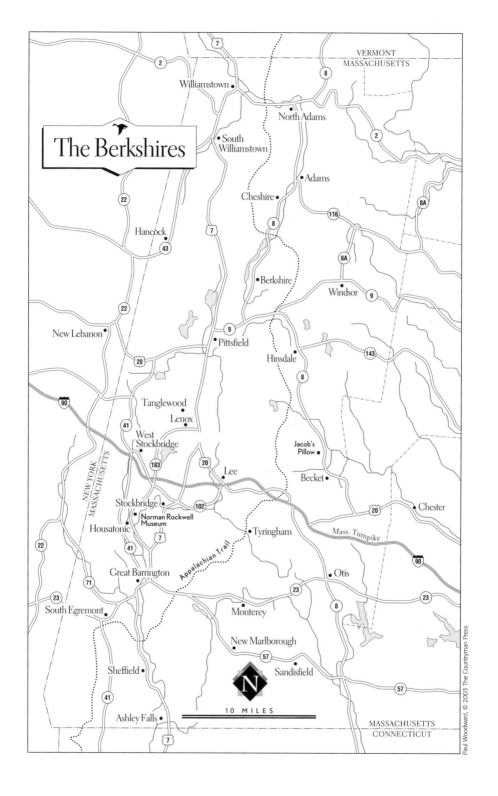

The Berkshires

VERMONT
MASSACHUSETTS

Williamstown

North Adams

South Williamstown

Adams

Cheshire

Hancock

Berkshire

Windsor

New Lebanon

Pittsfield

Hinsdale

Tanglewood

Lenox

West Stockbridge

Jacob's Pillow

Lee

Becket

Stockbridge

Norman Rockwell Museum

Chester

Housatonic

Tyringham

Mass. Turnpike

Great Barrington

Otis

NEW YORK
MASSACHUSETTS

Appalachian Trail

South Egremont

Monterey

New Marlborough

Sheffield

Sandisfield

Ashley Falls

N

10 MILES

MASSACHUSETTS
CONNECTICUT

Paul Woodward, © 2003 The Countryman Press

Expressway to the Saw Mill River Parkway, then the Taconic Parkway to the exit for Route 23 into the Berkshires. From Hartford, a beautiful drive takes you on Route 44 west to Route 183 north into New Marlborough, Massachusetts, and then Route 57 to Route 23 west into Great Barrington. It's a lovely, quiet route.

Getting Around

A car is the best way to get from town to town. There are several taxi companies if you plan to stay in one place and only need a ride occasionally.

SEEING AND DOING

The Berkshires attract visitors for many reasons. Mount Greylock in the north and Monument Mountain in the south are the major hiking mountains. Streams, like the Housatonic River, call to kayakers, canoeists, and anglers. There are lovely parks and scenic drives. Small lakes for swimming and stables for horseback riding can all be found.

In this chapter we focus on the cultural attractions.

Music

♦ **Tanglewood** (413-637-5165; in winter 617-266-1492), 297 West Street (Route 183), Lenox. To charge tickets through the BSO Symphony Charge, call 1-888-266-1200. Tickets are also sold through TicketMaster. You can order tickets online at www. bso .org. And if you want to buy tickets in person, they are sold at Tanglewood's box office beginning in early June 10–6 daily, noon–6 Sunday.

The Boston Symphony Orchestra's summer home is located on a beautiful green parcel of land actually named by Nathaniel Hawthorne (who wrote *Tanglewood Tales*). The summer concert series opens the July 4 weekend—or closest to it—and continues through August. Then the **Tanglewood Jazz Festival** kicks in at the end. The concerts are held in an open-sided building with marvelous acoustics known simply as "the Shed." More formally, the Koussevitzky Music Shed (Serge Koussevitzky was director of the BSO back in 1936 when the orchestra first came to the Berkshires) seats 5,000. If you don't have a reserved seat, you can always get a lawn ticket ($14.50–18, depending on the event), which some prefer. On a nice evening or Sunday afternoon, the lawn at Tanglewood is the place to be. People have been known to bring white linen and china and even to dress formally for their "picnic" at Tanglewood. Others, of course, spread out blankets and eat egg salad sandwiches. It can be very hot, rainy, or buggy at Tanglewood, and it's a good idea to prepare for exigencies.

In addition to the summer concert series on Friday and Saturday evenings and Sunday afternoons, there are Saturday-morning open rehearsals at 10:30 in the shed ($15) preceded by a 9:30 pre-rehearsal talk (free to ticketholders). This is a wonderful and more informal way for people to hear the orchestra—as it tunes up for the Saturday-night concert—and many people purchase subscriptions to the rehearsals.

Seiji Ozawa Hall is used for vocal recitals and a variety of chamber music concerts held during the week. In addition, the Boston Pops Orchestra has a concert or more during the summer at Tanglewood. Special musical events are also scheduled, including concerts by the Tanglewood Music Center students—emerging professional musicians of exceptional ability. Seiji Ozawa, the longest-presiding conductor in the history of the BSO, conducted his farewell concert in 2002. A series of interim conductors was expected to perform until the arrival of James Levine in 2004 as music director of the BSO. Levine has been the artistic director of the Metropolitan Opera. Concert tickets are priced $17–88. Up to four children 12 and younger can be admitted free to lawn concerts. Friday- and Saturday-evening concerts start at 8:30; the Sunday matinees begin at 2:30 PM.

♦ **Berkshire Opera Company** (413-644-9988), 40 Railroad Street, Great Barrington, MA 01230. This 18-year-old group purchased the Mahaiwe Theatre on Castle Street in Great Barrington in 2001. During the 2002 seasons, renovations were under way and the company had an abbreviated season with just one chamber opera offered in August. However, plans were to expand to a year-round schedule. Tickets, $20–60.

♦ **Aston Magna Festival** (413-528-3595; 1-800-875-7156), P.O. Box 28, Great Barrington, MA 01230. For more than 30 years, extraordinary baroque, classical, and early romantic chamber music concerts have been offered on five Saturdays in July and August. Concerts are given at St. James Church, corner of Main and Taconic Streets, Great Barrington, at 6 PM. Music is always played on period instruments. Daniel Stepner, festival director and violinist, leads a celebrated group of singers and players. The concerts have received excellent reviews by music critics. Tickets, $25.

♦ **Berkshire Choral Festival** (413-229-1999), 245 North Undermountain Road, Sheffield, MA 01257. Here is another long-lived music festival. For more than 20 years, the Berkshire Choral Festival has offered a series of five well-anticipated summer concerts. More than 200 voices (mostly experienced amateurs, along with some professionals) can be heard along with the Springfield Symphony. Performances are held in the open-air Rovensky Concert Shed on the lovely grounds of the Berkshire School. Picnicking is possible on the lawn before the concerts. The events take place on Saturday evenings in July and August. Tickets, $22–30.

Several music series are offered in area towns in summer. For example, Stockbridge Summer Music offers weekly concerts at Seven Hills Inn in Lenox (see *Where to Stay*).

Dance

♦ **Jacob's Pillow** (413-243-0745; fax 413-243-0749), 358 George Carter Road, Becket, MA 01223. (Mailing address: P.O. Box 287, Lee, MA 01238.) Order tickets online until 48 hours prior to performances, starting in spring, at www.jacobs-pillow.org. Known simply as "the Pillow" in the world of dance, this summer dance festival is preeminent in the country. Founded in 1933 by Ted Shawn—who with his wife, Ruth St. Denis, headed up the Denishawn Troupe of Dancers—the Pillow has attracted the greatest dance artists of the 20th and 21st centuries.

The Ted Shawn Theatre at the Jacob's Pillow Dance Festival

Shawn and his male dancers literally built the early buildings and blazed trails on the 150-acre site by hand. Mikhail Baryshnikov declared the place "one of America's most precious cultural assets," and the Pillow was recently named to the National Register of Historic Places. It is a magical place. The beloved 600-seat native pine Ted Shawn Theatre, constructed in 1942, hosts a different major dance company each week from late June through August. Now there is also the Doris Duke Studio Theatre—a 220-seat house with stage and seating areas that can be configured in many ways.

Often a performance at the Ted Shawn Theatre (designed by Joseph Franz, designer of Tanglewood's Shed) runs concurrently with a more experimental work at the Duke Theatre. Blake's Barn, an 18th-century barn moved in 1990 from Stockbridge, was a gift from Marge Champion, dancer and Berkshire resident, in memory of her son, Blake. It houses the box office, exhibits, and archives. The deck in back of the barn, known as Sommerspace, is used for Pillow Talks on Saturday, for Pre-Show Talks for the Ted Shawn Theatre (half an hour before performances), and as an informal rehearsal space. Inside/Out is an outdoor stage built in 1981. Every Wednesday through Saturday at 6:30 PM there's a free performance here featuring artists-in-residence, guest artists, and faculty and students at the school. On a nice night, against a Berkshires sunset, it can be a wonderful experience.

Food may be obtained at the Pillow Pub—with a full bar, snacks, and light meals (we picked up our picnic suppers there; they can be ordered ahead)—and at the Pillow Café, which offers fine casual dining under a striped tent before the performance. You can also bring your own picnic. There are several picnic tables and other spaces to set up. Jacob's Pillow celebrated its 70th anniversary in 2002 with a gala 99th birthday for theater artist Al Hirschfeld, who designed the cover of their program that year. Baryshnikov performed that season. Ted Shawn Theatre tickets, $40–50; Doris Duke Studio Theatre tickets, $20.

Theater

♦ **Berkshire Theatre Festival** (413-298-5576), 6 East Main Street, (Route 102), P.O. Box 797, Stockbridge, MA 01262. The Berkshire Playhouse—now the BTF—opened here in 1928. The building was designed by Stanford White in 1887 as a casino; 40 years later it was given by philanthropist Mabel Choate of Naumkeag fame to the Three Arts Society and moved to this site. The playhouse is well known in American summer theater. Works by top American playwrights have been performed here, including Tennessee Williams, Eugene O'Neill, and Thornton Wilder. Wilder's *Our Town* was produced here with Wilder himself in a featured role. A young Katharine Hepburn appeared here. Dustin Hoffman and Joanne Woodward also have been seen on the BTF stage.

Usually four major productions, including at least one musical, are presented in July and August in the main theater. The 100-seat Unicorn Theatre presents four newer or more experimental works concurrently. Interns and apprentices pursue a program of classes in acting, voice, dance, and design. Tickets, $28–47 for the major productions; $20–25 at the Unicorn Theatre.

♦ **Shakespeare & Company** (413-637-3353; fax 413-637-3160), 70 Kemble Street, Lenox, MA 01240. Tickets also may be ordered online at www.shakespeare.org. Under the artistic guidance of English actor-director Tina Packer, this theater company celebrated its 25th anniversary in 2002 at its expansive new 63-acre home at Spring Lawn, most recently the home of the National Music Foundation. Just a short distance from Edith Wharton's The Mount, where the company had performed since its inception, the new grounds offer a 428-seat Founders' Theatre as well as a smaller, 99-seat Spring Lawn space. Perhaps most exciting of all, the company plans to build a historically accurate reconstruction of the 1587 Rose Playhouse of Shakespeare's London on their new grounds (completion projected by 2007). For the project the company received a $1 million development grant from the U.S. government. Until then, the Rose Footprint Theatre, an outdoor space, is being used.

While the company is true to its name, it also honors the works of Edith Wharton and stages other productions. In 2002, for example, *Macbeth* was presented at the Founders' Theater, *Henry VI (Parts I, II, and III)* at the outdoor Rose Footprint Theater, and Edith Wharton's one-act plays, adapted from her stories *Roman Fever* and *The Other Two*. There was also an adaptation of Nathaniel Hawthorne's *The Scarlet Letter* later in the season at the Founders' Theatre. The beat goes on. This is already one of the most exciting Shakespeare festivals in North America. Tickets, $10–50.

♦ **Barrington Stage Company** (413-528-8888; fax 413-528-8807; www.barrington-stageco.org), Box 1205, Consolati Performing Arts Center, Mount Everett Regional High School, Great Barrington, MA 01230. A 1990s addition to the theater scene in the Berkshires, the BSC now has an ambitious summer program. The main stage presents three productions a season, with Stage II offering a couple of more experimental works. There are also occasional 1-night-only events. A summer acting program operates for kids aged 8–17. Preshow talks with artistic director Julianne Boyd are given on Thursday at 7:30 PM. Tickets, $24–40 for the main stage; $20–25 for Stage II; $8–13 for Youth Theatre.

Art

♦ **Norman Rockwell Museum at Stockbridge** (413-298-4100; 1-800-742-9450; fax 413-298-4142; www.nrm.org), Route 183, P.O. Box 308, Stockbridge, MA 01262. The new Norman Rockwell Museum—moved into this $4.4 million building designed by Robert A. M. Stern in 1993—always seems a tad pretentious to us, although its white-clapboard siding and fieldstone terraces are intended to evoke a New England feeling. No matter. It's what's inside that counts. Whether you view Rockwell as artist or illustrator (after a lengthy visit here, you may lean toward the former), there is much to see.

Norman Rockwell is simply one of the most beloved artists—and chroniclers of American life—in the country. He lived for many years in the village of Stockbridge, and his snowy holiday painting of Stockbridge Main Street is one of his most beloved. Prior to moving to this museum, his artworks were displayed at The Old Corner House, a classic white-clapboard house in Stockbridge. Since its move, the museum has become one of the most popular visitors' sites in the Berkshires.

At the center is a skylit gallery where Rockwell's *Four Freedoms* are on permanent display. Painted during World War II, they represent freedom of speech, freedom from fear, freedom of worship, and freedom from want. Rockwell had a long relationship with the *Saturday Evening Post*, and his images graced its covers for nearly half a century. Many of these covers are on display—as are later images done for *Look* and *McCall's* magazines. One of the most memorable is the view of federal marshals leading a young black girl to school in Little Rock, Arkansas, under court order.

In addition to Rockwell's works, the museum mounts special exhibits and sponsors special events.

The actual studio in which Rockwell worked has been moved to the grounds and is a short walk from the museum. It's free with museum admission. Here a tour guide is usually stationed who can explain some of the objects in the studio (recreated exactly as it looked at Rockwell's death). There are masks as well as paintings on the wall, and a fireman's helmet bought at a Parisian flea market that the artist referred to as his "humility helmet." The bookcases contain art books he used as references. It is a lovely place, one that helps you feel closer to Rockwell. On the grounds of the museum are sculptures created by the youngest of Rockwell's three sons, Peter.

There is a large museum store and a self-service Terrace Café under a tent, operated by the Red Lion Inn. Here you can get a cup of coffee or tea, a muffin or baked item, and sandwiches and salads at lunchtime. You can also bring your own picnic to the site. Open daily year-round, 10–5 from May to October; the rest of the year, 10–4 weekdays, 10–5 weekends. The studio is open May 1 through November 1. Museum free Thursday 5–8. Adults $12, students $7, kids free up to age 18.

♦ **Chesterwood** (413-298-3579; www.chesterwood.org), 4 Williamsville Road (off Route 183), P.O. Box 827, Stockbridge, MA 01262. This country estate with home, studio, garden, and museum gallery reflects the life and work of Daniel Chester French, creator of the *Seated Lincoln* in Washington's Lincoln Memorial as well as the *Minute Man* statue in Concord, Massachusetts. The site was discovered by French in 1895, when he was already widely regarded as a sculptor, having created

Norman Rockwell's studio on the grounds of the Norman Rockwell Museum in Stockbridge

the *Minute Man* at the age of 25. In 1969 the estate was donated by his daughter to the National Trust for Historic Preservation. The 17-room Colonial Revival house is a beautiful place, especially the wide central hallway through which Berkshire breezes still cool visitors. The original wallpaper in that hall, a landscape on Japanese rice paper, was recently taken off, treated by conservators, and reapplied to the walls. Gracious rooms are viewed with original furnishings. But the studio is the heart of this tour. Authentic to the time he worked there, it contains plaster casts used as models of the *Seated Lincoln,* as well as a beautiful statue of *Andromeda* that he was working on at the time of his death. There is a railroad track with flatcar on which sculptures could be placed and wheeled out to allow French to view them in natural light.

A barn gallery has an excellent display of French's sculptures and the process by which they were created. Maquettes for the four sculptures for the U.S. Custom House in New York City (Asia, America, Europe, and Africa) are on view here. Also here are casts of French's own hands, which he studied to establish the way Lincoln's would look. The gift shop has interesting items, including a small copy of the *Minute Man* statue in bronze ($900) and in resin ($179). Don't leave before you step out back to see resident sculptor Andrew DeVries at work. DeVries, whose studio is in Middlefield, Massachusetts, spends summers at Chesterwood, where he displays some of his fine bronze sculptures. On Saturday and Sunday, weather permitting, he gives a demonstration at 1:30 PM.

The gardens at Chesterwood are lovely. On the grounds, also, is **Meadowlark,** a cottage built by French as a second studio in 1905 to escape the distraction of visitors. He called it the "lower studio"—later given its name by his daughter—and used it to work on such commissions as the standing *Abraham Lincoln* for the State Capitol in Lincoln, Nebraska. After his death in 1931 the studio was adapted for use as a summer residence. It is now rented out for short stays. It has two bedrooms, a small kitchen, a spacious living room, and a full bath. There is also a large deck with views of Monument Mountain. Call the Red Lion Inn for information, because it handles reservations—(413) 298-5545.

Chesterwood is open from May through October, daily 10–5, with guided tours offered every hour on the half hour 10:30–3:30. There are picnic tables on the site. Adults $10, seniors $8, children 6–18 $5. Family group $20.

♦ **Frelinghuysen Morris House & Studio** (413-637-0166; www.frelinghuysen.org), 92 Hawthorne Street, P.O. Box 2256, Lenox, MA 01240. Here's a change of pace. Suzy Frelinghuysen and George L. K. Morris, husband and wife, were socialites and abstract artists from the 1930s to the latter part of the 20th century. They built this contemporary house in 1942 as an addition to an earlier studio that George had built for himself. Having studied art in Paris, he became a great fan of Cubism and continued to practice in the Cubist style through most of his life. Suzy also did Cubist paintings but was more eclectic—as the art on her bedroom walls will attest. She was also a trained opera singer and sang with the City Center Opera in New York City for several years.

Morris collected art and owned several Picassos, Legers, Mirós, and others of the period that are on exhibit here as well.

The house is sited a good distance from the road in a wooded setting carved from a piece of Morris's family property on the back side of Tanglewood. You park and buy tickets at a screened-gazebo, then walk or are shuttled the approximate half mile to the house itself. We gratefully accepted the ride. With its flat roof, glass brick facade, and square, low profile, the white concrete house is in the Bauhaus and art deco style. On one outside wall is a Cubist-influenced fresco by Morris called *The Battle of the Indians*—intended to portray some of the history and struggle for land in this part of the country. Inside at ground level are a dining room with predominantly blue Cubist frescoes by Suzy, a large living room with grand piano and frescoes by George, along with a marble bas-relief he designed and a small studio used by Suzy with a Matisse on the wall. George Morris knew the French artist.

Upstairs are the owners' two bedrooms, with adjoining bathrooms and a rather modest guest bedroom. (Another building on the property was also used as a guest cottage, we were told.) George's very large skylit studio has a Calder mobile, three Mirós, and several of George's own paintings.

Do wait to see the video at the end of the tour, which helps put the couple and their time in the art world into perspective. You learn that Morris's studio—built in the early 1930s—was the first modern structure in the New England landscape. Open July 4 through Labor Day, Thursday through Sunday 10–3; September through Columbus Day, Thursday through Saturday with reduced hours. You must tour in a group. Adults $9, children $3.

♦ **Naumkeag** (413-298-3239; www.thetrustees.org), 5 Prospect Hill Road, Stockbridge, MA 01262. The home of Joseph Hodges Choate, a wealthy New York lawyer, Naumkeag was named for the area around Salem, Massachusetts, that was Choate's birthplace. He and his wife had five children, and the family began summering in the Berkshires in 1884. This property was purchased that year—admired for its stunning view of Monument Mountain and the Berkshire hills—and a house was designed by Stanford White. It's a brick shingle home with turrets and walls, but one that does not seem pretentious.

Mabel Choate, the younger of the Choates' two daughters, inherited the property in 1929 and set to work on the gardens in earnest. She collaborated with landscape architect Fletcher Steele over a period of nearly 30 years to design exceptional outdoor "rooms" that spill down the hillside behind the house. These extraordinary gardens are the highlight of a trip to Naumkeag, so interesting that some people never step inside the gracious home. To the south, or left, as you exit the rear of the house, are the Outdoor Room and the Afternoon Garden. Oak pilings dredged from Boston Harbor were carved and painted to resemble Venetian posts. The marble-chip walks and four small fountains make for an intimate and picturesque spot. There are more elaborate and dramatic areas at Naumkeag, but this is my favorite. The Linden Walk, planned by the wife of Joseph Choate, is shaded by an archway of more than 50 trees. Behind the house, running down the center of the hillside, is an imaginative series of terraced steps known as the Fountain Steps. Water trickles as one pool flows to the next level and birch leaves shimmer from the trees flanking the steps. The Chinese Garden is a magical world of its own, enclosed by brick walls and filled with stone Buddhas, lions, dogs, and other carvings brought back from the Orient by Mabel Choate in 1935.

The tour through the 26-room house encompasses all three floors. Throughout are Stanford White–designed fireplaces. Naumkeag is under the auspices of the Trustees of Reservations. Open Memorial Day weekend through Columbus Day, daily 10–5. Guided tours of the house, 35 minutes; self-guided tours of gardens. Adults $9 for house and gardens, $7 gardens alone; children $3 for either or both.

The Mount (413-637-1899; fax 413-637-1899; www.edithwharton.org), 2 Plunkett Street, Lenox, MA 01240. Edith Wharton was the first woman novelist to win a Pulitzer Prize—for *The Age of Innocence* in 1920—but her first published book was one on interior decorating. *The Decoration of Houses*, published in 1897, is still in print. Wharton's summer home in the Berkshires, built in 1902 when she was 40, is her statement of how a house should be organized and decorated. Its design is based on precepts outlined in that first book, cowritten with interior designer and architect Ogden Codman Jr., who also was influential in helping decorate the

The Mount in Lenox, once writer Edith Wharton's home. It is now a museum.

house. The Mount celebrated its centennial in grand style in 2002. Seven internationally known interior decorators agreed to decorate one room each in the spirit of Edith Wharton. So the leopard-design carpeting that runs up the stairs is not necessarily what Wharton had when in residence, but was chosen for an interest, or an aspect of Wharton's personality, and as a way of emphasizing the hall's design.

Because the house was sold in 1911 and had several owners between then and 1980 when Edith Wharton Restoration (EWR) took over, personal furnishings of the author are not here. But the installations by the designers are expected to be in place for a few years, after which the hunt will be on to find original Wharton pieces. The restoration of Wharton's beautiful walled garden, paths and beds for her French-style flower garden, and the "lime walk" connecting the two has been completed.

Although the writer and her husband, Teddy Wharton, only resided here from 1902 through 1907, The Mount was a special place to Edith Wharton. She entertained notables here, including her close friend, writer Henry James. Wharton wrote her first best-seller, *The House of Mirth*, and the book *Ethan Frome* while in residence. "The Mount was my first real home . . . and its blessed influence still lives in me," she wrote in 1934 in France, just three years before her death. There is a shop selling all sorts of paraphernalia and many of the author's works. A terrace café operates 10–3, with beverages, snacks, and light lunches available.

Open early June to early November, 9–5; the grounds remain open until 6. Adults $16, students $8, children under 12 free if accompanied by an adult. Tours are in a group or self-guided. The gardens are self-guided.

♦ **Santarella Museum and Gardens** (413-243-3260), 75 Main Road, Tyringham. Looking like a gingerbread house from the exterior, this unusual place served as the art studio for sculptor Henry Hudson Kitson, who sculpted the *Minuteman* statue in Lexington, Massachusetts. Changing art exhibitions are mounted. Open from the end of May through October, daily 10–5. Admission $4; under 6, free.

♦ **Berkshire Botanical Garden**, (413-298-3926) Routes 102 and 183, P.O. Box 826, Stockbridge, MA 01262. Founded in 1934, this is an active horticultural center with diverse display gardens and special events. In 2002 the garden became especially interesting to art lovers when it sponsored a season-long installation of contemporary sculpture by the organization Sculpture Now called *Sculpture in the Garden 2002*. Otherwise, it's mostly of interest to gardeners. Allow 45 minutes for a visit. Open May to October, daily 10–5. Adults $7, seniors $5, students $5.

The Gilded Age

♦ **Ventfort Hall** (413-637-3206; www.gildedage.org), 104 Walker Street, P.O. Box 2424, Lenox, MA 01240. Saved from the wrecking ball in 1997 by a group of concerned Lenox citizens, Ventfort Hall was built in 1893 by George and Sarah Morgan (she was J. P. Morgan's sister and married a man with the same last name!) as a summer home. Costing $900,000, it was the most expensive Berkshire "cottage" at the time. It's described as an Elizabethan Revival mansion, constructed primarily of red brick with some stained-glass windows and dark wood accents. Rotch & Tilden, prominent Boston architects, were the designers.

The restoration is under way, albeit slowly. The main-floor dining room with woodwork of Cuban mahogany has been restored at a cost of $1 million. The soaring three-story great hall and staircase, with wood paneling, is occasionally used for special events. So far, these have been the only two rooms into which the public is allowed. The house served as the site of the orphanage in the movie *Cider House Rules* in 1998. Listed on the National Register of Historic Places, Ventfort Hall is intended to become a museum to showcase society during the period of the "Gilded Age." Open June to October, daily 10–3. Adults $8, children $4.

Shopping

It's fun to shop in the Berkshires. From tasteful (most of the stores) to tacky, you will find ways to spend what little you may have left—after paying your room, board, and ticket prices.

If you're looking for antiques, head immediately for the town of **Sheffield,** where good shops line Route 7 on both sides of the road. **Great Barrington** is another town with many antiques and collectibles shops, although you will find them in all towns, dotted here and there. Otherwise, here's a very personal list of shops I like.

In **Lenox, Colorful Stitches** at 48 Main Street (in a complex of stores; you can park in the back) is a knitting store with an unparalleled selection of yarns, patterns, and associated paraphernalia. Next door is the **B. J. Faulkner** art gallery with colorful, splashy paintings by the owner. There's definitely a Matisse influence here. **Cose d'Argilla** on Church Street is a shop with an interesting mix of all things Italian. **B. Mango & Bird** at 74 Main Street is a gift shop with everything from natural sponges and "Esther Williams" shower curtains to intriguing rugs and lamps. It's one of my favorites. Next door, **Berkshire Classic Leather & Silver** offers leather clothing, belts, and pocketbooks—even a leather director's chair!—as well as turquoise and silver jewelry from the Southwest. **The Gifted Child** on Church Street—and its sibling on Railroad Street in Great Barrington—have wonderful children's toys, costumes, games. **J. Warner Antiques** on the lower level of a brick building on Housatonic Street is fun to prowl; several dealers are represented. For women's clothes, by far my favorite is **Evviva** on Walker Street with truly unusual duds—you won't see yourself coming and going. Oh yes, there's a longtime **Talbots,** also on Walker, with its classic red door. **Tanglewool** has some gorgeous sweaters.

For music—sheet, CDs, tapes, and more—the **Tanglewood Music Store** just opposite the main gate at Tanglewood ought to be visited. The store especially stocks works by featured artists.

Great Barrington has some very interesting shops and restaurants on **Railroad Street,** off Main. **Gatsby's** has unusual and funky stuff for women, including nightgowns, Birkenstocks, even housewares. **Byzantium** has stylish and fun dresses, sweaters, blouses, and skirts as well as jewelry. **Seeds & Co. Inc.** has home and bath accessories—some quite original. On Main Street, just around the corner from Railroad, find two places to buy your CDs and tapes of classical, jazz, and blues. **Tune Street** at 294 Main Street also sells electronic gear. **White Knight Records** at

288 Main Street has been in town since 1979 and has an excellent selection of classical music. For books, **The Yellow House** on Main Street is fun to prowl—the emphasis is used books, but there are a few regional books that are new. For best-sellers, go to the **Bookloft** in the Barrington Plaza on Route 7 north of downtown.

In **Stockbridge** check out **The Pink Kitty**, the gift shop at the **Red Lion Inn**. You will find everything from souvenir mugs to books by Norman Rockwell for children. **Williams & Son Country Store** on Main Street is a classic general store with everything from jams and jellies to gifts, cards, gourmet foods, and some nostalgia items. **Sweaters Etc.** in a house behind the Red Lion Inn on Route 7 has an incredible collection of sweaters in wool and cotton.

In **Lee** wander the rooms in the big yellow house that is **Pamela Loring Gifts & Interiors**. Seasonal gifts and decorations are found here. **H A Johansson 5 & 10** on Main Street is a real old-fashioned five-and-dime store with a large sewing section. **The Upstairs Basement** on Main is an ongoing tag sale in a large double storefront. You never know what you'll find.

WHERE TO STAY

Call as soon as you have an idea you want to come to the Berkshires—winter and early spring are not too early to book for summer. Some people reserve rooms a year in advance, and we know one B&B where a faithful Tanglewood fan books a room for every single weekend in summer. Many—if not most—lodging establishments insist on 3 to 5 nights over holiday weekends, and sometimes there are 3-night minimums even for regular weekends. In addition to all the cultural venues, overnight camps in the Berkshires mean that parents will be in to drop kids off, visit kids, pick up kids, adding to the demand for rooms. Lodging prices in summer—the culture season—are among the highest in New England.

Full-Service Inns

♦ **Blantyre** (413-637-3556; fax 413-637-4282; www.blantyre.com), Blantyre Road, P.O. Box 995, Lenox, MA 01240. Want to live like royalty? You can, for a few days at least, at this castle—for that's what it is. When the original owner, Robert Paterson, acquired 220 acres here in the 1890s, he asked for a castle of "feudal architectural features," complete with towers, turrets, and gargoyles. The house was actually modeled after his wife's ancestral home in Scotland. In addition to the main house there were seven outbuildings, including an icehouse, stables for 16 horses, a carriage house, and extensive greenhouses.

In 1980 Jack and Jane Fitzpatrick of the Red Lion Inn in nearby Stockbridge bought the property, determined to restore it to its former elegance. They—and now daughter Ann Fitzpatrick Brown, who is the owner—have succeeded. Everything about Blantyre is tasteful, elegant, and not a bit glitzy. It is now recognized as one of the best small hotels in the world and is a member of the exclusive Relais & Châteaux group. Altogether 8 beautifully decorated, antiques-filled bedrooms and suites are located in the Tudor-style main house, 12 in the Carriage House and in four individual cottages, including the original icehouse. Beds might be four-poster or draped, and all but one are king or queen sized. Five rooms in the main house have a wood-burning fireplace, as do three cottages. Common rooms in the main house have dark wood paneling and furnishings that can only be described as regal; several ornately carved chairs and settees are upholstered in a cherry damask. The large Music Room at one end of the main house allows smoking.

Although there is no golf course on the 100-acre property, the Cranwell golf course is next door and Blantyre guests are accommodated with tee times (although golf is not complimentary). On the property are four Har-Tru tennis courts, two tournament croquet lawns, shuffleboard, and a secluded swimming pool. In-room massages may be scheduled. Horse-and-carriage rides are offered guests on Sunday morning. Continental breakfast is included in the rates, served in the conservatory off the dining room. Guests may order a larger breakfast off the menu. Dinner in a lovely intimate dining room is available nightly except Monday, with jackets and ties required (see *Where to Eat*). Children 12 and up are welcome. Doubles in the main house range $370–750 (the latter for the Paterson Suite, a large space with king-bedded bedroom, fireplaced living room, and two bathrooms). Carriage house rooms rent for $330–395. Cottages are $510–1,150 (for the Ice House, with two bedrooms, two baths, a sitting room with fireplace, screened porch, and patio). Open May to November.

♦ **Wheatleigh** (413-637-0610; fax 413-637-4507; www.wheatleigh.com), Hawthorne Road, Lenox, MA 01240. An Italianate villa on the back side of Tanglewood— restored to an elegant country manor house by owners Susan and Linfield Simon— is Wheatleigh. Originally built in 1893, it was given a complete redo in the mid-1990s. The mellow wheat-colored brick building with wrought-iron trim has a high-ceilinged entry area with formal, tasteful furnishings and mammoth fireplace. Everything is expertly arranged, even some Granny Smith apples in a large porcelain bowl that looked as if they ought to be broken apart by a cue stick. Altogether there are 19 guest rooms, about half with fireplace. All have TV with VCR, CD player, and two phones—one portable. Most have a separate tub and stall shower in the private bathroom. The most sought after, we're told, is the Aviary, a two-level suite with windowed downstairs sitting room, a glass-enclosed circular staircase to the upper-level bedroom, and a bathroom with antique soaking tub and separate shower area. It rents for $1,275 on Tanglewood and fall foliage weekends, $1,050 other times. There's an outdoor oval-shaped heated swimming pool in a treed area and a single tennis court. You can walk to Tanglewood if you want. Although breakfast is not included in the rates, it's served in the same wonderful windowed portico where dinner is offered nightly in summer and weekends off-season. Doubles, $465–1,275.

♦ **The Old Inn on the Green and Gedney Farm** (413-229-3131; 1-800-286-3139; fax 413-229-8236; www.oldinn.com), Route 57, New Marlborough, MA 01230. Gedney Farm is the accommodations portion of this extraordinary inn that unobtrusively dominates one of the quietest villages in the Berkshires. Leslie Miller and Brad Wagstaff, the couple who conceived and continue to create new sections of the property, have added a manor house to several options for where to lay your head. Gedney Manor is a stone guesthouse originally built in 1906 as a family estate, and more recently used as a private school. Located on a dirt road a bit northwest of the other properties in the complex, the manor house has a dozen guest rooms on the second and third floors, most with beautiful green views of the surrounding hills in summer. You enter the building and find yourself in a great hall with a huge fireplace, with a high-backed brown plush sofa and four large armchairs at one end, and with French doors that open out to a terrace furnished in teak. Original dark wood paneling has been restored in what is being used as the breakfast room to one side of the great room—so guests don't have to walk or drive all the way to the breakfast area in a barn on the east end of the complex, a couple of miles distant. You can, on the other hand, walk to the main buildings of the inn past a beaver pond and across high meadows anytime you want. Walking is one of the pleasures of staying out here in New Marlborough, and more trails are being developed.

Rooms at the manor all feel as if they might be stage backdrops for a movie set in an English country house. Room 502, a turret room, has a king bed with red-and-gold woven spread, a wood-burning fireplace, and an extra-wide stall shower in the bathroom. Off the second floor is a terrace with teak steamer chairs for reading, sleeping, or gazing at the bucolic countryside.

The actual inn on the green, dating from 1760, contains the candlelit dining rooms where four-star meals are served (see *Where to Eat*). But it also has five authentically restored and updated guest rooms, all with private bath, and one with a fireplace and porch. Gedney Farm rooms, in a renovated Normandy-style barn nearby, are ingeniously designed, both elegant and rustic, with a four-poster canopy queen bed, perhaps, and rough barn siding hung with an elegant Oriental carpet. Many of the 16 accommodations here have a fireplace. The Stebbins House is a four-bedroom Colonial house often rented by one family or group. Most elegant are the accommodations in Thayer House, next door to the inn itself, with five large, luxurious guest rooms and its own swimming pool. Four of the rooms have their own fireplace; bathrooms are elegantly appointed. Altogether there are 43 rooms, with a continental breakfast included. An on-site recreation director leads guests on hikes, bike rides, nature walks, and offers yoga, meditation, and chi gong in addition to kayaking, canoeing, and fishing. You can be as active or as lazy as you'd like. Doubles in the inn, $175–215; in Gedney Farm, $185–245; in Gedney Manor, $220–280; in Thayer House, $325–365. Stebbins House rooms, if rented separately and sharing baths, are $175.

◆ **The Red Lion Inn** (413-298-5545; fax 413-298-5130; www.redlioninn.com), 30 Main Street, Stockbridge, MA 01262. The inn's big wide porch overlooking Main Street is crowded all summer long, testimony to how center-of-the-action this venerable place is. The Red Lion's history dates back to 1773, although the imposing white inn on the corner of Routes 7 and 102 in the center of Stockbridge that you see today was completely rebuilt in 1897 and then added onto. The inn's prominence in a painting by Norman Rockwell of *Stockbridge, Main Street*, added cachet. Jane and Jack Fitzpatrick—and now their daughters, too—took over the inn in the late 1960s and made it what it is today. Their reach is wide—since then, the Fitzpatricks have taken over Blantyre in Lenox, Jack's Grill in Housatonic, the food concession at the Norman Rockwell Museum, and more. An adjunct business, **Country Curtains,** begun by Jane Fitzpatrick, has a retail outlet at the inn (and a larger store in nearby Lee). These old-fashioned curtains—some of them simple tiebacks reminiscent of what Grandma might have had—are found in all of the traditional and cozily decorated guest rooms in the inn and in several nearby houses in the village. Antiques and reproduction furniture are found in rooms, a good number of which have twin beds. Others have queens or doubles. All have TV and air-conditioning. Of the 109 rooms, just 14 share a hall bath; the consolation prize for these so-called bed & breakfast rooms is a complimentary continental breakfast. For pure luxury, you might rent out The Firehouse, once the Stockbridge Fire Station and transformed into a grand suite. It's located just across the parking lot from the inn.

The spacious, bustling inn lobby, the varieties of dining experience—including the large traditional hotel dining room and the flower-bedecked patio in back (see *Where to Eat*)—all make staying at the Red Lion fun. And while 2-night minimums are required on weekends, this is one place where—at the last minute—you might find a room for a single night. They have so many that there can always be a cancellation. Doubles, private bath, $105–205; doubles with shared hall bath, $80–105; suites, $180–345; The Firehouse, $300–385. Meadowlark, the former summer studio of sculptor Daniel Chester French, with two bedrooms, each queen bedded, plus kitchen and living room, rents for $355 per night and is available May to October.

Bed & Breakfasts

♦ **Garden Gables Inn** (413-637-0193; fax 413-637-4554; www.lenoxinn.com), P.O. Box 52, 135 Main Street, Lenox, MA 01240. The first in-ground swimming pool in Berkshire County, built in 1911 and at 72 feet still the largest, is just one of many comforts offered at this in-town inn. Located on busy Main Street, Garden Gables —consisting of an original gabled house to which wings and extensions have been added, plus a cottage to one side—is well back from the road on a shady and well-landscaped property. You feel secluded and cool and relaxed as soon as the car is parked and the welcomes said. Mario and Lynn Mekinda, originally from Toronto, are caring innkeepers who keep upgrading and polishing.

The Garden Gables Inn in Lenox

There are 18 rooms, all air-conditioned with private bath and phone. The four large, newer rooms in the cottage also have TV, VCR, and fireplace. Four rooms in the main inn are fireplaced. Three rooms have Jacuzzi tubs. Room 1 with its vaulted ceiling, wood floors, and fireplace can have its twin beds pushed together and made into a king. Room 15 with cathedral ceiling and fireplace also has a private balcony. Each space is different and charming. Airy, floral wallpapers predominate. Sherry in the living room, a full breakfast in a lovely dining room with blue-and-white china at each place, and tasteful decorating throughout are marks of Garden Gables. A wood deck around the pool has chaises and tables and chairs. If you want to play chess, Mario will take you on; the chess set is ready to go in the living room. Doubles, $110–275. Three-night minimum on summer weekends.

♦ **Applegate** (413-243-4451; www.applegateinn.com), 279 West Park Street, Lee, MA 01238. This magnificent white pillared Colonial is the site of elegant hospitality. Len and Gloria Friedman, New Yorkers, took on what was already a lovely property and have been upgrading energetically. Now in addition to the six original rooms in the main house, there are three elegant accommodations in the carriage house (two of them king suites) and two new luxury suites added to the second floor in the rear of the main house. All 11 accommodations have air-conditioning, fireplace or stove—most gas, but two wood-burning—and private bath. TVs with VCRs are found in the carriage house and the new luxury suites. Room 1 has an unusual, large steam shower. Common rooms include a very large living room with furnishings grouped for conversation. Once a year the Friedmans invite local artists to show their work, and for several months (usually summer into fall) the works are on the walls and for sale. A beautiful heated pool to the rear of the house allows guests to swim or sun. Across the street at the Greenock Country Club, they'll find tennis courts and a Don Ross–designed golf course. (In winter there are cross-country ski trails.) Bicycles may be borrowed for exploring country roads. Gloria loves to cook and delivers candlelight breakfasts in a pretty room with four separate tables set with Wedgwood china. These start with a fruit course (poached pears being a specialty) and continue with a hot entrée, such as a three-cheese baked egg casserole. Before bedtime, guests find Grenada chocolates on their pillows; Len's nephew owns the factory on the Caribbean island. Doubles, $95–300.

♦ **The Inn at Stockbridge** (413-298-3337; fax 413-298-3406), Route 7, Box 618, Stockbridge, MA 01262. Len and Alice Schiller laughingly say that "instead of having an empty nest we came to the Berkshires." Former New Yorkers with two adult daughters, they now have one of the most interesting B&Bs in the area. The Schillers offer 16 guest rooms in three buildings with exceptionally comfortable attributes. The main house, a 1906 Georgian mansion, sets the tone. The welcoming entry parlor has a stunning staircase that leads off to the right rear. Adjacent is the library, with shelves stocked with books and soft music playing. A small TV room can be used by guests whose rooms in the main house do not have televisions. Wicker chairs and tables furnish the wraparound porch; there are more chairs and tables on a back brick terrace. An outdoor pool is set a little distance from the main house.

All guests can use the new fitness/exercise room on the lower level of the Barn, a new lodging facility—or throw the ball for Mia, a standard poodle, to run after. Upstairs in the Barn are four high-end luxury suites with TV-VCR, gas fireplace, and double whirlpool. The Cottage—another outbuilding—adds four more elegant suites. "Provence" is decorated in red-and-white toile. Len does breakfast, served at one large table in a formal dining room or two smaller tables in a side room. In summer the repast sometimes moves outdoors. Sweet potato pancakes and butter rum muffins are two specialties. Doubles, $125–280.

♦ **Birchwood Inn** (413-637-2600; 1-800-524-1646; fax 413-637-4604; www.birchwood-inn.com), 7 Hubbard Street, P.O. Box 2020, Lenox, MA 01240. Ellen Gutman Chenaux has taken over one of the prettiest large houses in Lenox and made it better than ever. The huge sunken living room in this top-of-the-hill mansion is one of the loveliest I've ever seen. Decorated in deep yellow, green, and red, with area rugs on bare wood floors, its window seats, bookcases, fireplace, and comfortable sitting areas are all draws. A huge porch outdoors can also be pleasant, and the house is set far enough back from Lenox's Main Street to feel private and peaceful. Altogether there are 11 air-conditioned guest rooms, 2 of them in a carriage house out back. Room 5, the smallest, is still charming with cinnamon wallpaper, a bed with fishnet canopy, and a clawfoot tub in the bathroom. Room 7 up under the eaves has a king or twin beds, green-checked carpeting, and a bathroom with stall shower. Six rooms have fireplace and TV. Ellen loves to cook and usually has homemade cookies available. A full country breakfast is served in a pretty green dining room with several small tables; a cookbook, *Breakfast at Birchwood,* lists specialties like fruit upside-down French toast, a signature item. A guest pantry has an ice maker, refrigerator, and coffeemaker. The yard is spacious and has a hammock for relaxing. Doubles, $100–260.

♦ **Walker House** (413-637-1271; 1-800-235-3098; www.walkerhouse.com), 64 Walker Street, Lenox, MA 01240. Peggy and Richard Houdek, originally Californians, came to the Berkshires from the West Coast more than 20 years ago and now claim to have the longest tenure as innkeepers in Lenox. If you're serious about your music, this could be the place for you. "I sing and my husband is a music critic," says Peggy, who is a soloist at a Pittsfield church. He writes for the *Berkshire Eagle* and also puts together the multipaged *Walker House News,* by far the most interesting B&B newsletter we've seen. It's exceptionally useful, too. The Houdeks offer eight guest rooms in their rambling 1804 Federal close to the center of town. The house is showing a bit of age but has plenty of interesting aspects. Each guest room is decorated "in the spirit of the composer," so—for example—Tchaikovsky has somewhat dark wallpaper to account for his dark moods. Mozart is a very large room with a sketch or two of the composer. Several bathrooms have clawfoot tubs, and several rooms have fireplaces where fire logs may be used in-season. A very large dining room on the first floor—where a generous continental breakfast is served—leads to a wide porch out back with wooded views. A room on the main floor with large screen is used to show videos and movies. With five cats of their own, the Houdeks have no objection to well-behaved pets. There is a feeling of informality here, and the Houdeks are well versed in the goings-on about town. Doubles, $80–200.

♦ **The Gables Inn** (413-637-3416; 1-800-382-9401; www.gablesnox.com), 103 Walker Street, Route 183, Lenox, MA 01240. Frank Newton is a talker who loves to regale guests with tales of his years as a theater producer and to show photographs of famous show business people he has known. He and his wife, Mary, oversee this well-located B&B that once belonged to the mother-in-law of Edith Wharton. The writer actually used a room here for a few weeks while waiting for her own house, The Mount, to be ready nearby. Although the Edith Wharton Room is one of the smaller of 17 guest rooms, it is one of my favorites, done in rose hues and with a queen canopy bed and—Frank says—the very bathtub that Edith used (and a bit on the small side, too). There is also a fireplace. More elaborate is the Jockey Club Suite with its queen bed set into an alcove, a living room with wood-burning fireplace, a refrigerator, and a door leading to a deck. The Teddy Wharton Suite on the top level, done in shades of green, is the largest and most popular suite in the inn. In a separate enclosed building is a heated indoor swimming pool. You'll also find a tennis court and a garden with seats for reading or relaxing. The breakfast room—with delicate gold-painted chairs—has a long table where most guests can be seated for an expansive continental breakfast. Doubles, $90–250.

♦ **Apple Tree Inn** (413-637-1477; fax 413-637-2528; www.appletree-inn.com), 10 Richmond Mountain Road, Lenox, MA 01240. Its location—across the street from Tanglewood—makes this a favorite inn in summer. Yes, you can walk to the concerts quite easily, down the long driveway and across to the Tanglewood property. Just remember, it's *up* that driveway when you return home at the end of the afternoon or evening. The main inn's exceptionally comfortable and pretty parlor has graceful arched openings enclosing an inner space with comfortable seating areas. Because of the inn's hilltop location, views are terrific—from the multiwindowed, octagonal dining room with tiny white lights outlining each beam to the outdoor terrace across the front, where guests can enjoy the buffet breakfast. Possibly the best view of all is from the in-ground swimming pool, where you can sit and enjoy a glorious vista of the surrounding hills and even Stockbridge Bowl, a lake. Altogether there are 13 interestingly decorated rooms in the main house, a few with fireplace, and 20 more in a separate two-story building known as The Lodge. Room 2 in the main inn has a fireplace, good view, and four-poster queen bed. Rooms in The Lodge are more motel-like and some distance from the main house (and breakfast), but they have one advantage: They are much closer to the pool. The tavern room in the main inn is cozy with dark wood, a large fireplace, booths, and a bar, and is especially popular in winter. Owners are Sharon Walker and Joel Catalano. Doubles, $80–390.

♦ **Historic Merrell Inn** (413-243-1794; 1-800-243-1794; fax 413-243-2669; www.merrell-inn.com), 1565 Pleasant Street, Route 102, South Lee, MA 01260. I love this place! Former owners Charles and Faith Reynolds did a splendid job of turning a historic property into a viable bed & breakfast inn. Their successors, George and Joanne Crockett, are continuing in the same tradition with inspired touches of their own. George grew up in the innkeeping business—his parents ran what is now the Egremont Inn in nearby South Egrement. He and his wife spent several years in Ohio before returning to take over this long-running hostelry, dating from 1794 when it was a tavern. The building, a deep red brick with white pillars, has been restored to a true colonial feeling. There are 10 guest rooms on three floors, all with queen canopy or four-poster bed and private bath. Four of the rooms—including room 1 on the main floor—have wood-burning fireplace. Most bathrooms have been carved out of small closets and have a stall shower; two have a tub. While light fixtures and furnishings are chosen to give an authentic period feeling to the inn and the rooms, all guest rooms do have TV; a couple even have a VCR. The Riverview Suite in the back, with its own entrance, is spacious and has a king bed, parquet wood floors, and a good-sized bathroom. There's also a pullout sofa in the sitting room. The real bonus in this suite, however, is a back porch with a view across the deep yard to the Housatonic River. The Merrell Inn's location on the banks of the river—with a screened gazebo for enjoying the stream—is one of its best features. Guests sometimes put in kayaks or canoes from the property. George makes the full breakfasts, served in the old keeping room of the inn at tables for two. A recent menu offered a choice of omelets, eggs, blueberry pancakes, or French toast and sausage plus cold cereals, breads, and the like. Just across a parking lot next door is a good restaurant, the Sweet Basil Grille (see *Where to Eat*). Doubles, $90–225.

♦ **Auntie M's Bed and Breakfast** (413-243-3201; www.auntimsb.com), 60 Laurel Street, Route 20, Lee, MA 01238. Michelle Celentano and her husband, Phil, offer a wonderfully friendly B&B in a big old turn-of-the-20th-century gray house with white trim and big front porch. Set up on a hill from the main route, it offers porch-sitters a view of the busy traffic from which they are now comfortably removed. The location is terrific—on the road to Lenox but well positioned for Stockbridge, Lee, and Becket, as well. And the little town of Lee is getting more interesting all the time! The 1911 house was built by Thomas Boyne, general superintendent of Smith Paper Company Mills in Lee and the first person in town to own an automobile. Five Victorian-style bedrooms—all on the second floor—are named for nieces and nephews of Michelle and Phil. One room, the Anna Room, has a queen-sized canopy bed and private bath. The other four bedrooms share two full baths—one on the second, and one on the first floor. All rooms have air-conditioning. When we stayed in the Stephen Room—with twin brass beds, deep gold walls, and cranberry trim—all rooms were occupied, yet we never had to wait to use a bathroom. Guests gather on the big porch in good weather—where coffee is set out early in the morning—or the comfortable den with wood-burning pellet stove indoors for TV and games. The piano in the foyer is available for guests who might play—and some do. Michelle is a dynamic hostess and a wonderful breakfast cook whose stuffed French toast, crêpes filled with fresh fruit, and omelets "to your liking" are all favorite entrées. Guests gather together at the lace-topped dining room table, and the sharing of experiences can easily extend to midmorning. Doubles, $95–165. No credit cards.

♦ **Seasons on Main B&B** (413-298-5419; fax 413-298-0092; www.bedandbreakfast. com), 47 Main Street, Stockbridge, MA 01262. Greg and Pat O'Neill used to vacation with their two sons nearby in the Berkshires. When retirement was looming—and the sons were up and out—they relocated from nearby Connecticut to take over a wreck of a house that they turned into this beauty mostly with their own sweat equity. A gleaming white-clapboard house with dark green shutters and shiny red front door is the result. The house was built in 1862, and Pat has decorated with a simple Victorian feeling and a touch of Irish influence (lace curtains for the windows). All four guest rooms—one for each of the seasons—have air-conditioning, TV, and private bath. Two also have gas fireplace. Three large and comfortable common rooms on the main floor allow guests all the space they need to relax and

The Seasons B&B in Stockbridge

enjoy the house; there's also a porch to one side that's popular in good weather. Spring is a room with yellow, blue, and white color scheme including a yellow matelasse spread on the brass queen bed. Up one step and you're in the bathroom with clawfoot tub. A king sleigh bed in Winter is just across from the fireplace; an ingenious open floor plan offers a bathroom "en suite" with soaking tub and stall shower. Pat usually puts brandy in the guest rooms. She serves a full candlelight breakfast in the large dining room—where a fire blazes in chilly weather. Scones and Irish soda bread are often part of the meal. It's a cinch to walk into town from this house. Doubles, $135–255.

♦ **Seven Hills Country Inn** (413-637-0060; 1-800-869-6518; fax 413-637-3651; www.sevenhillsinn.com), 40 Plunkett Street, Lenox, MA 01240. The location of this venerable old inn—with a variety of rooms in different buildings—is its best feature. Sited next door to Edith Wharton's The Mount and just a few doors from the new Shakespeare & Company grounds, this inn is, quite simply, convenient. Innkeepers since 1994, Jim and Patricia Eder have upgraded the 57 guest rooms in three buildings, although the results are uneven. All rooms have private bath and TV, and some have air-conditioning. Manor House rooms, all on the second floor, tend to be more ornate and traditional. Number 5, also known as the bridal suite, has a nice view of the grounds, a king four-poster bed, and a fireplace where fire logs are used in cool weather. The two-story Terrace House looks rather motel-like, and yet a large new deck in front is a good place to sit and read or sun. Several rooms have been renovated and have two double beds or a king-sized bed. The six-unit Carriage House has the newest accommodations; rooms have king bed, air-conditioning, TV, and gas fireplace. Some have a kitchen area; all have at least a refrigerator. The grass around the Carriage House was badly in need of mowing when we stopped, however. On the extensive property are a swimming pool, two tennis courts, a volleyball court, and horseshoes. Breakfast is served in a large, pretty peach room with a rather formal feeling to it in the Manor House. In-season it's a full breakfast; off-season, a continental breakfast. Dinner is also available nightly here in-season and on weekends off-season. On Monday afternoon, lectures associated with The Mount are given here. On Monday and Tuesday evenings in summer, the Stockbridge Summer Music concerts take place here. Doubles, $85–339.

COFFEE AND . . .

Cliffwood Inn (413-637-3330; 1-800-789-3331; fax 413-637-0221; www.cliffwood. com), 25 Cliffwood Street, Lenox, MA 01240. Joy and Scottie Farrelly have one of the most pleasant places to stay in all of New England. This 1889 mansion built originally for a U.S. diplomat to France, Edward McEvers Livingston, is now a marvelous small inn with seven wonderful guest rooms. Six have wood-burning fireplace, one of which is in the bathroom (but can be seen from the bed)! All have private bath. They are named for ancestors of the Farrellys, and there's a short description of the person for whom the room is named in each one.

The Helen Walker Room ("She was my aunt," says Joy) has a king canopy bed, a sitting area in front of the fireplace, and a bright and cheery green-and-pink floral color scheme. A king canopy bed also crowns the Jacob Gross Room, with its fireplace to one side and a tub-shower combination in the bathroom. Joy and Scottie lived all over the world—including France, Belgium, Italy, and Canada—before settling here as innkeepers, and antiques and furnishings from around the globe are used throughout. They also have many Eldred Wheeler reproduction furniture pieces in the house that are for sale. All rooms have ceiling fan and air-conditioning; most have TV and VCR. There's also a TV in the living room.

Out back is a gorgeous swimming pool set amid Joy's lovely gardens. The Farrellys have also added a putting green with five holes beneath a huge shade tree. And there's a gazebo. Just inside the lower level of the house is a wonderful cedar-paneled room with a countercurrent pool that can be used all year. Joy used to serve full breakfasts, but decided it was time to cut back. Now guests have juice and coffee available in the dining room in the morning; they can go out for breakfast at any one of a number of in-town restaurants if they want to. Seat cushions, beach chairs—and a refrigerator to stock picnic supplies—are available for Tanglewood lawn concerts. Three- to 4-night minimums on summer weekends. Doubles, $114–254.

♦ **The Morgan House** (413-243-3661; fax 413-243-3103; www.morganhouseinn.com), 33 Main Street, Lee, MA 01238. Better known for its dining rooms (see *Where to Eat*), this old 19th-century stagecoach stop has 11 modest guest rooms on the second and third floors. These were renovated when the inn was taken over by current owners Wes and Kim Bookstaver in 1999. Four have private bath; there is one two-room suite with bath; and five others share two baths. All rooms are air-conditioned and, while several are on the small side, all have cheery quilts on beds and attractive decor. Beds are mostly kings and queens; two are standard doubles. A second-floor porch overlooking Main Street has chairs for sitting and relaxing. Doubles, $175 with private bath; $125 with shared bath in-season. Lower rates off-season. A full breakfast is included in-season.

Motels/Chains

♦ **Holiday Inn Express** (413-528-1810; 1-800-HOLIDAY; www.hiexpress.com), 415 Stockbridge Road (Route 7), Great Barrington, MA 01230. The new chain hotel—opened in 2002—offers 58 rooms on two floors plus six suites with Jacuzzi-style tubs. A couple of rooms have fireplace. A pleasant breakfast room on the main floor has a large-screen TV and a few rustic tables outdoors as well as indoor seating. A continental-plus breakfast is available buffet-style. Rooms have two queens or one king bed, TV in armoire, microwave oven, refrigerator, and coffeemaker. Dark wood traditional furnishings are the rule. A small indoor pool and fitness room are on site. Doubles, $189–325.

♦ **Laurel Hill Motel** (413-243-0813; fax 413-394-9878), 200 Laurel Street, Route 20, Lee, MA 01238. This one-level hilltop motel is well-located, clean, and convenient. The motel has 21 rooms with two queens or one king; one room has a king bed, Jacuzzi-style tub, and fireplace. All rooms have TV and refrigerator, and some have kitchen. Microwaves are available on request. There is an outdoor pool. The motel is owned by the same people who own the Yankee Home Comfort Inn on Routes 7 and 20 in Lenox. Doubles, $79–199.

WHERE TO EAT

Ah, the restaurants. Many are fine, sophisticated (and pricey)—so attractive that they become destinations in and of themselves. In order to thrive among the cultured summer crowd here, restaurants have to be good. New York and Boston prices prevail at the upper end. You can also find some less self-conscious eateries, but on the whole it's a good idea to make reservations ahead and expect to pay top dollar.

Big Night Out

These are restaurants where the meal is the star. Settle in and enjoy—without expecting to also rush to a concert or theatrical event.

♦ **The Old Inn on the Green** (413-229-3131; 1-800-286-3139), Route 57, New Marlborough. Here you'll find exceptional dining in a 1760 inn in candlelit dining rooms with fireplaces. While dinner is served nightly (except Tuesday) à la carte on the canopied dining terrace overlooking the gardens (and indoors in the taproom), it's the Saturday-night prix fixe dinners that are all the rage. Owners of the inn, Brad Wagstaff and Leslie Miller, know their way around a kitchen, but their long-time, excellent chef, Jeffrey Waite is in charge here. People drive for miles for the evening event (or lucky overnight guests just walk down the road). About 50 guests gather in three dining rooms with original wainscoting, antiques, and wall stenciling. A large mural of a dairy herd on one wall is charming. The Saturday-night repast begins with the chef's amuse—a little something to tease the palate. Then there is a choice of appetizer that might be chilled borscht with summer vegetables and apple horseradish crème fraîche; a peach "intensifier" salad with chilled roast-ed peaches, peach sorbet, and spiced peach glacé; or lamb and beef carpaccio served on arugula. Entrée choices recently were roast rack of lamb with grilled summer vegetables and Dijon spaetzle; chilled poached lobster with tomatoes, cucumber, and avocado; or farm quail grilled with rosemary and served with black-berries and crème fraîche. Finish with white chocolate mousse swans in a pool of passion fruit coulis or summer berry mélange with champagne sabayon. Saturday-night dinner, $58. The à la carte menu on other nights has entrées priced $22–27.

♦ **Blantyre** (413-637-3556; fax 413-637-4282), Blantyre Road (off Routes 7 and 20), Lenox. The elegant dining room at Blantyre has several tables set for dinner, each with different china and accessories—so no two are alike. Executive chef Christopher Brooks was sous chef here in 1995, left for a while, and returned to take over the top post. The three-course prix fixe dinner offers appetizers such as Maine lobster with crispy pancakes, spinach, mango, and ginger sauce; roast duck breast with baked apricot polenta and passion fruit; or asparagus soup with wild mushroom custard and white truffle oil. Summer entrées might be pan-seared sea bass with baby artichokes, tomatoes, basil, sweet corn, and olive oil; loin of rabbit with savoy cabbage, chanterelles, tarragon gnocchi, and carrot puree; or grilled veal chop with peach Tatin, spinach, and a lemon verbena sauce. White chocolate mousse might be the finishing touch. Dinner at Blantyre is a formal, elegant experi-ence, and men are expected to wear jackets and ties. After dinner a harpist some-times plays in the Music Room, where you might have an after-dinner drink. Lunch at Blantyre—usually served in the glass-windowed conservatory off the main dining room—is available in July and August. The three-course, prix fixe meal could start with a wild mushroom linguine with basil puree or a salad of watercress and frisée with local goat cheese and watermelon relish. Entrées might be warm lobster salad with beets, leeks, and a Thai curry sauce; seared rare tuna with aspara-gus, sweet corn, greens, and a lemon dressing; or tenderloin of beef with crispy romaine hearts, carrots, and a wasabi ginger sauce. Dinner ($80) served nightly in foliage season 6–8:45; closed Monday other times. Lunch ($43) is served daily except Monday in July and August. Reservations advised. Closed November through May.

♦ **Wheatleigh** (413-637-0610), Hawthorne Road, Lenox. The dining experience at this Italian palazzo—where guest rooms also are elegant—is meant to be memo-rable. The high-ceilinged dining room is formal with white-clothed tables and Chippendale chairs; next to it is the glass-walled conservatory. Dinner only is served in these main dining rooms with three prix fixe options: a three-course regular or vegetarian menu for $85 or a six-course prix-fixe degustation menu for $115. Starters could be grilled duck foie gras with pickled cherries and lychee fruit, or stuffed squash blossoms with razor clams and their flowers in tempura. The entrée choices could be grilled halibut with a confit of baby artichokes and a vanilla bean emulsion; rack of veal with sweetbreads, served with summer truffles and lettuce hearts; or a loin of lamb with millet griddlecake and Madras curry emulsion. One fish menu included Caspian caviar and French sea bass tartare; pan-seared prawns with green olive relish; char in a fennel and tomato broth; lobster with lemon verbena jus and saffron linguine followed by sheep's-milk cheese custard with poached figs and chilled rhubarb soup with lemon ice cream and crunchy rhubarb. The wine list is extensive. Lunch and dinner are served more informally in The Library—an attractive room off the main entrance foyer—from noon daily in-season. The all-day à la carte menu offers salads, soups, and entrées such as Tuscan pasta or roast chicken breast with asparagus and truffled potato puree (entrées are in the $20–28 range). Reservations are expected. Dinner is served nightly in summer and from Thursday through Sunday off-season.

Other Choices

♦ **Bistro Zinc** (413-637-8800), 56 Church Street, Lenox. Ever since Lenox native Jason Macioge, in partnership with Charles Schultz, opened this French-style restaurant in the late 1990s, it has been one hot spot. The name comes from the long bar in the back room, topped with zinc. There are tables here for dining, although the main dining room is in front on the street side—a mirrored room with tables so close together (and banquette seating on each side) that you're more or less forced to chat with your neighbors. People come here to see and be seen as well as enjoy great food. At our recent lunchtime visit, the Zinc SBLT (Scottish smoked salmon, smoked bacon, roasted tomato, arugula, and lemon aïoli) was being raved about by the couple next to us. We enjoyed a roast Dijon and tarragon chicken salad sandwich and an herb and goat cheese omelet with mixed green salad ($8–12). Dinner might start with a Moroccan lamb skewer with cucumber salad and curry oil, or fried oysters with celery root rémoulade ($10–16). Entrées ($21–28) may include French-style braised rabbit with smoked bacon, pearl onions, mushrooms, and red wine sauce; steak frites; oven-roasted halibut with leek crust; or grilled breast of duck leg with confit, mushroom cannelloni, and cider reduction sauce. During the week, there's a special each night; on Friday it's fish and on Saturday, lobster bouillabaisse. Wines are all from France. Open for lunch 11:30–3, dinner from 5:30 daily in-season; closed Tuesday off-season. Reservations are a must.

♦ **Spigalina** (413-637-4455), 80 Main Street, Lenox. Lina Paccaud, the chef, who opened this Mediterranean restaurant on her own, is now in partnership with her Swiss husband and baker, Serge Paccaud. The sunny colors of the Mediterranean countries—yellow-and-blue-patterned cloths and china, and sunny yellow walls— set the mood in two dining rooms inside a big old house. One architectural feature is a half-enclosed center fireplace—no longer usable, but a point of interest. Outdoors, diners can sit on the big wraparound porch, which is popular in summer and a place to watch the action out front. The flavors of Italy, Spain, southern France, Greece, and Morocco are presented in appetizers like fried calamari with aïoli, thinly sliced braised veal breast served with fennel, lemon, and herb salad, and the extremely popular kataifi-wrapped goat cheese on a bed of field greens with dried cranberries and toasted nuts ($6–12). Spanish seafood stew heads the list of possible entrées ($18–27), prepared with monkfish, shrimp, mussels, clams, rice, and Swiss chard. Other possibilities include veal Scallopini with green beans, semolina gnocchi, and Marsala sauce; salmon Niçoise with fingerling potatoes, green beans, asparagus, and an olive tapenade; and roast rack of lamb with Provençal ratatouille. For dessert ($6) you might try profiteroles, lemon mousse torte with hazelnut praline, or vanilla panna cotta with berry compote. The restaurant is open for dinner nightly in-season (sometimes they close a night or two in late fall); it shuts down from January to May.

♦ **Church Street Café** (860-637-2745), 65 Church Street, Lenox. Here's a restaurant that never seems to go out of style. On nice days, the canopied outdoor deck under the big shade tree is packed; indoors, three dining rooms fill quickly. Contemporary artwork fills the walls, and a young waitstaff buzzes about efficiently. A popular place for 20 years, Church Street Café changes its menu just enough to keep the interest up. At lunchtime we enjoyed a rock shrimp salad with cucumber, tomato, and watercress in a lemon dressing on organic greens, and a cornmeal-crusted New England cod sandwich on a roll with fries on the side. The charcoal-grilled "Church Street Hamburger" is always popular; other possibilities included an enchilada plate and roast salmon fillet ($12–16). In the evening, starters might be a tasting of local Berkshire cheeses with marinated olives and walnut bread, or warm eggplant, tomato, and goat cheese torte with black olive vinaigrette ($6–11). Entrées ($18–26) could include cornmeal-crusted trout with crabmeat and rock shrimp stuffing, served with lemon-pistachio rice pilaf, or grilled spice-rubbed pork loin with mashed sweet potatoes and barbecued beans. If the apple walnut crisp is on the dessert menu, try it. Open Monday through Saturday for lunch and dinner, and for dinner only on Sunday in summer; in the off-season, the restaurant often closes on Sunday and Monday.

♦ **Roseborough Grill** (413-637-2700), 71 Church Street, Lenox. Everybody's giving the Roseborough Grill high marks these days. Chef-owner Laura Shack Willnauer offers "creative American and international cuisine" in a sprawling wood house with front and back porches, bar, and a couple of good-sized dining rooms inside. Sponged rose walls with deep green below the wainscoting and dried hydrangeas in wall vases set a nice tone. Laura had a catering business in New York for 10 years and studied with James Beard before opening this spot in the Berkshires a dozen years ago.

For Sunday lunch my curried egg salad wrap with roasted cashews, golden raisins, and shredded carrots hit the spot, while my husband had a charcoal-grilled beefburger with bacon and cheese. Lobster rolls with coleslaw ($17), a marinated grilled chicken breast sandwich, and a grilled portobello mushroom sandwich with fresh buffalo mozzarella were also popular (most lunch entrées $9–12). In the evening a popular appetizer is the roast garlic plate with sun-dried tomato, goat cheese, Kalamata olives, and grilled farm bread ($8–11). "Francesca's fricassee of sea scallops" served over linguine is an entrée named for Laura's young daughter. Others might be charcoal-grilled whole Cornish game hen with garlic mashed potatoes, or grilled eggplant Parmesan served with crispy gnocchi ($16–22). In the evening you can get a bar menu on the back porch or in the bar; it includes many of the lunch entrées. Open for lunch Friday through Sunday in summer; nightly for dinner. Off-season, lunch is served on Saturday and Sunday only, and the restaurant closes on Tuesday and Wednesday.

◆ **The Old Mill** (413-528-1421), Route 23, South Egremont. Terry Moore, chef and founder of this immensely popular restaurant, presides over it still after more than 20 years. In a restored 18th-century gristmill, lucky diners (no reservations are taken except for large parties) enjoy both classic dishes and some surprising new twists. The atmosphere in the main dining room reflects the colonial heritage of the building in a nicely updated way. Some tall birch trees were set in place with bird-houses among the branches in this room when last we stopped; candles flicker on white-clothed tables, and a fireplace that can be viewed in both bar and dining room is popular in cool weather. Starters ($7–9) could be house-made duck liver pâté with cornichons and peasant toast; fresh figs and mozzarella served with baby arugula, roasted walnuts, and aged balsamic vinegar; or pan-seared scallops in blue-berry vinaigrette. Entrées—which happily come with a simple mixed green salad—could be chicken curry with almond-squash couscous; pan-seared calf's liver, a real favorite; or grilled lamb rib chops served with a fresh mint pesto and mashed Yukon gold potatoes. A bar menu is offered nightly except Saturday and includes a cheese-burger with fries, strip steak on garlic toast, roasted half chicken with herbs and mashed potatoes, and grilled salmon with a tomato-basil vinaigrette ($9–16). Here the salad is an extra $3.75. Dinner nightly in-season; closed Monday off-season.

◆ **John Andrew's** (413-528-3469), Route 23, South Egremont. This is one of the best and most romantic restaurants in the Berkshires. Chef-owner Daniel Smith and his wife, Susan, named the restaurant for her grandfather. A sophisticated red-and-green color scheme is used in the front dining room with fireplace; a rear porch is more contemporary with chrome and light wood chairs. Out back is a deck for dining amid flower gardens. Each dining space is appealing. Starters on the sophisticated menu ($8–15) might be crisp sweetbreads with morels and giant butter beans braised and served with prosciutto, or grilled lobster with leek and fen-nel terrine. Entrées ($16–25) could include spinach and ricotta gnocchi with sage and Parmesan; grilled sea scallops with wild rice, braised leeks, and asparagus; or the very popular sautéed duck breast served with crisp duck confit, mashed pota-toes, shallot jus, and balsamic syrup. A fruit crisp with vanilla ice cream or choco-late torte might be the finishing touch. Open for dinner nightly in-season; closed on Wednesday off-season.

◆ **Castle Street Café** (413-528-5244), 10 Castle Street, Great Barrington. Since 1989 chef-owner Michael Ballon has been doing well at this location next to the Mahaiwe Theater. The restaurant came first; in 1997 he added the Celestial Bar next to it—with a bar menu all its own and live musical entertainment on week-ends. The main dining room has white tablecloths and Windsor chairs. Here you can start the meal with fried shrimp dumplings and a dipping sauce; steamed mus-sels with tomato, white wine, and garlic; or perhaps a mesclun salad with local chèvre ($6–8). Pizza, pasta, and burgers are also available—the Castle Street Burger is half a pound of ground beef served with straw potatoes. Main courses, served with a mixed green salad, include the very popular sautéed calf's liver with glazed pearl onions and onion marmalade; warm duck salad with cashews and Asian slaw; and breast of chicken stuffed with spinach and portobello mushrooms and served with a shiitake mushroom sauce ($19–24). The bar menu has most of the appetizers plus burgers, burritos, and meat loaf with mashed potatoes ($8–12). Dinner nightly from 5, except closed Tuesday; the bar menu is served until 11 on Friday and Saturday nights.

♦ **Verdura** (413-528-8969), 44 Railroad Street, Great Barrington. Chef-owner Bill Webber opened his own restaurant on the Railroad Street "strip" in 2001, and it's definitely gotten the attention of locals and visitors. With a Tuscan atmosphere—rustic dark wood tables and chairs, and deep yellow walls—Verdura offers what one staffer calls "a creative take on regional cuisine." It has an Italian bent, and locally grown produce and other ingredients are used. The antipasti come in a selection of one to five ($5 each; $20 for all five) and include items like grilled prosciutto-wrapped asparagus and balsamic-marinated onions. First courses could be baby greens served with chèvre, hazelnuts, plumped figs, and citrus balsamic dressing; a fried whole artichoke with pine nut gremolata; or a risotto of lobster, sweet peas, and smoked bacon ($6–14). Pizzas that issue from the open kitchen have thin, deli-cate crusts and come with toppings like Gorgonzola, tomato, arugula, and figs ($12). Main courses ($18–25) might be porcini and foie gras risotto; wood-charred beef rib eye with roast mushrooms, truffle butter, and balsamic reduction; or braised lamb shank with rosemary white corn polenta and bitter greens. All pastas are made in house. There's a full bar. Dinner nightly in summer; closed Wednesday off-season.

♦ **Bizen** (413-528-4343), 17 Railroad Street, Great Barrington. Potter Michael Marcus hails from the Berkshires but became enamored of things Japanese during an apprenticeship there. This authentic Japanese restaurant and sushi bar also showcases his pottery—food is served on pieces made by Michael at his studio and kiln in nearby Monterey. The sushi menu alone is pretty intimidating, with several variations on more than 20 offerings including river eel, octopus, sea urchin, and wild bonito. Several combinations are offered as well as vegetable maki rolls. From the robata charcoal grill come dinner entrées ($14–17) such as charcoal-grilled Canadian sea scallops on fried sweet potatoes, salmon with a sweet teriyaki sauce, or organic vegetables, tofu, and tempeh served with ginger garlic sauce. Tempura and katsu are also available, along with a variety of noodle dishes. Wash it all down with Nagata Twig Tea, a form of green tea, or enjoy one of many estate sakes. Open for lunch and dinner daily.

♦ **From Ketchup to Caviar** (413-243-6397), 150 Main Street, Lee. Chef Christian Urbain and his wife, Lynne, made their mark at the tiny **Once Upon a Table** in

Stockbridge. This space is much larger, a big white house with yellow, green, and red trim featuring three inside dining rooms and an enclosed front-porch area. We were in the smallest dining room toward the rear with red damasklike wallpaper and plates mounted on the walls. You can start with house-cured gravlax with caviar vinaigrette and toast points or get a burger with Yukon gold fries and ketchup—in keeping with the unusual name. Appetizers ($7–9) include roasted Camembert with red onion chutney and mesclun salad mix. Entrées ($16–20) could be items like crisp seared salmon over lobster bread pudding with dill beurre blanc, Black Angus flatiron steak with cognac and fries, or Maine crabcake with basmati rice and chive beurre blanc. I had the pan-seared halibut, a special of the day, and my husband chose Florida red snapper. Both lacked flavor—perhaps an off night. For dessert we shared a crème caramel from a listing that included Boston cream pie, bread pudding, and the restaurant's signature profiteroles. Open for dinner nightly except Tuesday.

♦ **Once Upon a Table** (413-298-3870), 36 Main Street, The Mews, Stockbridge. Now this restaurant, tucked back from Main Street in a small group of shops, is owned by Nick Caplan, chef, and Alan O'Brient. The cute place with brick floor has about a dozen tables covered with beige cloths and set with mismatched bread plates. At lunch you can get a classic Caesar salad ($5), sandwiches like grilled pastrami or turkey Reuben, or a quiche of the day served with greens ($6–7.50). In the evening the appetizer of Prince Edward Island mussels steamed in white wine, shallots, and garlic is popular; you can also get smoked salmon with capers and red onion, or chicken liver pâté with armagnac and truffles ($7–9). Seared crabcakes with basmati rice and horseradish cream sauce are so popular as to be always on the menu. Ditto for roast baby rack of lamb with herbed jus. To these might be added Cajun-spiced pork tenderloin with honey mustard glaze or pecan-encrusted rainbow trout ($17–24). "World famous profiteroles" are one of the house-made desserts. Lunch is served daily in-season, 11–3. Dinner is served nightly from 5 except Tuesday. From November to April, dinner is weekends only.

♦ **Dream Away Lodge** (413-623-8725), 1342 County Road, Becket. "This is a theatrical event—it's a stage setting—there's a show going on." Pause. "It's edible performance art!" says owner Daniel Osman, who then cracks up at having finally described his restaurant-*cum*-entertainment-spot. The big white roadside restaurant (a former speakeasy) with neon signs and glass-enclosed front porch looms out of the dusk late in the day. You reach it via a tortuously winding road high into the Berkshire hills—you'd be wise to ask for directions. The Frasca family ran the remote spot for more than 50 years before Dan took over in the mid-1990s. On the Saturday evening we arrived hopeful of an early dinner, the place was sold out with people heading for the Pillow; we settled on meat loaf sandwiches from the bar menu and thought they were great. The dining rooms at one end of the house seat 60 at mismatched tables and chairs and with funky crockery and linens. A prix fixe $25 dinner includes soup or pasta, a choice of three to five entrées, salad, potato, and vegetable. From the bar menu, you can order à la carte items ranging $3–15 including burgers and other sandwiches. To the right of the main door is the Music Room, with beanbag chairs and floor pillows strewn all around; on Wednesday evening it's "open music" for anyone to come and play what they like. On Friday and Saturday musicians are booked, who play for dinner and tips—"and I work the crowd mercilessly," says Dan. A former actor, the owner welcomes music, dance, and theater artists, among other guests. On Sunday, brunch starts at noon and the specialty of the house is two fried eggs, two slices of bacon, and homefries served on salad greens. Open Mother's Day through Halloween, Wednesday through Saturday for dinner from 6; Sunday brunch from noon, with a slow changeover to bar menu and dinner. Fewer nights in winter; closed from January 1 through Valentine's Day. Reservations are a good idea, especially in-season.

♦ **Helsinki Café** (413-528-3394), 284 Main Street, Great Barrington. Deborah McDowell may not sound Finnish, but she is, and it's that part of her background that's honored at this funky and popular café-*cum*-nightclub. Finnish and Russian favorites make the menu particularly interesting. At lunch try a house favorite, Red Square Smelts—baby smelts lightly breaded and sautéed in extra-virgin olive oil, capers, and lemon—or Anni's Smorgasbord, "little bites from the land of the Midnight Sun like gravlax, dill sauce, cheeses, beets, salami, and more." Finnish-style dilled egg salad is served open face on anadama bread and topped with chopped red onion. Cheese blintzes, served with wild blueberry compote, are suggested with Russian tea ($7–12). For dinner, starters include the Helsinki salad with roasted pecans, red onion, cucumbers, apples, grated beets, shaved fennel, and chèvre-topped crostini, or borscht—a house special that can also be purchased by the quart. Entrées ($12–18) could be Finnish meatballs served with mashed potatoes and gravy and cucumber dill salad; horseradish-rubbed seared salmon with Swedish dill sauce; or natural chicken-apple sausage served with warm red cabbage slaw, potato latkes, and cucumber dill salad. Two dining rooms have quirky furnishings, bright cloths over chairs, and a feeling of the Old World. On weekend evenings, there's entertainment in the café. Open 11 AM–10:30 PM, with the hour between 4 and 5 used as the changeover from lunch to dinner.

♦ **The Sweet Basil Grille** (413-243-1114), 1575 Pleasant Street, Route 102, Lee. Rick and Lynn Penna operate this popular little Italian restaurant between Lee and Stockbridge—right next door to the Old Merrell Tavern. Burgundy cloths on tables upstairs may make that room slightly more formal than the main level, where place mats are used, but the menu is the same. Starters ($6–7) could be baked stuffed mushrooms or a spinach and artichoke dip with garlic rounds. Cream of roast garlic soup is a house specialty. Entrées include pastas like penne Pugliese—broccoli, mushrooms, and roasted red peppers tossed in garlic and olive oil and topped with Parmesan. Chicken, seafood, and veal dishes make up most of the menu, including shrimp with grilled sausage sautéed with broccoli, mushrooms, onions, and roasted peppers; and veal sautéed with garlic, onion, and fresh basil and simmered in white wine and fresh diced tomatoes, served over pasta. Entrées are priced in the $16–19 range. Salad, bread, and a vegetable come with all entrées. Open nightly 4:30–9.

♦ **Jack's Grill** (413-274-1000), Main Street, Housatonic. The Fitzpatrick family of the Red Lion Inn is behind this wonderfully retro restaurant, located in a big glass storefront space in the little hamlet of Housatonic. Shelves on either side of the former store are stocked with old toasters, cookie jars, and teapots. Old toys that a kid

The front porch of the Red Lion Inn in Stockbridge

could ride—like wooden airplanes—swing from the ceiling. These, we're told, are part of Nancy Fitzpatrick's collection—daughter of Jack and Jane. You'll find some 1950s comfort food on the menu, too. Jack's pot roast with pan gravy and mashed potatoes is the to-die-for dinner standard, and my husband was in heaven with his. It also comes as a sandwich. Appetizers include a classic wedge of iceberg lettuce with Russian dressing—so large you work to finish it—and sautéed salmon cakes served with lemon caper aïoli. The popcorn shrimp with Creole dip or cocktail sauce is popular. Main courses ($8–35 for a "jigantic" 28-ounce T-bone) include grilled center-cut swordfish, a burger with jack cheese or garden burger, and even spaghetti and meatballs. This is a wonderful place to bring kids; they can watch the little train that runs around on an elevated track, and there's a menu just for them. Desserts? Chocolate pudding is comforting, or have Toll House cookies, a root beer float, chocolate cake, or an oatmeal cookie and banana ice cream sandwich with chocolate sauce. Sunday buffet brunch is served 11–2; it's $6.95 for coffee, breads, and desserts; $14.95 for the whole thing. Dinner is served from 5 daily except Monday.

♦ **The Red Lion Inn** (413-298-5545), 30 Main Street, Stockbridge. This big old white hostelry will satisfy your hunger—one way or another. The main dining room—a large hotel-like dining space behind the dark red velvet drapes that separate it from the lobby—is preferred by many who want to be part of the action. Next door is the Widow Bingham's Tavern—rustic and more casual. Downstairs is The Lion's Den, a bar with a light menu. Out back is a flower-filled courtyard, a special place to dine in summer. Take your pick. Lunches ($9–15) include macaroni with Maine lobster, fisherman's stew, a turkey sandwich, or chicken potpie. Entrées in the evening ($20–32) include seared venison with Alsatian cabbage slaw, coriander-dusted salmon over summer vegetables, and prime rib served with a popover. The Widow Bingham Tavern has a lighter menu including grilled meat loaf. In The Lion's Den, starters like nachos and chili are popular, along with burgers and other sandwiches. There's also a daily entrée special.

The main dining room serves breakfast, lunch, and dinner; you can get lunch and dinner daily in the tavern and courtyard. The Lion's Den has lunch and dinner and serves straight through from noon.

♦ **The Morgan House** (413-243-3661), 35 Main Street, Lee. We arrived in Lee mid-afternoon famished and enjoyed lunch in the tavern room at this old stagecoach stop. The quiche combo platter—with a bacon, tomato, and onion quiche and a side salad—hit the spot. Our other choice was a burger served with coleslaw, also pronounced excellent. You can always get chili, sautéed Maine crabcakes, hot and cold turkey sandwiches, and a vegetarian wrap. At dinner there's a daily special (veal chop Thursday and lobster on Friday, for example) along with roast prime rib in two sizes, a roast turkey dinner, or more contemporary choices. Dinner entrées, $14–28. Lunch and dinner served daily.

Picnic Fare

♦ **Perfect Picnics** (413-637-3015) in Lenox has been around for 15 years now. For one picnic, it's $17; two for $30. You can get marinated chicken breast, medallions of beef teriyaki, a vegetarian special, or poached salmon (add $2) served with salad, roll and butter, fruit, and biscotti. You usually find the picnic people at an umbrellaed table on Church Street where you can place orders in person—or just call. You're all set for Tanglewood.

7 The Books of Boston and Cambridge, Massachusetts

No other city in New England has such a rich literary heritage and is so attractive to the writer and the reader as Boston, along with its "sister city" across the Charles River, Cambridge.

Why, here you can walk on the street where Henry Wadsworth Longfellow lived and wrote. You can visit his home, now a national historic site. You can stay in a hotel where Charles Dickens first read aloud his famous *Christmas Carol.* You can visit a bookstore devoted entirely to poetry for more than 70 years or one that sells only mystery books.

The first municipal free library supported by taxation in the *world* is the **Boston Public Library,** where a guided tour reveals all sorts of interesting facts about its architectural design and wonderful murals on its walls done by well-known artists. **The Boston Athenaeum,** a private membership library, welcomes the public to its renovated first floor and offers public tours and lectures at certain times. This is the library that owns the private collection of George Washington.

Did you know that **The John F. Kennedy Library and Museum,** designed by the great architect I. M. Pei, also contains some of the manuscripts and letters of Ernest Hemingway? Then there's the **Schlesinger Library** on the Radcliffe campus of Harvard University. Although devoted primarily to the history of women in America, it has a wonderful culinary collection that you can visit; you can even copy recipes!

Boston's exotic **Isabella Stewart Gardner Museum,** known for its art, flowers, and music, began as a rare-book collection with a copy of Dante's *Divine Comedy*—dating from 1485. Poet e. e. cummings and writers T. S. Eliot, Henry James, and Vladimir Nabokov all called Boston home at one time; Edgar Allan Poe was born here.

Children who've been introduced to Robert McCloskey's classic work *Make Way for Ducklings* love to visit the bronze replicas of the little ducklings in the **Boston Public Garden.** Another sculpture that pleases kids is the oversized bronze one from the enduring fable, "The Tortoise and the Hare." The Hare is shown sitting and scratching his ear, while the Tortoise continues along in a very determined manner. It's a tribute to all who have run the Boston Marathon—whose finish line is on Boylston Street, close to the square.

A major portion of the children's book *Trumpet of the Swan,* by E. B. White, takes place at the elegant and traditional **Ritz-Carlton Hotel** on Arlington Street. And Moss Hart's Broadway play *Light Up the Sky* was set in a Ritz-Carlton suite.

Practically everywhere you look, there is a literary reference in the city that is New England's largest, most vibrant and tradition-filled. A self-guiding **Literary Trail**—with a background book to help—has been inaugurated recently by the Boston History Collaborative. It includes a side trip to **Concord,** a suburb that was once home to Louisa May Alcott, Ralph Waldo Emerson, Nathaniel Hawthorne, and Henry David Thoreau.

This, then, is a chapter for the reader, the book lover, the literary lion. For the person who appreciates knowing that the first printing press this side of the Atlantic was set up in Cambridge and that Cambridge has the best concentration of bookstores anywhere in the country. (Boston has some fine bookstores, too.) For the person who—in this cyber age—still loves to hold a book in hand, or to think of the influences that caused one to be written.

Read on.

Getting There

Boston isn't so hard to get *to,* but it's devilishly difficult to drive *through.* The infamous "Big Dig" has made things much worse. Once we're there, we park the car and use public transportation whenever we can. The famous MBTA—the "T"—is the nation's oldest subway system but far from its grubbiest. It's quite efficient, with color-coded lines. Buses are also easy to take. A city bus travels Massachusetts Avenue from Boston directly to Harvard Square in Cambridge, crossing the Charles River en route.

By car: The Massachusetts Turnpike (I-90) leads directly into the downtown area from the west. (Take Exit 22 for Copley Square and the Prudential Center and gird your loins as you emerge from the tunnel into a labyrinth of mostly one-way streets.) Interstate 95 comes in from Maine and Rhode Island. Interstate 93 brings visitors south from Vermont and New Hampshire, and Route 3 is a fast route north from Cape Cod.

By train: Amtrak serves Boston, and South Station, the main terminal, was recently upgraded. The Acela train is the high-speed train from Boston to Washington, D.C. For information and reservations, call 1-800-872-7245.

By bus: Greyhound buses serve midtown terminals in Boston from all across the country. The number to call for information is 1-800-231-2222.

By air: Most major airlines fly into **Logan International Airport,** including many flights from Europe and overseas. A water taxi takes air passengers to Rowes Wharf on the downtown waterfront, and is one of the most expedient ways to get there.

♦ **Parking:** The underground **Boston Common** garage is probably the most rationally located and affordable place to park in center city. It has been renovated and is well lighted. Other commercial lots are available but expensive.

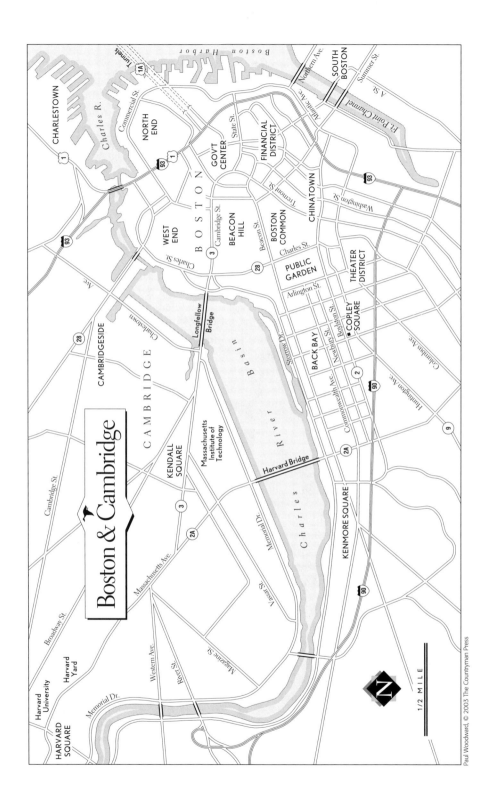

Boston & Cambridge

Boston Harbor

Boston

CHARLESTOWN

NORTH END

WEST END

GOVT CENTER

FINANCIAL DISTRICT

BEACON HILL

BOSTON COMMON

CHINATOWN

PUBLIC GARDEN

THEATER DISTRICT

COPLEY SQUARE

BACK BAY

SOUTH BOSTON

CAMBRIDGE

CAMBRIDGESIDE

KENDALL SQUARE

Massachusetts Institute of Technology

KENMORE SQUARE

HARVARD SQUARE

Harvard University

Harvard Yard

Charles River

Basin

Charles R.

Ft. Point Channel

Longfellow Bridge

Harvard Bridge

Commercial St.

State St.

Cambridge St.

Tremont St.

Charles St.

Beacon St.

Charles St.

Arlington St.

Commonwealth Ave.

Newbury St.

Boylston St.

Columbus Ave.

Huntington Ave.

Washington St.

Northern Ave.

Atlantic Ave.

Summer St.

A St.

Storrow Dr.

Memorial Dr.

Vassar St.

Charlestown Ave.

Cambridge St.

Broadway St.

Western Ave.

Magazine St.

River St.

Memorial Dr.

Massachusetts Ave.

1A

1

93

1

93

93

93

3

28

28

3

2A

3

2A

2

90

9

2A

90

Tunnel

1/2 MILE

N

Paul Woodward, © 2003 The Countryman Press

For More Information

♦ **The Greater Boston Convention and Visitors Bureau, Inc.** (1-888-SEE-BOSTON; www.BostonUSA.com). There are official visitors information centers at Boston Common, 147 Tremont Street; at the Prudential Center; and at the Cambridge Visitor Information Booth in Harvard Square. For information on Cambridge, contact the **Cambridge Office for Tourism** (617-441-2884; www.cambridge-usa.com). An excellent source of information about literary Boston is the book *Literary Trail of Greater Boston* by Susan Wilson for the Boston History Collaborative (Houghton Mifflin, $10).

SEEING AND DOING

The Literary Legacy

The first printing of a book in the English language in the English colonies took place in Cambridge in 1640. The *Bay Psalm Book* was printed by the Puritans to replace the disliked British version of the Psalms. The first press had been brought to the colonies in 1638 by Steven Daye and his wife. Steven perished on the voyage from England, but his spouse carried on. The first shop to sell books in Cambridge was the Steven Daye Press. Books were sold out of the print shop.

The first American poet is considered to be Anne Bradstreet, who lived in what is now Harvard Square in Cambridge. Her work was printed in England in 1650. Cambridge had the first library of more than 400 books in the colonies. It was donated by John Harvard to Harvard College in 1636.

Libraries

Boston and Cambridge have many libraries, several connected with colleges and universities in the area. Boston is, after all, a college town. Here are some particularly interesting ones to visit.

♦ **Boston Public Library** (617-536-5400; www.bpl.org), Copley Square, Boston. Founded in 1848, the Boston Public Library prides itself on being the oldest free library supported by municipal taxation in the country. It was also the first library to establish a separate children's room. The imposing central library complex in Copley Square is comprised of the original 1895 building designed by the architectural firm of McKim, Mead & White and the newer Phillip Johnson building, which was opened in 1972 and is the circulating library.

The library has more than 6.1 million books and 400 on-line databases, but if you take a public tour your guide will concentrate on the beautiful turn-of-the-century (the *past* century, that is) architectural designs and magnificent wall murals and statuary. This is the third home of the library and was designed to be "a palace for the people." The great sculptor Daniel Chester French, best known for his *Seated Lincoln* in the Lincoln Memorial in Washington, D.C., designed the bronze doors through which you enter from Copley Square. It was architect McKim's idea to ask well-known artists of the day to provide design work for various areas of the building. And so there are wonderful murals in the central staircase area by the French artist Puvis de Chavannes (who shipped them from Paris by boat); wall paintings on the history of Judaism and Christianity by portraitist John Singer Sargent; and *The Quest of the Holy Grail* murals by Edward Austin Abbey.

James McNeill Whistler was invited to participate by filling a large wall at one end of the Bates Reading Room on the library's second floor. Whistler was a testy guy, and while discussing the commission with McKim over lunch in Paris, he suddenly jumped up, threw his napkin on the table, and walked away. The space remains empty. The restoration of the McKim building to its original grandeur was completed recently.

The library is open Monday through Thursday 9–9, Friday and Saturday 9–5; Sunday (October to May) 1–5. Free architectural tours given Monday at 2:30 PM; Tuesday and Thursday at 6 PM; Friday and Saturday at 11 AM; and on Sunday when the library is open at 2 PM.

♦ **The Boston Athenaeum** (617-227-0270; www.bostonathenaeum.org), 10½ Beacon Street, Boston. Founded in 1807, the Boston Athenaeum is one of the oldest and most distinguished membership libraries in the country. By 1851, with 50,000 volumes, it was one of the five largest collections in the United States. It is the oldest cultural institution and largest membership library in North America. The Athenaeum helped establish Boston's Museum of Fine Arts, providing much of the museum's early artwork.

The building was designed by Edward Clarke Cabot and opened in 1849. It has beautiful arched ceilings, niches for white marble busts of famous figures, and extraordinary book collections, including volumes from the library of George Washington. One pays to belong and then has the privilege of borrowing from the collection or, perhaps, working at one of the beautifully situated tables or desks on a high floor—with its windowed views of the city. Members can also—in good weather—enjoy the outdoor terrace and even bring their lunch to eat there.

Those of us who don't belong to this distinguished library can still take a tour—or enjoy the recently renovated first floor of the library. Closed for renovations in 2001 and 2002, the library was expected to reopen with a dramatic change in the interior of the first and second floors, with the art gallery moved to the first floor and a room for lectures there, as well. This is good news and is expected to make the space more accessible to the public. The library has rich holdings in art, including works by John Singer Sargent and Gilbert Stuart. It's open Monday 9–8, Tuesday through Friday 9:30–5:30, Saturday 9–4 (September to May). Call for tour times. Free.

♦ **The John F. Kennedy Library and Museum** (617-929-4500; 1-877-616-4599; www.jfklibrary.org), Columbia Point (off Morrissey Boulevard), Boston. This presidential library enjoys a setting of stark grandeur overlooking the waterfront on the Boston campus of the University of Massachusetts. The sleek building has a soaring glass-walled pavilion that offers stunning views and houses the museum's café. Visitors view an introductory film showing John F. Kennedy from childhood to the time of his election. Twenty museum exhibits on a lower floor include furnishings of JFK's Oval Office as well as the office of his brother, Attorney General Robert F. Kennedy; special exhibits focused on crises during the Kennedy administration; exhibits devoted to Jackie Kennedy; and much more. All are enhanced by some-

The John F. Kennedy Library and Museum

times rare film footage. It's possible to sit and witness the whole of the inaugural address and Jackie Kennedy's televised White House tour.

The museum has a youthful vibrancy to it that reflects the time of Kennedy's presidency.

Open daily 9–5 except for Thanksgiving, Christmas, and New Year's Day. Special exhibits are mounted in main-floor galleries. Adults $8, seniors and students $6, children 13–17 $4; those 12 and under are free. Special exhibits sometimes have higher admission prices.

♦ **Schlesinger Library** (617-495-9647), 10 Garden Street, Cambridge. This library, on the campus of Radcliffe College (a part of Harvard University), is primarily a research library devoted to women and women's interests. The library's holdings document women's lives and women's issues, currently and retrospectively. Especially strong are areas of suffrage and women's rights, social reform, family history, health and sexuality, work and professions, culinary history, and gender issues.

The culinary collection is fun to visit, for here are hundreds of cookbooks, some going back to the early days of this country, as well as some European volumes that are even older. A small reading area was funded by Julia Child, the "French Chef," who lived for many years in Cambridge. It's possible to read the cookbooks and even to copy a recipe if you'd like. Open Monday through Friday 9–5. Free.

The Literary Trail of Greater Boston

The Literary Trail was inaugurated in 1999 by the Boston History Collective. Susan Wilson's guidebook Literary Trail of Greater Boston, a terrific and comprehensive volume, is provided to individuals who take the self-guided tour. Beginning at the Omni Parker House Hotel, and ending in the western suburb of Concord, this tour includes tickets to three museums with literary connections: The Gibson House (see below) in Boston and the Orchard House and Concord Museum in Concord. The Orchard House was Louisa May Alcott's home when she wrote Little Women. The Concord Museum has memorabilia from Ralph Waldo Emerson, Nathaniel Hawthorne, and Henry David Thoreau. In Concord followers of the trail can also visit Walden Pond, inspiration for Thoreau's famous tract and the site of the cabin where he lived for two years. (A replica is on the spot.) The cost of the tour is $19. Tickets can be purchased by calling (617) 350-0358. The web site for the tour is www.lit-trail.org.

Groups of 20 or more can arrange for guided group tours.

A *Walking Tour*

♦ **Walking Tour: Old Cambridge** is a well-thought-out stroll through the streets of the old city, encompassing the historic green, the Old Burying Ground (where printer Steven Daye rests, among many early presidents of Harvard and several veterans of the Revolution), and other interesting sites. You will walk past the Henry Wadsworth Longfellow house and also the Dexter Pratt House. Pratt was Longfellow's village blacksmith, about whom he wrote the famous poem "The Village Blacksmith," published in 1841. The attractively illustrated brochure can be obtained from the Cambridge Office for Tourism (617-441-2884) or the Cambridge Historical Commission (617-349-4683).

Cookbook Capers

♦ **Boston Cooks! Cookbook Dine Around.** If the books you like best to read are cookbooks, then pay attention to this annual event held from mid- to late January each year. Cookbook authors with local chefs prepare foods detailed in the authors' recent books. These are then served at Boston's finest restaurants. Call 1-888-SEE-BOSTON for information and a complete schedule.

Museums and Historic Houses

♦ **Isabella Stewart Gardner Museum** (617-566-1401), 280 The Fenway, Boston. The incredible Gardner Museum is a tribute to one woman's tastes, interests, and courage. When you visit this museum, designed and built in the style of a 15th-century Venetian palazzo, you will recognize that Mrs. Gardner was interested in art, music, and flowers. Indeed she was, but the Gardner Museum actually began as a rare-book collection and contains many manuscripts and rare volumes. Several years before she got into the serious acquisition of art, Isabella Gardner attended a fine arts class at Harvard taught by Charles Eliot Norton, who encouraged her to become a member of the Dante Society. Under his tutelage she became interested in rare books and manuscripts, collecting more than 1,000 rare volumes spanning six centuries. They included a 1485 edition of Dante's *Divine Comedy*.

Printed books in the collection include many early Venetian texts, letters, and photographs of great American writers of her time, including Emerson, Henry and

William James, Walt Whitman, and George Santayana—and a first edition of Nathaniel Hawthorne's *The Scarlet Letter*. There is in the museum a "Modern Authors and Actors' Case" (outside the chapel) with letters and photographs to Gardner from Sarah Bernhardt, George Sand, and Victor Hugo, among others.

The flower-filled courtyard of the museum is stunning. The nearby greenhouse is the source. Musical events are held in an acoustically superior hall on the second floor at regular times, including Sunday afternoon (tickets needed). The art in the collection includes paintings by Rembrandt, Titian, John Singer Sargent, Velazquez, and others of equal stature. Open Tuesday through Sunday 11–5. Guided tours on Friday at 2:30 PM. Adults $10 ($11 weekends), seniors $7, students $5, children under 18 free.

♦ **Museum of Fine Arts** (617-267-9300; www.mfa.org), 465 Huntington Avenue, Boston. This is Boston's major art museum and has been the site of blockbuster exhibits for the past several years. These are usually shown in the newer West Wing. The museum sprawls over an entire block and is really overwhelming to attempt in one visit. Its strengths include 19th- and 20th- century American paintings; European painting from the Renaissance through the impressionists; decorative arts; an Egyptian collection (including some mummies); and a major collection of Far Eastern art and architecture. Guided walks and gallery talks are offered frequently.

Book lovers should know that the museum shop prides itself on being "the largest art bookstore in the Northeast" and carries many antiquarian books as well. There is an art library on the second floor of the museum that has scheduled hours and may be used by researchers. The museum is open Monday and Tuesday 10–4:45, Wednesday through Friday 10–9:45, Saturday and Sunday 10–5:45. Adults $14, seniors and students $12, children under 6 free. "Pay as you wish" on Wednesday after 4 PM.

♦ **The Longfellow National Historic Site** (617-876-4491; www.nps.gov/long/), 105 Brattle Street, Cambridge. The popular American writer Henry Wadsworth Longfellow lived in this beautiful large yellow home for nearly half a century (1837–1882). (George Washington headquartered and planned the siege of Boston at this same house between July 1775 and April 1776.) Longfellow enjoyed great popularity during his lifetime, and he and his immediate and extended family and friends played a central role in the intellectual and artistic life of 19th-century America. Among those who visited here were Charles Dickens, Ralph Waldo Emerson, and Julia Ward Howe.

Longfellow spoke 8 languages and read 12. He was a professor at Harvard while he lived here with his family. Many of his most famous poems were written here, including "Paul Revere's Ride," "Evangeline," and "The Village Blacksmith."

The house, which reopened in 2002 after an extensive restoration, is a fine example of mid-Georgian architecture. Longfellow and his beloved wife, Fanny, meticulously preserved the character and style of the building. Fanny died here in a tragic fire in 1861. After the author's death in 1882, the family continued to preserve the property for 90 years until it was transferred to the National Park Service in 1972. Virtually all of the furnishings are original to the house, most dating from Henry Longfellow's occupancy. Longfellow is buried in nearby Mount Auburn Cemetery.

The Longfellow House in Cambridge

Open Wednesday through Sunday 10–4:30, with tours on the hour. Published poets read from their works on alternate Sundays in summer at 4 pm. On the other weeks, a musical program is presented. On Saturdays in summer, artists are invited to paint and draw in the gardens. Adults $2, children 17 and under free.

♦ **Nichols House Museum** (617-227-6993), 55 Mount Vernon Street, Boston. Henry James supposedly said Mount Vernon was the most proper of Beacon Hill's streets. Relatively few tourists seem to find their way to this house, attributed to architect Charles Bulfinch. Located at the crest of the hill, it has a splendid view down the street toward Charles Street. The house has been a museum for 30 years, willed as such by the never-married Rose Standish Nichols, a gracious hostess, landscape designer, and author. She wrote three books: *English Pleasure Gardens* in 1902, *Italian Pleasure Gardens* in 1931, and *Spanish and Portuguese Gardens* in 1924. She was also an originator of the Beacon Hill Reading Club. Any books in the house belonged to the Nichols family and—while never cataloged—can be seen in the first-floor library and in bookcases in various rooms. Our favorite feature of the house is the bookcase-flanked window seat on the third floor, with a glimpse of other brick facades on the street. The grounds are especially pretty in spring, when azaleas and many bulbs are in bloom. Open May to October, Tuesday through Saturday noon–5; Monday, Wednesday, and Saturday in winter. Tours on the hour. The house is closed for the month of January. Admission, $5.

♦ **Harrison Gray Otis House** (617-227-3956; www.spnea.org), 141 Cambridge Street, Boston. This beautiful home, designed by architect Charles Bulfinch, dates from 1796 and is both a museum and the headquarters of the Society for the Preservation of New England Antiquities (SPNEA). The organization operates many fine historic sites in the region. A brick Federal mansion, this is typical of the sort built for wealthy Bostonians following the Revolutionary War. Located in Boston's once fashionable West End, the house is now surrounded by motels, parking lots, and stores. But the building is magnificent and—jammed among less inspiring neighbors—seems to shine. It has been carefully restored to the period. We love the red, yellow, and green patterned carpet in the front parlor, the Classical Revival look to the dining room, and the "withdrawing room" upstairs with its flowery, feminine touches. The Otises were great party givers, and their famous punchbowl is displayed. It was a family tradition to invite friends in at 4 PM for a drink, possibly a precursor of today's cocktail hour. Otis was a congressman, mayor of Boston, land developer, and father of 11 children. A research library on site is open Wednesday through Friday 9:30–4:30 and is especially rich in photos and architectural drawings of old buildings. The public may do ancestral or architectural research by appointment. Open Wednesday through Sunday 11–5. Adults $5, seniors $4, children $2.50.

♦ **Gibson House** (617-267-6338), 137 Beacon Street, Boston. And now for the Victorian period. This well-preserved house was designed by Edward Clarke Cabot, the same architect who designed the Boston Athenaeum. Built in 1859, it's a great example of Back Bay housing during Boston's literary Golden Age. The bachelor son of the family who built the house, Charles Hammond Gibson Jr., was the author of two books, *Two Gentlemen in Touraine* and *Among French Inns*. His poems appeared in Boston newspapers and anthologies. Gibson kept the place just as it looked in its heyday—and it's still that way. The place is crammed full of things. The gilt-embossed linen wallpaper in the foyer is original to the house—and what a way to start. Check the Bavarian carved wooden umbrella stand. The dining room, its table set with family china, is located to the rear of the house and looks out on the narrow lot. Four floors above are filled with incredible, original pieces, among them a velvet pet pagoda, a genuine hand-cranked Victrola, a stereopticon viewer, and a magic-lantern slide projector. The library—on the second floor—has the family's books. The house acts as headquarters for the Victorian Society in America, New England chapter. It is a great place to visit. Open for tours Wednesday through Sunday at 1, 2, and 3 PM. Admission $5.

Bookstores

Boston and Cambridge have loads of interesting bookstores including the large chains. We suggest a few of those we find especially appealing.

IN BOSTON

♦ **Brattle Book Shop** (617-542-0210; 1-800-447-9595; www.brattlebookshop.com), 9 West Street. Kenneth Gloss, son of the man who bought this bookstore in 1949, describes the spot as "Boston's oldest and largest used-book shop." There are three stories of rare, used, and out-of-print books. "We specialize in not specializing," declares the owner. Next door to the store is a small empty lot filled with bookcases of bargain books where book lovers browse year-round. Open Monday through Saturday 9–5:30, Thursday 9–7, Sunday noon–5.

♦ **Peter L. Stern & Co.** and **Lame Duck Books** (617-542-2376), 55 Temple Place. These two stores share the same space. Lame Duck specializes in "intellectual history" books and foreign-language literature. Peter L. Stern is focused on English and American literature, 19th- and 20th-century mystery books, autographs, and manuscripts. The store has original art by writers such as e. e. cummings, Tennessee Williams, and Henry Miller. Among the original manuscripts I saw was a page from a recipe book in George Washington's own hand.

♦ **Trident Booksellers & Café** (617-267-8688), 338 Newbury Street. This bookstore, with an emphasis on psychology, self-help, and New Age books, calls itself "Boston's Alternative." It has a very relaxed atmosphere, loads of current magazines, and a café with two dining rooms and a counter, where breakfast, lunch, and dinner are available. You can get breakfast all day. Wine and beer are served. Open 9 AM–midnight daily.

♦ **Boston Globe Store** (617-367-4000), 1 School Street. Formerly the "Old Corner Bookstore," this was a meeting place for Emerson, Hawthorne, Stowe, and other authors. The *Boston Globe* currently owns the space and sells memorable front-page reprints (including the 1918 one that declares "Sox Win Championship"), maps, books about Boston, and other memorabilia. *Boston Globe*–published photos are also available. Open Monday through Friday 9–5:30, Saturday 9:30–5.

IN CAMBRIDGE

♦ A *Bookstore Guide: Cambridge* lists no fewer than 28 different bookstores within a small radius, most of them near Harvard Square. Here are a few of the more interesting.

♦ **Grolier Poetry Book Shop, Inc.** (617-547-4648), 6 Plympton Street. This is the oldest continuously operating poetry bookshop in North America, dating from 1927. There are some 15,000 current poetry titles on the high shelves. An annual poetry contest is held here, and there are autograph parties, readings, and a bulletin board. Daily noon–6.

♦ **Harvard Book Store** (617-661-1515), 1256 Massachusetts Avenue. Complete selection of new books, but go downstairs for the amazing remainders section with volumes at 50 to 80 percent off publishers' list prices. Book racks are also found outside the front door. Monday through Thursday 9:30 AM–11 PM, Friday and Saturday until midnight; Sunday 10–10.

♦ **WordsWorth Books** (617-354-5201; 1-800-899-2202), 30 Brattle Street. This big bookstore promises discounts on all books all the time—15 percent off all trade hardcovers and 10 percent off all trade paperbacks. Worldwide shipping and out-of-print searches are handled, as well. Open Monday through Saturday 9 AM–11 PM, Sunday 10–10. **Curious George Goes to WordsWorth** (617-498-0062), 1 JFK Street, Harvard Square, is the children's book division of this giant.

♦ **The Harvard Coop** (617-547-8855), 1400 Massachusetts Avenue. This is the official bookstore of Harvard. The coop (pronounced as in *chicken coop*) also carries university paraphernalia and textbooks, but the two main floors are a bookstore run by Barnes & Noble. There is a café for sipping as you read.

♦ **Schoenhof's Foreign Books, Inc.** (617-547-8855), 76A Mount Vernon Street, Harvard Square. French, Spanish, German, Italian, Portuguese, Greek, and

Russian literature, nonfiction, and children's books (I once bought a children's version of *The Odyssey* in Greek). Dictionaries, grammars, audio courses, and language-learning materials for some 400 languages and dialects are available. Mail-order services and worldwide shipping. Monday through Saturday 10–6, Thursday until 8. Closed Sunday.

♦ **Kate's Mystery Books** (617-491-2660), 2211 Massachusetts Avenue (in the Porter Square area). One of the country's largest selections of new and used mysteries. Housed in a freestanding red house with black trim and a "tombstone" on the front lawn. Fun to prowl and very well organized. Monday through Friday noon–7, Thursday noon–8, Saturday 11–5, Sunday noon–5.

There are many more. Just walk the streets of Cambridge and you're sure to bump into a few. Don't forget the great kiosk at the "T" station in Harvard Square that sells more magazines, out-of-town newspapers, maps, et cetera, than any other newsstand we know. It's a wonderful spot.

A Literary Cemetery

♦ **Mount Auburn Cemetery** (617-547-7105), 580 Mount Auburn Street, Cambridge. Founded in 1831 as the nation's first garden cemetery, this continues as an active cemetery with many notables buried here. Literary figures include Henry Wadsworth Longfellow, Julia Ward Howe, and Oliver Wendell Holmes, as well as Winslow Homer, the artist, and Mary Baker Eddy, the founder of the Christian Science church. Open 8–5; until 7 in summer. It's a beautiful, tranquil place to drive or walk through. The Friends of Mount Auburn Cemetery offer frequent activities, including memorial walks to the gravesites of famous people buried here, with readings and ceremonies to mark the event.

Universities

Readers enjoy wandering the grounds of universities, and Boston has many. Certainly Harvard Yard is a beautiful, historic place to stroll through. For information on Harvard events, check the **Harvard Events and Information Center** (617-495-1573) at 1350 Massachusetts Avenue, Cambridge. Free, student-led tours of the campus originate from this center.

WHERE TO STAY

IN CAMBRIDGE

♦ **The Charles Hotel** (617-864-1200; 1-800-882-1818; fax 617-661-5053; www.charleshotel.com), 1 Bennett Street, Cambridge, MA 02138. This luxurious hotel close to Harvard Square has a special feature for readers: Just call the concierge desk with a request for a book and someone will run up to the nearby bookstore, WordsWorth, to get you a copy and deliver it to the room. The bookstore also stocks the lobby library area, and guests are welcome to borrow books during their stay.

Harvard Yard in spring

A large painting of the Longfellow House on the wall of the expansive lobby area is another nod to things literary. The hotel's 252 rooms are furnished simply in light wood furniture with blue, beige, and white down quilts on beds that are reminiscent of Shaker designs. Bose radios can be found in all rooms; there's also a tiny TV in each bathroom. The walk to Harvard Square is interesting. The Regatta Bar in the hotel is a popular spot for a predinner libation, and Rialto, the main restaurant, is touted as one of the better places to dine in Boston and Cambridge (see *Where to Dine*). There's garage parking available next door. Rates vary with the seasons and special events going on in Boston, but a standard room can be as inexpensive as $169 on a weekend in midwinter; up to $550 for commencement weekend. The Presidential Suite goes for about $3,000 a night.

♦ **The Inn at Harvard** (617-491-2222; 1-800-458-5886; fax 617-520-3711; www.theinnatharvard.com), 1201 Massachusetts Avenue, Harvard Square, Cambridge, MA 02138. This hotel offers a tranquil, elegant setting in the midst of Harvard University, which owns the property. It's so close to Harvard Square and the bookstores on Massachusetts Avenue ("Mass Ave") that you can spend hours prowling the stores and other emporia conveniently. Then you can return to the inn, settle onto a sofa in the interesting atrium lobby, and start reading. Bookshelves line the lobby walls, and inn guests can peruse the books or borrow them and take them to their rooms. The atrium lobby also serves as the inn dining room with three somewhat pricey meals offered daily. The 113 guest rooms are serene spaces, decorated in neutrals with padded headboards, mostly queen beds, and wall-to-wall carpeting. They were being refurbished in 2002. A parking garage is located beneath the hotel, with valet service provided at $30 a day. Artwork from Harvard's Fogg Art Museum is seen in some public spaces and guest rooms. Also, photos of illustrious Harvard graduates line the public corridors. Doubles, $189–425.

◆ **Sheraton Commander** (617-547-4800; fax 617-234-1396), 16 Garden Street, Cambridge, MA 02138. The Sheraton Commander, a 175-room brick hotel adjacent to the Radcliffe campus of Harvard University, is the oldest hotel in Harvard Square. It opened in 1927. The George Washington ballroom in the hotel is the room where John F. Kennedy announced his candidacy for the U.S. Congress. Most rooms have two doubles, or a single queen or king bed. Furnishings are traditional with dark wood headboards, armoires with TVs, chairs with reading lights, and wall-to-wall carpeting. Bathrooms are generally on the small size but have tub-shower combinations. In-room coffeemakers are provided. A casual restaurant off the lobby serves three meals, including a breakfast buffet. Doubles are priced $189–329.

◆ **Hotel at MIT** (617-577-0200; www.hotelatmit.com), 20 Sidney Street, Cambridge, MA 02139. Cambridge's other university is home to this sleek, modern, high-tech hotel—whose bright colors, amenities, and special perks make it something of a bargain, pricewise. It isn't located in Harvard Square, but since the area is just off Massachusetts Avenue, between Boston and Harvard Square, it is convenient. The 218 guest rooms have two queens or a single queen bed and lots of work space. Bedspreads are bright and colorful, and desks have high-speed Internet access. Interior shutters on the windows are sleek and attractive. Robes are provided. In the center of the lobby is a machine from the MIT museum nearby—most recently a kinetic energy machine that was waiting for its inventor to come and fix it. The library/lounge off the lobby is particularly large and welcoming. We found on the shelves books ranging from a rather ancient *Mathematics for Electricians and Radiomen* and *Nuclear Reactor Theory* by Isbin to *Shakespeare in Art* and *Browning's Poetical Works*. There are tables and chairs for a hand of bridge and comfortable sofas and chairs just for relaxing. Parking is available in a next-door garage, and parking is sometimes included in special packages offered by the hotel. A restaurant on premises serves all meals. There is a rooftop garden. Doubles, $119–300. The Presidential Suite goes for about $2,000.

◆ **A Cambridge House B&B** (617-491-6300; 1-800-232-9989; fax 617-868-2848; www.acambridgehouse.com), 2218 Massachusetts Avenue, Cambridge, MA 02140. This Colonial Revival house dating back to 1892 is exquisitely—and extravagantly—decorated in the Victorian mode. It's directly across the street from Kate's Mystery Books in the Porter Square area and a 10-minute drive to Harvard Square. The main house has 15 individually decorated guest rooms, several with working fireplace. Out back a carriage house was renovated in 1999 to provide four more rooms, all with gas fireplace. An extensive buffet breakfast is served in two parlors on the main floor of the house each morning; it includes freshly baked goods, cereals, yogurts, fruits, and beverages. If more of a breakfast is desired, you can request eggs, waffles, and such. Hors d'oeuvres and beverages are served each evening in the parlor. Free parking. Doubles, $149–275.

IN BOSTON

◆ **Omni Parker House** (617-227-8600; 1-800-THE OMNI; fax 617-742-5729; www.omnihotels.com), 60 School Street, Boston, MA 02108. Boston's Omni Parker House Hotel—where Charles Dickens stayed when he was in town—claims to be the longest continuously operating hotel in the United States. It opened in 1856. In its early days, Boston Literary Club members gathered at the original Parker House. They included Thoreau, Emerson, Whittier, and Oliver Wendell Holmes. The Literary Trail inaugurated by the Boston History Collaborative starts here. Dickens stayed at the Parker House during his 1867–1868 lecture tour. During that period he gave a reading here of his famous holiday story *A Christmas Carol*, taking all the parts himself. These days his great-great-grandson comes across the "pond" from Britain to do one or two readings a year at the Shubert Theater during the holiday season. On the same day, the Parker House does a re-creation of a four-course dinner that Dickens would have enjoyed a century and a half ago. It quickly sells out. The hotel's 560 rooms and suites have been completely refurbished recently, and returned to authentic period style. Rooms have two double beds, or one queen- or king-sized bed, and vary in size. They have private mini bar, hair dryer, cable TV, and high-speed Internet access. The hotel has a health center and valet parking. **Parker's Restaurant**—where Parker House rolls and Boston cream pie originated— is a full-service dining room open for breakfast, lunch, and dinner. **The Last Hurrah,** the Parker House's famous bar, was resurrected in 2000. It has the ambience of a darkly wooded Irish pub. Doubles, $119–309.

♦ **XV Beacon** (617-670-1500; 1-877-XV-BEACON; fax 617-670-2525; www. xvbeacon.com), 15 Beacon Street, Boston, MA 02108. The books on shelves in the rooms are all covered in plain white, in keeping with the sleek contemporary decor at this very upscale boutique hotel. The color scheme is black, white, and neutrals. This 62-room hotel opened in 2000 in a turn-of-the-20th-century beaux-arts building. It is located across the street from the Boston Athenaeum, a short walk from the gold-domed State House, and close to the Boston Common. *Luxury* is the operative word with 300-thread-count Italian linens on four-poster queen beds and a gas fireplace with remote control in each room. Within a short time of arrival, a staff member knocks on the door with a treat—mulled cider and warm cookies when we stayed here—and service is attentive throughout your stay. One of two private hotel cars can be booked to whisk you to a restaurant for dinner—if you don't eat in the well-regarded on-site eatery, **The Federalist.** Here, white busts of the fathers of our country peer down as you dine. There's also a rooftop garden where you can lounge, relax, and enjoy a great view of the city. Doubles start at $395, suites at $1,200.

♦ **The Colonnade** (617-267-1607; 1-800-962-3030; fax 617-424-1717), 120 Huntington Avenue, Boston, MA 02116. You may not be able to stay there yourself, but book lovers will probably like knowing about the Author's Suite at this hotel. It claims to be the only custom-designed author's suite in Boston. Bookcases line one wall of the elegant space, which includes a large writing desk, overstuffed chairs, a king bed, and good views of the city from the eighth floor. There's an extensive collection of first editions by visiting authors. These include Spencer Johnson's best-seller *The One-Minute Manager* and Stewart O'Nan's *The Speed Queen*. The location is very convenient to the Boston Public Library. There are 285 rooms and 15 luxury suites with bathrobes, hair dryers, umbrellas, and mini bars. A rooftop swimming pool is open in-season. The French restaurant **Brasserie Jo** is just off the lobby. Doubles, $375–515, but ask for package plans in low season.

♦ **Ritz-Carlton Boston Common** (617-574-7100; 1-800-241-3333; fax 617-574-7200; www.ritzcarlton.com), 10 Avery Street, Boston, MA 02111. This new-in-2001 Ritz-Carlton (the second for Boston) is located in the emerging "Ladder District" between Tremont and Washington Streets in the old shopping district of the city. It isn't far from famous Filene's department store and its possibly better-known bargain "Basement." It's also close to many of the hottest restaurants in town—and the famous Brattle Book Shop is just a block away. The hotel occupies the lower 12 floors of the high-rise tower, with condominiums above. Many luxuriously appointed rooms have views of Boston Common; others look out over a landscaped rooftop. The lobby is large and elegant with huge fireplace, and tables and chairs for enjoying afternoon tea (a Ritz tradition) or cocktails. The 193 guest rooms range from standards—with two queen-sized beds—to luxury suites with separate living room and dining area. Colors are golds and greens with puffy feather duvets on beds and plush wall-to-wall carpeting. Bathrooms have good-sized tubs for soaking in addition to large glass-doored stall showers, marble counters, and marble floors. Bose radios are found in all standard guest rooms; in luxury suites, Bang & Olufsen sound systems have been installed. Half of one floor is devoted to smoking rooms. **JER-NE restaurant** on the second floor offers contemporary American cuisine with Asian influences. **JER-NE bar** at street level has a light dining menu 11:30 AM–11 PM. Complimentary membership to **The Sports Club/LA** is offered. This club is right next door and directly connected to the hotel. It has a junior Olympic pool, basketball, volleyball and squash courts, and fitness equipment. Doubles, $385–525.

♦ **Ritz-Carlton Boston** (617-536-5700; 1-800-241-3333; www.ritzcarlton.com), 15 Arlington Street, Boston, MA 02117. This is the grande dame of Boston's hotels, completely renovated and reopened in fall 2002. It has some fine literary connections, too. Part of E. B. White's story *The Trumpet of the Swan* takes place in the Ritz-Carlton, and Moss Hart's play *Light Up the Sky* was set in a Ritz-Carlton suite. Also, according to a hotel spokesman, when Tennessee Williams's *A Streetcar Named Desire* was having its Boston tryout, new material was conceived in a suite at this hotel. The building overlooks the Boston Public Garden where, in winter, ice skaters can be seen, and in summer the swan boats glide. Rooms are comfortably appointed with traditional furniture and floral bedspreads with matching draperies. The well-trained staff jump to attention to meet guests' needs. The main dining room, with its signature blue water goblets, overlooks the Public Garden. Afternoon tea is a ritual at the hotel. Shoppers find the Newbury Street proximity a plus. Boston Public Library isn't far. Doubles, $495–695.

♦ **Copley Square Hotel** (617-536-9000; 1-800-225-7062; www.copleysquarehotel. com), 47 Huntington Avenue, Boston, MA 02116. The location of this smaller (148-room) hotel in the heart of Copley Square makes it most convenient. There is an understated feeling, the kind of hotel you feel relaxed about entering. I remember happily the room we once had with bay window overlooking the square. The hotel has recently upgraded all of its rooms. Beds are king, queen, or two doubles. There are five family suites with two bedrooms; a king or queen bed is in one room and two doubles in the adjoining room. Furnishings are traditional but pleasant; most bathrooms have tub-shower combinations. Guests have use of the fitness center at the nearby Lenox Hotel. A coffee shop and a sports bar, the **Sports Saloon,** are off the lobby. Doubles, $225–405, but package plans are frequently offered.

♦ **The Charles Street Inn** (617-314-8900; 1-877-772-8900; fax 617-371-0009; www. charlesstreetinn.com), 94 Charles Street, Boston, MA 02114. This former apartment building and once the "model home" of a group of 19th-century town houses has been converted to an elegant nine-room bed & breakfast inn by co-owners Sally Deane and Louise Venden. The Charles Street Inn really takes note of Beacon Hill history. All of its rooms are named for literary and artistic figures who once lived in the neighborhood. These include Edith Wharton, Louisa May Alcott, Henry James, and Ralph Waldo Emerson. Each room is large with high ceilings and is individually and beautifully decorated. The room named for landscape architect Frederick Law Olmsted looks out onto a small parklike area to the rear of the building, appropriately enough. Several rooms have marble working fireplaces. With just two rooms per floor, there is a real sense of privacy. Deep whirlpool tubs with massage jets are found in the well-equipped bathrooms. Guests also have coffeemakers in case they can't wait until their breakfast is delivered to their room. Charles Street—with its wonderful shops and restaurants—is just outside the door. Parking? The garage under Boston Common might be your best bet. Doubles, $240–375.

♦ **Charlesmark Hotel** (617-247-1212; fax 617-247-1224; www.thecharlesmark.com), 655 Boylston Street, Boston, MA 02116. The fireplaced lobby—with tiny round tables for breakfasting—looks directly out on the facade of the Boston Public Library from this brand-new city hotel. Mark Hagopian, whose family owns the Newbury Guest House, and his friend, investor Charles Hajjar, joined forces to open this boutique hotel with 33 rooms in 2002. It's a bit of a narrow squeeze from the Boylston Street entrance down a hallway to the elevator, but once in the second-floor lobby, you feel comfortably cosseted. Rooms are efficiently organized on six floors and are contemporary in feel. They either have a queen bed along with a single pullout sofa or a double bed with built-in drawers below. Bathrooms, while small, have good-sized glass-doored shower stalls and handsome Italian tile and granite walls, floors, and sinks. A TV with VCR is found in every room, as well as a stereo system and selection of CDs. Work desks have Internet access. The hotel is just about opposite the finish line of the Boston Marathon, a race Mark Hagopian has run several times. A continental-plus breakfast is complimentary. Parking is available about a block away in the garage at Prudential Center. Doubles, $150–275.

WHERE TO EAT

IN CAMBRIDGE

There are all kinds of casual—and cheaper—places to dine in Cambridge, especially near Harvard Square. Here are a few more serious spots.

♦ **Sandrine's** (617-497-5300; fax 617-497-8504; www.sandrines.com), 8 Holyoke Street, Harvard Square. Raymond Ost, who is Alsatian, opened this cozy restaurant inspired by his homeland, along with partner Gwen Trost a few years ago. It's one of the most romantic, comfortable, and lovely spaces to dine anywhere. Walls are a soft blue-gray below the wainscoting and white above. Country-style plates and casseroles, vases with imaginative dried branches or flowers, and other touches—presumably from the Alsatian section of France—decorate walls and shelves. Tablecloths are white; chairs and banquettes red or red print. An open kitchen allows you to observe a serious chef staff at work. All ages—from students on dates to Harvard professors—make for a nice mixed crowd. Traditional *flammekueche*—like a thin-crust pizza/tart—can be a starter in the evening. These come with various toppings, the classic being hickory-smoked bacon, *fromage blanc*, and caramelized onions. Others could be mushroom, or smoked trout with Emmental cheese, or fresh asparagus.

Appetizers ($7–24, the higher price for a terrine of foie gras) include fresh chicken livers sautéed in port with fresh spinach in a Dijon vinaigrette, and Belgian endive salad with cucumber, tomato, spicy pecans, and red onion in a lemon olive oil dressing with feta. Entrées ($19–29) could be a grilled veal chop with Parmesan mushroom risotto and fresh asparagus; grilled pork chop with apple and maple syrup chutney and Calvados reduction; or a baby rack of lamb served on leek, carrot, and mushroom ragout with potatoes Anna, a delicious choice. Desserts include crème brûlée, poached caramelized white peach with ginger ice cream, and chocolate *kougelhopf* (a warm chocolate cake with caramel coulis, vanilla bean ice cream, and warm chocolate ganache)—priced $6–9. A prix fixe three-course menu at $29 includes mesclun salad or onion soup, mushroom ravioli, and crème brûlée. German Rieslings are among the nice range of wines offered. Open for lunch Monday through Saturday 11:30–2:30, and nightly for dinner from 5:30.

♦ **Harvest** (617-868-2255; fax 617-868-5422), 44 Brattle Street, Harvard Square. Harvest, located in the heart of Harvard Square—amid the shopping—is very popular for lunch and dinner. Harvest considers itself basically an "American" restaurant. Tim Lynch, one of the owners, says America is a melting pot—hence the wide cultural influences on the dishes. The space is serene and sophisticated, a white-tablecloth restaurant located in a contemporary building with shops and offices, and set back from the street. You can get a house-smoked turkey salad with dried cranberries, toasted walnuts, and blue cheese vinaigrette ($12) or the Harvest burger, served with a crock of Boston baked beans and french fries ($10) at lunch. Or even, if something more is required, a fennel-roasted pork tenderloin with olive oil mashed potatoes and oven-cured tomatoes ($14). In the evening entrées are

Christmas lights in Harvard Square

priced $20–30 and might be grilled veal flank steak with potatoes boulangère and roasted vegetables; roast fillet of salmon served on beluga lentils; or grilled rack of venison with braised red cabbage and a sweet potato soufflé. Starters include a chilled New England seafood sampler, caramelized Maine sea scallop on root puree with black truffles, or old-fashioned New England clam chowder with finnan haddie. Menus change frequently. Lunch Monday through Saturday noon–2:30; Sunday brunch 11:30–2:30; dinner nightly 5:30 to 10 or 11.

♦ **Rialto** (617-661-5050; fax 617-234-8093), 1 Bennett Street, in the Charles Hotel, Harvard Square. Jody Adams is the acclaimed chef at the helm of this more-than-a-hotel dining room. The space is contemporary, yet serene, with large, white-shaded floor lamps and comfortable banquette and table seating. There's also a long bar. At dinner, appetizers ($9–18) might include oysters on the half shell with seaweed salad and tempura scallions; spiced shrimp confit salad with sweet-and-sour squash, pine nuts, and spicy mint dipping sauce; or wild mushroom pasta spirals with porcini, Marsala, and Parmesan cream. Entrées are priced $22–36. They could be braised rabbit with red peppers, chickpea cake, garlic, and broccoli rabe; grilled leg of venison with Burmese rice, ginger-glazed carrots, chestnuts, leek, and baby bok choy; or Tuscan-style sirloin steak with sliced portobello mushroom, endive and arugula salad, and shaved Parmigiano Reggiano cheese with truffle oil. Finish with a dessert ($9–13) such as hot chocolate cream with hazelnut swirl ice cream and orange apricot sauce, or chèvre cheesecake in a gingersnap crust with cranberry coulis and sweet brandy crème fraîche. Adams is the author, with Ken Rivard, of *In the Hands of a Chef: Cooking with Jody Adams of Rialto Restaurant* (published in 2002). There is an exceptionally good wine list. Dinner nightly. **Henrietta's Table,** the casual bakery-*cum*-restaurant at the Charles Hotel, is also wonderful.

IN BOSTON

♦ **No. 9 Park** (617-742-9991; fax 617-742-9993), 9 Park Street. Barbara Lynch, one of the most respected and hottest chefs in Beantown, oversees this exquisite windows-on-the-world restaurant that overlooks the common and is close enough to the State House for the pols to patronize. The preferred tables are two in the large front windows, one of which was ours on a January afternoon with snow flurrying outdoors. A second, interior dining room is darker at lunchtime, but intimate in the evening. The marble-topped tables in the bar—to the left of the door as you enter—can be secured in the evening for a café-menu meal. The restaurant's signature drink is a pear martini (pear chips are sprinkled with sugar and then slowly baked before becoming part of this concoction). The serene space has white cloths on tables and soft green upholstered side chairs. Small glass chandeliers are mounted close to the ceiling. Deliciously chewy rolls are dispensed one at a time; as soon as one disappears, another replaces it. Gnocchi with lobster meat, served with mushrooms and peas, was a delectable offering (the chef loves to make gnocchi). Crabmeat salad with a fennel-flavored biscuit was also terrific. Lunch entrées, $13–19. In the evening, starters include a popular beet salad with Great Hill blue cheese and black olive croutons; hot and cold foie gras with lentils, apples, and brioche; and prune-stuffed gnocchi ($9–25). Entrées ($29–35) might be roast black bass with caramelized mushrooms, potato puree, and a seafood sauce; roast veal loin with a winter vegetable mélange and prune glaze; or bacon-wrapped short rib with mushroom fricassee and cooked and raw celery. A seven-course chef's tasting menu can be had for $85; a nine-course menu for $100. Desserts ($8–10) could be caramelized bananas with cranberry sorbet and cashew cake; Tahitian crème brûlée; or chocolate savarin made with a white chocolate soufflé. The café menu might offer bigoli with Bolognese sauce, Gorgonzola fondue with black olive coated lamb, or steak *au poivre* with sauce béarnaise ($16–24). Open for lunch Monday through Friday 11:30–2:30, and for dinner Monday through Saturday 5:30–10. The café menu is served until 11 PM Monday through Saturday.

♦ **Maison Robert** (617-227-3370; fax 617-227-5977), 45 School Street, in the old City Hall. For three decades this French restaurant has been part of the Boston scene, located so interestingly in the old City Hall in the center of the congested old downtown. The old corner bookstore, now the Boston Globe Store, is a few paces down the street. The statues in the courtyard out front are of Benjamin Franklin (hence the name *Ben's Café* for the more casual downstairs dining room) and of Josiah Quincy, second mayor of Boston. Ken Duckworth is the executive chef and Andree Robert—daughter of the founding chef, Lucien Robert—is now general manager. The main dining room, with high ceilings and formal drapery, has an elegant menu to match. The menu is printed in French and English. "Les Hors d'Oeuvre" might be corn and Parmesan soufflé with a Florida rock shrimp stew; lobster bisque with shrimp quenelle; or the restaurant's own smoked salmon with fried capers and dried apple chips ($12–24). Entrées might be as classic as pan-fried Dover sole with lemon butter or more contemporary butternut squash raviolis with pumpkin *au poivre* and arugula sauce. Roast rack of lamb and grilled filet mignon are also on the dinner menu ($19–35). Vegetables are à la carte. Desserts include upside-down apple tart with apple brandy sabayon, chocolate and Grand Marnier cake with raspberry coulis, and crêpes Suzette for two.

In the brick-walled café, a salubrious space with local artists' work on the walls and for sale, a somewhat more casual menu reigns. A warm Brie and mushroom tart or pasta of the day could be the appetizer. Entrées ($14–26) could be chicken in a casserole with pearl onions, potato, and mushrooms; calf's liver with onion or bacon; or a risotto with turnips, leeks, and mushrooms served in a cabbage leaf. The wine list is extensive. Lunch in the café, Monday through Saturday 11:30–2:30. Dinner in the café, Monday through Saturday from 5:30; in the main dining room, Tuesday through Saturday from 6.

♦ **Mantra** (617-542-8111; fax 617-542-8666; www.mantraboston.com), 52 Temple Place. A hookah den, an om bar with seats in a bank vault, and a huge dining space with marble walls that was once the main lobby of a bank—here's one of Boston's most exciting culinary and social spots. Located in the former Old Colony Trust Company building in the up-and-coming Ladder District, Mantra opened in 2001 to immediate acclaim. Chef Thomas John grew up in South India and graduated from hotel school in Delhi. He combines elements of American, Indian, French, and Southeast Asian cuisine—and Bostonians love it. Among his more creative starters at dinner are quail curry with eggplant and watercress; Jerusalem artichoke velouté with spiced pork rib confit and truffle oil; or golden beets and roasted sweet potato salad with endives, tangerines, and a cumin vinaigrette ($12–20). Entrées ($23–38) could be cabbage rolls of wild mushrooms with basmati rice, black-eyed beans, and corn ragout; clay oven roasted monkfish with braised leeks and a sweet pepper chutney; or seared veal tenderloin with cabbage and a ragout of root vegetables. Desserts are equally tantalizing: warm chocolate cake with hazelnuts, fennel, and Darjeeling tea; pistachio kulfi with candied kumquats and apricot coulis; or a spice-poached pear with vanilla bean ice cream ($9–12). A long marble bar draws the crowd that can't squeeze into the wood-ribbed hookah den, where you sits on low red cushions and smoke fruit-flavored tobacco from a hookah pipe while enjoying drinks. Downstairs, some of the seating at the dark om bar is in the former bank vault; the rest is around the perimeter of the room, centered by a star-shaped bar. It's all very au courant and popular. One waitress says the traffic from one part of the restaurant to another is crazy on weekends—it's an evening's entertainment! Open Monday through Saturday for lunch and dinner.

♦ **Limbo** (617-338-0280; fax 617-812-7908; www.limboboston.com), 49 Temple Place. A restaurant with a jazz club downstairs, Limbo is located across the street from Mantra and—since its opening in August 2001—lines have been out the door on weekend nights. The idea, according to Executive Chef Charles Draghi, is to sample a few plates at one sitting. Therefore, appetizers and entrées are not humongous portions, but rather geared—as the literature goes—to today's active lifestyle. Chef Draghi does not use cream or butter in cooking but relies on roasted vegetable juices, olive oil, and fermented fruits. The long, narrow space has a fascinating bar with lighted-from-within marble tables against banquettes, leather high-backed bar stools at the traditional bar, and two dining rooms, one in back and one on a mezzanine level. A disc jockey spins discs after dinner on the main level. Downstairs in the jazz club—where you can also dine with a reserved table—there is live entertainment 7 nights a week. It all adds up to an incredibly popular formula, especially with young professionals. And the food is highly rated. The tall, slim menu offers soups like fresh salmon poached in a light tomato water saffron broth with opal basil; salads such as arugula with shaved fennel, apples, and locally made goat cheese, or tomato with smoked prosciutto and a Zinfandel vinaigrette. Seafood, meats, and pastas are found on the menu. Singed sea scallops in a shell with a roasted yellow pepper and marjoram jus; grilled lamb with roasted red onion jus and spiced with scented geraniums; or lemon linguine with cockle clams steamed with leeks, arugula, and lemon thyme are priced $8–18. The wine list is extensive. Limbo is open Monday through Friday 11:30 AM–2 AM, Saturday and Sunday 5 PM–2 AM. Lunch is served 11:30–2; a café menu 2–5; dinner 5–11; and a late-night menu 11–1. The jazz club offers jazz, funk, Latin, and R&B every night 9–1. The DJ is in place on Thursday through Saturday nights 10–2 on the main floor.

♦ **Locke-Ober** (617-542-1340; fax 617-542-6452), Winter Place, Boston. Tradition! The menu for this venerable German restaurant in downtown Boston reads "established 1875." New life was breathed into the dark wood and the lace curtains in 2001 when dining room diva Lydia Shire took over, ably assisted by Jacky Robert—nephew of the founder of Maison Robert—as executive chef. Shire, already famous for her former restaurants **Biba** and **Pignoli,** kept much the same menu here as was famous for decades at Locke-Ober—along with the name. It still feels a lot like a men's club inside—for example, with heavy dark wood panels, leather chairs with nailed backs, and those half strips of lace at the window. The menu may not even *look* all that different, with such classics as steak tartare, Wiener schnitzel à la Holstein, and the restaurant's famous baked lobster savannah still on the menu. But it tastes better, say those who've dined here recently—and everything has been shined up and made to look less tired. Starters ($12–22) include crisp Cape scallops and bacon skewers, rosemary-scented mushrooms under glass, and escargots bourguignon. JFK's lobster stew (thick with chunks of lobster and one of the late president's favorite foods) is listed under the soups, along with lobster and finnan haddie chowder, and onion soup gratinée "with or without oxtail." Entrées are familiar fare for the most part ($29–48) and include duck with elderberry and ginger, veal chop Forestière, sweetbreads with chestnuts, and beef stroganoff with hand-cut noodles. The "limestone lettuce" on the salad portion of the menu is finer than bibb, comes from Kentucky, and copies an item popular 20 to 30 years ago. Among the famous desserts are Indian pudding with vanilla ice cream and macaroons. The restaurant is open for lunch Monday through Friday 11:30–2; for dinner Monday through Saturday from 5:30.

♦ **Beacon Hill Bistro** (617-723-1133; fax 617-723-7525), 25 Charles Street. The former Rebecca's near the corner of lively Charles Street and Beacon Street was given new life by Peter Rait, born in Buffalo, and his Swedish-born wife, Cecelia, in 2000. They opened this authentic French bistro—after having owned a French restaurant together in Lisbon for several years—with a small, 12-room European-style hotel above. A cheery fireplace greets you as you enter. The restaurant has dark wood walls, tile floors, and banquette seating with tables for two (that can be pushed together for larger parties). Three meals a day are served. For breakfast, standard egg dishes—with crispy chicken hash if you like—omelets, pancakes, waffles, and French toast are all on the menu. Lunch offers roasted beet salad with mint, farmer's cheese, and almond vinaigrette, or grilled flank steak salad with blue cheese and watercress. A burger, grilled chicken club with smoked bacon, or baked ham and cheese sandwich can be gotten. Entrées at lunch might be Breton fish soup with clams, leeks, and potatoes, or steak frites ($10–13). Starters at dinner might be veal short ribs with prunes, spaetzle, and *outarde violette*; a cheese tart with bacon, spinach, and poached duck egg; or pickled and smoked herring ($7.50–10). The entrées (priced $17–20) include confit of chicken with mushroom fricassee and baked onions; veal shank with roesti potatoes and Madeira; and roast salmon with lentils and bacon. Brunch is served on Saturday and Sunday. Breakfast is served 7–10; lunch 11:30–3; and dinner 5–11:30.

Patriotism and a Parade: Bristol, Rhode Island

8

The decorating begins in time for Memorial Day—red, white, and blue bunting and flags flying from just about every house and shop. By June 14, Flag Day, the town is decked out. It's all in anticipation of the Fourth of July, a holiday for which the entire town of Bristol, Rhode Island, gets revved up annually.

Bristol's Fourth of July parade is famous—and old. Bristolians who know their history are quick to point out that it's not necessarily the oldest Fourth of July *parade* in the nation, but simply the longest uninterrupted *observance* of the event. Bristol has been celebrating the independence of the nation since 1777.

"This is the flag-wavingest town in the country," says one resident.

The center stripe down the streets of town that form the parade route—Route 114 (Hope Street) and part of High Street—is red, white, and blue year-round, allowed by an act of Congress. The parade is a 3-hour-long extravaganza that everyone—it seems—turns out for. Picnics and parties follow. If you live in Bristol you more or less are expected to have open house.

The town itself is a picturesque, and historic, stage set for the parade. Named for a seaport in England, Bristol's origins date back to the Massachusetts Bay Colony, of which it was a part. Even the town common is said to be a "Massachusetts common" in style—a large open green. Although there are a couple of 17th-century homes in town, most date from the late 18th and early 19th centuries. (The British burned the town in 1776 as they marched through on the way to Newport.) The houses that line the gracious streets of Bristol today are beauties, bordering the parade route as if put there solely for that purpose. Some have wide porches on which people stand and cheer as the marchers go by.

Before white settlers came to the area, Bristol was the official headquarters for King Philip, the bellicose leader of the Wampanoag Indians. Wampanoag lands stretched east as far as Provincetown, Massachusetts, and west into what is now Connecticut. Philip's Native American name was Metacom (hence Metacom Avenue); his older brother, Wamsutta, was known to the English as Alexander. They were the sons of an Indian chief, Massasoit.

During the mid-1600s, Wamsutta went to Plymouth to meet with white men, and died suspiciously en route home. His younger brother, "King Philip," convinced that Wamsutta had been poisoned, banded many Native Americans together and went to war in 1675 against colonists. Philip was killed in Bristol as a part of that war, known as "King Philip's War," in 1680. After that, four Boston merchants with the names of Oliver, Byfield, Walley, and Burton settled Bristol. A school and a street are named for each of them.

These were children of *Mayflower* voyagers. The town appealed to settlers because it's at the very tip of a peninsula, with Narragansett Bay to the west and Mount Hope Bay to the east. A huge deep, natural harbor—Bristol Harbor—lies between two appendages of the town that extend like the thumb and forefinger of a mittened hand. This watery world was ideal for the merchant seamen who were its first inhabitants.

Bristol has the feeling of a real community. Residents have incredible civic pride. The town appeals to students attending Robert Williams University, to families, to retirees, and to tourists who come north from Newport or south from Providence and are floored by what they find. (Warren and Barrington, to the north of Bristol, aren't bad either.) The waterfront, the history, several fascinating museums, good restaurants, and places to stay—plus the simple beauty of the town—draw admirers.

Bristol is a perfect place for a weekend—small enough to feel as if you can see it, varied enough to appeal to many interests. And not only on the Fourth of July.

Getting There

If you're coming by **car,** take Route 114 south from I-195, then drive through Barrington and Warren to Bristol. The closest major **airport** is Green Airport in Providence. **Bus service** is provided from Providence via the Rhode Island Public Transport Authority (RIPTA)—(401) 781-9400.

For More Information

♦ **East Bay Chamber of Commerce** (401-245-0750; 1-888-278-9948; fax 401-245-0110; www.eastbaychamberri.org), 654 Metacom Avenue, Suite B, Warren, RI 02885. It's not a bad idea to pick up a copy of the weekly newspaper, the *Bristol Phoenix.*

SEEING AND DOING

The Fourth of July Parade

Should you want to attend this major annual event (and it's worth the effort), plan ahead. If you're traveling from a distance and need overnight reservations, make them several months ahead (see *Where to Stay*). On the day of the parade, people stake out viewing sites along the route beginning at 5 AM. Visitors should arrive in

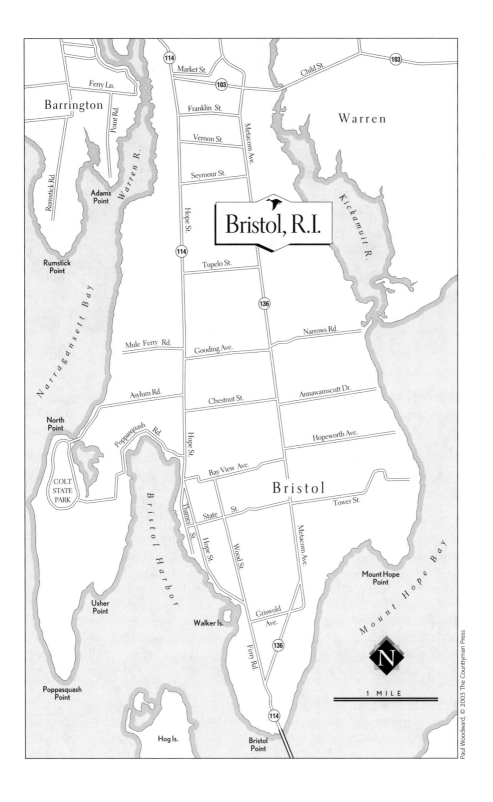

Bristol, R.I.

Barrington

Warren

114
Market St.
103
Child St.
103

Ferry Ln.

Point Rd.

Franklin St.

Vernon St.

Metacom Ave.

Rumstick Rd.

Adams
Point

Seymour St.

Warren R.

Kickamuit R.

Rumstick
Point

Hope St.

114

Tupelo St.

136

Narragansett Bay

Mule Ferry Rd.

Gooding Ave.

Narrows Rd.

Asylum Rd.

Chestnut St.

Annawamscutt Dr.

North
Point

Poppasquash Rd.

Hope St.

Hopeworth Ave.

COLT
STATE
PARK

Bay View Ave.

Bristol

Bristol Harbor

State St.

Tower St.

Usher
Point

Thames St.

Hope St.

Wood St.

Metacom Ave.

Mount Hope
Point

Mount Hope Bay

Poppasquash
Point

Walker Is.

Griswold
Ave.

136

N

1 MILE

Ferry Rd.

Hog Is.

114

Bristol
Point

Paul Woodward, © 2003 The Countryman Press

The Fourth of July parade in Bristol

Bristol via Metacom Avenue (Route 136), because Route 114 (Hope Street, the parade route) is closed early to cars. From Metacom, take State Street or Bay View Avenue to find off-street parking. From Wood Street, it's just a short two-block walk to Hope Street.

Bring folding chairs, hats, and cameras, and find a place along the parade route. Portable bathrooms are located throughout the downtown area, as are first-aid stations.

If you want to reserve an elevated site for watching the parade, you can get off-street parking, breakfast, lunch, and bathrooms by making a reservation through the historic house Linden Place, at 500 Hope Street. The number to call is (401) 253-0390.

The "parade before the parade" is part of the fun. Paradegoers deck themselves out in red, white, and blue and walk up and down Hope Street showing off their costumes before, during, and after the parade. Outrageous getups are not unusual. The parade steps off at 10:30 AM, rain or shine. Bands come from around the country to participate. There are floats and clowns and policemen on horseback in the parade. Kids love it. It's a very good idea to arrive *before* 8 AM if you want to get a place to park and to watch. Bringing your own coffee and muffins isn't a bad idea, either.

♦ **The Bristol Train of Artillery,** a 225-year-old military unit, always heads up the Fourth Division of the Parade, the historical division. Men in colonial uniforms with muskets march alongside some of the special historic guns and cannon, which are carried by truck. The B.T.A. has a museum/headquarters on State Street. For tours of its fascinating collection, including some rare specimens of military weapons and artifacts, contact Lieutenant Colonel Edward P. Smith at (401) 521-9136.

Historic Sites

While many of the houses and buildings in town are architecturally interesting and worth viewing from the outside, there are a few sites that are open to the public and merit a visit. Pick up the free pamphlet *Explore Historic Bristol on Foot*, produced by East Bay Chamber of Commerce, as a starter.

♦ **Linden Place** (401-253-0390), 500 Hope Street, Bristol. This is the one great home built by a successful merchant seaman in Bristol that is open to the public. Famed local architect Russell Warren was the designer, and the spiral staircase is noteworthy. The Federal mansion was designed and built in 1810 for General George DeWolf, a member of the seafaring DeWolf family of Bristol. The money came from the "triangle trade"—sugar, rum, slaves—that funded so much of Bristol's early prosperity. DeWolf's grandson, Colonel Samuel Pomeroy Colt, a later owner of the property, founded the U.S. Rubber Company (now Uniroyal). A guided tour of the house follows 177 years of occupation by five generations of the same family—with reference to its place in American history, including politics, business, philanthropy, and the entertainment world. (Actress Ethel Barrymore spent some summers here.) Located in the center of downtown Bristol, Linden Place is comprised of the mansion, sculpture-filled gardens, an 1825 carriage barn, and some outbuildings dating from 1750. Open May 1 through Columbus Day, Thursday through Saturday 10–4, Sunday noon–4. Open in December for some holiday events (call ahead). Adults $5, children $2.50.

♦ **Blithewold** (401-253-2707; www.blithewold.org), 101 Ferry Road, Bristol. Blithewold was built in the early 1900s in the style of a 17th-century English manor house. The stone-and-stucco mansion is decorated and furnished much as it was in the early years of the 20th century, when it was the summer home of Pennsylvania coal magnate Augustus Van Wickle and his family. For those who have just come from viewing the Newport mansions, Blithewold seems much more human in scale, and like a house that was actually lived in and enjoyed. The Van Wickles often had guests—hence the 32 sets of china.

The grounds at Blithewold are stunning. The 33-acre property overlooks Narragansett Bay and historic Bristol Harbor, where one of the family's Herreshoff steam yachts was kept. One of the earliest arboretums in America, it features 50,000 flowering spring bulbs, a Japanese water garden, an exotic bamboo stand, and a huge giant sequoia, more than 90 feet tall, the largest of its kind east of the Rocky Mountains. Daffodil time at Blithewold is spectacular.

Marjorie Van Wickle Lyons, daughter of the owners, spent summers at Blithewold until her death at the age of 93 in 1976. She bequeathed the property to the Heritage Trust of Rhode Island. Special events are great draws at Blithewold, including "Christmas at Blithewold," which takes place throughout the month of December. The house is decorated top to bottom and open to the public from Wednesday through Sunday. Check for hours. Otherwise, the mansion and gardens are open

Blithewold

from mid-April to mid-October, 10–4 Wednesday through Sunday and most Monday holidays. The grounds are open daily 10–5. Adults $10, seniors $8, youths 6–17 $6.

♦ **Herreshoff Marine Museum & America's Cup Hall of Fame** (401-253-5000; fax 401-253-6222; www.herreshoff.org), 1 Burnside Street at Route 114, Bristol. You won't have trouble spotting this place: A 12-meter yacht, *Defiant*, is on the front lawn. Serious boaters, and especially sailors, come to worship at the shrine of the Herreshoffs (pronounced *HER-shoff*). The Herreshoff Manufacturing Company, on the site of the present-day museum, produced the world's finest yachts—and several America's Cup winners—from 1863 to 1945. A genius of naval architecture, Captain Nathanael Greene Herreshoff, along with his business-oriented brother John Brown Herreshoff, made the boat manufacturing company tops in its field. The first U.S. Navy torpedo boats, fine lightweight steam machinery, pioneering fin-keel spade-rudder boats in the 1890s, and mammoth schooner yachts were among the boats and engines built. The Watch Hill 15 and the Buzzards Bay 25 are beamy sailing craft that are often passed down from generation to generation. The Herreshoffs constructed eight consecutive successful defenders of the America's Cup fom 1893 to 1934. "Captain Nat's" studio is re-created on site. There is a Hall of Fame of America's Cup winners and a Hall of Boats where those interested can spend hours. A model room with half models of boats is fascinating for viewing the differences in keel design, and so on. Herreshoff yachts are a vital part of the history of boating in America—and the history of Bristol, Rhode Island, as well. There are period rendezvous planned, and owners of Herreshoff yachts gather here for them. Open May through October, 10–5. Adults $5, seniors $4, students $2, children under 12 free.

♦ **Haffenreffer Museum of Anthropology** (401-253-8388; fax 401-253-1198; www.brown.edu/Facilities/Haffenreffer), 300 Tower Street, Bristol. Located on a high point in Bristol, on traditional Wampanoag Indian lands—and the site of the stone King Philip's Seat as well—this anthropological museum has rare treasures. The building is filled with beautifully crafted artifacts made and used by the Native peoples of the Americas, Africa, Asia, and the Pacific. Native American clothing, weapons, and household goods are included. Visitors enjoy viewing the wealth in four intimate galleries. The Haffenreffer belongs to Brown University and is considered one of the finest teaching museums in the Northeast. There are trails on the grounds open to the public and places to picnic. From here you also get nice water views. Open September through May, Saturday and Sunday 11–5; June through August, Tuesday through Sunday 11–5. Adults $3, children $1.

♦ **Bristol Historical and Preservation Society Museum and Library** (401-253-7223), 48 Court Street, Bristol. Artifacts covering 300 years of Bristol history are located in the cells of the former 1828 jail built of granite used as ballast in early sailing ships. The research library contains more than 1,800 books and documents. Ship models and children's toys are also found here. The library is open year-round on Wednesday 1–5; the museum June through September, Sunday 1–4. Donation.

Outdoors

♦ **Coggeshall Farm Museum** (401-253-9062), off Route 114 to Poppasquash Road, Bristol. This is a self-guiding historical farm museum with an 18th-century farmhouse (under restoration), a kitchen garden, pastures, hay fields, and a few small outbuildings. Costumed interpreters take care of vegetable gardens and animals. Two cows, two steer, a calf, and a few sheep were in the pastures when we stopped by. It's probably more interesting to visit on a weekend when a special event is planned—such as sheep shearing or a garden day. The place is breezy on a hot day and a good place for young children to run around. Open year-round, daily 10–6. Adults $1, children 50 cents.

♦ **East Bay Bike Path.** Nearly 15 miles in length, this paved path goes from Bristol to Providence, passing through Warren, Barrington, and Riverside as it heads into the state capital. People commute on it. The path follows the route of the old Penn Central rail line and never strays far from the water. Views are great. It cuts through several parks, including Colt State Park. Its starting (and ending) point in Bristol is waterfront Independence Park. There are places to leave a car in any of the parks along the route or in municipal parking lots. Walkers may also use the bike path. For information, call (401) 253-7482.

♦ **Environmental Education Center, Audubon Society of Rhode Island** (401-245-7500), 1401 Hope Street (Route 114), Bristol. Situated on a 28-acre wildlife refuge on Narragansett Bay, this center has Rhode Island's largest aquarium, environmental exhibits for the whole family (including a life-sized right whale), a tide pool tank, and other educational exhibits oriented toward the sea. May through September, daily 9–5; October through April, Monday through Saturday 9–5, Sunday noon–5. Adults $5, children $3.

◆ **Mount Hope Farm** (401-254-1745; 401-254-5059), 250 Metacom Avenue, Bristol. This 127-acre estate is open to the public for picnicking or walking/biking on roadways only. The main house, built in 1745, and other buildings are used for special events. There are 1,500 feet of waterfront on Church Cove. The site is listed on the National Register of Historic Places.

◆ **Prudence and Hog Islands Ferry** (401-253-9808), Church Street Wharf, Thames Street, Bristol. How about a ferry ride? Two islands just offshore are served by a ferry leaving from downtown Bristol. The larger island is Prudence, whose population swells in summertime with seasonal residents. The island can easily be seen offshore, and the ride is short (15 minutes or so) and sweet—especially for kids. If you have your own boat, you can take it out and dock at the south end of the island. Frequent ferry sailings mean you can do a round-trip in well under an hour. There are five or six ferries a day from Bristol to Prudence in summer, fewer the rest of the year. A separate ferry goes to Hog Island. Adult one-way tickets are $2.85; kids pay $1. **Rockwell Waterfront Park** next to the ferry landing has benches and is a nice place to sit and watch water activity for a while.

◆ **Colt State Park**, Route 114, Bristol. Free. This is a splendid park. The former Colt family farm, it has unimpeded views of Narragansett Bay from a circular 3-mile drive. Attractions include paths for hiking and biking, a tidal pond, many picnic sites, a boat-launching ramp, fishing docks, a stone barn, and all sorts of spring flowers. The **Bristol Town Beach** is accessed from the entry drive to the park. Turn to the right shortly after entering. The beach is open Memorial Day through Labor Day; parking weekdays for nonresidents is $4, on weekends $5.

Kayaking, Climbing, Biking

◆ **Ocean State Adventures** (401-254-4000), 99 Poppasquash Road, Bristol, specializes in kayaking, climbing, and biking instruction and adventures for the whole family. OSA also sells kayaks. Many different half-day or full-day kayak tours are offered.

Golf

◆ **Bristol Golf Course** (401-253-9844), 95 Tupelo Street, offers nine holes.

Shopping

This is **antiques** territory. State Street, leading to the harbor, and Hope Street (Route 114) are the two main shopping streets. We like **Alfred's** on Hope Street and **Alfred's Annex** (for overflow) a few doors south. These shops are crammed with goodies, including furniture, glassware, holiday ornaments, dishes, and so on. **Jesse/James Antiques** on State Street is also a good place to prowl. Specialties are lamps, textiles, furniture, and china.

Kate & Company on Hope Street is a great little gift and clothing shop. Also for sale are home items, gourmet foods, and jewelry. We liked the animal-print pocketbooks. **European Kitchen** on State Street has neat dishes and kitchenware from

France and Italy. **Claddagh Connection** is a large Irish shop near the new Bristol Harbor Inn at the end of State. Irish tweed suits, sweaters, capes, glass, Belleek china, and a large selection of Irish jewelry are for sale. **Good Books** on Hope Street also has picture frames, journals, and pottery. **Basically British** on State Street is a British and Irish foods shop.

Gift shops at **Linden Place** and **Blithewold** are worth a stop.

Want to buy a boat? **Eric Goetz Custom Sailboats** carries on in the tradition of the Herreshoff Manufacturing Company, making state-of-the-art custom boats and today's America's Cup challengers.

For the holiday season, the Bristol shopping district gets all dolled up. **Grand Illumination Night**—sometime after Thanksgiving—is the evening for turning on the lights. Shops stay open and people stroll about. It's the next-biggest Bristol event to the Fourth of July parade.

WHERE TO STAY

♦ **Bristol Harbor Inn and Suites** (401-254-1444; fax 401-254-1333; www.bristol-harborinn.com), 259 Thames Street, Bristol, RI 02809. This new little hotel is just what Bristol needed: a waterfront hostelry in a historic setting with easy access to center-of-town activities and restaurants. Three vintage buildings—including the original Bank of Bristol and a lumber building along the wharves—have been joined and turned into a boutique hotel with 40 classy rooms and suites on three floors. More than half the rooms have harbor views; the rest look toward town. The long taupe-clapboard building sits at right angles between the harbor and Thames Street, with an elegant, small lobby. Large black-and-white nautical maps of Narragansett Bay and a sailboat print on the lobby walls reference the marine setting. Rooms have one queen, one king, or two double beds and a spacious private bath with shower-tub combination. Eight "historic" rooms in the old 1797 bank building all have gas fireplaces, traditional mahogany furniture, chair rails, and small brass chandeliers. Other rooms and suites are more contemporary, with light wood furniture, pale blue walls, and neutral furnishings. Some have dormers, and a few are one-bedroom suites. The Observation Suite has four large windows with views of the harbor. A continental breakfast is served. Goff's on the harbor, in a separate building, is part of the Bristol Harbor Inn; it's a fancy bar with light food and a deck on top with killer water views. It's the place to be at sunset. Doubles, $139–219.

♦ **Bradford-Dimond-Norris House** (401-253-6338; 1-888-329-6338; fax 401-253-4023; www.bristol-lodging.com), 474 Hope Street, Bristol, RI 02809. When the British raided the town of Bristol in 1778, one of the many homes destroyed by fire was that of Rhode Island deputy governor William Bradford. In 1792 Bradford began work on this replacement, a gem located next door to the Linden House and convenient to major sites of interest. The Fourth of July parade passes by it. The house has a commanding presence with a large porch. Lloyd and Suzanne Adams (who also own the Bristol Harbor Inn with partners) are the helpful innkeepers. Each of four guest rooms is individually and attractively decorated and has air-conditioning and its own updated bathroom. All rooms—one on the first floor and three on the second—have queen beds. Two larger rooms have a separate dressing room with twin bed. An expanded continental breakfast is served in the dining room or out back on the veranda. There's always a home-baked item, sliced fresh fruit, yogurt, cereals, and breads. No children. Doubles, $95–120.

♦ **Rockwell House Inn** (401-253-0040; 1-800-815-0040; www.rockwellhouseinn. com), 610 Hope Street, Bristol, RI 02809. The lovely porch stretching across the front of this inn, close to the street and furnished with wicker, is one of the best vantage points for viewing the Fourth of July parade. Guests book up to a year in advance to secure this prime location. Giles Luther, the first recorded parade marshal, built the house in 1809. Debra and Steve Krohn, innkeepers, offer four individually decorated guest rooms with private bath. Three have king or twin beds; one has a queen bed, and there's definitely a romantic feel. Two of the rooms have a working gas fireplace, and all have terry robes, lighted makeup mirror, hair dryer, and air-conditioning. One room is on the main floor of the house, where you'll also find a high-ceilinged parlor and a dining room with a lace-cloth-covered table. Here Debra often serves her extravagant candlelight breakfasts. Among her specialties are a Dutch puffed pancake with cranberries, walnuts, and apples, and a baked sticky French toast. To the rear of the house is a 20-foot-long breakfast porch, used in warm weather. A "courting corner" with stone fireplace is also just outside the back door of the house. It was added by Charles Rockwell, a later owner, for his daughter to entertain suitors. In the deep garden out back there's a pond with waterfall. Doubles, $95–150.

♦ **William's Grant Inn** (401-253-4222; 1-800-596-4222; fax 401-253-4222; www. wmgrantinn.com), 154 High Street, Bristol, RI 02809. Warren and Diane Poehler, both in the teaching profession, came east from Arizona to operate this appealing B&B in Bristol. Joining them in the venture are their son, Matthew, and their daughter-in-law, Janet Poehler. The inn, painted deep blue with white trim, has five guest rooms. Three on the first floor have private bath; two on the second floor share. All but one have queen beds; that has a double. Each of the rooms is themed. The Nautical Room on the first floor has seafaring artifacts, a whirlpool bath, and a fireplace. Blithewold has a floral motif, while Sturbridge is decorated in a "historical" style. At two large tables just off the kitchen guests enjoy a full breakfast. "They watch me work," laughs Diane. She might prepare blueberry pancakes or a fresh spinach and mushroom omelet as the main course. Doubles, $75–105.

♦ **Hearth House** (401-253-1404; www.hearthhouse.com), 736 Hope Street, Bristol, RI 02809. A fireplace or wood-burning stove in each of three guest rooms makes the new name for this inn appropriate. Former New York City schoolteachers Angie and Tony Margiotta took over the former Parker Borden House in 2000. The Rose Room has a king bed, two fireplaces, and a view of Bristol Harbor. The Skylight Garden View Room has a wood-burning stove, private entrance, and view of gardens out back. The Harbor View Suite has two connecting rooms, two fireplaces, a private bathroom with Jacuzzi-style tub, and a water view. A common room on the second floor along with the guest rooms has a fireplace, satellite TV, and lots of books. This is the B&B closest to the start of the East Bay Bike Path across the street at Independence Park. It's also convenient to take a stroll by the water before turning in. Breakfast is hearty and includes homemade muffins. Doubles, $120–140.

♦ **Johnson & Wales Inn** (508-336-8700; 1-800-232-1772; fax 508-336-3414; www. JWInn.com), 213 Taunton Avenue (Routes 44 and 114A), Seekonk, MA 02771. This inn—just a 20-minute drive north of Bristol—is where we stayed one Fourth of July (Bristol inns having been reserved long before we made up our minds to go to the parade). The small hotel is operated by Johnson & Wales University, a Providence college specializing in culinary and hospitality programs. We found our suite with queen bed, whirlpool bath, and wet bar very comfortable. TVs are in armoires, and the separate living room makes these accommodations especially spacious. Several of the inn's 86 rooms have two double beds. **Audrey's Restaurant** is a serene space with a fairly ambitious menu; it was pretty empty, though, on the night we dined in mid-July. Entrées are $16–20 and may include pan-seared salmon with Gorgonzola butter and wild mushroom encrusted lamb loin. Doubles, $89–149.

WHERE TO EAT

♦ **Roberto's** (401-254-9732), 301 Hope Street, Bristol. Robert Myers is the chef and Robert Vanderhoof, the manager, so the name was a no-brainer. Locals all point to it as one of the finest places to dine in town. Ensconced in a tiny storefront space on lower Hope Street, the restaurant was due to expand within months of opening. The decor is simple: green arrowback chairs at white-clothed tables. At lunchtime, soups might be pasta e fagioli or beef barley. Other choices include a Tuscan bread salad, grilled chicken Caesar wrap, or specials like shepherd's pie or tortellini. At dinner, appetizers ($6–7) could be homemade polenta, pepperoni and cheese calzone, or portobello mushrooms sautéed with tomatoes and shallots. Dinner entrées (priced $13–20) can include tortellini with prosciutto, snow peas, and yellow squash in a cream sauce; penne pasta with lamb Bolognese sauce; tournedos of beef; or chicken or veal Piccata, perennially popular. And, says Bob Vanderhoof, "We have the best caramel flan in the world for dessert." Open for lunch Monday through Friday 11:30–2:30, for dinner nightly from 5.

♦ **Hotpoint American Bistro** (401-254-7474), 31 State Street, Bristol. James Reardon, chef-owner, worked at Newport's Clark Cooke House before striking out on his own. His grandfather got him started in the restaurant business quite young; at 12, he said, he was helping out in a family restaurant in Warwick, Rhode Island. This restaurant is next door to what was once an appliance store, and that's how Jim Reardon decided on the name. The narrow storefront space is in the historic waterfront area and close to everything. There's a tapestry hanging on one wall, as well as paintings and a mirror. Small tables and a tiny bar in the back fill the space. Reardon decribes his food as "fairly traditional" although he does quite a bit of game—including ostrich, venison, and elk—in fall. You can get a sandwich in the evening, including crabcake, hamburger, grilled pesto, and open-faced sirloin ($9–20). Sesame shrimp salad, and baby spinach salad with pears, blue cheese, pecans, and yellow and red tomatoes are included under "Light Fare." Fresh-cut french fries can be drizzled with a warm blue cheese sauce. Entrées ($14–20) include molasses-marinated pork tenderloin served with apple and house-smoked bacon mashed potatoes; lobster and asparagus fettuccine with a sage-Parmesan sauce; seafood pesto pasta; and chicken Marsala served over mashed potatoes with vegetables on the side. Dinner, Tuesday through Saturday, from 5.

♦ **Redlefsen's** (401-254-1188), 444 Thames Street, Bristol. This restaurant moved from the center of town to the west side by the water. There the owner ingeniously converted an old town garage into a very pretty space. A dark green awning shelters a small patio in front across the street from Independence Park. Inside, little white lights are looped as part of the decor. On one side there's a highly varnished wood bar with fireplace; on the other, bare wood dining tables with green chairs. Walter Guertler, who owns the restaurant with his wife, Sally, describes the venture as "retirement for a workaholic." A few German dishes appear at both lunch and dinner, and Oktoberfest is celebrated with gusto. At lunchtime salads, pastas, sandwiches, and light entrées—grilled trout with vegetables or Wiener schnitzel, for example—fill out the menu ($10–12 for the entrées). Dinner could begin with baked Brie *en croute* or Maryland crabcakes. A Black Angus burger with fries or ravioli is included with salads as "Light Fare." Dinner entrées ($15–20) might be twin grilled lamb chops with a maple brandy sauce, grilled bauernwurst and bratwurst served with sauerkraut, or baked scrod with rémoulade sauce. A variety of quality European beers is on tap, including Franziskaner Weissbier. From Memorial Day through Labor Day the restaurant serves dinner nightly from 5, and lunch Monday through Friday 11:30–2:30. During the off-season, Sunday dinner is served 2–8 PM and the restaurant is closed on Monday for dinner.

♦ **The Lobster Pot** (401-253-9100), 119–121 Hope Street, Bristol. The large windows across the front of the dining room have an unparalleled view of Narragansett Bay at this venerable restaurant. Dating to 1929, the restaurant was completely renovated in the mid-1990s. White linens and china make for a more formal seaside atmosphere than some. Dinner is served from quite early in the day, and entrées are in the $15–25 range—although you can get a 3-pound lobster for $60. There's also a lunch menu with omelets, a raw bar, several salads including lobster, Greek, and Caesar, and items like beef or chicken potpie ($8–10). The dinner menu offers a good selection of wines by the glass, appetizers like clams casino and fried calamari, and a raw bar with lobster (presumably not raw). Boiled, broiled, or grilled lobsters on the dinner menu come in sizes from 1 pound for $19.50 to the 3-pounder. The restaurant stresses seafood, such as baked scallops Nantucket with sherry and cheddar; scrod picante; and crabmeat casserole. You can also order filet mignon, roast duck, teriyaki chicken, or several versions of veal. All come with salad, potato, and vegetable. Dinner is served Tuesday through Saturday 3:30–closing, Sunday noon–9; lunch is served Tuesday through Saturday 11:30–3:30. Closed Monday.

♦ **S. S. Dion** (401-253-2884), 520 Thames Street, Bristol. The S. S. stands for Susan (the chef) and Steve Dion (her husband and host), who have had one of the more successful restaurants in town for the past 20 years. Captain's chairs and wood tables offer a simple setting indoors, and an outdoor deck with distant water views draws a loyal following. Starters include steamed mussels or clams in red (marinara) sauce or white (lemon, herbs, and wine); fried calamari; and stuffed mushroom caps. Pastas ($15–20) could be seafood fra diavolo or linguine Alfredo. Grilled fish (salmon, trout, or swordfish) can be topped with one of five toppings, such as dill and shallot mustard sauce. There are also veal and poultry dishes and some seafood classics like a seafood casserole and baked scrod ($14–20). A 10-ounce sirloin steak with three stuffed and baked shrimp constitutes "Surf and Turf." Dinner from 5 Monday through Saturday.

♦ **Quito's** (401-253-4500), 411 Thames Street, Bristol. Want to get close to the water and have some fried clams or a boiled lobster? This is your spot. Quito's is also a seafood store, and the fish is fresh. The location, at the water's edge and next to a town park overlooking Bristol Harbor, makes it extremely popular. Most sought after in summer are the tables under a large awning at the very edge of the dock; you can also eat at the booths or a few tables indoors. No reservations, so come early or prepare to wait. Fried dinners include fish-and-chips, a whole clam plate, scallops, and shrimp ($7–14). Side orders include coleslaw, fries, bread, and clam strips. Chowder (both New England and Manhattan), clam fritters, a lobster roll, or a fish sandwich are also on the menu. And for the kids there are hot dogs. Open May through September, daily except Tuesday 11:30–9; in March, April, and October through December, the place is open the same hours Wednesday through Sunday.

♦ **Aidan's Pub** (401-254-1940), 5 John Street, Bristol. This pale yellow building with a big American flag on the side has an outdoor terrace, but its water view is from a distance (across a street and a small park). Inside, there is the feeling of a traditional ale house, with dark wood tables and bar. You can get appetizers like pub fries, smoked Irish salmon served with chopped red onion, capers, and lemon, and fried mozzarella sticks with marinara sauce ($5–8). Rhode Island clam chowder (with clear broth) is available, along with a soup of the day and several salads. The burgers include the Limerick Burger topped with imported Irish bacon and cheese ($5.75). The "favorites" include bangers and mash, shepherd's pie, Dublin potpie, and a traditional corned beef dinner ($5–8). Newport Storm and Hurricane Amber Ale are on tap. Open from 11:30 to 10 or 11 daily.

♦ **Judge Roy Bean's** at 1 State Street is another popular pub with casual atmosphere and lots of beer on tap.

DEXTER'S GRIST MILL

To this Grist Mill, the early settlers of Sandwich brought
their corn to be ground into meal, their most important
food. you will see the old machinery with wooden gears
in full operation grinding corn - fresh ground meal is
available.

1654 · RESTORED · 1961

9 ◆ Cape Cod's North Shore

The thought of Cape Cod prompts visions of early American villages and beaches where you can stroll forever. Weathered gray houses with small-paned windows, village centers with classic New England greens, enticing shops, and artists' studios come to mind. Majestic lighthouses blinking their warnings and, on a foggy day, the low mournful sound of the foghorn. Fried clams, soft ice cream, and boiled lobster dinners.

The history of the Cape is compelling. The *Mayflower* first put down anchor here before continuing across the bay to Plymouth. Towns on the Cape developed early as an adjunct to Boston and the activity there. In addition to the beaches and the bistros, there is much to ponder about the early history of our country.

Among the most historic routes on Cape Cod is Route 6A. This road, the Old King's Highway, is the oldest route on the Cape and it is a beauty. The road roughly parallels Cape Cod Bay for 34 miles. Believed to have begun as a Native American trail stretching from Plymouth to Provincetown, the cart path eventually became the major east–west thoroughfare for early settlers. As colonial agricultural communities became more important on the Cape in the 1600s, it was the way to get products from place to place.

Lined by magnificent homes, many of them belonging to wealthy sea captains in the 18th and early 19th centuries, the Old King's Highway is a winding two-lane road related to its stagecoach past. Trees bend across the road in many sections, making it shady much of the way. There is a feeling of the country rather than of a summer resort. The water just north of Route 6A is Cape Cod Bay, with its tranquil beaches and picturesque harbors.

Sandwich was the first town to be incorporated on the Cape, in 1637. It is the first town of our chapter as well, a lovely atmospheric village that retains its serenity even when the rest of the Cape is pure madness. After Sandwich come Barnstable, Yarmouth Port, Dennis, and Brewster, each with its own personality and reasons to visit and stay.

Route 6A ties these towns together in a slowed-down way (partly because of

Dexter's Grist Mill in Sandwich still grinds cornmeal.

single lane of traffic in each direction, partly because of the bends in the road). It's good to be unhurried as you drive back and forth. Historic homes and house museums, antiques shops, vintage bed & breakfasts, ancient graveyards, and old churches add to the historic interest of the route.

You'll find restaurants that are rated the best on the Cape, fine artisans who open their studios, boutiques selling a wide range of unusual items. Scenic harbors, hidden beaches, and fine museums are worthy diversions. Once you manage to get across the Cape Cod Canal, you'll find your stressed-out self starting to relax. Many of the inns and restaurants along 6A are open year-round, meaning you can visit whenever the spirit moves. Come along with us to the best of the Cape at all times of year. Even—believe it or not—in summer.

Getting There

By car: Interstate 195 and Route 6 from the west and Interstate 495 and Route 3 from the Boston area are the major auto routes to Cape Cod.

By bus: Bus service is provided by the **Plymouth & Brockton bus line** (508-778-9767) to Harwich, Orleans, and other towns north to Provincetown. **Bonanza buses** (1-800-556-3815) serve Falmouth and Bourne from Boston, Providence, and New York City.

By air: You can reach the cape via **Cape Air** (1-800-352-0714), which flies from Providence, Boston, and New Bedford to Hyannis and also from Hyannis to and from Nantucket and Martha's Vineyard. **Cogan/USAir Express** (508-775-7077) has flights to the Cape from New York's LaGuardia Airport. The major airport on the Cape is **Barnstable County Municipal Airport** (508-775-2020; 508-778-7770) in Hyannis on the Cape's south coast. From there you will need a car.

TOWN BY TOWN

Five towns—Sandwich, Barnstable, Yarmouth Port, Dennis, and Brewster—comprise the focus for this chapter. They are situated from west to east along historic Route 6A. You may have tickets for the Cape Playhouse in Dennis one evening, or reservations at the famed Chillingsworth restaurant in Brewster, another. You may spend a half day or longer at Heritage Plantation in Sandwich at one time, or an entire sunny day at popular Sandy Neck Great Salt Marsh (and beach) in Barnstable. Yarmouth Port beckons for many reasons, but shopping and visiting its historic house museums are two. Here then, from west to east, are selections for things to do, places to stay, and restaurants to try in each of these charming North Shore towns.

Note: Many restaurants on the Cape do not take reservations—especially during the summer. Call ahead to check.

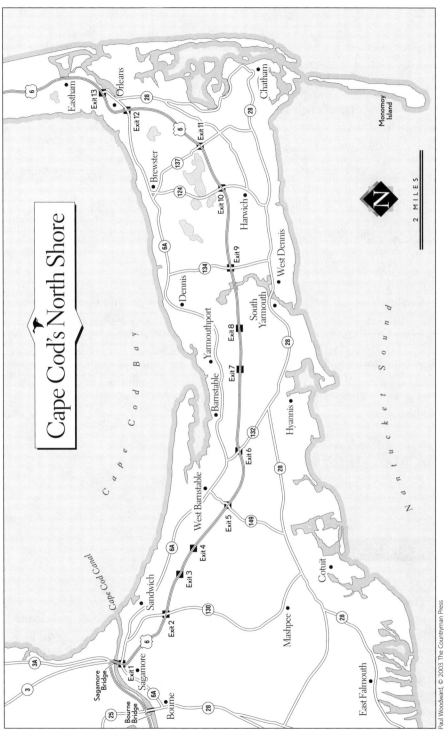

Cape Cod's North Shore

Cape Cod Canal

Cape Cod Bay

Nantucket Sound

Sagamore Bridge
Bourne Bridge
Saganore
Bourne
East Falmouth
Sandwich
Mashpee
Cotuit
West Barnstable
Barnstable
Yarmouthport
Hyannis
South Yarmouth
Dennis
West Dennis
Harwich
Brewster
Orleans
Eastham
Chatham
Monomoy Island

Exit 1
Exit 2
Exit 3
Exit 4
Exit 5
Exit 6
Exit 7
Exit 8
Exit 9
Exit 10
Exit 11
Exit 12
Exit 13

3
3A
25
6A
6
130
28
149
132
134
6A
124
137
6
28

N
2 MILES

SANDWICH

Ten men from Saugus, Massachusetts, were given permission by the governor of Plymouth Colony to settle the Sandwich area in 1637, making it the first settlement on Cape Cod. The site was close to the Manomet Trading Post operating in Bourne, and had plenty of salt-marsh hay to feed the settlers' cattle. Sandwich was an agricultural community until 1825 when Deming Jarves founded a small glass-making factory. Jarves's new enterprise was incorporated in 1826 as the Boston & Sandwich Glass Company. Local forests were the source of fuel for factory furnaces, and there was the salt hay for packing. In addition, Boston markets were but 50 miles distant by water. The glass-making factories shut down by the 1880s, however, due to competition from coal-fired glass-making factories in the Midwest coupled with a labor strike.

The Sandwich Glass Museum tells the history of Sandwich glass well.

Sandwich has other historic monuments. The Hoxie House, dating from 1680–1690 and on its original location, is an exceptional historic house museum. Dexter's Grist Mill still grinds cornmeal the way it did when the residents of town brought their corn to be milled in the late 17th century. It is restored and in its original location.

Sandwich—even at the height of summer—is one of the most peaceful towns on the Cape. The center of town is lovely to walk around—including a stroll by Shawme Duck Pond, whose waters turn the wooden waterwheel of Dexter's Grist Mill. The big red Dan'l Webster Inn dominates the center and serves as a meeting place. Shops on Main and Jarves Streets, especially, offer unusual wares. Although Route 6A passes through Sandwich, its village center is removed from the main thoroughfare, which aids its sense of quiet. Shady streets are graced with some very old houses.

For More Information

♦ **Cape Cod Canal Region Chamber of Commerce** (508-759-6000), 70 Main Street, Buzzards Bay 02532.

SEEING AND DOING

Historic Sites

♦ **Hoxie House** (508-888-1173), 18 Water Street, Sandwich. In terms of construction, this is a gem. It overlooks picturesque Shawme Duck Pond in a residential district not far from the center of town. Tiny Elizabethan casement windows and deep brownish gray weathered shakes are indicative of the age of the house. It was restored to its 17th-century appearance by the town in 1959. This is its original location. The house has a saltbox roofline, a loft reached by wide ladders (especially fun for children to contemplate), and an exceptional collection of Indian corn hanging on one wall. The restored interior of the house depicts the early colonial period. Amazingly, the house was lived in without electricity or plumbing until the middle of the 20th century. The house is named for Captain Abraham Hoxie, a whaling captain who owned it in the mid-1800s. Before that, it was home to descendants of the Reverend John Smith, who came to Sandwich in 1675. Gun stock posts, wide floorboards, chamfered beams, and other unusual architectural details are found in the structure, said to date to about 1680. Guided tours are given. Open mid-June to mid-October, Monday through Saturday 10–5, Sunday 1–5. Adults $2, children 12–16 $1; combined ticket with Dexter's Grist Mill, adults $3, children $1.50.

♦ **Dexter's Grist Mill** (508-888-1173), Shawme Duck Pond, Water Street. This mill dates from the mid-1640s and was used by original settlers of the town for grinding their corn into meal. The wheel is interesting in that it's an "undershot" wheel, meaning the water does not flow over the wheel but below it. Thomas Dexter, who built the mill, was one of the original 10 settlers of the town. An on-site guide describes the milling process, and you can buy bags of cornmeal to take with you. Open mid-June to mid-October, Monday through Saturday 10–4:45, Sunday 1–4:45. Adults $2, children 6–12 $1. Combined ticket with Hoxie House sold for $3 adults, $1.50 children.

♦ **Sandwich Glass Museum** (508-888-0251), 129 Main Street, Sandwich. The museum has been in operation since 1907 and is internationally known. Operated by the Sandwich Historical Society, it has chronological displays of thousands of beautiful glass objects, including candlesticks, tumblers, vases, pitchers, bowls, cake plates, and more. As the years went along, the designs and colors became increasingly elaborate. One particularly interesting exhibit shows how the colors were added to the glass. A new addition to the museum—begun in 2001—was to incorporate glassblowing demonstrations, a theater presentation, and more displays.

The museum also has a local history room with early furnishings and toys from Sandwich homes. Open April through December, 9:30–5; February and March, Wednesday through Sunday 9:30–4. Closed January. Adults $3.50, children $1.

The Sandwich Glass Museum sponsors **historic walking tours** from June to October on selected dates. "Stones of Time" is a 90-minute daytime tour that goes to the town's oldest cemetery and focuses on the artwork and design of gravestones, as well as the histories of some of the people buried there. On selected evenings the museum presents a "Lantern Tour of Historic Sandwich Village" that goes past some of the historic buildings and homes in the town. Both tours are free. For information and reservations, call the museum.

♦ **Benjamin Nye Homestead** (508-888-2368), 85 Old County Road, East Sandwich. Off Route 6A, this home, dating from 1685, belonged to one of Sandwich's first settlers. It has had many additions over the years, which makes it particularly interesting to students of architecture. At one time it was a saltbox; today it's a full Colonial. It isn't a perfectly pure restoration by any means, but you can see some old paneling and a few antique pieces of furniture. Open mid-June to mid-October, weekdays noon–4:30.

♦ **Friends Meeting House,** Quaker Road off Spring Hill Road (north of 6A). The 1810 weathered gray meetinghouse with large green doors in front is the third house of worship on the site. The original Sandwich Monthly Meeting of Friends was established in 1657 and is the oldest continuous Quaker meeting in North America.

Behind the building is the old graveyard with some ancient stones. The meetinghouse is flanked by carriage barns. A sign assures that VISITORS ARE ALWAYS WELCOME at the 10 AM Sunday meetings.

◆ **Heritage Plantation of Sandwich** (508-888-3300; www.heritageplantation.org), Grove and Pine Streets, Sandwich. This is not a historic site, per se, but is attractive to many interested in antique collections and early American art. The 76-acre site with several individual museums was founded in 1969 by Mr. and Mrs. Josiah K. Lilly III. Mr. Lilly was a descendant of the Eli Lilly Pharmaceutical Company family. The museum grounds are famed for an extensive collection of rhododendrons that bloom in late May and early

The Shaker Round Barn at Heritage Plantation in Sandwich

June, a wide range of unusual trees and shrubs, and nature trails. On the site is a replica Hancock Village Shaker Round Barn that houses antique automobiles (you can sit in the 1913 Model T). A short distance away is the military museum housing Josiah K.Lilly Jr.'s firearm and military miniature collection and a Native American exhibit. The Art Museum has a beautifully restored and operating 1912 wooden carousel that visitors young and old may ride. In addition, there's an excellent collection of primitive American paintings; special exhibits (landscapes by the late Boston artist Alvan Fisher when we last visited); and collections of Currier & Ives prints. Also on the property are a windmill, a museum store, a garden shop, and a café. The place is exceptionally clean and well tended. Open mid-May to mid-October, daily 10–5. Adults $9, seniors $8, children $4.50.

Outdoors

◆ **The Boardwalk in Sandwich.** Sandwich has a much-beloved boardwalk from which to view Cape Cod Bay. This one was rebuilt in 1991–1992 after a terrible storm hit the western part of the Cape. Individual planks were sponsored; some are memorials to townspeople. To find the boardwalk, wend your way north through the center of town. Take Town Neck Road off Route 6A to Freeman Avenue. You may see a great blue heron in the marshy area around the boardwalk if you're lucky.

♦ **Sandwich Hollows** (508-888-3384) is an 18-hole municipal golf course. **Sandwich Mini-Golf** (508-833-1905) on Route 6A is almost historic in its own right—a 50-year-old mini golf course.

♦ **Shawme-Crowell State Forest** (508-888-0351) on Route 130 allows you to walk, bicycle, and camp at some 285 campsites. Free day use.

♦ **Town Neck Beach** on Cape Cod Bay is off Town Neck Road and Route 6A. Facilities include changing rooms and rest rooms. The beach is fairly pebbly, and swimming is much better at high tide. There's a parking fee of $5.

Shopping

Among our favorite shops is **The Weather Store** on Main Street (directly across from the Dan'l Webster Inn), with unusual and fascinating items for weather-watchers. You can pick up a hurricane-watcher's graph and map; a fancy barometer; books on weather; and other instruments to help you play meteorologist. **Madden & Co.** on Jarves Street has a wide range of antiques, books, unusual gifts, and home decoration items. **Titcomb's Books** on Route 6A in East Sandwich offers atmosphere galore. On the main floor you'll find loads of books on the Cape (new and used), a great selection of children's books, old magazines, cards, and more. The shop at the **Dan'l Webster Inn** has all sorts of stuff.

WHERE TO STAY

♦ **The Dan'l Webster Inn** (508-888-3622; fax 508-888-5156; www.danlwebsterinn. com), 149 Main Street, Sandwich, MA 02563. This sprawling 54-room inn with red-clapboard facade and portico entrance is a village landmark. It has undergone an expansion and renovation of late. Newest among the rooms are the large Jarves suites on the second floor of a new wing, all with gas fireplace, king or queen bed, two-person whirlpool tub, TV in armoire, and heated tiles in the tub area. There is also a two-person walk-in shower in the bathroom. Two-room suites are found in the Fessenden House next door, and the Quinn Street House, both part of the inn. The main inn has 17 rooms on three floors, all decorated traditionally with repro-duction furniture; each has two double beds, a king, a canopy queen, or possibly twin beds. The outdoor pool and beautifully manicured grounds are pluses. Four restaurants (including a pub) on the premises provide a variety of meals (see *Where to Eat*). From here, you can walk to just about everything in the village. Doubles, EP, $109–399.

♦ **Belfry Inne & Bistro** (508- 888-8550; 1-800-844-4542; fax 508-888-8550; www. belfryinn.com), 8 Jarves Street, Sandwich, MA 02563. Innkeeper Chris Wilson has turned a rectory and church into one of the more charming Victorian-era inns at this end of the Cape. Known as the Drew House, the onetime rectory has eight appealing guest rooms, all with private bath. Even the belfry of the original house has been restored, and you can climb into the tower. Three rooms have gas fireplace, and a couple have whirlpool tub. We liked the Alice-in-Wonderland murals on one of the high-ceilinged third-floor rooms. We also liked room 5, a corner room with queen four-poster bed, single whirlpool tub, and flowered carpet. There are no TVs in individual rooms here, but a common room has one. The truly luxurious rooms at this inn are next door in the renovated church. The main floor has been turned into an elegant restaurant (see *Where to Eat*). Six guest rooms (named Monday through Saturday) on the upper level are exquisitely decorated. Saturday has deep-purple-striped walls, a Victorian loveseat at the base of a king-sized bed, light wall-to-wall carpeting, a step-up bathroom with double whirlpool tub, TV, and air-conditioning. How about the stained-glass window of St. Michael the Archangel staring down? I also liked Monday, with its yellow-striped walls, queen sleigh bed, two-person whirlpool, and fireplace. There's also a very private balcony. Doubles, $95–195.

♦ **Captain Ezra Nye House** (508-888-6142; 1-800-388-2278; fax 508-833-2897; www.captainezranyehouse.com), 152 Main Street, Sandwich, MA 02563. Harry and Elaine Dickson are stalwarts in the B&B business, having operated their bed & breakfast in an 1829 house for more than 15 years. The location—in the center of the village—is great. Accommodations are comfortable and clean but not flashy. The only TV is found in the Rose Suite to the rear of the house with its own entrance (and once a lawyer's office). The other five rooms are on the second floor of the house. All rooms have private bath and air-conditioning. The Peach Room is light and airy with king bed, white wicker furnishings, and an electric freestanding fireplace. One room has a wood-burning fireplace. Elaine whips up a full breakfast, possibly a cheese omelet served with banana bread or scones. Guests eat in a dining room or—in good weather—on a deck. "I like a big breakfast myself," says Elaine. Doubles, $90–125.

♦ **Bay Beach** (508-888-8813; 1-800-475-6398; www.baybeach.com), 3 Bay Beach Lane, P.O. Box 151, Sandwich, MA 02563. Want to be right at the water's edge? This beach house is contemporary in feeling with an open floor plan, decks, and views of Cape Cod Bay. Three exceptionally large and luxurious guest rooms all have king-sized bed, whirlpool tub, and fireplace. Two have direct water views and one a partial view. Guest rooms have their own private decks, but guests may also use a large rear deck on the house. Breakfast is set out at a large dining table on individual trays that can be carried outside or back to your own room, or you can stay and eat with other guests. Stocked refrigerators, phones, televisions with VCRs, and plenty of CDs to choose from are other amenities at this adults-only B&B. There's a beach directly at the end of a private boardwalk leading over marsh grass from the house. Beach towels are provided. Open May to October. Doubles, $245–325.

♦ **Spring Garden Inn** (508-888-0710; 1-800-303-1751; www.springgarden.com), 578 Route 6A, Box 867, East Sandwich, MA 02537. Window boxes filled with flowers, a well-landscaped outdoor pool area, and shaded seating out back overlooking a marsh make this former motel east of town something more. Innkeepers Stephen and Elizabeth Kauffman offer 11 comfortable rooms—all with air-conditioning, TV, and patio or deck overlooking the marsh formed around Scorton Creek. Two lower-level units in the back have full kitchen. The rooms across the front facing Route 6A have knotty-pine walls and ceilings that seem charmingly retro. These rooms have two double beds with tasteful spreads and a private bath with a tub-shower combination. A continental breakfast with home-baked breads is set out in the lobby each morning. Open April through November. Doubles, $72–114.

WHERE TO EAT

♦ **Genesis at the Belfry Inne** (508-888-8550), 8 Jarves Street, Sandwich. This is the most romantic place to dine in Sandwich. The nave of a former church has been converted ingeniously by Chris Wilson, owner and innkeeper, who also oversees this exquisite dinner-only restaurant. The bar is on an elevated platform. Queen Anne and slipper chairs surround white-clothed tables in the serene dining space. A fireplace—added by Wilson—has flickering candles in summer and a full blaze in colder weather. Several stained-glass windows pour golden light across the space in late afternoon. The walls are deep tangerine. Appetizers could be lobster bisque topped with crème fraîche and chives, lobster and scallops in a phyllo bag, or a vegetable spring roll ($5–9). The Belfry salad is fresh pears, Gorgonzola cheese, and toasted walnuts over arugula, tossed with tangerine vinaigrette. Entrées may include breast of duck served with mushroom risotto and a baked spiced apple, or rack of lamb roasted in a deep brown garlic sauce. Bouillabaisse is another favorite. Entrées, $25–27. The Belfry Pillow—Bavarian cream topped with pastry and fresh berries—is a favorite dessert. Dinner Tuesday through Saturday.

♦ **AquaGrille** (508-888-8889; www.aquagrille.com), 14 Gallo Road, Sandwich. The Zartarian family, owners and operators of The Paddock in Hyannis, opened this waterfront spot between the Sandwich town marina and the Coast Guard station in the late 1990s. John Zartarian—one of two sons of the original owners—is in charge. The wraparound porch with water view is the preferred spot for lunch; inside is a contemporary-style dining room with light wood furniture. There's also a good-sized bar. Aqua glassware and napkins give a nod to the name. At lunchtime salads (priced $3.25–7) include sautéed chicken livers with pecans, marinated balsamic red onions, Granny Smith apples, and fancy mixed greens, or fried scallops served on mixed greens with orange Thai vinaigrette. Fried scrod, calamari, scallops, and shrimp are accompanied by cabbage salad and french fries. You can also get a burger, a choice of sandwiches, a pricey lobster roll ($16.95), or some lunch specials. In the evening 1½-pound lobsters are available boiled or baked and stuffed at market price. Salmon burgers and smoked turkey wrap sandwiches are among a few items that remain on the evening menu. Entrées ($14–17) include items like fried Atlantic cod cakes with Boston baked beans; baked Atlantic scrod with lemon-flavored bread crumbs; and veal Scaloppine with a wild mushroom ragout and house-made German noodles. A German chef was also offering some Teutonic specialties. Open April through October, Thursday through Sunday in April and daily thereafter. Lunch is 11:30–2:30; a midday menu is served 2:30–5; dinner begins at 5 PM.

♦ **Amari Bar & Ristorante** (508-375-0011), 674 Route 6A, East Sandwich. Amari is a handsome and popular restaurant serving a variety of Italian specialties. Several dining spaces have high-backed booths as well as bare wood tables with arrowback Windsor chairs. Tile floors, soaring ceilings, an open wood-fired pizza oven, and a convivial atmosphere make this a popular choice. Starters might be Tuscan-style mussels sautéed in a garlic broth; twin crabcakes with mandarin oranges and crumbled blue cheese over greens; and a mixed antipasto ($8–12). Pizzas include the Rangoon with Alfredo sauce, ocean crab, and three cheeses. Among the pastas are the Verdura, grilled vegetables in a light herb broth; and Vongole, a rustic white clam sauce garnished with whole clams. All pastas can be served with spaghettini, fusilli, rigatoni, linguine, or fettuccine. Scampis, Piccatas, Marsalas, and Bonseras come with veal, chicken, or seafood. Grilled specialties include chicken Tuscany (oven roasted, then grilled, served over sautéed spinach and polenta triangles). Entrées are $14–19. Open from 4:30 for dinner Monday through Friday; from noon on Saturday and Sunday.

♦ **Dan'l Webster Inn** (508-888-3622), Main Street, Sandwich. A casual downstairs pub and several more formal main dining rooms—including one in a greenhouse—give you a choice of environments at this large center-of-town inn. Basically there are two menus, a casual-style one for the pub and a more formal menu for the other dining rooms. Pub lunches include lobster chowder, salads, beef burgers, pizzas, and sandwiches. Similar fare with a few specialties is available in the evening. Pub entrées—like applewood-grilled salmon served with rice and vegetables or grilled duckling topped with a tropical barbecue sauce—are priced in the $14–16 range. At lunchtime the main dining rooms offer the "lobster and lobster" special (also available in the pub) of a half sandwich of lobster salad with a cup of lobster chowder, accompanied by fruit at $12.95. Lunch entrées ($10–13) include chicken potpie, broiled scrod, shrimp cakes, and chicken and pasta. For dinner, starters ($8–10) might be baked oysters with leeks, garlic, and Brie and served on the half shell,or lobster and asparagus ravioli. Blue cheese salad Webster is a salad of specialty lettuces with fresh Gorgonzola, white raisins, and pistachios. Entrées ($18–25) might include roast rack of venison served over a chestnut and fig pesto; baked eggplant roulade served with pasta; or a semiboneless chicken breast pan-seared and topped with sautéed Cortland apples in cider. Open daily for breakfast, lunch, and dinner.

BARNSTABLE

Barnstable is almost as old as Sandwich, incorporated in 1639. It's also the Cape's largest town—with seven separate villages including Barnstable Village (and West Barnstable) along Route 6A and Hyannis and Osterville in the south. The Reverend John Lothrop, a Congregational minister, is credited with being town founder. Lothrop Hill Cemetery, just east of the village on Route 6A, is the burial site of the governor. It also contains the grave of Captain "Mad Jack" Percival, one of Barnstable's most famous citizens. He was captain of the warship *Constitution* (*Old Ironsides*) from 1844 to 1847.

Barnstable was settled by farmers. In addition to livestock, these early settlers raised crops of corn and rye. Fishing, shipping, and coastal trading became prominent in the 19th century. The Old Kings Highway continues to wind and dip as it passes through Barnstable and along Cape Cod Bay, remarkably free of commercial development. Instead, gorgeous old houses are sometimes turned into bed & breakfast inns — or else simply lived in.

For More Information
♦ **Hyannis Area Chamber of Commerce** (508-362-5230; 1-800-449-6647), Route 132, Hyannis 02601.

SEEING AND DOING

Historic Sites
♦ **West Parish Meetinghouse** (508-362-8624), Route 149 at Meeting House Way, West Barnstable. This is the second oldest surviving meetinghouse on Cape Cod and was the church of the Reverend John Lothrop. The congregation was actually organized in 1639, with the meetinghouse erected in 1646. This newer building was constructed in 1717 when Barnstable split into two parishes. A Paul Revere bell is in the bell tower. Until 1834, the meetinghouse doubled as a town hall. Sunday services are held at 10 AM.

♦ **Sturgis Library** (508-362-6636), 3090 Route 6A, Barnstable Village. The country's oldest public library building is the repository of fine genealogical records, more than 1,500 maps and charts, and maritime archives. William Sturgis, a self-made and self-educated man who went to sea as a teenager, was born in the original part of the house and deeded it to the town as a library. Open Monday, Wednesday, and Friday 10–5, Tuesday and Thursday 1–8, Saturday 10–4, and Sunday 1–5.

♦ **Barnstable County Courthouse** on Route 6A in Barnstable Village is a Greek Revival building built in 1831–1832. Barnstable has been the county seat of the Cape since 1685.

♦ **Donald G. Trayser Memorial Museum Complex** (508-362-2092), 3353 Route 6A, Barnstable Village. The Old Customs House (circa 1856) where cargoes in and out of Barnstable Harbor were laded became the headquarters of the Barnstable Historical Society in 1959. Downstairs from the Customs House activity was the town post office, in operation from the mid–19th century until 1959. The Customs House closed up shop in 1913 as the harbor became less active. Then this complex became a museum. In addition to the restored Customs House, the main building has exhibits of Native American arrowheads, nautical items, and children's toys. Outdoors is a small building with pieces relating to the fishing trade. There is also a shed with various vehicles including a wood-frame bicycle and an old horse-drawn hearse. And kids enjoy a section of the old gaol on the site. Open mid-June to mid-October, Tuesday through Sunday 1:30–4:30. Donation.

Whale-Watching

♦ The **Hyannis Whale Watcher** (508-362-6088; 1-800-287-0374). The only whale-watch that can be taken from this part of the Cape, Hyannis Whale Watcher leaves from Millway Marine, Phinney's Lane, off Route 6A daily from May to October. The 3- to 4-hour trips have naturalists aboard who can explain the differences among minke, humpback, and right whales. Adults $26, seniors $21, children $16.

Beaching

♦ **Sandy Neck Great Salt Marsh Conservation Area** lies mostly in Barnstable but is reached from Sandy Neck Road in Sandwich. Lifeguards are on duty weekends from Memorial Day to the end of June and daily until Labor Day. Parking is $10 at the public beach until 4 PM, after which there's no charge. You can pick up a map at the gatehouse to several different trails. The beach is managed jointly by the Town of Barnstable (508-362-8300) and the state Department of Natural Resources (508-790-6272). This is a 6-mile-long barrier beach, and it's one of the Cape's best—although there's not a lot of surf in the bay. There are changing rooms, rest rooms, and a snack bar at the public beach area. Four-wheel-drive vehicles are permitted on this beach (pick up a permit at the gatehouse). **Millway Beach** is a small beach just beyond Barnstable Harbor, limited to residents in summer.

Shopping

♦ **Maps of Antiquity** in West Barnstable specializes in maps of the 19th century and earlier, as well as prints and books of places all over the world.

WHERE TO STAY

♦ **The Bursley Inn** (508-362-0481; 1-800-552-5158; fax 508-362-0188; www.bursleyinn. com), 651 Old Kings Highway (Route 6A), West Barnstable, MA 02668. An old sea captain's home shaded by chestnut trees has been turned into a welcoming and taste-ful bed & breakfast inn by innkeeper-owner Kathy Jones. Lobby and breakfast room floors are painted with floral designs (a wreath of chestnut leaves in the lobby area; beach plum designs in the breakfast room) and highly varnished. Five guest rooms are offered, all with private bath, TV, VCR, and telephone. Three have a fireplace. The "Mad Jack" room on the main floor room has an original brick wood-burning fireplace that can be seen from the four-poster king bed (fire logs are provided). There's a double Jacuzzi-style tub in the bathroom. A stunning feature is the huge exposed brick fireplace in the center of the house, seen behind a glass window as you mount the stairs to the second floor. "Nostalgia" is a room with white cottage furni-ture and country touches. A full breakfast is served at separate tables in the breakfast room. Guests have the use of an outdoor patio. Doubles, $95–150.

♦ **The Charles Hinckley House** (508-362-9924), Route 6A, Barnstable, MA 02630. Miya and Les Patrick have created a romantic B&B in their 1809 Federal house where wildflowers and tall grasses run rampant in the front yard. The weathered gray house with burgundy trim offers four guest rooms, all with working fireplace. While the beds are reproduction four-posters (three queens and a double), most furnishings are antique and include Oriental rugs and wing chairs. Two rooms are on the main floor, and two are upstairs. Loveseats are set attractively before a fireplace in the parlor, magazines are spread on a green-painted animal feed box between them, and a decanter by the window is filled with sherry. The house is named for the great-great-grandson of the last governor of Plymouth Colony, whose it was. Miya, who used to run a catering business, makes great breakfasts—pancakes with strawberry topping on one of our visits. Fresh fruit, muffins, puff pastries, and eggs in various styles are all included in her repertoire. The Patricks like to cater to their guests on special occasions like anniversaries and might stock the room with a bottle of champagne or deliver breakfast in bed. Doubles, $139–169.

WHERE TO EAT

♦ **The Dolphin** (508-362-6610; fax 508-362-1666), 3520 Main Street, Route 6A, Barnstable. This center-of-town restaurant has been a Barnstable staple for years; Nancy Smith, the current proprietor, is a descendant of the original family who operated it. Everyone says the food is good. The taupe building with small-paned windows has a dining room with white-linened tables and bleached wood chairs, understated and sophisticated. Walls are knotty pine, and the bar toward the rear has a shiny granite surface; you can eat there, too. At lunchtime you can get salads (spinach, cobb, and lobster among them) and specialty sandwiches such as honey mustard grilled chicken (served on a Portuguese sweet roll with lettuce and tomato). Entrées ($9–13) include baked scrod, a fried scallop or clam plate, and chicken Marsala. For dinner, entrées are priced $17–23 and include steak *au poivre*; thick lamb chops with rosemary and sun-dried tomatoes; roast duck; and braised salmon with corn salsa. Appetizers and light fare (mussels in white wine or goat cheese with roasted peppers and olives, for example) as well as salads and a few sandwiches are also available in the evening. Lunch Monday through Saturday 11:30–3; dinner daily 5–9:30.

♦ **Barnstable Tavern & Grille** (508-362-2355.; fax 508-362-9012), Route 6A, Barnstable Village. This black-shuttered, white-clapboard inn is set back from the street with a brick courtyard where you can eat in good weather. The dining rooms, with light wood Windsor chairs and mismatched tables, are cozy and welcoming. At lunchtime, deli-style sandwiches—roast turkey, baked ham, corned beef, and tuna—are offered along with half-pound burgers, salads, and hot entrées. The dinner menu offers clam chowder, goat cheese salad, a cheeseburger or steak sandwich, or mostly seafood entrées ($12–17), including grilled swordfish or a fisherman's seafood platter with scrod, scallops, shrimp, and clams. Lunch is served daily 11:30–4, dinner from 4 to 9 or 10. Reservations are accepted.

♦ **Mattakeese Wharf** (508-362-4511), 271 Mill Way, Barnstable Harbor. The views of the harbor are so good here that the food is generally overshadowed by them. If you can get a table midsummer just before sunset, you might see fishermen bringing in their catches. Bob Benditti has been owner for more than 30 years. At lunch you can get a wide variety of salads and sandwiches, including a lobster and crabmeat roll ($12). At dinner, pastas (shrimp scampi over linguine, for example), seafood, and some meats are offered. Entrées ($15–26) include a broiled seafood platter with a half lobster on it. The bouillabaisse—offered in cup or bowl—is very popular. Open May to October daily. Lunch 11:30–4:30, dinner thereafter.

♦ **Mill Way Fish and Lobster Market** (508-362-2760), 275 Mill Way, Barnstable. The view is nothing to speak of (mostly parking lot), but the food served on the deck with its umbrellaed tables is raved about. The chef, Ralph Binder, makes a shellfish sausage that people love. Others stock up on buckets of clam chowder when company is coming. Basically this is a take-out restaurant. A few lucky people snag tables during the season to feast on fresh-grilled swordfish and tuna sandwiches, platters of oysters, scallops, shrimp, or salmon or other specials of the day. All platters come with coleslaw and a choice of french fries, potato salad, or pasta salad. Open April through Columbus Day, 11:30–6. The retail market remains open until December. This is very close to Millway Beach.

YARMOUTH PORT

Yarmouth—like neighboring Barnstable and Dennis—stretches all the way across the Cape to Nantucket Sound. Here along Route 6A tranquility prevails, and strict zoning laws keep out the kitschier aspects of tourism. Yarmouth Port is a tony village, several of its beautiful sea captains' homes turned into attractive B&Bs. And it's loaded with history. Yarmouth Port was founded in 1639 and on the early stagecoach route. Many ships sailed from its harbor to Boston in the 19th century. In fact, Yarmouth Port was immensely prosperous in the 1800s. The traveler today enjoys evidence of that magnificent past in its gracious homes, a couple of fine historic house museums, and a spacious town green. There are also good restaurants, tasteful shops, B&Bs in old sea captains' homes, walking trails, and even an old-time drugstore where you can get an ice cream soda (and check out a second-floor museum).

For More Information

♦ **Yarmouth Chamber of Commerce** (508-778-1008), P.O. Box 479, South Yarmouth, MA 02664.

SEEING AND DOING

Historic Sites

♦ **Winslow Crocker House** (508-362-4385), 150 Main Street (Route 6A), Yarmouth Port. In 1936 Mary Thacher, an avid collector of antiques, moved the house of a wealthy 18th-century trader, Winslow Crocker, to its present location in Yarmouth Port as a showcase for her antique furniture. The 1780 center-chimney Colonial with six fireplaces is surprisingly elaborate, with beautiful dentil molding over the front door and rich paneling in each room. But the furnishings are what draw visitors in particular. Here is an extraordinary collection of fine early pieces, including one of the earliest cradles made in America (a Pilgrim-era cradle made on Cape Cod) and a William and Mary chest-on-chest. There are examples of many early styles of chairs. The house is owned by the Society for the Preservation of New England Antiquities; it's open for tours on the hour 11–4 on Saturday and Sunday, June through mid-October. A special open house is usually held in September. Adults $5, seniors $4, children $2.50. During **Heritage Week** in June (a Cape-wide event), the site administrator for the Crocker House, Sara Porter, offers historic architectural tours of Yarmouth Port. For more information on Heritage Week, call (508) 362-0066.

♦ **Capt. Bangs Hallet House** (508-362-3021), 11 Strawberry Lane, on the common, Yarmouth Port. A fine example of the Greek Revival style of architecture, this house was built in the 1840s by Thomas Thacher, a descendant of Anthony Thacher, one of the three original founders of Yarmouth. Captain Bangs Hallet became the owner of the house in 1863. It has been refurbished and furnished in a manner reminiscent of the lifestyle of a prosperous, 19th-century sea captain. Open June to mid-October, Thursday through Sunday, with tours at 1, 2, and 3 PM. Adults $3, children $1.50.

♦ **Kelley Chapel,** behind the post office, off Route 6A, Yarmouth Port. For information, call (508) 375-6424. This tiny 1873 chapel was built by a Quaker man, David Kelley, for his daughter, Rosa, who lost a child. The chapel was a means of reawakening her interest in religion and the religious training of children, in which she had been active. Today the little building, with its potbelly stove and pump organ, is part of the Historical Society of Old Yarmouth. Although the chapel is not generally open to the public, it is frequently used for weddings and recommitment services (40 in the year 2000 alone). And it's open to the public for a Thanksgiving Day service.

♦ **Hallet's,** 139 Route 6A, Yarmouth Port. Here is a real old-time drugstore where you can now get an ice cream soda, a cone, a sandwich, and more, and sit up at an old-fashioned counter or at a traditional ice cream table to do so. Climb the stairs to the small museum upstairs, which displays items of times gone by, including old Coca-Cola glasses, ice cream sundae glasses, and historic photos of the site and of the town. It's not a terribly well-organized display, but that makes it seem all the more authentic.

Outdoors

Walking trails wander through approximately 50 acres of pine-hardwood forest in the center of town (between Strawberry Lane and Route 6A). The land was actually part of the original grant given to Anthony Thacher in 1639 when Yarmouth was founded. This piece and the Capt. Bangs Hallet House nearby were deeded to the Historical Society of Old Yarmouth in 1956 by Guido Perera, a Thacher descendant. Trails are laid out on approximately 1½ miles of the land and wend their way around Woodside Cemetery and Miller Pond. They also pass by the Kelley Chapel.

Beaches. Bass Hole or **Gray's Beach** is reached off Centre Street from Route 6A. It's a particularly good beach for kids, since it's protected. The Bass Hole Boardwalk extends across a marsh and a creek and is a popular place to walk. There's also a 2½-mile trail through conservation lands to the salt marsh.

Shopping

♦ **Parnassus Book Service** on Route 6A is one of a kind. Old (and a few newer) books are crowded into this big gray building; you can browse year-round at an open-air book stall to the side of the building. You may feel a bit disoriented when you first walk in; organization is not the defining attribute here. But, oh what fun! **Design Works** in the center of Yarmouth Port has wonderful home decor items—everything from Scandinavian country antiques to linens to wonderful accoutrements. The **Pewter Crafter** of Cape Cod is Ron Kusins, who uses time-honored methods and traditional tools for creating pewter pieces. He turns out traditional and contemporary designs in his shop behind a real-estate office at 933 Route 6A.

WHERE TO STAY

♦ **Wedgewood Inn** (508-362-5157; fax 508-362-5851; www.wedgewood-inn.com), 83 Main Street, Yarmouth Port, MA 02675. Gerrie and Milt Graham offer romantic getaways at this elegant nine-room B&B set up on a knoll overlooking the village. All six rooms in the main house have private bath; four have a working fireplace. The three newer rooms in the Carriage House out back are large, luxurious spaces also outfitted with wood-burning fireplaces—and the Grahams provide wood along with fire logs when the weather calls for it. Understandably this inn is popular in cold weather as well as warm. Furnishings are country-formal but far from stuffy. The house, built in 1812 for a maritime lawyer, has side porches for two main-floor suites, a built-in grandfather clock in the front hall, and handsome woodwork and moldings. Pencil-post beds in the rooms, antique quilts, period wallpapers, and distinctive art are characteristic of the decorating. Two of the rooms in the Carriage House (7 and 8) have their own deck, king-sized bed, TV in an armoire, and large soaking tub plus a spacious sitting area. Room 9 is on the main floor of the Carriage House, off a rustic, comfortable common area. All rooms are air-conditioned. Most rooms in the main house do not have TV sets. Guests help themselves to cold cereal, yogurt, muffins, and pastries from a sideboard in the dining room and then are served a main dish at their tables at breakfast. French toast is a favorite. Doubles, $135–205.

♦ **Liberty Hill Inn** (508-362-3976; 1-800-821-3977; fax 508-362-6485; www.liberty-hillinn.com), 77 Main Street, Yarmouth Port, MA 02675. Ann and John Cartwright were lawyers on Nantucket before moving to the Cape and taking over this charming inn located on the corner of Willow Street and Route 6A. The house was built by shipwrights in 1825; its high ceilings and interesting elliptical stairway in the front hall give it a special graciousness. Five rooms in the main house are furnished with period-style king, queen, or twin beds, and all have private bath, some with whirlpool tub. In the carriage house, all accommodations have a fireplace and full bath, some with whirlpool tub. A queen canopy bed is found in two of these rooms; there are other period touches. A large and slightly formal parlor is a comfortable space for guests to gather. The dining room has separate tables, and Ann serves a full breakfast including hearty casseroles (sausage and apple cobbler with corn bread topping is a favorite), baked French toast, or quiche. Doubles, $115–190. A 5-day honeymoon package is offered for $750–950 and includes a welcome basket of fruit and cheese and ferry tickets for a day on Martha's Vineyard.

WHERE TO EAT

♦ **Abbicci** (508-362-3501), 43 Main Street, Yarmouth Port. A low mustard-colored building beside Route 6A provides a sophisticated setting for a great meal. *Abbicci*, in Italian, is "ABC." Ancient maps of Italy have been reproduced in oversized scale on the walls of one dining room by the son of owner Marietta Hickey. Bottled water awaits on each white-clothed table; light Windsor-style or black chairs give a clean, uncluttered look. There is nothing spare about the food, however: Lunch and dinner menus are quite ambitious. The lunch menu stresses salads and panini sandwiches such as grilled salmon on mesclun greens, fresh tomato, and red onion with lemon and caper vinaigrette ($7–9). Entrées might be potato gnocchi with a tomato and cream sauce or homemade spinach and ricotta filled ravioli ($8–12). For dinner, start with fried calamari or carpaccio with truffle olive oil, shaved Parmesan, and baby arugula. Pastas include penne Bolognese, linguine with clams in the shell, and a risotto of the day. Other entrées ($24–29 range) might be sautéed veal Scaloppine with prosciutto and fresh sage served with sautéed spinach; seared salmon fillet with lemon and caper vinaigrette; or osso buco served with saffron risotto. Have a sweet tooth? Finish with pumpkin cheesecake, pear apple and dried fruit strudel, or layered chocolate and coffee mousse with Chantilly cream. Lunch daily 11:30–2:30 except for Saturday; dinner nightly 5–9.

♦ **Old Yarmouth Inn** (508-362-9962), 223 Route 6A, Yarmouth Port. An inn whose fortunes have risen and fallen regularly, this—claiming to be Cape Cod's oldest—was back in favor recently. The big white inn with blue shutters has several rooms for dining. Ours was an intimate room with navy blue walls with white trim. Four well-spaced tables were close to the fireplace. Another large windowed dining room is brighter and more open. Clam chowder and a soup of the day (beef barley when we stopped) are offered, along with salads, traditional sandwiches, and a good list of entrées at lunchtime. These might be chicken and broccoli with penne pasta or calf's liver with bacon, mashed potatoes, and vegetable ($9–14). For dinner, baked scrod, baked stuffed shrimp, grilled veal chop, and steak and cake (a beef fillet with a crabcake) are among the offerings ($15–25). A white and chocolate mousse cake or tiramisu were among the desserts. Lunch Tuesday through Saturday 11:45–2:45, dinner Monday through Saturday from 5; Sunday from 4. Sunday brunch.

♦ **Two other favorites. Jack's Outback** (508-362-6690) is a favorite of locals, owned and operated by Jack Smith. If you don't mind a little ribbing with your spare ribs, you may get a kick out of this place, located "out back" behind 161 Main Street. There's a certain do-it-yourself spirit here, and the food is good and affordable. Breakfast and lunch daily. **Inaho** (508-362-5522), the Japanese restaurant in the center of town, is also very popular, open for dinner only. The sushi is considered outstanding.

DENNIS

Dennis is—in some ways—the cultural center, as well as the geographic center, of this part of the Cape. America's oldest summer theater, the Cape Playhouse, is located in Dennis on Route 6A. On the same grounds are the Cape Cinema, showing art and international as well as independent films, and the Cape Museum of Fine Arts, with its newly expanded building site. Route 6A continues to roll through Dennis in its unpretentious way, governed by a historical commission that prevents the encroachment of too much commercialism. The center of town has a pretty white steepled church, an ancient graveyard, and a town green.

The oldest cranberry bog on the Cape is said to have been in Dennis. Resident Henry Hall cultivated the first berries early in the 1800s. The town was named for the Reverend Josiah Dennis, the first minister, who came in 1727 fresh from Harvard Divinity School. His home is now a museum open to the public and is worth a visit.

For More Information

♦ **Dennis Chamber of Commerce** (508-398-3568; 1-800-243-9920), Routes 134 and 28, West Dennis, MA 02638.

SEEING AND DOING

Historic Sites

♦ **Josiah Dennis Manse Museum** (508-385-3528), 77 Nobscussett Road, Dennis. Dennis was originally part of Yarmouth. In order to become a separate town, it needed a minister. Josiah Dennis, a young Harvard Divinity School graduate, was successfully recruited in July 1727 to serve the townspeople as minister. He headed up a congregation that worships today at the Dennis Union Church in the center of town and is buried in the Dennis Union Cemetery. This was his only ministry; he served for 37 years. The Reverend Josiah Dennis was a bachelor when he arrived in Dennis, but in 1736 this saltbox was built to accommodate the minister, his wife, and growing family. Three of his seven children were born here. The building is maintained as a colonial house museum, with costumed docents on hand. The only piece of furniture that belonged to the minister himself is a stand-up writing desk. Other furnishings are from early Dennis families. One of the most interesting parts of the museum is a maritime history room in an addition to the house. Here are models of several clipper ships built at the Shiverick Shipyard in East Dennis. There are also timbers from an old salt works in town. Next door to the manse is a 1770 **one-room schoolhouse** that can also be visited. Open mid-June through September, Tuesday 10–noon and Thursday 2–4. In September the house is also open on Saturday 2–4. Donation. The Old Manse is usually decked out on one Sunday in December for a Dennis Historical Society open house; traditional refreshments are then offered.

Dennis Union Church Cemetery on Route 6A is the burial place for many early citizens, including the Reverend Josiah Dennis.

Culture

♦ **Cape Playhouse** (box office 508-385-3911; business office 508-385-3838), 820 Route 6A, Dennis, MA 02638. "America's Oldest Professional Summer Theatre" brings in equity actors for 2-week runs through the summer. They perform in the atmospheric barnlike interior of a large white building just off Route 6A. Patrons sit on red cushions on long wood benches with wood backs (those familiar with the situation grab extra cushions on the way in to use as backrests). The theater was founded in 1927. Founder Raymond Moore wanted to create a summer theater close to Boston. He purchased land in Dennis and then had an old meetinghouse dragged down the road to use as the theater. The inaugural performance was of *The Guardsman* starring Basil Rathbone and Violet Kemble Cooper. Young unknown Bette Davis worked as an usher before returning the following summer to act. Others who've appeared over the years include Gregory Peck, Humphrey Bogart, Robert Montgomery, and Shirley Booth. This is Cape Cod's only professional theater, and it's a great place. A variety of shows are given through the summer—from mystery to comedy to straight drama. Productions run from late June to mid-September, Monday through Saturday at 8 PM and Wednesday and Thursday matinees at 2 PM. Tickets, $20–35.

♦ **Cape Cinema** (508-385-2503), on the grounds of the Cape Playhouse, shows art and international films. The ceiling of the building is rare—a mural done by Rockwell Kent that depicts a modernistic version of the heavens with comets, galaxies (including the Milky Way), and floating lovers. One of the famous films first screened here before being released to major cities was *The Wizard of Oz*. Movies are shown daily from mid-April to mid-October.

♦ **Cape Museum of Fine Arts** (508-385-4477), on the grounds of the Cape Playhouse. This 20-year-old museum was given a major renovation and expansion in 2001. It was rated "a star museum" by the *New York Times*. The museum aims to convey the role that Cape Cod and the islands of Martha's Vineyard and Nantucket have played in American art since the early 1900s. Changing exhibits highlight marine art, theater art from the neighboring Cape Playhouse, and work of artists who have found inspiration on the Cape—including the likes of John Singer Sargent, Childe Hassam, and Robert Motherwell. There's a fine sculpture gallery and a good museum shop where items made by Cape artisans and artists can be purchased. Open year-round, Tuesday through Saturday 10–5, Sunday 1–5. Adults

$7; children 18 and under are free. The annual **Secret Garden Tour** in late June is a fund-raiser that allows you to tour gardens and watch artists paint in them.

Outdoors

Tennis anyone? **Sesuit Tennis Center** (508-385-2200), 1389 Route 6A, East Dennis. The courts here are open to the general public on a pay-as-you-play basis.

Beaches

Corporation Beach off Corporation Road on Cape Cod Bay has low dunes. **Chapin Beach** off Chapin Beach Road is open to four-wheel-drive vehicles. **Mayflower Beach** off Beach Street has a boardwalk, rest rooms, and a concession stand. This is good for families with young children since the water is shallow. **Scargo Lake** is a lovely freshwater lake with public boat launches and two sandy beaches. Small Sailfish, kayaks, and canoes can be used on the lake.

Getting high. **Scargo Tower** off Scargo Hill Road from Route 6A. The view across Cape Cod Bay, all the way to Provincetown's distinctive Pilgrim Monument, is spectacular on a clear day. Scargo Lake, below, is a glacial gift. In fall there's a good view of the foliage.

Sesuit Harbor in Dennis is a small, picturesque harbor. There's a nice stone breakwater where you can sit. Reach it via Bridge Street off Route 6A.

Shopping

♦ **Webfoot Farm Antiques** on Route 6A, East Dennis, has four rooms in an old sea captain's house. **Scargo Pottery,** off Route 6A, Dr. Lord's Road, Dennis, is a wonderful place. A walk down a pine-needle path and through the woods leads to the studio of potter Harry Holl and his daughters. They make whimsical and very untraditional birdhouses, fountains, and architectural sculptures. Some look like castles that—when placed in water—seem to have moats surrounding them. One of their lovely creations sits outside the new Cape Museum of Fine Arts. This stoneware pottery is extraordinary. **Arm Chair Bookstore** at 619 Route 6A is a charming bookshop with a good children's collection. **Tobey Farm** on Route 6A is a colorful place, and owned by the same family for centuries. It's where to buy corn and produce in summer, a pumpkin or chrysanthemums in fall.

WHERE TO STAY

♦ **Isaiah Hall B&B Inn** (508-385-9928; 1-800-736-0160; www.isaiahhallinn.com), 152 Whig Street, Dennis, MA 02638. Located on a quiet side street, this 10-room B&B is comprised of an 1857 farmhouse with five guest rooms and an adjoining barn/carriage house with five more. Common rooms are comfortably cozy with an old-fashioned New England feeling. Handmade quilts or comforters cover the beds, some of which are iron and brass. Modern conveniences are found, too: TVs, VCRs, air-conditioning, telephones, and Internet access. One room has a wood-burning fireplace. "If we err, we err on the side of comfort," says longtime innkeeper Marie Brophy. Rooms in the barn have patios and are somewhat larger than those in the main house. A side porch is lined with rockers for relaxing. Out back are beautiful gardens. It's just over half a mile to Corporation Beach, and guests often walk. Beach towels are provided. Breakfast is continental-plus and includes yogurt, fruit, cereals, and home-baked breads. Open mid-May to October. Doubles, $96–150; $185 for a suite.

♦ **Scargo Manor** (508-385-5534; 1-800-595-0034; www.scargomanor.com), 909 Main Street (Route 6A), Dennis, MA 02638. From the fireplaced sitting room with deep brown velvet loveseats to the red-and-green breakfast room with lace-covered tables, this is a luxurious B&B. Seven rooms and suites are offered, all decorated tastefully. Captain Howe's Room on the second floor has a king canopy bed, separate sitting room with fireplace and TV, and private bath with tub and shower. The green-painted floors seem just right for the Cape. The Princess Scargo Room has its own deck from which you can see Scargo Lake. All rooms have queen or king bed, private bath, and TV. The property extends to the lake's edge, where there is a private beach. Kayaks, canoes, and other beach toys are available for guest use. A full breakfast is served, and the pumpkin-spice pancakes are especially popular. The house is next door to the Red Pheasant Inn (see *Where to Eat*), one of the Cape's finest restaurants. Open year-round. Doubles, $95–195.

WHERE TO EAT

♦ **The Red Pheasant Inn** (508-385-2133), Route 6A, Dennis. The Red Pheasant is a classic on the Cape. It has a loyal following among locals and visitors. The food is reliably good and the atmosphere, great. Behind an old red Cape Cod cottage is a long addition with two cozy dining rooms. It's a 200-year-old barn that was originally a ship's chandlery moved from Corporation Beach. One dining room is a long, porchlike area with white tablecloths that looks out onto lovely gardens. The interior room is separated by a low partition from a waiting area with sofas and chairs. Hurricane oil lamps, wall sconces, and frosted glass lights make for subdued, intimate dining. Chef-owner Bill Atwood Jr. changes the menu seasonally, but there's always a good mix of seafood and meats. Starters ($6–12) might include tomato and arugula tart, roast beets, house greens and avocado in an orange vinaigrette, or cherrystone clam and scallop chowder. Entrées ($18–30) could be crispy veal sweetbreads served with greens in a citrus vinaigrette and baked potato chips; tenderloin of beef wrapped in apple-smoked bacon and served with a red wine sauce; or butter-poached lobster from the bay. Dinner nightly from 5. Closed Monday and Tuesday in January and February. Reservations are an excellent idea.

♦ **Gina's By the Sea** (508-385-3213), 154 Taunton Avenue, Dennis. Take Taunton Avenue down toward Chapin Beach; just before you reach the water, you'll find Gina's. The small white-clapboard restaurant with blue-and-white-striped awnings has been a fixture here for more than 50 years. The original owner, Gina, has earned her heavenly reward. Larry Riley now handles the popular little spot where no reservations are taken and some are willing to wait up to 2 hours for a table in-season. The pine-paneled bar with a few booths is especially casual. The interior dining room with fireplace and the enclosed sunporch are pleasant places to dine. Nightly specials augment the standard Italian menu. You can get pasta with sausage or meatballs, baked stuffed shells, baked lasagna, and eggplant parmigiana ($5–12). There are also entrées such as chicken Dijon in a cream and mustard sauce with scallions, veal Scaloppine alla Milanese, and veal savoyard with Swiss cheese and a Madeira sauce ($17–20). These entrées are served with a choice of fresh vegetables or pasta and green salad. Specials appear each night on the blackboard. You can finish with spumoni, cannoli, or Mrs. Riley's chocolate rum cake. Open April through November, Thursday through Saturday in spring and fall and nightly from June to September.

♦ **Contrast** (508-385-9100), 605 Route 6A, Dennis. This bright and funky restaurant with multicolored painted tabletops, brightly painted walls, and innovative food is just the sort of casual yet with-it spot that Dennis needed. Stars and tiny lights hang from the ceiling. A bar with a few seats is a place for singles to feel comfortable or perhaps for couples who haven't remembered to get a reservation on a weekend night in summer. It's a small spot with two dining rooms in a long building with a couple of other shops. The menu tries to please everyone and seems almost too extensive. You can get salads with various toppings (like grilled chicken or shrimp), grilled pizzas and quesadillas, comfort foods (chicken potpie, meat loaf and mashed potatoes, moussaka), risotto du jour, and chef's specialties. The latter (priced $20–24) included grilled veal chop with a porcini mushroom demiglaze and sweet potato mousse, or pumpkin pecan and rosemary stuffed roast pork loin with a maple bourbon glaze. We settled on the meat loaf and the risotto (with sun-dried tomatoes and basil), both excellent. Open daily year-round, 11–3 for lunch and 5–9 for dinner. On Sunday, brunch is served 11–3.

♦ **Scargo Café** (508-385-8200), 799 Route 6A, Dennis. This multiroom restaurant in an old house is heavy on the wood—walls, tables, chairs, and more. But it's a warm and casual atmosphere and a popular spot. The menu is large. Advertised as the "house favorite" is Seafood Strudel at $16.99—crab, shrimp, and scallops baked in a pastry crust and covered with a Newburg sauce. Other entrées ($14–20 range) include grilled twin lamb loin steaks, pesto ravioli with spinach sauté, baked scallops, and grilled Salmon Siam with an Asian marinade. Starters include stuffed mushrooms, French onion soup, and sweet potato french fries served with a honey mustard dipping sauce. Sandwiches and salads are available at lunch and dinner. Families like it here, and there's a children's menu. Open for lunch Monday through Friday noon–3, dinner Monday through Friday from 5. On Saturday and Sunday the café is open from noon until closing without a break.

♦ **The Marshside** (508-385-4010), 25 Bridge Street, East Dennis, attracts locals year-round. Prices are fairly low and the offerings, predictable.

BREWSTER

Brewster is a favorite town of travelers, for it's loaded with fine places to stay and excellent restaurants. The town has eight public beaches, a marvelous library, good shopping (antiques, boutiques)—and it's a pretty spot. More and more retirees are calling Brewster home year-round.

The town was settled in 1659 and named for Elder William Brewster, who arrived at these shores on the *Mayflower*. It was a part of the town of Harwich until 1803. Salt making was big business in Brewster in the 19th century, when rows of saltworks were lined up on Brewster beaches with windmills providing the power to extract salt from the sea.

It's said that more ship captains per capita lived in Brewster than any other 19th-century town in America. Many of their homes have been turned into attractive bed & breakfast inns.

The fine Cape Cod Museum of Natural History resides in Brewster. So, too, does Nickerson State Park, one of the best and largest on the Cape. You can pick up the rail-trail here for a long bike ride. The Punkhorn Parklands are conservation lands in the center of town.

For More Information

♦ **Brewster Chamber of Commerce and Board of Trade United** (508-896-3500; www.brewstercapecod.org), P.O. Box 1241, Brewster 02631.

SEEING AND DOING

Historic Sites

♦ **Cape Cod Museum of Natural History** (508-896-3867), Route 6A, Brewster. What can be more historic than the actual geological and natural forces that brought Cape Cod into being? *The Cape Takes Shape* is a permanent exhibit at this wonderful museum. The exhibit explains geological and coastal changes—including effects from the age of glaciers—that actually shaped the Cape as it is. The museum is a great resource for learning about many aspects of the Cape's natural world. There are whale displays, tanks with lobsters, mollusks, turtles, and other marine creatures, photographs of fierce storms. Families love it here: There are many interactive hands-on exhibits for kids and special events, too. But it's also a suggested stop for adults. Three nature trails lead from the property. The longest and most intriguing is the 1⅓-mile John Wing Nature Trail (named for one of Brewster's early settlers) that leads north from the property through marshland directly to Cape Cod Bay. Two other trails, the three-quarter-mile South Trail through uplands and the short quarter-mile North Trail that kids can do, are also available. Open Monday through Saturday 9:30–4:30, Sunday 11–4:30. Adults $5, seniors $4.50, children 5–12 $2.

♦ **Stony Brook Grist Mill and Museum and Herring Run** (508-896-1734), 830 Stony Brook Road, Brewster. Here is a tranquil spot, and one of the most photographed and painted in the area. The original mill burned in 1870, after which a second structure was built on the original foundation. During the spring herring make their "run"—migrating from saltwater to fresh.

♦ **Brewster Historical Society** (508-896-9521), 3341 Route 6A, Brewster. Among the collections here are China trade memorabilia from Brewster shipmasters, ship portraits, a model of the the old Higgins Farm Windmill—it can be visited in Drummer Boy Park—plus the old East Brewster Post Office and Nate Black's Barbershop. It's an endearing local collection. Open in June on weekends 1–4, in July and August Tuesday through Friday 1–4. Free.

♦ **The Old Higgins Farm Windmill** and the **Harris-Black House** (508-896-9521), 785 Route 6A, Drummer Boy Park, Brewster. The Brewster Historical Society over-sees these two structures. The house is the smallest post-and-beam home to be seen anywhere on the Cape. It was moved here from its former site on Red Top Road. The windmill was originally located in East Brewster and is authenticated in town records to 1795. It's characterized by its octagonal design. Open July and August, Tuesday through Friday 1–4; in June, 1–4 weekends. Donations.

♦ **The Brewster Store** (508-896-3744; www.brewsterstore.com), 1935 Main Street (Route 6A). Normally, this would be among the "Shopping" entries, but this store has some real history to it. Built in 1852 as a church, the structure has been operat-ed as a store selling groceries and other general merchandise since 1866. It's a land-mark in Brewster, with just about everybody showing up here over the course of a few days. Red, white, and blue bunting decorates the front. Visitors love to sit on the benches outside, drinking coffee, reading the papers, solving the world's prob-lems. Inside, crowded aisles lead to kitchen gadgetry, cookware, tools, gifts, lamp parts, penny candy, and postcards of Cape Cod. You don't want to miss it. Open daily.

♦ **New England Fire & History Museum** (508-896-5711), 1439 Route 6A, Brewster. Kids really love this place. Set up around a 19th-century-style New England com-mon, the museum has a blacksmith shop, apothecary shop, antique fire-fighting equipment, and 30 working fire engines. There is also a picnic area. Open late May to mid-September, weekdays 10–4; mid-September through Columbus Day, week-ends noon–4. Adults $6, children 5–12 $3.

♦ **Brewster Ladies Library** (508-896-3913), 1822 Main Street (Route 6A), Brewster. This beautiful red, gold, and green library was originally established in 1852 by a group of book-loving young ladies. It was one of the first libraries on the Cape and is an example of the stick style of architecture. The building's original section dates from 1868—and has been restored. Two rooms are maintained as reading rooms but also have some museum artifacts, early portraits, and extensive genealogical materi-als. In 1997 a major addition tripled the size of the library. The exterior paint—dark red with gold and green trim—copies the original colors. Massachusetts residents may borrow materials free; out-of-staters can purchase a card for $10. The library is an active one with several Sunday concerts throughout the year, and a "mid-morn musicale" on the third Saturday of the month. There is an especially active chil-dren's program and a good children's room. Open year-round, Tuesday and Wednesday 10–8, Thursday 10–6, Friday and Saturday 10–4. Closed Sunday and Monday.

Outdoors

♦ **Nickerson State Park** (508-896-3491) has more than 2,000 acres of pine, spruce, and hemlock and wonderful walking, jogging, and biking trails, picnic sites, and sandy beaches. There is also a large campground.

♦ **Punkhorn Parklands.** In 1987 the town of Brewster acquired 800 acres of an area known affectionately as the Punkhorn, one of the last great tracts of undeveloped land on the Cape. Much of it is typical Cape woodland of pitch pine and mixed oak species, but the area is ringed by a necklace of ponds, old bogs, and streams. Park at the Eagle Point Conservation area off Run Hill Road. The Brewster Conservation Department sometimes offers interpretive walks.

Beaches

There are eight beaches on Cape Cod Bay in Brewster, but no lifeguards there. They range from Crosby Landing at the east end of town to Paines Creek Beach at the west. Lifeguards are on duty daily from July 4 through Labor Day at Long Pond Beach, a freshwater pond, accessible from Crowell's Bog Road off Route 124. Parking stickers are required for all beach parking and may be purchased by nonresidents for $8 a day or $45 for 2 weeks at the Brewster Town Office Building, 2198 Main Street, between 9 and 3 daily.

Biking

♦ The **Cape Cod Rail Trail** can be accessed from Brewster (Route 137) and from Nickerson State Park.

Canoeing and Kayaking

♦ Check the **Cape Cod Museum of Natural History** for naturalist-led trips to many areas of the Cape.

Walking

♦ **Namskaket Sea Path.** This 5-mile trail traverses portions of the Cape Cod Rail Trail and areas along the bay from Brewster into Orleans. Ask for a trail guide from the chamber of commerce.

Golf

♦ **Captains Golf Course** (508-896-1716), 1000 Freeman's Way, Brewster, is one of the premier golf courses on the Cape. The 36-hole golf course has two 18-hole courses designed by Brian Silva. Call for reservations.

Boating

♦ **Jack's Boat Rentals** (508-896-8556) at Nickerson State Park has canoes, kayaks, Sunfish, sailboards, pedalboats, and more in-season.

Culture

♦ **Cape Rep Theatre** (508-896-1888; www.caperep.org), off Route 6A, East Brewster. Two theaters, one indoors and one outdoors, are on the woodsy site. The indoor theater has five productions each season—comedies, serious plays, musicals. Each season is different. The outdoor theater offers general admission tickets sold only on the day of the performance; here you sit on bench seats with arms and backs. One major production is mounted each summer, but there are also daytime children's shows. The indoor theater operates Tuesday through Saturday in July and August, weekends in May, June, September, October, and November. Tickets average $16.

♦ **Dinner theater.** On Sunday evenings from mid-June to mid-September, the Cape Rep Theatre offers a Broadway musical dinner revue at the **Old Sea Pines Inn** in Brewster. All performances are at 7 PM and tickets are $42.50, including dinner, show, tax, and gratuity. For reservations, call (508) 896-6114.

Shopping

♦ **The Brewster Bookstore** is one of the more appealing on the Cape and hosts an ambitious schedule of special events in-season. **Kemp Pottery** in West Brewster has wonderful stoneware and porcelain designs by Steve Kemp. **The Underground Gallery** at 673 Satucket Road is an exceptional artists' gallery where the vibrant watercolors of Karen North Wells are shown, along with work by her architect-husband, Malcolm Wells. We love the handmade objects at **Handcraft House** in East Brewster, where paintings, pottery, birdhouses, candlesticks—you name it—can be found. **Pflock's Antique Shop** emphasizes copper and brass. **Spyglass Antiques** focuses on marine artifacts. **The Lemon Tree** is a popular shop with many items of pottery and other gift selections. The **Cook Shop** next door has all kinds of things for the kitchen, many of them European imports. The **Seaport Shutter Company** on Route 6A has some exceptionally interesting items for your home, many with nautical touches You will find many more wonderful shops along Route 6A.

Special Events

♦ In late April Brewster celebrates its thousands of daffodils with a festival known as **Brewster in Bloom.** Events include an arts and crafts festival, a parade, and a food fest.

WHERE TO STAY

♦ **The Ruddy Turnstone** (508-385-9871; 1-800-654-1995; www.sunsol.com/ruddy-turnstone/), 463 Route 6A, Brewster, MA 02631. This lovely weathered house, set back from the highway and overlooking Quivett Creek and marshlands to the rear, is one of the most comfortable and appealing B&Bs imaginable. Sally and Gordon Swanson lived on the Cape for many years and raised their kids here, then returned from a brief stint in New Hampshire to open this home to guests. They have five rooms with private bath, three in the main house and two in the barn across the way. A large living room and adjacent game room with Oriental rugs on the floors are well stocked with books, and very inviting places to hang out. All rooms have queen bed and private bath. The main-floor room has a queen four-poster, wide floorboards, and a tub-shower combination in the adjoining bath. On the second floor a common room with binoculars invites bird-watching. The large fireplaced room with beamed ceiling and gorgeous big window overlooking the marsh—the Bayview Suite—is our favorite. The rooms in the barn are rustic, with barn siding, braided rugs, and excellent views from a shared sitting area. Outdoors, chairs and hammocks invite relaxing. The nearest beach is about a mile away. Sally cooks a big breakfast served in the dining room of the main house. She often makes baked apple or blueberry French toast. Open April to mid-October. Doubles, $85–175.

♦ **The Captain Freeman Inn** (508- 896-7481; 1-800-843-4664; www.captain-freemaninn.com), 15 Breakwater Road, Brewster, MA 02631. This lime-green and cream Victorian-era inn—located right behind the Brewster Store and close to Route 6A—was built in 1866 by William Freeman, a Brewster sea captain. Rockers are lined up on the pillared front porch. Carol Edmonson, assisted by husband Tom, is a knowledgeable innkeeper who can direct guests to great little places on the Cape—that is, if you're inclined to leave the premises. An outdoor swimming pool with lounge chairs can be alluring in-season, and there are also badminton and croquet on the property. The Edmonsons provide bikes for guests; it's but a 10-minute walk to Breakwater Beach. Twelve rooms all have private bath. Six also have working fireplace (three wood, three gas), whirlpool tub, phone, refrigerator, and television with video player. All but one of the beds are queen sized; there's one standard double. Mashpee, on the main floor just beyond the breakfast room, is

The Captain Freeman Inn in Brewster

blue and yellow with a freestanding fireplace-stove, wall-to-wall carpeting, and a good-sized bathroom. Carol is an accomplished cook who makes the full breakfasts to be served indoors or on a screened-in porch. A cranberry and banana "smoothie" is a popular juice drink, and homemade cranberry granola is available in addition to the hot entrée. Doubles, $125–250. Carol also leads several cooking weekends during the year. Each concentrates on the cuisine of a particular region, prepared by the participants Saturday afternoon and enjoyed at a communal dinner on Saturday night. The price for two is $470–590, including 2 nights' lodging, two breakfasts, the class, a wine tasting, and a four-course dinner. The cooking school web site is www.capecodculinary.com.

♦ **The Candleberry Inn on Cape Cod** (508-896-3300; www.candleberryinn.com), 1882 Main Street (Route 6), Brewster, MA 02631. This large white Georgian-style inn with restored carriage house in back is a former residence of clipper ship captain Frank B. Foster and also of a onetime state senator from Brewster. Little white lights in the window are welcoming; the house has been used as an inn for more than 50 years. Wide floorboards, Oriental carpets, and antiques and family heirlooms are found in nine guest rooms. Six are in the main house—three with working fireplace—and three are in the renovated Carriage House. All have private bath and air-conditioning. Our Loft 1 room on the second floor of the Carriage House had striking orange walls, queen bed, TV, private bath with shower, and use of a semiprivate deck out back. TVs are found in Carriage House rooms but not in the main house. Common rooms include a comfortable parlor with fireplace, the large dining room with seating area, and a small parlor where sherry or wine is usually set out. Breakfasts are served at two large tables and one table-for-two in the dining room; we had French toast with bacon one morning and a poached egg with ham the second. Fresh fruit and yogurt are also set out. In good weather breakfast can be taken on a brick patio. Doubles, $95–205.

♦ **Old Sea Pines Inn** (508-896-6114; fax 508-896-7387; www.oldseapinesinn.com), Route 6A, Brewster, MA 02631. Huge baskets of flowers swing from the porch in summer at this onetime charm school for girls that now operates as a sprawling old-fashioned inn. Steve and Michele Rowan have been in charge for years and have really put their mark on the place. Set back from the road in a grove of pines, the inn has 24 guest rooms in three buildings. Fourteen of the rooms are in the main house and are decorated simply with old beds and antique pieces. Seven updated rooms named for flowers are found in the North Cottage; these have TV and bathroom with tub-shower combination. One is a suite with a wood-burning fireplace. The West Cottage is kid-friendly with three family suites. All rooms have private bath except for the five former classrooms in the main inn, sharing three baths. These are smaller rooms, four with double beds and one with twins. A large living room with old wicker furnishings and a log-burning fireplace is a gathering spot. Ellis Landing and Point-of-Rocks beaches are nearby, and beach towels are provided. A buffet breakfast with two hot entrées, fruit, cereals, bagels, and beverages is set out in a crisply decorated blue-and-white breakfast room. This is where the Cape Rep dinner theater operates on Sunday evening in-season. Open April through December. Doubles, $75–165; family units, $115–135.

◆ **Beechcroft Inn** (508-896-9534; 1-877-233-2446; fax 508-896-8812; www.beechcroft-inn.com), 1360 Main Street (Route 6A), Brewster, MA 02631. An English imprint has been put on this venerable hostelry by Paul and Jan Campbell-White. Paul says he operated a large hotel in England for several years before he and Jan came to the Cape, after a few years in Florida. All 10 rooms have plug-in electric pots and French coffee press pots so guests can make "a proper cup of tea or coffee" in their rooms, says Paul. China cups are provided. Flowery fabrics and wallpapers are seen throughout. Most rooms, on the first, second, and third floors, have king beds made from two twins pushed together. Two third-floor suites are cozy under-the-eaves places with a good-sized bathroom, a TV, and room to spread out. You must climb two rather steep old staircases to reach them. All rooms are air-conditioned. For TV, there are two common parlors on the first floor. Guests enjoy a full breakfast, usually with grilled tomato, toast, and eggs in keeping with the English tradition. They eat in the restaurant, the **Brewster Tea Cup,** which operates as a tearoom serving lunch and light supper as well as afternoon tea, scones, and clotted cream. A mural of the Mad Hatter's Tea Party on the wall was painted by a friend. Doubles, $115–165.

◆ **Poore House Inn** (508-896-0004; 1-800-233-6662), 2311 Main Street (Route 6A), Brewster, MA 02631. This house really was the original poor house for the town of Brewster, built in 1837 to house widows and orphans. It's operated as a comfortable B&B with five guest rooms on the second floor. One is a single with a twin bed—a boon for a person traveling alone. One room toward the back of the house with its own staircase is pet-friendly, and a well-behaved dog or cat is allowed. All rooms are air-conditioned and have private bath. Room 2 has a queen bed, working fireplace, and private bath with shower. A second fireplaced room has a bath across the hall. A full breakfast is served. Open late April to mid-October. Doubles, $110–145; single, $65–85.

WHERE TO EAT

◆ **The Brewster Fish House** (508-896-7867), Route 6A, Brewster. Brothers David and Vernon Smith run this small and hugely popular spot, which they refer to as "a nonconforming restaurant." Located in a weathered roadside building, the restaurant's interior is clean and crisp. Deep green tables with light wood Windsor-style chairs and bare wood floors are a simple setting for some inventive cuisine. Fish and nothing but fish is the order of the day, although there is the possibility of a hamburger or a chicken breast sandwich at lunchtime. At dinner, a vegetarian entrée is available. The lobster bisque is a staple, along with Fish House Chowder and, often, Portuguese kale soup. At lunch, a fish sandwich, fish-and-chips, crab-cakes, and a couple of entrées like grilled swordfish or cod are on the menu (entrées $9–11). At night, starters include steamed mussels Louisiana-style, dill and brandy cured salmon served with red onion and capers, and grilled squid marinated in soy, orange, ginger, and garlic ($7–9). A few pastas—perhaps spinach and sun-dried tomato fettuccine with a half lobster, squid, mussels, and shrimp—are offered.

Brewster Fish House restaurant in Brewster

Entrées might be sesame-crusted flounder served with gingered rice; grilled sea scallops with oven-roasted tomatoes; or grilled lobster with crispy leeks and a jicama slaw ($14–26). No reservations are taken; be prepared to wait for a table. Open daily for lunch and dinner from April to December.

♦ **Chillingsworth** (508-896-3640), Route 6A, Brewster 02631. Chillingsworth is the sort of place you'd select for a very special event. It is pricey and formal, and its contemporary French cuisine is considered tops in its class. In a restored 1689 house, Chillingsworth offers intimate, antiques-filled dining rooms, a bistro lounge and bar with lighter fare, and a gourmet food and gift shop. Chef-owner Robert "Nitzi" Rabin puts together a different menu nightly. His wife, Pat, a trained pastry chef, works the front of the house. While jackets aren't exactly required, it's the kind of place you'd wear one. The prix fixe dinner varies in price depending on entrée ($54–65). Appetizers might be grilled portobello mushroom with asparagus and radicchio in a warm sherry and shallot vinaigrette, or mascarpone, spinach, carrot, and fennel raviolis with truffle cream. Entrée choices could be seared salmon with tomato, leeks, orzo, greens, and fried potato hair; seared sea scallops with spinach, tomato coulis with tarragon, French beans, and leek hair; or seared duck breast with Parmesan grits, mango salsa, balsamic vinegar duck sauce, and snap peas. You might finish with roasted peach topped with caramel ice cream, a lemon tart with strawberry sorbet, or warm apple tart with cinnamon ice cream. The bistro menu offers entrées in the $16–25 range—things like mussels with grilled onions, smoked leek and spicy tomato broth, or grilled lamb chops with herbed risotto and fresh herbs. Open from Mother's Day weekend to Thanksgiving. Lunch daily in July and August except Monday. Dinner, Tuesday through Sunday in July and August, at 6 and 9 in the main dining room. June, September, and October, one dinner seating at 7 to 7:30 and lunch from Wednesday through Sunday, 11:30–2. Brunch is served on Sunday noon–2. Reservations are a good idea.

♦ **Peddler's Restaurant** (508-896-9300), 67 Thad Ellis Road, Brewster. This intimate little spot is a popular place among locals and visitors who manage to find it. (Turn south at the corner where the Brewster Book Store is located and go a few hundred feet.) Located in a small, weathered house, this spot isn't much to look at from outside. But what a great dining experience! Inside, in an L-shaped space, butcher-block tables are available for parties up to six in number. Maroon cloth napkins provide a touch of color. There's an open kitchen. Votive candles flicker on the tables, and olive oil is set out to use with crisp, chewy bread. Chilled tap water is brought to each table in a carafe. A large number of items is listed on a blackboard menu. Lobster bisque or escargots ($8) were available as starters. Among the entrées ($14–18 range) were seared sea scallops Provençal, which were plump and juicy; chicken Marsala; steak *au poivre*; and spaghetti Bolognese, thoroughly enjoyed by my husband. No reservations are taken, but there is a comfortable sofa area to wait in. That's not always enough. Open nightly in-season, Thursday through Saturday the rest of the year. Dinner only from 5.

♦ **Spark Fish** (508-896-1067), 2671 Main Street (Route 6A), Brewster. Opened in July 2000, this new restaurant prides itself on a wood-fired grill where many items are prepared. Steven Parrott, chef, and his wife, Mary Ann, who grew up in Brewster, oversee the popular place. Several dining spaces are available. There's a fireplace in one area for winter diners; in summer an outdoor patio under a maroon awning is popular. Early diners (between 4 and 6) can get half portions of entrées at half price. Appetizers include lobster or clam chowder, oysters on the half shell, clams casino, and a Cajun swordfish skewer ($7–11). Entrées (priced $15–25) include sautéed sea scallops in a saffron and garlic broth served with rice and grilled vegetables; wood-grilled swordfish or tuna; New Zealand rack of lamb; and a stack of grilled vegetables.

10 Portsmouth, New Hampshire

For a small city (population 21,000), Portsmouth packs a wallop. As New Hampshire's first settlement, it has a rich historic tradition and takes pride in its past. Yet waterfront redevelopment, the restoration of historic homes, excellent restaurants, and good places to stay also give Portsmouth an exciting present.

The town's original name was Strawbery Banke, an impulsive and appropriate choice by English settlers who arrived in 1630. They found wild strawberries growing in profusion on the banks of the Piscataqua River. Twenty-three years later the town was renamed Portsmouth. That suits, too, for it's an active port at the mouth of a grand river.

The old name, Strawbery Banke, lives on in a fine historic restoration in the city's South End. There a dilapidated but potentially rich neighborhood called Puddle Dock was saved from almost certain destruction in the 1950s. A few interested locals pleaded with the federal government not to raze buildings for the construction of subsidized rental apartments, but to help fund the restoration instead. The resulting Strawbery Banke will celebrate its 50th anniversary in 2008.

Elsewhere in Portsmouth you're forever bumping into construction crews who are retimbering some building or other. The entire city seems bent on the renovation and adaptation of its vintage houses and commercial buildings, and it has plenty to work on. After all, the reason the city was settled so early was because of the deepwater port it offered, and those early sea captains built some fine homes.

Several of Portsmouth's beautiful houses from the 18th and 19th centuries are open to the public as museums. The 1763 Moffatt-Ladd House, with its original formal English gardens out back, and the John Paul Jones House, built in 1758, are two favorites. Jones, whose ringing words, "I have not yet begun to fight," have inspired scores of schoolboys, rented rooms in town on two occasions while he oversaw the construction of vessels for the Revolutionary War.

Red tugboats, commercial fishing vessels, sight-seeing boats, pleasure craft, and massive freighters ply the waters of Portsmouth's harbor. On other side of the stream is the Portsmouth Naval Shipyard—for decades a major producer of naval warships, now relegated to the maintenance and refurbishing of atomic submarines. Officially it lies in the state of Maine, for the river is the dividing line. The Piscataqua is the second fastest tidal river in the United States navigable by ship, with 6 knots the average current and a 9-foot tidal range. It's interesting to sit out-doors on restaurant decks, or inside by windows in cooler weather, and check out the action.

Portsmouth has always been a year-round destination, but lately it is even more so. The historic development of Strawbery Banke now offers regular tours through the winter, and restaurants and lodging establishments are all open year-round. You may not be able to take a sight-seeing boat out around the harbor in February, but you can sit by a warming fire and sip a hot toddy, still with a view of the waterfront.

Getting There

Portsmouth is located at New Hampshire's northernmost seacoast point. It's easily reached by automobile via Coastal Route 1 or Interstate 95. The closest major **air-port** is in Manchester, New Hampshire, about 35 miles west, which offers increas-ingly active service from major U.S. cities. **Logan International Airport,** Boston, is about 45 minutes south of Portsmouth. There is frequent limousine service from the airport.

Vermont Transit/Greyhound (603-436-0163) provides bus service to Portsmouth directly from Boston and Portland, Maine, with connections from other cities nation-wide.**COAST** (603-743-5777) is a public bus company serving the New Hampshire seacoast towns of Exeter, Rochester, and Portsmouth.

Portsmouth is located less than an hour from Boston, under 3 hours from Hartford, and about 5 hours from New York City.

Getting Around

The **COAST trolley** provides convenient service from Market Square in the center of Portsmouth to many of the city's downtown attractions, and to free parking lots located in downtown. The trolley runs from the end of May to mid-September, Monday through Saturday 9:15–9:15. From mid-September to mid-October, it oper-ates on Saturday only. Fare is $1 for "hop-on passengers," $5 for a 3-day pass, and $15 for a monthly pass. Seniors pay half. Kids under 5 ride free.

If you park in one of the free public parking lots on the outskirts of the down-town area, you can ride the COAST trolley free. Parking is so tight in Portsmouth you may just want to do that.

About parking. This is one hard city to find a parking space in. Meters are for 2 hours and cost 25 cents per half hour. The parking garage on Hanover Street, just off Market, is closest to the action but fills fast. Once free of your car, you'll find that Portsmouth's historic downtown area is compact and walkable.

For more information, contact the **Greater Portsmouth Chamber of Com-merce** (603-436-1118; www.portsmouthchamber.org), 500 Market Street, Portsmouth, NH 03801.

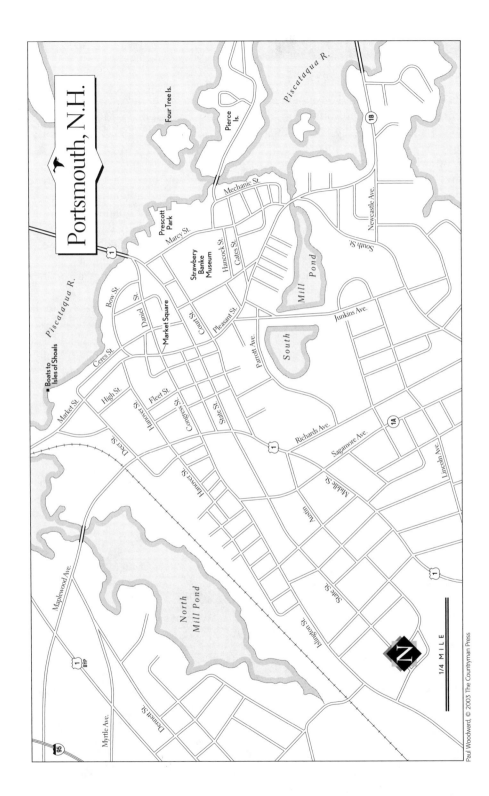

Portsmouth, N.H.

Piscataqua R.

Four Tree Is.

Pierce Is.

Piscataqua R.

1B

Mechanic St.

Newcastle Ave.

Prescott Park

Marcy St.

South St.

Strawbery Banke Museum

Hancock St.

Gates St.

South Mill Pond

Boats to Isles of Shoals

Piscataqua R.

Bow St.

Daniel St.

Market Square

Court St.

Pleasant St.

Junkins Ave.

Ceres St.

Parrott Ave.

Market St.

High St.

Hanover St.

Fleet St.

Congress St.

State St.

Richards Ave.

Sagamore Ave.

1A

Deer St.

1

Lincoln Ave.

Middle St.

Austin

Maplewood Ave.

Hanover St.

North Mill Pond

State St.

Islington St.

1

1 BYP

Myrtle Ave.

Dennett St.

N

1/4 MILE

95

Paul Woodward, © 2003 The Countryman Press

Historic Portsmouth

Historic restorations in Portsmouth can be appreciated from the exterior, but are more stimulating when you step inside. That's easy enough to do. More than 40 houses and buildings are open to the public in one way or another. The greatest concentration is at Strawbery Banke.

♦ **Strawbery Banke Museum** (603-433-1100; www.strawberybanke.org), Marcy Street, P.O. Box 300, Portsmouth, NH 03802. Open May through October, daily 10–5. Strawbery Banke is one of the most interesting historic restorations in New England. The approach is a little different here. Because most buildings extend well beyond the lives of a single generation, restorers at Strawbery Banke have sought to give a rounded picture of what the old Puddle Dock neighborhood was like over the more than 300 years it was inhabited. Therefore, buildings are returned not to one but to various periods. Virtually all of the buildings are on their original foundations, and the lives of real inhabitants are depicted.

Ten furnished homes and period gardens can be seen. The house restored to the most recent vintage—and one to which most Americans can personally relate—is the Shapiro House, home of immigrants. It represents life in the year 1919 and was the home of Russians Abraham and Sarah Shapiro and their only daughter, Molly. In addition to exhibiting the clothes and furnishings of the period, the house has extremely well-done video and audio presentations that bring the viewer into the lives of these hardworking immigrants in a very personal way. There's even a "Talk Back" board for visitors to sign, detailing their own immigrant histories. People from all over the country leave notes.

The Shapiro story is moving and authentic, and so are those of families of other restored homes at Strawbery Banke. You feel as if you know these people. They include the home of *Atlantic Monthly* editor and children's book author Thomas Bailey Aldrich, who summered here in the late 19th century. The Chase House is

Strawbery Banke Museum

Photo by George Barker, courtesy Strawbery Banke Museum

restored to the period 1815–1820, the Goodwin Mansion, to the Civil War era. The Drisco House is an imaginative attempt to contrast life in the 1790s with that in the 1950s.

The Abbott Store—almost exactly as it was in 1943, thanks to a local man who was a young clerk there at the time, and who could remember everything—is a popular stop. There are even ration books from World War II. Behind the store is a Victory Garden. A potter and a cooper regularly work at Strawbery Banke, and their products are sold on site. Other exhibits include woodworking tools, antique boats, and one showing the way the archaeological process is undertaken. Historical role players staff some of the houses.

Water no longer laps at the wharves in the neighborhood as it once did during high tide, but the green center lawn—and a good map—indicate where it would have been.

Visitors walk at their leisure and stop where they want. Several theme tours have been developed so personal interests—for example, gardening—can be focused on. Children love it here, for they get to experience the lives of kids their age. A good little restaurant, the **Café at the Banke,** offers soups, sandwiches, baked goods, and beverages. You can eat indoors in a period setting, or outdoors at picnic tables. You can bring your own lunch if you want.

Among the special off-season events are candlelight strolls, first 2 weeks in December; guided winter walking tours, November through April, Thursday through Sunday 10–2. These are half the regular admission price. Regular admission, adults $12, seniors $11, youths 7–17 $8; those 6 and under are free. Family rate: $28. Tickets are good for 2 consecutive days.

♦ **The Portsmouth Harbour Trail.** The trail was developed to showcase the many exceptional buildings and neighborhoods that tell the story of Portsmouth. The route is divided into three distinct loops, detailed in a color-coded map in a self-guiding pamphlet, and available for $2 from the chamber of commerce or at any of the sites on the trail. Bright blue banners fly from each stop. **St. John's Episcopal Church** on Chapel Street, brick with cream trim, is an especially beautiful building. It was built in 1807. **The South Church** at 292 State Street, home to Unitarian-Universalists, is Portsmouth's only granite church. It was completed in 1826 and is also worth a look.

You can take a **guided tour** of the Harbor Trail if you want. These leave from the information kiosk in Market Square and take about an hour or a little more. The tour features costumed role players. A "highlights tour" leaves at 10:30 AM Thursday, Friday, Saturday, and Monday and at 1:30 PM on Sunday. A "twilight tour" leaves at 5:30 PM Thursday, Friday, Saturday, and Monday. Adults $8, children $5.

Historic Homes

Ten historic sites, including Strawbery Banke Museum, are linked by the **Portsmouth Historic House Passport.** Purchase of the passport at any of the houses or at the chamber of commerce for $5 allows visits at a $1 reduction at each individual site. Most of the houses charge $5 admission.

♦ **Moffatt-Ladd House** (603-436-8221), 154 Market Street, Portsmouth. If you can visit but one historic house while you are in Portsmouth, make it this. A copy of an English manor house, it's beautifully situated high on the banks of the Piscataqua River—and it isn't hard to imagine lawns extending to the water's edge, as they once did. Today Market Street interferes, but out back extensive English gardens remain much as they were when laid out by Alexander Hamilton Ladd in the mid-1800s. The house was built in 1763 as a wedding gift from John Moffatt, an English sea captain, to his son. Later it was the home of John's son-in-law William Whipple, a signer of the Declaration of Independence. In 1776, after returning from Philadelphia, he planted the enormous horse chestnut tree that still stands.

Visitors are treated to three floors of exceptional 18th-century furnishings and architecture. The design of the house is unusual, from the cellar with its great brick arches leading to a secret passageway that once went to the wharves, to rooms with extra-deep fireplaces allowing for spacious closets on each side (a novelty in their day). Next door is the 1823 Counting House where Moffatt and Ladd cargoes were laded. Out back is a small herb garden. A used-book sale is conducted on an ongoing basis in the Coach House. Open mid-June to October 20, daily 11–5; last tour at 4. Sunday, 1–5. Adults $5, children $2. Gardens only, $2.

♦ **John Paul Jones House** (603-436-8420), 43 Middle Street, Portsmouth. John Paul Jones, the naval hero, was a bachelor who never owned a house. But he made this lovely yellow gambrel-roofed house his headquarters during two lengthy stays in Portsmouth. Sarah Wentworth Purcell, a widow, rented Jones a room in 1776–1777 when he was in town to oversee construction of the sloop *Ranger*, and again in 1781–1782 when he returned for the building of the *America*. A handsome man (note the bust of Jones in the house), he is reputed to have turned a few pretty heads during his stay. The second-floor room he occupied is a memorial. Built in 1758, the house has been headquarters of the Portsmouth Historical Society for many years and contains rich local collections. You'll love the costumes, the collection of canes in which weapons are concealed, and items from ships dismantled in Portsmouth. The kids will, too. Mid-May to mid-October, Monday through Saturday 10–4, Sunday noon–4. Adults $5, children $2.50.

♦ **Wentworth-Coolidge Mansion** (603-436-6607), Little Harbor Road, Portsmouth. This rambling yellow-clapboard structure of 42 rooms is situated on a point of land with a great view of Portsmouth Harbor. It was originally the home of Benning Wentworth, New Hampshire's royal governor, from 1741 to 1767, and contains the council chamber where the state's first provincial government conducted its affairs in the turbulent pre–Revolutionary War period. It's a handsome space, with low corner cupboards, unique to the house, and a splendid table surrounded by beautiful walnut Queen Anne chairs. When Benning Wentworth died in 1770, his widow married Michael Wentworth, a retired British army colonel. They entertained George Washington here in 1789. The house's many subsequent owners made changes and added rooms that contribute to its eclectic but not unattractive appearance. The grounds contain the oldest lilacs original to their property in the United States. The house is viewed primarily for its construction and history. Changing exhibits are also mounted. Open May to October, Tuesday, Thursday, Friday, and Saturday 10–3; Sunday noon–5. Adults $5, children $2.50.

♦ **Wentworth-Gardner House** (603) 436-4406, 50 Mechanic Street, Portsmouth. Considered one of the most nearly perfect examples of Georgian architecture in America, this house had an interesting succession of owners, beginning with a member of the ubiquitous Wentworth family and including the Metropolitan Museum of Art. The museum at one time planned to move the house to New York's Central Park. Fortunately, the plan fell through. The carving throughout the interior required 14 months to complete. Among items of interest are the great fireplace in the kitchen, original Dutch tiles, and the spinning attic on the third floor. Open June to mid-October, Tuesday through Sunday 1–4. Adults $5, children $2.50. The **Tobias Lear House,** a charming 18th-century hip-roofed mansion, was built before 1740 and is located close to the Wentworth-Gardner House, under whose aegis it operates. Lear was secretary to George Washington and tutor to Washington's adopted children. The plan is a "four-square" house with wide halls running from front to back on the first and second floors. Interesting early wall paneling is viewed. Open Wednesday 1–4.

♦ **Warner House** (603-436-5509), 150 Daniel Street, Portsmouth. The house is considered the finest example in New England of a brick urban mansion of the early 18th century. Among its treasures: six mural paintings on the staircase wall, an early example of marbleization in the dining room, and a lightning rod on the west wall, said to have been installed under the supervision of Benjamin Franklin in 1762. From 1748 to 1754 it was the home of Governor Benning Wentworth, who seems to have lived only in the best places. Guided tours are offered. Open June to October, Tuesday through Saturday 10–4, Sunday 1–4. Adults $5, children $2.50.

Other historical houses include the **Rundlet-May House,** the **Jackson House** (dating from 1664, it is Portsmouth's oldest), and the **Gov. John Langdon House** of 1784, with a wing designed by McKim, Mead & White in 1906. All three are operated by the Society for the Preservation of New England Antiquities (SPNEA). Call (603) 436-3205 for hours of operation or for more information.

Visitors at Strawbery Banke

Photo courtesy Strawbery Banke

Forts

There are several forts in the Portsmouth area, for it was a place to be defended against outside incursions, especially by the British during Revolutionary War times.

♦ **Fort Constitution** in nearby New Castle is open year-round, 10–5. It is close by the U.S. Coast Guard Station. The fort was originally built in the 17th century but gained prominence during the Revolutionary and Civil War periods. A 1774 raid by a large band of local patriots took the fort from the few British who manned it. This was one of the first direct attacks against England prior to the Revolution. Next to the fort is the still-important Fort Point Lighthouse, with occasional tours offered.

♦ **Fort McClary,** across the river in Kittery Point, Maine, is now a state park. You get a lovely vista of sea and coast. The fort has a six-sided blockhouse commanding impressive views of the river's mouth. Attractive paths lead to the edge of the bluff, from which you can look down on the sea. Picnicking is permitted. To reach the fort, take Route 1 to Kittery, then Route 103 or Kittery Point Road to the fort.

Books

Historians love the chance to research, and two libraries in Portsmouth afford ample opportunity.

♦ **Portsmouth Athenaeum** (603-431-2538), 9 Market Square, Portsmouth. The Joseph P. Copley Research Library and the Randall Room exhibition gallery on the third floor of the building at 6–8 Market Square (just left of the main entrance) are open to the public free Tuesday and Thursday 1–4, Saturday 10–4. The first-floor reading room at 9 Market Square is open to visitors on Thursday 1–4.

The Portsmouth Athenaeum was established as, and still is, a private subscription library similar to those in Boston and Newport. The first floor of the building has been used as a reading room and meeting place since 1808. In recent years the Portsmouth Athenaeum has become more accessible to the public, and its changing exhibitions—especially a recent one on local poet Celia Thaxter of the offshore Isles of Shoals—have been popular. Genealogical research is often done here. The collection is especially strong in maritime and navigation history, law, and arts and architecture. It houses 74 manuscript collections. The personal libraries of two men, Benjamin Tredick (1802–1877) and Charles Levi Woodbury (1820–1898) are maintained intact in special alcoves in the third-floor Library Room.

♦ **Portsmouth Public Library** on Islington Street is a fine and accessible public library. It was expected to be moving to a new site and expanded to meet the growing needs of consumers. Across the street in a big gold house is an interesting used- and rare-book shop.

A Historic Cemetery

♦ **North Cemetery** on Maplewood Avenue is one of the city's oldest and dates from 1753. It is the final resting place of many famous sons and daughters of Portsmouth, including Governor John Langdon, William Whipple (signer of the Declaration of Independence), Abraham Isaac, Portsmouth's first Jewish settler, and the Chase family, representing the city's mercantile class. You may want to visit on your own. If you are interested in a **guided tour,** contact Audrey and Irwin Bierhans, who give "Gravestones by Dusk" tours of the cemetery by appointment during the day on Sunday, or on Tuesday and Saturday at 5:30 PM. There are sometimes other times available. Call (603) 436-5096 to reserve a place. Cost: $10.

Horse and Carriage Rides

Are you into the historical mode enough to take a carriage ride? **Portsmouth Livery Company** has a carriage stand in Market Square and conducts day and evening sight-seeing tours from Memorial Day through Labor Day. Off-season, special tours—such as a ride along the waterfront and to the Strawbery Banke Museum— are offered by reservation. Call (603) 427-0044 for reservations, information, and costs. Prices are generally in the $20–25 range for the regular tour.

Special Attractions

Portsmouth is a city for walkers: Its streets are narrow, and the houses and shops easily viewable. One popular area for strolling is the Market Street–Ceres Street area near the riverfront, with shops and restaurants. Check out the Moran red tugboats tied up by the Ceres Street docks; they symbolize the city and are used to aid ships coming up the river. A map from the chamber of commerce or picked up at one of the commercial establishments is invaluable.

One walk we like begins at the Portsmouth Public Library on Islington Street (there's a public parking lot nearby). Walk along Middle Street to State Street and down State to Pleasant, passing the John Paul Jones House along the way. Follow Pleasant Street all the way to Marcy. Pass a park to the right and walk down through the greenery to the edge of Mill Pond. Continue on Pleasant past the Governor John Wentworth House at 346 Pleasant. Nearby is the Pleasant Street Cemetery dating from the mid-1750s. Turn left onto Marcy Street, which leads past Strawbery Banke Museum on the left and Prescott Park on the right.

♦ **Prescott Park,** at 105 Marcy Street, is located in an area that was once one of the seamiest in the city. Two civic-minded sisters, Mary and Josie Prescott, began to beautify the waterfront in the 1930s by establishing the oldest section of the park. They willed their fortunes for its further development. Formal gardens with lighted fountains have long been an attraction. The Prescott Park Arts Festival operates all summer long with a variety of special events, musical, theatrical, and otherwise. And it still has no fixed admission. Organizers suggest a $3 donation to attend an event. For more information on the arts festival, call (603) 436-2848 or access www.artfest.org.

♦ **New Castle.** This "suburb" of Portsmouth is filled with historic old homes and makes for one of the prettiest drives in the area. Take Route 1-B from south Portsmouth, head over the causeway, and drive along the single road. **Great Island Common** is a public park with rest rooms, picnic tables, and a small beach and pier. Nonresidents are charged a small fee. Continue to the site of the famous old resort hotel, **Wentworth-by-the-Sea.** If plans have progressed as promised, you may even see a new resort at the location (see *Where to Stay*).

♦ **The Isles of Shoals.** Ten miles of the coast of Portsmouth lie nine rocky islands first charted by Captain John Smith when he sailed past in 1614. They were, for centuries before that, used as a summer fishing base by the Abenaki tribe of Native Americans who peopled this region. Although Smith originally named them for himself—*Smythe's Isles*—they were subsequently used for many summers by European fishermen, who were attracted by the "shoals" or schools of fish. In the 1800s they became famous as summer resorts, especially the two largest, Appledore and Star Islands. Star Island was also center of a famed codfishing area. There's some not-so-nice history to the isles, as well. The Smuttynose Island murders of two women in 1873 was most recently referenced in the Anita Shreve bestseller, *The Weight of Water.*

The most famous daughter of the islands was poet Celia Thaxter, born in Portsmouth (a plaque on Daniel Street makes note of the spot) and raised out on the islands. Her father, Thomas Laighton, was the lighthouse keeper at White Island Light and later the first innkeeper on Appledore. To his hotel, the Appledore House, Celia attracted many artistic and literary figures of the day, including Nathaniel Hawthorne, James Russell Lowell, Henry Ward Beecher, and the artist Childe Hassam, who painted famous scenes of Celia's garden. Since early in this century, Star Island has operated as a religious conference center under the Congregational and Unitarian-Universalist Churches. Appledore today is used as the Shoals Marine Laboratory, a joint venture operated by Cornell University and the University of New Hampshire. A couple of the other islands have private ownership.

These days the state line between Maine and New Hampshire cuts right through the island group so that Appledore, for example, lies in Maine and Star Island in New Hampshire.

Boat Trips

While not directly on the ocean—and with no good beaches in Portsmouth to speak of—the city is definitely dominated by the water and its tricky, tidal river. That's what made the place. A boat trip is in order.

♦ **Isles of Shoals Steamship Co.** (603-431-5500; 1-800-441-4620), Steamship Dock at 315 Market Street. Parking $3. The *Thomas Laighton* makes several trips a day to the Isles of Shoals, not just for sight-seers. The shipping company is the lifeline to Star Island, bringing water (some 5,000 gallons daily) and supplies so that the conference center can operate in the summer season. But for the sight-seer, the trip is a wonderful one, complete with live narration on the legends and lore of the islands, as well as of Portsmouth Harbor. While the "Historic Isles of Shoals and Portsmouth Harbor Tour" is fascinating, even more fun is the "Star Island Stop-over" that combines the narrated tour with a chance to get off on the island for a few hours at lunchtime. This is obviously an all-day commitment, but worth it, we think. Other trips include a Star Island Sunrise Cruise that includes continental breakfast, and that leaves on Monday, Tuesday, Thursday, and Friday at 7:30 AM

The *Thomas Laighton* takes sight-seers to the Isles of Shoals

($12 adults, $6 children). The Star Island Stopover is offered daily at 10:55 AM, returning at 5 PM ($27 for adults and $18 for children). The regular narrated historic cruises leave at 10:55 and 2:25 daily ($20/$12). A Sunset Lighthouse Cruise leaves Monday at 4 PM, returning at 8 PM ($25/$15). Music cruises (rock on Monday, reggae on Wednesday) leave at 7:30 PM and return at 10:30 PM ($16, and you must be over 21). Whale-watches are offered daily ($27/$18), but times change depending on the day. The daily schedule operates June 16 through September 3. In fall, September 4–30, fewer cruises are offered. October is devoted to foliage cruises. Call for reservations and information.

♦ **Portsmouth Harbor Cruises** (603-436-8084; 1-800-776-0915), Ceres Street Dock, Portsmouth. These fully narrated cruises discuss many of the buildings around the harbor. They include the now defunct—but once very famous—Portsmouth Naval Prison, as well as the many lighthouses. Several cruises are offered daily. On Wednesday and Thursday an Isles of Shoals cruise is scheduled. In fall the boat offers an Inland Rivers Cruise. Prices range $10–17 for adults, $6–9 for children. Seniors get a $1–2 discount.

♦ **Isles of Shoals and Lobster Tours** (603-964-6446), Rye Harbor State Marina, Route 1A, Rye. The Isles of Shoals are a little closer to Rye than Portsmouth, and several boat trips are offered daily. The 10 AM trip is a 1-hour lobster outing. Trips at noon and at 2:30 PM go to the Isles of Shoals. The season is late May through September. Adults pay $14, kids $11 for the Isles of Shoals trip; adults $10.50 and children $8 for the lobster trip.

A Historic Ship Museum

♦ **USS *Albacore*** (603-436-3680), Albacore Park, 600 Market Street, Portsmouth. Built at the Portsmouth Naval Shipyard, the USS *Albacore* served with the U.S. Navy from 1953 to 1972. Her innovative teardrop hull design was a triumph, making her the world's fastest submarine at the time and becoming the model for contemporary submarines. Open Memorial Day through Columbus Day, daily 9:30–5; Columbus Day to Memorial Day, Thursday through Monday 9:30–3:30. Adults $5, seniors $3.50, kids $2.

Antiques

New Hampshire, including the Portsmouth area, is filled with antiques dealers and shops. Pick up a copy of the *Directory of New Hampshire Antiques Dealers* to find those that interest you.

Shopping

Portsmouth is a fun shopping town. Most stores are found near Market Square or close to the waterfront on Bow Street, Ceres Street, and Market Street. The "Macro" stores—**Macro Polo Inc., Wholly Macro!, Macroscopic,** and **Macrosonic**—offer toys and gimcracks for kids and adults, environmental items, clothing, gifts. They are located near one another in the strip of warehouses between Market and Ceres Streets. A newish crafts gallery located in an old bank building in Market Square, **Taylor-Kumminz,** has very interesting items. They included, when I was there, a wood table formed from the back of a tall giraffe sculpture. I couldn't think where we would put it. The **Dunaway Store** at Strawbery Banke Museum is chock-full of items for kids and adults, many of them historically oriented. **Gee Willikers!** has great stuff for children. **Byrnes & Carlson** on State Street is a chocolatier of

Market Square

high quality. **Serendipity** has always had a nice mix of gifts and clothing. **Tulips** sells American handcrafts on Market Street.

But you will find your own shops. They are sitting there, one next to the other, easily browsed.

WHERE TO STAY

Accommodations are varied in Portsmouth. The city boasts several charming B&Bs in vintage homes and a larger Victorian-era inn that all seem in keeping with the city's emphasis on reclaiming historic sites. A Sheraton hotel on the waterfront and several good motels at the Portsmouth traffic circle off I-95 offer alternatives.

Historic Inns and B&Bs

♦ **The Inn at Strawbery Banke** (603-436-7242; 1-800-428-3933), 314 Court Street, Portsmouth, NH 03801. Innkeeper Sarah Glover O'Donnell maintains a simple, truly historic feeling at this seven-room B&B. Built in 1800, the house is located in the heart of the downtown area and very close to Strawbery Banke Museum. All seven guest rooms have private bath and air-conditioning. There are no TVs or telephones —except in the two common rooms, one on the first and one on the second floor. The beds have simple bedspreads, and interior shutters on the windows, original to the house, make for a clean, uncluttered look. When my daughter and I stayed here, our second-floor room in blue and white was light and airy, with a queen and single bed. Six of the rooms have queen beds; one has a double. Three guest rooms are on the first floor and four, on the second. All guests enjoy a hearty breakfast served in a sunny, windowed breakfast room, an addition to the rear of the house. Sourdough blueberry pancakes are one specialty. Homemade breads, muffins, and coffee cake are always available. There's parking in the next-door lot. Doubles, $140–150.

♦ **The Martin Hill Inn** (603-436-2287), 404 Islington Street, Portsmouth, NH 03801. What a charmer this place is! The first of Portsmouth's B&Bs, it's run with care by Jane and Paul Harnden, corporate dropouts who work as hard at innkeeping as they ever did in the business world. Seven air-conditioned rooms with private bath in two buildings are tastefully decorated with mostly period furnishings. The main house, circa 1815, has three guest rooms; the second building, known as the Guest House, has four. They are linked by an exquisite city garden, an oasis of shade and color on a warm day, where the Harndens have also constructed a water garden. Two round tables with chairs invite lingering. The inn is on a busy street, a couple of miles from the historic waterfront section of town, but once here, you're in a world of your own. Wildflower and glycerin soaps are furnished—and can be purchased in gift packs as keepsakes. We like the suite with a greenhouse in the Guest House; it features lush plants and rattan furnishings. A first-floor room with pineapple-post twin beds in the main house is also special. Breakfast, served at a large table in a dining room amid lovely Sheraton furnishings, is delicious. Blueberry-pecan pancakes, omelets, and baked apples are among the most popular items. Doubles, $90–130.

♦ **The Oracle House Inn** (603-433-8827; www.nhhappenings.com), 38 Marcy Street, Portsmouth, NH 03801. This salmon-and-cream-colored structure built in 1702 was a restaurant before being converted into a three-room B&B in the mid-1990s. Owner Charles Godfrey of Kennebunk, Maine, a construction specialist, has a partner, Nan Milani, who serves as the on-site manager. She's a native of the area—back 12 generations, she claims—and knows how to steer guests to good dining, shopping, and such. The house has a great location, across the street from the waterfront and Prescott Park and a short walk to Strawbery Banke and restaurants in the downtown area. Each bedroom—one on the first floor and two on the second—has a wood-burning fireplace and air-conditioning, for any sort of weather. Fire logs are provided even in summer, when on a cold, rainy, or foggy night you might want to have your own blazing hearth. Oriental rugs on bare wood floors and period furniture decorate the rooms. We like the second-floor room with painted black floor and queen canopy bed dressed with red-and-white period print coverlet and checked dust ruffle. Its bathroom contains a large whirlpool tub. A light breakfast with fresh fruits, baked breads and croissants, juices, and beverages is served in a pretty garden or indoors in a breakfast room. Doubles, $150.

♦ **The Inn at Christian Shore** (603-431-6770; fax 603-431-7743; www.portsmouth-nh.com/christianshore), 335 Maplewood Avenue, Portsmouth, NH 03801. This handsome deep gold Federal house, circa 1800, is in a historic district of sorts—but not the downtown one. It's just up the street from the Jackson House, Portsmouth's oldest, and around the corner from the North Cemetery, one of the city's most historic. Mariaelena Koopman, who grew up in Argentina but lived for years in New York City, is the innkeeper. She has five guest rooms, all with private bath—although two are across the hall. All have TV and air-conditioning. Room 2 on the first floor is the largest, a very spacious room with Oriental blue-and-white carpet on the floor, queen bed, and period furnishings. Altogether there are three rooms with queen beds and two with doubles. Guests can relax in a charming breakfast/sitting room with wing chairs at small tables on one side, a huge hearth, and a large center table. Here Mariaelena whips up a full breakfast, with the main course possibly being caramel sugar French toast with tangerines, Spanish tortilla, or porridge "with a tot of whiskey." Tea and sweets are available in the afternoon. Doubles, $90–115.

♦ **The Sise Inn** (603-433-1200; 1-877-747-3466; fax 603-431-0200), 40 Court Street, Portsmouth, NH 03801. This small luxury inn with 34 air-conditioned guest rooms is owned by Someplaces Different, Inc., a Canadian organization. Opened in 1986, it was the group's first in the United States, although they now have a few others in New England. The house was built in 1881 by John Sise as a family home. There are 10 rooms in the original building, 2 in a carriage house, and the remainder in a rear addition. All have private bath, wall-to-wall carpeting, and TV hidden in an armoire. The mood is Queen Anne Victorian, and there are great oak beds, skylights, overhead fans, and a different-patterned wallpaper (usually floral) in each room. Room 203 with a sitting area and fireplace is particularly attractive; the fireplaces, however, are only to be looked at. A few bathrooms contain whirlpool tubs, and one suite in the carriage house has a sauna as well as a two-person Jacuzzi.

One suite also has a kitchenette and dining room. The inn is notable for the amount of richly varnished butternut wood in the lobby. A Victorian-style parlor is comfortable, and a cheerful breakfast room offers a full buffet breakfast including a hot dish such as quiche or waffles. Some special weekend packages are occasionally offered off-season. Doubles, $110–260.

♦ **Wentworth-by-the-Sea Resort** (1-866-240-6313), New Castle. Expected to open in spring 2003, a revival of the famous resort hotel of the early to mid-1900s on the island of New Castle was being handled by Ocean Properties, a franchisee of the Marriott hotel corporation. The original hotel was the site of the signing of the Treaty of Portsmouth ending the Russo-Japanese War in 1905. But it fell into sad disrepair, an eyesore to anyone who drove by. Plans were to add two wings (wings were lopped off after the hotel closed in the 1980s) and to offer 170 luxury rooms as well as a restaurant, full-service day spa, outdoor pool, and access to a nearby golf course. Because the fortunes of the hotel have been so uncertain, we can only wait and hope.

Other Choices

♦ **Sheraton Harborside Portsmouth Hotel & Conference Center** (603-431-2300; 1-877-248-3794; fax 603-431-7805), 250 Market Street, Portsmouth, NH 03801. This brick-and-granite hotel is all angles and interesting architecture, but alas—those big salt piles on the waterfront across the street prevent more than a few good harbor views. That may not matter too much, however, for this is a class operation, and interior spaces are comfortable and very attractive. Altogether there are 171 rooms, including 7 ultra-elegant Ports of Call suites named for historic figures in the area. The suites, individually decorated, have one or two bedrooms with queen or king beds, plus living room with gas fireplace, dining area, full kitchen, and exterior patio or deck. A continental breakfast is delivered to the room. One-bedroom suites, $500–600; two-bedroom suites, $650–850. For mere mortals, the remaining rooms have one king or two double beds, all covered with blue-gray quilted bedspreads, and with at least one blue wall in the room. Historic reproduction photos are on the walls. To accommodate businesspeople there are two-line phones, voice mail, and huge work desks. All bathrooms have tubs and showers. Parking is in a garage below the hotel. It's a short walk to the waterfront area of Portsmouth. The hotel has its own full-service restaurant, **Harbor's Edge,** located at the waterfront end of the large, open lobby. Doubles, $139–235.

♦ **Bow Street Inn** (603-431-7760; fax 603-433-1680; www.bowstreetinn.com), 121 Bow Street, Portsmouth, NH 03801. This well-located establishment operates the second floor of a brick building that is also home to the Seacoast Repertory Theatre. Getting there means trekking up a flight of steps in front and then taking a small elevator one floor, but once you've arrived, the digs are quite attractive and comfortable. Two of 10 rooms offer harbor views, but all are nicely decorated in pastels with Victorian touches. All have queen-sized brass bed, private bath, TV, and telephone. Parking is in a municipal garage nearby. Continental breakfast, served in a small but attractive breakfast room, includes home-baked breads. Doubles, $119–149. A large mini suite rents for $160 or $175.

Motels

These motel-style accommodations are all in the area of the Portsmouth traffic circle, right off I-95 and Route 1. You have to drive from here to most area attractions, but then again, you have free on-site parking and are out of the fray.

♦ **Anchorage Inn & Suites** (603-431-8111; 1-800-370-8111), Woodbury Avenue (off Exit 6 from I-95), Portsmouth, NH 03801. The Ramsey family runs this immaculate 93-room motel, and other members of the family have same-named inns in Rochester, New Hampshire, and in York and Ogunquit, Maine. An indoor kidney-shaped pool and hot tub room join the two sections of the motel. Each room has two doubles or a king bed—except for three 2-room suites with king bedded room, whirlpool tub, and separate living room. Family rooms have two doubles and an additional pullout sofa. A continental breakfast is served in an attractive breakfast area just off the lobby. Doubles, $59–199.

♦ **Fairfield Inn Portsmouth** (603-436-6363; fax 603-436-1621), 650 Borthwick Avenue, Portsmouth, NH 03801. A former four-story Susse Chalet was completely overhauled and opened as a Marriott Fairfield Inn in summer 2001. Attractive guest rooms have a queen or two double beds, bath with tub-shower, large 25-inch TV, telephone, and air-conditioning. The location is off the traffic circle via a couple of streets, making it seem very private and quiet. There's an outdoor pool for use in summer. A cheerful breakfast room off the lobby is the place for a buffet continental breakfast—cereals, juice, fresh fruit, coffee, tea, and muffins, bagels, and English muffins. It's a good value, too. Doubles, $79–119.

♦ **Wynwood Hotel and Suites** (603-436-7600), 580 U.S. Highway 1 Bypass, Portsmouth, NH 03801. The 169 guest rooms include 30 one- and two-bedroom suites featuring fully equipped kitchens, a king-sized or two double beds, a whirlpool tub, and a separate living room. All rooms have in-room coffeemaker, hair dryer, and refrigerator. There are an indoor and an outdoor pool. A new six-story tower contains the suites. There's a lot of activity at this site. A Bickford's Family Restaurant is next door. Doubles, $59.95–200; suites, $125.95–350.

WHERE TO EAT

Not all that long ago, Portsmouth was dubbed "the San Francisco of the East." It had little to do with the ocean and even less with the lifestyle. The comparison was to Portsmouth's restaurants, which—ever since James Haller created The Blue Strawbery in an old warehouse building down on Ceres Street in the late 1970s—has been hailed for its eateries. Bostonians regularly come for dinner.

Portsmouth's restaurants seem to be holding up, with new ones opening regularly and beloved old ones occasionally going out of business simply because the owners get tired. You have to be good to make it here, and most are. The following represents a cross section of some of the best, most interesting, or just plain most reliable. By the time you visit, there will, of course, be more. Even though some of these restaurants are elegant enough to be special-occasion places, the fact is that Portsmouth—like the rest of the world—is casual. You can dress that way, too.

Fine Dining

♦ **Anthony Alberto's Ristorante Italiano** (603-436-4000), 59 Penhallow Street, Portsmouth. Possibly the most romantic restaurant in Portsmouth—and certainly one of the very best—is this intimate dining spot ensconced in the cellar of the old Custom House. Down a set of stone steps is a dark, stone-and-brick-walled space with exposed ceiling beams, Oriental rugs on the slate floors, intimate booths, and well-spaced tables. Co-owner Tod Alberto (whose partner is Massimo Morgia) says engagements and anniversaries are often celebrated here; if you want one of the most intimate enclosures, ask for a "nook." Guests are served in several small dining rooms and spaces. Start with steamed mussels in a smoked Gouda broth with garlic, shallots, and tomatoes, or shrimp, scallops, and lobster wrapped in phyllo dough and covered with artichoke salsa and chive crème fraîche ($8–15). Pastas ($14–20) might include cannelloni of braised duck, radicchio, fresh peas, artichoke hearts, Reggiano cheese, and tomatoes with roasted duck breast and Kalamata olive sauce or the homemade ravioli of the day. A soup or salad can be ordered ($7 range) such as traditional Caesar or tomato, fresh mozzarella, and basil. "Second plates" (priced $18–28) could be olive-marinated grilled filet mignon with crispy potatoes, prosciutto-wrapped asparagus, and mushroom ragout, or a steamed whole lobster with pistachio rice stuffing, oven-roasted asparagus, tomato coulis, and cilantro avocado butter. If you have any room for dessert, you might order crème caramel or a fruit tart. Open for dinner nightly except Sunday.

♦ **Café Mirabelle** (603-430-9301), 64 Bridge Street, Portsmouth. Another romantic restaurant is this special second-floor space presided over by French-born chef Stephan Mayeux and his wife, Christine. They have established a fine reputation in Portsmouth, although the location of the restaurant is somewhat removed from downtown. A plus: the parking lot across the street. We lucked out on a Friday night without reservations (a cancellation had just occurred) while driving south from the northern part of the state and snagged a table in-season. Little white lights adorn branches on the ceiling and walls; tables are well spaced and service, attentive. Warm crusty bread arrived with a crock of butter and two glasses of wine to get us under way. Appetizers include baked Brie with walnuts and fresh thyme in a puff pastry and escargots with wild mushrooms ($5–9). The classic bouillabaisse—brimming with scallops, shrimp, salmon, mussels, and lobster in a saffron bouillion—is served with salad, vegetable, and wild rice ($23). My husband chose the Pork Pommery with spinach and wild mushrooms in a mustard brandy cream sauce, pronounced delicious. My swordfish steak sautéed with asparagus, roasted tomatoes, capers, garlic, and basil in a Muscadet wine and butter reduction was equally satisfying. Entrées come with a mixed green salad, vegetable, and starch. The restaurant usually celebrates Bastille Day (July 14) with a special prix fixe dinner around that date, for which reservations are needed well in advance. Dinner Wednesday through Sunday starting at 5:15.

♦ **43° North** (603-430-0225), 75 Pleasant Street, Portsmouth. Opened in February 2000 by Chef Geno Gulotta—whose previous credits include the Mansion at Turtle Creek in Dallas and Anthony Alberto's in town—this new spot was fast gaining loyal followers. Located in a cream-colored brick building with arched entry, the dining room is large and open; diners are seated in contemporary black chairs at small tables. Fine paintings on the walls and some antique furnishings help signal high-minded intentions. Although the chef refers to his restaurant as a "kitchen and wine bar," the menu is inventive and exciting. Among the starters on a changing list of offerings, the homemade gnocchi are always available, although the fillings change. Other starters might be lobster bisque, a Maine crabcake with sweet corn coulis, or baked oysters with warm bacon and blue cheese dressing ($7–9). Entrées (priced $17–23) might be crispy pancetta-wrapped pork tenderloin with tomato and bacon topping; red snapper roasted with goat cheese and spinach in a saffron mussel broth; or grilled lamb porterhouse with artichoke, Kalamata olive, and zucchini salad. Dessert offerings change daily. Open nightly from 5, except closed Sunday.

♦ **Lindbergh's Crossing** (603-431-0887), 29 Ceres Street, Portsmouth. The narrow brick-walled 18th-century warehouse across from the waterfront—with just enough room for an aisle between two rows of wall-hugging tables—was formerly occupied by The Blue Strawbery. Several owners share the honors but one of them, Jeff Tenner, is executive chef, and it is his creativity that people rave about. The place is dark and potentially intimate, but it can be very noisy. A group of six businessmen toward the back of the room was so loud that the rest of us could barely be heard. Upstairs there's a much more informal room with bar and windows looking out on the waterfront (which cannot be seen from the lower-level main dining room). Photographs of Lucky Lindy adorn the side walls and a single propeller blade is on the rear wall, but the reasoning behind the name is simply that the owners all are fascinated with aviation. It was such a warm evening when we ate here— although the space itself was comfortable—that we passed up the appetizers. We might have had mussels steamed in a white wine and shallot broth, a tapas plate of basil-marinated roasted red peppers, whipped chèvre and olive tapenade, or seared squid stuffed with curried rabbit ($7–10). From the main dishes one of us chose the seared steak salad over spinach and roasted tomatoes with creamy blue cheese and corn bread, while the other had the crispy duck breast with pistachio jasmine rice and an orange peppercorn gastrique. Both were good. Other choices ($15–25) might have been mussels in a white wine shallot broth served over linguine, salmon roulade of leeks and goat cheese with polenta, or mustard seed crusted halibut. We split a slice of lemon custard pie for dessert; the crust seemed tough but the filling was wonderful. Desserts are $6 and also included crème brûlée and summer berry tart with crème anglaise. Dinner nightly.

Seafood and Such

♦ **Jumpin' Jay's Fish Café** (603-766-FISH), 150 Congress Street, Portsmouth. This casual storefront space on a busy corner of town is indeed jumping. We ate here on a Sunday evening and the place was filled—mostly with young people who took over the oval stainless-steel bar, sat on benches along the walls nearby, and filled the small tables. Gray carpeting, deep coral walls below the wainscoting with white walls above, and loopy strings of lights made from old-style bulbs surrounded by metal reflectors tacked to the ceiling make for an informal atmosphere. Of course

Sailboats moored on the Piscataqua River

there are a few fish—sculptures, pictures, murals—here and there. This place is about fish, fresh-as-can-be-fish. Appetizers include pan-fried oysters over fingerling potato salad, sautéed calamari with hot peppers and tomatoes, and Maine crabcake with house aïoli ($5–9). Fish from around the country is brought in by owner Jay McSharry; the night we ate here the specials included grilled swordfish from Canada, Pacific halibut, yellowfin tuna from the coast of New Jersey, and Cajun-crusted catfish from North Carolina. Linguine Provençal-style can be had with scallops, mussels, chicken, shrimp, or a combination (at only $14–15). It is a magnificent presentation; I couldn't finish the large portion. My husband had haddock Piccata—pronounced excellent. Crusty warm bread came with olives and softened garlic and butter. Open nightly for dinner. Reservations are taken.

♦ **The Oar House** (603-436-4025), 55 Ceres Street, Portsmouth. This popular restaurant across the street from the waterfront draws crowds because of the location and ambience, as much as the food. On our latest visit, a couple arrived in a rainstorm and said they always had lunch here when on their annual trip through Portsmouth. The restaurant is located in what was once a warehouse for a local merchant. Brick walls, candles in hurricane lamps, and eclectic furnishings—believe it or not, one table features the brass headboard and footboard of a bed—add charm. A small deck, across the street and overlooking the river, is crowded on nice days. Always on the menu are clam chowder and onion soup au gratin ($5 cup, $7 bowl). Other choices might be shrimp cocktail, baked lobster and artichoke dip, or cherrystones or oysters from the raw bar. At lunch, try a BBLT (Danish blue cheese, bacon, lettuce, and tomato sandwich), tarragon tuna salad, or a lobster roll ($9–16). Entrées ($11 and $12) include fish-and-chips, broiled scallops, and boiled lobster. Dinner entrées ($20–29 range) might be tournedos of beef à la fromage, broiled haddock baked in white wine and lemon, or seafood scampi. Open daily for lunch 11:30–3, nightly from 5 for dinner.

♦ **Dunfey's Aboard the *John Wanamaker*** (603-433-3111), 1 Harbor Place beneath the Memorial Bridge, Portsmouth. Who wouldn't want to dine aboard this sleek yacht originally built by the city of Philadelphia for more than a million dollars many years ago? It's a great space, lots of wood and brass, but its food fortunes seem to rise and fall like the tide. At our last visit, things were once again looking up. Is there a better location for lunch than on the upper deck, with the action of the Piscataqua River spread out before you? The lunch menu ranges from appetizers like fried calamari and sweet potato fries, to soups and salads and sandwiches. These include grilled tuna melt, lobster roll, and burgers. In the evening three different dining spaces belowdecks take over—one of them in the bow of the ship. Appetizers ($10–15) include tuna carpaccio, a classic raw bar, and seafood antipasto. Spinach salad with shredded radicchio, shaved Parmagiano Reggiano cheese, and a lemon basil dressing might precede dinner. Entrées ($20–30 range) include pine nut crusted salmon with a lime beurre blanc ragout; grilled lobster; and roast chicken with a roasted corn flan. The light menu is served on the deck all day 11:30–9. Downstairs, dinner begins at 5 nightly.

♦ **Warren's Lobster House** (207-439-1630), Route 1, Kittery, Maine. Portsmouth locals and visitors are glad to walk over Memorial Bridge to the other side of the river and this more-than-popular seafood spot. The knotty-pine interior has been the same for years, and prime locations are the booths by the riverside windows. We used to grab lunch here when we were delivering or picking up our daughter from college in Maine. The fare is reliably good, if rather predictable. At lunchtime you can have clam chowder, lobster stew, onion rings, or lobster and corn chowder to start. A lobster roll, crabmeat salad sandwich, or fried haddock roll might please. Entrées include lobsters—baked, stuffed, or boiled. Raspberry-glazed salmon, fried haddock, and baked scrod are other possibilities ($8–11). At night the Down East shore dinner includes a cup of chowder, mussels, a lobster, french fries or onion rings, a trip to the salad bar, and dessert—at the market price. Fried fish dinners are popular, and salmon Oscar is topped with shrimp, asparagus, and béarnaise sauce ($11–16). Prices are good here, and that's part of the attraction. Open daily for lunch 11:30–4 and for dinner all day.

Other Choices

♦ **Porto Bello** (603-431-2989), 67 Bow Street, Portsmouth. This intimate second-floor, L-shaped dining room overlooking the water is given high marks for northern Italian cuisine. Tables are clothed in white, and exposed beams on the ceiling add to the ambience. Yolanda Desario and her mother cook up authentic and traditional dishes in the kitchen, preparing everything from scratch. Lunch is served only on Friday and Saturday and might be pasta with marinara sauce, veal Milanese, or grilled fish of the day. In the evening, starters include a mixed salad, grilled portobello mushroom, and grilled calamari ($8–10). Pastas are wonderful-sounding dishes like fettuccine alla Bolognese "simmered for hours in wine," homemade cheese ravioli, or lasagna layered with five cheeses. Second plates might be a half chicken roasted in garlic and olive oil, then slowly baked with onions, shallots, fresh porcini mushrooms, and white wine; lamb loin chops served with rosemary; or lobster tails basted with basil butter and lemon ($15–22). Cannoli might be on the dessert menu. Lunch Friday and Saturday noon–2:30, dinner Wednesday through Sunday from 4. Reservations are a good idea.

♦ **Portsmouth Brewery** (603-431-1115), 56 Market Street, Portsmouth. This is a lively and popular spot that sells more Smuttynose microbrew products than any other site in town. Light wood tables and chairs are used, and a couple of different levels break up the large space. Old Brown Dog and Shoals Pale Ale are among the favorite brews. The place is open all day, with dinner entrées not available until 5 PM. Before then, you can get char-grilled or veggie burgers, a steak salad, grilled chicken breast with honey ale mustard sauce on a bulky roll, or pizza. There are also nachos, chicken tenders, stuffed mushroom caps, and such. For dinner, entrées ($11–20) might be jambalaya with or without andouille sausage and chicken (to please the vegetarians among us); Old Brown Dog marinated London broil; or a seafood fra diavolo. Sides include black beans and rice, and tortilla chips and salsa. The restaurant's beer grain rolls are made especially for the restaurant by the local bakers at Me & Ollie's. Open 11:30 AM–12:30 AM daily.

Light Fare

Location, location, location is what the **Café Brioche** (603-430-9225) has—on Market Square with a double storefront space and loads of tables and chairs out front. The food is good, too. Longtime owner Paul Norton is a baker and pastry chef who turns out the delectable scones, croissants, muffins, and breads that people eat along with their lattes and cappuccinos all morning long. The café also makes boxed lunches for picnickers and has specials to go like baked chicken, lasagnas, casseroles, roll-up sandwiches, and soups. You can eat inside or out. The place is open 6:30 AM to 11 PM in summer, from 6:30 AM to sometime between 6 and 9 PM in winter. On Tuesday, Thursday, and Saturday there's live music in the evening, usually jazz.

♦ **Me & Ollie's** (603-436-7777, diagonally across Market Street from the Café Brioche, is renowned for its many varieties of fresh-baked bread. Owner Roger Elkis named it for his three sons, Max, Eli, and Ollie, hence Me & Ollie's. Big cinnamon buns, muffins, and coffees are on the menu early in the day. For lunch we had two great sandwiches—tuna salad with a mixture of finely diced vegetables on homemade white bread (called "honest white"), and chicken on whole wheat bread. There's a huge blackboard menu. Soups the day we were there were lentil, gazpacho, and tomato bisque. Hours are weekdays 7 AM–6:30 PM, Sunday 8–5.

 # 11 Block Island, Rhode Island

A friend says, "Just give me an island—any island." She says the moment she leaves the mainland, she changes her watch to Island Time, kicks back, and is a different person in a different world. The island she was referring to at the time was Block Island.

Block Island is a seascape in bright green, soft blue, and gray. The greens are the rolling hills; the blues, the sky and the sea; the grays, the weathered houses and old stone walls (2,042 miles of them by chamber of commerce count).

Located just a dozen miles south of the Rhode Island mainland, the island packs a visual wallop in its 7-by-3-mile-size. In many ways it is the state's crown jewel. Often likened to Ireland and to Bermuda for its rolling green hills, views of the sea at every turn, and stream of bicyclists, the island has managed—so far—to retain its sense of identity. It has not sold out to the McMansions and the McDonalds of the world.

Environmental and preservation groups already own or oversee nearly one-third of the island, with more promised. The goal is 50 percent. For its herculean efforts to keep from ruining what it has, Block Island was identified by The Nature Conservancy as one of the "Last Great Places" in the Western Hemisphere. (In this book the tidelands of the lower Connecticut River, Connecticut, are another.) As one visitor said, "This is one place that is trying to get it right."

Occasionally, of course, there are setbacks. Islanders dug in and fought the inauguration of a high-speed ferry all the way to the Rhode Island Supreme Court and lost. The passenger-only boat began service in summer 2001—taking half an hour instead of an hour to whisk people over from Point Judith, Rhode Island, to New Harbor on the Great Salt Pond.

The Great Salt Pond appears as a huge void on maps of the island. Once a large freshwater pond, it became an enormous protected harbor once a cut was made through to the sea for access. Boaters fill it all summer long. A large public dock, Payne's Dock, extends out into the pond. The area is known as New Harbor in contrast to the old original one on the east side of the island.

Old Harbor—officially New Shoreham, but nobody calls it that—is Block Island's one town. Most ferries land here. With its old Victorian-era hotels lined up to face the port, Old Harbor is where the action is. When I first visited the island in

Old Harbor, Block Island

1970, the Block (as it's affectionately known) was barely awakening from its postwar lethargy. Those big old hotels that had drawn crowds via steamer from New York City at the turn of the last century were boarded-up hulks. A guesthouse or two—notably the 1661 Inn—were just beginning to get into business again.

Yet among those who spent all or part of the year on Block Island, fierce loyalties developed. Block Island, in recent years, has experienced an incredible resurgence. Hotels are back in business, guesthouses and bed & breakfast inns are sprouting up everywhere, and the activity on summer weekends is intense.

There's a caste system, of course. Day-trippers are at the bottom of the heap. Up a notch are weekenders, superceded by homeowners. Year-rounders (about 800 at last count) have more clout. At the apex of this pyramid are the descendants of the island's original 16 settlers. Their names are listed on Settlers Rock near the north end of the island.

Before the settlers, the island's first inhabitants were the Manisses Indians, a Native American people who established here one of the earliest year-round settlements in southern New England. That was about 2,500 years ago. When European explorers (one of them Adriaen Block, the Dutch navigator for whom the island is named) first visited in the early to mid-1600s, they noted the island's heavy forestation. The trees are gone now, taken to build the first settlement in 1661 and used in years following for fuel. There's a windswept beauty in their place, with low shrubs and bushes and a chance to really see the undulations of the land.

The island is a serious stop for migratory birds. Audubon Society trips are scheduled in spring and fall. Hikers and walkers appreciate the many nature trails that lace the island. In-season, the local Nature Conservancy chapter offers guided hikes. A book newly published in 2001, *On This Island*, details the history of Block Island's stellar conservation effort and describes the trails.

Block Island really feels like an island. Wild roses and beach plums line the twisting roads that sometimes end in dirt pathways at a south shore beach or when they wind through the center of the island. Two- and 3-acre zoning outside the town of Old Harbor itself has limited the number of houses that can be built. It also preserves the vista of rolling green hills with distant views of the water (Block Island Sound to the north, the open Atlantic to the south). Artists love the island for its light, its sunsets, and the charm of its old buildings. Art galleries are, in fact, among the more recent serious establishments.

Block Island is for the carefree traveler, the kind who can be happy with a book on the beach or a bike ride to the far end of the island. They might be found in cutoff jeans and a T-shirt or, at most, a pair of casual pants. They don't expect, nor do they insist on, a TV and telephone in their room (although a very few of the newer places have them). They might actually leave their cell phones at home. If you're that kind of traveler, then Block Island is the place for you.

Getting There

By boat: The main port of embarkation for ferry service to Block Island is **Point Judith, Rhode Island,** from which **Interstate Navigation Company** (401-783-4613) offers year-round service. To get to Point Judith, take I-95 north to exit 92. Bear right

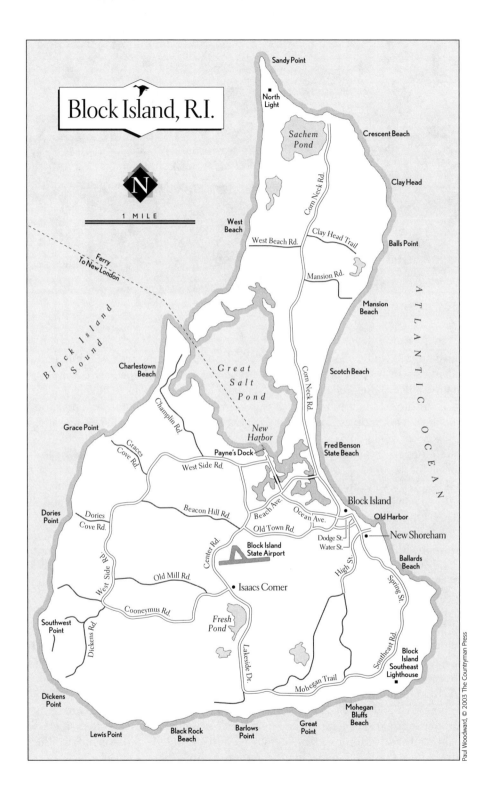

Block Island, R.I.

N

1 MILE

Sandy Point

North Light

Sachem Pond

Crescent Beach

Clay Head

Corn Neck Rd.

West Beach

West Beach Rd.

Clay Head Trail

Balls Point

Mansion Rd.

Mansion Beach

Ferry To New London

Block Island Sound

Charlestown Beach

Great Salt Pond

Corn Neck Rd.

Scotch Beach

A T L A N T I C   O C E A N

Champlin Rd.

Grace Point

New Harbor

Fred Benson State Beach

Graces Cove Rd.

Payne's Dock

West Side Rd.

Block Island

Old Harbor

Dories Point

Dories Cove Rd.

Beacon Hill Rd.

Beach Ave.

Ocean Ave.

Old Town Rd.

New Shoreham

Dodge St.

Water St.

Center Rd.

Block Island State Airport

High St.

Ballards Beach

West Side Rd.

Old Mill Rd.

Isaacs Corner

Spring St.

Cooneymus Rd.

Fresh Pond

Southwest Point

Dickens Rd.

Lakeside Dr.

Southeast Rd.

Block Island Southeast Lighthouse

Dickens Point

Mohegan Trail

Mohegan Bluffs Beach

Lewis Point

Black Rock Beach

Barlows Point

Great Point

A ferry ready to depart Block Island for Point Judith

on Route 2 to Route 78 south (the Westerly, Rhode Island, bypass). At Route 1, turn left and travel to Route 108 (signs to Point Judith and Galilee, the town). Travel south 3 miles to the Block Island boat sign and follow directions to the pier.

There are 8 to 10 trips a day each way from mid-June to September; ferries run less often at other times. The trip takes about an hour. Approximate one-way fares: adults $8.40, children $4.10, cars $27, motorcycles $16, bicycles $2.50. One-day round-trips are available at a reduced rate. Reserve well in advance to take a car during the summer.

Daily ferries also run in summer from **New London, Connecticut,** operated by **Nelseco Navigation Co.** (860-442-7891). The *Anna C* takes 2 hours to reach the island. One-way costs: car $28, adult $15, child $9.

Passenger-only ferries are run by **Interstate** (401-783-4613) in-season from **Newport, Rhode Island,** leaving Newport at 10:15 AM and returning from Block Island at 4:45 PM. The round-trip cost is $12.

There is a summer ferry from **Montauk, Long Island,** run by **Viking** (631-668-5700). One trip a day allows day-trippers from Montauk about 6 hours on the island. The ferry arrives in New Harbor. The round-trip cost is $40. No cars.

The new **high-speed ferry,** the catamaran *Athena,* runs from the Galilee State Pier in Point Judith, Rhode Island, several times daily in-season. The operator is **Hi-Speed Ferry** (877-733-9425). This is a passenger-only ferry that arrives at New Harbor in 30 to 40 minutes. Adults one-way $14, round-trip $26. Children $8 and $12. Bicycles are free.

By air: More and more people are reaching the island by air. **New England Airlines** (from Westerly 401-596-2460; on Block Island 401-466-5881) offers several flights daily and year-round service from **Westerly, Rhode Island.** Flights are also offered from **Groton, Connecticut** by **Action Airlines** (860-448-1646).

Getting Around

You don't need a car, particularly for a stay of 2 or 3 days and if you plan to be near town. There are several taxis. Getting car reservations on the ferry in midseason can be a hassle, so if you want to take a car, plan ahead.

Bicycles, leisurely and quiet, are the preferred mode of transportation. They can be rented for $15–25 a day. Mopeds are noisy and often the drivers are inexperienced, making for hairy adventures. Block Island has a love-hate affair with these two-wheelers. Should you feel confident, expect to pay about $60 for a single-passenger vehicle per day or $85 for a two-seater. The island limits the number of mopeds to a total of 150 to control their use. They are not to be driven after dusk. (Remember, there's no hospital on the island.)

Walking is recommended. If you stay in or near Old Harbor, you can walk to just about everything, including the beach.

A handy map of the island is available in the *Block Island Times,* the indispensable weekly newspaper. You usually can pick a copy up at one of The Block's two bookstores, Island Bound or the Book Nook or at your hotel or inn.

For More Information

♦ **Block Island Chamber of Commerce** (401-466-2747; 1-800-383-BIRI; www. blockislandchamber.com), Drawer D, Block Island, RI 02807.

SEEING AND DOING

Exploring the Island

Bicycling is often the way to do this. **North Light** at the end of Corn Neck Road (the Indians used to grow their corn there) at the northern tip of the island is a favorite cycling destination; you can picnic once you get there. Built of Connecticut granite in 1867, the lighthouse there has been restored recently. A small maritime museum inside is open 10–4 daily in July and August and on weekends in late spring and early fall. Admission, $3. The trip by bike to North Light is about 4 miles each way and is slightly hilly, but reasonably easy. Out by the freshwater **Sachem Pond** at this end of the island, you'll find **Settlers Rock** with the names of the 16 stalwart souls who settled the island in 1661.

Hardy sorts (you don't have to be *too* hardy) like to make a bicycle circuit of the island. Begin in Old Harbor and travel north along the shore to the intersection with Beach Avenue, then west past New Harbor with its marinas (you can find rest rooms here), the Block Island Historical Cemetery, and on to West Side Road. From West Side Road you can take any number of dirt roads to the water; we like Cooneymus Road to reach a wild, wonderful stretch of beach, often deserted. Retrace this dirt stretch to the paved portion of Cooneymus and follow it east to Lakeside Drive. Then head south to Mohegan Trail with its fabulous high views over Mohegan Bluffs (toward Montauk, Long Island) and on to **Southeast Light,** an 1874 brick lighthouse whose lantern can be seen 35 miles at sea. A very small museum at the lighthouse is operated by the Block Island Historical Society, but mostly there are souvenirs for sale. Every so often tours are led up into the light itself. Open in summer, daily 10–4. Donation.

This end of the island in particular has been likened to Ireland. Follow Mohegan Trail to Southeast Light Road, then head to Spring Street and back into Old Harbor.

If you aren't up to biking, you can take a taxi tour. Several companies offer them.

Walking is a particular pleasure on Block Island, for it's a compact place. The town of Old Harbor is fine for moseying. You can poke in the shops, watch the ferry come in, or visit the Block Island Historical Society or the Island Free Library.

Out on the island are several good places for walking. Delightfully meandering paths cut through 11 acres of natural growth at **The Maze** in the island's northeast corner. Located atop Clay Head, the area offers fantastic views out over the ocean, the surprise of hidden ponds, and many birds, since it's one of the Audubon Society's banding stations.

Rodman's Hollow, a wild and beautiful cleft in the rolling southwestern terrain, adjoins a 200-acre parcel of land managed by the Rhode Island Audubon Society. The cemetery on Center Road is an interesting place for exploring, and some of the tombstones bear unusual legends. Be watchful for ticks when you are walking around in shrubbery. Lyme disease has been a problem on the island.

Outdoors

Beaching. It is best and safest along the island's east coast. There are several names for what is essentially the same strand, from Surfer's Beach to Fred Benson State Beach to Scotch Beach and eventually Mansion Beach. The whole stretch is some-times referred to as Crescent Beach. The state beach section has the gentlest surf, plus a pavilion, snack bar, and lifeguards. It's great for kids. You can rent umbrellas and beach chairs here ($5 each) and buy snacks and grilled hamburgers and hot dogs. The water is crystal clear and inclined to be brisk, especially before mid-July.

Locals love Mansion Beach, reached via dirt road from Corn Neck Road. Charleston Beach on the west side of the island, just southwest of the Coast Guard Station, is more rugged and better for exploring and walking than swimming. We've found good driftwood here. Reach it via dirt roads from West Side Road. Ballard's Beach, on the other side of Ballard's Inn and Restaurant (a short walk from the ferry in Old Harbor), is the only other beach (other than the state beach) that is staffed with lifeguards. A volleyball net is up, and live music is sometimes scheduled on the beachside patio. But be careful; the surf can be rough here. The beaches are free.

Kite flying. Don't miss a chance to use the great island breezes and have some fun. You'll find a good selection of kites at the **Block Island Kite Company** on Corn Neck Road.

Sportfishing. This is big. Stripers, blues, and swordfish are caught in abundance in the waters off Block Island. You can find a charter boat easily by walking along the dock near Ballard's restaurant, not far from the ferry dock slip where several tie up. **Oceans and Ponds** (401-466-5131) on Ocean Avenue, an official outlet of Orvis of Manchester, Vermont, offers fly-casting lessons and fishing gear.

Boating. **Rowboats** can be rented at the **Twin Maples** on Beach Avenue, New Harbor. One marina where you can watch graceful sailboats and huge powerboats is **Champlin's.** You'll also find **kayak** rentals there. Rentals, lessons, and charters for sailors and would-be sailors are offered by **Sail Block Island** at (401) 466-7938.

Kayaking is coming on strong. You can rent one at **Oceans and Ponds** (401-466-5131) on Ocean Avenue and explore Trims Pond, the Great Salt Pond, Sachem Pond, and the waters around Mansion and Scotch Beaches. Kayaks are also for rent at **Fred Benson State Beach.**

Two-hour **sailboat cruises** on a 45-foot trimaran are offered daily from Block Island Boat Basin in New Harbor. Tickets ($40 each) may be picked up at the Oceans and Ponds store (401-466-5131).

Parasailing is relatively new on The Block and very popular. Call **Block Island Parasail and Water Sports** at (401) 466-5299. Or stop at the booth on the Old Harbor Dock next to Ballards.

Horseback riding is available. Guided trail rides are offered on beaches and through meadows by **Rustic Rides Farm** (401-466-5060).

Birding. This is big, especially in spring and fall when the island is directly on the migratory path of many species. The **Rhode Island Audubon Society** based in Smithfield, Rhode Island (401-949-5454), leads interesting walks. **The Nature Conservancy** (401-466-2129) sponsors various migration field trips in September and October. A network known as **The Greenway** offers 25 miles of trails with 11 access points that birders often like.

Indoors

♦ The **Block Island Historical Society** (401-466-2481), Old Town Road and Ocean Avenue. In addition to permanent historical exhibits portraying the island's farming and maritime past, there are changing exhibits from time to time. A video on the island is fun to watch. Robert Downie, who works here, has put together two impressive photographic books on the island. They are called *Block Island: The Sea* and *Block Island: The Land.* They're for sale here. Open in summer daily 10–5 and on weekends in spring and fall. Adults $3, seniors $2, children $1.

♦ The **Island Free Library** (401-466-3233), Dodge Street. This building is surprising for its contemporary design and is a beehive of activity, especially on a rainy day. It doubled in size in 2001. Leave a deposit and borrow a book. Flyers advertising island events are posted here. Tuesday and Thursday 10–7, Wednesday and Friday 10–5; Saturday 10–3, Sunday 11–3. Closed Monday.

Movies. The Oceanwest Theater near Champlin's Marina presents first-run movies including matinees on rainy days. The Empire Theater in Old Harbor changes flicks every 3 or 4 days and is a great old-time place to watch a movie. Matinees on rainy days.

Shopping

We used to dismiss the shopping on Block Island as unexciting. No more. Old Harbor has most of the stores and can occupy you the better part of a rainy day if you really get into it.

Our favorite two shops just might be **The Scarlet Begonia** on Dodge Street and **The Glass Onion** on Water Street. At The Scarlet Begonia, owner Molly O'Neil sells wonderful ceramics, fabrics, holiday ornaments, and jewelry and always has surprising new things. She carries Nicholas Mosse pottery from Ireland, too. The Glass Onion is one of the most tasteful and unusual gift shops on the island and has some good reading material—even the *International Herald Tribune* when last we stopped.

Joan Mallick's **Block Island Blue** pottery, displayed in a little Cape Cod–style house on Dodge Street, is especially attractive and quite affordable. **Watercolors** on Dodge Street is another favorite, with nice pottery, mobiles, and artwork.

The women's clothing store **Rags** carries Esprit and other good lines in casual summer wear and had terrific Block Island T-shirts the last time we visited. At the venerable **Star Department Store** on Water Street you can find T-shirts, shorts, and sundresses. Also ceramic lobsters, kids' games, beach toys, greeting cards, and wild bumper stickers.

Bruce Johnson's **Oceans and Ponds** on Ocean Avenue is the place to get Block Island baseball caps made of "Nantucket pink" heavy sailcloth with the island logo hand-embroidered in black. You can have the name of your boat embroidered here on a sweatshirt. A burgee (boat flag) can be made for you overnight. You can rent kayaks and canoes and sign up for a sailboat trip. This is a good place for water lovers, boaters, and anglers.

There are three wonderful **art galleries** above the new post office on Water Street just beyond the statue of Rebecca (the white statue erected by the Women's Christian Temperance Union in 1896 to encourage island sobriety—it didn't work, but it's a landmark). The galleries show work by local artists like Jessie Edwards, known for her monoprints; Cindy Kelly (large paintings of cows are a specialty and very intriguing); and the late William Sommerfeld.

The new post office building is an oasis of culture in other ways. On the main level are a few shops, including **Island Bound,** a really good bookstore, and **The Daily Market,** an exceptional gourmet food shop where you can have good sandwiches made to take to the beach. You'll also find good desserts, fine coffee, bagels, and such. There are a few tables on the patio out front; people love to hang out here.

The other, older, island bookstore is **The Book Nook** in the center of town on Water Street. Get newspapers here on Sunday.

You can buy wine, beer, and such at the **Red Bird Liquor Store** on Dodge Street, where the wine selection is quite adequate. **Block Island Grocery** on Ocean Avenue has a fairly extensive selection of foods.

The Three Sisters (Molly, Bridget, and Maria Price of New Jersey) have the best sandwiches and desserts at their tiny place on Old Town Road near the corner of Dodge and Ocean Avenue. People can eat at red picnic tables scattered around the lawn or take food to go.

Block Island honey from the **Littlefield Bee Farm** is sold in many shops and at inns. There's also honey mustard, cinnamon honey, and beeswax candles. If you can't find the stuff, call (401) 466-5364.

Accommodations on Block Island are found in simple summer hotels with rocking chairs on the porches, in refurbished Victorian hostelries full of pressed-oak furniture, and in increasingly sophisticated bed & breakfast inns. You can also rent houses by the week. Camping on the island is strictly prohibited. In summer it is imperative to have a reservation. Three-night minimum stays are common on weekends in-season.

To write for accommodations, simply address the establishment as listed, Block Island, RI 02807. Rates listed range from low to high season. Lower rates prevail during spring and fall. Midweek rates can sometimes be available even in high season. Just ask.

OUT OF TOWN

♦ **The Hygeia House** (401-466-9616; www.hygeiahouse.com), Box 464, New Harbor, Block Island. Lisa and Champ (for Champlin, an old island name) Starr have provided the most recent excitement in the hotel industry on Block Island. They refurbished and opened the 10-room Victorian inn that was once known as the Hygeia Annex to the long-gone Hygeia Inn, operated by Champ's great grandfather, Dr. John Champlin. The good doctor was both an innkeeper and island physician. He had his medical office in this building.

Located on a hill with sea views from every room (either of the Great Salt Pond to the west or of Old Harbor and ferry dock to the east), the now pale yellow and burgundy building with mansard roof was an eyesore for years. When Lisa and Champ finally obtained the property, they discovered many old iron and wood beds that were usable. The rooms are all named for Champlin family members. A ground-floor, handicapped-accessible room with queen bed, separate sitting room, and large bathroom honors the memory of Champ's mother, Annette, who had MS.

Upstairs are five guest rooms or suites on the second floor and four more on the third. Beds are doubles and queens. Some suites have pullout sofas or an extra single bed. Because of the exceptionally high ceilings and wide hallway on the top floor, we like these suites best. Most have a bedroom plus separate small sitting area. All rooms have private bath, and the decorating—with colorful coordinated wallpapers, hand stenciling, and tasteful touches—is lovely. You do have to walk up somewhat steep (but wide) staircases to get to the second and third floors.

A continental-plus breakfast, which sometimes includes the famous doughnuts from nearby Payne's Dock, is included. Yogurt and fresh fruit are commonly added. Breakfasts are served at long, common tables in the main-floor dining room. Guests also have use of a good-sized main-floor parlor with corner fireplace, where a puzzle is usually in progress on one of the tables. Although not air-conditioned (as is the general rule on Block Island), Lisa says "It's always breezy" because of the hilltop location. On the warm day we stopped, she was right. The Starrs offer kayak and canoe rental from their own dock. And kids are welcome (the Starrs have two young ones of their own). Doubles, $175–240. Open year-round.

♦ **Old Town Inn** (401-466-5958; fax 401-466-9728; www.oldtowninnbi.com), Box 1762, Old Town Road, Block Island. Lucinda and David Morrison, formerly of Glastonbury, Connecticut, took over this 10-room inn—after a couple years of its not being open at all—and refurbished it for opening in summer 2002. David, who had spent many summers as a young man working on the island and who is the breakfast cook, and Lucinda, who has a good eye for decorating, brought two young daughters with them for a real family adventure. The inn is composed of an old 1825 house, a new wing built in the early 1980s, and a three-bedroom efficiency cottage that rents by the week.

Although the inn is not in town or next to a beach, it isn't far for bicyclists or those with a car—your own or a taxi. It is quiet. Anyone flying in to the island airport will find this inn very close to the airport. David runs a van service a few times daily to the beach with drop-off and pickup.

All rooms have private bath. Four in the original house have double or twin beds; six in the newer wing have queen beds or (one room) twins. The Captain's Room in the old section has original flowered wallpaper, but most of the rooms are painted bright solid colors.

There's a large fireplaced common room in the new section of the inn, where guests gather. There is also an outdoor deck overlooking the rear yard and gardens. Breakfasts are served in a pretty creamy yellow room with hardwood floors and lighted paintings on the walls. Guests sit at a few separate tables. Baked goods, cereals, yogurt, fruits, and beverages are set out buffet-style along with one hot entrée. Egg-in-a-basket is served individually with egg, ham, and lemon sauce, and a blueberry cobbler is especially popular. Hors d'oeuvres and wine are served on the deck in the afternoon. Doubles, $125–200. Open year-round.

♦ **The Barrington Inn** (401-466-5310; 1-888-279-9400; www.blockisland.com/barrington), Beach and Ocean Avenues, New Harbor. Geri Ballard, daughter of the former owners, and Michael Shatusky took over this six-room B&B, located high on a knoll with a view of the Great Salt Pond, in 2001. They've stuck close to the original successful formula of Geri's parents. In addition to the main house, they also rent a couple of two-bedroom housekeeping apartments for about $1,000 a week in summer. The location is excellent, only a short walk into Old Harbor and down the street from the state beach. Around the corner is Payne's Dock in New Harbor, where there's always lots of action.

The innkeepers put out fluffy striped beach towels in the parlor for guests to use. A terrace with lawn furniture is good for lounging. I like room 4 in the main house, with its own deck overlooking the water. Every room but one has a water view, and furnishings are crisp and up-to-date. All rooms have private bath. For a TV, you can head to one of the two common parlors. A continental-plus breakfast is served in a large, bright room where most guests share one big table. The muffins are freshly baked, fresh fruit is served, and you can scoop up the inn's own granola with yogurt. Guests may rent kayaks and 18-speed bikes here. Doubles, $75–175. Open March through November.

♦ **The Atlantic Inn** (401-466-5883; 1-800-224-7422; fax 401-466-5678; www. atlanticinn.com), High Street, Box 188, Old Harbor. Situated on a grassy hilltop where it gets the best of the island's breezes and distant views of the sea, this large

Victorian hotel was totally redone recently. Under the care of Brad and Anne Marthens, innkeepers and owners, it is most welcoming, from the white Adirondack chairs and little tables scattered across the front lawn and on the front porch to Victorian sofas in the lobby. Check out the antique wooden phone booth with working pay phone. The main-floor bar is one of our favorites, outfitted with bentwood bar stools, Victorian settees, and sofas. It's a nifty place to sip sherry on a rainy evening, listening to classical music on tape. On most afternoons the porch is crowded for happy hour. The inn serves tapas on the porch in the late afternoon and evening, sophisticated fare like red wine braised squid salad or frittata of asparagus and corn. The attractive main dining room has the island's most sophisticated menu (see *Where to Eat*). There are 21 guest rooms, all with private bath and all decorated in Victorian style. Headboards and antique bureaus are often of pressed oak. Beds are doubles, queens, or a queen with a twin, often covered with patchwork quilts. Each room has a phone and floral carpeting. Some are small—room 8, for example, is a small double but seems especially cozy. In room 9 you must go up three steps to the bathroom with stall shower. Each has its own quirks, part of the charm of the establishment. A "fresh-baked" continental breakfast is served to inn guests. And custom gourmet backpack picnic lunches can be ordered by guests for a day at the beach or wherever. The inn also has two tennis courts and an "almost regulation" croquet court. Children are welcome. Doubles, $140–260. Open April to October.

♦ **1661 Inn, Guest House, Ball Cottage,** and **Hotel Manisses** (401-466-2421; 1-800-626-4773; fax 401-466-3162; www.blockisland.com/biresorts), Spring Street, Old Harbor. The Abrams family of Providence owns or operates all of these establishments. They broke ground by opening the **1661 Inn** in 1969. Since then, they have added and upgraded and taken over the large Victorian hotel **The Manisses** just down the street (which was a complete wreck before they restored it). The properties are a short walk from town. In 1996 they leased the nearby **Dodge Cottage,** with nine rooms, six of them queen-bedded with private bath; the other three are efficiencies. They also oversee the lovely six-room **Dewey Cottage** on Ocean Avenue. The nine plush rooms in the 1661 Inn are furnished in antiques and come with private bath and refrigerator. Beds are kings or queens, and five rooms have Jacuzzi-style tubs. Most also have private sundecks with ocean views. The **Guest House** next door to the 1661 Inn has the most affordable accommodations of all— all without TVs. There are a few shared baths, a few private ones, and a couple of rooms with ocean views. The three rooms in the **Nicholas Ball Cottage,** also next door to the 1661 Inn, have loft areas and wood-burning fireplace, as well as TV. In the Victorian hotel **The Manisses**, 17 rooms with private bath are attractively decorated with turn-of-the-20th-century furniture. Some have a whirlpool tub. The Chelsea is a main-floor, king-bedded room with an especially spacious adjoining bath. The large lobby here with light floral wallpaper is a terrific place to relax, and there's a huge TV set for those who must. All guests enjoy the same huge buffet breakfast (often including a whole bluefish) served at the 1661 Inn, although those at the Dewey Cottage have their own continental fare in the morning because of the distance. Children are welcome except at Manisses. An especially appealing perk for guests staying at any one of the locations is a free narrated tour of the island by van. Doubles, $60–300. Some rooms are available year-round.

◆ **Sea Breeze Inn** (401-466-2275; 1-800-786-2276; www.blockisland.com/seabreeze), Spring Street, Old Harbor. This weathered inn is comprised of several cottage-style buildings. Owned for some 20 years by New Yorkers Mary and Bob Newhouse, it used to be a boardinghouse. It exudes a true island feeling, and many fans return again and again. Several rooms have views or glimpses of ocean, but even if yours doesn't (and ours didn't) there are Adirondack chairs in a grassy area out back where you can sit and contemplate a lovely pond and marshy area beyond which is the sea. There are several comfortably padded chaises for sunning. Five of the 10 rooms have private entrance and private bath. The other five are in one building with its own living room and shared baths. Breakfast is delivered in a basket to the rooms with private bath, although there's a common area for breakfast in the larger building.

Decorating here is our idea of "summer cottage"—bare wood floors with scatter rugs, bright colors, a table and chairs where breakfast or a drink can be enjoyed. Baths have showers only. Towels for the beach are available. No TVs or phones in the rooms, although there's a phone for guest use. Plantings are somewhat random, in keeping with the casual spirit of the place. Doubles, $100–210. Although most rooms are open from mid-May to mid-October, two are available year-round.

◆ **Rose Farm Inn** (401-466-2034; www.blockisland.com/rosefarm), Box E, off High Street, Old Harbor. Judith Rose operates this attractive bed & breakfast inn located off a road behind the Atlantic Inn and with the same wonderful breezes and views. The original inn, once a farmhouse for the area, has a marvelous stone porch that has been enclosed and turned into a multiwindowed breakfast room. Eight rooms here have private tiled bath, and two share. Rooms on the inn's east side enjoy water views. A second, newer building with porches all around is the Captain Rose House. Located just across the drive, it adds nine quite large rooms with private bath. Although it lacks the charm of the original, it is comfortable, and one room offers handicapped access. Rooms on the first floor have two-person whirlpool tubs. Those on the second floor have distant water views. Cereal, fruit, yogurt, and homemade breads are set out for continental breakfast served in the farmhouse. Guests are provided beach towels for a day at the beach. Judith Rose keeps her gardens beautifully groomed. Daughter Janie operates Beach Rose Bicycles next door. A public bathroom with shower is available to guests after checkout, an especially nice feature. Open May to October. Doubles, $99–200.

◆ **The Sheffield House** (401-466-2494; 1-866-466-2494; www.blockisland.com/sheffieldhouse), High Street, Old Harbor. Nancy Sarah, who is skilled in personal and professional life coaching, is the innkeeper at this six-room B&B. The house dates from the 1880s and has colored glass panes in its main door plus a prominent turret at one front corner. Nancy refers to this as the "Crow's Nest"; you can climb up into it from the second floor for a great island view. There's enough room to settle in for a reading session.

Four guest rooms have private bath, and two share a hall bathroom. There are queen beds and ceiling fans—but no TVs or phones in the rooms. If you must see TV, there's one in a common area along with board games and books. One of the two first-floor bedrooms has floral wallpaper, a white matelasse spread, and an especially large shower. Terra-cotta walls in room 7 on the second floor—whose bed has a floral quilt—are very pretty. This is one of the rooms with shared bath. Nancy makes a full breakfast. The main dish can be quiche, French toast made with a babka fruit bread, or an "eggy cheesy thing." She accepts guests for holiday periods. Open year-round. Doubles, $70–185.

♦ **Anchor House Inn** (401-466-5021; 1-800-730-0181; fax 401-466-8887), Spring Street, Old Harbor. The 1800s Admiralty ship anchor on the lawn identifies this six-room B&B just around the corner from town and barely up the hill. Melissa and Edward O'Reilly, the young innkeepers, invite you to enjoy a rocking chair on the front porch along with recently refurbished rooms. All have TV and private bath. The first-floor back room has a view of the ocean and a private bath with tub and shower. Second-floor rooms are more compact, with TV mounted high on the wall and bathroom with stall shower only. Ceiling fans are used on the hottest days. A continental breakfast with bagels, muffins, juice, and hot beverages is served in the breakfast room, where guests sit at two large tables. Melissa's grandfather was born on Block Island and she spent a lot of time growing up here, so she's helpful in steering guests around. Open Memorial Day to October, weekends from March to May. Doubles, $120–200.

IN TOWN

♦ **The Surf Hotel** (401-466-2241), Box C, Dodge and Water Streets, Old Harbor. "Do we have a web site? We don't even have a computer," laughs Lorraine Cyr, who writes hotel reservations by hand into a big old ledger on the desk at The Surf. This grand old Victorian hotel, built in 1876, is perfectly situated between the activity of Old Harbor and the glorious beach that runs for miles along the island's east coast. You can walk to everything. To some visitors The Surf is synonymous with the island itself, and the Ulric Cyr family (Lorraine's parents) has run the hotel for more than 40 years. They keep things pretty much the same. You'll still find the rocking-chair-lined front porch, where people-watchers have their fill. Just about everyone on the island passes here sooner or later.

The oversized chess set and a color TV in the lobby are often in use. Out back is a porch with wicker furniture from which to contemplate the sea. There is also a deck with tables and chairs and ocean view where, one presumes, you can take your breakfast or a late-day drink. Climb down a staircase out back and you're right on the beach. All 35 rooms in the hotel share baths, but each has its own sink. In the Surfside Annex around the corner are three rooms with private bath and several that share. In the Back Cottage to the rear are five singles with shared bathrooms. A light buffet breakfast is included in the rates. The Surf requires a 6-night minimum stay in July and August, and pretty much fills up. Occasionally there are shorter periods available in high season. Doubles, $99–150. Weekly rate, doubles, $640–920.

♦ **The National Hotel** (401-466-2901; 1-800-225-2449; fax 401-466-5948; www.block-islandhotels.com), Water Street, Old Harbor. This imposing white hotel dominates your view of town as your arrive in Old Harbor by ferry. Its flag-topped cupola is a real landmark. Dating from 1888 but refurbished and restored after several years as

The National Hotel

a decrepit, nonfunctioning eyesore, it attracts crowds to its porch bar and restaurant. This is a real meting place; by four o'clock of a summer's afternoon it is sometimes all you can do to find a place to sit. The porch is high up off the street and grants a view of the downtown action, ferry arrivals, and everyone going by. If you want a quiet, off-the-beaten-track kind of place, this isn't it. All 45 rooms have private bath, TV, and telephone and are decorated in Victorian style with floral comforters on the beds. The "corner queens" are a bit larger and have good cross-ventilation. The Old Harbor Suite, a one-bedroom suite on the main floor, also boasts a VCR with TV, air-conditioning, and a quite large bathroom. The only drawback is one window looking out onto the porch, which can be so noisy. Floral blue-and-pink carpeting runs all through the hotel. A continental breakfast is included in the rates. Open May to October. Doubles, $79–229; suites–259.

♦ **The Blue Dory Inn** (401-466-5891; 1-800-992-7290; fax 401-466-9910; www.blockislandinns.com), Dodge Street, Old Harbor. Ann Law, an energetic innkeeper, oversees this 11-room in-town Victorian inn with a few cottages out back. She is also innkeeper of the nine-room Adrianna Inn located on Old Town Road just beyond the busy commercial center. Rooms at the Blue Dory are consistently described as "romantic," and there's an emphasis on plump pillows, floral wallpapers, lacy curtains and swags, brass and iron period beds. The front parlor of the Blue Dory sets the scene with a low red Victorian sofa, oval marble coffee table, dried floral arrangements, and wood rocking horse. Ann serves wine and snacks in the afternoon and often bakes her "very famous cookie" made with chocolate chunks and walnuts. All rooms have private bath. Some in the Blue Dory have TV and air-conditioning. A pretty brick walk winds among cottages, all blue with white trim, out back. The Adrianna is quieter. At the Blue Dory guests enjoy a full breakfast in an attractive stone-walled cellar room where food is set out buffet-style. The Adrianna has a continental breakfast. Doubles, Blue Dory, $65–235. The Blue Dory Inn is open year-round. Doubles, Adrianna Inn, $65–195; open May to October.

♦ **Gables Inn** and **Gables II** (401-466-2213; 401-466-7721), Dodge Street, Old Harbor. These two guesthouses with apartments are practically across the street from the beach and not far from the shopping area. Barbara Nyzio, a daughter of the owners of the Surf Hotel, is a Block Islander and a helpful innkeeper. Accommodations are done simply. Traditional wallpaper and antique furnishings are the rule. Some rooms have private bath, and others share. We stayed in one of the latter and could always find a shower or bathroom when needed. Tea and coffee are available all day, and there's a refrigerator in each building for guests' use. A continental breakfast is provided in the morning. Most guests carry theirs onto the front porch or lawn and watch the world of Block Island go by. Gables II is the building with efficiency apartments, each with its own outside entrance. Free use of items like chairs and coolers for the beach is a plus. Barbecue grills and picnic tables in the yard can be used for cookouts. Doubles, $55–125; efficiency apartments, $85–210. A cottage for four rents for $515–910 weekly. Open May to November.

WHERE TO EAT

Breakfast and dinner are the meals most often needed by weekenders—the former only if you're staying in an inn that doesn't serve breakfast (and that's rare). However, some visitors find that a continental breakfast stays with them for only so long—then they want to dig into something more substantial (in effect, making it their lunch).

For **lunch,** there are a few snack places where you can get a sandwich or hot dog, and there's a snack bar at the beach (they grill the hot dogs and hamburgers outdoors). You can pick up sandwiches at several spots, including the markets. Some of the restaurants listed under *For Dinner* are also open for lunch.

For Breakfast

♦ **1661 Inn** (401-466-2421), Spring Street. This venerable spot serves a buffet breakfast to its own guests and those of The Mannises hotel, and the public is welcome during the summer season. For $12.75 you'll feast on such specialties as corned beef hash, scrambled eggs, quiche, oven-roasted potatoes, and possibly a vegetable casserole or chicken tetrazzini. A whole bluefish on a platter is often a centerpiece. The dining room, to the back of the original inn, has indoor dining, covered-deck dining, and an open patio on a lower level. The ocean is seen in the distance. Breakfast midweek 8–11, weekends 8–noon.

♦ **Ernie's,** Water Street. Frank and Betty Jean Nicastro—he's the cook at the island school—leased this space for the summers of 2002 and 2003. Good thing. Ernie's was hands-down the most popular breakfast place on the island, and people are happy to have it back. Those who can get in eat at a counter, tables in the compact indoor space, or outside on the back deck with the view of the ferry's arrival. After 10 the deck must be vacated so that Finn's—which owns this space—can set up for lunch. All the standards are offered—pancakes, eggs, hash browns, French toast. Open 6–noon in-season.

♦ **The Bagel Works** at the corner of Old Town Road and Corn Neck Road—in the old post office building—is a place to get a light breakfast. The doughnuts from **Payne's Dock** are a Block Island tradition. **The Oar** on West Side Road serves breakfast. Most inns and B&Bs serve breakfast to their own guests.

For Dinner

♦ **The Atlantic Inn** (401-466-5883), High Street, Old Harbor. This is the most romantic and leisurely dining experience on the island. The $44 prix fixe four-course dinner (we'd call it three because of the sorbet that is slipped in between appetizer and entrée) is not overpriced. The meal is served in a pretty pink dining room with a somewhat subdued inner room and a windowed "porch." On a nice evening, if you dine before dark, do choose the porch: You get island and water views and more of a summertime feeling. White linens, fresh flowers in pottery vases, and flickering candles make tabletops attractive. A sun-dried tomato and herb spread with crackers appeared with our wine, a Château Bonnet white Bordeaux, which was light and dry. Bread that night (it changes with the whim of the pastry chef) was a cheddar Dijon loaf that at first sounded strong but was actually lightly flavored and delicious.

Executive Chef Ed Moon oversees an interesting menu. One of us had an appetizer of venison pastrami, pronounced outstanding, and the other, the saffron lobster broth that was light and lovely. Cranberry orange sorbet came in a tiny glass before our entrées—in one case, striped bass on a bed of fennel potatoes; in the other, salmon with saffron rice, fresh tomatoes, and olives. For dessert we had the crème caramel and strawberry shortcake, both excellent. Other entrées included coq au vin, grilled monkfish with cannellini and wild mushrooms, and roast pork with braised red cabbage. Dinner from 6 nightly in-season. Reservations suggested.

♦ **Eli's** (401-466-5230), Chapel Street, Old Harbor. Eli's motto used to be "Life's short—eat large," and founder David Silverberg's creative dishes came in very large portions. In 2002 Brad and Anne Marthens of The Atlantic Inn and Executive Chef Ed Moon became partners in Eli's when David left the island to pursue other ventures. Now portions are just a bit smaller but no less creative. Light wood tables and chairs and bright napkins and place mats—plus that screen door—give this a beachy, casual feeling. People just want to walk in. No reservations are taken and the place, which seats about 40 plus a few at a bar in the back, fills up by 7 when a waiting list is started. Among the popular starters are the fried calamari, sweet pepper and black hummus served with veggies and crackers, and a good selection of salads. Entrée choices ($15–20) include a chicken Gorgonzola tortellini, carpetbagger fillet—a 12-ounce piece of beef stuffed with fresh lobster meat, fresh basil, mozzarella, sun-dried tomatoes, and topped with béarnaise (at $37 the most expensive entrée of all)—or a spicy shrimp baked with tomatoes, avocado, peppers, sausage, and feta. There's a good wine list. Dinner nightly 5:30–10. Open March to November.

♦ **Hotel Manisses** (401-466-2421), Spring Street, Old Harbor. The restaurant at the Manisses is well regarded. The dining rooms are on the lower level of the big gray

Victorian inn, reached by outdoor stairway. The light and airy windowed gazebo overlooks the backyard. It's a more recent add-on and is one choice for dining. Or you can sit in the darker indoor dining room with something of the feeling of a library about it. The menu changes nightly in summer and has some creative touches. Fresh vegetables and herbs from the hotel garden show up in soups and in many of the main dishes. Appetizers might be oven-roasted quail, steamed littlenecks, or tenderloin of beef tamales ($10–13). Among recent entrées were grilled veal tenderloin, Atlantic swordfish with red and yellow bell pepper coulis, pistachio-encrusted rack of lamb, and New England–style bouillabaisse ($20–35). A lighter menu is offered at tables near the bar, known as The Gatsby Room. This includes appetizers from the main menu, salads, and a couple of entrées—such as spinach fettuccine—for $8–20. Lunch is also served here in-season. These might be a cold lobster plate, salad, or sandwich special. There is a full bar. In summer, lunch daily, dinner nightly 6–10; weekends only the rest of the year.

♦ **Winfield's** (401-466-5855), Corn Neck Road, Old Harbor. Winfield's is a subdued spot (compared to its companion next-door drinking place, McGovern's Yellow Kittens), and it has a definite following. White-clothed tables, Windsor-style chairs, fresh flowers, and candles—there's a romantic feeling here, although it has never seemed particularly island-y. The food is very highly rated and the menu creative. Starters could be crawfish gnocchi, pan-seared scallops, or duck confit ($9–13). The house salad (Boston lettuce, pistachio nuts, cucumbers, sun-dried cranberries, and Gorgonzola with raspberry-maple vinaigrette) is complimentary with all entrées. These could include lobster ravioli, tournedos of beef served with Saga blue cheese, roast rack of lamb with Swedish lingonberry demiglaze, and fettuccine napoli with sea scallops ($18–29). Open from the end of May through Columbus Day nightly for dinner 6–10. Reservations are a good idea.

♦ **The Oar** (401-466-8820), West Side Road, New Harbor. This small restaurant with a big deck overlooking the Great Salt Pond used to be a beery hangout for sailors at the nearby marinas. Not so anymore. With its takeover by the Abrams family (of the 1661 Inn and Manisses), its act has been cleaned up and the food is quite good. It's great to watch all the maneuvering of yachts and sailboats as you eat outdoors at one of the umbrellaed tables on the deck, where there's an L-shaped bar in one corner. The all-day menu is nicely balanced with appetizers and sides such as vegetarian chili, beer-battered french fries, rice and beans, and clam chowder. You'll also find club sandwiches (a lobster club at $12.95). Entrées ($8–26) include seafood cakes with corn salsa, fried scallops, grilled swordfish with roasted leek and tomato vinaigrette, and lobsters. Open daily in-season, 11:30 to 11 or midnight.

♦ **The Beachhead** (401-466-2249), Corn Neck Road, Old Harbor. Out by Crescent Beach, this wood building with large front porch for dining—plus a large bar area and inside dining room—is very popular. The location couldn't be better for beachgoers, and if you sit on the porch you can get a view of the dunes across the street and watch the beach traffic. The all-day menu has appetizers like steamed mussels, crabcakes with roasted red pepper and basil mayonnaise, and fried calamari ($7–10). Block Island chowder is a clear-broth Rhode Island version; you can also find chili and lobster bisque. Sesame ginger noodle salad is offered among other salads. The basic burger is always a hit. Or you can get sandwiches like a chicken tarragon salad wrap that was a special when we stopped and delicious. Entrées are on a short list of staples: fried or broiled scallops, clam strips, fish-and-chips, chicken Parmesan ($8–12). A full bar is here. Open daily 11:30–9:30 year-round.

♦ **Finn's Seafood Restaurant** (401-466-2473), Water Street, Old Harbor. Fred and Debbie Howarth have a reputation for serving fresh fish (from the seafood market next door), and this place is especially popular with locals. The restaurant on the lower level is reached directly from the ferry parking lot. The deck upstairs—where both lunch and dinner are served in addition to the main dining room and lower patio—gives you a good view of the action at the dock. A stone outline of Block Island is worked into a brick wall inside, which is about as fancy as things get around here. The fare is uncomplicated. Lobster comes in many sizes up to 3-pounders. Other possibilities are linguine with clam sauce, broiled swordfish, and broiled yellow- or bluefin tuna. Entrées ($10–20) can be ordered with coleslaw and fries or with corn on the cob, salad, and/or baked potato. Fruit pies and something called a chocolate suicide cake are on the dessert menu. The menu hasn't changed much in years. And the restaurant, last we knew, was for sale. Open in-season, Memorial Day through Columbus Day, daily 11:30–9:30.

♦ **Black Rock Café** (401-466-8500), Water Street, Old Harbor. The newest kid on The Block, this café and gourmet grocery is owned by John and Sandra Hopf, with son Bill as the head chef. The best clam chowder on the island, in our opinion, was available here when we stopped for lunch. It was milky and filled with clams and potatoes but not overly thick. People come here for everything from a coffee or cappuccino with muffin or coffee cake to great sandwiches. The Skinny Dipper is avocado, plum tomatoes, alfalfa sprouts, onions, cucumbers, pepper jack cheese, and balsamic vinaigrette on a pita. Sandwiches are $7–9, and everything can be taken out in case you're on your way to beach or the ferry. Three or four entrées are offered in the evening at $8–15. A few small tables are available inside, plus stools at a long counter. Kitchen gadgets and handsome crockery are also on sale here. Open in-season, May to October, daily 7:30 AM–9 PM.

Picnicking

We prefer to picnic at the beach. You can enter the sandy strand from many points along Corn Neck Road leading north from town, beginning just after the bend in the road where there are suddenly small dunes and beach grass. Or you can enter at the main entrance of Fred Benson State Beach with its pavilion and racks for bicycles. There is a snack stand here with drinks, sandwiches, ice cream, and outdoor grills where hot dogs and hamburgers are prepared. The grocery stores in town have provisions. **Three Sisters** and **Black Rock Café** are our choices for take-out.

Another popular spot for picnicking is at the North Light, about a 5-mile bicycle or car ride from town. It's also fun to sit on Payne's Dock in New Harbor, eating a sandwich and watching all the boating action.

12 Monhegan Island, Maine

Until around 1990 Monhegan Island did not have electric power—and it's still not completely electrified. That's just one of the charms for those attracted to the whale-shaped island off the Maine coast. There's incredible variety in its 1-by-2-mile confines. They include the highest cliffs on the Maine coast (160 feet high), deep pine woods, 17 miles of hiking trails, a regular community of artists (Jamie Wyeth owns a house here), a picturesque harbor, and no cars. There's also a good little museum and a good-sized art gallery.

Ironically, it was the inventor Thomas Edison's son, Theodore, who assembled enough property on Monhegan to protect its wild interior. In 1954 he helped organize Monhegan Associates, a nonprofit corporation dedicated to preserving the natural state of the island. Members take charge of the hiking trails, and we've seen them at work, hard work, clearing and opening up the paths that allow for such rewarding experiences and grand views for those hardy enough to hike them.

The lack of cars is particularly surprising to the modern-day tourist. The very few roads are rugged, and the only motorized vehicles are a few lumbering old trucks for transporting supplies from the little wharf and—in summer—luggage for tourists to island hotels or cottages. Although a generator now supplies electricity to those who opt for it, some cottages (especially of summer-only residents) do without. The dining room of one of the three major island hostelries serves meal by candlelight. *Low-key* is practically an overstatement.

Lying 10 miles east of the mainland, Monhegan was known to Europeans as early as the 1400s and to Native Americans probably long before that. The island attracted a small regular community of dwellers before the Pilgrims arrived at Plymouth. When explorer John Cabot stopped by in 1497, Monhegan was already well known as a rest stop and repair center for fishermen from Europe. Verrazano, the Italian navigator, made several references to the island in his notes of 1524.

In 1605 Captain George Weymouth of England anchored offshore long enough for his crew to collect fresh water and for the captain to perform a flag and cross-raising ceremony for the benefit of the British Crown. Other explorers

A cottage on Monhegan Island

of the New England coast, including Bartholomew Gosnold, Samuel de Champlain, and Captain John Smith, also dropped anchor. Smith stayed long enough in 1614 to build several ships and plant a garden. Later residents of Monhegan erected a bronze plaque in his honor. It was dedicated in 1914 (on the tercentenary of his visit) and can be seen near the wood-frame schoolhouse at one end of the village.

Permanent settlement began by 1619 and continued to the end of the 17th century, when the island was abandoned for nearly 100 years, prompted initially by the French and Indian War. Monhegan later revived, and while other larger coastal ports in Maine and Massachusetts now overshadow its prominence as a fishing site, it is an island to which visitors, especially artists, are drawn. Sketchers first came to the island in the mid–19th century, and Monhegan has a reputation among artists exceeding that of any other island off the coast of New England. Rockwell Kent spent years here.

Monhegan is one of just 14 true island communities left on more than 4,000 Maine islands. At the turn of the past century, nearly 300 were populated. Lobstering is the prime occupation of year-rounders. The lobster season lasts from early December to late June, and the lobster traps are piled high all over the village in summer. A 3-mile offshore perimeter marks the Monhegan Lobster Conservation Area and protects it for the local guys.

These days about 70 hardy individuals form the year-round population. Most recently there were five school-aged children attending the island school, for which a full-time instructor is brought in. Some 200 summer residents augment the year-round population, several of them artists who stay the season. Then there are the vacationers and day-trippers who take the ferry from one of three ports in Maine: Boothbay Harbor, New Harbor on Pemaquid, and Port Clyde.

Frankly, a few hours on the island (all that day-trippers can manage) is not enough to get a real taste. Monhegan's magic needs time to sink in. Serious walkers and hikers love the early morning and often get out for their constitutionals before the sun is fully up. Artists sometimes have easels set up by 6 AM to catch a certain light. During the day, it may be possible to peer over a shoulder to see how a painting is coming along or to stop at one of nearly 20 resident artists' studios, each of which is open at least a few hours each week, to view work and talk with the creator. There's a small beach for swimming, called Swim Beach, although the water's usually too cold for mortals (one very hot July day only little kids were braving it).

In the evening, after the last boat has left for the mainland, the island's serenity sinks in. It is then that you might sit on one of the rocking chairs of the long harbor-facing porch of The Island Inn, watching the few boats bob up and down on the waters between Monhegan and smaller, uninhabited Manana Island. The latter is a high rounded hulk just across the way that helps form the harbor. It was once the residence of a local hermit, Ray Phillips, who raised sheep and rowed over to the main island now and then for supplies. You can take a late-day walk up the short but steep road to the hilltop lighthouse for a marvelous view of the whole village below and later enjoy a leisurely dinner at one of a handful of dining rooms on the island.

Monhegan Island, Maine

Eastern Duck Rock

Middle Duck Rock

Western Duck Rock

Gulf of Maine

Green Point

Pebble Beach

Pulpit Rock

Seal Ledges

Cliff - 1

Fern Glen - 17

Pebble Beach - 14

Cliff - 1

Evergreen - 15

Station Hill - 18

Cliff - 1A

Deadmans Cove

Blackhead - 10

Blackhead

Nigh Duck

Ice Pond

Cathedral Woods - 11

Squeaker Cove

Red Ribbon - 9

Long Swamp - 12

Cliff - 1

Shining Sails B&B

Little Whitehead

The Island Inn

Lighthouse & Museum

Whitehead - 7

1A

Manana Is.

North End Market

Alder - 6

1A

White Head

Monhegan House

Gull Cove - 5

Trailing Yew

Burnthead - 4

Gull Cove

Monhegan Harbor

Lobster Cove Rd.

Underhill - 3

Burnthead

Lobster Cove

Cliff - 1

Gull Rock

Christmas Cove

Nortons Ledge

ATLANTIC OCEAN

Washer Woman

N

1/2 MILE

Paul Woodward, © 2003 The Countryman Press

Getting There

Passenger ferry is the only way to get to Monhegan—there is no airport. Three companies provide daily service in summer. The only year-round ferry service is that from Port Clyde. **From Port Clyde, Maine. The Monhegan Boat Line** (207-372-8848; fax 207-372-8547; www.monhegan-boat.com) operates two boats, the *Laura B.* and the *Elizabeth Ann*, providing three trips total each day from July 1 until just after Labor Day. From May through October, there is daily service, but it's sometimes only one or two boats a day and—in stormy weather—perhaps none. From November through April, there's service on Monday, Wednesday, and Friday, leaving Port Clyde at 9:30 AM and returning immediately to the mainland. The trip takes about an hour. Adults, $27 round-trip, $16 one-way. Children, $14 round-trip.

The little dock on Monhegan

From New Harbor, Maine. Hardy Boat Cruises (207-677-2026; 1-800-2-PUF-FIN; www.hardyboat.com) runs daily service aboard the *Hardy III* from mid-June through September, leaving New Harbor at 9 AM and returning from Monhegan at 3:15 PM. Round-trip fare is $27 for adults, $15 for children. Pay half for one-way fares. The trip takes a little more than an hour.

From Boothbay Harbor, Maine. The *Balmy Days II* (207-633-2284; www.anchorwatch.com/balmydays) provides daily service from late May to early October, departing from Boothbay at 9:30 AM and from Monhegan at 2:45 PM. The trip takes 85 minutes each way. Adults, round-trip $30, one-way $18. Children, round-trip $19. Half-hour cruises around the island—for a bargain $2 a head—are offered at 2 PM daily and are well worth it.

For More Information

Check out the web site: www.monhegan.com. You can also get information through one of the island hotels or the **Rockland-Thomaston Area Chamber of Commerce** (207-596-0376; 1-800-562-2529).

Monhegan is up and running for tourists from late spring until Columbus Day weekend, generally speaking. The three larger island hotels/inns (The Island Inn, The Monhegan House, and The Trailing Yew) are open from the end of May until October. If you have a hankering to be on the island in winter, Shining Sails

B&B is open year-round. The high season here is definitely July and August. But because this is such a relaxed and small place, Monhegan never seems overcrowded. And while air-conditioning is virtually unheard of on the island, the breezes can almost always be counted on to make Monhegan at least 10 degrees cooler than the mainland.

Packing. Because of the rough nature of only dirt roads and paths, bring low-heeled shoes. Sneakers, boat shoes, and hiking boots are best. Backpacks are useful, as are walking sticks or poles. Also, note that there's no resident physician on the island, nor a drugstore. Make sure you have enough of your medications with you. There *is* an ambulance and also an emergency medical team.

Facilities (or lack thereof). No bank operates on the island, although there is an ATM machine at the Barnacle, the small café near the wharf. Bring cash or personal checks; many places don't accept credit cards. The only public toilet facilities on the island are "pay toilets" in a small building behind the Monhegan House in the center of the island. You put your donation into an iron pipe. The last time we were over, we used these facilities on two different days and found them unacceptable—no toilet paper, no paper towels, wastebaskets full to overflowing. Monhegan needs better public rest rooms.

Smoking is strictly prohibited outside the village. The threat of a fire ever looms.

Attitudes. Monhegan has a love-hate relationship with visitors, although summer-long residents and serious artists are well accepted. An article in the July 2001 issue of *National Geographic* magazine about Monhegan was titled "Welcome to Monhegan Island, Maine. Now Please, Go Away." An outdoor message board at the Carina store—the most complete general store on the island and quite a sophisticated one at that—loves to pull tourists' legs. BEWARE OF BEARS, read one message. Another time, BEWARE OF LOCALS. Take it in the good spirit it's meant and you'll do fine.

WHAT TO SEE AND DO

Major activities are hiking, painting, reading, eating, visiting artists' studios, and, to a great extent, sitting and contemplating the sea. It is everywhere. No trail bikes may be used on Monhegan's hiking trails; bikes and strollers are strictly confined to the village. Be sure to pick up the small pamphlet *A Visitor's Guide to Monhegan Island, Maine* for a list of activities and rules and regulations.

The Trails

"Monhegan is a fragile, wild, beautiful island cherished for generations by artists, writers and nature lovers," begins the official Monhegan Associates Trail Map brochure. You need this piece of literature if you plan to hike at all on the island. It's available free or for a nominal fee in many places on the island or at the boat terminals. Even at that, the map and descriptions of walks can be tricky to follow. Outside of the village are roughly 17 miles of hiking trails, all named and numbered and varying in character. The trails are on the natural surface of the land—soil, rocks, grass, mud—and can be sometimes wet and often steep. Picking or uprooting any plants or mosses is strictly prohibited. If you plan to picnic during your hike, you must carry your supplies in and out.

On the "back side" of the island, away from the harbor, are the high cliffs. These are dramatic and beautiful, and there is a Cliff Trail that circumnavigates the island with many fine views of the crashing sea. It is *very dangerous* to go anywhere near the edge. Stay well back from the high-water mark on lower rocks since the "black rocks" are often very slippery and—were you to fall into the sea—you'd have an almost impossible time trying to climb out. The Cliff Trail isn't too difficult between Lobster Cove and Burnthead (we've done it twice), but there are very tricky sections at other points. Ask around.

Other popular trails include Cathedral Woods, with pine-needle-strewn paths under high fir trees. It can be dark and buggy depending on the season, but this trail is a favorite with all ages. Burnthead is the easiest route from the village to a panoramic view of the sea from a 140-foot headland. After you've climbed a short hill from the village, it's mostly flat meadowland until you reach the ocean, and only about a 20-minute walk.

Members of Monhegan Associates maintain the trails, but the trail map is deceptively simple looking. You can lose your way if you're not very careful. We have.

A popular destination is the walk from the village to Lobster Cove to see the wreck of the ship *D. T. Sheridan*. This isn't difficult—on a wide dirt road—and everyone seems to like to photograph the wreck.

Other trail highlights include Squeaker Cove, where you stand on rocks above a churning sea; Gull Cove, where you view the headlands from sea level; Whitehead, which gives a wonderful panorama on a clear day; and Pulpit Rock, an unusual rock formation.

Artists and Studios

Every year a list is printed of the artists in residence for much or all of the summer. It includes a simple map locating their studios and listing times when they welcome visitors. My daughter and I had a charming visit once with Sylvia Murdock, a watercolorist and oil painter who has been coming to Monhegan for nearly 20 years and who told us she is largely self-taught. Audrey had been doing a watercolor of the cliffs in fog, and Sylvia was most generous in spending time to comment constructively on the work. Her studio is just off the Burnthead Trail and easy to get to. On another occasion, my husband and I visited Fred Wiley in his studio on the main road. He does fine oils and watercolors and has lived year-round on Monhegan for many years.

The Lighthouse

At the top of a short but steep hill, the lighthouse was built in 1824, and although its beacon still shines it has not been manned since 1959. You can't go up into the light, but from the site you have a great view of the village, the harbor, Manana Island, and—on a clear day—the mainland, including the Camden hills. Benches are thoughtfully provided. The big bell outside the buildings was the predecessor

The village on Monhegan as seen from the lighthouse. Manana Island is visible to the rear.

to the island foghorn and was on Manana Island. Now there's a solar-operated foghorn on the island.

The Monhegan Historical and Cultural Museum

Housed in the former keeper's house on the lighthouse grounds, recently added to the National Register of Historic Places. It is truly worth a stop. You'll find an interesting and expansive collection of island memorabilia—including old paper dolls played with by island children, Christmas cards designed by island artists, and a room devoted to fishing and lobstering. There's an exhibit of the "touch me" sort on the sea that appeals to children. You will also see displays of island flora, birds (Monhegan is on the Eastern Flyway), ecology, and history. There's a special exhibit on Ray Phillips, the recluse who lived on Manana Island for many years. Across the grassy area from the main museum is a restored assistant lighthouse keeper's house with a terrific large art gallery. Every year a show is mounted honoring one of the many artists who have worked on Monhegan. Catalogs are sometimes printed. The donation for the museum is $3. Except for a director and assistant, the museum is staffed by eager volunteers. P.S. There are new public rest rooms at this museum, open during museum hours. Open July through September, daily 11:30–3:30.

The Monhegan Library

Take a left after getting to the main road of the village from the ferry dock. The library will be on your right in a small frame building. In its collection are several histories of the island, an extensive 1992 land-use survey of Monhegan, fiction, nonfiction, and children's books. It's open to all. Summer hours are Tuesday, Thursday, and Saturday 1–4, and Monday, Wednesday, and Friday evenings. It's a great little spot.

The harbor at Monhegan Island

Boat Trips

You may have had enough boating on the ferry ride over. However, **Hardy Boat Cruises** (207-677-2026; 1-800-2-PUFFIN) offers "Monhegan Puffin Watch" trips between May and mid-August three times weekly. These 2-hour trips take passengers to Eastern Egg Rock, about 5 miles away, where the puffin colony is. Recently up to 50 puffins have been nesting here. They leave around the middle of August. Call ahead to check the schedule and make a reservation. Adults $12, children $8.

If you'd like to be ferried across the harbor to visit Manana Island (perhaps to look back at Monhegan to photograph or paint it, or just to walk up to the top of this "submerged mountain"), you can. Hire a young boy or girl from the village to take you over in a rowboat. They charge $5 or so one-way. Ask at your hotel or at one of the general stores.

Fish Beach

Clustered around this beach in the village are the fish houses that serve as workshops for many of those who fish and lobster. You may be amazed by the height of lobster pot piles along the main road. There are about 15 full-time lobstermen on the island who are active in-season.

Swim Beach

This small strand is considered the only safe place to swim on the island. Reached just off the main road, and a part of the harbor, it's famous for its cold water and swift tides. Be sure that someone on the beach knows you're swimming—if you dare.

The Meadow

In the heart of the village is a meadow that serves as the site of the public water supply via underground springs. People used to see deer browsing here, but the entire deer heard on Monhegan had to be eliminated due to concerns about Lyme disease, carried by the deer tick.

The Bulletin Board

Next to the meadow is the rope shed that serves as a bulletin board for island activities. Everything of note is posted here. A folk concert was being held at the schoolhouse (the site of many activities) one evening while we were in town; a sculpture and porcelain show was scheduled the day after we had to leave. Lectures are sponsored throughout the summer, as are other musical or cultural events. Regularly scan for information. You may find a whimsical announcement or two, as well.

The Ice Pond

In back of and not far from the schoolhouse is the old ice pond. Although the last harvest of ice was in 1974, the pond is an excellent spot for bird-watching and a favorite skating area in winter. Ice cutting was a major island industry for many years.

The Monhegan Church

This nondenominational gray wood church sits in the center of the village. It is surprisingly large and attractive in a simple, New England way. An overhead light fixture, which still uses kerosene, has been maintained even though the church now has electricity. In winter an island touring minister comes once a month for a service (he or she travels to other islands as well). In summer there is usually a Sunday-morning service arranged by the summer community with visiting clergy. This is a lovely place to sit quietly. Many clergy are Episcopalian, but other denominations are welcome, too. Monhegan maintains it was the first New World site of an Anglican service—in 1608.

Harbor Seals

Harbor seals may be seen best at half tide on some of the Duck Rocks near the Pebble Beach area (check your trail map).

Shopping

There's not a lot. **The Lupine Gallery** represents Monhegan and coastal Maine artists and has a beautiful array of works for sale. The book *Monhegan, the Artists' Island*, by Jane and Will Curtis and Frank Lieberman, is available here and is a treasure. An oversized softbound book, it has beautiful color reproductions of many of the artworks made on Monhegan as well as a fine history of the island. You can buy art directly from artists in their studios, and you often see pieces packed and going back on the ferries. **Winter Works** is an attractive small gift shop on the road leading from the ferry dock where items made by Monhegan residents are sold. These include sweaters, hats, T-shirts, jewelry, notecards, and the like. Hours are a bit casual, but during the season this shop is usually open afternoons. **Carina,** the store in the weathered building with pink trim, carries books by island poets and writers as well as other reading; wine and beer (you have to take your own to island restaurants); daily newspapers (including that day's *Boston Globe* and *New York Times*), and picnic supplies. You can also get coffee and pastries early; the place is open by 6. The **Duck Trap** is a gift shop with all sorts of items you might like to take home as mementos, although many are made off-island.

WHERE TO STAY

There's a limited choice. This is another reason the island is so special. It's simply not overrun with tourists. Make reservations well in advance.

♦ **The Island Inn** (207-596-0371; fax 207-594-5517; www.islandinnmonhegan.com), Box 128, Monhegan Island, ME 04852. Our favorite is certainly this large white inn with dormered roof and a cupola with a flag flying from the top. It overlooks the harbor and is closest to the ferry landing. Englishman Philip Truelove and American Howard Weilbacker are partners in the venture, and since taking over in the mid-1990s they've been upgrading nicely. Krista Lisajus is the helpful front desk manager. There are 33 accommodations in all: 27 simple summery rooms and suites on the second and third floors of the main building, and 4 rooms plus 2 suites in the Pierce Cottage next door. Seven rooms and two suites in the main inn have private bath, as do the two suites in the Pierce Cottage. The rest share baths. Pierce Cottage suites have a queen bed, a separate living room, and a bathroom with stall shower. If you want a tub, choose a suite in the main inn. Our room, on the second floor of the inn, shared baths—which we found not to be a problem, because there were two large bathrooms directly across the hall, each with stall shower and lots of room for changing clothes. Also, our room had its own sink, a real plus. We slept in twin beds pushed together and covered with puffy white duvets. A painted floor, built-in pine closets and sink enclosure, and plenty of counter space were appealing features. White tieback curtains at the window, overlooking the harbor, gave a real summery feeling.

The long porch with rockers on the front of the inn, plus Adirondack chairs scattered around the lawn, gives everyone plenty of opportunity to view the harbor and ferry dock activity. There are no TVs, phones, or air-conditioners. Breakfast is included and served in a large, airy dining room with water view. Choices included cinnamon brioche French toast and inn-made granola. The inn has a truck to take luggage up the short hill to its door. The dining room here is terrific (see *Where to Eat*) and serves all three meals. Doubles with breakfast, $120–185; suites, $105–250. Open Memorial Day weekend through Columbus Day weekend. Credit cards accepted.

♦ **The Trailing Yew** (207-596-0440; 1-800-592-2520), Monhegan Island, ME 04852. Named for a ground-creeping type of juniper, this is a group of four large houses and a private cabin (with its own bathroom facilities) for a total of 37 rooms spread over a hillside. The complex is off the one main road leading from the village toward Lobster Cove. It isn't a terribly long walk, but it's about the farthest of the major accommodations from the wharf where the boats arrive. A truck transports your luggage up and back. Most room share baths—an average of five rooms per bath—and furnishings are rustic. White Adirondack chairs are set about the grounds, and you're apt to see flowers planted in old tree stumps. There's a flag in the center of the grassy area and a horseshoe pit. While one full building and all bathrooms are electrified here, the dining room is not. Candlelight dinners—served family-style at large tables in two large dining rooms—are part of the deal. Typical rooms have double or twin beds with chenille bedspreads and wood-paneled walls. No TVs, phones, or air-conditioning are available. Those who stay here must take breakfast and dinner on the premises. When there's room, the public can make reservations for dinner (see *Where to Eat*). This is a little like camp, and the group staying here gets to know one another easily. Sometimes whole groups of artists or writers taking workshops will bunk in here. Guests are told to bring flashlights to get around after dark, and sleeping bags in spring or fall since there is no heat. The Trailing Yew definitely has its devotees—many of them—but it's not for everyone.

Rates are per person, per day, and include breakfast and dinner. Adults $64, children 12 and under $10–55, depending on age. Taxes and gratuities are included. No credit cards. Open from mid-May to mid-October.

♦ **Monhegan House** (207-594-7983; 1-800-599-7983; fax 207-596-6472), Monhegan Island, ME 04852. This big brown weathered building is right in the middle of the village. It's directly across from the church and next to the Burnthead Trail, leading to a great view of the ocean. The hotel isn't on the water, but it's high enough that some upper-level guest rooms have water views. Open since 1870, the Monhegan House had new owners, Holden and Susan Nelson, in 2001. A welcoming lobby has a huge stone fireplace that gets lighted in the chilly season. All 33 rooms on the four floors (top-floor rooms are singles) share a bathroom annex on the second floor. Here are several different spaces, some with toilet only, some with sink, some with shower. Rooms have double or twin beds, pressed-oak furniture, pastel walls, and white bedspreads. They are basic but functional. The hotel has electricity. The Monhegan Café is a full-service restaurant located along one side of the building with a wall of windows looking out toward the center of the island. It serves three meals a day. No meals are included in rates. Open Memorial Day through Columbus Day. Doubles, $99–105, EP. Credit cards are honored.

♦ **Shining Sails Guesthouse** (207-596-0041; fax 207-596-7166; www.shiningsails. com), Box 346, Monhegan Island, ME 04852. This weathered house off the lane leading from the ferry dock—and with great water views from most of its accommodations—is a B&B with two guest rooms (both with private bath) and six efficiencies (one studio and five one-bedroom apartments). Room 5 is a one-bedroom apartment with queen bed, gas fireplace, and great view. Our unit had a wonderful little wood deck with table and four chairs off the kitchen/sitting room where we could enjoy the breezes and the ocean view. There was a queen-bedded bedroom, a pullout sofa in the sitting area, and a bathroom with a cedar-lined shower stall. All accommodations can be rented on a short-term basis or for longer periods. Shining Sails is open year-round.

Continental breakfast comes with all accommodations, including the efficiencies, which is a plus. It's served in the large common room of the inn, a pleasant space you step down into. The room has a large wood dining table, sofas, comfortable chairs, and other places to settle. For breakfast there's a choice of juices and hot beverages, a bowl of fruit, cereal, and bagels. One day there was also a basket of home-baked muffins. Owners John and Winnie Murdock have been island residents for more than 25 years and are experts on island activities. John is also a lobsterman. And they handle cottage rentals on a weekly or longer basis. Doubles, $80–95; efficiencies and one-bedroom apartments, $100–130.

Cottage rentals. At least 25 cottages are available to rent for a week or longer. They vary in size, price, and amenities, and some do not have electricity. Weekly rentals range $600–2,000 (for a three-bedroom cottage on the waterfront). **Shining Sails Rentals** (207-596-0041) handles most of these.

WHERE TO EAT

The three main inns are all open to the public for dinner. The Island Inn and Monhegan House also serve breakfast and lunch. There are a couple of other casual eating options such as **The Barnacle** at the ferry dock where coffee, pastries, and baked goods and sandwiches are available. Inns and restaurants do not serve liquor, but you're welcome to bring your own. You can pick up alcoholic beverages at **Carina** or **North End Market,** or bring them from home.

♦ **The Island Inn** (207-596-0371). The dining room at The Island Inn is the best on Monhegan. It's also a very pleasant, large, and breezy space with windows along both ocean and island sides. Tablecloths are white, topped with blue-plaid overcloths for breakfast. There are light maple captain's chairs. Small bouquets of flowers are on each table. It has a good summery feeling. The food is far more sophisticated than you might first expect. For dinner you can start with a chunky lobster bisque (yes, real lobster chunks), tuna and shrimp on a skewer over a bed of sautéed veggies, or a hot spinach dip with tortilla chips. Lobster pie has huge pieces of the crustacean. Have a salad such as wilted spinach with red onion, plum tomato and chopped egg tossed with warm bacon vinaigrette dressing, or perhaps a Caesar salad with garlic croutons. Several pasta and vegetarian entrées are offered—possibly tricolored tortellini with diced tomato, cream, mozzarella, and Parmesan cheese, or grilled eggplant with ratatouille served with a tomato basil sauce. Boiled lobster is always available. We found the blackened swordfish with dirty rice delicious. You can also get grilled filet mignon or haddock. Dinner entrées, $17–24. There's a $3-per-bottle corkage fee for wine. At lunchtime try items like lobster stew, salads, and sandwiches. Breakfasts offer a full range of items. All three meals are offered daily.

♦ **The Trailing Yew** (207-596-0440). Family-style dining at painted wood tables with fresh flowers and lots of colorful crockery is fun. The dinner bell rings at 5:45—partly to take advantage of the light, because there's no electric power. Tall white candles burn on each of several tables. We were placed in a group of six— two other "outsiders" and a couple who were overnight guests. Two entrée choices are offered—ocean catfish or roast lamb the night we dined here. The full-course, prix fixe dinner started with pea soup (rated "just okay" by the crowd), a mixed salad with vinaigrette dressing, the entrée with peas and a baked potato, and a choice of dessert—blueberry pie or cantaloupe. But for the price and the conversation—which was terrific—who can go wrong? Entrées, $17, except lobster, which is $27. This is a campy, fun place to eat. You can usually stop by to make a reservation the morning of the day you want to dine here. No credit cards.

♦ **Monhegan House** (207-594-7983). This long, narrow dining room has high-backed blue Victorian chairs and tables marching down one side of the room next to the windows plus a few other tables on the other side. There is an Old World feeling here. Breakfast, lunch, and dinner are available to houseguests and the general public. Lunch choices ($8–11) include a cheeseburger, lobster roll, baked stuffed sole with Newburg sauce, and turkey club sandwich. For dinner you might have stir-fried chicken, pan-fried steak *au poivre*, baked haddock, or char-broiled salmon (all served with bread, salad, vegetable, and starch) for $15–24. Open nightly from 5:30. Credit cards are accepted.

♦ **The Barnacle** at the wharf is a great little café run by The Island Inn. Scrumptious sandwiches and pastries, café lattes and cappuccinos, iced teas and fruit drinks are all to be found here. Soups and good salads that can be eaten here or taken out and eaten back at your room, efficiency, or cottage are also available. Open daily in-season 7 AM–8 PM.

♦ **The North End Market and North End Pizza.** This is a good little store where you can pick up cold drinks, bottles of cold water for hiking, sandwiches or sandwich makings, basic provisions, and take-out pizza. There's a picnic table nearby where, if you're lucky, you might eat it as well.

Lake Sunapee, New Hampshire

Sunapee is a lovely lake, its irregular shoreline creating many picturesque bays and harbors. At 1,100 feet above sea level, the 9-by-3-mile lake is so clean that it's the source of drinking water in the area.

Several islands dot the surface, the largest of them—Great Island—having 22 summer cottages. But for all its beauty and desirability, Lake Sunapee and the nearby town of New London were once much busier as a tourist destination than today. Six steamboats at one time—in the late 1800s and early 1900s—took hundreds of passengers from Boston, New York, and other eastern hubs to large summer hotels around the lake. People stayed for weeks. Not one of these hotels remains today. Instead, the shoreline is almost entirely given over to private cottages and homes, only 20 percent of them used as year-round residences by owners.

Lake Sunapee and a few nearby smaller lakes—Little Lake Sunapee and Pleasant Lake in the tony town of New London, and Kezar Lake in rural North Sutton, for example—comprise a low-key resort and retirement area. The area contrasts strongly with the more commercial "fun and games" atmosphere of New Hampshire's biggest lake, Winnipesaukee. You won't find theme parks, water slides or outlet stores, huge hotels or late-night goings-on here. About as wild as it gets of a summer evening in New London is going to dinner and a show—usually a musical—produced at the decades-old summer theater, the Barn Playhouse.

Sunapee Harbor is perfectly charming if a little hard to find (it's reached off Route 11 on the west side of the lake, but signs are small). It, too, is low-key. You'll find a lakefront restaurant (the only one directly on the lake), a few small, individual gift shops, a very local history museum, a gazebo and bandstand, and a town beach. The lawn of a waterside town park is manicured, the flower beds tended. A modest-sized cruise boat , the M.V. *Sunapee*, takes visitors on narrated tours of the lake in-season. A second boat offers buffet dinner cruises.

The Lake Sunapee area is quite decentralized with small towns—even tiny villages—popping up as you drive the winding mountain roads. These include New London, the largest; Newbury, Georges Mills, Sutton Mills, North and South Sutton,

Sailing is a favorite activity on Lake Sunapee

Bradford, and Warner. Two major peaks—Mount Sunapee at the southern end of the lake, and Mount Kearsarge several miles to its northeast—dominate the skyline. Driving around, you head up and down long, hilly grades as the clouds cast shadows on the mountain ranges. Like small jewels of blue, the lakes sparkle among them.

The word *Sunapee* was taken from the Native American *Soonipi*—meaning "landing place of the wild goose." White settlers came to the area in the 1770s, many of them during or just after the Revolutionary War. These towns often harnessed the power of mountain streams for saw- and gristmills. Sutton Mills, a picturesque spot today, was settled by Moses Quimby in 1773, and had both types of mills. The last one closed in 1939. Georges Mills at the north end of Lake Sunapee was another mill town.

New London is the largest town in the region. It is home to pretty Colby Sawyer College, whose redbrick buildings overlook Main Street (Route 11). Along this main route are the restaurants, shops, and commercial establishments of a town with year-round vibrancy. Retirees have established themselves in attractive condominium complexes as well as beautiful old homes. College kids, families, and businesspeople work, live, and play here.

While these lakes are at their best and busiest in summer, when boaters, swimmers, and holiday seekers enjoy their charms, autumn is spectacularly beautiful. Country innkeepers light fires in big old lobby fireplaces, and breakfasts get heartier. Foliage is brilliant and the scenery can take your breath away. The first snow cranks up the large downhill ski area, Mount Sunapee, as well as a couple of good cross-country ski centers nearby. Spring comes late.

Sunapee appeals for its understated charms. Most lodging establishments and restaurants are comfortably sized, shops small and select, and diversions personal and accessible. For the weekender with a desire to "get away from it all," this is one place to do so.

Getting There

I-89 is the major route to and through the region, with access from I-91 in the Lebanon area, or from I-93 in Concord (the route from Manchester and Boston). Hartford is south via I-91, about 2½ hours away. Boston is less than 2 hours from Lake Sunapee.

The closest major **airport** is located at Manchester, New Hampshire, served by several major carriers. **Vermont Transit** (800-451-3292) has **buses** daily to New London from Boston.

For More Information

Contact the **New London–Lake Sunapee Region Chamber of Commerce** (603-526-6575; 1-877-526-6575; www.lakesunapeenh.org) or the **Newport Chamber of Commerce** (603-863-1510). Pick up the *Kearsarge Shopper,* available weekly at supermarkets, drugstores, post offices, and the like for the latest information on events and activities in the area.

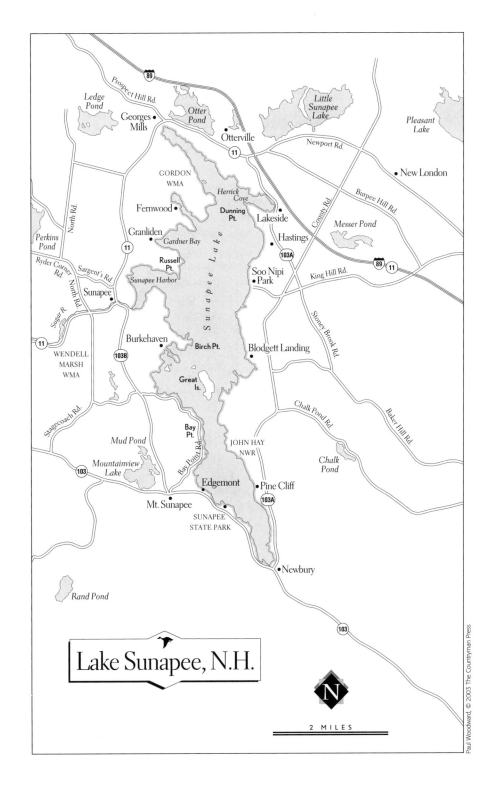

Lake Sunapee, N.H.

2 MILES

Paul Woodward, © 2003 The Countryman Press

Getting Around

Once here, you really need a car. The area consists of far-flung towns on mountainous terrain. Only bikers in excellent condition should attempt biking the region.

On and Near Lake Sunapee

The lake is the prime attraction, for it's the largest in the area and the most active. It is also somewhat frustrating to view, for no road follows the perimeter closely and virtually all the property—except for Sunapee State Park—is privately owned. Therefore, it's a good idea to get out on the lake via private boat or on an excursion tour. Sunapee Harbor is fun to prowl around, and Mount Sunapee State Park offers a wide sandy beach, play equipment for little kids, and rest rooms.

◆ **M.V. *Mount Sunapee* II** (603-763-4030; www.sunapeecruises.com), P.O. Box 345, Sunapee, NH 03782. This comfortable tour boat with an open upper deck operates 1½-hour cruises with live narration by the captain (ours thought he was a comedian, but we enjoyed it). It's a great way to get out onto the lake, to learn a little about its history and particularities, and to see the islands and private homes along the shore. Some are quite extravagant—mansions really—but most are not. We learned that the lake has one area that is 110 feet deep. There are three small lighthouses. Fishing is good for landlocked salmon and lake trout. The lake is spring-fed and clear as glass. Tours from mid-May to mid-June and from Labor Day to mid-October are offered at 2:30 PM on Saturday and Sunday. From mid-June to Labor Day, two tours a day operate, one at 10 AM, the other at 2:30 PM. Adults $12, children $7.

◆ **Dinner cruises** are offered daily in summer aboard the **M.V. *Kearsarge*** (603-763-4030). On Monday the dinner cruise leaves at 5:30 PM; Tuesday through Sunday two cruises are offered, at 5:30 and 7:45 PM. A buffet is provided, with carved beef, perhaps chicken, various salads and hot dishes, and a choice of desserts. Cocktails and wine are available at an extra cost. $26 per person. Call for reservations.

Sunapee Harbor. The charming harbor area—reminiscent of a seaside fishing village—slopes down to the water off Route 11 on the west side of the lake. Here are found **The Anchorage,** the only true lakeside restaurant on Sunapee (see *Where to Eat*); a waterfront town park with small sandy beach; a parking area, some shops, and a museum. The gazebo/bandstand on the hill above the harbor is used for concerts in summer. A delicatessen across from the water has breakfast, lunch, and ice cream cones. There's a public boat launch. **Sunapee Water Sports and Marine** (603-763-4030) has kayak and canoe rentals and sales.

◆ **Sunapee Historical Association Museum** (603-763-4418), Sunapee Harbor. An old stable has been turned into a local history museum with a range of goodies—from the pilot house of the steamer *Kearsarge* that you and the kids can step into, to photographs and postcards of Lake Sunapee's Victorian heyday as a resort. There's a dugout canoe dating from around 1800 and brought up from the bottom of the

The tour boat *M.V. Mount Sunapee II* prepares to board

lake, an old milk wagon, a raketooth machine, and a hot-air engine used to pump water from the lake into a cottage owner's reservoir. It's all somewhat disorganized, but fun. Open mid-June through Labor Day, Tuesday and Thursday through Sunday 1–4 PM; Wednesday, 7–9 PM. Donation.

♦ **The Fells** (603-763-4789; www.thefells.org), Route 103A, Lake Sunapee, Newbury, NH 03255. The John Hay National Wildlife Refuge is spread along 3 miles of lake frontage of Lake Sunapee. The big white house on the property was the summer home of American writer and diplomat John Hay. He served as private secretary to Abraham Lincoln, ambassador to Great Britain, and was secretary of state under Presidents William McKinley and Theodore Roosevelt. Roosevelt visited in 1902; the room he stayed in is pointed out on the short tours of the house offered on weekends and holidays between Memorial Day and Columbus Day. Unfortunately the furniture was sold at auction; rooms are bare except for the library, where a few copies of the original books fill floor-to-ceiling shelves.

It's the property that's important here. With gorgeous gardens, trails, and plantings, the site is jointly owned by the U.S. Fish and Wildlife Service and the Society for the Protection of New Hampshire Forests. Emphasis is on appreciating the flora and fauna via streamside nature trails, gardens, and woodlands. The gift shop is small but quite nice. Special events—such as Hay Day in June—are occasionally scheduled. Open daily, year-round, dawn to dusk. Adults $3, children $1.

♦ **Sunapee State Park** (603-263-4642), Route 103, Newbury. Open mid-May to mid-June on weekends, and daily from mid-June through Labor Day. Lifeguard on duty in summer only. A lovely sandy beach with grassy area, picnic tables, a snack bar, rest rooms, and a changing facility. Fee.

Around the Region

Elsewhere in the area you can pursue a variety of activities, with the emphasis on the out-of-doors.

♦ **Mount Sunapee Resort** (603-763-2356; www.mtsunapee.com), Route 103, Newbury. The mountain is in full gear in winter, but it's a pretty pleasant place in summer, too. Several trails are great for hiking—particularly those that lead to **Lake Solitude,** a beautiful little jewel on the backside of the mountain. In summer an **in-line skate park** operates daily from the end of June to Labor Day, and weekends in late spring and early fall. The cost is $5 for 1 hour; $10 for 5 hours; and $12 for a full day. Hours are 10–5. **Sky rides** to the summit are always offered on the weekend of the big **crafts fair** (See *A Special Event*) and on foliage weekends in fall. They are available on some other selected weekends. (If you take the sky ride, the walk to Lake Solitude is less than a mile.) Trails are closed to mountain biking.

♦ **Skiing and skateboarding** are offered at Mount Sunapee between November and April. An all-day adult weekend lift ticket is $49. Seniors 65 and older pay $33. The resort has invested several millions in new lifts, trails, and a new base lodge recently. It's operated by the same company that operates Okemo Mountain in Vermont.

Museums

♦ **Mount Kearsarge Indian Museum** (603-456-2600), Kearsarge Mountain Road, Warner. Open May through October, Monday through Saturday 10–5, Sunday noon–5. This museum is a find, the collection of one man—Bud Thompson— who fell in love with Native American lore and artifacts as a young boy. He bought a former indoor riding arena and converted it to display the excellent pieces he collected over many years. Here are incredibly beautiful baskets made of ash, sweet grass, and honeysuckle vine woven by the Cherokee, Seminole, Penobscot, and Passamaquoddy tribes, among others. There are several different designs of snowshoes, a Hopi wedding vase, dugout canoes of cypress from the Seminoles, and birchbark canoes from northern woods Indians.

Guides take visitors on 45-minute to 1-hour tours because the founder did not want people to miss important concepts by just reading labels. Our guide was excellent, interpreting and explaining the beliefs and lives of Native Americans as she led us from room to room. This would be a wonderful place to take children.

We also enjoyed the walk through the Medicine Woods outdoors—a stone-lined path through a shady grove, with medicinal plants identified for the walker. A printed guide is helpful. In an outdoor garden the museum is experimenting with growing several types of early corn and other plants known to Native Americans. Adults $6.50, seniors $5.50, children $4.50.

♦ **Enfield Shaker Village,** Enfield (see the "Shaker Weekend" chapter).

♦ **Muster Field Farm Museum** (603-927-4081; 603-927-4276; www.musterfield-farm.org), Harvey Road, North Sutton. (Take Route 114 to North Sutton and follow signs.) This mostly outdoor museum includes the childhood home of two brothers, Congressman Jonathan Harvey and New Hampshire governor Matthew Harvey. It's an 18th-century farmhouse listed on the National Register of Historic Places. The house is an example of rural Georgian architecture, little altered from its 1787 appearance. The 250-acre site—on a plateau 200 feet above Lake Kezar—also includes a collection of historic farm buildings and a working farm that produces vegetables, flowers, hay, cordwood, and maple syrup. Special events are scheduled throughout the season such as Harvest Day in fall, when the grounds are open 10–4. The homestead is open Sunday 1–4 in June, July, August, and September. Admission (on event days only) is $4 for adults, $2 for children. The grounds and historic farm buildings are open year-round. Hiking in summer and use of marked cross-country skiing and snowshoeing trails in winter are permitted. The farm stand is open noon–5 in summer.

Hiking

Trails lead up both **Mount Kearsarge** and **Mount Sunapee.** The view from the top of **Mount Kearsarge** is considered one of the most dramatic in New England. Hikers can take a 2-mile trail (the Northside Trail) from Winslow State Park on the northern side of the mountain. Those who want an easier trip can drive up Kearsarge Mountain Road from the center of Warner to Rollins State Park. Here the Northside Trail to the summit takes off from the picnic area and ends on smooth rock ledges—just a half-mile trek. On **Mount Sunapee,** there are several interesting trails. To reach **Lake Solitude,** hikers can take the **Andrew Brook Trail** (just under 2 miles) from a marked trailhead up Mountain Road, off Route 103. The **Summit Trail** is a 2-mile trail beginning on the right side of the Lower Ridge Ski Trail. The **Eagles Nest** is an overlook reached by a short trail off the lower portion of the **Newbury Trail**—it offers an excellent view of Newbury Harbor and Lake Sunapee.

Biking

♦ **Bob Skinner's Ski & Sport** (603-763-2303), at the Mount Sunapee traffic circle, Route 103, Newbury, has bicycles and accessories for sale as well as bike rentals.

♦ **Outspokin' Bicycle & Sport** (603-763-9500), Route 103, Newbury Harbor, has rental bikes.

Golf

♦ **Country Club of New Hampshire** (603-927-4246), Kearsarge Valley Road, North Sutton. An 18-hole championship public golf course and driving range located at the base of Mount Kearsarge. *Golf Digest* called it one of America's 75 best public courses.

Fishing

♦ **Dickie's** (603-938-5393) on Route 103 in South Newbury is a place to buy fishing tackle and to find out where to use it.

Beaches

♦ **Sunapee State Park** off Route 103 in Newbury has an excellent beach on the shores of Lake Sunapee. It's very popular. Less crowded is the beach at **Wadleigh State Park** on Kezar Lake in Sutton, reached from Route 114. There's a bathhouse, a shaded picnic area, and a nice beach with a gentle slope.

Leaf-peeping

Foliage can be exquisite in the Lake Sunapee area. If you get close enough to the water of the many lakes, the reflection of the brilliant trees is marvelous. A famous **Fall Foliage Festival** has been held in the town of Warner for more than 50 years. Usually it's on Columbus Day weekend, and all sorts of events are planned.

Indoor exercise and swimming

♦ **Hogan Sports Center** (603-526-3600) at Colby-Sawyer College in New London —with an indoor pool, fitness center, aerobics room, and walking/jogging track—is open to the public for a use fee. A swim in the pool is $5 per visit. A pass to use the exercise equipment in this new building is $10.

Culture

♦ **New London Barn Playhouse** (603-526-6710), Route 11, New London. This venerable summer theater—dark red wood with white trim—has been entertaining vacationers and area residents for more than 60 years. Most shows are musicals and run for 2 weeks; occasionally a pure comedy is offered. Showtimes are Tuesday through Saturday at 8 PM, Wednesday matinees at 2 PM and Sundays at 5 PM. Evenings $21 or $25 for box seating. Wednesday matinees, $19 adults, $12 kids.

Band concerts take place on Friday evenings at 7 in summer at the Haddad Memorial Bandstand on the common in New London. A variety of visiting bands and groups is scheduled.

Cross-Country Skiing

♦ **Norsk Cross Country Ski & Winter Sports Center** (603-526-4685), Country Club Lane, New London. Cross-country skiing on woodland trails, snowshoeing, tubing, and skating.

Shopping

The **Morgan Hill Bookstore** is a terrific independent bookstore in New London, where you can also buy sheet music, cassettes, and CDs. Elegant sweaters and other sophisticated women's duds—plus some gifts—are found at **The Lemon Twist** in New London. **Artisan's Workshop** at 186 Main Street has a wonderful selection of jewelry, handcrafted scarves, pillows, and other unusual gift items. **Serendipity** in the New London Shopping Center has casual women's clothing, jewelry, gifts, and cards. **Cricenti's** is an upscale supermarket in the same shopping center. **Mesa Pottery** at the Elkins Business Loop off Route 11 is a pottery outlet with items from Europe as well as the United States. The **Dorr Mill Store** between Newport and Sunapee is a bit retro, but has good-quality woolen fabric, blankets, children's items, and some adult clothing. **Priscilla Drake Antiques** is a barn full of furniture, china, glassware, and accessories open in-season on New London's Main Street. The **Deck Dock** in Sunapee Harbor is our favorite store for household decoration, including wreaths, candles and holders, pithy signs (GUESTS OF GUESTS MAY NOT INVITE GUESTS), outdoor fireplaces, dried floral arrangements, all sorts of goodies. You can get penny candy and stuffed animals at **Wild Goose Country Store,** also in Sunapee Harbor.

A SPECIAL EVENT

The annual **League of New Hampshire Craftsmen's Fair** is a weeklong event held annually at Mount Sunapee Resort in Newbury early in August. Hours are 10-5 daily, and admission is $7 adults, $5 seniors, and free to children 12 and under. Exceptional quality can be expected from these juried craftspeople who create items of stained glass, woodenware, quilts, leather, lamps, clothing, and gifts of all sorts.

WHERE TO STAY

Options include small B&Bs, modest-sized inns, and a few motels.

By the Water

◆ **The Follansbee Inn** (603-927-4221; 1-800-626-4221; www.follansbeeinn.com), Route 114, North Sutton, NH 03260. Dave and Cathy Beard were Denver lawyers before taking over this country inn in 1999. They searched from the West to the East Coast before settling on this spot. The combination of small country town, lakeside inn, and year-round appeal proved too much to pass up. The four-story white building with green trim dates from 1840 and has been an inn continually since 1880. Private frontage on Lake Kezar—just across a side road from the inn—has a dock, float, and kayaks, canoes, and rowboats for guest use. Guests swim or sun here. The picnic table beckons for a light lakeside snack or early-evening cocktail. Cathy hands out buckets with neck straps so that—in summer—guests can row over to a small island in the lake and pick blueberries. The inn itself has an old-fashioned feeling. No TVs or room phones, but lots of quilts (one for each bed) and board games. Two first-floor common rooms have fireplaces, and the Beards planned to add some to bedrooms. There are 20 guest rooms on the second and third floors, 16 with private bath. Carpeted halls are unusually wide, and each room

Boats at Sunapee Harbor

has been individually decorated. Personal touches include some family items like Cathy's baby shoes in one bedroom. Two suites, Rebecca and Sarah, have lake views, queen-bedded rooms, and cozy sitting areas under the eaves along with updated bathrooms.

Cathy is the breakfast cook, serving guests at comfortable wood tables with captain's chairs in the dining room. Coffee, tea, juices, and homemade granola are set out buffet-style. Strawberry crêpes, gingerbread waffles, and lobster and asparagus frittatas are among her specialties.

A bicycle built for two is among the bikes available for guest use, and Dave usually points adventuresome sorts toward the 10-mile Valley Trail leading to the summit of Mount Kearsarge. In winter guests can strap on their cross-country skis for a trip across the frozen lake to trails in the nearby state park. Open year-round. Doubles, $110–130 with breakfast; suites, $165.

♦ **The Inn at Pleasant Lake** (603-526-6271; 1-800-626-4907; www.innatpleasant-lake.com), 125 Pleasant Street, New London, NH 03257. Chef-owner Brian MacKenzie, a graduate of the Culinary Institute of America, has made this charming inn with access to Pleasant Lake famous for its dining room (see *Where to Eat*). But he and his wife, Linda, have also given 10 guest rooms—all with private bath— a very personal, and comfortable, feel. The rooms, located on the second and third floors of this steeply gabled white house, have white matelasse spreads on almost all queen beds. Room 4 on the second floor has a king bed, a view of the lake, and an attached sitting room. Four guest rooms have a whirlpool tub; just one has a double bed. On the main floor, in addition to the flagstone-floored dining room, are a spacious living room with overstuffed furniture and fireplace, plus a smaller, cozy reading or game room. Down by the lake—located across a grassy field—are a rowboat, two canoes, a small beach, volleyball net, and basketball hoop for guests to use. This inn is located out of town so bicycling is safer. Hiking trails are nearby. Open year-round except for 2 weeks early in November. Doubles, $110–135; suites, $165 with a full breakfast and afternoon tea.

♦ **Lakeview Motor Lodge** (603-763-2701), Route 103, Newbury, NH 03255. Touting "the best views of the lake" this small, 12-unit motor lodge is well located and does have high unimpeded views of Lake Sunapee. It's not directly on the waterfront, but Sunapee State Park—with its sandy beach and changing facilities—is just a few minutes by car. Rooms are on two levels. Ours, on the upper level, had two double beds (one definitely firmer than the other), a picture window with the great view, a screened-in porch overlooking the lake, a TV, and phone. The small bathroom had a tub-shower combination, and everything was very clean. Lower-level rooms have a patio instead of porch. A continental-plus breakfast is serve-yourself in the office of the motor lodge. Bananas, yogurt, bagels, muffins, juice, hot beverages, and cereal are offered. You fill up a tray and take it back to your room or to a small outdoor terrace behind the office. Open year-round. Doubles, $59–99.

♦ **Best Western Sunapee Lake Lodge** (603-763-2010; 1-800-606-5253; www.sunapeelakelodge.com), Route 103, Newbury, NH 03255. Just a short walk from Sunapee State Park, this two-story motel has a small indoor pool and mini gym. Although it's close to the lake, rooms do not have lake views. Rooms come in three styles: standard with two queen or one king bed; deluxe with king bed and queen pullout sofa, microwave oven, and refrigerator; and two-room suites with either two queen beds plus two queen sleepers, or king bed and two queen-sized pullout sofas. The suites all have an oversized jet tub, microwave oven, and refrigerator. In winter free ski shuttles to nearby Mount Sunapee are offered. A fireplaced lobby breakfast area is the place for continental-plus buffet breakfast in the morning. Doubles, $89–229. **Murphy's Grille** next door serves lunch and dinner. It is under the same ownership. A new 55-room Best Western hotel was to be built directly across the street from this one and was also to be under the same management. Estimated opening is winter of 2003–2004.

Other Choices

♦ **Rosewood Country Inn** (603-938-5253; 1-800-938-5273; www.bbonline.com/nh/rosewood/), 67 Pleasant View Road, Bradford, NH 03221. Lesley and Dick Marquis have made a destination inn of this big gray Victorian with dark pink shutters. You drive through the little town of Bradford and up a long country road before coming to the inn, which has maintained an AAA three-diamond rating. The building dates from the late 1800s, and its turrets and porches are emblematic of the era. Eleven distinctive guest rooms have king or queen bed and private bath. Most have in-room fireplace, and several also have a Jacuzzi-style tub. The Marquises pride themselves on their "candlelight and crystal" breakfasts—Lesley is the cook, and Dick waits on tables. A fruit course, a bread course (homemade muffins or scones), and a hot entrée such as Belgian waffles or a tomato basil egg soufflé set guests up for a day of exploring the area.

Personal touches are everywhere in the inn. Lesley did the stenciling of walls in five common rooms where guests have plenty of room to relax. A pond on the property is used for ice skating in winter and fly-fishing in summer. Cross-country skiing, snowmobiling, and snowshoeing are all cold-weather pursuits. The inn sponsors a couple of moonlight snowshoe weekends when guests are led through the woods by a knowledgeable guide. Mother-daughter, Dickens Christmas weekends and a pre-Halloween weekend with an event like ghost tales around the fire might be other special weekends each year. Children over 12 are welcome as guests, but this is a romantic spot preferred by couples. The newly decorated Abigail Adams Room has a chaise in the turret area of the room, a queen canopy bed, an in-room fireplace, and a lace shower curtain in the bathroom. Whispering Pines is done in darker colors with plaid patchwork comforter on the queen bed, a large bough of bare branches with a birdhouse in one corner, and a step-up bathroom with paisley shower curtain for the tub-shower. Wine and hors d'oeuvres are served on Friday evening. Doubles, $109–229.

♦ **Colonial Farm Inn & Antiques** (603-526-6121; 1-800-805-8504; www.colonial-farminn.com), Route 11, New London, NH 03257. Three-in-one—an attractive bed & breakfast inn, a dining room of distinction, and an antiques shop—are all found in this country complex painted white and owned by Bob and Kathryn Joseph. He is a chef and she has overseen the tasteful decorating. The center-chimney, 1836 Colonial inn is the site of the intimate first-floor dining rooms (see *Where to Eat*) and of six charmingly decorated guest rooms. Five are on the second floor, where our favorite is Wauwinet, named for the resort in Nantucket. That's the island where the Josephs were married. It has a queen-sized bed and a particularly large bathroom with pedestal sink. Laura Ashley prints are used in some rooms, and in the first-floor room—equipped for handicapped guests—is a queen bed with a floral spread to match the draperies. The rooms have radio but no TV. The only common room is a front parlor that must be shared with guests arriving for dinner. A full breakfast is served in the dining room to houseguests. Open year-round. The antiques shop next door has well-displayed wares from several dealers and is fun to browse in. Doubles, $110–125.

♦ **The Back Side Inn** (603-863-5161; fax 603-863-5007; www.bsideinn.com), 1171 Brook Road, Goshen, NH 03752. Bruce Hefka honed his hospitality skills at Walt Disney World in Florida, and his wife, Mackie, knew how to cook. They combined these forces to open their own place in 1984 on the "back side of Mount Sunapee." Bruce had vacationed in the area as a kid and fantasized about owning his own inn. Possibly best known for its dining (see *Where to Eat*), the inn has 10 simple rooms, 8 with private bath (a couple across the hall from the room itself). All baths have a stall shower. One suite has a queen-bedded room plus a room with twin beds and shares a bath—it's good for families. The remaining rooms have king or queen beds, painted plank floors, and simple furnishings—reminiscent of an old ski lodge, which this is in winter. The first-floor common rooms are spiffed up and have a TV for those who want to check in with goings-on in the "outside world." There's a great front porch for sitting and reading or watching the traffic, plus a hot tub out back. Across the street is Audrey Nelson's used-book shop; you can walk to the public beach at Rand Pond for a swim in summer. Full breakfasts are a feature here, and cinnamon French toast and eggs Benedict are specialties. Open year-round with brief breaks in April and November. Doubles, $75–85.

♦ **Hide-Away Inn** (603-526-4861; 1-800-457-0589; fax 603-526-4258), Twin Lake Villa Road, P.O. Box 1249, New London, NH 03257. Keep going past the big old buildings of the summer-only Twin Lake Village to find this large white house with wide porch and swinging baskets of flowers. Originally built in the 1930s for poet and author Grace Litchfield, it's now owned by Lori and Michael Freeman, who also run a **dining room** open to the public. The main lobby with huge stone fireplace and high ceilings is especially attractive. Upstairs are six appealing guest rooms, including one suite. Two have gas fireplace. All have beaded walls of Oregon spruce. Room 1—with fireplace—has a queen bed tucked in beneath bookcases and a bathroom with footed tub. Room 3 is quite large with plaid quilt, antique bureau, and a stall shower in the bathroom. Lori says guests can use Backlin Beach on Little Lake Sunapee where there are kayaks, canoes, and paddleboats as well—it's not far. Doubles, $95–135 with full breakfast; suite, $160.

♦ **New London Inn** (603-526-2791; www.newlondoninn.com), 140 Main Street, New London, NH 03257. This big white inn in the center of town has a terrific location. Built in 1792, it's next door to Colby-Sawyer College and within walking distance of restaurants and shops. It is usually quite busy. Several common rooms with beamed ceilings—a couple with fireplaces—stretch across the front of the inn, and there's a good-sized dining room. A total of 23 guest rooms on the first, second, and third floors vary in size and appeal. All have private bath and shuttered doors leading to the rather wide hallways. Painted floors with scatter rugs are found in most rooms—although some looked as if they needed a touch-up. A few rooms have TV and air-conditioning, but not all. Room configurations vary widely. Room 21, for example, had two double beds, one on each side of a room split partway by a wall and a small bathroom. Open year-round. Doubles, EP, $95–140.

♦ **Maple Hill Farm** (603-526-2248; 1-800-231-8637; fax 603-526-4170; www.maple-hillfarm.com), 200 Newport Road, New London, NH 03257. Longtime innkeepers Dennis and Roberta Aufranc run a 10-room B&B in a rambling old country house that can be especially appealing to families. It's located very close to Exit 12 off I-89. Six rooms with private baths (some quite small, carved from closets) are found on the first and second floors; the third floor has four bedrooms sharing two baths. There's a basketball court in the barn out back and a hot tub on the outdoor deck. A walk through the back of the property actually brings you to the shore of Little Lake Sunapee. Breakfast is served in a large pine-paneled room in the center of the house. Guests have a choice of four different breakfasts including blueberry pancakes and eggs, bacon and fried potatoes. Doubles, $80–125.

♦ **The Village House** (603-927-4765; www.villagehousebnb.com), Sutton Mills, NH 03221. Marilyn Paige, an artist, and her husband, Jack, a blacksmith, open three rooms with private bath in their 19th-century home. The house, white with dark green trim, and located at the top of a steep flight of granite steps, dates from 1857. Two guest rooms on the second floor and one on the first have a queen bed; one queen-bedded room also has a twin bed. A small sitting room with TV on the second floor and a parlor on the first are used by guests. A full breakfast—among the specialties are lemon waffles with bacon, and cheese and sausage strata—is served in a dining room. Guests enjoy visiting their hosts' studio and workshop in the brown barn at the street level below the house. This is also where you park. This is not a handicapped-accessible facility. Doubles, $90.

♦ **Shaker Meetinghouse B&B** (603-763-3122), 176 King Hill Road, New London, NH 03257. Set far back from the road, this new building is a replica of a Moses Johnson meetinghouse from the Shaker community at nearby Enfield, New Hampshire (see "A Shaker Weekend"). New in 2001, it's run by Laura Chowanski Walters and her parents, John and Louise Chowanski. The colors of Shaker meetinghouses—white walls with blue trim—are used, and floors are bare, softly buffed wood in warm honey tones. On the main level is a sitting area with two plaid loveseats in front of a fireplace. At the other end of the open space is a long Shaker-style table with ladderback chairs, where guests gather for breakfast. Laura says she whips up a full morning meal with scones, muffins, homefries, eggs, and bacon as examples. Upstairs are four guest rooms—three available when we visited. All are in the blue-and-white Shaker colors with an up-to-date private bathroom and air-conditioning. Quilts on reproduction Shaker queen beds have a little color in addition to the blue. All furniture is reproduction Shaker-style. Rooms are named for Shaker communities in New England: Enfield, Hancock, Harvard, and Canterbury. Doubles, $85.

WHERE TO EAT

Finding a place to eat isn't a problem in the Lake Sunapee area. From formal to casual, there are excellent spots to choose from.

♦ **The Inn at Pleasant Lake** (603-526-6271; 1-800-626-4907), North Pleasant Street, New London. A large, spacious dining room stretches across the front of the inn, with distant views of the lake. Chef-owner Brian MacKenzie, an alumnus of the Culinary Institute of America, serves what many feel is the finest dinner in the area. This is often a place to go for a special occasion. The prix fixe five-course meal offers a choice of meat or fish as the entrée, after a soup, salad, and entremezzo (sorbet or fruit). Dessert follows. Soup might be wild mushroom bisque with parsley oil, or bisque of Granny Smith apples and butternut squash with cinnamon crème fraîche and fried leeks. Salad choices have been organic baby greens with Stilton dressing, bibb lettuce with creamy lemon caper dressing, or organic baby spinach with balsamic vinaigrette. A different bread is served each night—ranging from country white, to sun-dried cherry bread with honey butter, to sourdough French. Entrées could be marinated tenderloin of beef with tomato basil concassé, or wood-smoked breast of duck served with lingonberry demiglaze and red onion confit. Fish entrées might be grilled salmon with basil coulis, pan-seared swordfish with dill beurre blanc and tropical chutney, or grilled red grouper with citrus vinaigrette. The dessert of the evening could be baked chocolate pudding over Grand Marnier crème anglaise or individual cheesecakes with raspberry coulis. Prix fixe at $46.

♦ **La Meridiana Restaurant** (603-526-2033), Route 11, Wilmot. Piero Canuto, a native of the northern Italian Alpine town of Sabbia, has run this charming Italian eatery for more than 15 years. A huge fieldstone fireplace—pressed into service during the long, cold winter—dominates the dining room at this roadside spot. Tables have white cloths, and chairs are high-backed wood. Lunch, dinner, and Sunday brunch are served. At lunchtime, soups can be had for $2—perhaps chicken broth, minestrone, or pea. A salad ($3–6) could be romaine with strawberries and hazelnuts or a classic Caesar. Entrées include pastas like lobster ravioli, homemade pasta with Bolognese sauce, panini with various toppings, a smoked fish platter, and chicken Scaloppine ($8–18). Dinner features pizzas among the pasta dishes like gnocchi alla Piemontese (potato and flour dumplings served with sage, butter, and tomatoes). Specialties can be a risotto with Parmesan cheese, saffron, porcini mushrooms, and chicken stock, or veal chop baked with Fontina cheese and mushrooms ($11–19). Fresh asparagus served with butter and lemon, and fried eggplant baked with mozzarella and tomato sauce are side dishes. Sunday brunch brings raviolis, agnolottis, salads, plus some classic brunch items like five-grain buttermilk pancakes, omelets, and French toast ($6–13). Lunch Monday through Friday 11:30–1:30, dinner Monday through Saturday 5–9, Sunday, 3–7; Sunday brunch 11:30–1:30. There is a full bar.

♦ **Colonial Farm Inn** (603-526-6121; fax 603-641-0314), Route 11, New London. Two small dining rooms and a porch out back overlooking a pond and perennial gardens provide an engaging setting for some of the best food in the area. Bob Joseph is the chef-owner who offers five or six entrées such as sautéed boneless breast of chicken filled with Boursin cheese; beef tenderloin with a roasted shallot and port wine sauce; or boneless rack of lamb with a pecan crust, topped with red wine sauce ($16–25). Side dishes the evening we dined here were garlic mashed potatoes and asparagus. Entrées are not huge, but ample. We skipped the appetizers, but shared mixed green salads. Eggplant and mozzarella filled ravioli or sautéed crabcakes were other choices for starters ($5–6). Warm bread pudding with a creamy custard—topped with blueberries or not, as you chose—was a fitting ending to our meal. The fireplace is used in cold weather. Dinner Wednesday through Saturday 5–9.

♦ **Millstone Restaurant** (603-526-4201; fax 603-526-2933), Newport Road, Route 11, New London. Tom Mills is the owner of this and the **Four Corners Grille** in the New London area. Locals are faithful to this spot, a pretty place with two pink-walled dining rooms, plus a bar where you can also dine. Tablecloths are white, and napkins are green. Lobsters—available in several guises—and crab pie are among the classics here. At lunchtime you can have a burger, an omelet, or a hot entrée like the crab pie with lobster sauce or rack of lamb ($13–20, with a jumbo lobster going for $39.95). At dinner the range includes fried calamari or hummus with pita bread, lobster bisque or a soup of the day, lobster, fruit and green salads. Entrées ($13–23, except lobster) might be calf's liver, Bavarian schnitzel, or a roast half duckling. Twin lamb chops are marinated in rosemary, garlic, and olive oil and grilled to order. Open daily for lunch 11:30–2:30; for brunch and lunch on Sunday 11:30–2:30; and for dinner 4:30–8:30, except 5–9 on Friday and Saturday. Reservations are a good idea.

♦ **The Back Side Inn** (603-863-5161; fax 603-863-5007), 1171 Brook Road, Goshen. During the spring, summer, and fall, innkeeper and chef Mackie Hefka fires up the range and offers dinners Thursday through Saturday evenings to the public. In addition, there is the Wednesday-night pasta feast offering seven different pastas from which guests fill their plates. Salad comes in one large bowl family-style. There is also Italian soup. The meal costs $17.95. Bring your own bottle of Chianti. On Thursday through Saturday evenings, a traditional dinner menu is available. Since only 35 can be seated at tables on the glassed-in porch and main dining room, it's a good idea to reserve ahead. The meal includes a platter of hors d'oeuvres, cup of homemade soup, salad, and bread and butter for the price of the entrée ($27–31). Among entrées available you might find oven-roasted boneless breast of duck served with a red currant Merlot sauce; center-cut boneless pork chop served with homemade apple butter; or baked scallops seasoned with lemon. In the winter season dinner is available nightly to houseguests, who are usually so exhausted from skiing they'd rather stay in and dine. These family-style dinners cost $20–22 each.

♦ **Peter Christian's Tavern** (603-526-4042; fax 603-526-4443), 186 Main Street, New London. Established in the New London area in 1975, this cozy Colonial-style tavern is possibly the most popular place in town. It was sold by founder Murray Washburn to employees and their spouses in the late 1990s and is now owned by two couples, Tom and Kathi Brown and Russ and Kathie Sarles. The restaurant, located in the old 19th-century Edgewood Inn, features intimate booths with high wood backs, exposed-beam ceilings, lots of green plants. There's also a patio for summer dining. The all-day menu includes appetizers like a cheese and meat board of assorted cheeses, sliced ham, roast turkey, and roast beef with warm bread and PC's mustard (so famous it's sold separately), and Parmesan artichoke dip with fresh vegetables ($4–9). Beef stew can be had in a cup or mug, and onion soup, vegetable soup, and a soup of the day are available. Caesar salad includes artichoke hearts and marinated chicken breast. One sandwich has been on the menu forever—Peter's Mother's Favorite (baked ham, roast turkey, Vermont cheddar, and tomatoes with PC's mustard sauce and mayonnaise). Like other sandwiches, it can be had in half or whole sizes. Heartier fare includes shepherd's pie, beef stew, mustard chicken cordon bleu, and Tavern Chicken, the latter a chicken breast stuffed with Boursin cheese and spinach and baked with crisp bacon ($9–11). You can always find a rich chocolate dessert. There's a full bar. Open 11–10.

♦ **New London Inn** (603-526-2791), Main Street, New London. This good-sized and somewhat formal dining room has a reputation for good—if not extraordinary—food. Its location makes it popular. A wall of windows overlooks gardens and lawns outside. New England fare is the rule; we enjoyed broiled haddock and veal Piccata. Other possibilities might be garlic and cracked pepper crusted lamb finished with lemon rosemary sauce; seafood bouillabaisse; or veal Gregoire—dipped in Parmesan egg batter and topped with sautéed lobster and asparagus. Entrées are priced $17–23. Open 5–8:30 nightly. Lunch ($7–10) is offered 11:30–2, and pot roast is a favorite.

♦ **Four Corners Grille** (603-526-6899), Route 11 and 114, New London. Panoramic views of Mount Kearsarge from the big windows on the south side of this casual restaurant can take your breath away on a clear day. We enjoyed lunch on just such a day, the sun warming our shoulders as we enjoyed our window table. Bare wood tables with captain's chairs invoke a casual mood. A special the day we

The Anchorage Restaurant at Sunapee Harbor

dined was the French Connection—house-smoked ham and Brie with apple on a croissant—which was delicious. Other items on the all-day menu range from an ale and onion soup to sesame chicken salad, fish-and-chips, several styles of burgers and entrées. In the latter group—called Main Street Fare—are grilled marinated lamb, New England scrod, and a steak marinated in stout ($12–15). Next door in the same building is the **Flying Goose Brew Pub**, with entertainment on Thursday evening in fall and winter. **Kearsarge Mountain Coffee Roasters** is another business in the group located here. You can buy the coffee to take home. Open daily 11:30–9.

♦ **MacKenna's Restaurant** (603-526-9511), New London Shopping Center, Main Street, New London. This is a casual daytime restaurant serving breakfast, lunch, and early dinner, and it's a classic in New London. Prices are low. Possibly as well known for its ice cream desserts and homemade pies (you can buy one to take home) as its regular meals, MacKenna's commands a loyal following and is busy all day. Start your morning with Texas-style French toast ($3.99), a plain omelet ($4.15), or two eggs, toast, and homefries ($2.95) and go on from there. Lunchtime brings burgers, specialty sandwiches (pepper steak, fried chicken, egg salad, tuna salad), and entrées—roast lamb dinner at $9.95, Yankee pot roast for $9.25, or chicken and biscuits for $7.65. There are also pastas. Homemade pies include strawberry-rhubarb, apple, blueberry, mince, pecan, chocolate or banana cream, and coconut cream. Grape-Nut custard, tapioca, and bread pudding are time-honored, and the brownie sundae is a bellyful at $3.90.

♦ **Jack's Coffee** (603-526-8003), 180 Main Street, New London, is one in a group of three of these casual spots where not only coffee and newspapers, but also sandwiches, salads, soups, and specialties of the season can be enjoyed. The atmosphere is very comfortable, funky—a place to hang.

Water Views

♦ **The Anchorage** (603-763-3334), Sunapee Harbor. For the only lakeside dining around, this is the place to get close to the water and the action. On a nice afternoon or evening, there's nothing better than establishing yourself at a table on the outdoor deck, where you can watch the boating activity. In lieu of that, try for a window booth inside. We wish we could be quite as enthusiastic about the quality of the food. We've eaten here a couple of times and still say the view is what it's all about. The all-day menu includes third-of-a-pound burgers, TLC (tomato, lettuce, and chicken) sandwiches, quesadillas, nachos, and veggie wraps. For more substantial fare, you can turn to the section on the menu titled "Harbor Specialties" and order white veggie lasagna, Yankee pot roast, lobster-stuffed chicken, or corn bread stuffed pork chops ($12–15). There's a full bar. Open May to mid-October, 11:30 AM–closing.

♦ **M.V. *Kearsarge* Restaurant Ship** (603-763-4030), Sunapee Harbor. This dinner cruise ship is a popular way to go on a nice evening. Dinner cruises are offered on Sunday and Tuesday through Friday at 6, and at 5:30 and 7:45 on Saturday. No cruises Monday. Guests dine buffet-style on cheese and crackers, a salad bar, a deli platter, salads, a top round of beef carved fresh, vegetable lasagna, hot veggies and potatoes, and coffee and tea. There's a complete liquor license. The cost is $26 per person, and reservations are important. The cruise takes a little less than 2 hours.

14 ► Mount Desert Island, Maine

The island that is home to Acadia National Park is a mountainous place, its peaks carved by glaciers some 8,000 years ago. The most famous—and highest—of these is Cadillac Mountain, whose summit is the destination of most who visit the park and Mount Desert (pronounced *dessert*) Island. From the top of Cadillac on a clear day (and not all of them are because of the prevalent ocean fog) you can get a magnificent view of Frenchman Bay and the coast.

Actually, getting to Acadia doesn't seem much like going to an island. Mount Desert is really more like a huge peninsula, separated from the mainland by the Mount Desert Narrows and approached by a relatively short bridge. This marvelous piece of land, located halfway up the coast of Maine and connected by a low span built in 1836, is particularly attractive to outdoor types. Climbing, hiking, kayaking, canoeing, boating, biking, camping—what isn't here?

Mount Desert is a fascinating piece of real estate. It lays claim to the only true fjord in North America—Somes Sound. The picturesque sound bisects the island, separating the northeasterly half from the southwesterly. Acadia National Park, covering more than a third of the entire area, stretches over both sections. It also spills onto nearby Isle au Haut, an offshore island, and north to a portion of Schoodic Peninsula.

The serious park visitor—hiker, kayaker, rock climber, walker, biker, or camper—can easily fill most of his or her time engaged in park activities. Acadia provides a glorious natural environment, especially enticing because of both wooded and seaside terrain. The first national park established east of the Mississippi, it was also the first composed of nothing but privately donated land. Large tracts were given by several of the island's wealthy summer inhabitants, including John D. Rockefeller Jr., who built the 57 miles of carriage roads that lace the park. These are limited to hikers, mountain bikers, horseback riders, and horse-drawn carriages. No cars on carriage roads.

A bit of history. Although Mount Desert Island was mapped in 1604 by the intrepid explorer Samuel de Champlain, its remote location protected it from

Bikers check out a menu at a Bar Harbor restaurant

development until discovery by landscape artists in the 19th century. Images by Thomas Cole and Frederic Church were widely distributed, and before long the tourist rush was on.

Most of the 19th- and early-20th-century summer residents of Mount Desert—known as "rusticators"—chose to settle here in lieu of Newport and the Berkshires because it offered a more low-key, natural experience. Not that they were exactly "roughing it." They built mansions—some 200 of them—on the streets of Bar Harbor and along the coast. A devastating fire in 1947 swept away 67 of those "cottages" and five hotels. But Bar Harbor, the commercial center of the island, and Acadia itself recovered admirably.

On August weekends the place can be downright mobbed—cars driving bumper to bumper along the park's magnificent Loop Road or through the streets of Bar Harbor in search of hard-to-find parking spaces. Yet even during this most visited month in Maine, there are areas of MDI that are quieter and more peaceful. The outer villages of Northeast Harbor and Southwest Harbor, Somesville, Seal Harbor, Tremont—for example—are always less frantic.

During the rest of the year, the whole place is quite manageable. June and September can be glorious, and winter is a world unto itself. Of course "the season"—from mid-June to early autumn—finds most of the hotels and inns and restaurants open, the park in full gear, the shops stocked. It's when most people want to visit.

Getting There

Most visitors arrive **by car,** many with kayaks, canoes, or bikes strapped to the top. From Brunswick, Maine, and south (including New York), the shortest route is I-95 north to Bangor and then I-395 and Route 1A southeast to Ellsworth, the access point on the mainland. From there you take the short bridge over to Mount Desert Island. Driving from Connecticut, we like to pick up I-495 in Portland, which swings slightly to the west of I-95 and joins up with it farther north near Gardiner, Maine. It's a less traveled and, hence, more peaceful route and takes only slightly longer. You can, of course, take Coastal Route 1 north to Ellsworth: very commercial, highly trafficked, and apt to be frustratingly slow. If you have all the time in the world, however, it's fun to drive through Maine's coastal towns and stop wherever you want. It's better to do this off-season.

By air: Bangor International Airport (207-947-0384) is 26 miles north of Ellsworth. It's served by several different airlines and connects with most American cities. Among the airlines serving Bangor are USAirways, American, Delta, and Northwest. **Hancock County and Bar Harbor Airport** (207-667-7171; 1-800-428-4322) provides daily service to and from Boston. It's 12 miles from downtown Bar Harbor.

By bus: Vermont Transit (1-800-451-3292) serves Bar Harbor seasonally with one bus daily from Boston. The bus leaves Boston around noon, arriving at Bar Harbor about 6:40 PM. The return trip leaves Bar Harbor early in the morning. **Concord Trailways** (1-800-639-3317) serves Bangor from Boston (South Station or Logan Airport) and continues with summer shuttle service—ending Labor Day weekend—to Bar Harbor.

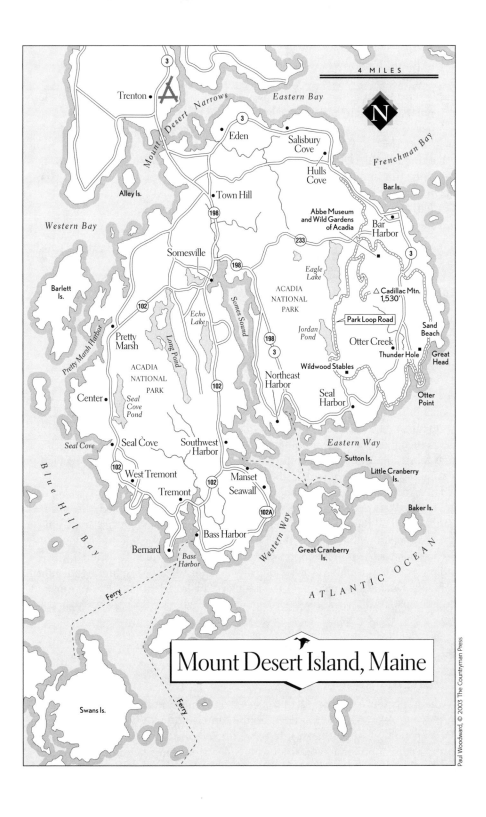

Mount Desert Island, Maine

Getting Around

♦ The **Island Explorer** (207-667-5796) is a system of large bright white buses with blue and green stripes operating on seven routes a day. This popular (and free) shuttle serves most of the island. Stops include Blackwoods Campground, the ferry terminal, Sand Beach, Southwest Harbor, Eagle Lake, and Jordan Pond.

A new **Great Meadow Loop Trail** permits foot access to Acadia directly from Bar Harbor. Just walk on into the park.

Parking is hard to find in Bar Harbor in summer. There are a few downtown lots. Once you find a space, cherish it. Park the car and walk. The village is compact and quite easy to traverse. Northeast Harbor and Southwest Harbor can be crowded, but we've never had trouble finding a parking space.

For More Information

♦ **Bar Harbor Chamber of Commerce** (207-288-5103; 1-888-540-9990; www.Bar-HarborMaine.com), 93 Cottage Street, P.O. Box 158, Bar Harbor, ME 04609-0158.

THE PARK

Today one of the most visited national parks in the country, Acadia was created from parcels of land assembled by many wealthy and foresighted individuals around the turn of the 20th century. In particular, Harvard University president Charles W. Eliot and Boston textile heir George Dorr assembled acreage for public use. Dorr was the man who went to Washington to persuade the federal government to accept the land and create a public park. He spent his entire fortune purchasing lands for Acadia, and he urged others to contribute land as well. In 1919 Acadia became the first national park in the East.

The park's 40,000 acres may not rival, sizewise, the giant parks out west, but the variety of scenery and terrain are exceptional. Acadia includes forested valleys, a rocky coastline, and all the major mountains of Mount Desert Island. Hiking trails and carriage roads open up the interior of the park for anyone willing to travel by foot, by bike, on horseback, or in a horsedrawn carriage. The Park Loop Road offers a thrilling 27-mile ride along a marvelous stretch of coastline before turning inland and eventually reaching the peak of 1,530-foot-high Cadillac Mountain. For information about the park, call the Acadia Information Center (207-667-8550; 1-800-358-8550).

SEEING AND DOING

Highlights

♦ The **Hulls Cove Visitors Center** located off Route 3 just north of Bar Harbor is the place to start your visit. It's open from mid-April through October. Here you climb up a long flight of stairs (if you are disabled, head up the short road at the nearby intersection for a parking lot with easier access) to a handsome glass-and-stone building. An introductory film about the park is shown every half hour. You can pick up a free map and the current *Beaver Log*, which lists all naturalist activities. If you want, you can sign up to participate in ranger-led programs scheduled from June through September—many of them at the amphitheaters of the two park campgrounds (Blackwoods and Seawall). There's an information desk and book sales area. You can also purchase a pass for the Loop Road (see below), although this can be bought at other spots along the way, too.

The Park Loop Road is a beautiful, serpentine 27-mile road that no one should miss. It's so scenic and curvy that it has been used in many automobile commercials. While it officially begins at the Hulls Cove Visitors Center, the Loop Road can be entered at many points along the way. Much of the road is one-way. Plan to stop along the way, for there are many interesting sites. The park entrance fee is $10 per car (including all occupants) for a 7-day pass.

These stops are listed in order and are just some of the highlights:

Sieur de Monts Spring, Abbe Museum, Wild Gardens of Acadia, and **Nature Center.** Pull into the good-sized parking lot for this grouping of sites. The **spring** is the least impressive in that there's not much to see. A pretty little octagonal building covers the location where a spring was once the source of commercially bottled water. It was purchased by George Dorr in 1909. Apparently no fresh water flows through anymore, for it looked pretty fetid and unappetizing when we stopped. You observe the spring through glass panels.

Robert Abbe Museum. This small, private museum has huge collections of Native American artifacts, only a tiny fraction of which can be on view in this tiny building with a surprising Spanish tile roof. That's why a new building for the Abbe Museum opened in downtown Bar Harbor in 2001 (see *Bar Harbor*). The museum—founded by Dr. Robert Abbe, a plastic surgeon—is said to have the largest collection of Maine Indian baskets in the world, and the few on view were indeed lovely. There are also birch-bark canoes, harpoons, animal bones, and other artifacts. In this little original building, the gift shop (with baskets and such for sale) is as large as the exhibit area! Admission $2.

The **Nature Center** is a small brown building at the end of the parking lot that requires no more than a quick look. It has a few small exhibits on flora and fauna in the park. Rangers are on hand to answer questions. And there are rest rooms. The **Wild Gardens of Acadia** nearby showcase more than 500 species of plant life native to Mount Desert. The garden, while not large, is divided into several different sections to model the range of habitats present on the islands. It is an easy walk.

Sand Beach. Ten miles into the Loop Road is one of two natural sand beaches found on the island (the other is located in Seal Harbor). Climb down a large granite stairway to the water's edge. Rest rooms and changing areas are available, but remember that the temperature of the water rarely exceeds 55 degrees during the hottest part of summer. Three wonderful hikes commence here: Great Head Trail, Ocean Trail, and Beehive (see *Hiking*).

Thunder Hole. This might be everybody's favorite stop. The geological phenomenon is a formation of rock with a narrow passage in the granite that—when hit by the right waves at the right time—produces a booming sound. The water rushes in and air is compressed in a small cave at the far end. If the pressure becomes great enough, the trapped air explodes outward in a thunderous spray of surf. Our children were fascinated by this when younger. Many visitors are disappointed in Thunder Hole because it seems so tame. The best opportunity for a real show comes halfway between high and low tide—you'll have to check tide tables to time your visit. Or go after a storm.

Jordan Pond House. The tradition of popovers and tea at the Jordan Pond House dates back to 1895 when private owners of a farmhouse on the pond, Thomas and Nellie McIntire, offered picnic meals, including hot popovers, to hikers in the area. They ran a restaurant here until 1945. By that time John D. Rockefeller Jr. had purchased the farmhouse and donated it to the park. But the tradition of serving popovers continued. The original Jordan Pond House burned in 1979. The modern replacement offers indoor and outdoor seating for dining—although on a nice day, the tables out on the lawn are *primo*. They offer a gorgeous view of the pond and of the glacially formed "Bubbles" beyond—two rounded mountains looking for all the world like a woman's breasts.

We had to sit indoors on the recent rainy day we stopped, but having tea and hot popovers seemed all the more appropriate. College students from around the country in blue shirts and khaki skirts or pants comprise the waitstaff, and bring a pot of tea, butter, strawberry jam, and hot popovers (two to each person). The best part is that the popovers are delivered piping hot, the second one only after you've finished the first. "You're always thinking, who needs a popover?" said Sarah, our waitress, a student at the University of North Dakota.

Lunch and tea are served 11:30–5:30; dinner is served from 5:30 to 8 or 9. (See Jordan Pond House under *Where to Eat*.) In summer reservations are a good idea. The gift shop at the Jordan Pond House is one of the best in the park.

The Carriage Roads

John D. Rockefeller Jr., one of Acadia National Park's most generous benefactors, was afraid that the automobile would drive the horse off the road. He provided for that not to happen on the 57 miles of "carriage roads" that wend their way through the park. Begun in 1913, the roads took more than 200 men 27 years to build. The last one was completed in 1940. You may enjoy the roads on foot, bike, or horse. They open up hidden forest stretches. The roads are bordered with huge square granite boulders, and through the network are 16 unique stone bridges that are truly picturesque.

We took one of the carriage rides offered by Wildwood Stables close to Jordan Pond. Our 1-hour ride in an open wood carriage—with a dozen other riders—took us to Day Mountain. Had our weather not been gray and foggy, we would have been able to see the ocean from a high spot. Nonetheless, there is something lovely and timeless about bumping along on a gravel road at the pace of a pair of Belgian draft horses. The sunset ride to Day Mountain—a 2-hour ride—is deservedly popular on a clear day.

If you'd like to take a carriage ride—the way the roads were originally intended to be used—contact **Wildwood Stables** at (207) 276-3622. Several rides are offered each day, and reservations at least a day or two in advance are advised. The cost of a

1-hour ride is about $14 per adult. If you have your own horse, you can keep it at Wildwood Stables.

Many hikers use the carriage roads as trails. Useful reading, if you plan to go this route, is Diana Abrell's *Pocket Guide to the Carriage Roads of Acadia National Park*, available at shops in the park.

Cadillac Mountain

The Park Loop Road ends at Cadillac Mountain, Acadia's highest, after a 3½-mile ascent. Once at the summit—and on a clear day—the visitor is treated to 360-degree views of the Maine coast. Sunrise and sunset are especially popular times to be atop Cadillac. Because of its elevation, Cadillac is the first spot in the United States to catch the morning sun. But evenings are even more beautiful, when sunset is viewed across Eagle Lake. If you go then, plan to arrive early, because parking can be tight.

SCHOODIC POINT

About an hour's drive north of Mount Desert Island, at the end of the Schoodic Peninsula, is another section of Acadia National Park. To reach the peninsula from Route 1 in Gouldsboro, take Route 186 south to Winter Harbor and keep driving, keeping a lookout for the sign on the right directing you to Schoodic Peninsula. Schoodic Point faces open water, and the waves can be impressive. Driving down to the point past Winter Harbor is pleasant and relaxed and even when MDI is crowded, Schoodic is apt not to be. Only 1 in 10 park visitors ever gets here. A relatively short one-way road wraps around the peninsula. It's fairly level and has glorious views, making it perfect for biking. The **Frazier Point Picnic Area,** reached soon after you enter the park area, has several picnic tables and grills and offers a terrific view over Winter Harbor. If you want to bike around the peninsula, you can leave your car here. Schoodic Point itself beckons with its mostly flat rocks leading down to the edge of the ocean. Sit on the rocks in the sun and watch the waves. There's a large parking lot here. Farther on, the 1-mile **Anvil Trail** rises to the top of Schoodic Head, the highest point on the peninsula. To get there, continue about a mile past the point on the one-way road. There's a small parking area; the trail starts across the road. Views of Mount Desert Island and Winter Harbor are great.

Hiking in Acadia

Two-thirds of the more than 3 million annual visitors to Acadia National Park take at least a short hike. Acadia's trails evolved over centuries of human use and settlement on the land. American Indians, white settlers, and 1800s "rusticators" all added to the network of paths and trails up mountains, through the woods, and along the ocean shoreline. The first extensive trail plans were drafted in 1891.

Hiking is wonderfully varied in the park and ranges in difficulty from an easy, level walk around Jordan Pond (the Jordan Pond Loop Trail) to the very steep and challenging Precipice Trail. For the latter, you climb up the sheer rock face of Cadillac Mountain and use a series of ladders and iron rungs along the way. It is not for the faint of heart or someone fearful of heights. I did not do it.

A short but challenging hike is the 1½-mile **Beehive Trail.** Although it's less than a mile up and only 540 feet in height, it's a nearly vertical climb over rock steps and along steep ledges. There are some steel-rung ladders embedded in the rock. You reach the trailhead from the Sand Beach parking lot. The 4-mile climb to **Norumbega Mountain** is also considered challenging—even grueling. And several trails lead up to Cadillac Mountain, especially the **North Ridge** trail and the **West Face** trail, the first considered moderate; the latter, strenuous. Both can be accessed from near Bar Harbor.

Several pocket guides and maps detail the hiking trails in the park. A *Walk in the Park* by Tom St. Germain is a particularly helpful guide to the trails in Acadia.

Biking

You can mountain bike the Carriage Roads or road bike the Park Loop Road in Acadia. A popular short ride on the carriage roads is a 4-mile loop around Witch Hole Pond and Paradise Hill. The 6-mile ride around Eagle Lake provides up- and downhill stretches. Then there's the 26-mile Around the Mountain loop, which will take you the better part of a day and lots of stamina. Fire roads on the western side of the island can also be used for mountain biking.

Bike rentals are available in Bar Harbor from **Acadia Bike & Canoe** (207-288-9605), 48 Cottage Street, and **Bar Harbor Bicycle Shop** (207-288-3886; 1-800-824-2453), 141 Cottage Street, among others.

Rock Climbing

Some people just can't get enough of those adrenaline rushes. We're not among them, personally, but if you want to give it a try, there are places to get good instruction and equipment. Contact the **Atlantic Climbing School** (207-288-2521), P.O. Box 6003, Bar Harbor; it's located in Cadillac Mountain Sports on Cottage Street). **Acadia Mountain Guides Climbing School** (1-888-232-9559) is located in summer at 198 Main Street, Bar Harbor.

Kayaking

Sea kayaking—and kayaking on the lakes of Acadia National Park—is more and more popular. The following are rental sources: **Coastal Kayaking Tours** (207-288-9605), 48 Cottage Street, Bar Harbor; **National Park Sea Kayak Tours** (207-288-0342; 1-800-347-0940), 39 Cottage Street, Bar Harbor; **Loon Bay Kayak** (207-288-0099; 1-888-786-0676), 184 High Street, Ellsworth.

Swimming

Sand Beach and **Echo Lake** are the two lifeguarded beaches within Acadia National Park. Echo Lake is accessible from Route 102 near Southwest Harbor and is well marked. The water is frigid.

Camping

Two campgrounds are within the park. One is **Blackwoods Campground** located on Route 3 about 5 miles south of Bar Harbor. It's open year-round; reservations are required from June 15 to September 15. The cost is $18 per night per site. Contact the National Park Reservation Service for reservations by calling (800) 365-2267 or writing NPRS, P.O. Box 1600, Cumberland, MD 21502. Specific sites cannot be requested. Blackwoods is first-come, first-served from September 16 to June 14. Fees vary during the off-season.

    Seawall Campground is located on Route 102A 4 miles south of Southwest Harbor. It's open from late May to late September. It's first-come, first-served, and sites are $12–18 per night. In late July and August lines form early each morning. Pets are allowed but must be leashed and attended at all times.

Winter Sports

Acadia is favored in warm weather, but **cross-country skiers** and **snowshoers** enjoy use of the park's carriage roads in winter. Some intrepid sorts also try **ice climbing.**

Additional Reading

Acadia Revealed by Jay Kaiser is a helpful book. The gift shops in the park have many other books for sale.

ELSEWHERE ON MOUNT DESERT ISLAND

Acadia National Park justifiably demands the most attention on Mount Desert Island. But the towns and villages outside the park are interesting also. Here's a quick run-down of things to see and do, plus information on staying and dining in **Bar Harbor, Northeast Harbor,** and **Southwest Harbor,** the three major towns on the island.

BAR HARBOR

This is a small, crowded, and quite commercial town, especially in summer. It is closest to the main entrance to Acadia, and also to the bridge that gets you onto the island in the first place. Because of that, it's the center of island life. When visiting MDI, we prefer to stay in Northeast Harbor or Southwest Harbor, out of the fray. Many of the shops in Bar Harbor—and there are lots of them—are of the ceramic lobster refrigerator magnet sort, although there are exceptions. Fine restaurants exist amid quite ordinary sorts; the same is true of inns and motels. On a rainy day in July or August the place is barely manageable because of the crowds. But then there are bright spots. Bar Harbor has a few fine museums including the new **Abbe Museum** with Native American artifacts. There is the lovely **Shore Path** for a coastal walk. You can hang out at the **town green** and people-watch. How about an **ice cream cone** from Ben & Bill's at the intersection of Main and Cottage Streets (where they even have lobster ice cream)? Don't forget to **walk the Bar**.

SEEING AND DOING

The Great Outdoors

♦ **The Shore Path.** This is a smooth and level path that skirts the eastern shore of Bar Harbor, passing beaches, parks, and huge mansions. Begin at the Town Pier at the end of Main Street. Just step onto the asphalt sidewalk in front of the Bar Harbor Inn and head away from the shops of town. After passing the Bar Harbor Inn, you'll be rewarded with sweeping views of Frenchman Bay and the Porcupine Islands. You will pass Grant Park and Balance Rock—a striking, 15-foot-high rock placed by glaciers thousands of years ago. After crossing a small wooden bridge, the Shore Path comes to an end at a chain-link fence. You can turn right and head toward Main Street or reverse directions and enjoy the walk all over again.

♦ **Walking the Bar.** Bar Island—one of the five Porcupine Islands—is actually connected to Bar Harbor by a natural sandbar that is exposed at low tide. Twice a day there's an opportunity to walk out to the island via the sandbar, but be careful not to tarry too long or the water will cover up your return path. Follow West Street away from the Town Pier, take a right onto Bridge Street, and you will come to the water's edge and the beginning of the sandbar.

♦ **Whale-watching.** Several boats leave from Bar Harbor. Check with **Acadian Whale Watcher Co. (207-288-9794)** and **Bar Harbor Whale Watch Company** (207-288-2386). Most also take you to see puffins. The trips generally last from 2 to 4 hours and travel about 25 miles offshore to see the big mammals.

♦ **The Cat** (207-288-3395; 1-888-249-7245). This is the high-speed ferry between Bar Harbor and Yarmouth, Nova Scotia. The trip takes just 2¾ hours each way so you can go over to Nova Scotia for the day. There are a café and a casino on board. If you take the early ferry to Yarmouth, you can spend up to 8 hours in Nova Scotia before returning the same day. A special 1-day round-trip costs $55. Otherwise, one-way fares are $55 for adults, $25 for children. It costs about $100 to take a car each way. Nova Scotia is in the Atlantic Time Zone and is 1 hour later than Bar Harbor. Runs mid-May to mid-October.

Indoor Activities

♦ **Abbe Museum** (207-288-3519; www.abbemuseum.org), 26 Mount Desert Street, Bar Harbor. This handsome newly renovated YMCA building (plus new section) offers 17,000 square feet of exhibit and office space. It's open year-round (unlike its small 2,000-square-foot counterpart in Acadia National Park). Finally a much larger portion of the museum's 50,000 artifacts can be displayed. The museum—dedicated to furthering the understanding and appreciation of Maine Native American cultures, history, and archaeology—was founded by the late Dr. Robert Abbe, a New York surgeon who summered in Bar Harbor. Most pieces in its large collection are from tribes in Maine and the Maritimes. Attached to the downtown building is a new circular structure known as the Circle of the Four Directions, a distinctive space that reflects the importance of the circle in Native American cultures. Open year-round. Memorial Day to mid-October, daily 10–5; until 9 PM Thursday through Saturday. From mid-October to Memorial Day weekend, Thursday through Sunday 10–5. General admission is $4.50 for adults, $2 for children.

♦ **Bar Harbor Oceanarium** (207-288-5005), Route 3, north of Bar Harbor. Exhibits and information pertaining to the Maine lobster are the focus here. During the day there are lectures presented by a real lobsterman who talks about the famous Maine crustacean and will answer questions. There is a working lobster hatchery. Outdoors there is a marsh walk. Open mid-May to mid-October, 9–5.

♦ **College of the Atlantic** (207-288-5015), Route 3, Bar Harbor. This small and pretty college for liberal-arts students specializing in ecological studies is also home to the **Natural History Museum.** Exhibits include the skeleton of a rare true-beaked whale and dioramas of plants and animals of coastal Maine. There is a hands-on discovery room where you can touch real baleen, fur, wings, and animal bones. Open mid-June to Labor Day, daily 10–5; otherwise, Thursday, Friday, and Sunday 1–4, Saturday 10–4. Adults $3.50, teens and seniors $2.50, children $1.

♦ **Bar Harbor Historical Society** (207-288-0000; in winter 207-288-3807), 33 Ledgelawn Avenue, Bar Harbor. The collection and exhibits include photographs, paintings, and costumes of the "gilded age" of Eden (the town's name was changed in 1918), plus hotel registers, ribbons won at horse shows, and huge scrapbooks documenting the disastrous fire of 1947. Open mid-June to mid-October, 1–4, and by appointment the remainder of the year.

Culture

♦ **Films** are fun to watch at the vintage **Criterion Theatre** (207-288-3441) on Cottage Street in Bar Harbor. The **Arcady Music Festival** is an ambitious summer-long series of classical music events in various Maine towns, including Bar Harbor. Events are held at several locations. For information and tickets, call (207) 288-2141.

Shopping

For outdoor types, **Cadillac Mountain Sports** on Cottage Street is a must. Readers will want to stop at **Sherman's,** a bookstore and more on Main Street. **Island Artisans** has some wonderful handmade pottery, textiles, and other items. **The Black Bear** has good socks and T-shirts.

Gift shops at the **Abbe Museum** and at **Acadia National Park** are also good places to browse.

There are thousands of guest rooms in Bar Harbor. We have made a selection based on those that will appeal to active travelers and those that simply appeal to us.

♦ **Nannau** (207-288-5575; fax 207-288-5421; www.nannau.com), a seaside B&B, 396 Lower Main Street, P.O. Box 710, Bar Harbor, ME 04609. Ron and Vikki Evers are the consummate hosts at this well-located inn south of town and out of the madness. It's a bit hard to find; you must look carefully for the number on the mailbox. From there a long driveway leads you through woods to the house itself, a shorefront estate built in 1904 as a summer "cottage." The 5-acre property includes perennial gardens and its own beach although, admits Vikki, the water is just too cold. Four guest rooms, one a suite, are located on the second and third floors and have queen-sized bed, private bath, and ocean views. Down comforters and feather pillows are standard. The suite also has a room with twin beds. Two rooms have a working fireplace for use in fall only. Main-floor common rooms are high ceilinged and gracious, decorated—as are the guest rooms—with William Morris wallpapers and fabrics. While individual rooms have no TV sets, there is one in a parlor. Breakfasts are served at an extraordinary large table with regal high-backed chairs— possibly omelets, almond-filled French toast, or croissants baked by the owners. Open mid-June to late October. Doubles, $145–195.

♦ **The Inn at Bay Ledge** (207-288-4204; www.innatbayledge.com), 1385 Sand Point Road, Bar Harbor, ME 04609. A guest lies beneath a light blanket on a sofa, reading, in an attractive and comforting common room. What could be better on a cool and rainy afternoon in late June? Jack and Jeani Ochtera provide for good and not-so-good weather days at their seafront B&B north of Bar Harbor. This inn is away from the madding crowd and close to the sea—just the sort of retreat needed after a day of activity. Seven rooms in the main inn—all but one with a deck or picture window looking out toward Frenchman Bay—and three private cottage accommodations in a pine grove across the road comprise this well-organized property. Guests love the location. Famed Cathedral Rock on the coast sits adjacent to the inn; an 80-step staircase leads down from the rock to a private beach. There are also terraces overlooking the sea and an outdoor swimming pool, sauna, and steam shower. A wicker-filled porch to the rear of the inn looks past the lawns and out to the bay. Designer linens, down comforters, and feather beds are used in all rooms. A breakfast room with light wood tables and chairs is the setting for extravagant breakfasts such as Bay Ledge hash with salsa, blueberry breakfast pudding with English custard sauce, or baked puffs with fresh berries. Homemade granola is also available. In the afternoon tea or lemonade is served with goodies. Jeani makes Nantucket baskets in several styles for sale. Open May to October. Doubles, $100–350.

♦ **Manor House Inn** (207-288-3759; 1-800-437-0088; www.barharbormanorhouse. com), 106 West Street, Bar Harbor, ME 04609. Malcolm "Mac" Noyes and James Dennison have expanded this 17-room bed & breakfast establishment from the original 1887 Victorian main house with the addition of three striking outbuildings. "Slowly but surely we're filling the property with buildings," laughs Mac. The latest, built by James, is the lovely Acadia Cottage to the rear of the property with three luxurious guest rooms. This building, taupe with gray shutters, offers accommodations with a king or queen bed, gas fireplace, wet bar, and whirlpool tub in a well-appointed private bath. One suite also has a large living room. The main inn, yellow with green trim, is decorated with striking Victorian wallpaper and period antiques and has nine guest rooms, all with private bath, on the first and second floors. In addition, three rooms in the chauffeur's cottage to the rear, and two in individual gingerbread cottages to the side, all have private bath. Two of the suites in the chauffeur's cottage have Franklin fireplaces. One is a flowery bower with floral wallpaper, cathedral ceilings, king-sized bed, and refrigerator. Rooms 4 and 5 in the main inn also have a fireplace. Everyone has a big breakfast in the manor house itself, once known as Boscobel. It's served buffet-style in the elegant double parlor with its grand piano, where a specialty of the house is baked stuffed blueberry French toast. A front porch with wicker chairs allows guests to sit and watch the comings and goings on West Street, the most elegant in town. Open April to November. Doubles, $75–225, with seasonal fluctuations.

♦ **The Holland Inn of Bar Harbor** (207-288-4804; www.hollandinn.com), 35 Holland Avenue, Bar Harbor, ME 04609. An 1895 farmhouse was personally restored by Evin and Tom Hulbert. This in-town inn has five guest rooms and suites, one on the first floor and the rest on the second. All are bright, airy, and impeccably clean—each one named for one of the hikes in Acadia National Park. All have private bath, TV, and ceiling fan. The largest single room in the house is Precipice (also the most challenging hike in the park), with five windows overlooking the front yard and Holland Avenue. There's a queen-sized pencil-post bed, a bright sitting nook, and a twin bed for a child or travelers who prefer separate beds. Bubbles, the smallest room, has a built-in queen captain's bed that seems like the coziest sleeping accommodation ever. Beehive is a two-room suite with two private baths with showers. Evin loves to cook and serves up a full breakfast on the sunporch, where guests dine at individual tables. Among her specialties are blueberry-stuffed French toast and avocado quiche. Open year-round. Doubles, $60–145.

Motels

♦ **Atlantic Oakes By-the-Sea** (207-288-5801; 1-800-33-MAINE; www.barharbor.com), Route 3, Bar Harbor, ME 04609. Located close by the high-speed ferry to Nova Scotia and not far from the main entrance to Acadia National Park, this motel complex is very popular. Altogether there are seven buildings spaced amid 12 acres, including a onetime "cottage" known as the Willows. The Willows operates as a B&B inn, while the other buildings have standard motel rooms with one king bed or two doubles. Families love the place for the amenities: good-sized indoor and outdoor pools, five tennis courts, a pebble beach, a pier and float. Many rooms have ocean views, and guests keep an eye on the comings and goings of *The Cat* along with boating on Frenchman Bay.

The Willows has 14 guest rooms, all with private bath and several with ocean views. A continental-plus breakfast is served in a breakfast room in the building. While breakfast is not included in the rates for regular motel guests, they can opt for a continental breakfast at $4.50 per person or a full breakfast for $7 served in the breakfast room. All motel rooms have TV, telephone, and balcony or patio with ocean views. Doubles, The Willows, $78–237. Doubles, motel rooms, $92–159. Open year-round.

◆ **The Bayview** (207-288-5861; 1-800-356-3585), 111 Eden Street (Route 3), Bar Harbor, ME 04609. This large white motel building on the water has 29 ocean-view rooms, most with two double beds and five with king-sized bed. The building is particularly close to the water, and expansive views are offered. An outdoor pool sets into a deck outside overlooking the bay. Rooms are attractively decorated with flowered bedspreads and draperies. A complimentary continental breakfast of fresh fruit and pastries is served. Doubles, $125–250. Open mid-May to mid-October.

Cottages

◆ **Emery's Cottages on the Shore** (207-288-3432; 1-888-240-3432; www.emerys-cottages.com), Sand Point Road, (off Route 3) Bar Harbor, ME 04609. This immaculately kept cottage complex on the waterfront has been run by the Gray family for more than 30 years. The 21 cottages all have refrigerator; 13 also have kitchenette. Most have queen or king bed and some, an extra twin. All have electric heat and cable TV. Linens, dishes, and cooking utensils are included, and the coffeepot is on for everyone in the community building in the morning. Picnic tables, lawn chairs, barbecue grills, and a stove for cooking your own lobsters are provided. There is a small private pebble beach. Most units are rented by the week only in-season ($500–800 per week), but they are often available for a couple of days in spring or fall. Doubles, $52–107.

WHERE TO EAT

◆ **The Burning Tree** (207-288-9331), Route 3, Otter Creek. This summery place with several dining rooms—and a wood-burning stove for cool nights—is located between Bar Harbor and Northeast Harbor. Take a drive out of town and be rewarded with one of the best meals on the island—and plenty of space to park your car. Elmer and Alison Beal have been in charge for many years; the name was taken from a song written by Elmer, a guitarist. Appetizers might be crispy kale and oven-roasted little-neck clams with garlic pine nuts and chèvre, or country pâté with Madeira, rosemary, thyme, and summer savory served with fresh grapes and homemade melba toast ($6–8.50). Entrée choices could include broiled halibut served with a browned Pernod and green peppercorn sauce; local crabcakes served with a roasted jalapeño tartar sauce; or—among several vegetarian dishes—cashew, brown rice, and Gruyère terrine served with sautéed mushrooms. Entrées, $18–23. There's a nice wine list. Open mid-June through Labor Day for dinner nightly (except Tuesday) at 5.

◆ **Café This Way** (207-288-4483), 14½ Mount Desert Street, Bar Harbor. This small white building—set back off the street close by the town green—is a favorite of locals. The environment is a bit funky—a wall of bookcases along one side, mismatched tables and chairs, a few lounging chairs and sofas. Breakfast and dinner are served seasonally. The morning meal—the perfect way to prepare for a rig-

The Café This Way in Bar Harbor

orous day of activity—can be a Country Breakfast with two eggs, two pancakes, ham, homefries, and toast for $6.95, eggs Benedict with several accompaniments, granola with spiced yogurt and blueberries and bananas, or corned beef hash. At night, starters include grilled duck sausage with apples and onions; a plate of tapas, smoked salmon, and capers; and Maine crabcakes ($6–9). Several salad choices ($6–8) include grilled Belgian endive served warm over greens with grilled Maine shrimp, smoked Gouda, and a peppery strawberry vinaigrette. For your entrée, you have choices like cashew-crusted chicken over sautéed greens (or substitute cashew-crusted tofu); a Thai seafood pot; grilled tuna served with sautéed apples and smoked shrimp; and baked boneless pork chops ($13–21). There's a full bar, and reservations are taken. Breakfast is served Monday through Saturday 7–11, Sunday 8–1; dinner is served 6–9 nightly.

♦ **Havana** (207-288-CUBA), 318 Main Street, Bar Harbor. This restaurant feels more sophisticated than some because of its clean lines and spare decor. But that's just the background for one very good meal, we are told. The emphasis is on Caribbean, especially Cuban, cuisine. Starters include the classic Cuban black bean soup with cilantro crème and tomato sauce ($5.50). The house salad is fresh lettuces with pecans, red onions, and crumbled goat cheese with a raspberry vinaigrette. Among the appetizers are tenderloin sauté with mushrooms and garlic, and grilled shrimp marinated in brown sugar and rum ($8–10). The main dish might be Jamaican black bean stew with roasted sweet potatoes, served with yellow rice; or brined and roasted double-cut pork chop with rum, chilies, and garlic, finished with a papaya coulis. Entrées, $16–29. Reservations taken. Open from 5:30 nightly.

♦ **Thrumcap** (207-288-3884), 124 Cottage Street, Bar Harbor. The former Porcupine Grill has the same owner, Tom Marinke, but a new name since 2000. The name comes from the spiked-fir crown in the center of small Maine rock-bound islands. The emphasis now is on "smaller portions of upscale cuisine" and the atmosphere—dark wood tables with Chippendale chairs and forest-green napkins—is both luxurious and sedate. There's quite an emphasis on wines, with a huge wine cellar downstairs and many wines offered by the glass. Starters might be grilled marinated quail with plum sauce; Maine clam chowder with smoked salmon crème fraîche; or halibut and salmon mousse ravioli ($9). For entrées, try seared halibut with pine nut and crumb crust and an arugula walnut sauce, or a wild mushroom or crab risotto ($14–18). Finish with caramelized phyllo hazelnut triangles with coffee ice cream or red wine sorbet. Open nightly in-season; weekends only rest of year.

♦ **Mache Bistro** (207-288-0447), 135 Cottage Street, Bar Harbor. Chris Jalbert (the chef) and his wife, Maureen Cosgrove, own this popular little place in town. Chris worked in the kitchen at the renowned Fore Street restaurant in Portland for several years before striking out on his own. This 40-seat spot is busy in-season; reservations are advised. Starters might be native lobster cakes with citrus vinaigrette, mussels with lemon truffle butter, or sautéed shrimp and garlic over greens ($7–10). The main course (priced $16–20) is usually chosen from five to six offerings—possibly hanger steak with port and shallot infused jus; salmon fillet with orange and balsamic vinegar; or a crisp duck breast with orange-infused sauce. Open nightly from early July through Halloween; weekends until January 1. Closed winter and spring.

♦ **Galyn's Galley** (207-288-9706), 17 Main Street, Bar Harbor. This is an old-timer. If you find yourself down near the Town Pier on lower Main Street and want a good meal, here's one place to head. The narrow restaurant, located in a restored 1890s boardinghouse, is tucked between storefronts. It's especially popular locally and is open year-round. An antique mahogany bar is a feature of the **Galley Lounge,** where cocktails, appetizers, or casual dinners are offered. Otherwise, diners choose from a variety of small dining rooms on two floors. Fresh fish is featured. Most recently, an "early lobster special" served between 4 and 6 was going for $13.95. Starters include lobster bisque, clam chowder, and lobster or shrimp cocktail and mussels in a broth of Dijon mustard, white wine, garlic, and herbs ($5–7). Dinner entrées (priced $13–26) include a spicy bouillabaisse known as Frenchman Bay stew, seafood pasta, stuffed pork chop, and tarragon chicken in a mustard cream sauce. All dinner entrées come with garden salad and fresh bread. Among popular desserts are blueberry-apple crisp, Mississippi mud pie, and a cappuccino sundae. Open 11:30–2 for lunch, 4–10 for dinner. Closed January.

♦ **Lompoc Café** (207-288-9392), 36 Rodick Street, Bar Harbor. Now for something a little more casual. Kristin Klint and Patti Savoie own this laid-back café where beers are a specialty. Atlantic Brewing Company ales are on tap and include Bar Harbor blueberry ale—not as sweet as you'd think. Several other beers are on draft; you can get hard apple cider, too. There's a pleasant outdoor terrace with wrought-iron tables. Inside are three different rooms. Several specials appear on the menu each day—such as the pear and Brie quesadilla with sautéed scallops and orange and cranberry sauce, served with a garden salad for lunch when we stopped. At $7.95, it was delicious. Other light possibilities are asparagus and Swiss served open faced with a hot Dijon mustard; shrimp and corn cake sandwich; and a hummus wrap. Appetizers can include stuffed grape leaves, baked spinach and artichoke gratin, or spicy Dijon mussels ($5–8). Pizzas are available. Entrées ($13–18) might be pan-fried trout with hazelnut lemon butter, haddock with sour cream and lime, or asparagus pesto pasta. Open May to November, daily 11:30–3 for lunch, 3–5 for snacks, and 5–9 for dinner.

♦ **Miguel's Mexican Restaurant** (207-288-5117), 51 Rodick Street, Bar Harbor. A brick patio out front, a large bar, and two good-sized dining rooms attract a youngish crowd to this well-established and colorful place. Chairs are blue, napkins red, and tables have a colorful Mexican tile in the center. Fajitas for two (chicken, steak, and shrimp) served on a sizzling platter go for $24; carne Asada is also popular—marinated steak, char-grilled and served with enchiladas ($14). Dinners can be had for as little as $6.95 for two large tacos and go up to about $15. The usual suspects are here, including quesadillas with a variety of fillings, chili with cheese, empanadas, and burritos. A tostada salad is a crispy tortilla shell with refried beans topped with salad and guacamole. Open March to November, nightly from 5.

NORTHEAST HARBOR

Northeast Harbor (so called because it's "northeast" of Southwest Harbor—more on that later) is considered by some the toniest community on Mount Desert Island. It's known for its affluence, its multimillion-dollar summer homes. It became *the* place to be around the turn of the past century when some of the cottagers in Bar Harbor found the place overcrowded and too commercial. The town's deep, sheltered harbor is said to be one of the best along the entire coast of Maine. During the summer months it's filled with gorgeous yachts. But—if you don't have one of your own—there are several ways to sail from Northeast Harbor.

The town is much quieter than Bar Harbor. Yet access to Acadia National Park is quite easy from here, and the Jordan Pond House in the park is close to Northeast Harbor, as are the Wildwood Stables. Shopping is limited to a fairly brief stretch along Main Street, where elegant boutiques and art galleries are found. Some fine public gardens are interesting to visit. Elegant inns and good restaurants make Northeast Harbor a good choice to settle in. From here it's quite easy to explore the rest of MDI.

For more information, contact the **Mount Desert Island Chamber of Commerce** (207-276-5040), P.O. Box 675, Northeast Harbor, ME 04662. Pick up a copy of **Mt. Desert Village/Island Guide & Northeast Harbor Port Directory.**

SEEING AND DOING

Northeast Harbor is renowned for its harbor, its gardens, and its shopping.

Boating

♦ **Sea Princess Cruises** (207-276-5352). Several cruises—with naturalist on board— leave from Northeast Harbor using the tour boat *Sea Princess*. A morning trip with an official Acadia National Park naturalist as narrator leaves at 9:45 and takes about 3 hours. Adults $15, children $10. A similar afternoon trip leaves at 1 and spends a little more time traveling up Somes Sound. The price is the same. A Somes Sound fjord cruise at 3:45 PM takes an hour and a half (adults $12, kids $8). The sunset dinner cruise leaves at 5:30 and takes passengers to a restaurant on Little Cranberry Island where dinner is enjoyed. Adults $12, children $8 for boat only. Trips run seasonally.

♦ **Sailing aboard the** *Chamar* (207-276-3993; winter 207-244-9159), Great Harbor

Charters, P.O. Box 788, Mount Desert, ME 04660. Maggie and Bill Johnston provide explanations of basic sailing and navigation to those who sail aboard their 33-foot sailboat. The full-day cost is $90 per person for a 10 AM to 4 PM trip. The half-day cost is $45 per person for a 9:30 to 12:30 sail or 1 to 4 sail. You can participate in the sailing as much or as little as you want.

♦ **Friendship Sloop** *Blackjack* (207-288-3056). Four 90-minute trips are offered daily (at 10, noon, 2, and 4) from the Town Dock in Northeast Harbor. This 33-foot sloop carries a maximum of six passengers.

♦ **Mailboat to the Cranberry Isles** (207-244-3575). Ferry service to the nearby Cranberry Isles is operated by Beal & Bunker Inc. The boat leaves several times daily from Northeast Harbor. The boat goes to Great Cranberry and Islesford year-round; in summer Sutton Island is also included. Those who take the boat can stay a while, hiking or biking around an island. The round-trip fare is $12 adults, $6 children. You pay $3 per bike.

Biking

Rent bicycles at the **Northeast Harbor Bike Shop** (207-276-5480), Main Street, Northeast Harbor.

Gardens

♦ **Asticou Azalea Gardens,** Routes 3 and 198, Northeast Harbor. Open May to October, sunrise to sunset. More than 50 varieties of azales, rhododendrons, and laurels are in full bloom in this gorgeous spot in early summer. New varieties are added regularly in a garden funded by John D. Rockefeller Jr. The garden is located directly across the street from the Asticou Inn. Stone benches set out for contemplation make this an especially peaceful place.

♦ **Thuya Garden** (207-276-3344), Route 3, Northeast Harbor. Open July through September, daily 7–7. Considered the loveliest public garden on the island, Thuya Garden is located on a hill overlooking the harbor. The grounds are part of a land trust that was set up by a Boston landscape architect, Joseph Henry Curtis, who summered nearby. His cottage is now open to the public with an extensive collection of botanical literature. The name comes from *Thuja occidentalis*, the American white cedar found throughout the area. You can take a small, somewhat steep trail by foot or drive in a car. The path starts on the stone walkway across from the Asticou Terraces parking lot. If you drive, continue past the parking lot and take your first left up Thuya Drive. Follow the road until you reach the cul-de-sac at the end.

A Museum

♦ **Great Harbor Maritime Museum** (207-276-5262), the Old Firehouse, Main Street, Northeast Harbor. A collection of model ships, small boats, and historical artifacts is found here. The number of items is small but growing. Open June through Columbus Day, Monday through Saturday 10–5. Small fee.

Shopping

In the center of Northeast Harbor are lovely shops. The **Holmes Store** has the classic Nantucket pink—here called "Breton red"—pants and Bermuda shorts for men, plus other preppy clothes for men and women. **Island Artisans**—with the work of local craftspeople—has a shop at 119 Main Street. The **Kimball Shop** on Main is fabulous, with several rooms of china, furniture, and kitchen accoutrements. The **Smart Studio and Art Gallery** has lovely paintings and craft items. **Sherman's Bookstore,** located in Bar Harbor, has a branch here. **The Romantic Room** is a stunning shop with all sorts of things for summer cottagers, including, when we were last there, a display of Lilly Pulitzer's pink and green duds. **Pine Bough** is an antiques shop sharing space with **Wikhegan Old Books.**

WHERE TO STAY

♦ **Harbourside Inn** (207-276-3272), Route 198, Northeast Harbor, ME 04662. Great wood-burning fireplaces are found in 9 of the 14 rooms and suites in this turn-of-the-20th-century summer inn. Ours had one, and on the cool and rainy June weekend we spent here we used it gratefully both nights. Built as a summer hotel in 1888, in the shingle style of architecture so popular at the time, the Harbourside Inn was taken over in 1977 by the Sweet family. Gerrie summered on Mount Desert and couldn't wait to bring her U.S. Navy husband, John, back after retirement. Their kids and spouses lend a hand. The inn is maintained in a wonderfully old-fashioned style. There are no TVs, although phones have been added recently.

Lest you expect a water view, the vista has been obscured by trees and construction since the original structure was built. But the harbor is close enough. Rooms are large; a few have separate entrance and all have private bath—some with marble sink and clawfoot tub. Fireplaced accommodations are on the first and second floors. The innkeepers set the fires and provide plenty of wood.

Some rooms have kitchenettes; suites have sunporches. Fresh flowers brighten the space. White Cape Cod–style curtains flutter at the windows, and Oriental rugs adorn some of the wood floors. You may find a king four-poster, a queen-sized bed, or twin beds. Wicker furniture and comfortable chaises on sunporches invite long afternoons of reading.

Guests enjoy homemade blueberry muffins, juice, and coffee or tea on a large first-floor sunporch each morning. A footpath from the property leads directly into Acadia National Park. The minimum stay is 2 nights. Doubles, $125–140; suites, $175–190. Open mid-June to mid-September.

♦ **Grey Rock Inn** (207-276-9360; fax 207-276-9894; www.greyrockinn.com), Route 198, Northeast Harbor, ME 04662. A mother and two sons—Janet, Adam, and Karl Millett—oversee this elegant bed & breakfast inn. Set high off the road on 7 lush acres, the inn's property has trails that lead directly into Acadia, one of them particularly challenging. Built in 1910 as one of the great summer homes of MDI, the house became an inn in 1975. Eight accommodations are offered on the second and third floors, all beautifully decorated and with views of the harbor. "There's not a square room in the house," says Karl. The architect was Fred Savage, well known in the area. The gracious public rooms and a few guest rooms have fireplaces. Beds are queen or king sized, and furnishings include antiques. There are no TVs or telephones, but there is a wonderful selection of reading material. A full breakfast is served at individual tables and includes fresh fruit, a selection of three hot entrées, and beverages. Children 7 and older are welcome. Open mid-May to late October. Doubles, $155–375.

♦ **Asticou Inn** (207-276-3344; 1-800-258-3373; www.asticou.com), Route 3, Northeast Harbor, ME 04662. One of the more famous inns on Mount Desert Island, this classic hostelry has been in continuous operation for more than 100 years. The inn is named for a long-forgotten local Indian chief. Situated at the head of the harbor, with wonderful views from many guest rooms, its dining rooms, and several cottages nearby, the Asticou gives visitors an old-fashioned sense of summer by the sea. Altogether there are 47 rooms, 16 in outlying buildings—including the Cranberry Lodge with 3 rooms. There are also two rooms in each of several surprisingly modern circular cottages that overlook the water, known as Topsiders. Room 103 in the main inn is typical: a not-large room with floral wallpaper, queen-sized bed, gorgeous view of the harbor, and telephone but no TV. Rooms have private bath. A deck stretching the length of the main inn overlooks the harbor and is a place to enjoy lunch or cocktails. Three meals a day are served in summer in the main dining room, with its mural-decorated walls and Windsor-style chairs (see *Where to Eat*). Clay tennis courts and a heated outdoor pool are on the well-landscaped property. Tea is served in the afternoon. Breakfast is standard with all rooms; dinner may be added for an additional charge. Open mid-May to late October. Doubles, B&B, $130–285; MAP, $292–362. Suites, B&B, $175–325; MAP, $282–402.

♦ **Kimball Terrace Inn** (207-276-3383; 1-800-454-6251; fax 207-276-4102), Huntington Road, Northeast Harbor, ME 04662. Most of the 70 rooms in this motel-like establishment have water views of beautiful Northeast Harbor; the others have so-called forest views out back. Rooms have two double beds, TV, and private bath. Most also have private balcony—many with water views.

There is a good-sized outdoor pool on the property, and public tennis courts are nearby at the marina. The **Main Sail** restaurant is attached and offers three meals a day. Doubles, $70–150. Open April through October.

WHERE TO EAT

♦ **151 Main Street** (207-276-9898; fax 207-276-5188), 151 Main Street, Northeast Harbor. New in 2001 was this charming storefront restaurant opened by Northeast Harbor native Nicene Pascal and his chef-wife, Emily Damon Pascal. A specialty bakery augments the dinner-only restaurant, allowing for custom cake orders and such. A few high-backed booths, several small tables with bentwood chairs and banquettes, and a long bar—where dinner can also be eaten—set the comfortable tone. There are nautical charts on the walls. Comfort foods—including chicken potpie, meat loaf, and meatballs (as a starter)—seemed part of the attraction early in the season. And the prices were right. The place was packed on a Friday night. Small plates (appetizers) included Maine crabcakes and "limies" (bacon, onion, and cheese broiled on crispy English muffins) — $4–8. A garden or Caesar salad was offered at $5. Thin-crust pizzas topped with veggies (caramelized onion, spinach, mushrooms, and cheese) or white clams and bacon, for example, were $8 or $9 and served two or three. "Large plates" included the excellent chicken potpie, shrimp Gambino (sautéed in butter, shallots, and bread crumbs, and served with linguine), and a 10-ounce hand-cut sirloin steak with garlic mashed potatoes. Open for dinner Tuesday through Saturday 5–9. Dinner is also offered on Sunday in summer.

♦ **Jordan Pond House** (207-276-3316), Park Loop Road, Acadia National Park. The tradition of dining at the Jordan Pond House extends back to 1847. Prior to that, Mr. and Mrs. Thomas McIntire presided over a restaurant with birch-bark dining rooms and massive fieldstone fireplaces from 1895 to 1945 in the same spot. In 1946 it became part of Acadia National Park. After a fire in 1979 the current, more contemporary building was erected, still with a massive stone fireplace in the center of the dining room. Tea and popovers are served 11:30–5:30 daily ($7). (You can now substitute cappuccino for tea, and pay a dollar extra.) Lunch offers lobster stew and popovers ($12 cup, $15 bowl); a salad of mixed greens, tomatoes, olives, local feta, and balsamic vinaigrette for $7.50; a $14.25 lobster roll; and entrées ($11–18) like grilled Maine salmon and baked scallops. From 5:30 to 8 or 9, dinner is available. A complete dinner special includes soup or salad; a lighter portion of one of four regular entrées (salmon, chicken, scallops, pasta) with rice or potato, vegetables, and popovers; and a choice of homemade ice cream or blueberry crisp, all for $19. Entrées, priced $16–20, include prime rib, Maine crabcakes, steamed lobster, and a bowl of lobster stew. Popovers can be had for dessert with Jordan Pond ice cream for $5. Reservations are recommended in summer. Open mid-May to October, daily 11:30 to 8 or 9.

♦ **Asticou Inn** (207-276-3344), Route 3, Northeast Harbor. The dining room at the Asticou is managed by the New England Culinary Institute. All three meals, plus cocktails, are served. Lunch on the harborside deck is available in July and August. Lobster and crabmeat rolls for $12.95 or a chicken breast sandwich at $7.95 are among the offerings. At night, candlelight dinners in the main dining room are a soothing end to an active day. Start with sliced smoked duck breast with rhubarb chutney and bitter greens, baked stuffed clams carbonara, or oysters on the half shell ($8–12). Entrées ($19–27) include wild mushroom and eggplant roulade, lobster stew, baked stuffed lobster, and rosemary rack of lamb with white bean ragout. Dinner nightly when the inn is open.

♦ **The Docksider Restaurant** (207-276-3965), 14 Sea Street, Northeast Harbor. This casual family restaurant under the management of two sisters — Brenda and Gail Webber — for more than 20 years is a local favorite. Light pine booths and tables inside — and a small deck outside with tables and chairs — set the scene for fresh fish and all kinds of lobster. Actually, you can get almost anything here, including hamburgers, PB&J, hot dogs, chicken salad, and grilled cheese sandwiches. The clam chowder is great — not too floury — and the Islander special includes a cup of it, a boiled lobster, a choice of sides, and blueberry pie or ice cream for $17. A shore dinner ups the ante with steamed clams and comes to $21. You can get a lobster cocktail as a starter. Dinners include chicken potpie, seafood crêpes, fried or grilled haddock, jumbo sautéed lobster, and a cold shellfish plate ($9–25, with the sautéed lobster the highest). Wines and beers are available. Open late May to early October, 11:30–9. Sometimes hours are abbreviated in the off-season.

♦ **Abel's Lobster Pound** (207-276-5827), Route 198, Somes Sound. This is probably the most elegant of the lobster pounds on MDI in that you don't have to wait for your number to be blared out and then do your own hauling. Abel's has a waitstaff. After a busy day, we enjoyed kicking back with a beer and ordering our lobster dinners from a cheerful and energetic Bates College student. Abel's is located in a boatyard with picnic tables amid pine trees on the lawn overlooking Somes Sound. However, we all opted for the indoor wood-paneled building with long picnic tables on two levels because it was a foggy, chilly night. There are still views through the big windows. Lobster dinners are priced by size (small at $19.45, medium $22.95, and large $24.95) and come with coleslaw and baked potato. Pies (apple or blueberry) are $5 a slice. You can also order chowder, steamers, and other usual accompaniments. Open Memorial Day through June, 5–9; July and August, noon–10; September through Columbus Day, 5–9. Reservations are recommended in the evening.

SOMESVILLE

En route to the town of **Southwest Harbor,** you will pass through **Somesville.** Stop at **Port in a Storm Bookstore** (207-244-4114) at the head of Somes Sound—a delightful two-story bookstore, with places to sit and read. Many special events, including author signings, are scheduled. **Somesville Museum** (207-244-5043) at 2 Oak Hill Road has exhibits on Mount Desert Island history. It's open June 15 through September, Tuesday through Saturday 10–5. You can pick up a self-guided tour pamphlet of pretty Somesville with its Greek Revival houses here. This museum is run by the Mount Desert Island Historical Society.

SOUTHWEST HARBOR

Southwest Harbor is so called because it lies southwest of Bar Harbor. Then along came Northeast Harbor, which designated its location in relationship to Southwest Harbor. No wonder visitors get confused! Southwest Harbor is located on the half of Mount Desert Island that is across Somes Sound, south of Somesville. Route 102 gets you there. It's a busy community, the next liveliest to Bar Harbor, with an active shipbuilding trade, stores, restaurants, and places to stay. This is the so-called quiet side of MDI.

During the mid-1800s, Southwest Harbor was the center of life on Mount Desert. It was the island's commercial hub. Hotel development flourished. It's possible the fish-canning industry (and the odors created by it) steered tourists away from Southwest Harbor. But now there are no more fish canneries and Southwest Harbor is a great little town to visit. The **Hinckley Yacht Company** is the best known of the boatbuilders in town. Operating since 1932, Hinckley is thought by some to build the finest yachts and motorboats in the world. A small store near the boatyard (on Mansell Lane, off Route 102A) sells nautical and sailing equipment.

For more information, contact the **Southwest Harbor/Tremont Chamber of Commerce** (207-244-9264; 1-800-423-9264), Route 102, P.O. Box 1143, Southwest Harbor, ME 04679.

SEEING AND DOING

♦ **Wendell Gilley Museum of Bird Carving** (207-244-7555), Route 102, Southwest Harbor. Wendell Gilley was a resident of Southwest Harbor who took up wooden bird carving as a hobby. Eventually, he was considered one of the country's best folk artists. The museum displays eagles, puffins, bluebirds, loons, and other birds carved by Gilley. There are also video presentations, lectures on environmental topics, wildlife art exhibits, and a museum shop. Carving demonstrations and workshops are popular. June through October, Tuesday through Sunday 10–4; May, November, and December, Friday through Sunday 10–4. Adults $3.25, children $1.

♦ **The Oceanarium** (207-244-7330), Clark Point Road (next to the Coast Guard Station), Southwest Harbor. More than 20 exhibits and displays focusing on the sea life in local waters. Informal tours and discussions. Open mid-May to mid-October, Monday through Saturday 9–5. Adults $5.95, children $4.25.

♦ **Oktoberfest.** In October more than 20 Maine microbrewers gather in Southwest Harbor for the annual celebration. Beer, food, and music are the focus of the all-day event. For this year's date, contact the chamber of commerce at (207) 244-9264.

Boating

♦ **Schooner *Annie McGee*** (1-888-818-8234) is a charter vessel—smallest of the windjammers—available for all-day sails. Six-person maximum. The vessel costs $500 for exclusive use for a full day. Per-person tickets are $100 each. Departs from Southwest Harbor July to October, daily except Friday.

Hiking

The chamber of commerce has a terrific trail map/hiking guide called *Take a Hike on the Quiet Side*. Call (207) 244-9264.

Shopping

The Dogwood Tree advertises "fun clothing and gifts." **Hot Flash Anny's** has some neat stained-glass pieces. Great breads and other bakery items can be found at **Little Notch Bakery. MDI Sportswear** has clothing and accessories, some for the sportsman.

♦ **The Claremont Hotel** (1-800-244-5036; fax 207-244-3512; www.acadia.net/ clarement), Clark Point Road, Southwest Harbor, ME 04679. Established in 1884, the yellow-clapboard Claremont is on the National Register of Historic Places. The main inn, with gorgeous views of Somes Sound, has 24 recently renovated rooms. On the 6-acre waterside site are also 12 housekeeping cottages, each with wood or gas fireplace; the Phillips House with six guest rooms including two with fireplace; and the Clark House with its own suite. The newly constructed Cole Cottage includes a ground-floor efficiency and two second-floor guest rooms with water views. The old-fashioned fireplaced lobby sets the tone for the inn, which retains a sense of timelessness and old-fashioned charm. Two other common rooms invite reading; one is a game room with board games. Everything is meticulously maintained. Rooms are light and breezy, traditionally furnished, with private bath but no TVs. Since 1977 the hotel has hosted an important tournament of nine-wicket croquet during early August. Guests may participate or simply watch. The weeklong event culminates in a lively buffet dinner with entertainment on Saturday. There are a clay tennis court, bicycles, a dock, rowboats, and a library. The Claremont dining room (see *Where to Eat*) is well regarded, and jackets are required. Doubles, B&B, $95–169; MAP, $145–229. Open Memorial Day through October.

♦ **The Inn at Southwest** (207-244-3833; www.innatsouthwest.com), Box 593, Southwest Harbor, ME 04679. This high-mansard-roofed house in the village is a charmer. Sandy Johnson and Andrea Potapovs took over as innkeepers in 2001, making a few cosmetic changes to what was already a lovely Victorian-era inn. Among the changes was the installation of gas log stoves in several rooms, and the conversion of a couple of spaces into suites. All rooms are named for historic Maine lighthouses. They have private bath, down comforter, and ceiling fan. A full breakfast is included in the rates—things like crab potato bake and Belgian waffles. Winter Harbor is a two-room suite with bay window, queen four-poster canopy bed, and shower bath. French doors lead to a sitting room with wood floors and a gas log stove. Egg Rock is small and cozy with full-sized bed, shower bath, and writing desk. There's a window seat under a chapel window in Owl's Head. Open May 1 to early November. Doubles, $70–160.

♦ **Lindenwood Inn** (207-244-5335; 1-800-307-5335; fax 207-244-3643; www.lindenwoodinn.com), 118 Clark Point Road, Southwest Harbor, ME 04679. Australian Jim King owns this exceptional 21-room inn, and has enlisted the assistance of Esther Cavagnaro, who knows how to run an inn, as manager. She has had experience in a number of high-level places on MDI. Teak seating on the front porch can be used for cocktails or appetizers before dinner, since the Lindenwood is aiming to make its dining room into a separate destination. The attractive small reception parlor sets a sophisticated tone for the inn. Rooms all have private bath and include a range of options, from standard rooms with double or queen bed to housekeeping suites with fully equipped kitchens and gas fireplaces. All accommodations have TV, and several have harbor views. If yours doesn't, it's easy enough to walk from the property to the waterfront. A heated in-ground pool and whirlpool are available for guest use. A full breakfast is included, served in the dining room. Doubles, $75–185. Open year-round.

♦ **The Moorings Inn** (207-244-5523; 1-800-596-5523; www.mooringsinn.com), Shore Road, Southwest Harbor, ME 04679. Nautical touches fill the old-fashioned public rooms of this family-run inn on the water south of town. The location is great, and prices are a bargain for the area in-season. That may be because some of the rooms are on the rustic side. Our twin-bedded room with small screened-in porch over-looking the water was that way—the porch especially needed to be given a little attention. The Moorings doesn't promise breakfast, so perhaps we should not have been disappointed in the store-bought doughnuts, available with coffee and juices. Once you get beyond those little quibbles, this is a terrific spot for families, for those who want to be out of the fray, and for those who enjoy the use of rowboats and canoes, which can be rented. There is a restaurant next door, which adds to the convenience. Altogether 10 rooms in the main inn, another 3 rooms in a motel unit out back, a two-bedroom Pilot House, and three efficiencies in Lookout Cottage comprise the property. The King family has been in charge for 40 years and offer attentive service. Most units are heated, and The Moorings is open year-round. Doubles, $60–150.

WHERE TO EAT

♦ **Preble Grill** (207-244-3034), 14 Clark Point Road. A bright southwestern look sets the scene for this popular, casual restaurant located in the heart of the village. A redbrick fireplace offers warmth in the cool months. Booths are set around the perimeter of the restaurant. The food is billed as Mediterranean/regional. At lunchtime, have a house-roasted turkey breast, Maine cranberry chutney, bacon, and Swiss cheese sandwich; a lobster roll; or honey-glazed salmon wrapped with rice, roasted peppers, and Asiago cheese in a tomato tortilla ($5–13). There are also soups and salads. In the evening starters can be lobster ravioli or a grilled pizza topped with pesto and four cheeses ($8–10). Pastas ($14–17) include shrimp with artichokes and feta over farfelle, and Mediterranean meat sauce over penne. A fish of the day, lobster, chicken Marsala, pork tenderloin with mango shallot sauce, and grilled Angus steak are on the entrée list ($15–22 range). Desserts change daily. Open year-round, 11:30–2 for lunch, 5–9 for dinner.

♦ **Fiddlers' Green** (207-244-9416), 411 Main Street, Southwest Harbor. Chef Derek Wilbur grew up in town; he and his wife opened this quickly popular spot in a big house on the main drag in 1999. In 2001 they expanded with a raw bar and martini bar deck to one side. We ate here the first season and found the food inventive and good. Since then the place has blossomed. Diners eat in one of two rooms toward the rear of the house, overlooking flower gardens. One has deep yellow sponge-painted walls. Appetizers might include grilled veal sausage with a three-onion fennel sauté and mole sauce, or mussels steamed in Guinness, garlic, and shallots ($7–9). Entrées, including house salad, home-baked breads, and a potato or grain, could be roasted wild boar and scallops atop green cabbage with Damson plum sauce; pan-seared yellowfin tuna; or seared and roasted duck breast with a pomegranate glaze ($21–27). Finish the evening with a dish of pineapple coconut sorbet, maple-iced layer cake with almond buttercream, or crème brûlée. Open mid-May to mid-October for dinner only. Reservations suggested in midseason.

♦ **The Claremont** (207-244-5036), Clark Point Road, Southwest Harbor. The view from the dining room at the Claremont Hotel is about as good as it gets—a beautiful panorama of Somes Sound. You can have a drink first on the deck of the Boathouse, then saunter over to this old-fashioned dining room where jackets are required for gentlemen. White tablecloths and bentwood chairs set the tone. Starters could be salt cod cakes with bacon and chive oil, smoked salmon pâté, or shrimp cocktail ($7–8). French onion soup is offered with a soup of the day. Entrées include roasted free-range chicken with cranberry pine nut stuffing, shell-fish linguine, and Atlantic sea bass served with risotto and fresh avocado, red onion, and apricot. Entrée prices range $19–21. Dinner nightly, late June through early September.

♦ **Beal's Lobster Pier** (207-244-3202; 1-800-245-7178), Clark Point Road, Southwest Harbor. You sit right out on a pier and watch all the boating action while waiting for them to call your number so you can pick up your lobster and the trimmings. Crabmeat rolls are also available. You have to head to a second location to order a beer or other beverage, but once you've got it all done, this is a great place to linger in the evening, with the sun going down and the day coming to an end.

15 ◆ Newport, Rhode Island

Talk about ritzy! Newport takes the crown—for here more than anywhere else in the United States the gentry came to play, to be seen, and, incidentally, to vacation. In Newport during the late 1800s and early 1900s, the Gilded Age was truly celebrated. Extravagant houses, dress, and parties were in style. Those who came created their own little world, the main ticket of admission being *wealth*.

Why Newport? The place had long been fashionable—in one way or another. Newport is actually one of the earliest colonial communities in the Northeast. The town was founded in 1639 by a small band of Boston colonists who left Massachusetts—attracted in part by Newport's excellent natural harbor and setting. Those first settlers laid out their port and immediately began to build ships and wharves. By the mid–18th century the town was at its height of maritime prosperity. Gorgeous Federal-period homes attest to that success, including Hunter House, the very first home renovated and opened by the Preservation Society of Newport County.

Even after Newport's post–Revolutionary War mercantile decline, the town was attractive for its setting and its marvelous climate. Southerners came, as well as New Yorkers, Bostonians, and visitors from Baltimore—all in search of cool, breezy, watery summer vacations. At first they boarded at farms. The first true hotel went up in the mid-1820s just off Bellevue Avenue. The earliest summerhouses were built in the 1830s. It is to this period that Kingscote belongs; it is one of the mansions opened by the Newport Preservation Society.

The most imposing "cottage" to be erected in the 1850s is Chateau-sur-Mer. This Italian stone villa is also open to the public and maintained by the preservation society.

Gradually—and certainly by the 1860s—it was no longer fashionable to stay at a Newport hotel for the season. One had to own or rent a "cottage." As the Civil War depleted visitors from the South, cottagers from New York and Boston began to dominate summer society. And Bellevue Avenue was the street of streets—most mansions were either on it or very close by.

Visitors tour The Breakers in Newport

The Newport season—while it attracted certain writers and artists—was very much a season of sport. Riding, coaching, tennis, croquet, fishing, sailing, polo, and golf were all enjoyed. In 1879 the Newport Casino (with tennis courts, a theater, and other recreational facilities) was built by James Gordon Bennett Jr., publisher of the *New York Herald.* He built it across the street from his cottage on Bellevue. It was an immediate hit and remained a center of the daytime activities for the "cottage set" for decades.

From the 1880s to the 1900s the cottages became what truly may be called mansions—larger, grander, more opulent than anything conceived of in America before. They made Newport the most important resort of the Gilded Age. These mansions included Marble House, built by William K. Vanderbilt as an anniversary gift for his wife and clad in shimmering white marble. It was soon eclipsed by The Breakers, the summerhouse of his older brother, Cornelius II. This mansion—modeled on the idea of a European palace—has never been surpassed. It's among the 10 most visited tourist sites in all of America.

The mix of beautiful Colonial architecture and fancy Victorian summer "cottages" makes the town one of the most interesting in New England architecturally. Just walk the streets to the north and east of the downtown area and notice all the plaques proclaiming the age of the buildings plus—in many cases—their inclusion on the National Register. What's even better is the fact that most are in use today: as homes, offices, and small inns or restaurants.

Newport lies on the southernmost section of Aquidneck Island, and Newporters are always saying "Here on the island." Its watery environs—from a deep natural harbor on the Narragansett Bay side to a wild southern shore facing the open Atlantic—have influenced its fortunes all along. From its early days as home to a fleet of merchant ships, to its era as a yachting capital for the rich and famous, to its days as site of a major establishment of the U.S. Navy, Newport's economy has been much dependent on the sea.

So it is, still. Tourism reigns in this small city of just over 30,000 residents—with more than 4 million visitors arriving annually. The mansions are a major draw, and so is the water. Visitors almost always take a drive along the dramatic and scenic oceanfront road known as Ocean Drive or amble along the Cliff Walk, which runs behind many of the largest mansions along the edge of the sea. They pack the wharves to have a meal with a view of the water, or simply to walk and shop where they also can see boats bobbing at anchor. If they are lucky, and can afford it, they may even book a room with a water view.

Newport can be pricey. It's home to the largest concentration of high-style B&Bs and inns—for a town of its size—in New England. Many of its restaurants offer fine dining with menu prices to match. Shopping in Newport is fun, but can also do damage to the wallet.

Newport is a place to indulge yourself. Imagine staying in a room with its own fireplace, double Jacuzzi tub, and rooftop deck with hot tub and view of the entire waterfront. (You can.) Consider dining on a classically prepared French meal at a beautifully decorated, chef-owned restaurant. Enjoy the opportunity to buy trendy fashions or fine antiques.

Newport can, however, be frustrating to visit. Its narrow streets (many of them

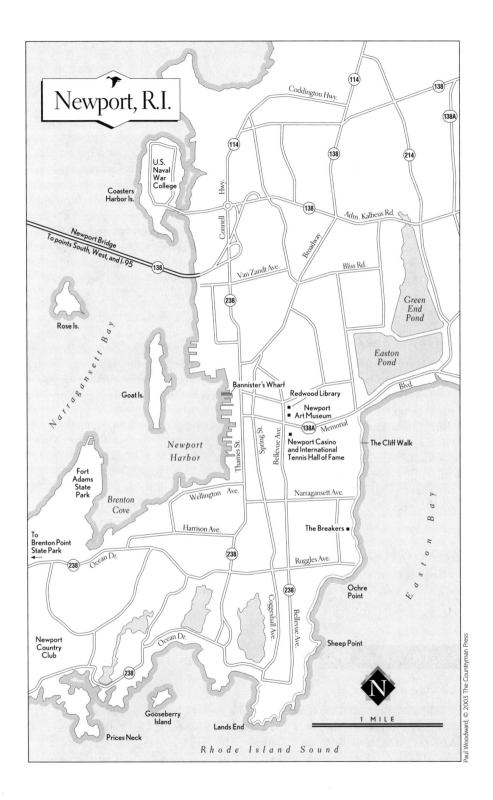

Newport, R.I.

U.S. Naval War College

Coasters Harbor Is.

114

Coddington Hwy.

114

138

138

138A

214

Connell Hwy.

Newport Bridge
To points South, West, and I-95

138

Adm. Kalbeus Rd.

Broadway

138A

Van Zandt Ave.

Bliss Rd.

238

Rose Is.

Narragansett Bay

Goat Is.

Green End Pond

Easton Pond

Blvd.

Bannister's Wharf

Redwood Library

Newport Art Museum

138A Memorial

Newport Casino and International Tennis Hall of Fame

The Cliff Walk

Newport Harbor

Thames St.

Spring St.

Bellevue Ave.

Fort Adams State Park

Brenton Cove

Wellington Ave.

Narragansett Ave.

To Brenton Point State Park

Harrison Ave.

The Breakers

Easton Bay

238

Ocean Dr.

238

Ruggles Ave.

238

Ochre Point

Newport Country Club

Ocean Dr.

Coggeshall Ave.

Bellevue Ave.

Sheep Point

238

N

Gooseberry Island

Lands End

1 MILE

Prices Neck

Rhode Island Sound

one-way) weren't laid out for today's crowds. This makes the town a nightmare to negotiate by auto on weekends in July and August. Finding a parking place is a high-stakes game. If you're fortunate enough to get one, leave the car and walk. The downtown is compact.

You can also visit off-season. Spring, fall, and winter are wonderful times to be in Newport. Snow is relatively rare, because of the ocean's influence. Some Newport mansions—plus many other sites of interest—are open year-round. Many of Newport's inns and B&Bs offer fireplaced guest rooms and elaborate afternoon teas. There is something quite magical about spending a bracingly cold winter day by the ocean, followed by a warming dinner—perhaps in front of a fireplace. Then you can return to your own luxurious digs where you can have your own fire, falling to sleep in front of its flickering flames.

Whenever you go, you will find Newport a town of discovery—with new places to explore each time you visit. In this chapter we concentrate on the moneyed face of Newport—its history as a resort of distinction where American high society congregated and played. We look at some of its more luxurious inns and B&Bs, its upscale restaurants, its lovely shops. It's time for a splurge.

Getting There

By car: From New York City, take I-95 to the third Newport exit, picking up Route 138 east and crossing the Newport toll bridge ($2) just north of the downtown district. From Boston, you can take Route 24 through Fall River and then pick up Route 114 into town.

By bus: Bonanza Bus Lines (401-846-1820) buses come right into the center of town to 23 America's Cup Avenue at the Gateway Center. This is also the location of the tourist information center.

By air: T. F. Green/Providence Airport (401-737-8222) in Warwick, south of Providence, handles national flights into the state. From the airport, a shuttle operates to Newport ($20). Call (401) 737-2868 for information and booking.

For More Information

♦ **Newport Convention and Visitors Bureau** (401-849-8048; www.GoNewport. com), 23 America's Cup Avenue. **The Preservation Society of Newport County** (401-847-1000; www.NewportMansions.org) has information on most mansions.

SEEING AND DOING

The Mansions

The following properties are operated by The Preservation Society of Newport County: The Breakers, Marble House, The Elms, Rosecliff, Chateau-sur-Mer, Kingscote, the Isaac Bell House, Chepstow, Hunter House, and Green Animals Topiary Garden. Three properties are open from January 2 through April 12: The

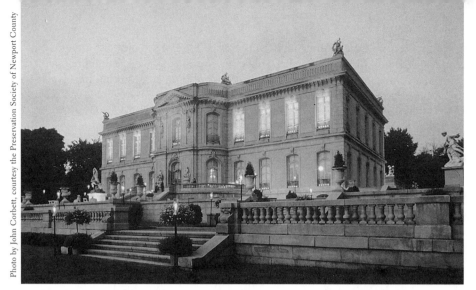

The Elms

Breakers is open daily, and Chateau-sur-Mer and The Elms are open on weekends.

From mid-April to mid-May, the Breakers, the Elms, and Chateau-sur-Mer are joined by Marble House and Rosecliff and open daily, usually 10–5. From mid-May to mid-October, all properties are open daily. From mid-October to early November, The Breakers, Chateau-sur-Mer, The Elms, Marble House, and Rosecliff remain open daily, while the others close. Throughout November, The Breakers, The Elms, and Marble House are open daily. From late November to January 1, Christmas decorations are seen at The Breakers, The Elms, and Marble House, which remain open daily. Some holiday evening events are held in December.

Admission: single house except The Breakers, $10; The Breakers, $15; Rooftop and Behind-the-Scenes Tour at The Elms, $15; Bellevue Avenue Walking Tour (offered late May to mid-October, Thursday and Sunday at 11 AM), $25. Several combination tickets are available. Call The Preservation Society of Newport County at (401) 847-1000 or visit www.newportmansions.org.

Other mansions open to the public and operated separately are The Astors' Beechwood, Belcourt Castle, and Rough Point.

♦ **The Breakers, Ochre Point Avenue.** This four-story limestone palace with 70 rooms epitomizes the Gilded Age. Cornelius Vanderbilt II, grandson of Commodore Vanderbilt, engaged architect Richard Morris Hunt for the design, modeled after Renaissance palaces of Turin and Genoa. Work was begun in 1893 and completed in just over 2 years. The dining room could seat 34 in red upholstered chairs; an upper and lower loggia had gorgeous views of the ocean and were open-air spaces. There were 26 fireplaces along with central heating; taps in the bathrooms could be turned to hot or cold salt or fresh water. More than 95 percent of the house is original with the furnishings, too, so you get to see The Breakers as it looked when the Vanderbilts were at the top of their game, so to speak. A children's playhouse outdoors is interesting and the view of the water, magnificent.

♦ **Kingscote, Bellevue Avenue at Bowery Street.** One of the oldest summer cottages still standing in Newport, Kingscote dates from 1839—well before the Civil War put a damper on summer visits by wealthy southerners. It was built for George Noble Jones, a well-to-do plantation owner from Savannah, Georgia. Designed by the well-known architect Richard Upjohn (who designed New York's Trinity Church), the house is in the Gothic Revival style. It was later added onto by subsequent owners David and Ella King, with the addition designed by Stanford White. Peaked roofs, gables, and stained glass all figure into its design; there are parquet floors and twin parlors furnished with family pieces.

♦ **The Elms, Bellevue Avenue at Dixon Street.** Here is a massive place, built for the coal magnate Edward Berwind of Pennsylvania by Horace Trumbauer, a young architect from Philadelphia. It is a copy of an 18th-century French château, surrounded by a 10-acre park with beautiful plantings. The grand staircase is of white marble with an elaborate wrought-iron and bronze railing. An airy conservatory with fountain, a Venetian-style dining room with large wall murals, and a ballroom used for lavish entertaining are among its features. A behind-the-scenes tour of The Elms is especially interesting—and takes you to the downstairs boilers that heated the house, to the kitchens, and even up onto the roof.

♦ **Chateau-sur-Mer, Bellevue Avenue at Shepard Avenue.** This mansion was built for William Shepard Wetmore, who settled in Newport after making a fortune in the China trade. Completed initially in 1852, it was designed as a romantic Italianate villa. After Mr. Wetmore's death in 1862, the house became the property of his only son, George Peabody Wetmore, who hired Richard Morris Hunt to rebuild the house. Steep mansard roofs were added and a huge billiard room was designed.

♦ **Rosecliff, Bellevue Avenue.** This mansion has the largest ballroom in Newport, a 40-by-80-foot space that was the scene many lavish balls and dinners hosted by Theresa Fair Oelrichs, wife of the American agent of the North German Lloyd steamship line. The most famous of her entertainings was the Bal Blanc, given on August 19, 1904, to celebrate the Astor Cup race. For the event the house was transformed into a world of white—white hydrangeas and hollyhocks in the vestibule; white roses, orchids, and lilies of the valley in the ballroom. Women guests dressed in white and powdered their hair. All the male guests wore black. Parts of the movie *The Great Gatsby* were filmed here. Its exterior rose garden has been restored.

♦ **Marble House, Bellevue Avenue.** No surprise, this mansion is built of white marble with four towering Corinthian columns at its entrance. It's a dramatic place, built for Alva Vanderbilt, wife of William K. Vanderbilt. The architect was Richard Morris Hunt, and the house was begun in 1888 in great secrecy. Laborers were mostly French and Italian and directed not to communicate about the job. Modeled after the Petit Trianon at Versailles, the house has the most ornate ballroom in Newport, called the Gold Ballroom. Unfortunately, 2 years after the house was built the couple divorced. There is also a wonderful Chinese Teahouse on the estate.

♦ **The Isaac Bell House, Bellevue Avenue.** This is one of my favorites to visit in Newport, for its renovation is "in process." One of the best surviving examples of shingle-style architecture in the nation, it was erected in 1881–1883 by the firm of

McKim, Mead & White as a summer residence for Isaac Bell Jr., a wealthy cotton broker. It blends English Queen Anne architecture with New England Colonial and Oriental influences. Huge outdoor porches, peaked roofs, and unique exterior shingle patterns are all of note.

♦ **Chepstow, Narragansett Avenue.** This cottage originally was built for Edmund Schermerhorn in 1860–1861 as a summer residence. The architect, George Champlin Mason Sr., was a Newport native. Schermerhorn, a bachelor, retired permanently to Newport after a few seasons and was reported to be Newport's richest year-round resident. The estate was later purchased by Mrs. Emily Morris Gallatin in 1911, and it was she who provided its current name. The house contains Gallatin furnishings along with a collection of important 19th-century American paintings.

♦ **Hunter House, Washington Street,** in The Point section of town. This beautiful house comes from another era. It's a fine example of mid-18th-century architecture and was the first house to be saved by the preservation society. The Point area was the focus of Newport's marine trade, and the house was built for Jonathan Nichols, a merchant in the shipping trade. The house was added onto by its later owner, Colonel Joseph Wanton, and is now a two-and-a-half-story dwelling with four rooms on each floor. It's noted for its interior woodwork and fine furnishings, including many pieces from the local cabinetmaking firm of Townsend and Goddard. Many original pieces are gone, but authentic Queen Anne, Chippendale, and Hepplewhite pieces made by Townsends and Goddards and other Rhode Island craftsmen fill the house today.

♦ **Green Animals** is a charming seaside estate in nearby Portsmouth, Rhode Island. Its topiary garden is wonderful—with hedges carved into the shapes of animals and other dramatic designs.

♦ **The Astors' Beechwood Mansion** (401-846-3772; www.astors-beechwood.com), 580 Bellvue Avenue, Newport. For many visitors this mansion tour is a favorite. Here actors take the roles of servants, guests, and family members of Caroline Astor, Mrs. John Jacob Astor I, whose home this was. House administrators refer to it as Newport's "only living history museum." Caroline Astor was *the* Mrs. Astor, and the famous term *Four Hundred* referred to the number of people who could fit into her ballroom in New York City. The guides provide lively and humorous sketches of life at the time the mansion was occupied by the Astors, beginning in the 1880s. Most Tuesday evenings in-season there are "Astor balls," with a promenade involving tourists and staff and exhibition dances. Most Thursday evenings there are murder mystery tours, but check first—the schedule can change. Open from mid-May to early November, daily 10–5. Adults $15, seniors and children $10, family pass for two adults and up to four children $45.

♦ **Belcourt Castle** (401-846-0669; www.belcourtcastle.com), 657 Bellevue Avenue, Newport. Belcourt Castle was constructed in 1891–1894 for Oliver Hazard Perry Belmont, who inherited a fortune from his father, August Belmont. He married the divorced Alva Vanderbilt in 1896, giving her the deed to Belcourt as a wedding present. The house is now owned by the Harold B. Tinney family, but is opened to the public for tours. Designed by Richard Morris Hunt, the house contains 60 rooms, each done in a different period of French, Italian, or English design. A large collection of stained glass is a highlight. The center courtyard, where the Belmont horses were exercised daily, is of interest. Open daily year-round except Wednesdays in March. (Check for times, which can vary.) Adults $10, seniors $8, children $5. Candlelight and/or ghost tours, available some evenings, cost $15.

♦ **Rough Point** (401-849-7300; www.newportrestoration.org). The most recent of Newport's grand houses to be opened to the public is the estate of tobacco heiress Doris Duke, who was also founder of the Newport Restoration Foundation. Visitors must take a shuttle bus from the Gateway Information Center to visit the house; the round-trip plus tour of the house takes about an hour and a half. This vast Gothic-style house was built by Frederick W. Vanderbilt in 1889 on a windswept promontory overlooking the Atlantic Ocean. It was purchased by Doris Duke's father in the 1920s. The house preserves the memories of Newport's Gilded Age and its architects as well as showcasing the collections of art acquired by Miss Duke. It is furnished as it was at the time of her death in 1993. Visitors tour almost the entire first floor and can also view Doris Duke's second-floor bedroom and a music room on that floor. Plans were being made to exhibit some memorabilia of Miss Duke's, including clothing and jewelry. Open mid-May through October, Tuesday through Saturday 9–4. Adults $25, children $24.

Tours

For an overview of Newport, you can take a 90-minute trolley tour of town by **Viking Tours** (401-847-6921), 23 America's Cup Avenue at the Gateway Center. Tours are offered daily April through October; from November through March, on Saturday only. The tour takes riders past 150 attractions. The cost is $20 for adults, $10 for children. You can tack on a tour of a mansion or two if you want for an additional charge. In that case, you're dropped off at the mansion and picked up by another trolley when the tour is over. All tours are first-come, first-served. In the busy summer season, you should get there 20 to 30 minutes ahead of time.

Sites of Interest

♦ **Museum of Newport History** (401-841-8770; 401-846-0813), 127 Thames Street in the Brick Market at the foot of Washington Square. This is a wonderful small museum and as good a place to begin a weekend visit to Newport as any. With engaging exhibits, the Newport Historical Society—operator of the museum—puts into perspective the highlights of the city's fascinating history. The building itself is fascinating, completed in 1771 and used for years as a place where goods from seagoing ships were sold. Exhibits on *Newport and the Sea* and *Neighborhoods of Newport* are well done. There are old advertisements for steamboats to New York City, account books of 18th-century merchants, boat models, even a video on a torpedo station from World War II. You can sit high in an 1890s "omnibus" and view a video about the Gilded Age and Bellevue Avenue. Open in-season daily (except Tuesday) 10–5, Sunday 1–5. In winter, hours may be abbreviated. Adults $5, seniors $4, students $3.

♦ **International Tennis Hall of Fame** (401-849-3990; 1-800-457-1144; www.tennis-fame.com), 194 Bellevue Avenue, Newport. Located in the **Newport Casino,** the national historic landmark built in 1880 by Stanford White, this international tennis museum is a beauty. The 6-acre complex has 13 grass tennis courts, a royal tennis court—for playing the medieval version of the game, Court Tennis—the Bill Talbert Stadium Court, and the interactive and interesting museum rooms themselves. Founded in 1954, the Tennis Hall of Fame honors legends of the game (recent inductees: Ivan Lendl, John McEnroe, and Martina Navratilova). A copy of the original patent for the sport granted by Queen Victoria in 1874 hangs here, along with all sorts of memorabilia—trophies, apparel, artifacts, even a rare 18th-century "bottoir," the oldest tennis racquet known. The game, you learn, was first played in monasteries. Court Tennis or Royal Tennis is played on a specially sized indoor court—and visitors here can take lessons and play on such a court, adhering to rules of the ancient medieval game. (You must make reservations. That is also required for playing on the grass courts, which are open to the public. For the latter, call 401-846-0642 for daily times.) The casino originally included 60 acres and was considered the largest men's social club in the world at the turn of the past century. It was a center of social life for Newport during the Gilded Age. The building—now with a restaurant and several classy boutiques—is fully restored and is a fine example of Victorian shingle-style architecture. The tennis museum is open daily 9:30–5, except Thanksgiving and Christmas. Adults $8, children under 16 $4, family $20.

♦ **The Museum of Yachting** (401-847-1018; www.moy.org), Fort Adams State Park, Newport. If there was another passion enjoyed by the socialites who summered in Newport, it was yachting. Here's the museum to learn about that. The *Mansions and Yachts* exhibit is a fascinating look at that aspect of Newport history. The museum, housed in a restored brick livestock barn once used by the fort, is a multi-faceted spot with volunteers who show up year-round to use the woodworking shop and build small boats (later auctioned off as part of the fund-raising efforts of the

A demonstration of lawn tennis at the International Tennis Hall of Fame

A 12-meter yacht heels dramatically at the Museum of Yachting

museum). The 12-meter yacht *Courageous,* winner of the America's Cup in 1974 and 1977, is permanently moored here in summer. Other boats from the museum's collection also bob at anchor; volunteers are assigned to keep up a particular vessel and get to sail it. Yachting, you will learn, is simply "pleasure boating." If you sail a Sunfish, you're a yachtsman. An exhibit on the America's Cup race documents the famous sailing contest from its inception in 1851—remember, it was usually held off Newport, and for most of its history the cup was proudly held by the New York Yacht Club, sponsor of the American cup challenger. The cup was most recently won by New Zealanders. Also in this interesting museum is an exhibit on single-handed sailors like Joshua Slocum and Howard Blackburn. The American Sailboat Hall of Fame inducts two boat types each year. Fort Adams is a 100-acre park. There's plenty of parking and cool breezes out here, even on the hottest, most crowded day in town. An annual Labor Day weekend regatta is fun to watch. Open mid-May through October 15, daily 10–5. Adults $5, children $4.

♦ **Samuel Whitehorne House** (401-849-7300), 416 Thames Street. This Federal-style house is actually a showplace for fine furniture—much of it by Goddard and Townsend—acquired by Doris Duke and her Newport Restoration Foundation. There are also silver and pewter pieces made by Newport silversmiths between 1740 and 1840. The house itself was built in 1811. Guided tours are given from the end of April through October. The house is open Monday, Thursday, and Friday 11–4, Saturday and Sunday 10–4. Adults $8, children $3.

♦ **Redwood Library and Athenaeum** (401-847-0292; www.redwood1747.org), 50 Bellevue Avenue. The library was organized in 1747 by 46 proprietors who obtained a charter for a library whose claim was "having nothing in view but the good of man." This was the first community library building in the country. Abraham Redwood donated 500 pounds sterling to purchase books from England for this "public" library, and Peter Harrison, now considered America's first architect, designed and oversaw construction of the building. Original books—purchased in 1749—reside in the initial library building (behind wire cages). Among the titles are *Maitland's History of London* and *Wilson's Surveying*. Today the Redwood has more than 162,000 volumes, archives, and manuscripts and an important collection of fine and decorative arts. Portraits by Gilbert Stuart—and a life mask *of* Gilbert Stuart— are among the treasures. Many early portraits were gifts to the library by Cornelius Vanderbilt II's daughter, Countess Laszlo Szechenyi. This is a membership library— with membership open to all—and during the Gilded Age many of the wealthy summering Newporters belonged. The reading room is a lovely space, inviting you to sit and peruse magazines and books—which you may do. Open Monday, Friday, and Saturday 9:30–5:30, Tuesday through Thursday 9:30–8, and Sunday 1–5. Free.

♦ **Newport Art Museum** (401-848-8200; www.newportartmuseum.com), 76 Bellevue Avenue. Located next door to the Redwood Library, the main building for the art museum is a prime example of mid-Victorian stick-style architecture and was designed by the architect Richard Morris Hunt. The museum has regular exhibits in its four galleries, including the adjacent formal Cushing Gallery. The gift shop, known as the Griffon, is interesting. Here are sold antiques and consign-ments. The items, including furniture and jewelry, that are placed on consignment in the shop are reduced in price monthly for 3 months, at which point the owner can take back the piece or donate it to the shop. Open from Memorial Day through Labor Day, daily 10–5; the rest of the year, Tuesday through Saturday 10–4 and Sunday noon–4. Donations.

Churches

Rhode Island is known for religious tolerance, and the nation's first colonies of Jews and Quakers were established in Newport. **Touro Synagogue** at 72 Touro Street is the oldest house of Jewish worship in North America and a national historic site. It's a beautiful building, designed by colonial master builder Peter Harrison. It's open June through Labor Day, Sunday through Friday 10–5. **St. Mary's Church** at the corner of Spring Street and Memorial Boulevard is the oldest Catholic parish in Rhode Island. A Gothic-style red-stone church, it is possibly best known as the site of the 1953 wedding of Jacqueline Bouvier to then U.S. senator John F. Kennedy. A brass plate marks the pew where the family sat. Jacqueline Bouvier spent summers in Newport at her family's **Hammersmith Farm,** once but no longer open to the public. Rhode Island's first Anglican church is **Trinity Church,** whose graceful white spire is one symbol of the town. It's located at the corner of Church and Spring Streets.

Outdoors

Ocean Drive is a 10-mile drive that takes you past gorgeous oceanfront mansions and offers spectacular views of the crashing Atlantic. Brenton Point State Park is along the drive; you can park here and enjoy a picnic or just sit and feast your eyes on the water views.

♦ **The Cliff Walk** is a gift. Who would expect to be able to walk behind the mansions—getting an up-close look of their grounds, the backs of the houses, and—on the other side—the crashing sea? Well, you can, on this 3½-mile walkway. The Cliff Walk can be accessed from various points, including Narragansett Avenue where you approach the ocean on the Forty Steps, and also from Memorial Boulevard near Easton's Beach. You don't have to do the whole walk, although you may want to. This is simply one of the most enjoyable things to do on a visit to Newport.

♦ **Fort Adams State Park** is a terrific resource. Located on Fort Adams Road (off Harrison Avenue), it's a wonderful hilly point that juts out into the bay. Often when Newport is crowded beyond belief, this lovely and breezy park is relatively empty. It's a great place for strolling, picnicking, watching sailboats, and flying kites. The fortification itself was established to protect the head of Narragansett Bay and was in use from 1799 to the mid-1900s. There are scheduled guided tours of the fort during the summer season.

The beaches. Yes, you can go to the beach in Newport. Not to **Bailey's Beach**, which is where all the rich folk went and which is still private. Nearby, though, on Ocean Drive is **Gooseberry Beach**, a public/private beach where you can pay to park your car and use bathhouses. **First Beach** (also known as **Easton's Beach**) is a nice strand extending from the start of the Cliff Walk on Memorial Boulevard to the Middletown line. There's an amusement area and a parking fee per car.

On the Water

It's hard to be in Newport and not think about getting out on the water. **Harbor cruises** are offered several times daily by different tour operators. They include Viking Tours (401-847-6921), whose ship, the ***Viking Queen,*** takes passengers on 1-hour narrated cruises of the harbor and bay several times daily. Adults $10, seniors $8, children $5. It leaves from the Goat Island Marina. One-hour narrated cruises are also offered by the **M.V.** *Amazing Grace,* which leaves from Oldport Marine (401-847-9109) on Sayer's Wharf. Adults $9, seniors $7.50, children $5.50.

♦ **Sightsailing of Newport** (401-849-3333; 1-800-709-7245; www.sightsailing.com) offers sailing lessons, an opportunity to charter a sailboat, and 2-hour sails around Newport Harbor on sailboats ranging in size from 22 to 50 feet long. A private charter for two people (with captain) can cost $200 for the entire boat. Individuals pay $30–35 apiece for 1½- to 2-hour sails. The boats leave from 32 Bowen's Wharf. You can make reservations ahead.

A 78-foot schooner, ***Adirondack II,*** leaves several times a day from the Newport Yachting Center (401-846-3018) on America's Cup Avenue for sails around the harbor and Narragansett Bay. The cost is about $30 per person. Several other charter boats are available and can be assessed by walking the wharves in the waterfront area.

Small boats may be rented for sailing from **Sail Newport** (401-849-8385) at Fort Adams State Park. J-22s and Rhodes 19s are available for 3-hour stretches (9–noon, 12:30–3:30, and 4–7). You must be "checked out" (at a cost of $10) before you will be allowed to take out one of these keel sailboats. The J-22s are $110 for 3 hours; the Rhodes 19s, $70.

Music in the Mansions

♦ **Newport Music Festival** (401-846-1133; www.newportmusic.org). Chamber music concerts with American debuts as well as performances by world-class artists are offered over a 2-week stretch in July. Now 35 years old, the festival uses the gorgeous Newport mansions as venues for the concerts, which might be offered in the morning, afternoon, evening, or even—as they have been a few times—at midnight! Box lunches or suppers can sometimes be ordered. This is a very special series with a loyal following.

Shopping

Shops come and go in Newport, but there are always lots to choose from. Two main shopping areas are Bellevue Avenue, near Memorial Boulevard, and lower Thames Street.

On Bellevue, in the Newport Casino building, are boutiques like **Michael Hayes** for men's, women's, and children's fashions; **Papers** for stationery, cards, wrapping paper, fine pens; and **The Runcible Spoon,** a wonderful kitchen shop with pottery, tabletop items, linens, and holiday items. Check out, too, **Cabbages and Kings** for fine china. Across Memorial Boulevard on the other stretch of Bellevue is **Karen Vaughan** for well-chosen pillows, toys, baskets, candles, and such. Across the street from the Redwood Library is **Miniature Occasions and Dolls,** 57 Bellevue, where you can find wonderful dollhouses (including one in the shape of a lighthouse), fantastic marionettes, lovely toys, handmade porcelain dolls, and miniatures. You can spend hours here.

Downtown Newport along the wharves is the place to find **The Museum Store** run by the **Preservation Society of Newport County,** with local books, replicas of small pieces or dishes from the mansions, jewelry, and such. Of course each mansion has its own shop as well. **The Ball and Claw** is famed for reproduction furniture, some copies of Townsend and Goddard pieces.

On Spring Street, find **Boulangerie Obelisk,** the wonderful little pastry and food shop operated by the owner of the fine restaurant Asterisk and Obelisk. You can find tasty breads, soups, and specialty foods here. **Rue de France** is an exceptional shop selling all things French at 78 Thames Street (that's upper Thames, out of the usual shopping area). The shop began 20 years ago as a place to buy French fabrics; you can still find yard goods upstairs in this shop, but now there are also baby items, select pieces of furniture, pottery, glassware, table linens, and so on. There's a catalog now, too, but the shop is a terrific place to see the items firsthand.

Cadeux du Monde at 26 Mary Street—across from Vanderbilt Hall—sells the folk art of some 40 developing nations. The brightly painted house in which the shop is located is hard to miss; inside are several small rooms and galleries with unusual items —pillows, jewelry, sculpture, more. On lower Thames Street we love **The Armchair Sailor,** where you can purchase nautical charts from all over the world and nautically oriented books. **Aardvark Antiques** is also fun to prowl around. **The Gourmet Dog** has premium dog biscuits and other canine specialties. **The Gilded Age** specializes in Victorian accoutrements. **Karol Richardson** on Washington Square has trendy clothes for women. **Sole Desire** in the Brick Market Shops is a good shoe store.

There are loads of places to stay in Newport—from large hotels like the Marriott to timeshares to private homes offering a couple of rooms. There are also less expensive places than the ones we offer, and the Newport Convention & Visitors Bureau can be of help there (see *For More Information*). We think it's most fun, however, to stay in an elegant small hotel or B&B in order to experience Newport in a grand way. Remember, this is a splurge.

♦ **Vanderbilt Hall** (401-846-6200; fax 401-846-0701; www.vanderbilthall.com), 41 Mary Street, Newport, RI 02840. This 52-room luxury mansion hotel has a history that connects it directly with the Gilded Age. The original redbrick building was built in 1909 as a YMCA by Alfred Vanderbilt and donated to the town of Newport. Somewhat removed from the mansions of Bellevue Avenue, it lies on a narrow street in the heart of the old town and can be a bit daunting to find. But once here, with your car safely parked, it's an easy walk to just about anywhere. The public rooms are gracious and welcoming, especially the glorious Main Hall with comfortable chairs and tables grouped for tête-à-têtes and a good-sized fireplace and grand piano. A solarium off the living room is a small, bright, and beautifully elegant space. All the rooms and suites are individually and creatively decorated. The only one with an in-room fireplace is the first-floor Cornelius Suite, with a wood-burning fireplace in the sitting room and a single whirlpool tub in the bathroom. But other rooms are charming, as well—if you can find the elevators, obscured by clever trompe l'oeil painting, to reach them. Some rooms are split levels with a small study below and queen-bedded bedroom above; junior suites have a separate sitting area with television. The Lighthouse Tower room really does feel as if you're inside a lighthouse. A rooftop deck offers a grand view of the harbor; guests sometimes take drinks up there. In the basement is the original YMCA swimming pool, now located in a pillared space that almost feels like a Roman bath. Afternoon tea is served in the common rooms on the main floor. The main dining room, **Alva,** has a bit of a masculine feel to it with dark wood doors and columns and deep green walls. Brandy and cigars may be enjoyed in the billiard room on the lower level. This is one of the most charming smaller hotels in New England. Doubles, EP, $220–795. Occasionally B&B packages are offered in the off-season.

♦ **Chanler Hotel** (401-847-3620), 117 Memorial Boulevard, Newport, RI 02840. This oceanfront property—site of the former Cliff Walk Manor close to Easton's Beach—was being turned into an elegant 19-room hotel by John Shufelt and his wife, Jean. Shufelt is the owner of the Mission Point Resort on Mackinac Island, Michigan; he and Jean also own the LaFarge Perry House in Newport (401-847-2223). Reconstruction dragged on, however, and the hotel—originally set for a 2001 opening—had been pushed back to spring of 2003. Stay tuned.

♦ **The Francis Malbone House** (401-846-0392; 1-800-846-0392; fax 401-848-5956; www.malbone.com), 392 Thames Street, Newport, RI 02840. Location! This gorgeous Colonial brick house offers high-style accommodations on one of Newport's most active streets. Park your car in their lot out back and walk to shops and restaurants—a true luxury in this crowded town. You are right across the street from the wharves, and some rooms even have water views. We stayed in one of the fireplaced guest rooms in the old section of the house with deeply recessed windows, wide floorboards, and queen four-poster bed. Newer garden suites out back have whirlpool tub and fireplace as well as a small terrace. There are two ultraspecial suites in the Benjamin Mason House to the rear of the parking lot—with fireplace, whirlpool tub, and a common living room. The common rooms in this bed & breakfast inn are special. They are fireplaced, have Oriental carpets on the floors, and offer plenty of seating and reading materials. People often get an early cup of coffee and relax here before heading for breakfast. The breakfast room has a huge wood-burning fireplace (it was too windy to use when we visited) with several tables. Guests pick up yogurt, cereal, fresh-baked breads, and beverages; a hot entrée is brought to the table. On one morning we had exquisite stuffed French toast with pecans and caramel sauce. Doubles, $175–395 with full breakfast.

Legendary Inns of Newport. These three inns, owned by Win Baker of Connecticut, offer exceptional accommodations in Newport. They are:

♦ **Cliffside Inn** (401-847-1811; 1-800-845-1811; fax 401-848-5850; www.cliffsideinn. com), 2 Seaview Avenue, Newport, RI 02840. Formerly the home of American artist Beatrice Turner—whose self-portraits are amazing and many of which grace the walls of this house—this Second Empire Victorian became a B&B in 1980. Its 16 guest accommodations are located in the main house and in the Seaview Cottage on the property. The three suites in Seaview Cottage are premier accommodations; one has a glass-walled steam shower with pulsating jets and a color TV for watching while washing. All rooms have at least one fireplace, telephone, air-conditioning, private bath, and cable TV. The Governor's Suite in the main inn has a see-through fireplace that can be viewed from the bedroom or the elegant bathroom with double whirlpool tub. The parlor at the Cliffside is especially welcoming with its bright orange drapes and varying shades of pink in fabrics and walls. Here's where a full breakfast is served, and also afternoon tea. Guests have a choice of 11 newspapers to be delivered in the morning, including the *Wall Street Journal* and the *Boston Globe*. The inn is out of the downtown area—but just one block from the famous Cliff Walk so you can get in an early-morning constitutional. Doubles, $245–495.

♦ **Adele Turner Inn** (401-847-1811; 1-800-845-1811; www.adeleturnerinn.com), 93 Pelham Street, Newport, RI 02840. This inn is located in the heart of the downtown area. A 146-year-old Victorian inn, the house features glorious 10-foot-high arched windows overlooking a collection of historic homes on a historic street. The decorators have wisely "played to" these windows so that they are beautifully dressed and brighten the guest rooms. The most popular room in all of the three sister inns is here: the Harbor View Spa room on the third floor. Although not the largest room in the house, it has a queen-sized bed, fireplace, and French doors opening to an adjoining private outdoor deck with year-round hot tub and 180-degree vista of Newport. Roof decks are hard to come by in this town, so this is justifiably prized. The third-floor Tycoon Suite with its king-sized four-poster bed,

canopied whirlpool tub with sky-light above, and sitting room with fireplace is elegant. Guests enjoy a fireplace in each room, TV with VCR, telephone, and air-conditioning. All rooms have private bath and complimentary morning coffee and newspaper room service. The main-floor parlor is where a gourmet break-fast and afternoon tea are enjoyed. Doubles, $200–450.

♦ **Abigail Stoneman Inn** (1-800-845-1811; fax 401-848-5850; www.abigailstonemaninn.com), 102 Touro Street, Newport, RI 02840. The most luxurious of rooms—just five of these beau-ties—are found in the newest property to be converted by innkeeper Win Baker. Opened in spring 2002, the Abigail Stoneman Inn was built in 1866 by renowned Newport architect

Afternoon tea at the Adele Turner Inn

George Champlin Mason as a private home. Abigail Stoneman was an unusual Newport woman of the colonial era and the first woman in town to own an inn. With major renovations, five huge suites have been carved out in this in-town house, just two doors away from Newport's famous Touro Synagogue. Possibly the most extraordinary of the accommodations is the third-floor suite, with five rooms including two bedrooms, a library with fireplace and media center, a kitchen/dining area, and an elegant bathroom known as a "bathing salon." For $525 a night, it can be yours. The first-floor suite known as Vanity Fair is also enticing with 11-foot-high ceilings, an ornate king-sized bed, a bay-window read-ing area, and period antiques. The two-person whirlpool tub in the bathroom is within sight of a large two-sided fireplace that also faces a sitting room. Shell out $425 for this one. Two second-floor rooms are $325 each. Guests can select from a 17-pillow "menu" (so you get just the right pillow to put your head on at night) and also enjoy a "water bar" with a full array of "designer" waters. There is also a small "Tea-for-Two Room" where you and your special friend can sit practically knee to knee. A full hot breakfast, afternoon tea, and morning newspapers are brought to your room. A 2-night minimum (3 nights on holiday weekends) stay is required.

♦ **Castle Hill Inn and Resort** (401-849-3800; 1-888-466-1355; fax 401-849-3838; www.castlehillinn.com), 590 Ocean Drive, Newport, RI 02840. The romance of Castle Hill is in its setting. The weathered gray main house—and three other outbuildings with accommodations—are located on a 40-acre peninsula south of the city of Newport proper but with smashing views of Narragansett Bay. There are a private beach and hiking trails. With its own highly rated dining room and atmospheric bar, it provides an away-from-it-all feeling and the option for just staying put. Forget the mansions, the restaurants, the Cliff Walk. This is a place to rest, relax, and recharge. The main house was built in 1874. Today it has nine guest accommodations upstairs from the elegant main floor, characterized by extensive butternut wood paneling. A small sitting room on the second floor is enjoyed by house guests. Room 6 has a view of the ocean, gas fireplace, canopy king bed, and elegant sofa. A soaking tub and original brick fireplace in the bathroom are appealing. The Harbor House just a few steps from the main inn has six identical accommodations. All have a summery feel with cottage-style furniture, king beds, soft green decor, and a ship's picture on the wall. Each has a small porch with Adirondack chairs from which to enjoy a water view. Guests can walk to what the innkeeper refers to as "our Grace Kelly beach" because the star once visited. The Beach Houses, put up in the summer of 1999, are premier accommodations. These eight large spaces are side by side in a Nantucket-style gray building with white trim. Each has a king iron bed, queen leather pullout sofa, good-sized deck with direct ocean view, gas fireplace set into a high stone wall, TV, and CD player. The bathrooms have two-person whirlpool tubs and showers. You feel as if you are in your own cottage. Guests can walk or drive up to the main house for breakfast, which is a few hundred feet distant. The final two accommodations are in a chalet close to the main inn. Room rates include a full hot breakfast served in the attractive main dining room of the inn. Ten rustic summer cottages rent by the week only and are spartan but popular since they are directly on a sandy beach. The **dining room** at Castle Hill generally is well regarded; chef Casey Riley has been in charge for several years. Among his specialties are wood-grilled Atlantic salmon in tahini butter crust with sticky rice, and aged beef tenderloin with green chile, potato-saffron, and artichoke aïoli. The dining room is open to the public for breakfast, lunch, and dinner daily, and also for Sunday brunch. The lounge with bay view opens at 5 PM and is a great place to settle in for a drink. Doubles, $145–750. Beach House suites can be rented by the week at $4,550 per week.

♦ **Ivy Lodge** (401-849-6865; 1-800-834-6865; fax 401-849-0704; www.ivylodge.com), 12 Clay Street, Newport, RI 02840. Eight elegant rooms with private bath and all sorts of comforts are offered by Daryl and Darlene McKenzie in this Stanford White–designed 19th-century "cottage." The house is characterized by its 33-foot-high Gothic oak entry hallway with wraparound balconies. A high, pointed turret pokes into the sky. The Turret Room is the highest priced. It has bright gold walls and blue wall-to-wall carpeting, a king-sized bed in dark mahogany, and a gas fireplace. There are two wing chairs for reading and a double whirlpool-style tub, plus a shower stall, in the adjoining bathroom. TVs hide in armoires. The first-floor Library Suite off the entry foyer was the original library of the house. Done in gold and red—with a red bedspread on the queen sleigh bed—it has a fireplace with blue tiles and an antique bureau. A two-person whirlpool tub and large shower are in the adjoining bathroom. There is a tucked-away, romantic feeling here. Common rooms include a large and gracious living room, a smaller sitting room, and a large wraparound porch with wicker furniture that is favored in warm weather. The dining room, with one long table, is the place for a full breakfast—possibly gingerbread pancakes with lemon sauce or raisin-stuffed French toast with apples and cream cheese. Here a small refrigerator and honor bar are available to guests all day. Hot teas, cocoa, coffee, cookies, and fresh fruit are set out. Doubles, $99–319.

♦ **Wayside Guest House** (401-847-0302), 406 Bellevue Avenue, Newport, RI 02840. Stay right on Bellevue Avenue, practically across the street from The Elms? You can at this former summer cottage, a beige-brick home with modest pillars to mark the entrance. It's now a 10-room B&B with guest rooms on three levels. The Post family has been operating this place since 1975. Rooms range in size; some are huge. Room 5 has two queens and a single bed and can take a crowd. Recently updated, room 7 has a queen bed set on an angle and fresh yellow-and-blue decor. The first-floor Library, my favorite room, has a queen canopy bed and separate— predominantly blue—sitting area. It's the room most convenient to the pretty heated in-ground pool, for you walk through French doors onto the terrace above the pool. All rooms have private bath and television. A two-bedroom apartment over the Carriage House out back was being renovated. With a full kitchen, queen, and two twin beds, it would be an ideal place for a family to settle in. Children are welcome here. A pretty dining room is the place to have a continental-plus breakfast in the morning before setting off for a day of exploring. The Wayside is one of Newport's more affordable spots, especially considering its great location among the mansions. It's a 7-minute walk to the Cliff Walk. Doubles, $75–175; housekeeping apartment, $220.

♦ **The Inns of Newport** (401-849-7397; 1-800-524-1386). Rick Farrick and his wife, Tamara, operate four bed & breakfast inns within close proximity of one another and the center of town. Three—**The Cleveland House, The Clarkeston,** and the **Admiral Farragut Inn**—are next to or across the street from one another on Clarke Street, just a few steps from the intersection with Mary Street and Vanderbilt Hall. The fourth, **The Wynstone,** is at 232 Spring Street—not far away. Altogether there are 50 rooms, with the top of the line being the five deluxe, fireplaced rooms at The Wynstone. Here are double Jacuzzi-style tubs in large bathrooms, cable TVs, and a sense of privacy. The 21-room Cleveland House is the largest—and also where the office is located. Guests check in here. Rooms in this inn range in size, and a continental breakfast is offered. Across the street at The Clarkeston, 5 of 10 rooms—including the first-floor Doris Duke Room—have fireplace, and all have private bath. The Admiral Farragut also has 10 rooms on three floors, 5 with fireplace. Several were being reconfigured and updated in 2002. The Admiral's Quarters was going to have a king bed, gas fireplace, and spacious bathroom when finished. "We're upgrading all the time," said the wiry, energetic Rick. Full breakfasts are served at the Admiral Farragut, The Clarkeston, and The Wynstone. Doubles, $85–385.

IN "THE POINT" SECTION OF TOWN

This is a very old and historic part of town, one of the first developed sections along the waterfront. It's now quietly residential. The area juts out into the water just south of the Newport-Jamestown bridge. The Hunter House, which is open the public in-season and one of the finest colonial restorations in the country, is located here.

♦ **Sarah Kendall House** (401-846-3979; 1-800-758-9578; fax 401-849-2811; www. sarah kendallhouse.com), 47 Washington Street, Newport, RI 02840. Fran and Bryan Babcock offer five deluxe rooms in this exceptional Victorian house, which they opened to the public in the early 1990s. Isaac Kendall, who was in his 70s at the time, built the house in 1873–1875 for his second wife, Sarah Kendall. This period predated most of the mansions, and this was one of the largest Victorians in town. The guest rooms are on the second and third floors and have working gas fireplace, air-conditioning, cable TV, bathrobes, hair dryer, and king-, queen-, or double-sized bed. The deep green house with white trim and a turret has recently had its large enclosed cupola rebuilt and furnished with sofa and chairs. With its killer view of Narragansett Bay, it's a popular spot for guests to spend time. Water views are also available from a couple of the guest rooms and from the wide wraparound porch, which gets breezes from the bay all summer long. A full breakfast is served and always includes fresh bagels from the owners' bagel shops in town. Afternoon tea is put out in-season. Guests enjoy the use of a large living room on the first floor, furnished with a mix of 18th- and 19th- century antiques and family heirlooms. The house is open daily throughout the season and weekends only in winter. The owners sometimes take a few weeks' vacation in February or March. Doubles, $125–275.

♦ **Stella Maris Inn** (401-849-2862; www.stellamarisinn.com), 91 Washington Street, Newport, RI 02840. Stella Maris was a convent occupied by the Sisters of Cluny prior to its 1989 purchase by Dorothy and Ed Madden for conversion into a B&B. The huge brownstone mansion was built in 1861 by Edward Meyer, a New York businessman. It's now on the National Register of Historic Places. Of eight guest rooms on the first, second, and third floors, five have working fireplace—with fire logs provided September to April—and all have private bath. There is an elevator. All rooms are named for Irish playwrights and poets. The Parnell Room on the first floor is huge, having once been used as a chapel by the nuns. Two club chairs face a marble fireplace, and a queen bed is dramatic against Chinese red walls. The room has access to its own porch in summer, and a huge floor-to-ceiling windowed area lets in light. The James Joyce Room on the second floor is wallpapered in beige with a purple-and-green vertical flower design; its fireplace is easily viewed from the queen bed. A TV in the large common living room is for use by all guests; individual rooms do not have TVs. A buffet breakfast—described as "complete continental"—is set out in the dining room and consists of fruits, cereals, homemade breads, and muffins. Lemon bread and prune coffee cake are two specialties. Guests eat in the sunroom or on the large porch. Many rooms have water views, and a small park, Battery Park, is just across the street. You can sit there and watch the boats. Open April through December. Doubles, $125–195.

Newport has loads of good restaurants. The ones I've selected lean toward the high end; you can also find sandwich shops and hot dog carts.

♦ **Restaurant Bouchard** (401-846-0123), 505 Thames Street. Chef Albert Bouchard and his wife, Sarah, operate one of the most romantic and classically French restaurants in Newport. The sprightly mural on one long wall is of St. Tropez; the items on the menu are very Gallic. There are two dining rooms—one at the front of the restaurant with tapestry-covered seats overlooking the busy street, and the other in back with shield-back chairs and some banquette seating. Both have a feeling of intimacy. You might start with lobster bisque, warm mousse of artichoke with tomato and garlic beurre blanc, or escargots in phyllo dough with tomato tarragon ($8–10). A Caesar salad or a mesclun salad with a red wine vinaigrette could come next ($7.50–8.50). Entrées ($24–28) include possibilities like roasted Dover sole with a sorrel sauce, Atlantic salmon with a Thai crust and lemongrass sauce, sliced fillet of beef with a port-flavored demiglaze, and duck breast sautéed with a coffee crust and finished with a brandy balsamic sauce. Cappuccino, espresso, and chai accompany individual dessert soufflés or other lovely French creations. Open nightly 5:30–9:30, except closed on Tuesday.

♦ **Asterisk & Obelisk** (401-841-8833), 599 Thames Street, Newport. A converted garage with star-shaped lights in bright colors hanging from the ceiling is a creative setting for equally innovative cuisine. Owner John Bach-Sorenson also has the popular Boulangerie Obelisk—bakery and prepared foods—on Spring Street. The restaurant offers a large, convivial environment. More than 50 vodkas can be made into cocktails, and the list of single-malt Scotches is also impressive. Appetizers ($7–12) might be crabcakes rémoulade, smoked trout with lemon pepper dressing and cucumber, steak tartare Parisian-style (with aquavit, capers, and horseradish), or a warm frisée salad with braised celery, blood oranges, toasted walnuts, and Stilton cheese. Entrées ($18–28) could be butter-roasted lobster tails with a creamy lobster and corn broth; barbecued double rib lamb chops with cassoulet of summer vegetables and parsley pan jus; steak *au poivre* with spinach and pommes frites; or veal Scaloppine with mashed potatoes, fava beans, and tarragon butter. Finish with a cadeau of chocolate (with caramel and white chocolate sauce); an iced tiramisu parfait; or raspberry crème brûlée. Dinner nightly.

♦ **White Horse Tavern** (401-849-3600), 26 Marlborough Street, Newport. This dark red building is one of America's oldest tavern buildings, originally constructed before 1673 as a two-room, two-story residence. The building was later the meeting place of the colony's general assembly, criminal court, and city council (whose members could dine here and charge their meals to the public treasury). A tavern license was obtained in 1687. The tavern was meticulously restored in 1957 and has been owned by O. L. Pitts for more than 20 years. I love to eat here on a rainy or cold day; the huge wood-burning fireplaces cast a glow over main-floor and second-floor dining rooms. (It's up to the waiters to keep the fires going.) Among the traditional fare that is always on the menu, you'll find clam chowder and raisin bread pudding with bourbon butter sauce. Peach barbecue-glazed quail, veal sweetbreads in a Marsala wine cream sauce, a ragout of wild mushrooms, and baked Maine oysters topped with prosciutto, spinach, caramelized leeks, and bell peppers are mouthwatering starters at dinner ($9–14). A smoked chicken and Danish blue cheese salad over mesclun greens or a baby spinach salad may also be ordered. Entrées include citrus pepper grilled swordfish; veal loin chop roasted and served with swiss chard, Saga blue cheese whipped potatoes, and Granny Smith apples; or an individual beef Wellington ($28–35). In addition to the bread pudding, you might finish your repast with crème brûlée, cheesecake, or Triple Silk, a three-layered chiffon mousse that is a house specialty. Brunch on Sunday includes such possibilities as eggs Benedict, lobster salad, and cinnamon raisin French toast. Jackets are required for men at dinner and are provided if you've forgotten yours. Open for lunch Wednesday through Saturday 11:30–2:30, brunch Sunday 11:30–2:30, and dinner nightly 5:30–9:30.

♦ **La Petite Auberge** (401-849-6669), 19 Charles Street, Newport. Three small and romantic dining rooms plus a more casual Courtyard Café to one side of the restaurant are located in the historic deep green Stephen Decatur House at the edge of downtown. The tiny kitchen is the domain of chef-owner Roger Putier of Lyon, France, who has owned the restaurant with his wife, Martine, since the mid-1970s and established a reputation for serving fine French food. Lace tablecloths over darker undercloths add to a feeling of romanticism in the main dining rooms, and this is the perfect environment for celebrating a special event. Jackets are not required but are suggested.

Starters include the house specialty, escargots with cépes, goose liver pâté, or mussels in light cream sauce ($8–9). A salad of Belgian endive with apples and almonds or tossed greens with house dressing is a possibility. Entrées ($22–29) might be lobster tails with truffles; frogs' legs in garlic butter; duck with raspberry sauce; or veal medallions with morels and a cream sauce. A saddle of lamb for two with garlic sauce is $56. Finish the meal with baked banana flambée served over ice cream; crêpes Suzette (except Saturday); ice cream; pears in chocolate sauce; or a cake of the day. The Courtyard Café serves a lighter menu ($10–29), including a burger with caramelized onions and roasted red peppers; roast chicken with creamed leeks; and pork tenderloin with prunes and armagnac. Dinner nightly from 6; from 5 on Sunday.

♦ **Tucker's Bistro** (401-846-3449), 150 Broadway. In what is fast becoming a new restaurant district—away from the harbor and the mansions and on a busy thoroughfare—is Tucker Harris's romantic and popular spot. Three intimate and quite dark dining rooms—they give you a small flashlight to help you read the menu—stretch across former storefronts. Tiny white lights twinkle on the ceiling. Our dinners were excellent, from the warm goat cheese and mesclun salad we split to entrées of salmon in a creamy leek sauce and a special of chicken livers crostini. Sarah Vaughan and Frank Sinatra sang to us while we dined. Other starters ($7–10) could be steamed mussels with garlic, shallots, fresh basil, and grape tomatoes in a white wine broth; fried calamari with hot banana pepper butter sauce; or beef tartare with capers, red onions, and white truffle oil served with grilled French bread. Entrées ($17–25) might be wild mushroom penne with toasted almonds and a touch of nutmeg; caramelized ginger sea scallops with brown sugar and sake; pan-seared breast of duck with a vanilla-bourbon demiglaze; or vegetarian Wellington made with sweet potatoes, spinach, artichokes, and wild mushroom mascarpone mousse in a pastry shell. We skipped—but noted—the white chocolate, sun-dried cherry, and pecan bread pudding. All desserts are made in house. Open nightly for dinner, and for Sunday brunch in summer.

♦ **Puerini's** (401-847-5506), 24 Memorial Boulevard. The Puerini family operates what many think is the best Italian restaurant in town. All pasta is homemade, and the menu is simple: appetizers, veal dishes, pasta with chicken or beef, and a couple of seafood and vegetarian meals. The little restaurant with lace curtains covering half the windows has two smallish dining rooms and a feeling of warmth and conviviality. Since no reservations are taken, it can sometimes mean a wait. Wine and beer are served. As starters, try sweet roasted red peppers in oil and garlic served with sliced provolone; mushrooms sautéed with spinach, zucchini, red peppers, and pignoli nuts with balsamic vinegar; or antipasto ($4–9). Veal dishes (all $19.95) could be made with Marsala, alla cacciatora, sautéed with Gorgonzola cheese, pignoli nuts, and scallions in a rich cream sauce, or sautéed with roasted red peppers, artichoke hearts, chopped garlic, and prosciutto. All are served with a half order of fettuccine. Chicken may be substituted for veal. Chicken also comes as a boneless breast with artichoke hearts, sautéed in olive oil, red wine, and herbs, and served over spinach fettuccine. Lasagna, fettuccine Bolognese, and homemade linguine or penne with semihot sausage may also be ordered. There are also vegetarian plates. Open for dinner nightly from 5. Dan Puerini also recently opened a tapas bar called **Pop** on 162 Broadway (401-846-8456). The fireplaced space with high ceilings and one orange wall was was a hit from the start.

♦ **Scales & Shells** (401-846-FISH), 527 Thames Street. The freshest fish—most of it described on a large blackboard menu—is featured here, and everybody agrees it's the best fish place in town. Sit up at the horseshoe-shaped bar and enjoy a few oysters or raw clams with a drink before heading to the table for food expertly prepared by chef-owners Andrew and Debra Ackerman. The feeling is that of a fish market, with tile floor. The open kitchen is impeccably clean and well organized. Lobster fra diavolo for two ($42) is a signature dish. Other choices might be swordfish with green olive butter; tuna with soy sauce; shrimp scampi; shrimp, scallop, or monkfish Marsala; or mesquite-grilled halibut, red snapper, or scallops ($16–22). If you can't or don't want to eat fish, you can have pasta primavera. With entrées comes a choice of one of the following: house salad, french fries, vegetable kabob, or pasta. In summer **UpScales** opens upstairs. Here reservations are taken (unlike Scales & Shells), and the atmosphere is a bit more formal. The menu might include appetizers like chilled lobster cakes, mixed seafood salad, or deep-fried calamari ($8–12); entrées ($17–25) like pan-roasted sea bass, grilled salmon with red pepper and red chili puree, or macadamia-crusted codfish. No credit cards are taken at either restaurant. Scales & Shells is open for dinner nightly year-round from 5; on Friday and Saturday, from 6. UpScales is generally open late May to September.

♦ **The Black Pearl** (401-846-5264), Bannister's Wharf. The painted black interior— including black chairs and tables—of this wharfside tavern draws legions of faithful for the great dill-flavored clam chowder, the popular pearl burger in pita bread with mint salad, the chicken potpie, or specials like Irish lamb stew. Sandwiches are $6–8; entrées, $16–20. At night you can start with a swordfish brochette, country pâté, or fried Brie and have an entrée of calf's liver, baked cod, or sea scallops with bacon, mushrooms, and cream ($14–24). In the more upscale **Commodore Room** next door the small-paned windows look directly out on the harbor, and white-clothed tables are set with ladderback chairs. Here appetizers include shrimp, crab, and lobster cocktail with three sauces ($10.50); Maryland crabcake; and Scottish smoked salmon. Pear endive salad with Roquefort cheese can also be a starter. Entrées ($19–35) could be twin lobster tails with lump crabmeat; medallions of veal with mushrooms and champagne sauce; soft-shell crabs; or rack of lamb with roast-ed garlic and rosemary. Dinner is served in the Commodore Room from 6; jackets required. The tavern is open 11:30–10. Closed early January to mid-February.

♦ **Twenty-two Bowen's** (401-841-8884), 22 Bowen's Wharf. New in 2001, this wine bar and grill is located at the end of the wharf where the old Chart House stood. The views of the harbor are still pretty good through large glass windows on the first floor; they're even better from tables one flight up. Main-level floors are brick, tables dark with green place mats at lunch. White tablecloths go on for dinner and brass lamps burn with a kerosene flame in the evening. Walls give the impression of New England white clapboard above dark wainscoting. This eatery, owned by the Newport Harbor Corporation—which also owns Castle Hill Inn and The Mooring restaurant—specializes in prime beef from Allen's Steak House in Chicago, we're told. In designing the space, the feeling of "an old gentlemen's club" was sought, and there is a masculinity to the place. Some items are on both the lunch and din-ner menus and include appetizers such as lump crab cocktail with mustard sauce, smoked salmon tart, and thick-cut fried Cajun onion rings with horseradish cream sauce. Lobster bisque, the signature soup, came in a large shallow bowl but had finely minced pieces of the crustacean (instead of the lumps we would have pre-ferred). You can also get clam chowder and French onion soup. At lunch you might get an open-faced prime rib-eye sandwich with blackened onions and horseradish cream, or a burger with Havarti cheese. There are also entrées ($13–25) such as grilled tuna steak with tropical fruit salsa, and East Coast cioppino. For din-ner, entrées ($21–31) include shrimp scampi, pork tenderloin with apricot-sausage stuffing, and grilled filet mignon with Maytag blue cheese and roasted shallot mashed potatoes. Open from 11:30 daily, with the dinner menu kicking in at 5.

♦ **Le Bistro** (401-849-7778), Bowen's Wharf. Climb the stairs to the second- and third-floor dining rooms and be rewarded by a wall of windows and views of the busy wharf and harbor below. There's an open feeling and also a somewhat removed one—the result of being a level or two above the chaos on the wharf, I guess. Here things are quiet, almost sedate. French food is emphasized, although you can get a burger for lunch. The Bistro burger comes with wild mushrooms and béarnaise sauce. Escargots bourguignon and L'Assiette de Charcuterie (sausages and prosciutto with cornichons) are appetizers at both lunch and dinner. At night you can also start with asparagus and wild mushrooms in puff pastry, the chef's pâté, littleneck clams steamed in white wine, or clam chowder. Entrées ($19–25 range) might be baked scrod with asparagus butter, half a roast duck served with fresh blueberry sauce, sea scallops sautéed with red peppers, corn, fresh mint, and tequila, or Newport bouillabaisse. Open from 11:30; lunch served until 5, dinner thereafter. On Sunday, brunch is available 11:30–3:30.

♦ **Clarke Cooke House** (401-849-2900), Bannister's Wharf. The second floor of this multilevel establishment has one of Newport's fancier dining rooms—although on a cold, windy night in late winter it still seemed awfully summery, with wicker chairs and bright pillows on banquettes. The wood-burning fire was what attracted us, and they kept a reservation promise to seat us very close. In summer an open-air porch extends from this level and has views of the harbor. You might start dinner with a pricey appetizer ($12–17) such as ravioli of lobster and wild mushroom, carpaccio of yellowfin tuna, or pan-seared breast of squab with a roasted corn pancake. Entrées ($28–40) include steamed native gray sole with leek puree and truffle vinaigrette, twin lobsters steamed in a court bouillon, and rack of lamb persillade with caramelized onion, potato-turnip gratin, and minted tarragon glaze. If you've room or money enough for dessert, you might try banana caramel mousse, crème brûlée, or fresh fruit terrine with mandarin sorbet. Open for dinner nightly in-season 6–10; weekends in the off-season. **The Candy Store and Grille** at street level is a more casual spot for less expensive food—things like burgers, sandwiches, pasta, or lunch entrées like chickpea crêpes or chicken sautéed with wilted spinach and served with roesti potatoes. At dinner downstairs, entrées are $12–22 and include a single steamed native lobster, braised lamb shank, and wood-grilled sirloin salad. The Candy Store is open daily for lunch and dinner in-season; on weekends in winter.

Casual restaurants to consider are **The Mooring** on Sayer's Wharf, where dining on the deck in summer gets you as close to the boats as anywhere; **LaForge Casino Restaurant** in the Bellevue Avenue area, where the turkey and cranberry sandwich is terrific; and **Norey's,** a spot on Broadway.

16 ◆ Woodstock, Vermont

Woodstock's elliptical town green, surrounded by gorgeous, well-kept Federal houses and the tony Woodstock Inn & Resort, is one of the most admired in New England. The rest of town isn't bad either. For its size—fewer than 4,000 year-round residents—Woodstock carries itself proudly. Lovely homes, many with elegant white picket fences bordering the street, make a walk through town a pleasing exploration. High-end restaurants, fine art galleries, and impressive antiques shops are all nearby. It seems as if success came to this town early and stayed. That's not far off the mark.

Historians credit the naming of Woodstock as the shire town of Windsor County—in the 1790s—for the way the town developed. As the county seat it was deemed the place to be, and the professional class rushed to build homes. Later, its location by the strong Ottauquechee River proved fortuitous. The river, rushing east to empty into the Connecticut River, brought power to 19th-century mills.

The early settlers—influential attorneys, bankers, and merchants—built many of the fine houses in town. But it was three men who occupied the same "house on the hill" just outside the village proper who made the greatest impact on Woodstock.

They are George Perkins Marsh, an early conservationist; Frederick Billings, a lawyer and railroad tycoon who returned to his native Woodstock after the San Francisco Gold Rush; and Laurance S. Rockefeller, a grandson of John D. Rockefeller, who married Frederick Billings's granddaughter. His wife's interests, and her town, soon claimed his attention. Rockefeller created the Woodstock Foundation that has underwritten many town preservation efforts, and he owns the center-of-town Woodstock Inn & Resort.

The stories of the Marsh, Billings, and Rockefeller contributions to Woodstock and the conservation movement in general are told at Vermont's only national park—opened in 1998 on the site of the big brick house that was their home. A visit to the house and its gardens is a good way to put the place into some kind of perspective.

For all its sophistication, Woodstock is hardly stand-offish. It has been a resort town since early on, and traditions of hospitality are well established. The state's first golf course was opened in 1895 at the Woodstock Country Club. The fine

One of Woodstock's handsome brick homes with a picket fence

18-hole course was redesigned by Robert Trent Jones Sr. and is now operated by the Woodstock Inn. The first ski tow in the nation was installed in 1934 at Suicide Six, just north of town. It is now also run by the Woodstock Inn.

People may come to Woodstock to golf or ski, but there are many who just seem to enjoy being there. They meander the streets of town, browse in the upscale shops and art galleries, and eat in some of the finest restaurants in Vermont. They enjoy luxurious lodging options. The Woodstock area is home to many fine inns and B&Bs, including the exclusive complex that has been rated by one survey as the top small hotel in the entire country.

Nearby are Quechee, with its spectacular gorge carved by the Ottauquechee River, and the towns of Barnard, Bridgewater, and Killington. Woodstockers think nothing of hopping into the car and heading to a nearby town for dinner, to shop or take friends on a junket. Travelers will find they can do the same, exploring the beautiful mountain roads and making discoveries of their own. They make the best stories for the breakfast table at your B&B — or to share on your return back home.

Getting There

Most people drive. Take I-91 north to the intersection with Route I-89. From I-89, take Exit 1 onto Route 4. Route 4 leads directly into Woodstock.

The nearest **airport** is in Lebanon, New Hampshire, 15 miles distant. USAir flies in from Boston and Philadelphia. From across the country or the world, most visitors fly into Boston's Logan Airport and rent a car.

Getting Around

Parking can be tough to find and regulations are enforced, especially on weekdays. Feed the meter! If you want to mosey around town without worrying, check out the free parking lot off Pleasant Street by the river.

For More Information

♦ **Woodstock Area Chamber of Commerce** (802-457-3555; 1-888-4-WOOD-STOCK; www.woodstockvt.com), 18 Central Street, Woodstock, VT 05091. The chamber's brochure, *Window on Woodstock*, gives a helpful overview. The chamber operates an information center on the green from June to October.

SEEING AND DOING

♦ **Visitors Center for the Marsh-Billings-Rockefeller National Historical Park and the Billings Farm and Museum**, Route 12, just north of the village of Woodstock. The center serves both the national historical park with the Marsh-Billings-Rockefeller house and the model farm. A theater shows a film about Marsh, Billings, and Rockefeller called *A Place in the Land* as an orientation. The center is open late May through October, daily 10–5.

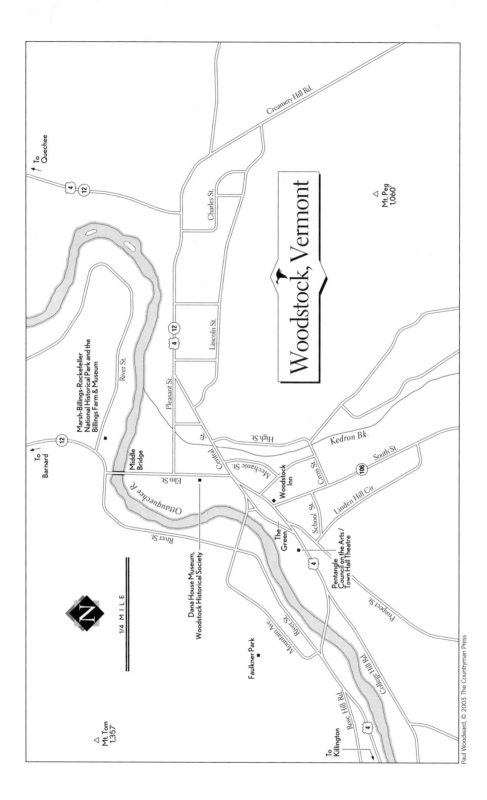

Woodstock, Vermont

To Quechee

Creamery Hill Rd.

Charles St.

Mt. Peg 1,060'

Marsh-Billings-Rockefeller National Historical Park and the Billings Farm & Museum

River St.

Lincoln St.

Pleasant St.

Central St.

High St.

Kedron Bk.

Mechanic St.

South St.

106

Woodstock Inn

Cross St.

Linden Hill Cir.

Elm St.

Middle Bridge

Ottauquechee R.

To Barnard

12

School St.

The Green

Pentangle Council on the Arts / Town Hall Theatre

Prospect St.

River St.

Dana House Museum, Woodstock Historical Society

Mountain Ave.

River St.

4

College Hill Rd.

Faulkner Park

Rose Hill Rd.

To Killington

4

N

1/4 MILE

Mt. Tom 1,357'

The Marsh-Billings Rockefeller mansion

♦ **Marsh-Billings-Rockefeller National Historical Park** (802-457-3368; www.nps
.gov/mabi), Route 12, north of the village. Tours of the mansion are offered on the
hour between 10 and 4 daily in late May and June, and on the half hour from July
through October. They are limited in size, so it's best to make reservations ahead
for a specific time. Tours last about an hour and a quarter. Park at the visitors center
and cross Route 12 into the park. It's laced with carriage roads and trails leading up
Mount Tom, which are open year-round and free for anyone to use. The mansion
tours start in the beautiful dark wood **Carriage Barn,** where an exhibit helps to
explain Marsh, Billings, and Rockefeller and their place in conservation efforts.
There is a nice reading area with a huge table where books on conservation,
including some for children, can be perused. The park is the only one in the
nation specifically dedicated to telling the story of conservation. The tour takes you
through the main floor of the brick Queen Anne–style home and out back to a
beautifully tended garden. Originally built in 1805–1807, the mansion was expanded
to its present size in the late 1800s by Frederick Billings. It is viewed as it was when
the Rockefellers used it as a part-time home—with some gorgeous original artwork
from Hudson River School painters on the walls. There are Tiffany glass windows,
19th-century furnishings, and, best of all, interesting tales of the people who inhabited it.

George Perkins Marsh, the first, was born and raised in the house. By the age of
7 he had nearly ruined his eyesight from reading and was encouraged by doctors
and parents to "play outside." There he studied the natural world, learning the
names of indigenous plants and animals. Marsh went on to become a U.S.
congressman and ambassador to Turkey and Italy, where he became horrified at the
despoilment of lands around the Mediterranean. He wrote a very influential book,
Man and Nature, that is considered seminal in the conservation field.

Lots of people read Marsh's book, including Frederick Billings, another Woodstock native. Billings was a lawyer who went to San Francisco at the time of the Gold Rush and made his fortune as the city's first lawyer. He returned to his home and bought the "house on the hill" he had admired. He transformed the house into the mansion of today, planted trees all over the hillsides, and created carriage roads. He also created a model dairy farm on his property (importing pure-bred Jersey cows), which also can be visited (see Billings Farm & Museum).

Frederick Billings's granddaughter Mary Billings French married Laurance Rockefeller in 1934, and they eventually came to live in the brick mansion. The Rockefeller family was already well known for its devotion to conservation efforts and the gifts of much of the land for several national parks, including Acadia in Maine. This was the joining of two great conservation families. Rockefeller was about preserving more than the estate, however. He purchased the beloved old Woodstock Inn, razed it, and rebuilt in the same location the 142-room hotel you see today. He upgraded the Suicide Six ski area and had Robert Trent Jones redesign the golf course of the Woodstock Country Club. His Woodstock Foundation preserved other sites in the area. Mary and Laurance Rockefeller made the gift that established the Marsh-Billings-Rockefeller National Historical Park as the first national park in Vermont.

After viewing the house, visitors go outdoors to beautiful gardens. Efforts are at work to preserve the plants in the most benign way—hence the little bars of soap that swing over some of the vegetation to discourage deer.

Open late May through October, 10–5, although the last tour may go out some-what earlier. The carriage barn is open free. The house tour fees are $6 for adults, $3 for seniors and children.

♦ **Billings Farm and Museum** (802-457-2355; www.billingsfarm.org), Route 12, Woodstock. The Billings Farm was established in 1871 by Frederick Billings. He imported cattle from the Isle of Jersey, maintained careful records of milk produc-tion, and bred selectively to improve his herd. He also planted the hillsides with trees in an expansive reforestation project. Today visitors see a working dairy farm and a living museum of Vermont's rural past. Exhibits explain the many tasks of farm life: plowing, seeding, cultivating, and harvesting crops, making cheese and butter, woodcutting, maple sugaring. The Farm House, built in 1890, has been restored. It is seen as a "model home" that served as the hub of the farm and forestry operation. The cows are milked daily. There are special events year-round such as Thanksgiving weekend, December weekends, and sleigh ride weekends scheduled in January and February. Kids love the place. Open late May through October 31, 10–5. Adults $9, seniors $8, 13–17 years $7, 5–12 $4.50, and 3–4 $2.

♦ **Dana House Museum, Woodstock Historical Society** (802-457-1822), 26 Elm Street, Woodstock. This 1807 brick-and-frame house was originally the home of Charles Dana, a dry goods salesman, his wife, and seven children. It remained in the hands of descendants until 1942. The house is decorated in the Federal and mid-Victorian periods. The old kitchen/keeping room with original granite hearth is used to display early cooking implements. A hutch built by John Dana, brother of Charles, is interesting for its mahogany veneer with inlays of ivory. Thirteen pieces of glass in the fanlight over the front door represent the original 13 colonies. (Vermont was not one of them; it became the 14th state in 1792.) The primitive portrait of the Titus Hutchinson family of Woodstock showing husband, wife, and six children is terrific. The children's room has lots of dolls and two dollhouses. The permanent museum exhibit in an attached section is interesting and shows early ski industry artifacts, county fair ribbons, and other historical items. Open May through October, 10–5. Admission $3. Tours of 40 to 45 minutes take place on the hour.

A PRESIDENT'S BOYHOOD HOME

President Calvin Coolidge State Historic Site (802-672-3773; www.historicvermont. org), Route 100A, Plymouth Notch. People think nothing of taking a 30-minute trip from Woodstock to this rural Vermont village that was the boyhood home of the nation's 30th president. Coolidge, then vice president of the United States, was vacationing here with his wife, Grace, when he got word of the unexpected death of President Warren Harding. At 2:47 on the morning of August 3, 1923, Coolidge took the oath of office administered by his father, John, a notary public. The oath was taken by the light of a kerosene lamp, and the Coolidge Homestead—restored to the exact way it looked when Calvin, his sister, and his parents lived there—is also lighted primitively. It may seem a little dark, but it is authentic. Most furnishings are as they were when the Coolidges lived here. The rest of the village is interesting as well. You can visit the Wilder Barn with an extensive collection of 19th-century farm implements and horse-drawn vehicles on display; the Wilder House, the childhood home of President Coolidge's mother, Victoria Josephine Moor (now a coffee shop); the Calvin Coolidge birthplace, a small house where the president was born; and the Florence Cilley General Store, which was owned by the president's father. The Union Christian Church with its beautiful hard pine interior was built in 1840 and rededicated in 1900. Services at 11 AM are held on the first Sunday of the month in July, August, and September with visiting ministers. The Plymouth Cheese Factory was once owned by the president's father, and later by his son, John Coolidge. You can buy many kinds of Vermont cheddar and other cheeses made in Vermont. Bring a picnic or have lunch at the Wilder House, whose restaurant operates 9:30-2:30 daily in-season. If you're just thirsty, you might get a cold Moxie for 85 cents at the General Store. Calvin Coolidge loved the stuff. Open late May to mid-October, daily 9:30-5:30.

♦ **Vermont Raptor Center/Vermont Institute of Natural Science (VINS)** (802-457-2779; www.vinsweb.org), 27023 Church Hill Road, Woodstock. The center has been located at this address, 1½ miles south of Woodstock, for some time. However, it was due to be closed to "drop-in visits" by the public in late 2002 and moved to Quechee (off Route 4, west of Quechee Gorge) for reopening in 2004. If you would really like to visit, please call ahead and they will try to fit you in during the interim. It's a great place—an educational center and clinic devoted to birds of prey needing rehabilitation. Bald eagles, peregrine falcons, snowy owls might all be

The Woodstock green

in residence at one time. Usually there are 70 to 100 birds of 20 or so species. In its Woodstock location, birds were kept in large enclosures off a woodland path, and you could take a walk to see them. There were also special opportunities daily including raptor-in-flight demonstration and a guided raptor center tour. All of this and more are expected to be available in the new Quechee location. VINS also operates a nature and gift shop across the road from the Simon Pearce complex in Quechee. Open year-round.

♦ **Covered bridges.** There are three in Woodstock: the **Lincoln Bridge** on Route 4 in West Woodstock; **Middle Bridge,** in the center of the village close to the green; and the **Taftsville Bridge** off Route 4 east.

♦ **Pentangle Council on the Arts** (802-457-3981; www.PentangleArts.org), 31 The Green, P.O. Box 172, Woodstock. This 27-year-old cultural organization brings movies and more to Woodstock year-round. Films are presented in the **Town Hall Theatre** September to April, Friday through Monday at 7:30 PM ($7 adults, $6 seniors, $5 children). Other special theater events are held on the main stage on occasional weekend nights (when you can scratch the movies). In summer, special events take place in the town hall or at one of the churches in town. A popular noon "Brown Bag Series" is held on Thursdays in summer on the green and is free. Look for the lively brochures put out by the group.

The Active Life

The active vacationer has much to enjoy in the Woodstock area. Here's a sampling.
♦ **Woodstock Health & Fitness Center** (802-457-6656), Route 106, Woodstock. You don't have to leave all your health club benefits at home. Owned and operated by the Woodstock Inn & Resort, this fitness center has two indoor and 10 outdoor

tennis courts, a squash court, racquetball court, indoor lap pool, exercise room, steam bath, sauna, and whirlpool. Spa manicures, pedicures, and facials are available in addition to Swedish or deep tissue massages. All facilities are available to the public on an à la carte basis.

Biking

♦ **Woodstock Sports** (802-234-1568) at 30 Central Street, Woodstock, has bike rentals. They give out a free bike map of the village; for $2.50 you can purchase another of the region.

♦ **Bike Vermont** (802-457-3553; 1-800-257-2226; www.bikeVermont.com), 51 Pleasant Street (Route 4), Woodstock. The state's best guided bike tour organization is located right in town in a little white house. You're welcome to stop in to inquire about weekend, or 5- to 7-day tours. Rental equipment is available. About 15 different itineraries are offered in Vermont. They also do tours in Scotland and Ireland.

Boating

♦ **Silver Lake State Park** in Barnard (802-234-9451) has rowboats and paddleboats for rent. **Canoe and kayak trips** are offered by **Wilderness Trails** (802-295-7620) on local lakes and ponds. They also have rentals.

Fly-Fishing

♦ The art of fly-fishing—lessons and guided trips—is offered by the **Vermont Fly Fishing School** (802-295-7620), located at the Quechee Inn at Marshland Farm.

Golf

♦ The **Woodstock Country Club** (802-457-6674) has an 18-hole Robert Trent Jones course. Rentals, lessons, and a driving range are all here.

Hiking/Walking

There are three marked and mapped trails within the village; you can get maps at the information booth on the green. You'll find trails on **Mount Peg** behind the Woodstock Health & Fitness Center. You can make it to the summit on a fairly easy trail and have views west toward Killington. Walk to the 1,250-foot summit of **Mount Tom** on a marked 1½-mile trail from Mountain Avenue in the village, through Faulkner Park. You can also walk the back side of Mount Tom via 30 miles of footpaths that are wide and sturdy—they were originally carriage roads—at the Marsh-Billings-Rockefeller National Historical Park. These trails are used in winter as cross-country ski trails. For information, call (802) 457-3368.

In addition, the Appalachian and Long Trails are not far; get guides to these in local bookstores.

Horseback Riding

♦ Saddle up at the **Kedron Valley Stables** (802-457-1480) in South Woodstock. Lessons are offered by appointment, trail rides organized, or you can take a horse-drawn ride in surrey, carriage, wagon, or sleigh. Nearby is the **Green Mountain Horse Association** (802–457-1509). One of the oldest equine organizations in the United States, the GMHA has more than 100 annual events at its large South Woodstock facility where spectators are welcome. (No horses for hire.)

Ice Skating

♦ Vail Field in Woodstock and on the green (January and February) skating areas are maintained. If it's cold enough you can also ice skate at Silver Lake in Barnard.

Picnicking

♦ Take your lunch to **Silver Lake State Park,** off Route 12, in Barnard; to the top of Mount Tom or Mount Peg (if you've the legs for it); or just to one of the benches on the village green. There is also a wonderful little spot by the Ottauquechee River on Central Street in the village. Look for the bridge with the flower boxes and scoot down a couple of steps to the lower level. It's wonderfully cool here. Or take any road and you'll discover your own beautiful spot.

Swimming

♦ **Silver Lake State Park** (summer 802-234-9451; January to May 1-800-299-3071). There are nice beaches, a grassy play area for children, picnic tables, changing facilities, and a snack bar. Also campsites.

Skiing

♦ Ski **downhill** at the nation's oldest ski area, **Suicide Six** (802-457-6661), just north of the village. With two double chairlifts and about 20 trails, this is a good area for those who don't want the hassles of the big mountain, **Killington,** located just 18 miles west. Rates are $44 per adult per day on holidays and weekends; $25, weekdays. Kids and seniors pay $28 and $20. **Cross-country skiing** at the **Woodstock Ski Touring Center** (802-457-6674) at the Woodstock Country Club (Route 106). Some 60 km of trails are tracked and groomed. Terrain is varied and includes gentle to upland and forest areas. Rentals and lessons are available.

The Nordic trail system on **Mount Tom,** mostly made of carriage roads, is pretty spectacular. It climbs all the way to the summit (rather gently), from which you can get a good view of Woodstock. Of course, then you have to ski down.

Shopping

Woodstock has excellent shopping. Just walk Elm and Center Streets to find classy boutiques, art galleries, antiques shops, bookstores, and more. Among the **art galleries,** I especially like the whimsical **Stephen Huneck Gallery** at 49 Central Street. Animals (especially dogs and cats) have the attention of Huneck, whose studio is in St. Johnsbury. Here you'll see furniture with playful animal drawer pulls, jewelry in the shape of cats and dogs (my cat pin has wings; it reminds me of my dear, deceased Panda), paintings, and even books illustrated by Huneck. The **Gallery on the Green** shows the works of more than 40 northeastern artists, among them Cape Ann favorite Donald Mosher. We also liked the oils by Bernard Coney and portraits by the Italian painter Pino, who lives in New Jersey.

Two **handmade furniture** showrooms are across from one another on Elm Street. One is the showroom for furniture maker **Charles Shackleton,** whose beautiful wood armoires, tables, and chairs (most of cherry) share space with the exquisite pottery done by his wife, **Miranda Thomas.** I am wild about the black pear design she uses on vases, plates, pitchers, and bowls. Even better is to take the short ride west to Bridgewater Corners where Thomas and Shackleton have their workshops, a much larger showroom, and where you get a chance to buy seconds in pottery. Shackleton, Irish by birth, first worked out of the Simon Pearce complex in Quechee and later struck out on his own.

The other furniture maker whose showroom is in Woodstock is **Clear Lake Furniture Makers,** whose handsome beds, benches, and tables are on view. Their main factory is in Ludlow.

Nearly 20 **antiques shops** are located in and around Woodstock. Pick up the helpful guide *Antiquing in and around Woodstock, Vermont,* and plot your course. Itching to knit? The **Whippletree Yarn Shop** on Central Street can probably satisfy your needs. Handcrafted wooden toys are also sold here. **Morgan-Ballou** on Elm Street is a store that sells classic women's clothing and handloomed sweaters. A few men's items, like ties, are for sale, too.

Charles Shackleton in his workshop

The Yankee Book Shop, 7 Central Street, is a wonderful small-town bookstore with a good selection of Vermont and New England titles. **Shire Apothecary** on Elm Street has suntan oil and mosquito repellent, and daily newspapers from Boston and New York.

Aubergine on the lower level below Bentley's restaurant is a great kitchen store with all sorts of kitchen tools and gadgets, epicurean foods, wine openers and racks, nifty napkins, and tableware.

F. H. Gillingham & Co. on Elm Street is one store you can't miss. Billing itself as "Vermont's Oldest General Store," it has been run by the Billings family for more than 100 years. It's quite a sophisticated spot up front, with good wines, cocktail foods, lovely pottery, Clarendon hardwood bowls for salads (and a pallet of local strawberries on the day I stopped). If you want plain old hardware items—say, a towel rack for the bathroom—find these items out back. There's a large selection of fresh produce. The **Village Butcher** on Elm has great deli sandwiches among its many offerings (which include a fine selection of domestic and imported wines and cheeses, Vermont maple products, breads, and pies).

Out of the village proper, head for the **Woodstock Farmer's Market** on Route 4 west for marvelous goodies. High-quality commercial/organic produce, fresh breads, cheeses, plants from the greenhouse, and gardening paraphernalia are to be found here. They'll make a sandwich or pour a cup of java for you. The **Taftsville Country Store** on Route 4 is the center of life in little Taftsville. Upscale Vermont foodstuffs are here, plus the staples you'd expect. You can buy wine and books, too, and some gift items. **Simon Pearce's** fantastic glass and pottery are found in the expansive showroom above the workspace in **The Mill at Quechee.** Pearce himself is a designer and blower of glass who worked for 10 years in his native Ireland. He moved his operations from Ireland to this historic mill in Quechee in 1981 where he revived the traditions of glassblowing, creating clear pieces of the highest quality. He's a good marketer; he now has retail stores throughout the Northeast. Stay for a meal at the **Simon Pearce Restaurant** (see *Where to Eat*). Across the street from the mill, check out the nature and gift shop run by the **Vermont Institute of Natural Science (VINS).** There are all sorts of nature study gifts for kids, some fine jewelry, and—my favorite—Lithophane Luminaires, lamps made with genuine porcelain three-dimensonal carved shades.

WHERE TO STAY

The top small hotel in the country—rated so by Zagat's, at least—is located in Barnard, just a 10-mile drive up Route 12 from Woodstock. High-style bed & breakfast inns, the center-of-town Woodstock Inn & Resort, and the Kedron Valley Inn in South Woodstock offer the traveler excellent options for a pampered stay.

♦ **Twin Farms** (802-234-9999; 1-800-894-6327; fax 802-234-9990; www.twinfarms. com), Barnard, VT 05031. Exact directions will be sent once you confirm reservations at this luxurious, yet tastefully understated, retreat in the Vermont woods. Located on a 235-acre property, once owned by the writers Sinclair Lewis and Dorothy Thompson, Twin Farms is—simply—the ultimate get-away-from-it-all spot.

The main dining room at Twin Farms

"Imagine," said the marketing manager Anne Black Cone, "leaving New York in the morning and being here in the afternoon."

We were, at the time, exploring one of Twin Farms' nine exquisite cottages, Orchard Cottage. Set in the midst of an old-farm apple orchard, the cottage is a large, high ceilinged space with Asian influences. As with all 15 accommodations (for a total of 30 guests at one time), this has a king-sized featherbed with duvet, at least one fireplace (in this case two hand-carved granite fireplaces), TV/VCR/stereo, trays with a coffee press and an electric teapot—and Harney & Sons teas to choose from. There are two sinks in bathrooms, terry-cloth robes, and a large selection of all-natural toiletries. In this cottage, as with all the cottages, there is a large screened-in porch. Trail maps and some trail mix have been placed on a table. One popular "sport" among the Twin Farms crowd is quiet walks along well-carved trails through the property.

The latest—and priciest—accommodation at Twin Farms is Chalet, an expansive cottage with sunken living room above which is a balcony with dining table. This is the first space to have his-and-her bathrooms. His has the circular mosaic tiled shower; hers, the soaking tub. A fireplace is surrounded with hand-done ceramic tiles and can be seen from the bed. A deck off the bedroom allows for luxurious sitting and viewing the surroundings. There is a screened-in porch with stone Jacuzzi. And another outdoor sitting area.

Four large rooms in the 1795 main house are appealing. Dorothy's Room has a Russian turn-of-the-20th-century influence with a ceramic tiled fireplace in the sitting area, plus a double soaking tub. The walls, paneled in pumpkin pine, are hung with watercolors. Although the smallest of the spaces at Twin Farms, at 700 square feet, it is cozy and welcoming.

Guests can swim in a sandy-bottomed spring-fed pond or borrow a mountain bike for a ride through the woods. They can ski on their very own downhill ski area (equipment is available) with five runs and one Poma lift or they can play a game of croquet on a velvety piece of lawn. Stave puzzles are available for intellectual exercise.

The tab is high for an overnight stay, but it includes all meals and beverages and virtually all activities. The only extras are the spa treatments. Massages are done in the privacy of your own room or cottage.

Dinner is served in a rustic dining room, with black-and-cream-square rug—to look like tiles—where tables are set for two. Many guests choose to dine in their own cottage or room.

Twin Farms was created by the Twigg-Smith family of Hawaii, who are owners of the Kona coffee plantations. Now Thurston Twigg-Smith heads up the corporation known as The Twin Farms Collection. More inns may be in the offing.

Doubles, $900–2,400 for Chalet. Closed during the month of April. Two- to 3-night minimums. The whole place may be rented for $20,000.

♦ **Woodstock Inn & Resort** (802-457-1100; 1-800-448-7900; www.woodstockinn. com), 14 The Green, Woodstock, VT 05091. The most central location in town is enjoyed by this 142-room white-brick inn built and owned by Laurance S. Rockefeller. The huge fieldstone fireplace in the lobby—seen the moment you enter—is a gathering place and a welcome sight on a chilly Vermont day. It's large enough to burn 4-foot logs. Rooms are not grand, but comfortable. The 1991 addition , known as the Tavern Wing, provides 34 rooms, 21 of them with in-room wood-burning fireplaces. Four suites in the Tavern Wing have king beds, a separate living room with fireplace, and a deep green and cherry-red color scheme. A TV hidden in an armoire, a Bose radio, and bookcases filled with books might inspire you to go no farther. The bathrooms have tub-shower combinations. The deep green color scheme extends to most of the rooms at the inn, many of whose beds have the same dark green painted headboards reminiscent of window shutter construction. Two "porch rooms" are popular in summer for their outdoor decks overlooking the gardens. Many rooms have two queen-sized beds.

The Woodstock Inn is close to just about everything. When staying here you get preference for a golf time at the spectacular 18-hole Robert Trent Jones Sr. course at the Woodstock Country Club, owned and operated by the inn. Suicide Six, the small but serviceable downhill ski area that was the nation's first in 1934, is also under the inn's umbrella. A health and fitness club on Route 106—south of the inn—is owned by the Woodstock Inn. Packages involving these satellite operations sometimes are offered.

Guests can take a guided walking tour of the village on Saturday morning. Or they can spend half the day cooking with the chefs in the AAA four-diamond kitchen for $40. Kids can also have an hour's lesson in the kitchen.

Public rooms are comfortable. We especially like the library with its sink-into chairs and dark wood desks where you can read or work. The dining room is well rated (see *Where to Eat*). More casual fare is available in the Eagle Café, bright and cheerful with yellow wallpaper and serving three meals a day; and the dark, convivial Richardson's Tavern, where you can get a burger, soup, or a limited number of entrées. Here you can dine inside or—in summer—on the outdoor terrace. Live entertainment is offered most weekends.

An indoor and an outdoor pool are available to guests. Hiking trails start from nearby. And it's an easy walk into town to shop or dine. Doubles, $195–375, EP. MAP plans are available. Ask about weekend packages.

♦ **The Jackson House Inn** (802-457-2065; 1-800-448-1890; fax 802-457-9290; www. jacksonhouse.com), 114–3 Senior Lane, Woodstock, VT 05091. This 15-room country inn offers a quiet getaway (the sound of a clock ticking in the side-by-side parlors, for example) as well as luxurious amenities. Located a short distance from the center of the village, it's a destination in itself with a fine-dining restaurant on the premises (see *Where to Eat*). Innkeepers Carl and Linda Delnegro raised seven children and then turned their attention in 2000 to innkeeping. "We were fans of the property," explained Carl in their choice of the Jackson House. Built in 1890, the gold-clapboard house with black shutters and welcoming porch is listed on the National Register of Historic Places. In a nod to its age, some decorating—but not all—is in the Victorian mode. Since the Delnegros' arrival, four luxurious suites have been added. These have gas fireplace, large bathroom with whirlpool tub and stall shower, TV in an armoire, stereo, and CD player. French doors lead to a private patio in the two first-floor suites in the new wing. Rooms are all individually styled. The third floor under-the-eaves Gloria Swanson Suite in the main inn has a photograph of the star smoking a cigarette. The first-floor Josephine Bonaparte Room is wallpapered in a classic gray pattern with urn design and has formal gold floor-to-ceiling drapes. Bathrooms can be on the small side in the original house, but all have glass-enclosed tub-shower combinations.

Guests are pampered. An elaborate assortment of hors d'oeuvres is offered with wine or champagne in the evening. Breakfasts are large with cakes, yogurt, fresh

The Jackson House Inn

fruit, breads, and housemade granola on the buffet. You then order an entrée from the menu—the day we stopped it was hotcakes with candied Georgia peaches, toasted almonds, and bacon, or poached eggs Florentine served with potato hash. The grounds are lovely. A maze comprised of dwarf Alberta spruce trees is intriguing and has tables and chairs where guests may lounge. These are innkeepers who know what they are doing. Doubles, $195–395.

♦ **The Maple Leaf Inn** (802-234-5342; 1-800-51-MAPLE; www.mapleleafinn.com), Route 12, P.O. Box 273, Barnard, VT 05031. When Janet and Gary Robison came to Vermont from Texas to be innkeepers, they couldn't find exactly what they wanted—so they built their own place from the ground up. It is a Victorian-style inn with peaked roof, front porch, and loads of large windows, set back from the road in a grove of birches. And because Gary was frustrated by the few "fireplace nights" in the Lone Star State, he put wood-burning fireplaces in all five luxurious first- and second-floor guest rooms, and in the parlor and dining room, too. Since then they've added two more guest rooms on the third floor that are without fireplaces, but are also less costly. All guest rooms have king bed, TV in armoire with VCR, large bathroom with either whirlpool tub or—in the third-floor bathrooms—soaking tub for two, and plenty of space. There's always a sitting area with two comfortable chairs.

Janet did the wall stenciling in each room—meant to tie in with the room's name. Winter Haven, for example, has a darling little village with snowcapped roofs on houses painted above the fireplace mantel. A floral motif is used in the first-floor handicapped-accessible room named Country Garden whose bed has a picket-fence-style headboard. We liked our view of our fireplace in Autumn Woods, where it's directly across from the bed. All beds have white matelasse bedspreads for a crisp, clean look, and quilts to match quilted shams on the pillows. Sheets are lace edged. A whole closet full of varying pillows is available for anyone who needs a different firmness.

Janet loves to cook and is known for her three-course breakfasts. Her buttermilk scones are often requested by returning guests. Tables for two are set up in the bright dining room, where various versions of the LOVE postage stamps have been embroidered and framed by Janet. This *is* a romantic destination; a soon-to-be-married man was booking one of the rooms for his wedding night when last we stopped. Plenty of movies are available for guests' use from a collection in the library. Again, in Janet's view, they are "romantic movies—no shoot-'em-ups."

The Robisons will provide after-dinner treats in guests' rooms. Janet calls them "movie munchies"—maybe fresh fruit with Vermont cheeses and crackers, or a chocolate brownie sundae with two spoons, or maybe just popcorn and a soft drink. Janet and Gary can also deliver wine or beer to guests' rooms since they have a wine/beer license. Doubles, $130–230.

♦ **Kedron Valley Inn** (802-457-1473; 1-800-836-1193; fax 802-457-4469; www.kedron valleyinn.com), Route 106, South Woodstock, VT 05071. When recently departed innkeepers Max and Merrily Comins took over this inn in 1985, they upgraded by adding lots of working fireplaces. Now 20 of the 28 guest rooms in three buildings have fireplaces or wood-burning stoves. Merrily also brought her wonderful antique quilt collection, and many old quilts grace walls and guest rooms where they can be admired. Both enhancements seemed perfectly appropriate since this is one of Vermont's oldest inns: dating from the 1830s. In June 2002 the Cominses handed over the keys to a Rowayton, Connecticut, couple, Jack and Nicole Maiden. Merrily said she'd be working side by side with the new innkeepers and she and Max were going to live in South Woodstock.

The main inn is a mellow, aging brick with a large porch. To the left of the entrance is a parlor with small bar. To the right is the check-in area with wicker furnishings. Down the hall is the atmospheric beamed dining room, where chef James Allen presides. He was to stay on with the new innkeepers. In addition to the main inn, rooms are located in the Tavern Building next door and in a log motel-style building to the rear of the property.

Most rooms have queen canopy beds; two have king beds in the mission style, and there are four rooms with double canopy beds. All rooms have TV and private bath, and a third are air-conditioned. Room 2 in the main brick inn is a corner room with four windows, rockers before the fireplace, and a bathroom with tub and shower. The room is pale yellow, large, and comfortable. In the Tavern Building next door, room 24 is on two levels, with bathroom and sitting area with wicker pullout sofa as you enter, and a queen bed in the sleeping loft above. In number 26, also in the Tavern Building, you step down a couple of stairs into a large open space with five windows, queen bed, fireplace, air-conditioning, and bathroom with tub and shower. Ten of the rooms have a private outdoor sitting space. On the grounds is a spring-fed pond with two sandy beaches, where guests may swim in summer. Dogs are accepted at the inn with advance approval and must be leashed.

Although the inn is not connected with the Kedron Valley Stables, guests often head to the nearby spot for horseback riding. South Woodstock is about 5 miles from the village of Woodstock. Doubles, with breakfast, $135–260.

♦ **The Quechee Inn at Marshland Farm** (802-295-3133; 1-800-235-3133; fax 802-295-6587; www.quecheeinn.com), Quechee Main Street, Quechee, VT 05059. This place looks just like the Vermont you imagine: a big white inn with a red barn out back. Inside, things are comfortably familiar. The building was built in 1793 and was originally the home of Colonel Joseph Marsh, Vermont's first lieutenant governor. The living room, with low beamed ceiling and barnwood walls, is furnished with Windsor-style and wing chairs and low coffee tables, arranged into seating groups. Period antiques grace the inn's 22 guest rooms and two suites. Floors are often bare wood with wide floorboards, covered with small braided rugs. Beds are canopied. All rooms have TV and private bath. Off the second-floor hallway guests have access to an open porch where they can sit and enjoy the country views. Guests are able to get equipment and lessons for fly-fishing, kayaks, and rental bikes from the Vermont Fly Fishing School and Wilderness Trails center, both on the property. In winter 18 km of cross-country trails are groomed. A full buffet breakfast with fruits and cereals, eggs and bacon, muffins and breads is complimentary to guests and served in the **dining room.** This atmospheric room—with a few outdoor tables—is the setting for dinner, served nightly. On a recent menu (entrées, $18–25) were crispy Long Island duck with a dried apricot and passion fruit sauce, and horseradish-crusted Atlantic salmon. Doubles, $90–240.

♦ **The Charleston House** (802-457-3843; 1-888-475-3800; www.charlestonhouse. com), 21 Pleasant Street, Woodstock, VT 05091. Dieter (Dixi) and Willa Nohl offer warm hospitality at this brick 1835 Greek Revival town house. There's nothing southern about the Nohls (he comes from Austria and managed ski areas in Vermont; she is a native of Montreal), but previous owners, who named the house, were from the South. No matter, laughs Willa, pointing to her husband's nickname. Nine guest rooms—five in the original house and four in a new wing to the back—all have private bath and air-conditioning. The four newer rooms are very large, with a Jacuzzi-style tub in the bathroom and small TV set. Ours, Mount Peg (named for the nearby mountain), had a four-poster queen bed and two wing chairs for relaxing. Rooms in the main house are a bit more old-fashioned and do not have TVs, except for the second-floor Pomfret Hills. There's a large communal TV set in the lovely front parlor, furnished with chintz-covered sofas and mahogany tables. A first-floor bedroom, Antique Store, is cozy in soft green and peach with a star quilt on the bed. Baths have large black-and-white-square-tiled floors in the main house; this had a tub-shower combination and pedestal sink. Beds are high enough so that steps are provided to climb in.

Willa is an exceptional cook and prepares beautifully arranged plates for breakfast in the dining room. One morning we enjoyed lighter-than-air pancakes; the second morning, a delicious quiche. Also on the plate are fresh fruit, homemade muffins, and a breakfast meat. Dixi keeps the coffee cups filled and is the server. Doubles, $110–225.

♦ **Applebutter Inn** (802-457-4158), Happy Valley Road, Taftsville, VT 05073. This B&B is located in the tiny village of Taftsville, just up the road from the Taftsville General Store. Bev and Andrew Cook spent 15 years developing this charming and pristine B&B, where all five guest rooms are named for apples and all have private bath. Then, in summer 2002, they handed over their creation to new owners and retreated to their house on a hillside nearby. There they planned to open two large suites, call them Apple Hill, and work with the new innkeepers jointly to fill the rooms. The common rooms at Applebutter Inn are gracious and include the large breakfast room to the back of the house and two front parlors, one an inviting yellow room with wood-burning fireplace. All have warm pine floors with wide floorboards. The first-floor guest room, Winesap, is a real charmer with a private entrance overlooking barn and orchard, king-sized bed, and adjoining bath. The large kitchen is in the center of this house, causing guests to walk through it to get from one end to the other. Bev liked that; it was her way of getting to see the guests. Doubles, with breakfast, $75–150.

♦ **Canterbury House** (802-457-3077; 1-800-390-3077), 43 Pleasant Street, Woodstock, VT 05091. Bob and Sue Frost operate a Victorian B&B where all the rooms are named for Chaucer's *Canterbury Tales*. They are an unusual pair in that they had never been in Vermont, or in a B&B, before they decided to buy a Vermont B&B. That was a few years ago, and they like the life. American and British flags fly out front, and the English theme is carried out in the dining room where wallpaper is of teapots. Two large breakfast tables accommodate guests from the seven guest rooms. Sue's the cook, and she prepares large breakfasts—often with French toast or pancakes as the centerpiece. Sue said she thinks of her guests as coming to "that favorite aunt's old house." Guest rooms, all air-conditioned, are decorated with antiques and wicker, and lots of floral fabrics and wallpaper. Squire's Tale on the second floor has a country pine queen bed, and a private sitting room furnished in wicker with a TV set. On the third floor, up a narrow staircase, Chaucer's Garret has a king bed at one end and a sitting area with TV at the other. It's quite cozy. The bathroom has an angled ceiling and tub-shower combination. Monk's Tale to the back of the house has its own entrance, a queen bed, and a small gas fireplace. It's done in blue florals. The Frosts, who have no children of their own, welcome guests for Christmas when they say it's like a big house party. Sue decorates a huge tree and puts it into the bay window of the living room. Doubles, $120–175. No children.

♦ **Three Church Street** (802-457-1925; fax 802-457-9181), 3 Church Street, Woodstock, VT 05091. Eleanor Paine and a bevy of young assistants welcome guests into this Federal brick period house close to the green and the center of town. *Faded elegance* might be the best way to describe the house, with 11 guest rooms, 6 with private bath. A spacious and somewhat formal sitting room with grand piano and an elegant foyer—with a bust of Lafayette in one niche—are testimony to the original grandness of the house. All rooms are on the second floor of the original house and a wing added later. Most are simply furnished with white spreads, wall-to-wall carpeting, and simple bureaus or side tables. They have king, queen, or twin beds. There's a large back porch to sit on with a view of the grounds and toward Mount Tom. The rates are good for Woodstock. Surrounding the house are 2 acres of gardens and lawns with swimming pool and clay tennis court that can be used by guests. Large breakfasts are served in two side-by-side dining rooms with separate tables. Pets are permitted. Children, too. Doubles, $85–125.

♦ **The Carriage House of Woodstock** (802-457-4322; 1-800-791-8045; www.carriage-housewoodstock.com), 455 Woodstock Road (Route 4), Woodstock, VT 05091. Debbie and Mark Stanglin, who call themselves "corporate refugees," operate this B&B just a mile west of the Woodstock green. The big gold house with turret was built in 1865 as a boardinghouse for a nearby mill. All nine rooms—varying in size—have queen bed, private bath, and air-conditioning. They are all named for Vermont covered bridges. The decor is Victorian, so you might find a high oak bed or a brass and iron painted bedstead plus floral, flouncy curtains. Rooms vary in size, with seven on three floors of the main house, and two larger rooms in the walkout area beneath the rear carriage house. These have whirlpool tub, TV, and doors to the outside. The larger of the two has a king bed and fireplace. Debbie whips up a snack in the afternoon and makes full breakfasts with homemade breads or muffins in the morning. The wicker-furnished porch is a popular place to sit. Doubles, $95–185.

♦ **The Shire Motel** (802-457-2211; www.shiremotel.com), 46 Pleasant Street, Woodstock, VT 05091. Under the same ownership for nearly 20 years, this blue-gray, two-level motel is a good choice for anyone who craves a view. Most motel rooms look out over the Ottauquechee River, which runs behind the structure. The 36 motel rooms have two double beds, a king or two queen-sized beds, TV, and the usual amenities. In an older village house next door, purchased recently by the motel owners and overhauled, are three spacious suites with Jacuzzi-style tub, fireplace, and king bed. One very attractive room has a king spool bed, gas fireplace, double Jacuzzi-style tub. This room can be rented with an attached complete kitchen. To the rear of the property, a new building was under construction that would add five more luxury king-bedded suites. It was expected to open in late 2002. Doubles, $88–148; luxury suites, $150–300.

WHERE TO EAT

Fine dining is available in the Woodstock area but, like everywhere else, casual fare and dress are creeping in and gaining in popularity. Here are our favorites, with the emphasis on the high end.

Serious

♦ **Hemingway's** (802-422-3886), Route 4, Killington. For a special event, or just for a great meal, Woodstock residents happily travel the 20 to 30 minutes west to this restaurant. Ted and Linda Fondulas—he's the chef—have operated their spot in the red 1860 Asa Briggs House for more than 20 years. Many think it is the best restaurant in the state. Ted has won many awards—most recently the Robert Mondavi Culinary Award of Excellence in 2001—after which artist Delmar Ochsner was commissioned to do his portrait. The large, bright painting of Ted in chef's duds hangs in the main peach dining room with the stunning floor-length black-and-peach floral draperies and crystal chandeliers. The *Wine Spectator* Award of Excellence has been bestowed upon the wine list since 1990. The guy knows his stuff.

Ted and his wife met as literature majors while studying at Syracuse University. They named the restaurant for Ernest Hemingway, a favorite writer. Linda said their idea was to express—in culinary terms—the same simplicity, yet fine artistry, that Hemingway does in his books. "We walk the line between modern and classic," she said.

Nothing has been left to chance. While the restaurant is located in what was once a stagecoach stop and boardinghouse for weary travelers, and the period look retained outside, each of three dining rooms inside is atmospheric, romantic, and stylish. In addition to the main dining room, there's the brick-floored Garden Room, with yellow bentwood chairs and a fireplace that burns on chilly evenings. Two tables in the fireplaced lounge area—a space distinct from the bar—are popular, especially in cool weather. An intimate stone-walled wine cellar downstairs is set with a few tables as well.

While the menu is sophisticated and inventive, Hemingway's does not stand on ceremony. Jackets are not required for men, which makes sense in a ski area.

Several different prix fixe meals are available: the regular three- or four-course dinner, at $50–60; a six-course feasting menu with smaller portions and more items to sample at $65–75; a wine tasting menu at $75–85; and a vegetable menu for about $45.

Ted is known for his "birds." Quail or pheasant are almost always on the menu, and others as available seasonally. Fish is big, and Ted is a stickler about preparing and serving only wild fish. Wild sea bass and wild sockeye salmon were on the menu when we last visited.

The chef never seems to tire of coming up with fascinating combinations. A recently popular appetizer was the fallen goat cheese soufflé, prepared with aged goat, sheep, and blue cheese, all from Vermont, prepared with a Spanish quince paste and served with a date pecan tart with candied fennel and port sauce. Other starters might be chilled spring pea soup with lemon cream and yam crisps, or roasted tomato and olive tart with organic greens in a basil vinaigrette. Entrées might be wood-roasted wild salmon with baby green beans, sun-dried tomato, caramelized shallots, and crisp potatoes, or mushroom-crusted sirloin of lamb with eggplant, zucchini, and red lentils. A confit of rhubarb and strawberry with lovage ice cream made here was a star on the dessert menu, along with blueberry brioche pudding with candied lemon and bourbon cream.

Open Wednesday through Sunday, 6–9 midweek and until 10 on Friday and Saturday. Closed Monday and Tuesday except Labor Day, when the annual "mushroom forage" is held. "We go out hunting mushrooms, then have lunch and a lecture," said Linda. It's popular.

Reservations are strongly recommended at Hemingway's.

♦ **The Barnard Inn** (802-234-9961), Route 12, Barnard. Will Dodson and Ruth Schimmelpfennig, spouses and chefs, are the proprietors at one of the area's top restaurants. The handsome brick house in which the restaurant is located may seem to be out in the country, but fans of good food aren't the least distressed by the ride. The restaurant has had a fine reputation for many years under at least two prior regimes. That continues.

The more formal restaurant occupies three fireplaced rooms, including the large keeping room of the former house with a huge wood-burning fireplace. The beamed ceiling adds to the atmosphere. In two smaller front rooms, with yellow walls, white trim, and Oriental carpets on wood floors, there are gas-burning fireplaces. Starters here could be slow-roasted tomato bisque with Vermont cheddar and herbs, or leek and potato soup served with shaved black truffle. Other appetizers might be smoked rainbow trout with a sweet corn pancake, or beef carpaccio with black pepper and capers, served with a simple salad ($8–12). A salad of mesclun greens was dressed up with candied walnuts and Danish blue cheese and tossed in a maple-balsamic vinaigrette. Entrées ($25–31) could be wild sockeye salmon with asparagus and whipped potatoes, lobster and shrimp gnocchi, or roast pork tenderloin prepared in a tarragon marinade and served with baby carrots.

At the back of the house, Max's Tavern is a place for more casual fare. With only four dark wood tables, set with captain's chairs, this is a spot that has gained great popularity among the locals. This is also the room with the bar. You need to arrive early, since reservations are not taken for this room. On the menu you'll find a few of the items from the main menu—the soups, for instance—plus entrées such as penne pasta primavera, pan-roasted chicken breast with mashed potatoes, or sautéed cod with lemon caper butter and veggies ($11–15).

The main restaurant serves dinner Wednesday through Saturday in-season, sometimes weekends only off-season. Max's Tavern opens at 5 PM, with dinner served 6–9. The restaurant usually closes briefly in April and again in November.

♦ **The Prince and the Pauper** (802-457-1818), 24 Elm Street, Woodstock. Chris Balcer, chef-proprietor, has been providing Woodstock with its very own fine dining

Simon Pearce restaurant and workshop in the Mill at Quechee

for the past 20 years. This in-town restaurant, located down an alley off Elm Street, is a favorite of locals and visitors alike. A beamed ceiling, high-backed wood booths with a lovely painting over each, and tables with white tablecloths are in the main dining room. A few more tables with woven green place mats on bare wood are by the bar, which fills up with the local gentry. The effect is a nice mix of comfort with sophistication. Vince Talento, part owner, may show you to your table and point out menu classics, like Carre d'Agneau Royale—boneless rack of Australian lamb, grilled and baked in puff pastry with spinach and mushroom duxelles. My husband chose that dish and pronounced every bite wonderful. I settled on an appetizer, pan-seared scallops served with a chive beurre blanc, and a green salad with crumbled blue cheese. Everything was delicious.

Other starters might be prosciutto and melon; the house pâté made with pork, chicken livers, port-soaked cherries, and pistachio nuts; or Asian-cured salmon sliced thin and served with sesame toast and a cucumber yogurt sauce ($6–9). Entrées can be scallops of veal sautéed with artichoke hearts, spinach, Marsala wine, and balsamic vinegar; crisply roasted duck with a cherry sauce; or grilled tuna with Thai ginger sauce and wasabi garnish. Entrées, $24 range. A prix fixe dinner is $39. A bistro menu, served in the bar, offers burgers, Maine crabcakes with roasted red pepper aïoli, Chinese barbecued ribs, and the like ($13–19). Open nightly 6–9; the lounge opens at 5.

♦ **Simon Pearce Restaurant** (802-295-1470), The Mill, Quechee. Located in the large brick mill building where Simon Pearce glassblowers create some of their wondrous designs, and where the large showroom for glass and pottery are also housed, this restaurant has one of the most dramatic locations in the area. From many of the large windows you get a great view of the thundering falls of the Ottauquechee River—once used to power the mills. In fact, one room is built out over the river with windows all around. From some points you also get a good view of the covered bridge that crosses the river just downstream. Light wood tables and simple woven-seat chairs are an appropriately simple background for the dramatic views and food. Pottery "seconds" are used for dining. Many chefs here have trained in Ireland at the Culinary Institute in Ballymaloe, others in the States. We've never had a bad meal here.

At lunchtime you might find shepherd's pie; a falafel and hummus roll-up sandwich served with a cucumber-dill sauce; a pulled pork sandwich with coleslaw and maple baked beans; or grilled flank steak with romaine lettuce, new potatoes, and Caesar dressing ($9–12). Lamb stew is another favorite. Dinner might begin with appetizers such as spicy tuna and salmon tartare served with a yellow beet coulis, lightly curried peekytoe crab and avocado, or a spice-crusted gravlax salad with fennel, horseradish oil, and scallion pancake strips ($8–12). Main dishes could be horseradish-crusted cod with herb mashed potatoes; roasted lamb loin with gingered black beans and kohlrabi greens; crisp roast duckling with vegetable fried rice and mango chutney sauce. Desserts are equally scrumptious. Open daily for lunch 11:30–2:45, and 6–9 for dinner.

♦ **Jackson House Restaurant** (802-457-2065), 114–3 Senior Lane, Woodstock. For a vintage inn, the Jackson House surprises with a many-windowed, fresh, somewhat contemporary restaurant. A large room added to the rear of the Victorian-era inn, it has sponged peach walls, cathedral ceiling, and tables with white cloths covered with champagne-tinted overcloths. In summer the beautiful gardens are the focus; in cooler weather a see-through granite fireplace warms the space. Owner Carl Delnegro said a Victorian conservatory complete with plants would soon be added since "everyone wants to eat in the gardens."

Chef Marty Holzberg offers an eclectic menu with an emphasis on Mediterranean dishes. You can order a six-course tasting menu at $65; a vegetable tasting menu for $55; or a standard three-course dinner at $55. First course on the three-course dinner might be lobster cassoulet combining Maine lobster, Tuscan white beans, duck confit, and mesclun greens ($21, à la carte); fried baby squid with a potato galette; or a crispy duck confit salad with mission figs and crisp potatoes. Entrées include the very popular veal and chicken carciofi, Parmesan-crusted chicken and veal with homemade pasta and sautéed baby artichokes. Other choices ($32–38 à la carte) could be pan-seared Copper River salmon with lemon-scented risotto, shiitake mushrooms, and grilled prawns, or a grilled hanger steak with black truffle whipped potatoes, beef marrow, and whole-grain mustard jus. For dessert; a chocolate almond truffle tartlet comes topped with vanilla bean ice cream, and Grand Marnier panna cotta is a served with sweet cream buttermilk custard and orange caramel sauce. There's an excellent wine list. Dinner 6–9 nightly except Tuesday. Inn guests have a full breakfast in the dining room.

♦ **Woodstock Inn & Resort** (802-457-1100), 14 The Green, Woodstock. The main dining room at the inn is a serene space with a AAA four-diamond rating. Putty-gray carpeting with discreet floral design stretches underfoot, and at one end of the room an arrangement of tree branches holds tiny white lights. Chairs are upholstered and edged in dark wood, and tablecloths are white. Jackets are not required. Diners might start with fried wild mushroom ravioli with Vermont goat cheese; oysters Rockefeller (said to be owner Laurance Rockefeller's favorite recipe); or New England lobster and crabcakes with a mustard crème fraîche ($7–10). Woodstock Inn Caesar salad adds diced tomatoes and Kalamata olives to the classic. Entrées can include bacon-wrapped veal tenderloin with a sun-dried cherry bread pudding; char-grilled salmon with tomato and artichoke topping and orzo; or roasted rack of lamb served with a lentil ragout and caramelized winter vegetables (entrées, $26–29). Desserts are a selection from the pastry chef. Dinner nightly and Sunday brunch are served.

In the more casual **Eagle Café,** where yellow wallpaper with red and green figures and off-white-painted furniture contribute to a lighter, more casual effect, three meals a day are served. Soups, salads, and sandwiches are emphasized at lunch. Dinner ranges from a sirloin burger platter and pizzas to roast turkey dinner, veal Parmesan, and a char-grilled New York strip steak (entrées $10–20). **Richardson's Tavern,** the bar, opens at 5 nightly. With its wood-burning fireplace and dark wood paneling and furniture, it's a cozy space. Several can crowd into one of the half-circle booths against the wall. Light dinner can be found here, including burgers, crabcakes, salads, and so on.

♦ **Parker House** (802-295-6077; www.theparkerhouseinn.com), 1792 Quechee Main Street, Quechee. Walt and Barbara Forrester, both chefs, came east from Chicago to operate this inn and restaurant. The restaurant is the star here, and Barbara reigns as head chef. Walt is the breakfast cook for guests in the inn's seven rooms. Son Jay serves as food and beverage manager. Queen Anne chairs and white tablecloths lend a formality to the two side-by-side dining rooms. There's also a pleasant pub where dinner may be eaten and—in summer—dining on the deck with views of the Ottauquechee River out back. Starters ($5–9) might be wild mushroom filled ravioli with sage and garlic brown butter sauce, smoked salmon served with a horseradish-flavored potato pancake, or puree of garlic soup with a poached egg. Baby spinach tossed with smoked bacon vinaigrette and garnished with mushrooms, red onion, and Maytag blue cheese is a favorite salad. Entrées ($19–24) could be spice-crusted pork tenderloin finished with brandy and whole-grain mustard sauce; steak tenderloin grilled and served with roasted garlic; or New Zealand rack of lamb with a rosemary-Cabernet sauce. Seven rooms on the second and third floors all have private bath and rent for $115–150 with breakfast.

More Casual

♦ **Corners Inn and Restaurant** (802-672-9968), Route 4, Bridgewater Corners. Chef-owner Brad Pirkey commands a loyal following at this comfortable spot a few miles west of Woodstock. One warm summer evening we enjoyed dinner on the wraparound deck; there are also two dining rooms inside. When have you last had a crock of cheese (spicy shallot flavored in our case) and crackers brought to you with your drinks? That's the kind of personal touch that people like here. Beer from the nearby Long Trail brewery is on tap, and we enjoyed large glasses after a hot day. Home-baked bread arrives with rosemary-flavored olive oil. Starters could be seafood cakes with mango chutney, warm cabbage salad with prosciutto, pine nuts, and Gorgonzola, or a five-onion soup ($4–7). We shared a salad of mixed baby greens before our entrées—shrimp scampi over a bed of angel-hair pasta, and blackened halibut with corn sauce, served with sugar snap peas in a curried carrot sauce. Both were delicious. Other possibilities might be pasta Bolognese or lobster ravioli in a sun-dried tomato and pesto cream sauce (salads come with the pasta dishes), salmon with raspberry glaze, cioppino over linguine, or mixed grill—strip steak with a mustard chive sauce, three large grilled shrimp, and a small seasoned lamb tenderloin. Entrées are $13–19. Dinner is served Wednesday through Sunday from 5:30. The restaurant closes in April and in November.

♦ **Pane e Salute** (802-457-4882), 61 Central Street, Woodstock. Caleb Barber and Deirdre Heekin met while students at Middlebury College, married, and spent a year in Tuscany. Caleb also gained a few years of experience as a chef and baker here and there before he and Deirdre, a writer, opened this evolving bakery and restaurant in the mid-1990s. (Their cookbook, *Pane e Salute*, was published in 2002.) The intimate space in a little house at the east end of the village has cases filled with delectable pastries, a refrigerated case with cheeses, and wood shelves behind the counter for various breads. The rustic Roman sourdough is especially praised. At lunch we enjoyed the salad Veronese (radicchio with pancetta, goat cheese, and walnuts) and a special, marinated and dried beef served with a mound of greens both in a balsamic vinaigrette. They were excellent, as was the crusty bread brought to the table. Tap water comes in a large clear bottle that you can pour yourselves, or you can order Italian bottled waters. Other luncheon possibilities included macaroni and cheese, Roman-style; spaghetti Bolognese; and risotto, which changes daily. Wines and beers are available, and desserts are usually selected from the display case. Dinner offers antipasti in both vegetarian and meat versions; pastas such as penne with fresh ricotta, peas, and basil ($12); and entrées such as breaded halibut with green sauce and aïoli, roast chicken in egg and lemon sauce, and pork loin braised with bay leaf and garlic ($16). Desserts include assorted truffles and praline with fresh fruit, a selection of three cheeses, or the house specialty: pears poached in Pernod ($7–9). Several different types of pizza are also available. Sunday brunch includes frittatas, Belgian waffle with berries or bananas, and rosemary lemon roasted chicken with a mixed salad and roasted potatoes ($6–11). Naturally, you can also order cappuccino, espresso, or café latte along with teas and American coffees. A 17 percent gratuity is automatically added to all meals. Open Monday and Thursday through Saturday for lunch noon–2:30; Sunday brunch 10–2; and dinner on Friday and Saturday 6–9. The place opens at 7 AM weekdays to sell coffee, pastries, and breads.

♦ **Bentley's** (802-457-3232), Elm Street, Woodstock. This multilevel restaurant, decorated in the Victorian mode, throbs with activity day and night. Bill Decklebaum and David Creech, partners, opened the restaurant more than 25 years ago. Commanding the busiest corner of town, it is the place to see and be seen. With an eclectic mix of furnishings—from floor lamps with fringed shades to wing chairs and tables of all sizes and shapes—the restaurant also has potted palms and hanging plants. It's fun and a little frantic at times. At lunch you can have a warm spinach salad, a BBQ pulled pork sandwich, the Greenbriar (chicken salad with grapes, walnuts, and sage on a toasted croissant), or Bentley's Famous Hamburger (half a pound in size). Prices are in the $7–12 range. At night the dinner menu has salads and other starters such as lobster bisque, deep-fried calamari, or bruschetta. Dinner entrées ($17–20 range) could be maple mustard chicken rolled in pecans and served with a maple mustard sauce; duck glazed with a cranberry-Chambord sauce; or fettuccine with tomatoes, basil, and spinach. Lunch daily 11:30–3; dinner 5 to 9:30 or 10; Sunday brunch 11–4. You can get late lunch between 3 and 5.

♦ **Woodstock Country Club** (802-457-6672), South Street, Route 106, Woodstock. Lunch only is served at this pleasant restaurant on the second floor of the club building. In summer a shady umbrellaed deck is available in addition to the large room inside. I had the Painter's Palette, a lovely arrangement of colorful fruits with cottage cheese and two sandwich wedges (how long since you've had cream cheese on date and nut bread?). Our other choice was "The Mighty Slice," grilled ham, cheese, and egg salad with black olives on country white bread. Both were excellent. Other possibilities are curried chicken salad, the "chowder of the day," and a char-grilled burger on a kaiser roll with red onion, lettuce, and tomato. A Golfer's Express Lunch in summer includes a cup of soup and deli sandwich (or half deli sandwich). There's a full bar. Open for lunch daily in golf season. Call to be sure of hours.

Picnics

Well, picnics are the best, aren't they? Pick up picnic fare at the **Woodstock Farmers' Market** on Route 4 west of town, where you can find meals to go, soups and sandwiches, cookies and other bakery items. **The Village Butcher** on Elm Street in Woodstock is also a fine provider of deli sandwiches and baked goods. **The Barnard General Store**, Route 12, across the street from Silver Lake, will also provide you with picnic supplies—you can eat in Silver Lake State Park.

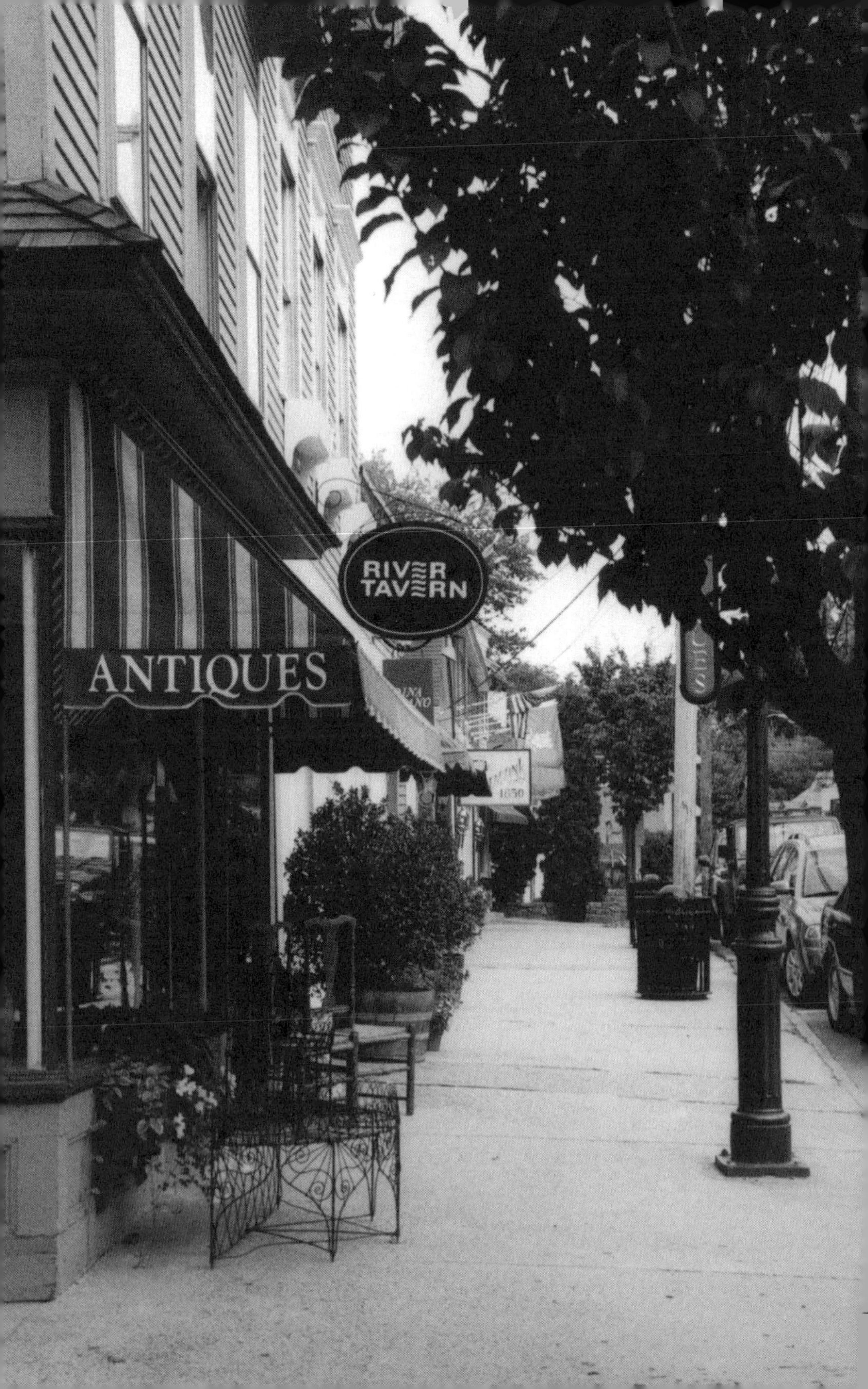
RIVER
TAVERN
ANTIQUES

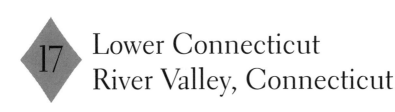

17 Lower Connecticut River Valley, Connecticut

As it travels south in its 400-mile journey through New England, the Connecticut River cuts a wider swath—and increasingly dominates the landscape. From East Haddam to Old Saybrook, Connecticut, as it prepares to empty into Long Island Sound, the river becomes a major factor in the lives of the towns on either side. A wide, island-studded delta fans out where the river meets the sound. Yet because of major sandbars here at its mouth, navigation was never as easy as would have been necessary for the development of a commercial center.

Instead, charming river towns—mostly residential, but with homegrown industries—developed. The riverbanks stayed green, and the hillsides are banked with trees. The Nature Conservancy recently named the tidelands of the Connecticut River one of the "Last Great Places" in the Western Hemisphere (in this book Block Island is another) because of the many natural areas that have been preserved and the attention paid to keeping the river clean. The Connecticut chapter of the Conservancy lists more than 15 locations within the region where you can enjoy nature in a special, set-apart way.

Yet the lower Connecticut River Valley is hardly a bucolic backwater. This is a sophisticated area. That's due to influences such as an early major art colony, top summer theater venues, and extraordinary shopping and dining. Although there's not an overabundance of places to stay, most are excellent. New Yorkers, who form a large part of the tourist trade, would hardly settle for less.

Famous people have lived here—temporarily or permanently. When the Old Lyme Art Colony of American impressionists flourished in the early 1900s, artist Childe Hassam was among them. Actress Katharine Hepburn, daughter of a Hartford doctor, spent childhood summers in Fenwick, an exclusive summer colony that is part of Old Saybrook, the town farthest south on the river's western side. She came home to Fenwick to retire.

The late TV newsman Charles Kuralt had a home in the area's yachting capital, Essex. Contemporary artist Sol LeWitt and his wife are major property owners in tony Chester, where she also runs a shop selling Italian and Portuguese pottery.

The main street of Chester, Connecticut

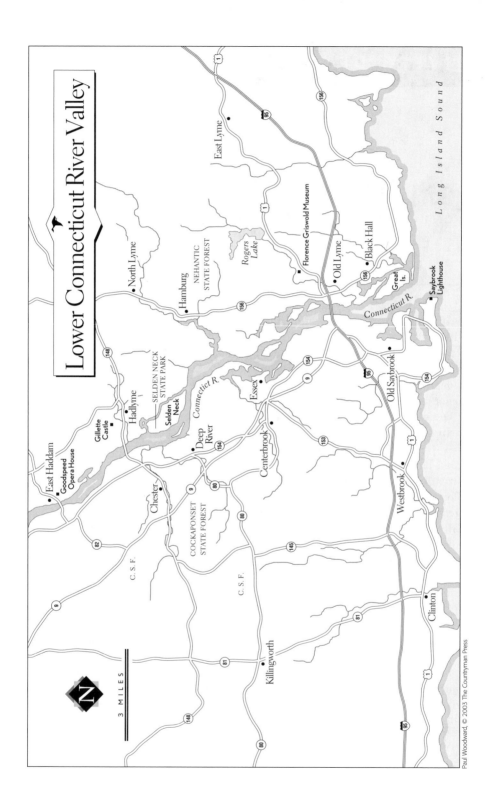

Lower Connecticut River Valley

N
3 MILES

Long Island Sound

Connecticut R.

East Lyme
North Lyme
Hamburg
NEHANTIC STATE FOREST
Rogers Lake
Florence Griswold Museum
Old Lyme
Black Hall
Great Is.
Saybrook Lighthouse
SELDEN NECK STATE PARK
Selden Neck
Hadlyme
Gillette Castle
Deep River
Essex
Old Saybrook
Centerbrook
East Haddam
Goodspeed Opera House
Chester
COCKAPONSET STATE FOREST
C. S. F.
C. S. F.
Westbrook
Killingworth
Clinton

Paul Woodward, © 2003 The Countryman Press

A crew of professional actors and actresses settle in East Haddam in summer and fall when they are on stage at the Goodspeed Opera House.

The opera house, a frothy white Victorian buildings on the river's banks, dominates sleepy **East Haddam.** Since Goodspeed's renovation and reopening in 1963, it has been home to more than 100 different musicals. Possibly the most famous have been *Annie, Man of La Mancha,* and *Shenandoah*—all of which had long Broadway runs as well.

South of East Haddam, on the same side of the river, is **Gillette Castle,** the amazing retirement home of Victorian actor William Gillette. The stone edifice is intended to look like one of those ruined German castles overlooking the Rhine. Closed for 3 years for a complete renovation, Gillette Castle reopened in 2002 and is a must-see attraction for visitors between May and October. Also on the east side of the river, **Old Lyme** is most famous for its turn-of-the-20th-century artists' colony, the site now for the famous Florence Griswold Museum and brand-new Krieble Gallery. They are home to many works of Connecticut impressionism. The Florence Griswold house is interesting, too, as a former boardinghouse for artists.

Cross the river on the I-95 bridge to **Old Saybrook,** where you can dine—and stay—on the water. North of Old Saybrook on the western bank are river towns with great appeal for visitors. **Essex,** home of the well-known Griswold Inn, has a harbor filled with exquisite boats. **Centerbrook** and **Ivoryton,** two sections of Essex, are known for dining and for the Ivoryton Playhouse summer-stock theater. In **Deep River,** just north, you'll find a wonderful waterfront park, a quiet Main Street with some funky little stores and restaurants, and a good B&B. **Chester** is the place to shop and dine. Exceptional boutiques are here along with fabulous restaurants. Chester is also home to the Norma Terris Theatre, where experimental plays try out under the aegis of the Goodspeed. Farther north, in **Haddam,** you can eat at the river's edge in a little restaurant where the style is casual and the food, delicious.

Although summer is the busy season, virtually all the restaurants and inns—and the museums—are open year-round. Even the Goodspeed goes full-tilt from April to December. In January bald eagles from Canada come to this part of the Connecticut River to nest; eagle-watching trips are run by local excursion boats and the Audubon Society.

The best part about the lower Connecticut River Valley may be a genuine relaxed feeling. There are no traffic jams—except for the few minutes you have to wait while the swing bridge between East Haddam and Haddam opens for a tall mast. People are generally unhurried. This is a weekend when you can slow down, kick back, and—quite simply—enjoy.

Getting There

Take I-95, to get to the area from New York or Boston. Take Exit 69 to Route 9, a limited-access highway that connects many of the Connecticut River towns on the west side of the river. To go directly to Old Lyme, hop off I-95 at Exit 70.

Private **planes** can land at the **Chester Airport** or **Goodspeed Airport** in East Haddam. **Amtrak's** shoreline route between Boston and New York has a stop in Old Saybrook. For train information, call (800) 872-7245.

Getting Around

The local road running north and south on the west side of the river is Route 154—take it all the way from Fenwick in the south to Haddam. On the east side of the river, Route 156 goes north from Old Lyme to Route 82, which takes you to Gillette Castle and into East Haddam. You can take a little ferry from Chester on the west to Hadlyme on the east via Route 148. It is known, logically enough, as the Chester-Hadlyme ferry and is run by the state of Connecticut. Public transportation is not easily obtained among the towns, but you can rent a car near the train station in Old Saybrook and some inns will pick you up there.

For More Information

♦ **Connecticut River Valley and Shoreline Visitors Council** (860-347-0028; 1-800-486-3346; www.cttourism.org), 393 Main Street, Middletown, CT 06457-3309. Phones and web sites for individual towns include: **Chester** (860) 526-2077 or www.visit-chester.com; **Deep River** (860) 526-4056 or www.deepriverct.com; **Essex** (860) 767-3904 or www.essexct.com; **Old Lyme** (860) 434-1575 or www.oldlymect.com; **Old Saybrook** (860) 388-3266 or www.oldsaybrookct.com.

SEEING AND DOING

River Access

The Connecticut River and its estuaries are very attractive to **canoeists** and **kayakers.** Several canoe/kayak trails have been developed by the Connecticut River Estuary Regional Planning Council, and elaborate maps and descriptions of these routes are available from local information bureaus and chambers of commerce. Kayak and canoe **rentals** are available from **Black Hall Marina** (860-434-9680), 132 Shore Road, Old Lyme. You can access the 500-acre Great Island Wildlife Management area directly from the marina.

Be aware that the river is tidal throughout the area. When canoeing or kayaking anywhere on the river or its creeks, know what time high and low tide will occur. Strongest currents, both outgoing and incoming, occur halfway between low and high tides. Each tidal cycle is about 6 hours. Add time to upriver trips due to paddling against the southerly flow of the Connecticut River. Wear a personal flotation device at all times.

♦ **Ferry Landing State Park,** Ferry Road, Old Lyme. (From Exit 70 off I-95, go south until you hit Ferry Road; follow it to the end.) The state Department of Environmental Protection is headquartered here, and just beyond is a good-sized parking lot. You can enjoy picnic tables and gazebo with an unsurpassed view of the wide Connecticut River, which seems gigantic at this point. Follow a boardwalk around and south under the old railroad bridge and to its end, probably encountering fishermen along the way. Birders like it here, too. There are benches to sit on and—at the end—an observation platform that can be reached up an easy set of stairs. Roger Tory Peterson, the great birder, lived in Old Lyme, and the area is dedicated to his memory. The spot is not well known, and once here you are quite removed from the everyday bustle of life. The name derives from the fact that this was once the point of a ferry route between Old Saybrook and Old Lyme.

♦ **Haddam Meadows State Park,** Haddam. This 175-acre park is in the Connecticut River floodplain and it is, therefore, quite flat. A loop road provides access to both the meadow and the Connecticut River. Activities include picnicking, fishing, boating, cross-country skiing, and mountain biking. Located 3 miles south of Higganum off Route 9A.

♦ **Hurd State Park,** East Haddam. Situated on the high east bank of the Connecticut River, this 884-acre park provides a scenic view of the river in spring and summer and of foliage in autumn. Hiking, picnicking, cross-country skiing, field sports, boat camping, rock climbing, and mountain biking. Located 3 miles south of Cobalt center on Route 151.

♦ **Nature Conservancy preserves.** For more information on the following preserves, contact The Nature Conservancy's Connecticut chapter (860-344-0716; www.nature.org/connecticut), 55 High Street, Middletown, CT 06457.

The preserves in the lower Connecticut River Valley include **Turtle Creek,** Essex, with a mile of trail through mountain laurel thickets and along a cove on the Connecticut River; **Selden Creek,** Lyme, a 394-acre preserve that is a critical site for wintering bald eagles; **Chapman Pond,** East Haddam, a 50-acre tidal freshwater pond just east of the Connecticut River with more than 500 acres around the pond.

Culture

♦ **Florence Griswold Museum** (860-434-5542; www.flogris.org), 96 Lyme Street, Old Lyme. Old Lyme was an art colony of note at the turn of the past century. Henry Ward Ranger, a known artist in New York, is credited with "discovering" Old Lyme as a place to paint in 1899. He took rooms at the boardinghouse run by Florence Griswold, or "Miss Florence," and others followed. The museum is comprised of the Florence Griswold House, where many of the artists had rooms and which is seen today as both a house museum (first floor), and art gallery (upstairs), as well as a new contemporary gallery to the back of the property. In the house the dining room is of particular note: The artists removed panels and painted them, then replaced them all around the room. Behind the house are historic gardens, re-created to look much as they did at the time the artists were in residence.

The Florence Griswold Museum in Old Lyme, Connecticut

The new Krieble Gallery at the Florence Griswold Museum

A rich bequest in the late 1990s was the collection of 188 paintings formerly owned by the Hartford Steam Boiler Inspection & Insurance Company in Hartford. The collection concentrates entirely on works by American artists who lived or worked in Connecticut and spans a period from the late 18th to early 20th century. That gift led to a donation from the Krieble Foundation in the name of the late Nancy and Robert Krieble (he was founder of the Loctite Corporation) to build a new gallery to house and display these paintings. Opened in 2002, the Krieble Gallery for American Art, a contemporary building with sawtooth roof and turret at one end, is an interesting construction. Galleries, lighted by means of skylights, offer salubrious spaces for the viewing of art. The Lieutenant River runs behind the museum and was often depicted in paintings by the Connecticut impressionists who worked here. One studio, that of the artist of William Chadwick, was relocated to the grounds of the museum from another site in Old Lyme and can be viewed in summer. This is a lovely spot to visit; have a picnic if you'd like, but bring your own picnic cloth. Artists may paint on the grounds at any time. Open April through December, Tuesday through Saturday 10–5, Sunday 1–5; January through March, Wednesday through Sunday 1–5. Highlight tours are offered daily at 2 PM. Adults $7, seniors and students $6, children 6–12 $4.

♦ **Lyme Art Association** (860-434-7802), 90 Lyme Street, Old Lyme. Just down the street from the Florence Griswold Museum is a building in which artists have been exhibiting their work for more than 80 years. It was organized by the Old Lyme colony of artists; the building opened in 1921. "Miss Florence" was the first gallery manager and remained so until her death in 1937. Approximately six juried shows are presented annually with most works for sale. There are three large exhibition spaces. Open Tuesday through Saturday 10–4:30, Sunday, 1–4:30. Suggested donation $4.

♦ **Goodspeed Opera House** (860-873-8664; box office 860-873-8668; www.goodspeed.org), Box A, Goodspeed Landing, East Haddam. This white Victorian confection with pillared front porch and high mansard roof was built in 1876 by William H. Goodspeed, a shipping and banking magnate and avid theater lover. Originally it housed a theater, professional offices, steamboat passenger terminal, and general store. After a period of neglect, it was reborn in 1963 as the Goodspeed Opera House, home of musicals—some of which have really made names for themselves. Fifteen productions of more than 100 have gone on to Broadway. Three musicals are produced each season under the direction of Michael P. Price. The house is fun to be in—at intermission the audience can stroll out on the riverfront balcony and enjoy night reflections on the water and the swing bridge that spans the river in East Haddam. The theater revives old musicals and also works to develop new vehicles to add to the repertoire—the latter are first tried out at the **Norma Terris Theater** in nearby Chester, with three productions annually. Tickets for both theaters are purchased through the Goodspeed box office.

♦ **Ivoryton Playhouse** (860-767-8348), 103 Main Street, Ivoryton. This claims to be the nation's oldest professional self-supporting theater, and it is a classic on the strawhat circuit. The old theater has been updated recently and sports jaunty striped awnings, new siding, and an air-conditioned interior. These days the River Rep players—with headquarters in New York—stage a full summer season of comedies, dramas, and musicals, Tickets are in the $25–30 range.

♦ **Gillette Castle State Park** (860-526-2336), River Road, Hadlyme. After 3 years of extensive renovations—and the construction of a new visitors center—this favorite Connecticut destination is once again open. Hartford native, actor, and playwright

The Ivoryton Playhouse is a venerable old summer theater.

William Hooker Gillette had the castle built in 1914–1919 as his retirement home. Gillette made his name in theater with his portrayal of Sherlock Holmes over a period of some 30 years. One story claims he was committed to building a home on Long Island, but when returning home on his little boat, the *Aunt Polly*, he anchored below the site where he would ultimately build his castle and was smitten by its beauty. The southernmost of seven hills on the east side of the river, the estate was officially called Seventh Sister. Gillette not only directed the construction company but also designed built-in furniture (including an ingenious bar that he could lock in such a way as to keep his guests out when he was not there). He also designed the heavy wood locks for all 80 windows and more than 40 heavy oak doors. The place is incredible. So is the site, high above the Connecticut River with a gorgeous view of the stream from the terrace outside. A whimsical stone dragon's head greets visitors as it did in the days of Gillette, and two hand-carved wooden cats are on the roof of a nearby open-air pavilion because the actor loved cats so much. He used to have a miniature train on the property, with which he entertained and sometimes terrorized guests, but that was sold long ago to Lake Compounce Amusement Park in Bristol. Picnic areas and hiking trails are part of the 125-acre park. The park is open Memorial Day through Columbus Day, daily 8–7; the castle is open for self-guided tours between 10 and 4:30. Park free. Castle $4 adults, $2 children.

♦ **Connecticut River Museum** (860-767-8269; www.connix.com/~crm), 67 Main Street, Essex. One of the best things about this museum is its location—at the very end of Essex's Main Street, overlooking the water. There's a patch of grass next to it and benches, too, where you can sit and watch all the water activity—and there is plenty in this boating town. The museum seeks to tell the history of the river. Changing exhibits may focus on one aspect or another—all the way from its northern origins to its emptying out into Long Island Sound. A former steamboat warehouse, and a National Register landmark, the two buildings housing the museum are just the permanent aspect of what has become an active place with special events like boat shows through the year. For the year 2003, it was hoped to have an excursion boat leave from the museum and travel around the harbor and out onto the river. A full-scale working reproduction of the *Turtle*, the first submarine, built as a "secret weapon" for the Revolutionary War, is a prized possession. There are also scale models of river steamboats that once traveled between Hartford and New York. Boats built and used on the river are shown in the adjoining boathouse. Adults $5, seniors and students $4, children $3. Open year-round Tuesday through Saturday, 10–5.

Boating, Training, Planing

You see that water—you want to get out onto it, be near it, float above it. Well, you can.

♦ **Mark Twain cruises, Deep River Navigation Company** (860-526-4954; www.|deeprivernavigation.com), Dock 'n' Dine restaurant, Old Saybrook. Daily, mid-June to Labor Day. Weekends in September. The jaunty *Aunt Polly* sails four times daily from the dock outside the Dock 'n' Dine restaurant in Old Saybrook. From 11 to 1, the 2-hour Essex Harbor cruise is held. From 1:30 to 2:30 and 5:30 to 6:30, the

1-hour Lighthouse Cruise is offered. It goes along the Old Saybrook waterfront and out into Long Island Sound, turning at the Outer Light. The Duck Island Cruise is scheduled from 3 to 5 PM. You sail westward to Cornfield Point and Duck Island. All cruises feature narration; refreshments and snacks are available. Two-hour cruises, $12 adults, $6 children. One-hour cruises, $8 adults, $4 kids. **Winter eagle-watch cruises** from Essex are also offered. Call for information.

♦ **Camelot Cruises, Inc.** (1-800-522-7463; www.camelotcruises.com), 1 Marine Park, Haddam. On Tuesday and Wednesday all-day cruises are offered to Greenport, Long Iisland, on a 400-passenger ship. They leave Haddam at 9:30 AM, arrive in Long Island at noon, leave at 3 PM, and return home by 5:45 PM. Adults $27.50, children $10. Dinner theater—with a murder mystery to solve—is held on many evenings, Thursday through Sunday. Call to check on dates. Departure is at 7 and return at 10 PM; the price is $60 per person. On selected Fridays and Saturdays there are dance parties from 7 to 10 with rock 'n' roll oldies and dinner. $60. Sunday brunch buffet cruises from noon to 2:30 cost $29; in fall the price goes up to $35.

♦ **Essex Steam Train and Riverboat** (860-767-0103; 1-800-377-3987), 1 Railroad Avenue, Essex. Railroad buffs, kids, and anyone who enjoys a rollicking ride on a smoke-spewing old steam train will enjoy this excursion. Leaving from a railroad depot in the Centerbrook area of Essex (just outside the village), this train takes you through the woods and along the river as far as Deep River. There you can connect to a riverboat for a 1-hour excursion on the Connecticut River, with the boat heading as far north as the Haddam Swing Bridge and Goodspeed Opera House. But you don't have to. You can do just the train portion of the ride if that's all you want. Trains leave several times a day, and not all connect with the boat, so do inquire. In fall there are foliage excursions, and in December there's a Santa Special. For the train alone, adults pay $10.50 and children, $5.50; for train and boat, adults pay $18.50 and children, $9.50.

Deep River landing, where you can transfer from the Essex steam train to a riverboat.

♦ **Chester-Hadlyme Ferry,** Route 148, Chester or Hadlyme. This car-carrying ferry has a history dating back to the late 18th century. It goes "on demand" and cars line up and wait to make the short 4-minute crossing. Up to nine cars can squeeze on. It's a marvelous way to go from Chester to Hadlyme and then on up to Gillette Castle, which towers above. April to November. Car and driver, $2.25 one-way; passengers or foot travelers, 75 cents.

Biplane Rides

♦ **Chester Charter** (860-526-4321; 1-800-PLANES-1), Chester Airport, 61 Winthrop Road, Chester. Want to return to the golden age of flying? You can take a ride in an authentic 1941 Boeing Stearman. Scenic tours of the lower Connecticut River Valley and Connecticut coastline are offered. Call for details.

Shopping

As elsewhere in New England, antiques shops are everywhere. Especially on Route 154 between Old Saybrook and Chester, you will find one after the other. **Brush Factory Antiques** is a 30-dealer shop in Centerbrook. **Old Saybrook Antiques Center** at 756 Middlesex Turnpike, Old Saybrook, has 125 dealers exhibiting furniture, porcelain, jewelry, and paintings. We like **Luxe** on 174 Main Street, Old Saybrook, with a variety of items including mirrors, home furnishings, antiques, things for the garden—a little of everything. **The Wise Owl,** calling itself a "parent-teacher store" in Old Saybrook, has lots of interesting-looking educational toys. **Mirabelle** on Main Street is a French patisserie with luscious-looking items. **North Cove Outfitters** is a big store with items for outdoorsmen, women, and children.

In **Chester,** our favorite river town for shopping, you'll find classy and individualistic women's attire at **Sarah Kate.** Good birthday cards, napkins, toys, and little things for your home are found in **Interiors.** At **Soleiado,** France rules in Provençal prints, tableware, place mats, candleholders and candles, pillows, and more. Trisha Ginter, a graduate of the Fashion Institute of Technology, designs and makes wedding gowns and headpieces, as well as dresses and other outfits. Her shop is called **Lillian's,** named for her grandmother. In the same stone building at 4 Water Street is **The Hammered Edge,** with incredible jewelry and the beads to make your own. Nearby, vintage clothing is sold at **The Willow Tree. Simon's Marketplace** on Main Street is a fun place to prowl for soaps, gourmet foods, napkins, aprons, all kinds of interesting discoveries. They'll make you a sandwich, too. They'll do the same at **Wheatmarket** next to the restaurant **Fiddlers.** The iced coffee comes with ice cubes made of coffee so your drink doesn't get watered down. **Ceramica** has wonderful, colorful Italian pottery. **Queen of Tarts** is a bakery to beat all; Laurel Roberts is a Culinary Institute of America pastry graduate who used to work at **Restaurant du Village.** She specializes in pies (blueberry and tart cherry when I stopped), but also has lots of other goodies, everything made from scratch. Little white iron tables and chairs in a terraced backyard are the perfect place to sip a cappuccino and nibble on an apple tart.

Essex seems to be sprouting more real estate offices than shops. We still like **The Red Balloon** in the square across from **The Griswold Inn** for wonderful children's clothes. In the same little square is **Olive Oyl's** for delectable take-out salads, pastries, hot dishes, and sandwiches. Plus gourmet foods. **Red Pepper** has interesting clothes and knickknacks at pretty high prices. **Aegean Treasures** has offered Greek jewelry and clothing for years. **The Clipper Ship Bookstore** has a nice selection, especially things nautical. **Phoenix** is a store that is a mélange of all sorts of stuff—including wonderfully aromatic carpet spray for holiday-time when I stopped once.

Bed & Breakfasts

♦ **Bishopsgate Inn** (860-873-1677), Goodspeed Landing, P.O. Box 290, East Haddam, CT 06423. Built in 1818 by a merchant and shipbuilder, this Colonial house is tended with care by Jane and Colin Kagel and their son and daughter-in-law, Colin and Lisa. Three-year-old Noah is now part of the scene. The house is located about one long block from the Goodspeed Opera House. Over the years the Kagels have added gardens with seating areas and a hammock out back. The living room in this house, with its huge fireplace, stacks of magazines and books, and comfortable chairs and sofas, is one of those rooms you'd rather not leave. Lisa is usually in charge of breakfast—two favorites being blintz soufflé and waffles. In summer guests often eat in the garden, but the long table with built-in seating in the kitchen is popular, too. Six guest rooms, all with private bath, are offered. Two are on the first floor—the one with the bath in the hall has a screen to shield it from the common area. On the second floor, The Director's Suite takes the cake. It has a king iron bed, a porch overlooking the gardens in back, and a bathroom with double sink, stall shower, and sauna. This room is large enough to put in a single folding cot with featherbed so that an extra person can be accommodated. A couple of rooms have fireplaces that get lots of use in winter. Doubles, $105–165.

♦ **123 Main** (860-526-3456), Chester, CT 06412. This large yellow house with wraparound porch and gorgeous flowers all around is set high up off Main Street at the edge of the downtown area. Chris and Randy Allinson offer five guest rooms, three with queen bed and private bath and two sharing. The two that share—a single and a double—can be reserved as a two-room suite. Bright artworks by local artists—especially the work of Sonya Gill—fill the walls. Guests gather for breakfast at a large table in the dining room, where coffee is set out for early risers. A full breakfast is served on weekends and "a hearty continental breakfast" during the week. An asparagus, goat cheese, and red onion frittata is one of Chris's specialties. Room 1 is especially pretty with a queen sleigh bed and an oval flowered loop rug. And that wraparound porch with plenty of chairs and tables is a spot for whiling away hours—and for enjoying breakfast. Children over 10 are welcome. Doubles with private bath, $125–145; with shared bath, $95–105.

♦ **Riverwind** (860-526-2014), 209 Main Street, Deep River, CT 06417. We popped in on new innkeepers Monique and Roger Plante just days after they had taken over this wonderful B&B in July 2002. Former owner Barbara Barlow—who had set the tone, and overseen the construction of an addition—returned to her native Virginia with husband Bob Bucknall. The Plantes lived in an 1820 Victorian in Wrentham, Massachusetts, and had been looking for an inn for two years. She was formerly in health care, and he is a painter and paperhanger who "can do anything" says his wife. Riverwind has eight guest rooms, three on the first floor and five on the second. Two side-by-side dining rooms, where a full breakfast is served, and a very atmospheric keeping room with gigantic fireplace are spots for guests to relax. There are also a front parlor and a wide front porch. A study on the second floor with beamed ceiling from which hang dried herbs has couches, games, and books for guests to enjoy. All guest rooms have air-conditioning and private bath. A TV is found in a common room. The Quilt Room on the second floor has two handsome double four-poster beds covered with blue-and-maroon quilts and a bathroom with deep blue tiled floor. Champagne & Roses is a very large room to the back of the house; its adjoining bathroom has a whirlpool tub as well as a stall shower. All the rooms are charming, and Monique was looking forward to cooking up full breakfasts for guests. Doubles, $95–175.

♦ **Deacon Timothy Pratt B&B** (860-395-1229; fax 860-395-4748; www.connecticut-bed-and-breakfast.com), 325 Main Street, Old Saybrook, CT 06475. Energetic young innkeeper Shelley Nobile puts her talents toward running one of the most appealing B&Bs on the shoreline. The gray house with white trim dates from 1746, when it was built by a carpenter and deacon. It has been attractively restored. Shelley also acquired one of Old Saybrook's most loved landmarks next door, the James Gallery & Soda Fountain, which she operates during the summer and where she has additional guest rooms. Five guest rooms in the main house all have queen bed, TV, stereo CD player, air-conditioning, and private bath. Most have a fireplace and/or a Jacuzzi-style tub. The Suite on the second floor has a huge bathroom with Jacuzzi, and a bedroom with painted floor. Two front rooms have queen canopy beds and fireplaces where fire logs are provided in winter. Next door on the second floor above the James Soda Fountain, Shelley was planning to renovate what was now an efficiency guest suite into two luxurious guest rooms. A massage therapist is on call to provide a massage in guests' own rooms. The rear yard has a rope hammock, a fountain, and shady sitting areas. A full three-course breakfast on weekends, and expanded continental on weekdays, is served at a long table in a dining room where chairs are Duncan Phyfe lyre-back designs. Beach passes are provided to guests in season. Doubles, $140–225.

Inns with Restaurants

♦ **The Bee and Thistle Inn** (860-434-1667; 1-800-622-4946; www.beeandthistleinn.com), 100 Lyme Street, Old Lyme, CT 06371. When Marie Abraham was a student at nearby Connecticut College in New London, she visited this inn once and fell in love with it. Years later, married to a chef, Phil Abraham, who was looking for an inn with a restaurant to run, incredibly she ended up with this property. Since taking over in 2000, they have painted the former mustard-colored building a light, bright yellow. Eleven guest rooms on the second and third floors have private bath. Slowly the Abrahams are redoing the rooms, but still keeping the homey, traditional look. Room 1 has a queen canopy bed and a bathroom with old-fashioned hexagonal tiles on the floor; there are Subway tiles above the tub. Room 3 has twin beds with pristine white coverlets. One room has a queen bed and gas fireplace. Breakfast does not come with these rooms, since it's available every day downstairs in the public restaurant. A self-sufficient cottage with fireplace is also rented out. The comfortable parlor of the main inn—with its blazing wood-burning fireplace—is turned into a tearoom from mid-November to December. Otherwise two glassed-in side porches and a rear dining room form the restaurant (see *Where to Eat*). Doubles, $79–189.

♦ **Old Lyme Inn** (860-434-2600; www.oldlymeinn.com), 85 Lyme Street, Old Lyme, CT 06371. Keith and Candy Green, who've had a home in Old Lyme since the 1980s, took over this well-known inn in 2001 and are dynamically changing it. Attention was first being paid to the dining rooms, which have been expanded and given two "personalities." (See *Where to Eat*.) A total of 13 guest rooms, 5 in the original building and 8 in the newer wing, all have private bathroom. Four luxurious new rooms were to come on line in August 2002 in Rooster Hall, the Greens' own home at 2 Lyme Street—a house Keith Green says is "one of the most beautiful on Lyme Street." Breakfast is served to guests in the taproom of the main inn. In the newer wing of the main inn are good-sized rooms, and the Four Poster Room is fireplaced and has a large bay window. Decorating is pleasant if not exceptional. Guests do not really have the use of common rooms here since those are turned over to the restaurant. There are a few benches on the lawns outdoors. Doubles, $135–225.

♦ **The Copper Beech Inn** (860-767-0330; 1-888-809-2056; fax 860-767-7840), 46 Main Street, Ivoryton, CT 06442. The Copper Beech changed hands in 2002 when Ian and Barbara Phillips of Rowayton, Connecticut, took over from longtime innkeepers Sally and Eldon Senner. Ian had previously overseen a renovation of The Bradley Inn in New Harbor, Maine, and then sold it. As soon as he was in charge, he began to upgrade The Copper Beech, which was in need of updates. Gardens, guest rooms, and common rooms in the main inn got the first attention. A new chef was in place (see *Where to Eat*). Four main inn guest rooms, on the second floor, have queen or king bed, new bathroom, and traditional furnishings. One has smashingly painted walls in deep red and Victorian-style furnishings. Room 1, a very large room, has a bay window with chairs and table, and new beige wallpaper with stylized flowers. Fireplaces in guest rooms were to be returned to working order. Carriage House rooms have open-air decks. Some have cathedral ceiling, and all have TV and private bath with whirlpool tub. These were to be upgraded, and—eventually—more rooms added. A complimentary buffet breakfast is set out in the main inn. The Victorian-style conservatory in the inn is used by guests for a drink before dinner or sometimes just for sitting and relaxing. Doubles, $105–325.

♦ **Saybrook Point Inn** (860-395-2000; 1-800-243-0212; fax 860-388-1504), 2 Bridge Street, Old Saybrook, CT 06475. Here is the ultimate waterside location—right in the midst of a busy marina. In fact, if you manage to book the Lighthouse Apartment—a separate unit built onto the marina dock—you feel as if you're on a boat! This apartment has a kitchenette, living room with TV and pullout sofa, bedroom, and private bath, and is designed with a little lighthouse turret (unfortunately not accessible). The views are fabulous, although you may feel a little self-conscious in the midst of the marina action in midsummer. The remaining 81 luxurious rooms and suites are located in a large gray-clapboard main building that loosely references Cape Cod architecture. Just step inside and a smashing coral lobby with floral carpets and a seating group before the fireplace sets the tone. I wish the chlorine aroma from the indoor pool hadn't drifted quite so strongly into the lobby on the day I last stopped, however. Both indoor and outdoor pools are offered, plus fitness center, whirlpool, and steam room. There's also a spa. Most rooms have a king or two full beds, reproduction mahogany furniture, spacious seating areas, bedside clock-radio consoles that control lights, air-conditioning, and such. The baths are large and marble. Most rooms have a balcony just large enough to step out onto. Two-thirds of the rooms have water views of the busy marina; 50 have fireplaces for which fire logs can be requested in-season. The Terra Mar Grille, the inn's restaurant, is well rated (see *Where to Eat*). The inn offers complimentary bikes for guest use—and this flat area of shoreline is a perfect place to pedal. Doubles, $159–649 for a two-bedroom suite. The Lighthouse Apartment rents for $429 on weekends from April through October and is not available in winter.

♦ **Griswold Inn** (860-767-1776), 36 Main Street, Essex, CT 06426. The historic Griswold Inn in Essex dates back to 1776. This old inn is best known for its atmospheric Tap Room and dining rooms (see *Where to Eat*). It also has 30 rooms, some small and simply furnished, others much more spacious. Nine are in the main inn, four in the Hayden House next door. Deluxe and superior suites are the Fenwick and Garden Suites across the way in separate buildings—the Fenwick has a fireplace in the bedroom. The least expensive rooms are in The Annex—whose rooms are inclined to be smaller, with a variety of double, twin, or queen-sized beds. All rooms have air-conditioning, private bath, and piped-in music. Most have been upgraded of late. The Griswold Inn has been catering to guests for more than 200 years—and it feels that way, too. Floors might be uneven and hallways narrow. Stairways in the main inn tend to be steep. A complimentary continental buffet breakfast is served to overnight guests. Doubles, $95–200.

♦ **Gelston House** (860-873-1411; fax 860-873-9300), P.O. Box 456, East Haddam, CT 06423. Although primarily a restaurant, the Gelston House has four accommodations, two of them rather large suites with river views, on the third floor of the big white structure. All rooms have private bathroom, queen-sized bed, and a mix of antique and contemporary furnishings. A complimentary continental breakfast basket is brought to the rooms. The main floor of the inn is dedicated to the restaurants. Doubles, rooms, $100; suites, $225.

♦ **Liberty Inn** (860-388-1777), 55 Springbrook Road, Old Saybrook, CT 06457. Some people simply prefer a motel. This independently owned 22-room two-story motel was renovated in the late 1990s. Rooms have one king or two double beds. Microwaves and refrigerators are available in several rooms. A complimentary continental breakfast is offered in the lobby. Doubles, $68–98.

WHERE TO EAT

Some of the best restaurants in Connecticut are located in these riverside towns, and more seem to be opening all the time. Here, more or less in the order of our preference, are ones we like. Since it's a short trip from one town to the next, it's not an issue to stay in one town and head to a nearby one for a meal.

♦ **Restaurant du Village** (860-526-5301), 59 Main Street, Chester. The deep blue facade, the red-lettered name, the white curtains in the front windows, the overflowing flower boxes out front—these are what to look for when searching for this fine little French restaurant. For nearly 15 years chefs and spouses Michel and

Cynthia Keller have owned and operated this lovely eatery in the center of the village. Inside, white-clothed tables occupy a main dining room, with four more for overflow in the colorful, cozy bar. Everything is made from scratch in the small, serious, and very well-organized kitchen where Michel, originally from the Alsatian region of France, presides. He makes his own bread, a signature item wonderfully crusty and chewy, served warm in a basket with sweet butter. Michel and Cynthia, a graduate of the esteemed Culinary Institute of America, keep their standards exceptionally high. (We have been thanked more than once for sending a graduating senior from Wesleyan and her Chicago family to this restaurant to dine; until they ate here, she said, her father thought Chicago restaurants had no peers.) Soup is always among the starters—possibly onion or perhaps chilled potato soup with fresh sorrel, garnished with crème fraîche. Other fine choices could be cassoulet of shrimp with a light curry and white wine sauce; a tart of leek, tomatoes, and Roquefort cheese; or rustic veal and pork pâté studded with pistachios and served with a quince and port wine sauce ($9–15). A not-too-long list of entrées ($28–33) changes nightly and could include pan-seared salmon steak with tiny French green lentils in a Pommery mustard vinaigrette; a half duckling crisply roasted and served with a brandied apricot sauce; or boeuf bourguignon, prepared traditionally and served in a puff pastry shell. For dessert on one summer evening, a cheesecake with strawberry-rhubarb compote and what Michel called a sunflower—brioche dough filled with pastry cream, with apricots forming the petals and blueberries in the center—were being offered. A fine wine list is available. Open Wednesday through Sunday from 5 for dinner.

♦ **Steve's Centerbrook Café** (860-767-1277; www.stevescenterbrookcafe.com), 78 Main Street, Centerbrook. Chef-owner Steve Wilkinson has reconfigured his restaurant in this small house in the Centerbrook section of Essex more than once. But he hit pay dirt when he landed on this casual concept a few years ago. The once white house with latticework outside is now an olive green with colorful trim; three dining rooms inside are the setting for fine food. Affordability is stressed immediately, with several wines at $6 a glass or $20 a bottle featured along with $4 beers. Of course, you can order a pricier wine—and a good list is available—but if you want a night out at rational prices, you can have that, too. Appetizers could be Parma ham with fresh figs served with olive oil and balsamic vinegar reduction, or chilled cantaloupe and strawberry soup ($6–9). A black mission fig and farmhouse blue cheese salad, served on field greens, tempts. Under the "Pasta" heading, you might find sweet potato ravioli or angel hair with shrimp, basil, and native tomatoes. Other entrées could be grilled veal chop with polenta, sautéed broccoli rabe and fresh tarragon butter, or lamb curry with fresh peach and mango chutney ($16–20). The most famous dessert is Steve's marjolaine, a four-tier almond and hazelnut torte with crème fraîche, praline, and bittersweet Belgian chocolate, but you might opt for crème brûlée, plum anise soup, or white peach parfait ($6–8.50). Dinner from 5:30 Tuesday through Saturday; from 4:30 on Sunday.

♦ **River Tavern** (860-526-9417; fax 860-526-9478), 23 Main Street, Chester. Jonathan Rapp grew up in Essex, then hit Manhattan to partner with family members in an Upper West Side eatery called Etats-Unis. He returned to this part of the world in late 2001. "I grew up in the business" is the way he put it, his father having been a restaurateur. This space, formerly that of The Mad Hatter, has been converted to look oh-so-citified. Bright gold walls gleam above gray-white wainscoting. Black-and-white photographs by a local artist were being displayed. Dark stained wood-topped tables are set close to one another against a banquette, and there's a large, communal table up front across from the bar—where diners are also welcome. In the two front windows diners can perch on cushions to face their partners over small tables. Dinner only is served and reservations advised. From the menu there's always a prix fixe three-course offering, priced one evening at $29 and another at $35. It includes two specially chosen wines. Appetizers could be a cool seaweed, cucumber, and sesame salad, a bowl of fresh steamer clams with melted butter, or a plate of cured meats and salamis with mustard. One intriguing salad was golden beet, grapefruit, walnut, and tarragon, although Jonathan admits the "classic Caesar salad" has been on the menu since opening. Entrées could be handmade spaghetti with spicy pork meatballs, basil, and Parmesan; grilled wild striped bass with slowly simmered tomatoes, garlic, and herbs—served with a spicy coleslaw; or roast rack of lamb with herbs and garlic, served with a roasted sweet pepper sauce ($19–24). The dessert menu might bring a chocolate pot de crème, vanilla bean and rum pound cake with key lime curd and berries, or chocolate almond plum tart ($7). An international selection of wines is offered, with a good price range. Dinner nightly.

♦ **Fiddler's** (860-526-3210), 4 Water Street, Chester. Nathaniel von Staats, who worked in the kitchen at Steve's Centerbrook Café, took over this popular seafood eatery—run so successfully by Paul McMahon for years—with his wife, Roselle, in summer 2002. The two small dining rooms were simplified even more, with plain white tape-edged curtains, beige walls, white tablecloths, and pale bentwood chairs. The emphasis remains seafood, with only a couple of items for those who cannot or will not indulge in *fruits de mer.* Nathaniel considers tuna, swordfish, and salmon among his stellar presentations. Appetizers on one dinner menu were lengthy and included tuna tartare with caramelized pineapple, served with ginger, white anchovies, and chives; oyster stew; fried calamari with a light tomato jus; and oysters on the half shell with champagne vinegar, tobiko, and tarragon. Lobster bisque or clam and black bean chili soup were offered. The house salad is field greens tossed in sun-dried cherry and apricot vinaigrette. Entrées ($16–22) could be flame-seared swordfish with Kalamata olive sauce, carrot puree, and jasmine rice; lobster *au peche* with shiitake mushrooms, peaches, and cream; Asian BBQ-glazed ahi tuna; or grilled fillet of salmon with golden yucca cake and radish salad. A grilled rib steak and a roast half chicken were also available. Desserts are made in house and included coconut flan, fried cheesecake with smoked blueberry reduction, and lemon crêpes with key lime mousse ($5 and $6). Lunch Tuesday through Saturday 11:30–2; dinner Tuesday through Saturday 5:30–9, Sunday 4–8. Closed Monday.

♦ **Copper Beech Inn** (860-767-0330), 46 Main Street, Ivoryton. Exciting changes were under way at the venerable Copper Beech, where the dining room has always been considered one of the best in the area. New executive chef Bill von Ahnen, who spent years as a chef at Chantecleer on Nantucket, and his wife and Culinary

Institute of America classmate, Jackie, were turning things around in July 2002. For the time, dinner only—and Sunday brunch—were being served, although a return to lunch was contemplated. At the same time, one of the dining rooms, the Copper Beech Room, was to be transformed into a taproom with lighter menu. The transitional menu gave hints of their strengths. Appetizers ($10–26) included escargot ravioli; an assortment of wood-smoked fish with an aïoli sauce; soft-shell crab meunière; and chilled pheasant galantine served with Cumberland sauce. Among the entrées ($24–38) were grilled sea scallops and shrimp with a Pinot Noir sauce and wild mushrooms; "Injected Lobster"—roasted lobster injected with champagne and saffron beurre blanc and served with pesto risotto; and coq au vin from Burgundy garnished with bacon, mushroom, and pearl onions. From Jackie, the pastry chef, came chocolate hazelnut praline gateau with espresso sauce; hot apple tart served with Calvados ice cream; and classic crème brûlée. Dessert soufflés were soon to join the menu. Open from 5:30 nightly, except closed Monday. Brunch Sunday noon–2. Check for hours.

♦ **Rosemary & Sage** (860-388-1166), 1080 Boston Post Road (Route 1), Old Saybrook. When the popular French spot Café Routier moved to larger space in the next town, Westbrook, this small restaurant was taken over by Michael (Mickey) and Wendy Josephs, formerly of Hanover, New Jersey. The Josephs came from Israel several years ago and trained in New Jersey restaurants. Walls are a deep melon color, and green half shutters are closed on a bank of windows. The cheerful lunch and dinner menus start off with "Let's Begin" for the appetizer section. At lunchtime, several specials were offered; one of us had the plate of coin-shaped pasta with chicken sausage and the other, a special salad with field greens, strawberries, Gorgonzola, and walnuts—both delicious. Other choices were homemade gnocchi in lamb-fused tomato puree with pecorino cheese, and tilapia fillet, shrimp, clams, and mussels in a tomato, herb, and wine sauce ($10–13). At dinner, starters can be a cannoli shell filled with peppercorn-crusted, pan-seared tuna; oysters stuffed with crabmeat and spinach in a brandy sauce topped with béarnaise; or spinach soup. Among several pastas ($15–19) were penne with grilled eggplant, roasted peppers, tomato, basil, mushrooms, Bolognese sauce, and pignoli nuts; and linguine with half a lobster, shrimp, and clams in light tomato wine sauce. Other entrées ("The Main Event!") could be breast of chicken stuffed with fresh spinach, feta, and pine nuts in a white wine sage sauce, or crusted rack of lamb in peppercorn brandy cream sauce. Open for lunch Monday through Friday 11:30–2; dinner Monday through Saturday from 5. Closed Sunday.

♦ **Bee and Thistle Inn** (860-434-1667), 100 Lyme Street, Old Lyme. Even though new innkeeper Philip Abraham has a Culinary Institute of America degree, he's happy to have Francis Brooke-Smith as executive chef in this three-meal-a-day dining room. People love to take a drive to Old Lyme and wind up at this lovely yellow inn. Dining is on two glass-enclosed side porches and in a back room. Tables are covered with calico undercloths and a solid cloth on top, and are perfectly in tune with the spirit of a country inn. Breakfast is available daily, so should you be out and about early in the morning you might stop in for a Bee & Thistle Popover—filled with scrambled egg, bacon, and cheese. Lunch offers entrée salads such as grilled chicken with mango and sesame beef salad in addition to hot entrées ($10–15) such as mussels in Thai green curry, grilled lamb chops with a tomato mint chutney, or scallops in cassoulet served with mashed potatoes. Dinner entrées ($21–30) could be grilled medallions of pork on a plum-Syrah sauce; seared tuna on wasabi mashed potatoes; or rack of lamb coated with Dijon mustard and parsley crumbs and served with sautéed spinach—a house favorite. The very popular Sunday brunch provides roast leg of lamb with cheddar mashed potatoes; basil scrambled eggs served on sautéed spinach; and waffle tropicale with grilled pineapple and roasted banana ($14–18). Breakfast daily; lunch Wednesday through Sunday; dinner daily except Tuesday; Sunday brunch.

♦ **Old Lyme Inn** (860-434-2600), 85 Lyme Street, Old Lyme. The dining room has always been well respected at this inn, and under the new ownership of Keith and Candy Green, the restaurant is being given even more prominence. One weekday lunch in July, the place was booming. The front taproom, with its long bar, the parlor across the way, a hallway to the rear, and a lower-level library space all have been handsomely outfitted as The Grill. This is open for lunch and dinner daily. The main dining room, down one level with white-clothed tables, is open for Friday- and Saturday-night dinner as a more elegant space. The menu is the same. Lunch brings a mixture of sandwiches (Italian sausage on baguette, salmon BLT on toasted brioche bread, and open-faced classic Reuben, for example)—for $10–15. Salads might be pear and Maytag blue cheese on field greens with walnuts, or a warm goat cheese salad. Entrées include jumbo lump crab and corn cake with mango salsa tossed in a plum vinaigrette, long a specialty of the house; and steamed mussels ($8–16). For dinner, starters ($8–14) could be pepper-crusted tuna with pickled ginger and English cucumbers served with wasabi mayonnaise or portobello napoleon layered with tomatoes and herbed goat cheese. Entrées at night ($24–38) might be batter-fried lobster tails with apple-corn fritters and honey-mustard dipping sauce; grilled pork tenderloin with chorizo sausage, black bean, and smoked corn relish; or oven-roasted salmon topped with homemade pesto. A separate Steaks and Chops menu offers seven different prime meats including New York strip, filet mignon, and three double-thick lamb chops. Lunch and dinner daily.

♦ **The Gelston House** (860-873-1411), 8 Main Street, East Haddam. The Gelston House is three different restaurants under one roof (and an awning). Views of the Connecticut River are spectacular from the top-level River Grille, open for dinner; and from The Beer Garden, where light lunches and dinners are served. Inside the big white building is the Tavern, described as a "New American Bar & Bistro" with several agreeable rooms. The Carbone restaurant family of Hartford took over this restaurant in 1995 and have showed it can be done; others had faltered, especially when the next-door neighbor, the Goodspeed Opera House, is not open in winter. The River Grille, the "dress-up" room with huge windows overlooking the river, serves dinner most nights and lunch prior to Wednesday theater matinees. Starters could be grilled baby vegetables with a warm polenta cake, seafood cocktail with tropical marinade, or smoked red deer carpaccio with mesclun greens, caper berry, and aged Reggiano. Entrées ($24–29) could be pistachio-encrusted pork tenderloin served with purple potato salad; duck breast in a grapefruit vinaigrette; or filet mignon with truffled veal jus and a wedge of Gorgonzola. Lemon roulade with citrus curd is one popular dessert. A prix fixe, three-course dinner, is offered at $32 and is a good value. The Tavern serves an all-day menu that includes nachos, cheese fries, stuffed blue crabs, tuna and spinach salad, burgers, and a surf 'n' turf special. (Entrées here, $12–16.) In The Beer Garden, in addition to all sorts of brews, you can get a steamed lobster, barbecued chicken, cheddar burger, raw bar, clam chowder, and such. Entrées are served after 3:30 and priced $10–15. The Gelston House is closed on Monday and Tuesday. The Tavern is open Wednesday through Sunday from 11:30 through dinner; the Beer Garden opens at 11:30 and adds dinner entrées at 3:30 from May to October. The River Grille serves dinner only Wednesday through Sunday and lunch on Wednesday matinee days. The Grille and the Tavern are both open year-round.

♦ **Anne's Bistro** (860-434-9837; fax 860-434-FOOD), Old Lyme Marketplace, Halls Road, Old Lyme. Anne Haviland, a Culinary Institute of America graduate, has been running this popular little eatery in a shopping center for more than half a dozen years. The attractive space has high-backed pressed-oak chairs at small tables facing banquette seating, a few separate tables, bright artwork on the walls, and—new in 2002—a wine bar. Tapas are available all day, things like asparagus tart (asparagus and escarole with Manchego cheese and custard); roasted clams with garlic; and artichoke hearts, white beans, and cheese served warm on a baguette ($2–7). Lunch offers ever-changing soups, a classic spinach or Caesar salad, plus Anne's Favorite salad (mesclun greens, sliced pear, Gorgonzola, and caramelized walnuts in balsamic vinaigrette). There are also sandwiches and a lobster roll ($12) with fresh lobster chunks in a lime tarragon mayonnaise. At dinner, entrées ($17–25) might include olive-crusted rack of lamb served with wilted spinach, couscous, and crème fraîche, or pan-roasted halibut over rice noodles and veggies in an Asian lobster broth. The Shore Dinner, most expensive at $25, is lobster, mussels, corn on the cob, and red bliss potatoes; it is offered on Friday and Saturday evenings only. Open for lunch Tuesday through Saturday 11–2, dinner 5:30–8:30. Closed Sunday and Monday.

♦ **The Blue Oar** (860-345-2994), Snyder Road at the Midway Marina off Route 154), Haddam. The word is out—this is a wonderful place to dine at the very edge of the Connecticut River on a good day. A side road leads down a short but steep hill and through a marina to this tiny yellow former snack shack and an arrangement of outdoor seating. Rainy days tend to be washouts—the only covered tables are those on an open wraparound porch high up on the snack shack building, plus those in a separate small outbuilding on the grounds, enclosed on three sides. Elsewhere are colorful picnic tables and—right next to the river—a raised platform with several tables for two, where we snagged one. It's all first come, first served and bring-your-own. Some guests were surprisingly dressed up the night we ate here; we surmised they had theater tickets. But the food is up to any sort of dress. Jim Reilly and his wife, Jody, had the vision in 1997. You climb up a staircase to an enclosed room where you check out the blackboard menu and place your order—a surprisingly long selection the evening we stopped (with entrées in the $10–17 range). Then you're given a number, and wait to have the food delivered. At the end you take your number up to the cashier and pay. One of us had the pork tenderloin with grilled potatoes and zucchini and the other, warm lobster roll (bathed in butter) served with a side of pasta salad—both excellent. Our chilled Chardonnay was just right (bring your own glasses, too), and we listened to the water lap the rocks as we ate. Lots of folks were ordering the heaping bowls of steamers. You can also get entrées such as grilled salmon in a wine sauce. Burgers and hot dogs are on both the lunch and dinner menus as well. Desserts—displayed in a case next to the order desk—are made by a woman in Middletown and are wonderful. Almost everything seemed to be chocolate when we were there—turtle cheesecake being one choice. Open from early May to October daily except Monday for lunch 11:30–5, and dinner nightly from 5. No credit cards.

♦ **Terra Mar Grille** (860-388-1111), Saybrook Point Marina, Old Saybrook. This pretty dining room overlooking a marina is one of the dressiest waterside spots around. Chinese Chippendale chairs at well-spaced tables signal an elegant dining experience, and in general the dining room's reputation is solid. Lunch brings burgers and salads along with entrées such as lime-marinated salmon served with lo mein noodles or petite filet mignon with portobello mushrooms and fries ($9–17). For dinner, the classic shrimp cocktail is offered as a starter, along with Prince Edward Island mussels and crispy duck leg confit. Entrées ($18–25) might be panroasted monkfish with celery root puree, chanterelle-encrusted chicken breast with golden beet risotto, or grilled frenched pork chop with mashed sweet potatoes. This is a nice location for Sunday brunch, when a buffet is available at $29.95 for adults, $16 for children. Lunch Monday through Saturday 11:30–2:15, dinner 6 to 9 or 9:30.

♦ **The Griswold Inn** (860-767-1776), 36 Main Street, Essex. For atmosphere alone, the Gris is one of Connecticut's best-loved venues. The busy Tap Room with its potbelly stove, aromatic popcorn machine, and that ever-present Christmas tree—dressed to honor each season—is a great place to settle in for a cool drink in summer or a hot toddy when the sea winds blow. Banjo players are sometimes strumming, or sea chanteys being sung. The dining rooms are dark and atmospheric. The Covered Bridge dining room, just behind the Tap Room, fashioned from a real New Hampshire covered bridge, has steamboat prints all over the walls—most of them Currier & Ives—and a huge fireplace at one end. This is the largest dining room; two others, including the library (our favorite) are smaller and more intimate. The menu is a mix of seafood, sausages, pastas, and—at lunch—lots of egg dishes. Steamboat sandwiches claim to be copies of legendary overstuffed sandwiches served aboard steamship liners at the turn of the last century—they can be fresh beef, corned beef, or pastrami. Dinner entrées ($18–29) could be seared sea scallops and sherried leeks in puff pastry, maple-basted smoked pork chop, or prime rib, a Gris favorite. On Sunday the Gris offers a famous Hunt Breakfast, a buffet at $14.95 each with the usual suspects kept warm on a steam table. Lunch Monday through Saturday 11:30–3, dinner nightly from 5:30; Sunday brunch 11–2:30.

♦ **Dock 'n' Dine** (860-388-4665), Saybrook Point, Old Saybrook. Another very popular spot—for its location overlooking the point at which the Connecticut River enters Long Island Sound—is this venerable place. The three-sided windowed dining room that juts out into the water is the draw, but the bar always seems busy, and then there's a little outdoor terrace where drinks and light fare can be enjoyed along with the view of the water. For lunch there's a predictable assortment of clams casino, chicken wings, tuna or lobster salad sandwiches, crabcakes, and grilled London broil (top entrée about $10). For dinner, entrées ($12–18) include baked cod with potato crust; baked or fried sea scallops; oven-roasted salmon; grilled tuna; and a couple of pasta and steak dishes. Lunch, daily in-season, 11:30–3, bar menu 3–4, dinner 4–10. Closed Monday and Tuesday off-season.

♦ **The Short Stop** (860-526-4146), 165 Main Street, Deep River. This popular little local restaurant looks as if it's been around since the 1950s. Maybe it has. The point is, the breakfasts and lunches are delicious, the service prompt, and the locals flock here. Breakfast plays out the baseball theme with its specials: The "Grandslam" is two eggs, two pancakes, corned beef hash, and toast ($6.50); the "Error" is scrambled eggs in a flour tortilla with tomato, onion, melted cheddar, and sour cream served with salsa ($5.50). The muffins are very large, and the coffee keeps coming. At lunchtime you'll find familiar fare like roast beef and Swiss with horseradish grilled on rye; turkey Reuben on rye; and egg salad with bacon, lettuce, and tomato on a hard roll. Roast turkey is served (along with other specials) Thursday evening, the only night the place is open for dinner. So the turkey salad sandwich on Friday is excellent—served with slaw made from red cabbage. Open on Sunday 5:30 AM–noon, Monday through Friday 5:30 AM–2 PM; Saturday 5:30 AM–12:30 PM, Thursday evening 5–7. Breakfast is served until 11:30; after that, it's lunch.

18 Boothbay Harbor, Maine

It's all about the ocean in the Boothbay Harbor region of Maine's legendary and craggy seacoast. Water views await at nearly every turn in this section of midcoast Maine, with harbors, coves, bays, and inlets created by long fingers extending into the ocean from the mainland. Boothbay calls itself "the boating capital of New England." On Windjammer Days (sometime in late June or early July annually) several passenger-carrying schooners add their tall-masted glory to the hundreds of smaller boats that crowd around. The water is so compelling here that you may want to get out onto it. Fortunately there's a long list of excursion boats from which to choose.

Yet those who drive along Coastal Route 1 in Maine—thinking this will take them to the seashore at every point—could miss the area entirely. They need to know enough to pick up the access road, Route 27, and head southeast a dozen miles toward the sea and into the little town itself.

The Boothbay Harbor area is primarily defined by three craggy projections that jut far out into the ocean. These are the long, narrow island of Southport, at whose end is Cape Newagen to the west of Boothbay; Ocean Point, on the far east side of region; and Spruce Point, a more rounded piece of land that forms the actual eastern shore of Boothbay's inner harbor. At the end of each of these spruce-crowned and rock-edged projections is a major resort: The Ocean Point Inn, the Spruce Point Inn, and the Cape Newagen Seaside Inn. Talk about location.

Offshore are islands, some inhabited, some not. The most famous is probably Monhegan, located a dozen miles out to sea (see the separate "Monhegan Island" chapter). This primitive place, with a year-round population of about 70 souls, can be reached by a public boat from Boothbay Harbor.

Settled in the 17th century by Scotch-English fishermen, the Boothbay area was one the Pilgrims of Plymouth turned to for help their first winter. They sent a vessel up to obtain supplies. Eventually Native American hostility drove the Europeans away, but by 1729 many people had returned and the area began to grow.

Vacationers have been coming to the Boothbay region since shortly after the

Lobster traps behind Lawnmeer Inn, West Boothbay

Civil War, initially by steamship. By the turn of the past century, the place was already a summer destination of note. And by the beginning of the 21st century, it hasn't slowed down a bit.

The downtown section of Boothbay Harbor proper—with its narrow, irregular, and hilly streets; tightly arranged shops, restaurants, and lodging establishments; and busy-as-can-be waterfront—is a popular, crowded place. It sports a somewhat carnival atmosphere in summer. Streets are so narrow and parking spots so hard to find that you are best advised to do your exploring on foot. (If you must drive, get into town early enough to find a space in one of the municipal or waterfront lots; they fill fast.)

Boothbay's tremendous appeal lies in its variety, the views it affords of harbor and ocean, the sense that this is the picturesque Maine we all dream of. It is easier here than anywhere else we know to get out on the water for sight-seeing, fishing, whale-watching, or sailing trips. The shops are filled with both tasteful items and pure kitsch: salt and pepper shakers in the shapes of lobster claws, T-shirts with stupid sayings on them, infinite amounts of blueberry-decorated pottery, even a toy moose dressed up in the sou'wester outfit of a fisherman. Right in the center of the commercial district is a 55-year-old log building, the Romar candlepin bowling lanes, run by the same family since the mid-1940s. It anchors the place with a sense of timelessness, of summers gone by, of summers to come.

In counterpoint to the tourism of Boothbay Harbor itself are the less crowded, more rural areas of Southport, East Boothbay, and Ocean Point. Shipbuilding is still big business in the region—the yards now specialize in yachts, big steel fishing vessels, ferries, and tugs. Although overfishing has put many fishermen ashore, lobstering is big. You'll certainly want to indulge while you're in the area, for the mighty crustacean is found on just about every menu and even in a local ice cream flavor.

From East Boothbay, Route 96 leads down to Ocean Point, where you can walk the waterfront and even climb onto some large boulders. There is a small beach. Driving around the region is one of the joys of visiting, and it takes a good while to see the whole place. As you head west, across the drawbridge and down Southport Island to Cape Newagen, be sure to stop off at Cozy Harbor, one of the most picturesque little harbors in the entire area. There's a homey bed & breakfast inn here, too, with fabulous views of the water.

Most of all Boothbay Harbor is about summer by the sea. This is the season, no doubt about it. Not long ago, they say you could roll a bowling ball down the center of the main street on Thanksgiving Day and not hit a soul. Most restaurants and hostelries close up shop by October, and the 1,500 or so year-round residents give a collective sigh of relief that things have returned to normal. Yet times are slowly changing. A few B&Bs and some restaurants have begun to stay open year-round, and so does the local chamber of commerce. Fireplaces are being installed in guest bedrooms for the off-season visitor. And because the seacoast has less snow, generally, than inland, a winter weekend can be a peaceful time to take a walk along the water, eat a warming meal, and settle down before a fire with a good book. It can be a time of restoration.

Whichever you prefer—the summer frivolity of a busy seaside resort, or the exceptional quiet of a winter weekend by the water—the Boothbay Harbor region well may have what you want.

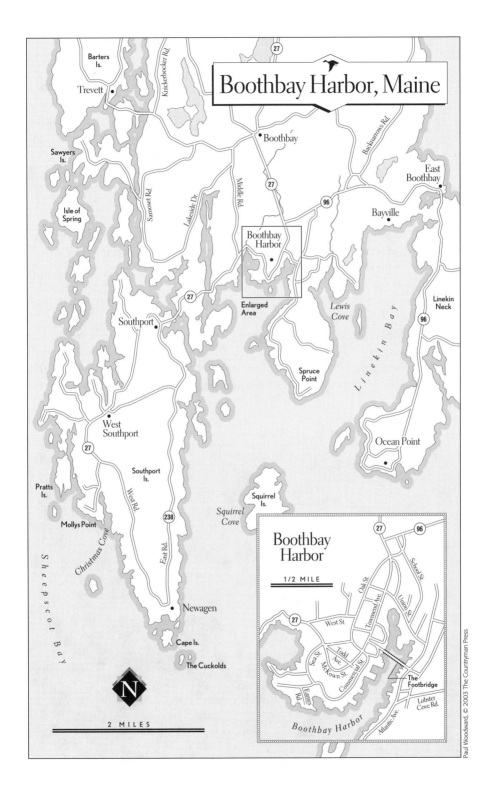

Boothbay Harbor, Maine

Barters Is.

Trevett

Knickerbocker Rd.

27

Boothbay

27

96

East Boothbay

Sawyers Is.

Samoset Rd.

Lakeside Dr.

Middle Rd.

Bayville

Backnarrows Rd.

Isle of Spring

27

Boothbay Harbor

Enlarged Area

Lewis Cove

Linekin Neck

96

Southport

27

Spruce Point

Linekin Bay

West Southport

27

West Rd.

Southport Is.

Pratts Is.

Mollys Point

Christmas Cove

East Rd.

238

Squirrel Cove

Squirrel Is.

Ocean Point

Newagen

Cape Is.

The Cuckolds

Sheepscot Bay

N

2 MILES

Boothbay Harbor

1/2 MILE

27

96

Oak St.

School St.

Townsend Ave.

Union St.

West St.

Sea St.

Todd Ave.

McKown St.

Commercial St.

Eames Rd.

The Footbridge

Atlantic Ave.

Lobster Cove Rd.

Boothbay Harbor

Paul Woodward, © 2003 The Countryman Press

Getting There

Boothbay Harbor is located about one-third of the way up the Maine coast from the New Hampshire border. Take I-95 north to Exit 22 (Coastal Route 1) and follow Route 1 just past Wiscasset. After crossing the broad Sheepscot River, look for Route 27, which leads southeast for 12 miles directly into Boothbay Harbor.

The area is 166 miles from Boston; 270 miles from Hartford; 379 miles from New York City. Bar Harbor, Maine, is another 125 miles north of Boothbay.

The closest major **airport** is at Portland, Maine. Private planes may fly into the Wiscasset Airport.

Getting Around

Courtesy trolleys run from mid-June through Labor Day between 10 AM and 5 PM. A harbor shuttle operates in July and August from 7 AM to 11 PM. Some resorts provide their own shuttles into town; be sure to ask when booking rooms.

For More Information

♦ **Boothbay Harbor Region Chamber of Commerce** (207-633-2353; www.boothbayharbor.com), P.O. Box 356, Boothbay Harbor, ME 04538. An information booth is located during the summer on Route 27 as you enter the region. The main office and information center, open year-round, is on Route 27 next to the Shop 'n Save supermarket.

A windjammer sets sail from Boothbay Harbor

The many waterfronts of the region are its prime attraction. Getting out on boat is a must. Call for reservations ahead of time.

THE BOATS

Windjammer Eastwind (207-633-6598). This 64-foot windjammer departs from Fisherman's Wharf four times a day in midseason. The 2¹/₂-hour cruises take passengers to the outer islands and seal rocks. $20 per person.

Windjammer Sylvina W. Beal (207-633-1109). An 84-foot-long schooner built in 1911 in East Boothbay, the Beal takes morning, afternoon, and sunset sails of 1¹/₂ to 2 hours in duration. The sunset sail often includes live music. $22 per person; kids $14. She sails from Pier 1 near the footbridge.

Balmy Days cruises (207-633-2284; 1-800-298-2284; www.balmydayscruises. com), sailing from Pier 8 in the downtown area. Captain Bill Campbell operates four different boats. Trips are to Monhegan Island aboard the *Balmy Days II* (adults $30, children $18 round-trip); the harbor tours aboard the *Novelty* (several 1-hour tours daily; adults $9, children, $4.50); mackerel fishing aboard the *Miss Boothbay* (several trips daily in-season; adults $20, children $16); and sailing trips aboard the *Bay Lady* for 1 1/2 hours several times daily ($18).

Boothbay Whale Watch (207-633-3500). Leaves daily from Pier 6 aboard the *Harbor Princess.* Adults $28. children $15.

Cap'n Fish's Sightseeing Boat Cruises (207-633-3244; 207-633-2626). For more than 75 years these Boothbay Harbor natives have taken vacationers out on various cruises. They include a whale-watch cruise daily in-season; a Little Bit O'Maine 2-hour trip on Monday, Tuesday, and Friday that includes seals; a Cap's Special trip of 2 hours to lighthouses, harbors, bustling boatyards, and so on; a 2-hour cruise to the Pemaquid Point Lighthouse; a Lobster Trap Hauling and Seal Watch trip; and puffin trips. Trips leave from Pier 1. Call for a complete schedule and fees.

Sportfishing aboard the Breakaway (207-633-6990). Captain Peter Ripley, a Registered Maine Guide, takes two half-day trips out daily in search of blues and stripers. The cost is in the $50 range with a minimum of three persons required. Pier 6 at Fisherman's Wharf.

Other charters are offered, including **Redhook charters** (207-633-3807) that go from the docks at the Tugboat Inn, Boothbay Harbor.

Kayaking

♦ **The Tidal Transit Company** (207-633-7140) located by the footbridge in the Chowder House building, Boothbay Harbor, offers guided kayak, lighthouse, wildlife, and sunset tours. You can also rent kayaks by the hour, half day, full day, or for several days. **Bikes** are also rented here.

Kayaks are available also from the **Gray Homestead Campground** (207-633-4612) in Southport at $12 an hour single, $20 an hour double.

A fishing boat sets out from Boothbay Harbor

Wooden Boat Rental

Traditionally built wooden boats—sail, oar, and power—are rented by the hour, day, or week from **Finest Kind Wooden Boats** (207-633-5636), Harborfields, West Boothbay Harbor.

Fishing

Fishing tackle may be purchased in the **Tackle Shop** (207-633-3788) at the White Anchor Motel, Route 27, Boothbay.

Golf

♦ **Boothbay Country Club and 19th Hole Lounge** (207-633-6085). This 18-hole course is open to the public daily from mid-April to mid-November. Greens fees, $65 for 18 holes and $45 for 9 holes; prices include cart. Tee times are required.

Swimming

Maine waters are cold, and most visitors don't brave them. Besides, there are devilishly few beaches where the public can take a dip. **Hendricks Head Beach** near Cozy Harbor on Southport Island is said to be open to the public. There is a beach at **Townsend Gut**, just beyond the drawbridge leading to Southport Island, off Route 27. **Grimes Cove Beach** near Ocean Point is a tiny piece of sand you might try. If you're especially lucky, your hotel or inn will have a swimming pool, but few do. The excellent **Boothbay Region YMCA** (207-633-2855) has a large indoor swimming pool open to the public, in addition to programs for all ages.

Bowling

♦ **Romar Bowling Lanes** (207-633-5721). The Rowe family has owned this eight-lane candlepin bowling alley in a log-and-frame building in the center of town—and with a view of the harbor—since 1946. On rainy summer days or evenings, the wait for a lane is sometimes pretty long. There are also pinball machines, a billiard table, and a luncheonette where you can get both Eastern (ham and egg) and Western (ham, egg, and onion) sandwiches, hamburgers, and hot dogs. You can order a root beer float, too. Open noon–11 PM.

Miniature Golf

For the kids, there are two miniature golf courses, both on the main road, Route 27. **Treasure Island** is in Boothbay Harbor and **Dolphin Mini Golf** is in Boothbay.

More Diversions

♦ **Maine Resources Aquarium** (207-633-9559), McKown Point Road, West Boothbay Harbor. You supposedly can pet a live shark, see skates, sportfish, and lobsters, and generally get a taste of marine life at this small but pleasant spot. The aquarium is sponsored by the Maine Department of Marine Resources and the U.S. Fish and Wildlife Services. If you bring a picnic lunch, you can enjoy it with a view of the harbor—the aquarium is situated on a point of land with water all around. Open Memorial Day weekend through September, 10–5. Adults $3, seniors and children $2.50.

♦ **Boothbay Railway Village** (207-633-4727; www.railwayvillage.org), Route 27, Boothbay. This is Maine's only 2-foot, narrow-gauge railway, preserved and made part of a very popular museum. Visitors take a 15-minute ride on the train through woods, over a bridge, past railroad yards, and into a turn-of-the-20th-century village of 24 buildings. In the village is a collection of some 60 vintage automobiles. In July there's a mammoth annual antique auto meet, and at Halloween a Ghost Train is operated. During the season, the train operates about every half hour, with the last train leaving at 5 PM. Open in summer, daily 9:30–5; weekends off-season. Adults $7, children $3.

♦ **Boothbay Region Historical Society** (207-633-0820), 72 Oak Street, Boothbay Harbor. Located in the 1874 Elizabeth F. Reed house and grounds, the collection of the society consists of Reed family heirloom furnishings, local historical mementos, and documentary collections. There are seven display rooms. Among the treasures are the Fresnel lens from the Ram Island Light, relics of bygone vessels, nautical instruments, and early tools such as those used in ice cutting. An elegant model of the Gulf of Maine shows varying depths of water and where different species of fish were caught. Open in July and August on Wednesday, Friday, and Saturday 10–4; year-round, Saturday 10–2. Donation.

♦ **Coastal Maine Botanical Gardens** (207-633-4333), Barter's Island Road, Boothbay. The office is located at 1 Oak Street in Boothbay Harbor. This 28-acre property is operated by a young, nonprofit organization. Self-guided nature trails wend past tidal shoreline, and wetland garden plants are identified. Open daily dawn to dusk. Free.

♦ **The footbridge.** The famous footbridge across the harbor—first built in 1901— isn't quite as practical as it seems for those already in Boothbay Harbor. There's not an awful lot on the east side of the harbor—other than a few motels and restaurants—once you walk over. For those on that other side of the harbor, though, it's a practical way to get into town without a car. And the footbridge is a good place to use your camera. Many people just like to walk over and back. In Boothbay Harbor you can find it close to Andrews' Harborside Restaurant.

♦ **Hendricks Hill Museum** (207-633-1102), Route 27, Southport. The history of Southport is preserved in this small museum run by a local volunteer crew. A boat shed out back has old wooden boats on display. The Cape Cod–style house with the main collection contains mementos from the old Southport post office, old whale oil lamps, fishing industry tools, ice cutting paraphernalia, and so on. Open July and August, Tuesday, Thursday, and Saturday 11–3. Donation.

Shopping

There are loads of interesting shops in the Boothbay Harbor area, with everything from fine art to baseball hats. For women's clothing, we particularly like the swingy dresses and sophisticated separates at **Calypso** in a barnlike building on Commercial Street. More preppy types might turn to the classic clothes at the **House of Logan,** a large white building in the center of town. **Edgecomb Potters** have their main facility on the access road coming into Boothbay, but their beautiful glazed wares are also sold at **Hand in Hand Gallery** in town. **Abacus** is an excellent gallery with unusual items, including some exceptional sculpture. **Gimbel & Sons Country Store** with myriad items is next door to the famous gift store, **The Smiling Cow** (with a sister shop in Camden).

For books, magazines, art supplies, business needs (computer supplies), and such, check out the large, two-level **Sherman's.** Maine and American handcrafts are sold at **The Mung Bean. Boothbay Harbor Artisans** at 11 Granary Way is a cooperative of Maine craftspeople and artists—with everything from stained glass, jewelry, pottery, baskets, and baby clothes to ceramics, bird feeders, soaps, and dried flower wreaths. Blueberry pottery made by the same Maine artist for more than 25 years is offered at **The Custom House.** T-shirts can be found just about anywhere.

For serious **antiques enthusiasts,** it might be worth a stop in nearby **Wiscasset,** south on Route 1, where the main street is lined with some very fine shops.

WHERE TO STAY

Boothbay Harbor has been in the business of catering to vacationers for many years. There's a full range of options—from small and personal B&Bs to large, full-service resorts and major motels. Here's a selective sampling:

B&Bs

♦ **The Greenleaf Inn** (207-633-7346; 1-888-950-7724; fax 207-633-2642; www.
greenleafinn.com), 65 Commercial Street, Boothbay Harbor, ME 04538. Jeff Teel,
who summered in Boothbay Harbor "my whole life," left the world of accounting
to pursue his true vocation as an innkeeper with his sidekick, a faithful dog,
Metro, in the late 1990s. The large white Cape-style home is 150 years old, located on a knoll at the south end of Commercial Street, and in the center of the
action. Once inside the tastefully upgraded inn, you feel as if you are in a world
apart, quiet and comfortable. The view of the harbor activity from the wicker-furnished front porch makes you want to sit there all day. Either that, or you might
opt for the oversized hammock on the front lawn. Seven rooms and suites—two
on the first, three on the second floor, and two newer ones above a wing—have
TV, VCR, private bath, and telephone. Four have a gas fireplace. The suite on
the main floor is decorated breezily with a fish decor and with coastal art on the
walls. One room on the second floor has both a double and a single bed; room 5
has a huge bathroom; and most rooms have water views and queen bed. Two
have their own balconies.

Jeff makes the full buffet breakfasts, sometimes serving gingerbread waffles or
baked French toast as the entrée. Guests pick up their breakfast in the fireplaced
Great Room with library—a good place to hang out—and dine either inside or out
on the porch. Open year-round. Doubles, $105–155.

♦ **Anchor Watch** (207-633-7565; www.anchorwatch.com), 9 Eames Road, Boothbay Harbor, ME 04538. Diane Campbell, a native of the area, and her daughter,
Kathy Campbell Reed, keep this immaculate and well-located five-room B&B running smoothly. Situated just around the corner from the commercial downtown
area on a quiet little street, it offers an "away-from-it-all feeling" while being close
enough to town to walk. The inn owns shady, well-landscaped property across the
street leading to the water and its own dock; we had a terrific picnic lunch beneath
a big old tree there one day, watching harbor activity. Since the Campbell family
(Diane's son Bill is in charge) runs the Balmy Days cruises, they can fix you up
with a boat trip easily. Our king-bedded room on the first floor had its own
entrance, parking just outside the door, and a view of the water. Known as the
Balmy Days Room, it also had a gas fireplace for cool-weather stays and was the
only room with TV. Cross-ventilation and an overhead paddle fan kept us comfortable during a hot stretch in late June. A second-floor room with new balcony offers
a water view from the balcony that's just wonderful; two third-floor rooms have
expansive water views. These rooms have queen beds. Diane is a wonderful cook,
and guests eat breakfast overlooking the water in a windowed parlor/dining room
combination. Her open kitchen is close by. A cheese and egg pie, fresh fruit,
muffins, and hot fruit cobbler plus juice and hot beverages got us off to a good start
one morning. Open year-round. Doubles, $90–150.

♦ **Welch House** (207-633-3431; 1-800-279-7313; www.welchouse.com), 56 McKown
Street, Boothbay Harbor, ME 04538. High atop McKown Hill in the center of town
with an unbelievable 180-degree view of the water from its rooftop deck, this 16-
room B&B is run by Texans Wood Livingstone and Wes Garlington, who got their

start in the airline industry. So they know about pleasing the public. The glass-enclosed breakfast/sitting room has individual wood tables for dining, a stone fireplace, and comfortable sofas. It acts as a place to gather as well as enjoy a full breakfast—set out buffet-style. Just outside is a deck with umbrellaed tables, and then there is that large top-of-the-world sundeck with spectacular views of the harbor. The house has rooms on a lower level and three floors, all of them with private bath (some shower only, some with tub); there are double, queen, and king beds. Decor is a tasteful mix of old and new. While there's no air-conditioning, every room has cross-ventilation. TVs—but no phones—are provided. The gardens outside are beautifully tended, and it's an easy walk down the hill into town, a bit harder puffing uphill at the end of the day. No smoking. Open April through October. Doubles, $90–165.

♦ **Cozy Harbor Bed & Breakfast** (207-633-3546), P.O. Box 225, Pratt's Island Road, Southport, ME 04576. This small two-room B&B—with views from both rooms and from a front porch of picturesque Cozy Harbor and the Sheepscot River across the way—offers a true old-fashioned B&B experience. Just 10 minutes from downtown Boothbay Harbor on the island of Southport, you feel as if you are far away from everyday life. Sandra Seifert, a former schoolteacher who retired to this antique 19th-century farmhouse with her husband, acts as the innkeeper. The immaculate and large guest rooms on the second floor of their own wing share a bath and a half. One room has a king bed, the other a queen. There are no TVs, but good reading lights and plenty of books to borrow. There is a TV (if you must) in the comfortable parlor with woodstove that's used by guests. If you want to put something in the house refrigerator, you can. A full breakfast is served in a pleasant room off the kitchen. Hendricks Head Beach is nearby, and there's a lobster pound not far off. Open May through Columbus Day. Doubles, $85.

♦ **Linekin Bay Bed & Breakfast** (207-633-9900; 1-800-596-7420), 531 Ocean Point Road, Route 96, East Boothbay, ME 04544. This gleaming white house with fuchsia-shaded petunias spilling from baskets across the front porch is a welcoming B&B with distant views of—but not direct access to—Linekin Bay. On the quiet eastern side of the Boothbay region, the four-room B&B is run by a former police officer, Larry Brown, with help from his wife, Marti Booth, a schoolteacher. The most luxurious accommodation is the main-floor Holbrook Suite with four-poster king-sized bed set in the middle of an extra-large room, with large bathroom and a lovely private side porch. We rather liked the second-floor Rhapsody in Blue, a long room carved from two smaller spaces. A chaise lounge set by a window with a view of the water looked inviting. All guest rooms have TV and phone. Three have water views, and all but one have stove or fireplace. A brand-new space out back on the main floor with skylights and a view of the water was being furnished as a breakfast room and parlor. Larry makes the full breakfast, and touts his baked French toast or sour cream waffles. In the afternoon a variety of homemade sweets are set out on the dining room table along with something to drink. Adirondack chairs on the expansive back lawn with the water view are tempting. Open year-round. Doubles, $85–175.

Inns

♦ **Lawnmeer Inn** (207-633-2544; 1-800-633-SMILE; www.lawnmeerinn.com), Route 27, P.O. Box 505, West Boothbay Harbor, ME 04575. Advertising itself as one of the oldest operating inns in the area, dating back to 1898, Lawnmeer offers comfortable lodgings in the main inn and two adjacent motel-like structures. Its restaurant is well regarded (see *Where to Eat*). The white building complex with yellow shutters is located just beyond the drawbridge on Southport Island, and the rear lawns overlook a small harbor known as Townsend Gut. The ingenious gardener has planted flowers amid old wooden lobster pots. Guests love to sit on the lawn and watch the boats come and go.

Rooms in the main inn are cozy and traditionally furnished, with a stuffed teddy bear on every bed. Baskets filled with teddy bears are also to be found in wicker-furnished common lounges on the second floor of the main inn. Room 1 in the main inn has a queen bed with floral comforter, a small TV, and dark wicker furniture. All rooms have private bath and TV. Room 3 has a four-poster queen bed, a bath with stall shower, and a gorgeous water view. Altogether there are 33 rooms, 13 in the main inn and 20 in two renovated motel structures (each room here having two queen beds with bright printed quilts and its own balcony overlooking the water). There's also a cottage for two with a deck at water's edge. Main-floor public rooms in the inn include a dramatically wallpapered parlor in green-and-white stripes and a bar with mostly green decor. Guests may have a full breakfast in a room with wood captain's chairs and tables, although the meal is not included in room rates. Owners Lee and Jim Metzger are constantly

Water views are everywhere in Boothbay Harbor.

upgrading the inn; Lee herself has done some of the stenciling on the walls. Open late May to mid-October. Doubles, $95–180. The private cottage rents for $160 a night in-season.

♦ **Five Gables Inn** (207-633-4551; 1-800-451-5048), Murray Hill Road, P.O. Box 335, East Boothbay, ME 04544. Although not, strictly speaking, an inn (it lacks a public restaurant), this is much more than your average B&B. The beige Victorian hostelry with cream trim and dark green shutters offers 16 beautifully decorated guest rooms on three floors. All overlook Linekin Bay, as does the well-furnished wraparound porch. From here, on the east side of the region, you can drive into downtown Boothbay Harbor in 10 minutes. Five of the rooms have a working fireplace but one—on the first floor—has a whimsical trompe l'oeil fireplace painted on a brick chimney. The inn is aptly named for the five steep peaks that characterize the architecture of the 130-year-old building. It was run as a low-key guesthouse for years, then totally renovated by former innkeepers the Morrisettes. De and Mike Kennedy purchased the inn after they'd spent the better part of a year crewing on a yacht in French Polynesia and then backpacking through Southeast Asia. Their creative touches are enjoyed—De's crocheted afghans on some of the beds (all but one are queen sized, the last king sized), and Mike's culinary expertise in the bountiful buffet breakfasts set out in the spacious lobby/dining area. A specialty is fresh tomato and basil frittata. From this room, a staircase leading to the second floor has a pottery bird on each step, a charming touch. Inn literature claims there's saltwater swimming across the way; there is a public boat launch nearby. There's a relaxed feeling here of summer by the shore. Open mid-May through mid-November. Doubles, $120–155.

Resorts

A major resort commands each of three points of land at the end of a peninsula with water all around. The locations of all three are superb.

♦ **Newagen Seaside Inn** (207-633-5242; 1-800-654-5242; fax 207-633-5340; www. newagenseasideinn.com), Cape Newagen Road, P.O. Box 29, Newagen, ME 04576. Rattan furniture upholstered in deep red and neutrals plus bare wood floors in the large fireplaced lobby signal a new air of sophistication for this time-honored inn. Indeed, new innkeepers Corinne and Scott Larson arrived from Atlanta, Georgia, at the end of 2000 and were quickly putting their own touches—especially Scott's expertise as an event planner—on the property. When we stopped in, an artist's workshop was being held, one of many scheduled during the summer. The Portland String Quartet does workshops at the beginning and end of the season, and "weddings and special events" are now mentioned prominently in the literature. The main inn has 26 well-appointed rooms, often with a queen and twin bed, decorative coverlets, and bare, polished wood floors. All have private bath, but no TV or air-conditioning. A few rooms have a balcony. The appeal of Newagen lies in its self-contained aspect; you really don't need to leave unless you want to. Surrounded on three sides by the waters of Sheepscot Bay, with its own pool and hot tubs, tennis courts, rowboats, and bikes, this is a place to settle in. A 1½-mile nature trail leads through the property, and there are wonderful views from the rocky shoreline. The dining room is highly regarded. A full breakfast is included in the rates. There are three separate housekeeping cottages that rent by the week only. Open mid-May to mid-October. Doubles, $95–205.

♦ **Spruce Point Inn** (207-633-4152; 1-800-553-0289; fax 207-633-7138; www.spruce-pointinn.com), Atlantic Avenue, P.O. Box 237, Boothbay Harbor, ME 04538. The Spruce Point Inn—located on 12 spectacular piney acres at the end of a private peninsula stretching into the harbor—is the toniest place to stay in the area. Co-owners Joseph Paolillo and Angelo DeGiulian oversee a property that includes 20 buildings and 85 accommodations ranging from 9 well-appointed rooms in the main inn to junior and regular suites—all with fireplace—and several cottages with one, two, and three bedrooms. There are also Oceanhouse condominiums with two or three bedrooms and full kitchen, living room, and dining room. The Admiral's Suite in the main inn is truly luxurious, a very large space with built-in window seat, a balcony with a gorgeous view of the harbor, and a living room on the upper level with king-bedded bedroom area below. Most rooms have ocean views, a large TV set in an armoire, refrigerator, and phone. Many have a fireplace. Some have a kitchenette. The real draw here may be the extraordinary features available to all guests. They include a saltwater swimming pool with whirlpool set in rocks above the harbor; a second heated freshwater swimming pool in an area where families are often housed; planned activities for children during July and August so parents have time to themselves. There are also weekly lobster bakes followed by sunset cruises ($50 a person), and dining rooms that are acclaimed (see *Where to Eat*). Har-Tru tennis courts, a regularly scheduled shuttle bus to town and to the Boothbay Region Country Club golf course, and lawn games like croquet, horse-shoes, and shuffleboard are popular. Although meals do not come with standard room rates, they may be added at $14 for breakfast for an adult, $5 for a child; $40 for dinner for an adult, $10 for a child. Complimentary coffee and muffins are available in the main lobby foyer—furnished with dark wicker pieces and smashing dark plaid cushions. The resort is reached via a pretty road through a shady residential section. Spruce Point Inn is open from late May through October. Doubles range $125–350; cottages $295–550 daily with a minimum stay of 6 nights. Condos range $295–565 with a 6-night stay in summer. To this add hotel charges and gratuities of 10 to 15 percent. Package plans are available.

♦ **Ocean Point Inn** (207-633-4200; 1-800-552-5554; www.oceanpointinn.com), Shore Road, Route 96, P.O. Box 409 East Boothbay, ME 04544. This inn, white with green trim, has a dramatic setting at the entrance to Linekin Bay, with ocean traffic passing in front of its many buildings. Altogether 61 accommodations are available in 15 buildings strung along the shore. They range from nicely updated rooms in the main inn done in "woodsy" color schemes of dark green and neutrals, to simpler rooms in motel units near a large swimming pool. These rooms have two queen beds apiece, and families love them. Other accommodations might be in duplex or single cottages or the lodge, a two-floor 10-room building across from the pier. Beds are king, queen, or twins. Some rooms have a balcony, some have air-conditioning, and all have TV, heat, private bath, and mini refrigerator. A line of Adirondack chairs is set along the shore to take advantage of the exceptional views.

The dining room has big windows with views of the water (see *Where to Eat*). The big rocks are fun to sit or sun on in front of the inn, and there's a small beach nearby. The adjacent neighborhood, with big summer cottages, is also interesting to stroll around. Some package plans are available. Open late May to October. Doubles, $69–159. Cottages rented by the week only are priced $650–1,114 per week, depending on size.

Motels

♦ **Smuggler's Cove Inn** (207-633-2800; fax 207-633-5926; www.smugglerscove-motel.com), Route 96, East Boothbay, ME 04544. Five motel buildings contain 60 guest rooms in this appealing motel complex tucked in a quiet cove not far from the Ocean Point Inn. One of the buildings is actually set on pilings and juts out over the water. Most have ocean views and balcony (although some views can be impeded by other buildings). Anchor, which faces the water, and Lantern, the building that sits right over the water, are probably your best bets for a good view. Most rooms have two doubles or two queens. There's a small sandy beach, pool, TV in the units, and rowboats. Families like this place. A full-service restaurant, the **1820 House,** is next door, serving breakfast and dinner. Open late May to mid-October. Doubles, $99–169.

♦ **Rocktide Inn** (207-633-4455; 1-800-ROC-TIDE), 35 Atlantic Avenue, Boothbay Harbor, ME 04538. Ninety-eight rooms in four buildings on the east side of the harbor are popular places to stay. Some rooms have private balcony, and many have water views. All have two double beds or one queen, a private bath, carpeting, air-conditioning, TV, and phone. An indoor swimming pool is a plus. There are also four **dining rooms** on the property ranging in sophistication—two require that men wear jackets. The location is just 100 feet from the famous footbridge into town, a real plus. This place always seems to be very busy. Open mid-June to mid-October. Doubles, including full buffet breakfast, $92–162.

♦ **Tugboat Inn** (207-633-4434; 1-800-248-2628), 80 Commercial Street, Boothbay Harbor, ME 04538. This five-building complex puts you in the heart of the tourist area in downtown Boothbay, and the adjoining **restaurant** is convenient as well as offering more smashing waterfront views. The red tugboat signals that you have arrived. Rooms have light wood furniture, views of the harbor, air-conditioning, and king or queen bed. You'll also find TV, telephone, and hair dryers. Some have a private balcony and deck area. Altogether there are 62 accommodations with 2 suites. Complimentary coffee and pastries in the morning. Open mid-April to mid-November. Doubles, $75–180.

Camping

♦ **Gray Homestead Campground** (207-633-4612; www.gwi.net/~gray), 21 Homestead Road, Southport, ME 04576. This is the only campground in the area that's directly on the ocean. Not all sites are waterfront, but those that aren't are woodsy and it really feels like camping. Altogether there are 40 sites, with electrical hook-ups for RVs and a few tent sites. There's a small private beach, and you can buy lobsters here to cook at your campsite. In addition, kayaks are rented here. Campsites, $19–27 a night.

Cottages

If you want to rent a cottage in the area, you can contact the **Cottage Connection of Maine, Inc.** (207-633-6545; 1-800-823-9501), Route 27, P.O. Box 662, Boothbay Harbor, ME 04538. They claim to have more than 150 cottages to choose from.

WHERE TO EAT

Plenty of lobster pounds are available in the Boothbay Harbor area. And lobsters are on the menu in most other places, too. But there's more to life than lobsters, right? Here is a range of possibilities.

♦ **Christopher's Boathouse** (207-633-6565), Head of the Harbor, 25 Union Street, Boothbay Harbor. They call it "New World Cuisine," and Christopher Russell, a graduate of the Culinary Institute of America, and his wife, Marie, present lunches and dinners at the top-rated place in town. The location could not be better: a large white former boathouse with full-length windows overlooking the waters of the harbor. Inside, all is sophisticatedly simple: white-clothed tables set about with light wood Windsor-style chairs. There are also a couple of booths formed from old church pews. A deck outside is the preferred spot on warm evenings, although the candlelit interior is romantic and peaceful. Christopher and staff work over a wood grill in an open kitchen.

At lunch, offered in June, July, and August, you might start with the lobster and mango bisque (for which the restaurant is famed), chilled gazpacho, or fried calamari with dipping sauces. Lunch can be a Caesar salad with anchovies, as it should be, and topped with either grilled chicken or grilled scallops; a Boathouse burger served with lettuce, tomato, and red onion—and Maytag blue cheese if you want; or a fresh fish sandwich of the day. Lunch entrées are in the $6–10 range.

For dinner, offered year-round, appetizers might be a napoleon of crispy potatoes and wild mushrooms served with an herb cream sauce, or a summer salad of duck confit with dried cranberries and orange segments. A typical menu also offers oven-roasted monkfish; pan-seared veal Scaloppine layered with duck prosciutto and topped with truffle oil; rum and spice painted salmon with Maine shrimp and ginger strudel; and the ubiquitous split and grilled lobster served with a roasted red pepper tarragon coulis and asparagus risotto. Dessert might be a fruit-flavored flan. Entrées, $20–27.

Next door to the restaurant is **Christopher's Wine Cellar,** a retail store with a fine selection of wines and cheeses.

♦ **Spruce Point Inn** (207-633-4152), Atlantic Avenue, Boothbay Harbor. A large oceanfront dining room is appealing for a fine meal at this resort, but there are other possibilities, including a newish bistro with lighter fare and an outdoor pavilion where food is served in good weather. In the dining room, appetizers ($5–10) might be fresh fruit compote, crabcakes served with a spicy peanut and Thai sauce, or wild mushroom strudel. A la carte salads include the "inn salad" of greens with cucumbers, carrots, and tomatoes; Caesar; and a portobello napoleon. Entrées include halibut choron, with the halibut first seared, then oven poached and served on a bed of julienned vegetables; shrimp scampi Dijonnaise; duckling à l'orange; or chicken saltimbocca. Of course there's lobster, steamed or baked and stuffed. (Entrées, $19–29.) Desserts include strawberry rhubarb pie, triple chocolate mousse cake, coconut crème brûlée with wild berry compote, or chocolate decadence torte ($6). Lobster bakes on Wednesday or Thursday night are open to the public at $50 per person; reservations are essential.

The bistro menu is served in the adjacent **Whistling Whale Lounge** and ocean-front deck when weather permits. Here entrées ($12–23) include a Baja seafood quesadilla; swordfish chunks with mushrooms, onions, and peppers served on rice; and a sirloin steak served with jumbo baked potato and crisp onion rings. The restaurant is open seasonally, as is the resort.

♦ **Newagen Seaside Inn** (207-633-5242), Cape Newagen, at the tip of Southport Island. The longtime chef, Eric Botka, continued on at this acclaimed dining room after new owners took over in 2000. The room has water views on two sides and is simple and summery, the main feature being the fine food. Dinner might start with lobster cakes (lobster, scallops, sweet potato, and red pepper with a spicy lobster sauce), mussels marinara, or mushroom caps topped with cheese ($5–9). Entrées include pan-fried sole with capers and lemon, a rack of lamb roasted with a touch of Dijon mustard and herbs, oven-roasted semiboneless duck served with raspberry coulis and bordelaise sauce, or boneless breast of Tuscan chicken, served with artichoke hearts and sun-dried tomatoes ($14–25). Apple strudel and various cheesecakes are often on the dessert menu. Dinner is served nightly except Tuesday, mid-May to early October. Reservations required.

♦ **Lawnmeer Inn** (207-633-2544), Route 27, West Boothbay. Everybody wants the front row of waterside tables in the dining room at this venerable inn, but you can get a pretty good view of the water from anywhere. You'll observe activity on Townsend Gut (a *gut* being a narrow passage or channel of water) to the rear of the inn. High dark ladderback chairs are set at tables topped with pale green and maroon cloths. A single candle in a hurricane lamp flickers as you dine. We shared an order of Maine crabcakes served on a bed of fresh spinach that was delicious. Other starters can be the inn's seafood chowder, Maine mussels steamed in white wine with garlic and tomato, or escargots in puff pastry ($6–8). Entrées might be native haddock fillet baked with lemon, butter, and fresh herbs; a grilled chicken satay with spicy peanut sauce; or an 8-ounce filet mignon with an herb crust and green peppercorn butter. A diner nearby was exclaiming over London broil of grilled venison the night we dined here ($16–20). Desserts are popular at this inn, especially key lime pie, bread pudding, and crème brûlée. Dinner nightly 6–9, mid-June to Labor Day; fewer nights in spring and fall.

♦ **Ocean Point Inn** (207-633-4200), Shore Road, Ocean Point. A long ride down the peninsula to dramatic Ocean Point, and a waterside dining room with views of Linekin Bay are almost reasons enough to dine in the teal-carpeted, oceanside dining room at the Ocean Point Inn. The older section has knotty-pine walls; chairs are ladderback or Windsor, with white-clothed tables. The inn claims fresh Maine salmon fillets as its signature item—they are offered in four different versions—and seafood definitely dominates the menu. Other entrées include shrimp scampi served over linguine, broiled sea scallops served with white wine and butter, and char-grilled swordfish served with an herb sauce. For landlubbers, several choices of char-broiled steaks are offered, as well as chicken, pork, and a grilled duck breast with bigarade orange sauce (entrées $13–19). Caesar salad with lobster meat can make a meal for $11.95. Lobster stew is also on the menu. Open nightly for dinner in-season.

♦ **Carriage House** (207-633-6025), Route 96, East Boothbay. "Not a bad place to bring friends since May, 1987" reads the menu for this venerable restaurant on the east side of the Boothbay region. George Bourette, the owner, really did find an old carriage house on the local hospital grounds that he transported here. The place is not on the water, but nautical references and paraphernalia abound—portholes, a bar made out of a dory and called the S.S. *Belly Up* on the second floor, and even a sign for the fantasy Perch Island Yacht Club. A casual atmosphere prevails, with knotty-pine walls and some booths downstairs; meals are also served in the second-floor bar area. Beloved by locals, the restaurant offers blue-plate specials each evening—BBQ ribs and chicken on Tuesday; roast turkey on Thursday; and fish fry on Friday, for example, at $8.95. In fact, Bar-B-Que Ribs are something of a specialty, with a half order available nightly for $10.95, and a full rack for $16.95. Other entrées include baked or deep-fried haddock dinner, grilled salmon with sour cream dill sauce, fresh fried oysters, and baked seafood Newburg ($13–19 for entrées). All are served with choice of potato, vegetable, salad or coleslaw, and bread. From the charcoal grill come chicken breasts, pork chops, and Delmonico steaks. Pastas and pizzas are also available. And if you're not too hungry, you can have a chicken or fried haddock sandwich, a cheeseburger or no-frills burger, or a grilled portobello and blue cheese sandwich ($7–10). Open year-round for dinner, Tuesday through Saturday 5–9:30. Lunch is served on Thursday, Friday, and Saturday. The place usually closes for 6 weeks in the dead of winter—January to mid-February.

♦ **The Carousel Marina & Restaurant** (207-633-6644), 125 Atlantic Avenue, Boothbay Harbor. This waterfront dining spot with a small deck and chairs outside is another favorite of locals. You find it by turning right directly after the big yellow statue of the fisherman at Brown Brothers Wharf; it's located next door to the Carousel Marina and overlooks the harbor from the east side. There's parking avail-able. "We have the best sunset views," claims Linda Allen, the new chef since the restaurant transformed from the former Cap'n. Groovy's. The large space with bar toward the rear is surrounded by huge glass windows, and views of waterfront activi-ty are available from many tables and booths. There are also outdoor umbrellaed tables. At lunch you'll find hamburgers, hot dogs, and sandwiches like turkey, bacon, and avocado, along with clam chowder and French onion soup. For dinner seafood reigns, with creamed haddock (a Dijon cream sauce) and Carousel had-dock (broiled, with a sherry crabmeat cream sauce) two popular favorites. Black Angus tenderloin and—on Friday and Saturday—prime rib are also available. Entrées range $10–19. Desserts include a five-layer chocolate cake with local ice cream; bourbon bread pudding; and tiramisu. Open year-round, lunch 11–3:30, dinner 5–9. A light bar menu is also available. Days and hours may be somewhat limited off-season. The restaurant takes a month off in the dead of winter.

♦ **Andrews' Harborside Restaurant** (207-633-4074), at the footbridge, Boothbay Harbor. From its signature plate-sized cinnamon rolls at breakfast to Maine blueberry cobbler after dinner, Andrews' provides satisfying and popular fare in the center of the downtown area. There's sort of a view of the water, but you must look past a crowded parking lot to enjoy it. Craig Andrews opened here in the mid-1970s and has provided breakfast, lunch, and dinner in-season ever since. Three-egg omelets, pancakes, French toast, and spinach quiche are also on the breakfast menu, served 7:30–11. Lunch kicks in at 11:30 and goes until 2:30 with lobster stew ($7.25 cup, $14.25 bowl), Maine crabcake sandwich, fried sea scallops with fries and coleslaw, salads, and traditional sandwiches. A crab roll is $8.95. At dinner, 5:30–8:30, you might start with steamers or a fried shrimp cocktail, opt for a lobster and crab salad platter ($21.95), or try house specialties like stuffed haddock with seafood Newburg, broiled haddock, or chicken pie ($14–22).Finish up with Granny's Apple Crisp, hot fudge sundae cake, or lemon cake pudding with raspberry sauce. Wine and beer are served. Open daily for breakfast, lunch, and dinner from mid-May to mid-October.

♦ **Lobsterman's Wharf** (207-633-3443), off Route 96, East Boothbay. What can be better than sipping a cold brew, slurping steamed clams, and sitting at a red picnic table amid boatbuilding shops overlooking the harbor? This is our favorite lobster pound in the Boothbay area, although there are many others. It's fun to watch small boats tie up at the float and boaters climb up to the open deck out back for their meals. The immaculately cared-for restaurant also has indoor dining in booths and at tables in a nautically inspired dining room. At lunchtime you'll find steamed clams or mussels, scallops wrapped in bacon, deep-fried artichoke hearts, and crabcakes as appetizers. Clam chowder, lobster stew, spinach salad, a grilled blackened tuna Caesar salad all beckon. You can get a lobster club sandwich, crab roll, hamburgers, or a shore dinner. In the evening the same options are available, to which are added entrées like baked fillet of sole on spinach, covered with tomatoes and cheddar cheese; lazy lobster over linguine; salmon fillet with hollandaise sauce and sirloin steak; or veal Piccata (entrées $15–25). There's a full bar and a convivial feeling here. Open 11:30 to 9 or 10 daily mid-May to mid-October. Dinner starts at 5.

♦ **Cabbage Island Clambake** (207-633-7200). This sounds like fun. Altogether you devote 4 hours to a real Maine clambake on an island, beginning with a half-hour boat trip. Then you get to watch lobsters and steamers prepared in seaweed at water's edge. Depending on weather, the clambakes are offered daily between late June and Labor Day weekend. Reservations are a must. $39.95 per person.

♦ **Picnic fare.** Get excellent sandwiches and goodies for picnics at the **Blue Moon Café** in downtown Boothbay Harbor on Commercial Street. You can also eat there, with a view of the water. Or pick up a good sandwich at the **East Boothbay General Store.** Hankering for a hot dog? **Brud's hot dog cart** has been a fixture in town for more than 50 years. Sweet tooth? Stop in at **P&P Pastry Shop** on McKown Street in the downtown area for delectable pastries.

19 Canterbury Shaker Village and Other New England Shaker Sites

Canterbury Shaker Village in Canterbury, New Hampshire, was home to an active community of Shakers—formally known as the United Society of Believers in Christ's Second Appearance—for 200 years. It was the 6th of 19 self-contained communities to be formed by the Shakers, a Utopian society organized by a young English immigrant, Ann Lee, in the 1770s.

Amazingly, Ann Lee started with but seven followers, and Shakerism, at its height, numbered 6,000 members. What is it about this spiritual, celibate society that fascinates us so? In an age of sexual freedom, are we simply amazed that people could survive, even thrive, without it? In this time of stressful living, do we look at these peaceful, removed communities and long for their quiet? Do we simply love the products: the clean lines of the furniture, the beauty of the architecture, the healthfulness of the foods?

At Canterbury, followers of Shaker beliefs came together on the farm of Benjamin Whicher as early as 10 years before the community's official founding. The first building on the hilltop site was erected in 1792. Precisely two centuries later, in 1992, the last Canterbury Shaker, Sister Ethel Hudson, died in her room in the Dwelling House at the age of 96.

Believers reached a national strength—with communities extending from Maine to Kentucky—by the mid–19th century. Eleven of these Shaker villages were in New England. Only one active Shaker community remains today. It is at Sabbathday Lake, Maine, where a small band of Shakers work and worship.

Canterbury Shaker Village is one of the best Shaker sites to visit in order to get a sense of the society and how its members spent their time. At its height in the 1850s, It was home to 300 Shakers, men and women who lived in community under what they believed to be a mother/father God.

Shakers took their name from their frenzied dances while worshiping, and for their origins in Quakerism (actually they were called "shaking Quakers"). They are considered by far the most successful experiment in Utopian living in America ever.

The Shakers believed in Christianity, pacifism, communal living, equality of

The Dwelling House with Revere bell tower at Canterbury Shaker Village men and women and of the races, and celibacy. People often assume it was the last that brought about their demise. Undoubtedly it played a part. But the industrial revolution was probably more impacting. Men then left the farm and craft communities in droves to take jobs in mills.

Canterbury Shakers, like Shakers everywhere, attempted to create a community that was "heaven on earth." Each village had a spiritual name in addition to its everyday name. Canterbury's was *Holy Ground.* Meetinghouse colors in all Shaker communities were white walls and blue trim, believed to be "celestial colors." On Sunday the public, or the "World's People," were invited to attend services, sitting on benches placed around the perimeter of the room. The Shakers danced, sang, and professed their beliefs in somewhat elaborate dances in the center of the room.

The founder of the Shakers, Ann Lee, died in 1784 while her group of followers was still small. It was Joseph Meacham of Enfield, Connecticut (site of another Shaker community), who—with female leader Lucy Wright—fashioned the loose band of believers into a well-ordered society.

Although they themselves did not procreate, the Shakers grew as a religious sect when unmarried adults, or even whole families, joined up. It wasn't a bad life in a pre-industrial society where jobs and financial security were uncertain. The Shakers took in and educated orphans or children of single-parent or poor families when asked to do so. The children were brought up lovingly and educated well. They could stay or leave when they reached adulthood.

"It was a very secure way of life," says Scott Swank, current director of Canterbury Shaker Village.

Following Mother Ann Lee's motto, "Put your hands to work and your hearts to God, and benefits will befall thee," the Shakers lived a life of industry and simplicity. They dressed alike. The men often wore pants of blue, long vests of deeper blue, stout shoes, and gray stockings. They usually wore broad-brimmed hats. The women wore a white or drab dress and, over their neck and busts, white kerchiefs. They wore white caps on their heads.

Members rose early in the morning, ate when summoned by a bell, and went to daylong tasks separated by gender. Men farmed the land, raising crops and livestock and overseeing a rather large dairy herd, ran the mills (seven in Canterbury), chopped wood, constructed buildings, made brooms, and packaged seeds and medicinal herbs. These would be sold to the World's People to help sustain the community financially. Women cooked, did the laundry, made baskets, taught the children. Young girls were raised by their Shaker "mothers"; boys, by their Shaker "fathers." The community had its own infirmary and dentist. If a Shaker man or woman required surgery, leaders did not hesitate to authorize bringing in a surgeon from the outside world to operate.

The Shakers made furniture that is known the world around for its simplicity of design, usefulness, and comfort. In Canterbury they did not actually sell furniture, as in some other communities. Here the Shakers had a large textile business. They made and sold Shaker cloaks (the wife of President Grover Cleveland wore one to his 1885 inauguration) as well as sweaters. They even loomed "letter sweaters" for college students. The selling of medicinal herbs was also very important. Canterbury's famed Syrup of Sarsaparilla, developed by Dr. Thomas Corbett, a

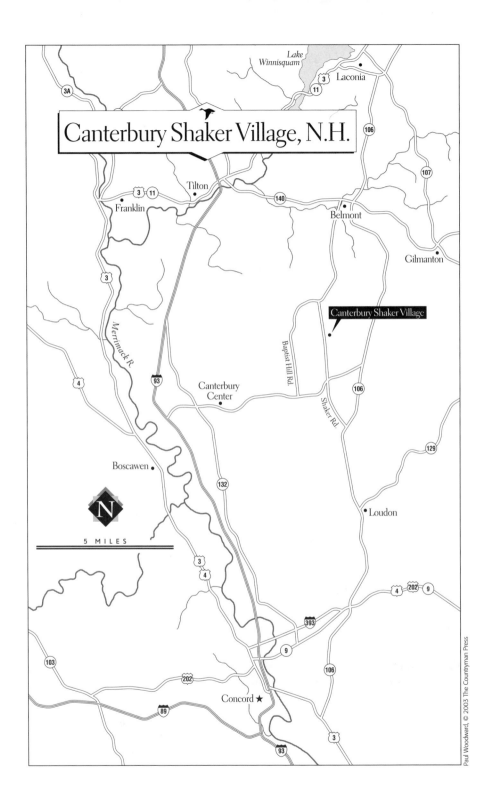

Canterbury Shaker Village, N.H.

Lake Winnisquam

Laconia

Tilton

Franklin

Belmont

Gilmanton

Canterbury Shaker Village

Merrimack R.

Baptist Hill Rd.

Canterbury Center

Shaker Rd.

Boscawen

N
5 MILES

Loudon

Concord ★

Shaker, was said to cure no fewer than 10 illnesses including "jaundice, indigestion, and chronic eruptions of the skin."

The Shakers were always searching for better ways of doing things. They did not eschew modern inventions. Shakers are credited with the invention of the flat broom and circular saw; they were the first to package garden seeds. The drying racks for clothes in the laundry at Canterbury alone are amazing. The community secured the rights to manufacture an industrial washing machine that they then sold to hotels, hospitals, colleges, and other large institutions.

Like other Shaker communities, Canterbury experienced a severe decline in numbers after the Civil War and especially prior to the turn of the past century. One community after another closed. At Canterbury, a Shaker sister—seeing that the end was in sight—incorporated the remaining land and buildings as a museum in the late 1960s. Canterbury is a rare Shaker site that was never out of Shaker hands, passing directly to museum status.

These days Canterbury Shaker Village is once again growing—as a museum. A major restoration effort has made the four-story Dwelling House structurally safe for visitors. With its Revere bell tower, it dominates the village. It is the only Shaker dwelling in public hands embodying two centuries of unbroken Shaker habitation. A new Visitor Education Center—built on the foundation of the old horse barn/distribution center—opened in fall 2001. The Millennium Campaign to raise funds for this new spurt of activity will fund the restoration of other buildings and the gardens. The hope is, that when completed, "the public will enter for the first time a Shaker environment of unique intimacy" according to a campaign description. It is already a wonderful place.

Getting There

Canterbury Shaker Village is located a few miles northeast of Concord, New Hampshire, in the approximate center of the state. Take Exit 18 off I-93 and follow the signs to Canterbury Shaker Village—about 7 miles from the exit. It's well signed. The village itself is set high on a hill, surrounded by fields and stone walls.

The closest major **airport** is at Manchester, New Hampshire.

For More Information

♦ **Canterbury Shaker Village** (603-783-9511; www.shakers.org), Canterbury, NH 03224.

VISITING CANTERBURY

The village is open daily May through October, 10–5, and weekends in April, November, and December, 10–5. Admission, $10 adult, $5 children. Guided tours are offered on the hour. These usually include visits to 3 or 4 of the 23 buildings on site. In addition, several buildings are open for self-visitation. Changing displays are mounted in the new Visitors Center, and there is museum space above the large Gift Shop. Traditional Shaker crafts demonstrations are generally given daily in one or two of the buildings.

The buildings you see in Canterbury were used by the Church Family. (Each community included several different self-sufficient "families.") They are simple white-clapboard structures, grouped comfortably close together with fields and gardens all around. Although now empty of Believers, the buildings seem friendly and welcoming. Visitors seem to lower voices instinctively and move quietly as if they are, indeed, on holy ground.

The huge **Laundry** at Canterbury is fascinating. This is where clothes and linens for the entire community were washed, ironed, and distributed back to the originating spot by an ingenious system of lettering and numbering for buildings and rooms. Huge drying racks on tracks were pulled out from the wall to hang clothes. When the racks were pushed back into place, the items dried quickly by steam heat. Young girls being raised by the Shakers would come to the laundry after school to have cookies and milk; it was then their job to distribute the baskets of fresh laundry.

The first **Meeting House,** dating from 1792, is a plain space with two identical doors for entering—one used by the men and the other by women. Here a guide usually explains Shaker spiritual beliefs and dancing.

A larger winter meeting room was incorporated into the four-story **Dwelling House** as a later addition and was used in cold weather. That Dwelling House, with its distinct red-roofed cupola, is open to the public after several years of restoration. Instead of returning the building to one particular era, it is seen as it would have appeared at various points through the years.

The children raised by the Shakers studied at the **Schoolhouse.** Blackboards with original writings by Shaker sisters have been covered with Plexiglas to protect them. Visitors can sit at desks and learn of Shaker teaching styles. Shaker schools were often considered among the best in their area; non-Shaker children sometimes attended. Other buildings at Canterbury include the **Sisters' Shop** of 1817, a textile workshop; a **Horse Barn** with horse-drawn vehicles; and extensive vegetable and herb gardens. There is a **Bakery** where goodies like molasses cookies are baked and can be purchased, and the **Syrup Shop** where the medicinal syrup production took place. A short walk or drive north on the main road brings you to the **graveyard,** with one single tombstone reading SHAKERS. Individual headstones were banned early on because the Shakers wanted to be in death as they were in life: not individuals as much as part of a community.

The **Sowing Spirit Trail** is a half-mile route through the gardens and part of the village, with a beautifully written discussion of Shaker life in the explanatory brochure. It can be picked up at the village.

The **Creamery** restaurant offers delicious lunches between 11:30 and 2:30 on days when the village is open (see *Where to Eat*). Dinners are offered on Friday and Saturday evenings and are a special event. On Saturday they are preceded by a 1-hour village tour. Reservations for the Shaker dinners must be made by calling the village ahead of time (603-783-9511).

Workshops and Events

Canterbury Shaker Village is a lively place. Workshops in traditional Shaker crafts are held frequently throughout the year and range from "stone wall building" to "oval box making" and "baking herbal breads." These change annually, and it's important to get a schedule ahead and also to register in advance. Most workshops are offered on Saturday and Sunday.

Special events are held throughout the season and are often on Saturday. These include Family Memory Day in May; an Herb and Garden Day in June; Mother Ann Day close to the foundress's birthday in early August (with Mother Ann Cake served); Wool Day in September; Harvest Day in October; and a Canterbury Craft Festival in November. All events are subject to change, and new ones are sometimes added.

Local Craftspeople

Canterbury probably attracts more high-level artisans to its environs than any other Shaker site in New England. Many of the wares—but not all—are carried in the excellent Gift Shop at the village. Here you can purchase Shaker-style furniture, oval boxes, brooms, books on Shakers, cards with Shaker sayings, and other compatible items like handmade pottery. Some craftspeople in the area open their homes/studios/shops to the public, but not all. A listing of some of the fine artisans now working in the Shaker tradition, as well as a couple of local shops that are complementary to the Shaker way of life and work, follows. Some craftspeople are difficult to locate, on back roads that are not well marked. Enjoy the adventure and call to make an appointment (asking for clear directions) if you are seriously interested in seeing a certain artisan's work.

♦ **David H. Lamb, Cabinetmaker** (603-783-9912), 228 Shaker Road, Canterbury, NH 03224. Fine furniture in the Shaker design and traditional American styles are made by this top craftsman. He is often scheduled many months ahead and sees people only by appointment. There is no public showroom.

♦ **North Woods Chair Shop** (603-783-4595), 237 Old Tilton Road, Canterbury, NH. The Shaker-style chair hanging upside down on a peg on a building across the road is a sign that you have reached the home of Brian Braskie and Lenore Howe. Brian makes beautiful wood pieces—not only chairs—in the Shaker style. Samples are on display in their home, and Brian will also fabricate pieces to order.

♦ **Cindi L. Bailey, Ash Baskets** (603-783-9001), Carter Hill Road, Canterbury, NH 03224. Cindi's handmade baskets are sold at the village gift shop.

♦ **Shaker Pine Crafts Center** (603-783-4403), 418 Shaker Road, Canterbury, NH 03224. This barnlike shop is close to the village and has two somewhat cluttered showrooms. David Emerson is the top craftsman, who works with apprentices to make small furniture pieces, boxes, and wooden toys.

♦ **Canterbury Woodworks, Steve Allman,** Shaker Road, Canterbury, NH 03224. Allman is a fine craftsman who only sells his work (oval boxes and accessories) through the Canterbury Shaker Village shop.

♦ **Olde House Smoke House** (1-800-339-4409), 335 Briar Bush Road, Canterbury, NH 03224. Matthew Bush offers a wide variety of country-smoked products, including ham, bacon, turkey breast, beef, and several varieties of cheese and almonds. The smokehouse is located on a dirt road off another dirt road north of the Shaker village. Next door is an **antique radio museum**, the large collection of Matthew's father, and absolutely fascinating. Don't miss it.

♦ **Hackleboro Pottery and Quilts** (603-783-4079), 376 Hackleboro Road, Canterbury, NH 03224. Traditional cobalt-blue decorated stoneware (some in Shaker motifs) and quilted wallhangings are offered by Kate Goegel. Open weekends only.

WHERE TO STAY

Small bed & breakfast inns seem appropriate as part of a Shaker experience, and there are two fine options in nearby Loudon. We wish there were more. Many visitors stay in larger inns or chain motels in Concord. Canterbury Shaker Village contemplates opening its own on-site B&B in the future.

♦ **Wyman Farm** (phone and fax 603-783-4467), 22 Wyman Road, Loudon, NH 03307. Judith Merrow opens her 200-year-old home on a hilltop to those lucky enough to get a reservation. Three charming rooms, all with private bathroom and separate sitting room or area, are offered. The largest has a bedroom with queen canopy bed, a full bathroom with old tin bathtub encased in wood, plus a shower, and a large fireplaced parlor (the fireplace is filled with candles). This room has a beautiful blue-and-rose Oriental-style rug as well as a collection of cranberry glass. Our room had a queen canopy bed, in-room sink, small lavatory with stall shower, and separate sitting room overlooking the back meadow. The smallest accommodation is a twin-bedded room with shower-bath and compact sitting area. Antiques and Oriental rugs make the rooms especially attractive. All have TV. A full breakfast is served at one large table in a dining room at the far end of this 18th-century add-on house—once Judith's grandmother's—where we had bowls of fresh fruit, pancakes with bacon, juice, muffins, and hot beverages. A screened-in gazebo on the property is filled with wicker, and our hostess brought us a tea tray with fruit and cookies there in the afternoon. Open year-round. Doubles, $60–90, including state tax.

♦ **Lovejoy Farm Bed and Breakfast** (603-783-4007; 1-888-783-4007; fax 603-783-8389; www.lovejoy-inn.com), 268 Lovejoy Road, Loudon, NH 03307. Art Monty and Rena Samard offer comfortable accommodations in a 1790 Georgian Colonial that Art almost single-handedly renovated, plus an attached carriage house with several more guest rooms. Altogether eight guest rooms with private bath are offered. Three in the main house are somewhat more formal, with antique furnishings. Two have a working fireplace. Guests have the use of two parlors in the main inn, one more like a family room off the large kitchen, and the other, filled with traditional furnishings. You can watch TV there. The Lovejoy Suite in the main inn is especially pretty with queen bed with fishnet canopy, braided rugs on painted floors, and a good-sized bathroom with double sink. Carriage House rooms range in size up to a large suite accommodating six people in single beds with two bathrooms. A full breakfast is served in a pretty blue dining room with working fireplace. Queen Anne chairs are set about a large mahogany table. Doubles, $89–99 except big NASCAR race weekends at the nearby Loudon track. Then the rates jump to about $130 with 2-night minimums. Open April 1 to early January.

♦ **Centennial Inn** (603-227-9000; 1-800-267-0525; www.someplacesdifferent.com), 96 Pleasant Street, Concord, NH 03301. This Civil War–era brick building with turrets and impressive woodwork throughout was taken over by the Canadian hotel group Someplaces Different, completely renovated, and opened in 1997 with 32 guest rooms. All of the beautiful woodwork in the lobby area and public rooms was restored to its original sheen. Wallpapers are smashing, many with large floral prints or designs. I don't know why hallways are so dark, but the guest rooms are brighter and well appointed with king or queen bed, TV in an armoire, phone, comfortable sitting area, and private bath with tub-shower combination. Rooms located in the rounded turret areas have extra space and, sometimes, private porches. A well-regarded dining room (see *Where to Eat*) is a plus. Full breakfasts are included. Doubles, $139–250.

♦ **Comfort Inn** (603-226-4100; 1-800-228-5150; fax 603-228-2106), 71 Hall Street (Exit 13 off I-93), Concord, NH 03301. This member of the national chain is nicely located, well kept, and has certain amenities such as an indoor pool and fitness room that are especially appealing. The 100 rooms have two double beds or one king, TV, phone, and private bath. There are even a couple of whirlpool suites available. A complimentary continental breakfast is served in an attractive breakfast area off the main lobby. Doubles, $59–179.

WHERE TO EAT

♦ **The Creamery** (603-783-9511), Canterbury Shaker Village, Canterbury. The restaurant on the grounds of the Shaker village is one of the best around. Lunch is served at four long tables set with low-backed Shaker taped chairs. This is much more than your average sandwich and soft-drink spot. Pitchers of Shaker spiced grape drink are set out on the tables; if you want to have some, you pay for your first glass and refills are free. Clam chowder, gazpacho, and chilled minted strawberry soup were available as starters on the summer day we visited. Entrées are a mix of Shaker foods and others, including applewood-smoked farm ham served as a sandwich or as part of a hot plate with baked beans and brown bread. Also offered were smoked pork ribs; a vegetarian dish of assorted vegetables with penne pasta; and a shrimp salad. You can get sandwiches such as a lamb-burger, meat loaf sandwich topped with smoked Gruyère cheese, or grilled chicken salad. Desserts made on site change daily and included a pecan raisin torte, brownie à la mode, and chocolate cheesecake when we visited. Entrées, $7–10. Open 11:30–2:30 on days the village is open. **Friday and Saturday dinners** at the Creamery are served during the summer and fall to as many as 48 people who make reservations in advance. The four-course candlelight dinners begin at 6:45 PM. On Saturday they are preceded by a 1-hour tour from 5:30 to 6:30. Three entrées are offered—possibly a roast half duckling with pecan and thyme sauce; steamed sole with roasted red pepper cream sauce; or braised veal osso buco. A soup (cream of mushroom, perhaps) is a starter, followed by a salad of greens grown in the village garden. With the entrée come vegetables. Dessert might be a strawberry and cream cheese tart or an almond cream apple tart. Beer and wine are available in the evening. The price is $32 for a four-course meal with taxes and gratuities included on Friday. On Saturday, when the tour precedes dinner, the prix fixe is $40.

♦ **Angelina's** (603-228-3313; www.angelinasrestaurant.com), 11 Depot Street, Concord. Richard Dennison, a graduate of Johnson & Wales University in Providence, is the chef-owner at this attractive little Italian bistro on the lower level of a storefront on a side street. Diners enter from the back into a room with rosy pink-painted brick walls, black bentwood chairs, white-clothed tables, and burgundy napkins. "It's meant to look like a little place in the North End of Boston," says the owner, and it does. Dennison, a native of Concord, dishes up antipasti such as sea scallops wrapped in prosciutto and topped with crumbled Gorgonzola, or mussels simmered in a spicy marinara sauce ($4–10). Pastas include penne Bolognese, Angelina's Primavera (fettuccine, angel hair, or penne served with garden-fresh vegetables), and shrimp and scallops limone, sautéed with plum tomatoes and scallions and served with a lemon butter. Veal in various guises (Marsala, Piccata, saltimbocca, Cassanova, parmigiana) are on the entrée menu, along with chicken Francese, osso buco, and eggplant Romana ($13–18). Desserts, perhaps tiramisu, are made here. There is a full bar. Reservations are a good idea on weekend nights. Open for lunch Monday through Friday 11:30–2, dinner Monday through Saturday from 5.

♦ **The Barley House** (603-228-6363; www.TheBarleyHouse.com), 132 North Main Street, Concord. Across from New Hampshire's attractive gold-domed State House, this restaurant is a natural for pols who prefer to make their deals over a good ale or beer. A former brew master is one of the owners and at least a dozen beers are on tap, including Warsteiner Pilsner and Redhook Hefe Weizen, an unfiltered wheat ale with a rich, creamy texture according to the menu. Hard ciders and a host of other beers in bottles, including La Fin du Monde, make this one of the savviest brew restaurants in the Northeast. To go with the beer, you can get appetizers like spinach dip with chips; "bangers" and mustard; and "Biggie Fries," large-cut potatoes deep-fried and served with bacon bits, cheddar, and ranch dressing. (Leave the diet at home.) Burgers and sandwiches such as an Irish whiskey steak sandwich served open faced are offered. From 5 PM entrées include New England fish stew, New Orleans jambalaya, vegetable lasagna, and honey chipotle glazed salmon ($10–16). The large place sprawls over two storefront spaces and has dark wood booths and tables, wood floors, and sponge-painted yellow walls. There are café tables out front on Main Street in nice weather. Wine is offered along with the brews. Open daily except Sunday from 11 AM to about 10.

♦ **Centennial Inn** (603-225-5301), 96 Pleasant Street, Concord. The Franklin Pierce dining room at this big center-of-town redbrick inn is the place to go for a special occasion. It's quite a formal space, with white tablecloths and wood slat-backed chairs. Original wood moldings and wood-enclosed fireplaces enhance the room. At lunchtime you might try chef's salad or grilled fajita chicken salad; a Philly cheese sandwich or a Reuben; or an entrée such as vegetarian pasta or baked scrod ($7–11). Starters at dinner include wild rice pecan spring rolls, shrimp and scallop seviche, and lobster ravioli ($7–9). Baby spinach and arugula salad with raspberry balsamic vinaigrette is one of the special salads. Entrées ($17–22) might be veal medallions sautéed with shiitake mushrooms and shallots and served with a stuffed artichoke bottom and basmati rice; or a seafood medley pan-sautéed in a Chardonnay herb cream sauce. Pork tenderloin is oven roasted with applewood-smoked bacon and served with a raspberry Chambord sauce and Yukon gold pota-toes. The inn serves lunch Monday through Friday and dinner nightly from 5:30. Sunday brunch is served except in July and August.

♦ **Makris Lobster & Steak House** (603-225-7665; www.lobster-makris.com), Route 106, Concord. East of the city not far from the big NASCAR racetrack in Loudon is a local favorite, a restaurant with a huge bar, outdoor porches, and several inside dining rooms that seem always to be packed. The atmosphere is casual—Formica-topped tables with captain's chairs. You can get almost anything on the all-day menu, from a good BLT (my dinner one night) to lobster prepared many ways. The literature says they'll ship lobsters anywhere; the owners of the restaurant also oper-ate a retail seafood store. The menu is large, with everything from shrimp cocktail or stuffed mushroom caps to start, to chowders (seafood, clam) and stews (oyster, lobster). Salads include chef's, cobb, and asparagus. Scallops, swordfish, haddock, crab, and salmon are all on the seafood menu. Prime sirloin, filet mignon, prime rib, and New York shell steak are among the items for "beef lovers." My husband found the small-sized prime rib plentiful and just rare enough. There's pasta, too, and a refrigerator case filled with pies, puddings, and cakes for dessert. Entrées, $10–15. Open daily from 11 AM to 9 or 10.

♦ **The Common Man** (603-228-DINE), Exit 13 off I-93, Concord. The newest member of a popular New Hampshire chain—started 25 years ago—opened in 2000 and was off to a roaring start. Early American decor (with just about every item available from a company store in Ashland, New Hampshire, or from smaller shops at the restaurants) features Windsor-style chairs and large round tables in the dining room. Comfortable sofas, chairs, and old sea chests for coffee tables furnish the upstairs lounge. Lighter fare is served in the lounge—salads, sandwiches, chow-ders. While you wait, you can play architect with a tin full of small wood blocks. There's a lighthearted approach to the dining experience complete with New England jokes on tape in the lavatories while you're washing up. For lunch you can have an "oven sandwich" like a "crab feast" or tuna melt; a regular lobster roll, BLT, or meat loaf sandwich; a burger; or salad. Hearty lunches ($8–10) include chicken potpie, macaroni and cheese, and country meat loaf. For dinner try grilled salmon, chicken Kiev, hazelnut-crusted chicken, roast prime rib in four sizes, and that good old country meat loaf. Dinners include salad, fresh-baked bread, vegeta-bles, and potato. Entrées are $11–20.

OTHER SHAKER VILLAGES IN NEW ENGLAND

Of the Shaker villages originally founded in New England, only one remains an active Shaker community. That is **Sabbathday Lake, Maine,** about half an hour northwest of Portland. Other Shaker sites include **Hancock Shaker Village** in Hancock, Massachusetts, with its famous round stone barn, and **Enfield Shaker Museum** in Enfield, New Hampshire. There is a single Shaker building on the grounds of **Fruitlands Museums** in Harvard, Massachusetts. Harvard and nearby Shirley, Massachusetts, were the locations for Shaker villages, and some buildings—especially in Harvard—can still be viewed from the exterior. They are owned privately.

SABBATHDAY LAKE, MAINE

Sabbathday Lake offers the unusual and moving experience of participating in a Shaker worship service in the 1794 Meeting House every Sunday at 10 AM. The small band of six Shakers at the Sabbathday Lake community lead the assemblage (about 30 when we worshiped on one Sunday in August). The hourlong service consists of readings, testimony, and a cappella singing of Shaker songs. The simplicity of the approach and the warmth of the Shakers and their neighbors are memorable. The Meeting House is located on the main road, Route 26, that cuts through the Shaker village. As is traditional, the interior has white walls with deep blue woodwork. The woodwork has the original paint, in remarkably good condition.
♦ **The Shaker Museum** (207-926-4597; www.shaker.lib.me.us), 707 Shaker Road (Route 26), New Gloucester, ME 04260. Open Memorial Day through Columbus

The Shaker Meeting House at Sabbathday Lake, Maine

Day, Monday through Saturday 10–4:30. Closed Sunday except for the worship service (see above).

Two versions of guided tours (introductory and extended) are offered. The introductory tours are $6 adults, $2 children. Extended tours are $7.50 adults, $2.75 children. The introductory tour takes people into the 1794 **Meeting House,** the 1839 **Ministry Shop,** and through 12 exhibit rooms on the Shaker Way of Life. Those who extend the tour also visit some workrooms in the herb department of the Sisters' Shop and an apple orchard exhibit in the Spinning Shop.

The community at Sabbathday Lake was organized in 1794. The Ricker family, who developed the nearby Poland Spring resort, exchanged land in Alfred, Maine, for acreage down the road from Sabbathday Lake. The Shakers then created a village in Alfred—about an hour distant—as well as the Sabbathday Lake community in New Gloucester. The Poland Spring resort and eventually the industry of bottled water was developed a few miles up the road from the Shaker community.

All Shaker communities developed reputations for particular industries. At Sabbathday Lake the Shakers were known for their herbs, garden seeds, brooms and

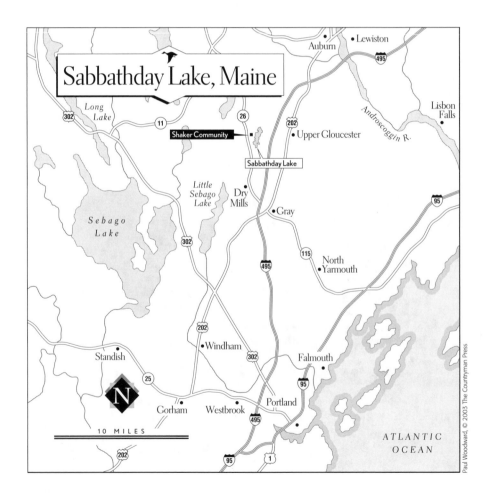

woodenware (including oval boxes, grain measures), and for their lumber. They operated a lumber mill as well as a carding mill (to which local farmers brought wool from their herds of sheep). The Shakers themselves had a small, 36-head herd of dairy cattle, Guernseys and Jerseys, and also kept sheep.

They had a school that was well regarded. The spiritual name for their community was *Chosen Land*.

The Shaker Library. On the property at Sabbathday Lake is an important Shaker research library. It contains more than 100,000 individual items. The collection documents Shakers from all over the United States in the 11 states where they had communities. In the collection are manuscripts including diaries and journals, periodicals, scrapbooks, photographs, an audio-video collection, and an index to more than 15,000 names of people who were, at one time, Shakers. The library is open on Tuesday, Wednesday, and Thursday year-round for research 8:30–4:30. Appointments are required by calling (207) 926-4597.

The **apple orchard** at Sabbathday Lake was important and still is. In fall, three successive Saturdays in late September and early October are designated Apple Saturdays. Visitors can walk through the apple orchard and pick their own apples. There is an apple pie sale. Gifts relating to apples—such as applehead dolls—are sold. Cider and homemade doughnuts are available.

The **Shaker Christmas Fair** at Sabbathday Lake is held on the first Saturday of December annually. It is an extremely popular event. For sale are homemade breads and fruitcake, herb and evergreen wreaths, Shaker herbs, and other gift items.

A Shaker store operates during the season; herbs are sold as well as other Shaker-related items.

During the season, **workshops and craft demonstrations** are scheduled at Sabbathday Lake, usually on Saturday. Topics such as a chair kit assembly workshop, a small bench workshop, a session on planning and planting the garden, chair caning, and culinary skills have been included in recent years. The schedule for the events—taught by Shaker brothers and sisters or by experts in the field—is usually available in early spring. Registration is required, and some workshops fill quickly. The office at Sabbathday Lake remains open year-round, and you can request a brochure and/or registration form at any time. The number to call is (207) 926-4597.

Perhaps the most thrilling part of a visit to Sabbathday Lake is in knowing this is the last place in the world where practicing Shakers still live and work. The half a dozen Believers who are at Sabbathday Lake know that Ann Lee, their foundress, began with a tiny band of seven. They lecture widely and hope for converts. When we visited, two potential members were trying out the life.

WHERE TO STAY

If you want to visit the Shaker community at Sabbathday Lake, you can easily stay in Portland, Maine, less than an hour away; see the "Portland" chapter in this book. Close by—and open from May to October—is the **Poland Spring Inn** (207-998-4351; www.49weekend.com), a 182-room American-plan resort with golf course just a few minutes up the road. However, it restricts stays to 3-day or 5-day packages, including meals. Prices range $100–258 for the 3-day period, per couple.

◆ **Hancock Shaker Village** (413-443-0188; www.hancockshakervillage.org), Route 20, Hancock, Massachusetts 01202. Open mid-May through late October, 9:30–5, for self-guided tours. Adults $13.50, children $5.50, family (two adults and two children) $33. Tickets are valid for 2 consecutive days. Guided tours of selected buildings are available late October to mid-May from 10 to 3. Phone ahead in winter months for tour times. Admission prices, October to May, adults $10, children free. Adults may visit galleries only for $5 in winter.

Famed for its round stone barn, a masterpiece of inventive engineering, Hancock Shaker Village in Hancock, Massachusetts, is an extremely active and well-organized village museum on the site of an important Shaker community. Known as the *City of Peace*, the village was an active Shaker community from 1783 to 1960.

Hancock Shakers were primarily farmers. They had a 3,000-acre farm and a large dairy herd, for which their beautiful stone barn was specifically designed and constructed. These days visitors have a special opportunity to view heritage breeds of livestock at Hancock. These include red Tamworth pigs, Silver Laced and Dominique chickens, wrinkly Merino sheep, and Durham cattle. These specific and unusual breeds represent those kept by the Shakers during their 200 years of farming this land.

Through a collaboration with the New England Heritage Breeds Conservancy, a variety of these special breeds of livestock are pastured in areas outside the village, as well.

Twenty buildings are restored and maintained at Hancock Shaker Village. The 1826 **Round Stone Barn** and the 1830 **Brick Dwelling** are both especially interesting. The village has recently opened the **Laundry/ Machine Shop.** Demonstrations and talks here highlight the use of 19th-century waterpower technology. The engineers in your group will be especially interested in the reproduction 1858 French Wheel water turbine that provides the raw energy to power a lathe and a late-19th-century bandsaw. Hancock Shaker Village is the only Shaker site with an operating water turbine system.

Visitors experience late-19th-century education in a one-room country schoolhouse. Among the most recent of the village's first-person programs to be put into place, the **reproduction 1820 schoolhouse** is brought to life with lessons taught by a costumed

The Deaconess' Room in the 1830 brick dwelling at Hancock Shaker Village

© M. Fredericks, courtesy Hancock Shaker Village

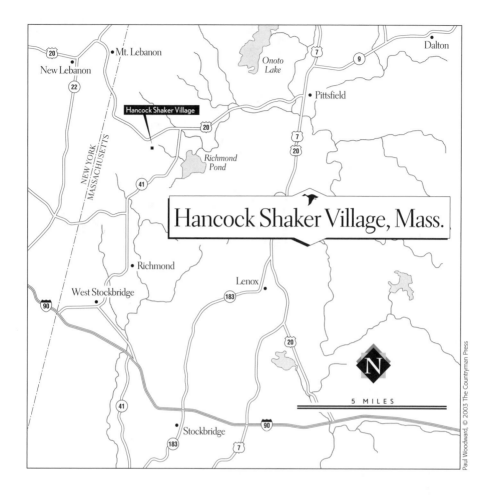

Hancock Shaker Village, Mass.

5 MILES

Paul Woodward, © 2003 The Countryman Press

staff person portraying a Shaker schoolteacher. Visitors use quill pens and slate boards to prepare lessons; recess means playing games of the period.

Hancock houses the largest collection of Shaker artifacts available to the public at an original Shaker site. More than 10,000 objects are owned—and the majority on display—in the historic buildings in this rural setting.

Among the riches at Hancock are a collection of "gift drawings"—spiritual artwork drawn by the Shakers and believed to be received as a gift from God. The Shaker Tree of Life design is probably the most famous of these, but there are many others, and several are usually on display.

At Hancock you go on your own and at your own pace. This has particular appeal for those traveling with children or with older family members. You can select what you want to see and stop and rest when you feel like it.

Several heirloom vegetable and seed gardens representing different periods in Shaker history as well as a demonstration herb garden with 100 different herbs grown and utilized by the Shakers for cooking and medicinal purposes are of particular interest.

Tours of the Round Stone Barn and of the Brick Dwelling are offered several times during the day. The kitchen at the 1830 Brick Dwelling is especially interesting—and was state-of-the-art when it was built.

Arts and crafts of the Shakers are demonstrated by various specialists, including blacksmiths, furniture makers, oval box makers, and broom makers. In the 1874 **Ministry Shop** basket makers create Shaker-style baskets.

Many Shaker wares—from boxes to furniture to clothing—are for sale in the excellent gift shop at the Hancock Shaker Village. It is open during village hours.

The 1830 brick dwelling at Hancock Shaker Village

A café on site offers breakfast and lunch items—salads, sandwiches, beverages, and light fare.

Shaker Harvest Dinners are offered on several Saturday evenings in September and October. These offer a wonderful opportunity to experience the village in a more intimate and detailed way. The evening begins with a brief tour of three or four buildings, is followed by dinner in the dining room of the Brick Dwelling, with Shaker foods featured, and ends with entertainment—sometimes singing of Shaker songs and sometimes demonstrations of Shaker dances. The per-person cost is $40. Reservations are required; call (413) 443-0188.

Events at Hancock

Hancock Shaker Village has an ambitious schedule of special events. They include the following, but new ones crop up all the time.

February—A Winter Weekend with hands-on ice harvesting, sleigh rides, crafts demonstrations, and an opportunity to visit the village's buildings.

April—Plowing Day, as fields are prepared for planting.

May—Sheep and wool weekend with an opportunity to see the entire sheep-to-shawl process of hand shearing, spinning, weaving, dyeing, and so on.

July—Major crafts show.

August—The Hancock Shaker Village Antiques Show—one of the most widely attended events of the year, held at the Round Stone Barn.

September—A barn dance and country auction. Also a country fair and crafts festival.

December—Community Christmas at Hancock Shaker Village.

Nearby—Another Shaker Site

Just down the road on Route 20 west of Hancock Shaker Village is the Darrow School, a private school on the grounds of what was the former Mount Lebanon Shaker community. Just over the line in New York State, this was the lead Shaker community of all, and Shakers were required to visit annually. Although most of the buildings are used by the school and not open to the public, there is a movement afoot to preserve and open more of the Shaker buildings. Just riding through the campus is a treat, however. Look for the Shaker buildings. You may be able to walk through the large building once used as the laundry. The Meeting House with its side-by-side entrance doors is quite recognizable.

WHERE TO STAY

♦ **The Inn at Richmond** (413-698-2566; 1-888-968-4748; fax 413-698-2100; www.inn-atrichmond.com), 802 State Road (Route 41), Richmond, MA 01254. A barn removed from the Hancock Shaker Village serves as a horse barn on a section of the property at this luxurious B&B inn. And Jerri Buehler—who owns and manages the inn with her husband, Dan—has used Shaker baskets and oval boxes to decorate. The historic white pillared building is just over 2 miles from Hancock Shaker Village and within easy striking distance, as well, of Tanglewood and other Berkshire cultural attractions. Seven guest rooms and suites and three full housekeeping cottages (rented by the week in summer, and the weekend off-season) comprise the accommodations. All have private bath, queen or king-sized bed, air-conditioning, TV, and telephone. Hair dryers, irons, and ironing boards—in case you want to get into an industrious Shaker mode—are provided. The Nantucket Retreat is a romantic corner room on the second floor with views of the gardens and Berkshire hills. The Victorian Room is furnished with family antiques and heirlooms of the era. It's decorated in aqua and rose hues and has an elegant iron queen-sized bed. Guests enjoy chairs by the reflecting pool outdoors, and hiking nearby trails. The horse barn is used for lessons, and activities there can be observed by inn guests. A full breakfast is included in the rates—possibly Amaretto blueberry French toast or smoked salmon and asparagus frittata. Doubles, $110–325.

See "The Southern Berkshires" chapter for more places to stay and dine in the area.

ENFIELD SHAKER MUSEUM, ENFIELD, NEW HAMPSHIRE

♦ **Enfield Shaker Museum** (603-632-4346; www.shakermuseum.org), 24 Caleb Dyer Lane (Route 4A), Enfield, NH 03748. The museum is open from Memorial Day weekend through the month of October. Hours are Monday through Saturday 10–5, Sunday noon–5. Admission is $7 for adults, $6 seniors, $5 students, and $3 for those aged 10–18. Children under 10 visit free. Take Exit 11 off I-89 to Route 4 east to Route 4A to reach the museum.

The Shaker village at Enfield, New Hampshire—located 12 miles south of Hanover, New Hampshire—was founded in 1793. At their height in the mid-1800s, the Shakers of Enfield controlled 3,000 acres and had three families, the Church family, the North family, and the South family. Located on the shores of beautiful Lake Mascoma, it is the Church family's property—or a portion of it—that is being preserved as a museum today. At this writing seven buildings are owned by the museum organization. Much less extensive than the Shaker villages at Canterbury and at Hancock, the Enfield site is nonetheless interesting, especially for its **1841 Great Stone Dwelling,** which was the largest Shaker building ever built. It has 500 built-in cupboards and 800 built-in drawers. Today it operates as an inn and a restaurant, thereby being the only place in New England where you can actually sleep in a Shaker room and go down to breakfast, as the Shakers would have, to the dining room they used. The inn is open year-round. (See *Where to Stay and Dine*.)

Because the Shakers sold their property in the 1920s to the French missionary order the LaSalettes, there is an unusual mix of structures on the property—some built by the Catholic order. Especially jarring (in Shaker terms) is the 1930 stone chapel with stained-glass windows that adjoins the Great Stone Dwelling Place and connects to it via a covered stone walkway. A trustee of the museum says the site must be viewed as a New England religious site, rather than a pure Shaker historical site. The LaSalette order still operates a Roman Catholic shrine next door to the Shaker site.

The Shakers of Enfield named their property *Chosen Vale*. They made a living through a medicinal business and the sale of herbs from extensive herb gardens—

An unusual Shaker cemetery near Enfield Shaker Village

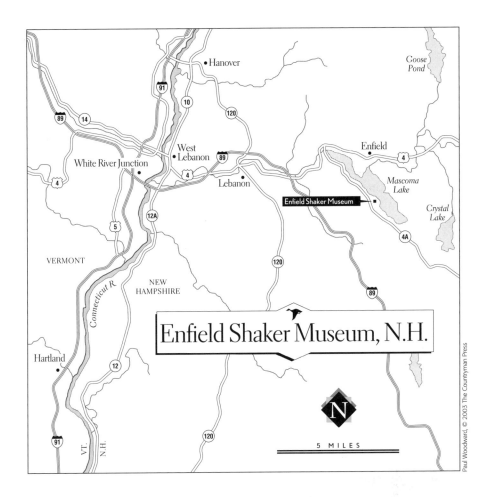

Enfield Shaker Museum, N.H.

N

5 MILES

Paul Woodward, © 2003 The Countryman Press

especially the herb valerian. They sold seeds and made furniture, buckets, tubs, and other fine crafts. They also made long flannel underwear.

The Shakers interacted with the town on the other side of the lake all the time. They built the Shaker Bridge across the center of the lake to make it easier to get to town, where they operated a factory and employed a good number of non-Shakers. Today's bridge is a replacement for the original, but is located on the same site.

Visitors start at the museum building and gift shop. An introductory video is helpful. Shaker artifacts are on display in the museum rooms. Of particular interest is a very graceful Shaker chair known to have been made in Enfield. You can walk around the site, visiting the **Brethren's Shop**—which is not restored, but is used as exhibit space. When we were there, a photography exhibit was on view.

The Great Stone Dwelling House is of great interest. So is **Mount Assurance**—the holy feast grounds of the Enfield Shakers. This is a three-quarter-mile walk uphill to a plateau. Shakers would go to the feast grounds twice a year for a spiritual meeting and celebration. There was once a marble stone carved with words holy to the Shakers in the center of the feast ground. It proclaimed the site a Holy Hill of

Mount Zion, sacred to the true Believers, and was removed when the Shakers ceased outdoor worship in the mid-1800s. Each village had a feast grounds, but many are difficult to reach.

The last eight Shakers of Enfield left the property in 1923 and joined the Canterbury Shaker community to live out their days.

We drove a short distance in search of the unusual Shaker cemetery once belonging to the South family of Enfield. You take a left on Route 4A from the Shaker museum, and drive about a mile to Bassy Lane (across from the Wilson Mobile Home Park). Take a left onto Bassy Lane. On the right, surrounded by a metal wire fence and tucked into a quiet space off the road, we saw three rows of identical headstones, mossy from age. The latest seemed to date from the late 1800s. There were about 40 in all. Each had the name of the person, town of origin, birth and death date. Most Shaker cemeteries have but one single stone, as does the main cemetery for the Enfield site, so this is unusual indeed.

Enfield Shaker Museum conducts workshops and special events. Several evenings of contra dancing were being held in the museum's stone mill one summer. Workshops in basket making, chair taping, and wreath construction were also planned. Call (603) 632-4346 for information or to register.

The gift shop on site has a variety of items, including Shaker books, oval boxes, cards, and other gifts. The booklet *A Walking Tour of Chosen Vale* is useful.

Shaker furniture. Reproduction Shaker furniture—or pieces inspired by Shaker designs—is constructed next door to the museum at **Dana Robes Wood Craftsmen** (603-632-5377). Located in a reproduction Shaker meetinghouse structure, the artisans at the furniture shop turn out chairs, tables, beds, nightstands, armoires, chests, and other handsome pieces. Not all the lovely wood pieces are Shaker in design. This is worth a stop. Weekend woodworking classes in the Shaker tradition are offered by the Robes furniture makers. Call for more information and to register.

WHERE TO STAY AND DINE

♦ **The Shaker Inn at the Great Stone Dwelling** (603-632-7810; www.theshaker-inn.com), Route 4A, Enfield, NH 03748. Here is the place to stay if you want a more in-depth Shaker experience. Owned by the Enfield Shaker Museum, the 24-room inn and restaurant is operated by Historic Inns of New England. It is on the National Register of Historic Places. Guest rooms are on the third and fourth floors (you have to walk up, but staircases are wide). Rooms are very large, as they once accommodated three or four Shaker brothers or sisters. Most have two queen-sized reproduction Shaker-style beds (although a few have one queen bed), two wing chairs and a table, and usually a bookcase with books for reading. Built-in cupboards from the Shaker days are interesting. Simple windowpane quilts cover the beds. Each room has a private bath with tub-shower combination or just a shower. A few have a clawfoot tub. At the end of each hall is a sitting area with Shaker furniture. The halls are exceptionally wide, and there's a simple peacefulness about the place. Open year-round. The **dining room** offers lunch in June, July, and August and dinner nightly in the same room once used by the

Shakers. Entrées ($10–25) range from pan-fried buttermilk chicken breast with Shaker smothered onion sauce to roast rack of lamb and rack of venison. The least expensive item on the menu is a vegetable risotto prepared with Shaker herbs. Doubles, $125–135.

See the "Lake Sunapee" chapter for more places to stay and dine.

20 Camden/Rockland, Maine

In 1876 the lighthouse keeper at Owls Head Light, the entrance to Rockland Harbor in Maine, counted more than 4,000 graceful coastal schooners entering the harbor. Today there are but 16 of these beauties sailing the coast of Maine, but the good news is they've been fitted out for passengers and are going strong. Landlubbers can leave their jobs and lives behind and head out to sea for a 3- or 4-day weekend or even for a full 6-day trip.

Windjammer cruises set out from one of the side-by-side coastal towns of Camden, Rockport, or Rockland. By the time you've reached these three picturesque seaports on Maine's long and interesting shoreline, you are headed Down East. No longer are you flirting with sandy beaches and amusement parks. This is the real thing: the Maine that legends are made of. Foggy mornings and cool nights, the clanging of bell buoys and the groans of fog horns. Lobster boats chug out to sea first thing in the morning, and the delectable crustaceans appear that same night on restaurant menus.

All three towns have impressive harbors. Camden's is probably the most famous, jammed with sailboats and with a small island at its entrance. I am somewhat partial to Rockport, where the harbor can be viewed from high above, set like a dark blue jewel into the shore. Rockland—with a broad waterfront easier for maneuvering—is actually the town from which most of the schooners set out. The windjammers sail the waters of Penobscot Bay, dotted with rock-edged, fir-crowned islands and considered one of the finest sailing grounds in the world. Maine writer Sarah Orne Jewett referred to this part of Maine as "the country of the pointed firs."

Windjamming allows as much or as little activity as you'd like. Snoozing aboard ship on a placid day—and there are plenty of them—is perfectly acceptable. You can also help hoist sails, store equipment, and assist in the galley. Four of us joined forces on one of these trips and all of us helped raise the sails each day. There was time to look for petrels and whales, to get to know our companions, even to steer the ship. I spent some time in the galley, washing salad greens and cutting fruits. We also explored islands where we stopped.

A windjammer under sail

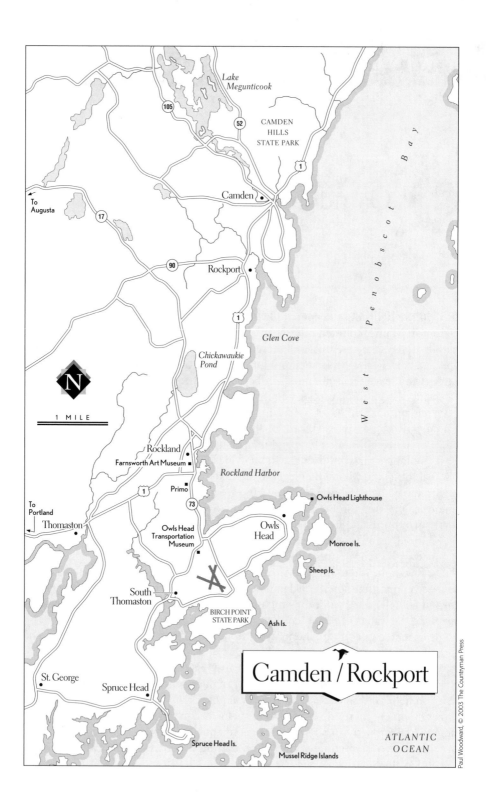

Lake
Megunticook

CAMDEN
HILLS
STATE PARK

105

52

To
Augusta

17

Camden

90

Rockport

1

Glen Cove

Chickawaukie
Pond

N

1 MILE

Rockland

Farnsworth Art Museum

Rockland Harbor

Primo

Owls Head Lighthouse

1

73

To
Portland

Thomaston

Owls Head
Transportation
Museum

Owls
Head

Monroe Is.

Sheep Is.

South
Thomaston

BIRCH POINT
STATE PARK

Ash Is.

St. George

Spruce Head

Camden / Rockport

Spruce Head Is.

Mussel Ridge Islands

ATLANTIC
OCEAN

West

Penobscot

Bay

Back on the mainland, there is much to do. The small inns of Camden are among the best in New England, and fine restaurants are found in the towns. Most emphasize seafood, as fresh as that day's catch. Outdoorsmen and -women are drawn to the hiking, kayaking, sailing, and biking opportunities. Shop-till-you-drop types scarcely can get their fill of small, independent, and interesting boutiques in all three towns, but especially in Camden and Rockland.

The Farnsworth Art Museum in Rockland is a world-class museum with a relatively new Wyeth wing, devoted to the art of three generations of Wyeth artists—N. C., Andrew, and Jamie. Art galleries, especially near the Farnsworth, are fun to poke around in.

Those who prefer a quiet weekend can find it. They might pick up a book in one of the fine independent bookstores in the area to take with them on their sailing adventure or to read at an amiable coastal inn. Early to bed and early to rise is the general rule of windjamming, although staying in bed late can be managed at your on-shore B&B.

The windjammers go out from May to October, a time when this part of Maine is at its busiest. However, this section of the coast remains open through the year. You may want to return for a fireside room and meal, and a toboggan ride down the hills at Camden Snow Bowl in winter.

Getting There

By car: It's a 4-hour drive to Camden/Rockland from Boston. Take Route I-95 north from Boston to Maine, continuing as far as Brunswick (Exit 22). This takes you to Coastal Route 1. Continue north on Route 1 to Rockland, Rockport, and Camden, in that order.

By bus: Concord Trailways (1-800-639-3317) offers service from Boston to Camden and Rockland. Buses leave from downtown Boston or from Logan Airport.

By air: The closest major airport is the **Portland Jetport,** served by many major airlines. From there you can rent a car and drive two hours to Camden/Rockland. Or you can contact **Mid-Coast Limo Service** (1-800-937-2424; www.midcoastlimo. com) to be picked up at the airport and driven to your windjammer or B&B. Rockland has a small airport with connections to Boston via **USAirways Express** (1-800-428-4322).

For More Information

♦ **Camden-Rockport-Lincolnville Chamber of Commerce** (207-236-4404; 1-800-223-5459), P.O. Box 919, Camden, ME 04843. For Rockland, contact the **Rockland-Thomaston Area Chamber of Commerce** (207-596-0376; 1-800-562-2529; www. midcoast.com/~rtacc). The **Maine Windjammer Association,** under whose banner 14 of the 16 windjammers sail, call be reached at 1-800-807-WIND or www.sailmainecoast.com.

The Windjammer Experience

Windjammers are graceful multisailed ships that ply the island-dotted waters of Maine's gorgeous Penobscot Bay. The ships range from 64 to 132 feet in length and take from 10 to 40 passengers plus crew. Windjammer cruises are for people of all ages except infants and small children. Vessels are well maintained and under Coast Guard scrutiny.

Long weekend trips—of 3 or 4 days—have surpassed the weeklong journeys in popularity. You can still find 6-day cruises. They all have certain aspects in common. Passengers are generally free to participate in many aspects, including hoisting sails, taking a turn at the wheel, navigating, or helping out in the galley.

"Schooner-cooked" meals are served family-style and generally are hearty and delicious. That salt air kicks up an appetite! Menu items include fresh seafood, roasts, pastas, garden salads, chowder, and homemade breads and desserts. A lobster bake on a Maine island is featured on every 6-day trip and on many of the shorter cruises as well. Ours took place on a deserted island where we gathered seaweed and driftwood and where our captain showed us how to eat roasted barnacles. It was such a warm day, we also took a swim in chilly Maine water.

Accommodations are simple except on three more luxurious schooners, the **Kathryn B.**, the **Ellida,** and the **Mistress,** most of whose cabins have a private head. On the other boats, the experience is akin to "camping on water" with simple bunk-style berths in cabins for two and a head shared by several. A duffel bag is about all the room there is for gear, so pack lightly. There is a warmwater shower available on all ships—although some are more primitive than others. Ours was rigged on the main deck for people to wash their hair, wearing bathing suits. Only about half of us braved the somewhat public trek to and fro.

Seasickness is usually not a problem because the vessels cruise in protected waters. No one was sick on our 4-day junket.

Windjammer trips usually involve setting sail after breakfast, lunching on board, and stopping at an island late in the afternoon. There's often a chance to explore the island a bit before or after dinner, with passengers taken from the schooner by smaller dinghy. Sometimes the ship will stop at an interesting port in the middle of the day and allow a couple of hours' exploration. Everybody goes ashore for the island lobster bake and helps with the preparations.

Costs range from $395 per person for a 3-day weekend, all expenses included, to $1,500 for 6 days on one of the more luxurious ships. The trips are so popular that many people return again and again. You can get yourself in the mood for all of this by reading the book *Windjammer Watching on the Coast of Maine* by Virginia L. Thorndike.

The Boats

Fourteen of the 16 schooners currently operate under the umbrella of the **Maine Windjammer Association,** a marketing group. Two others go it alone. The toll-free number of the Windjammer Association is 1-800-807-WIND. People there are help-

Spotting other schooners is part of the fun when aboard ship

ful in steering you to a ship that may suit your style. Or you can contact the individual ships and get colorful brochures for planning your trip. It's fun to look them over, check the ship's layout, and plan the adventure. The following ships are members of the Maine Windjammer Association. The others are listed later. The annual **Windjammer Weekend** when the tall-masted ships crowd Camden Harbor is usually held early in September.

♦ *American Eagle* (207-594-8007; 1-800-648-4544; fax 207-594-1001; www.schooner-americaneagle.com), Captain John Foss, P.O. Box 482, Rockland, ME 04841. Built in 1930, this 92-foot schooner can take 26 passengers. The *American Eagle* was built in Gloucester, Massachusetts, and was for 53 years a member of the famed Gloucester fishing fleet before being converted for passengers.

♦ *Angelique* (207-785-3020; 1-800-282-9989; fax 207-785-6036; www.sailangelique.com), Captain Mike and Lynne McHenry, Box 736, Camden, ME 04843. Built in 1980, this 95-foot boat can take 31 passengers. A ketch-rigged ship, she was built for windjamming in 1980 and patterned after the 19th-century sailing ships that fished off the coast of England.

♦ *Grace Bailey, Mercantile,* and *Mistress* (207-236-2938; 1-800-736-7981; fax 207-236-3229; www.mainewindjammercruises.com), Ray and Ann Williamson, Box 617, Camden, ME 04843. The *Grace Bailey* dates from 1882 and was originally engaged in hauling timber and granite, and participating in the West Indian trade until 1940 when she began to carry passengers. She can take 29. The *Mercantile* was built in Little Deer Isle, Maine, in 1916. She carried fish, barrel staves, and firewood until 1942 and can take 29 passengers. Both are listed as national historic landmarks. The *Mistress,* 60 feet long, has three cabins and takes just six passengers. Two cabins have a double bed; one has bunks; all have a private head. Built in 1960, the ship was restored in 1992.

The schooner **Mercantile** cruises among the islands of Penobscot Bay. It is part of the original fleet of windjammers that started carrying passengers in the 1930s.

♦ *Heritage* (207-594-8007; 1-800-648-4544; fax 207-594-1001; www.schonerheritage. com), Captains Doug and Linda Lee, P.O. Box 482, Rockland, ME 04841. This 95-foot schooner was built by her owners in Rockland in 1983. She was built in the tradition of a 19th-century coaster and can take 30 passengers.

♦ *Isaac H. Evans* (207-594-7956; 1-877-238-1325; www.midcoast.com/evans/), Captain Brenda Walker, P.O. Box 791, Rockland, ME 04841. The *Isaac H. Evans* was built in 1886 in Mauricetown, New Jersey. After 85 years as an oyster schooner on Delaware Bay, she joined the windjammer fleet. She is a national historic landmark and can take 22 passengers.

♦ *J. & E. Riggin* (207-594-1875; 1-800-869-0604; fax 207-594-4921; www.riggin.com), Captains Jon Finger and Anne Mahle, 136 Holmes Street, Rockland, ME 04841. Built in Dorchester, New Jersey, in 1927, the schooner won the first and only oyster schooner race ever held on Delaware Bay. A national historic landmark, she takes 24 passengers.

♦ *Lewis R. French* (207-236-9411; 1-800-469-4635; fax 207-236-2463; www.midcoast .com/~windjam/), Captains Dan and Kathy Pease, P.O. Box 992, Camden, ME 04843. Built in 1871 and launched in Christmas Cove, Maine, the 64-foot-long *French* claims to be the oldest documented windjammer in America. For more than a century she freighted fish and bricks. A national historic landmark, her passenger load is 22.

♦ *Mary Day* (207-236-2750; 1-800-992-2218; fax 207-785-5760; www.schoonermary-day.com), Captains Barry King and Jen Martin, P.O. Box 798, Camden, ME 04843. The *Mary Day* was the first windjammer built specifically to carry passengers. That was in 1962. The 90-foot boat can take 29 guests.

♦ *Nathaniel Bowditch* (207-273-4062; 1-800-288-4098; www.windjammervacation. com), Captain Gib and Terry Philbrick, Box 459, Warren, ME 04864. This ship was built as a racing yacht in East Boothbay and won class honors in the Bermuda Race in 1923. The 82-foot-long boat served in the Coast Guard during World War II. She can take 24 passengers.

♦ *Stephen Taber* (207- 236-3520; 1-800-999-7352; fax 207-236-0585; www.stephentaber. com), Captains Ken and Ellen Barnes, 70 Elm Street, Camden, ME 04843. Built as a coasting schooner in Glen Head, New York, in 1871, this 68-foot-long boat is the oldest documented sailing vessel in continuous service in the United States. A national historic landmark, she takes 22 passengers. Her captains also own a handsome B&B, the Capt. Lindsey House, in Rockland.

♦ *Timberwind* (207-236-0801; 1-800-759-9250; fax 207-236-3639; www.schoonertimberwind.com), Captain Rick and Karen Miles, Box 247, Rockport, ME 04856. The *Timberwind*, built in 1931, served as a pilot boat for 38 years before being converted to a cruise schooner in 1969. She has never left Maine waters. She takes 20 passengers.

♦ *Victory Chimes* (207-265-5651; 1-800-745-5651; www.victorychimes.com), Captains Kip Files and Paul DeGaeta, Box 1401, Rockland, ME 04841. Built in 1900 in Bethel, Delaware, to carry lumber along the Chesapeake Bay, the three-masted *Victory Chimes* is the largest passenger schooner in America. She is a national historic landmark and carries 40 passengers.

The following two windjamming schooners are operated independently and take smaller groups of passengers in more luxurious style.

♦ *Ellida* (207-549-3808; 1-888-807-6921; fax 207-549-4519; www.maineclassic-schooners.com), Captain Paul and Kristina Williamson, 178 East Pond Road, Jefferson, ME 04348. This 80-foot-long marconi-rigged schooner was built in 1922 for a wealthy physician. During the Second World War she served as a submarine patrol boat. She takes 10 passengers in five cabins, three with double-bedded accommodations and a private head and sink; the other two cabins have two single bunks, sharing a bathroom. The *Ellida* sails from Rockland. $390–950.

A crew member aboard the **Nathaniel Bowditch** prepares a buffet lunch.

♦ *Kathryn B.* (207-763-4255; 1-800-500-6077; www.kathrynb.com), Captain Gordon and Kathryn Baxter, 391 Hatchet Mountain Road, Hope, ME 04847. Built in the 1990s specifically for passenger cruising, this newest of the windjammers stresses luxurious accommodations and takes just 12 guests in double or queen-bedded cabins, most with a private head and shower. The 105-foot, three-masted schooner sails from Rockland. $695–1,500.

Camden/Rockland, Maine ♦ 439

Exploring the Area

Camden, Rockport, and Rockland are such compelling destinations that passengers on windjammer cruises often allow a couple of extra days at one or the other end of their trips to do a bit of exploring. Stay if you can. Here are area highlights.

Other Boat Trips

If you haven't had your fill of the sea on a windjammer trip, or if you'd like something requiring a little less commitment, there are many ways to get out on the water in the midcoast area. Here are just a few:

Lobster Fishing

♦ The **Lively Lady Too** (207-236-6672) leaves three times a day from the Bay View Landing Wharf in Camden for what is billed as a 2-hour educational trip to see how lobsters are caught. Kids usually find this especially fascinating. Trips head out Monday through Saturday. Adults $20, children $5.

A Daysail

Several schooners take passengers on 2-hour sails from Camden—a good way to test your interest in the sport if you've never sailed. A sail is also a refreshing way to escape a hot day.

♦ The 57-foot **Surprise** (207-236-4687) heads out from the Camden Public Landing on 2-hour trips a few times a day during the summer. The ship was built in 1918 in Gloucester and is on the National Historic Register. Passengers pay $28, which includes refreshments and a color photo of the ship.

♦ The two-masted schooner **Olad** (207-236-2323) heads out from the Public Landing in Camden on 2-hour sails several times daily. The cost is $25 adults, $12 children.

♦ The schooner **Lazy Jack** (207-230-0602) also heads out from the Camden Public Landing. The 1947 schooner has four 2-hour trips a day.

♦ **The North Wind** (207-236-2323) sails at 10 am daily in-season from Rockland Public Landing Middle Pier. A naturalist is on board to help explain how the Maine coast was formed, as well as identify sea life seen on the 2-hour trip. Adults pay $20, children less.

A traditional beachside lobster bake is a highlight of a windjammer cruise.

© Fred LeBlanc, courtesy Maine Windjammer Association

Ferries to the Islands

Regular ferry service is provided between Lincolnville (just north of Camden) to the island of **Isleboro** and from Rockland to the island of **Vinalhaven** year-round. The number to call for Islesboro information is (207) 789-5611; for Vinalhaven, (207) 596-2202. The trip to Vinalhaven is longer—just under 2 hours. Even if you can't spend much time on the island, it is a lovely ride.

Sea Kayaking

One of the largest organizers of sea kayaking trips—and also a fly-fishing school—is **Maine Sport Outfitters** (207-236-9797; 1-800-722-0826) in Rockport. From 1-day trips, such as a tour of Camden Harbor, to several-day trips guides work to get you acclimated to kayaking in the ocean. Call for information and to register.

Lighthouses

Maine has loads of lighthouses—the most of any coastal state in the United States. **Rockland Light** and **Owls Head Light** in the Rockland area are both accessible to walkers and picnickers. Rockland Light can be found just north of Rockland. From Route 1, you follow Samoset Road to the end. The Owls Head Light is north of the Owls Head Transportation Museum (and south of Rockland). This 1825 lighthouse is set atop cliffs, but there are safe trails down one side.

Other Outdoor Activities

♦ **Camden Hills State Park** (207-236-3109), Route 1, Camden. Entrance fee, $2 adults. The poet Edna St. Vincent Millay wrote glowingly of her hometown of Camden, especially the view from Mount Battie, one of the peaks in this beautiful park just north of town. Hikers like to climb it. From the top—reached these days by hiking *or* driving—you get the most glorious view over Camden Harbor, with its sailboats and the (from here) tiny Curtis Island at its mouth. Camden Hills State Park is a 6,500-acre park with picnic area and several other peaks, including Megunticook, Bald Rock, and Ragged Mountain. You can get a printed hiking guide at the entrance. **Campers** can reserve sites at Camden Hills State Park by calling (207) 287-3824 anytime between January 2 and late August. There are 107 campsites, flush toilets, hot showers, a picnic area, and 25 miles of trails. In winter people cross-country ski at Camden Hills, weather permitting.

♦ **Marine Park,** Rockport. This great little waterside park has picnic tables and grills where you can have lunch and enjoy the goings-on. Kayakers often put in from here, and there's boating activity of all sorts. Some restored lime kilns dating from 1817 (and on the National Register of Historic Places) are from the days when processing and exporting lime was a major industry here. At one time Rockport was the nation's third largest producer of lime. There is also a sweet sculpture of Andre the Seal, who took up residence in Rockport Harbor and entertained the crowds on summer afternoons. He died in the late 1980s. This harbor is quieter than that at Camden, a very restful place to read and relax.

The **harbor park** just to the north of Camden Harbor is a great place for enjoying a book, a lunch, and a view of the scenic harbor. There's a lovely manicured slope that leads down to the water, forming an amphitheater where concerts and special events are sometimes held. **Laite Memorial Beach Public Park** out on Bay View Street is a place to be quiet, have a picnic, and maybe stick your toes into the water.

Hiking
Besides Camden Hills State Park, there are several other areas for hiking, including the Tanglewood area in Lincolnville, just north of Camden.

Biking
Bikes can be rented from many places including **Brown Dog Bikes** (207-236-6664) in Camden. Route 1 is a scary place for bikes; better are the back roads and inland routes like 17 and 90.

Scenic Drive
A great drive is the back way from Camden to Rockport (instead of taking Route 1). Follow Bay View to Calderwood; it will bring you into Rockport close to its pretty harbor.

WINTER

You may be inspired to return in winter. If so, here are a few things to keep you busy.

♦ **Camden Snow Bowl** (207-236-4418), John Street, Camden. Ten trails from beginner to expert (although we would say "intermediate") offer great views of Penobscot Bay and the islands from the summit. A double chairlift and two T-bars are available. Snowmaking machines and lighted trails for evening skiing make this little area popular. The only public toboggan chute in Maine is here, also.

♦ **Cross-country skiing.** Ski touring is available on the rolling terrain of the golf course at the Samoset Resort in Rockland. Skiers may also used ungroomed trails at the Tanglewood 4-H Camp in Lincolnville, operated by the University of Maine Cooperative Extension Service.

♦ Cross-country ski lessons and tours are given by **Maine Sports Outfitters** (207-236-8797) in Rockport.

♦ **National Toboggan Championships.** These are held annually at Camden Snow Bowl. The races attract tobogganers from throughout the East and Canada. An annual chili and chowder festival is part of the fun, which also includes horse-drawn sleigh rides, dogsled races, ice skating, and snow tubing. The event is held on a weekend in late January or early February. For information, (207) 236-3438.

♦ **Ice skating** is available (weather permitting) on Hosmer Pond at the base of Camden Snow Bowl.

Museums

♦ **Farnsworth Art Museum and the Wyeth Center** (207-596-6457; fax 207-596-0509; www.farnsworthmuseum.org), 356 Main Street, Rockland. Founded in 1948 by local businesswoman Lucy Copeland Farnsworth, this fine museum specializes in American art with a focus on work related to Maine. The Farnsworth has a rich collection of material by three generations of Wyeths, many of them displayed in their own building, the former Pratt Memorial Methodist Church. This is an agreeable space, located at the corner of Union and Elm Streets, behind the museum. The family of N. C. Wyeth summered for years in a house in nearby Port Clyde. Son Andrew and grandson Jamie have island houses just off the coast near Port Clyde.

Also showcased are works by the premier 20th-century sculptor Louise Nevelson, who grew up in Rockland before moving to New York City. A photo on the wall of one gallery captures her as captain of the girls' basketball team at Rockland High School in 1916. She donated many of her works and personal papers to the Farnsworth, along with a major piece of sculpture. There are works by some of the great names in 18th- and 19th-century art history, including Gilbert Stuart, Thomas Eakins, and Fitz Hugh Lane. The museum has a good collection of pieces by American impressionists, including Childe Hassam, Maurice Prendergast, John Henry Twachtman, and Willard Metcalf. The museum is open Memorial Day through Columbus Day, daily 9–5. Winter hours are Tuesday through Saturday 10–5, Sunday 1–5. Adults $9, seniors $8, students 18 and older $5, 17 and under free.

The Olson House in nearby Cushing—which Andrew Wyeth painted often, and the location for his famous *Christina's World*—is owned by the museum and open in summer. So is the Farnsworth homestead to the rear of the museum. Call to ask about times to visit. The museum gift shop is top-notch.

♦ **Shore Village Museum** (207-594-0311; curator's residence 207-785-4609), 104 Limerock Street, Rockland. Calling itself "Maine's lighthouse museum," this is a fascinating place for those of us who are intrigued by lighthouses, lightships, lighthouse keepers, and all else relating to these important coastal beacons and those who manned them. The museum claims the largest collection of lighthouse and Coast Guard artifacts on display in the country, and the little building is chock-full. The Coast Guard exhibit rooms contain machinery from lighthouses, buoys, and lifesaving gear for search and rescue missions. A collection of early Fresnel lenses is impressive. Get on the mailing list for a fascinating newsletter about lighthouses all over the country. Open June 1 to October 15, daily 10–4. Free, but donations are appreciated.

♦ **Owls Head Transportation Museum** (207-594-4418; fax 207-594-4410; www.ohtm. org), Route 73, Owls Head (2 miles south of Rockland). Men especially love this museum. It is known for its collection of pioneer-era (pre-1930) aircraft, along with a display of historically significant automobiles, carriages, bicycles, motorcycles, and engines. The majority are maintained in operating condition and demonstrated at special events. These are usually on weekends between late May and October and include music, a chance to see antique airplanes in flight—aircraft like a 1916 Sopwith Pup or a 1917 Curtiss Jenny—plus other activities. Call for a schedule. There are also auctions of antique vehicles and several car meets throughout the summer and fall. Open April through October, 7 days a week 10–5 ; November through March, 10–4. Adults $6, children 5–12 $4, family rate of $16 covers two adults and as many children as they have with them.

Shopping

For many years Camden has been a shopping destination. Its center-of-town stores are independent boutiques and include gift, clothing, books, and more. Now Rockland has come onto the scene, as well. Although it still plays second fiddle to Camden's variety and quality, the town is expanding its offerings, especially with art galleries. These are a nice adjunct to visiting the Farnsworth Museum.

Many artists and craftspeople live in the area, and their works are shown in local shops and galleries. Among the more interesting are **Duck Trap Decoys,** creator of award-winning decoys, with a shop a mile north of Lincolnville Beach (just north of Camden). **Windsor Chairmakers** on Route 1 in Lincolnville produces high-quality reproduction furniture, including—of course—Windsor chairs. They also make exquisite beds, tables, and other household accoutrements. Their showroom is in two stories of a barn.

In downtown Camden we like **The Owl & The Turtle,** a major independent bookstore backing up to the harbor in the center of the shopping area; **ABCD Books** on Bay View Street for used and rare books; and **Meetingbrook,** a bookstore billed as "a place of collation and recollection on Camden Harbor." It offers coffee and pastries and, in winter, a fireplaced nook for reading spiritual and sensitive books from all faiths and ways of life. Also worth a stop is **Second Read Bookstore & Café** in Rockland.

Admiral's Buttons on Bay View has traditional men's and women's clothes. At **Surroundings** on Main Street you can find neat household items. The famous gift shop **The Smiling Cow** on Main Street has everything from refrigerator magnets to books about Maine (and a great back porch with a view over the harbor). **Once a Tree** is filled mostly with wood products, many of them very original in design. **Unique One** has incredible sweaters and knitting supplies. **Local Color** is a branch of the Northeast Harbor store, filled with hand-designed women's clothing. **Wild Birds Unlimited** offers a fantastic array of bird feeders, houses, and seed as well as other environmentally sound items. An array of ecofriendly and fun items from clothing to toys to jewelry is found at the **Planet** stores that are now found on both sides of Main Street. We found the best T-shirts at the **Atlantic Cotton Company** on Bay View Street. Check out **The Village Store** for good chocolates and maple sugar candy.

You can catch a movie at **The Bay View Street Cinema.**

In Rockland **The Grasshopper Shop** has tasteful women's clothing, kitchenware, jewelry, and gift items. Trendy women's clothes are also found at **Mace's** on Rockland's Main Street. The street itself has been placed on the National Register of Historic Places.

WHERE TO STAY

IN CAMDEN

◆ **Maine Stay** (207-236-9636; fax 207-236-0621; www.mainestay.com), 22 High Street, Camden, ME 04843. An inn can be entirely comfortable and still have an old-fashioned, authentic Down East feeling. So it is at Maine Stay, where innkeepers Juanita and Bob Topper keep televisions out of most guest rooms and provide an extra blanket at the foot of the bed for those cool Maine nights. Windows in original inn rooms are held open with old-fashioned notched sticks in summer. My daughter and I stayed in the antique twin-bedded Matthews Room, a comfortable corner room on the front of the inn. A new bathroom is spacious and up-to-date. The Stitchery Suite occupies the entire third floor of the inn. There's a queen-sized bed in the main bedroom with a single bed in a separate room. The sitting room has TV and coffeemaker. You can really settle in here. The ground-level Carriage House room is especially appealing, with queen bed, private bath, lots of books, a Vermont Castings stove, and French doors opening out to a stone patio.

Located on Camden's beautiful historic Main Street strip of homes—most on the National Register—Maine Stay is convenient to downtown, and guests can quite easily walk to shops and restaurants, no small convenience. Juanita, who was born in Austria and grew up in New Jersey, is the breakfast cook. Full breakfasts are served in a pretty room with several tables. During the winter and spring Maine Stay is a cozy retreat with wood fires aglow in twin front parlors. Doubles, $140–195.

♦ **The Hawthorn** (207-236-8842; fax 207-236-6181; www.camdeninn.com), 9 High Street, Camden, ME 04843. British-born Nick Wharton and his American wife, Patty, have been upgrading this marvelous yellow Victorian-era house with interesting turrets and angles. Well located in the historic district high above the harbor, it offers some smashing water views—albeit at a slight distance—from several rooms. Five guest rooms are in the main house—four on the second floor and a suite on the third. Four more are in the Carriage House out back. They have some extras—double Jacuzzi-style tub, TV, VCR, and individual fireplace. Glass doors in each of these rooms open onto a private deck that overlooks the harbor or the lawns and gardens below. A particularly good view of the water is from Norfolk.

In the main house our favorite room is Turret. We long to stretch out in the white wicker chaise lounge in the turret itself, from which Mount Battie in Camden Hills State Park can be seen. This room has a queen and a twin bed. Regency, also on the second floor, has a forest-green decor, and there's a soaking tub as well as oversized shower stall in the adjoining bath. There's also a small deck for watching the sunrise. For all this elegance, rooms are quite affordable.

The house itself, built in 1894, is a Victorian Queen Anne. A comfortable double front parlor is for the use of all guests, and a large dining room—where napkins are held with teapot-shaped napkin rings (you can purchase some to take home)—is where guests gather for a full breakfast most of the year. In summer the rear deck of the house is also used. Tea is served in the afternoon. Patty has an extensive breakfast repertoire, but one item her guests repeatedly ask for is her Roasted Red Bell Pepper Casserole served with Spicy Bacon. Doubles, $100–240.

♦ **The Hartstone Inn** (207-236-4259; www.hartstoneinn.com), 41 Elm Street, Camden, ME 04843. Mary Jo and Michael Salmon offer beds, breakfasts—and dinners for gourmets, if you want to dine here as well. Their mansard-roofed inn in the center of town has 10 rooms and suites, all with private bath, air-conditioning, phone, and queen-sized bed. Wood-burning fireplaces are available in two guest rooms. Two bilevel suites at the back of the inn with private entrances appeal for their seclusion. These have a living area with TV and gas fireplace and a sleeping loft with bathroom. The suites also have outdoor patios. Two third-floor rooms have high ceilings under the mansard roof and are especially spacious. Public rooms are decorated beautifully; the dining porch plus interior **dining room** have Chippendale chairs and dining tables with fresh flowers for an elegant setting. A $38.50 prix fixe four-course menu might begin with Maine crab and shrimp cakes; continue with baby greens with snow peas and crisp rice noodles in a ginger dressing; have an entrée of pan-seared duck breast with scallion smashed potatoes; and conclude with a dessert such as blueberry-hazelnut soufflé with toasted hazelnut crème anglaise. A full breakfast and afternoon tea are included in the rates. Doubles, $85–160.

♦ **The Whitehall Inn** (207-236-3391; fax 207-236-4427; www.whitehall-inn.com), 52 High Street, Box 558, Camden, ME 04843. This classic white inn with green shutters on the edge of the historic district draws return visitors who think it's the only place to stay in Camden. (We know one couple who wouldn't dream of staying anywhere else.) Owned and run for many years by the Dewing family, the inn offers a distant view of Penobscot Bay from huge green rockers with rush seats on the front porch. Guests often carry their breakfast coffee out here to sit and stare out to sea or simply to plan the day ahead. The building itself dates to the middle 1800s and is associated with the New England poet Edna St. Vincent Millay. A native of Camden, she gave a poetry reading here in 1912. Off the spacious main lobby, a Millay memorabilia room displays her high school diploma and several photos. The Stephen King movie *Thinner* used the lobby for one scene; the 1950s movie *Peyton Place* set a scene at the inn as well.

The Whitehall Inn is still a place out of another era. The innkeepers make no bones about the fact that most original fixtures are intact, including the hand-operated switchboard in the lobby. There's a shuffleboard court and tennis courts, but otherwise you're expected to make your own fun—perhaps by doing a puzzle or reading a book. The main inn has 40 rooms, and two Victorian houses across the street have five rooms each. King and queen beds have been added lately. The rooms feature old-fashioned small-print wallpaper, hobnail bedspreads, and some clawfoot tubs in the bathrooms. All but eight rooms have private bath. Breakfast is included, and dinner may also be taken in the country **dining room.** Possibly the best-known menu item is Chicken St. Millay, made with shallots, mushrooms, wine, and cream. The Spirits Room is furnished with old pedal-operated sewing machines. The inn is listed on the National Register of Historic Places. Doubles, with breakfast, $70–165. Gratuities are added (10 percent for rooms, 15 percent for food and beverages), so that no tipping is necessary. MAP rates are available on request. Open from late May to mid-October.

♦ **The High Tide Inn** (207-236-3724; 1-800-778-7068; www.hightideinn.com), Route 1, Camden, ME 04843. This inn, motel, and cottage complex keeps getting better. Innkeeper Jo Freilich has a real flair with decorating, and she has been upgrading the accommodations at this oceanfront site continually. On 7 waterfront acres north of town are a main house with five smallish but well-decorated inn rooms, two motel-style buildings (one next to the water) with 17 units in all—2 units in a duplex cottage and 5 attractive freestanding cottages. Most rooms have water views, and all have private bath. There are spacious lawns with chairs and tables and a private beach. The main house has a welcoming fireplaced living room for the use of all guests, as well as a library with fireplace. A continental-plus breakfast is served in a glassed-in dining porch with view of the ocean. There are TVs in the cottages and the motel rooms. Doubles, $55–205. Open May to mid-October.

♦ **The Lodge at Camden Hills** (207-236-8478; 1-800-832-7058; www.acadia.net/lodge), Route 1, P.O. Box 794, Camden, ME 04843. Fourteen modern, motel-style units in six buildings are set back from the highway in a hilly wooded setting. This assures privacy and, in most cases, offers distant bay views. The property is just a mile north of Camden and has an away-from-it-all feeling for those who prefer to be out of the hubbub. Several suites have a queen bed, sitting room with wood-burning fireplace, efficiency kitchen, and full bath, some with Jacuzzi-style tub. All have TV; in some cases, two. Light wood furniture gives a somewhat contemporary feeling. A few guest rooms offer two doubles or one queen bed, a refrigerator, and a private deck. Four cottages have a queen bed, whirlpool tub, kitchen, fireplace, and private deck. In-room coffee and tea help you to get the day under way until you can drive up or down Route 1 to find a breakfast spot or can prepare your own. These rooms are cool and green in summer, warm and cozy in winter. The lodge is family owned and run by Linda and John Burgess and John's father, Jack. Cottages, $175–249; suites and studios, $150–185; guest rooms, $99–165.

♦ **Lord Camden Inn** (207-236-4325; 1-800-336-4325), 24 Main Street, Camden, ME 04843. You can't get more center-of-town than this brick inn over the shops on Main Street. Altogether 31 rooms and suites are found on the second, third, and fourth floors. Upgraded recently, the rooms have two doubles, one queen, or in a few cases a king-sized bed. Several fourth-floor rooms have full harbor views; other rooms have balconies overlooking a river to one side or the town to the other. Many rooms have exposed brick walls; beds have white bedspreads, and there's wall-to-wall carpeting and air-conditioning. TVs are in armoires. The parking lot is about a block away, but once settled, you can easily walk to every place in town. In a comfortable second-floor breakfast room you can make your own Belgian waffles, try the inn-made granola, or have pastries and coffee. Open year-round. Doubles, $89–219.

IN ROCKLAND

♦ **Capt. Lindsey House Inn** (207-596-7950; 1-800-523-2145; fax 207-596-2758; www.lindseyhouse.com), 5 Lindsey Street, P.O. Box 864, Rockland, ME 04841. The Barneses, who operate the windjammer *Stephen Taber*, also own this elegant B&B, right in downtown Rockland. On a bright, hot summer's day, everything seems dark and restful inside. The gold-painted brick building was constructed in 1832 by sea captain George Lindsey. It was he who transformed his home into what is said to be the town's oldest inn, complete with a livery stable and popular tavern. It was restored by the Barneses several years ago. A small oak-paneled breakfast room with plaid-upholstered banquette seating is a cozy place to start the day with a country-style continental breakfast. Nine guest rooms and suites have stunning wallpapers, bedspreads, and Oriental carpets for a luxurious feeling. All are air-conditioned and have TV, phone, and private, well-appointed bath. A well-stocked library enables you to choose a book for relaxed reading, and the common fireplaced parlor is an elegant space filled with antiques and down couches. Doubles, $65–175.

Camping

For camping, see Camden Hills State Park.

WHERE TO EAT

From casual to more upscale, the Camden-to-Rockland area has restaurants that appeal.

IN CAMDEN

♦ **Boynton-McKay Food Co.** (207-236-2465), Main Street. Phil McElhaney, a former chef at the Waterfront restaurant and a resident of Camden since the early 1980s, is the proprieter at this drugstore-turned-restaurant in the center of town. A striped awning out front signals the spot where locals and visitors go for breakfast, lunch, snacks, and "grab 'n' go meals" to take home. The big clock on the wall says COFFEE TIME—CAMDEN, and smaller clock faces give times in Hong Kong, Paris, Chicago, and San Francisco. There are wood floors and old-timey booths where you can sit to enjoy old-fashioned ice cream sodas, creamsicle smoothies, and flavored coffees and cappuccinos. For breakfast an order of "huevos rancheros" ($5.50) or breakfast wraps ($3.50) with eggs, cheese, and homefries makes a good starter. Lunch might be a Caesar salad with ginger aïoli, wontons, and cashews; a chicken salad wrap with grapes, red onion, and herb mayonnaise; or a quesadilla with black beans and avocado ($4.50–5.50). Cookies, brownies, pies, tarts, strudel, and cheesecake are all made here. When we stopped, you could take home chicken cacciatore or dirty rice with pork and shrimp for $4.95. Open Memorial Day through October, daily 7–6 (until 9 PM in July and August); November to Memorial Day, closed Monday.

♦ **Bayview Lobster** (207-236-2005), Bayview Landing. Opened in 1997, this wharf-side lobster pound was packing them in the night we stopped. For one thing, it's a great location, where outdoor tables overlook the harbor. And there are the lobsters steaming away in vats at one end of the dock. You can also find other goodies that make for good seacoast dining: clam or seafood chowder, lobster stew, baskets of fried scallops, clams, shrimp, or fish-and-chips. Sandwiches—haddock, hamburgers, BLTs, lobster rolls (and deluxe lobster rolls, too)—are served all day. So are lobster dinners, priced according to size of crustacean and served with choice of potato and green salad or coleslaw. After 5, dinner entrées are available and include baked stuffed sole, fisherman's platter, shrimp plate, baked scallops, steak, and chicken ($9.95–16.99). Beer and wine are available. Open March to December, daily 11–10.

♦ **Cappy's Chowder House** (207-236-2254), 1 Main Street. For more than 20 years Cappy's has been a fixture in town, located at the corner of Main and Bay View. Dark and nautically decorated indoors, it's just the kind of cozy seaside tavern that you think of on a blustery night near the coast. Pull up a bar stool at the big wood bar as you enter, go right into a main-level dining room where green pool table lamps hang over the tables, or head upstairs to the Crow's Nest for a view of the harbor. The all-day menu has headings like Deck Munchies, Bountiful Burgers, or

Main Sheets (entrées served after 5). There's a full range of crowd pleasers. A house salad, Mexican salad (served in tortilla bowl), or "Jo's Health Watch" (grilled salmon on an English muffin with red onion, tomato, and hot mustard, plus a salad) are on the Lite but Lively section of the menu. Entrées include seafood pasta with shrimp, lobster, scallops, roasted veggies, artichokes, and pesto at $17.95; baby back ribs with fries, $15.95; and chicken Margarita (citrus-marinated grilled chicken breast topped with cranberry chutney and served over a cranberry almond orzo salad) for $9.95. Cappy's chowder is famous and comes in small or large mugs or in cans to take home. Champagne Sunday brunch is served 11–4. There's a seasonal bakery around the corner with great breads, cookies, pastries, picnic lunches, and so forth. The restaurant is open in-season, daily 11–9 (until 11 in July and August); closed Wednesday in winter.

♦ **Frogwater Café** (207-236-8998), 31 Elm Street. Two graduates of the New England Culinary Institute in Vermont—the husband-and-wife team of Joe Zdanowicz and Erin Carey—headed out West for a while and then returned to New England to open this popular and innovative storefront restaurant. Little white lights sparkle in the windows, and simple wood tables and chairs are well spaced inside. In 1999 Erin added a bakery with a full range of baked goods. Joe is the restaurant chef who comes up with creative and affordable lunch and dinner items. Appetizers ($6–7) include sweet potato and leek cakes topped with shrimp in a shallot-vermouth sauce; fried crawfish tails with sweet-and-sour sauce; and mushroom strudel. For entrées, the garlic ziti is especially popular. The dish contains sautéed chicken, mushrooms, sun-dried tomatoes, and prosciutto tossed with ziti in a roasted garlic Parmesan cream sauce. Other possibilities ($14–25) include roast salmon served with vegetable paella and topped with an olive and sun-dried tomato tapenade; grilled lamb loin over sautéed leeks, cherry tomatoes, endive, and artichoke hearts; and grilled eggplant slices rolled up with vegetables and ricotta cheese. At lunchtime you can have a crabcake salad, Caesar salad with chicken or shrimp, BLT, or perhaps a pesto flatbread with shrimp and ricotta cheese. Maine microbrews and a nice selection of wines are available. Desserts, described as "decadent," might be chocolate hazelnut layer cake, or a bread pudding with butterscotch sauce. Open daily for lunch 11–3 and dinner 5–9 in-season. Closed Wednesday in winter.

♦ **The Waterfront Restaurant** (207-236-3747), Bay View Street. This restaurant, located directly on picturesque Camden Harbor, is probably the best known in town. Location alone accounts for much of its popularity, but we've always found the food to be excellent. And it has year-round appeal. It's fabulous in summer, when many patrons eat outdoors on the huge deck/dock under peaked gray awnings, entertained by all the goings-on among the boaters. It is marvelous in winter when the two-sided fireplace warms both a cozy bar and one of the dining rooms. While we were forced to accept an indoor table on a hot July evening (or wait more than an hour to eat outdoors), we found that the high ceilings and paddle fans kept us relatively comfortable. A casual feeling is managed through exposed rough beams and bare wood tables with Windsor-style chairs. Huge photographs of fish and a wooden bird or two hanging from the ceiling are part of the decor. One of us had a fruit plate and enjoyed a huge assortment of cantaloupe, strawberries, blueberries, apples, peaches, and more, plus lemon sherbet and two slices of luscious lemon bread. The other chose clam chowder (not too thick and loaded with clams) and a spinach and chèvre salad with grilled portobello mushroom in a balsamic vinaigrette dressing. Had it been cooler, we could have opted for roasted sea scallops topped with sauce of fresh orange, gingerroot, Chablis, shallots, and butter; baked haddock with lobster-scented oil; or a grilled baseball-cut top sirloin steak. Entrées are priced in the $16–25 range. At lunch you can find sandwiches, salads, lobster rolls, or fried fish plates. Lunch 11:30–2:30, dinner 5–9:30, daily year-round.

♦ **Atlantica** (207-236-6011), 1 Bay View Landing. Another waterfront restaurant joined the Camden scene in the late 1990s and has been making waves ever since. Owned and operated by chef Ken and Del Paquin, it has a smallish but very popular outdoor deck, main-floor dining room, and small upstairs dining space. Artwork by local artists brightens the walls. Atlantica's menu with Italian and Asian influences—as well as New England favorites—is popular with locals and visitors. In summer, reservations are an absolute must for dinner. At lunchtime, appetizers include lobster and haddock cake served with fresh greens and mango vinaigrette; pan-steamed mussels with garlic, parsley, and saffron broth; and clam and leek chowder. A crabmeat burger, grilled tenderloin sandwich, or fresh fish sandwich will cost $8–10. At dinner a house specialty is sautéed scallops in a ginger and brown sugar glaze with citrus vinaigrette, absolutely scrumptious. Other possibilities ($19–30) are pan-roasted halibut with lemon-orange beurre blanc; roast rack of lamb with wine and fresh mint sauce; or macadamia-crusted breast of chicken with apricot chipotle sauce. Scallion mashed potatoes and *haricots verts* were accompaniments the night we dined here. We had an excellent Hess Chardonnay with our dinner. Profiteroles and lemon tarts were light and luscious finishes to the evening. Open for lunch and dinner daily year-round, although a spring break—possibly the month of March—is sometimes taken.

IN ROCKPORT

The very popular **Sail Loft** restaurant was closed in 2002 after a long run of more than 40 years. Here's hoping someone will reopen it soon.

IN ROCKLAND

♦ **Wasses,** 2 North Main Street. Since 1972, this year-round hot dog stand has been dishing up frankfurters and little more to an admiring audience. You can eat in the car, or take your lunch down to the waterfront, but there's no indoor dining. A hot dog was $1.30 last we looked; a bacon cheese hot dog, $1.90. How about a brownie (80 cents) for dessert? Drinks are available from a cooler.

♦ **The Brown Bag** (207-596-6372), 606 Main Street. Sisters Claire Holmes and Debbie Ortz operate this very popular breakfast and lunch spot (with a bakery, too). There are three rooms and a low-key storefront atmosphere—exposed brick walls, for example. You order at the counter. Breakfast could be a two-cheese omelet; a tostada with jack cheese, scrambled eggs, onions, and peppers in a floured tortilla; four-grain pancakes; or hot oatmeal with brown sugar ($3–5). Lunch includes sandwiches like roast beef, egg salad, PB&J, or the Brown Bag Ham Sandwich (grilled ham, Havarti cheese, capers, artichoke hearts, and a special sauce) for $2–4 a half; $2.50–7 for a whole. Soups and salads are also available. From the bakery comes everything from pecan sticky buns to scones to cinnamon biscuits. Breakfast 6:30–11, lunch, 11–4, bakery all day Monday through Saturday. Closed Sunday.

♦ **Café Miranda** (207-594-2034), 15 Oak Street. This bright spot on one of Rockland's side streets, close to Main Street shopping and the Farnsworth Museum, has been going strong for several years under the creative husband-and-wife team of Kerry Alterio, chef, and Evelyn Donnelly, who works the front of the house. The restaurant is located in a small green house where two pink flamingos peered from the windows recently. Dinner only is offered, both indoors at different-sized wood tables with brightly painted chairs, and outdoors in nice weather on a small patio with awning cover close to the street. An amazing number of high-quality items are created in the small, open-to-view kitchen where the cook staff works furiously. The large menu includes a list of more than 20 appetizers including chicken wings with ginger, lime, cilantro, and scallion; baked Brie with whole roasted garlic; Thai spiced ground pork with lime, cilantro, and lettuce wrap; and seafood cakes sautéed with fresh tomato, sour cream, and lemon. Entrées ($14–18) could be fresh tuna sticks coated with cornmeal and sautéed rare with fresh chipotle salsa, cilantro, and black beans; pasta Niçoise; chicken and eggplant curry; or duck breast Chinois. Open from 5:30 PM Tuesday through Saturday year-round.

♦ **Primo** (207-596-0770), 2 South Main Street. The name says it all. The aspirations of Culinary Institute of America graduate Melissa Kelly and her partner, Price Kushner, the pastry chef, are exceptionally high. Located in a house set well back from the road with plenty of land about it, this restaurant is European in feeling, with all the vegetables and salad items grown in kitchen gardens to the rear and side of the restaurant. "We grow all of our own things," says Melissa. The restaurant opened in April 2000 and was such a hit that people were driving from Portland and farther just for dinner. Three small dining rooms with white-clothed tables make for a somewhat formal atmosphere on the first floor. Upstairs, bistro-style dining is offered at bare mahogany tables in a room with tile floor and wood bar. The menu changes daily and offers a pleasing variety of items—including wood-fired pizzas with toppings such as grilled eggplant, spinach, balsamic onions, and ricotta salad. Starters might be bread and fish soup with local fish and leeks; seared foie gras with a rhubarb compote; roasted beets in an orange vinaigrette; or lobster and asparagus salad with curried lime vinaigrette ($7–14). Pastas could be seared scallops and linguine tossed with Maine shrimp, pancetta, garlic, and tomatoes, or hand-cut pappardelle with sautéed wild mushrooms, garlic chives, and spinach. Main courses ($19–27) could be sautéed cod on a bed of lobster, shrimp, garlic chives, and corn risotto; grilled duck breast and potato gnocchi with chanterelles and thyme; pesto tuna served with eggplant caponata and fresh tomato coulis; or roasted "Sunday" chicken with Tuscan bread salad tossed with arugula, currants, pine nuts, and mustard vinaigrette. Open for dinner only from 5:30 nightly in-season. In winter the restaurant is closed Tuesday or Tuesday and Wednesday.

21 The Mount Washington Valley, New Hampshire

Looking for winter? Head to New Hampshire's White Mountains. Even if the streets of Boston or Providence are bone dry, it's likely you'll find snow up here. And loads of things to do in it. Surprisingly, it's been only relatively recently that visitors have "wintered" in these highest of New England mountains. For many years the glorious peaks—the Presidential Range among them—were considered a summer destination only. Inns and hotels shuttered themselves right after foliage season and didn't reopen until May or June.

No more. The mountains now cater to winter vacationers. Even the huge red-roofed Mount Washington Hotel in Bretton Woods, for nearly a century a summer-only resort hotel, began to open in winter in the late 1990s. It attracted guests in higher-than-expected numbers right off the bat.

There is so much for the active visitor to do. Snowshoeing dates way back to the time of the trappers and of the Native Americans, whose only way to get through the sometimes hostile region was on foot, and it's in vogue again. Down-hill skiing came to these rugged peaks in the mid-1930s, about as early as it came to any other place in the country. Cross-country ski trails were carved in the 1950s. Ice skating, snow sculpting, sledding and tobogganing, snowmobiling, horsedrawn sleigh rides, winter hiking, ice climbing—even winter van rides up the side of Mount Washington itself. It's all here for the hardy traveler, the sort whose evening pleasure at the fireside is enhanced by having a few outdoor adventures to share.

Mount Washington is, at 6,288 feet, the highest mountain in the Northeast— famous for having one of the most unpredictable and rugged weather environments anywhere. (The highest wind speed ever clocked in the *world* was recorded atop its summit: 231 miles per hour.) Its snowcapped peak is usually seen against a blue sky from early autumn until late into the spring. Altogether the White Mountains have 48 peaks higher than 4,000 feet. The Presidential Range, of which Mount Washington is the headliner, includes eight mountains, all but one higher than 5,000 feet. (Mount Eisenhower is just under.)

Taking a challenging run on Wildcat Mountain
© Brooks Dodge, courtesy Wildcat Mountain

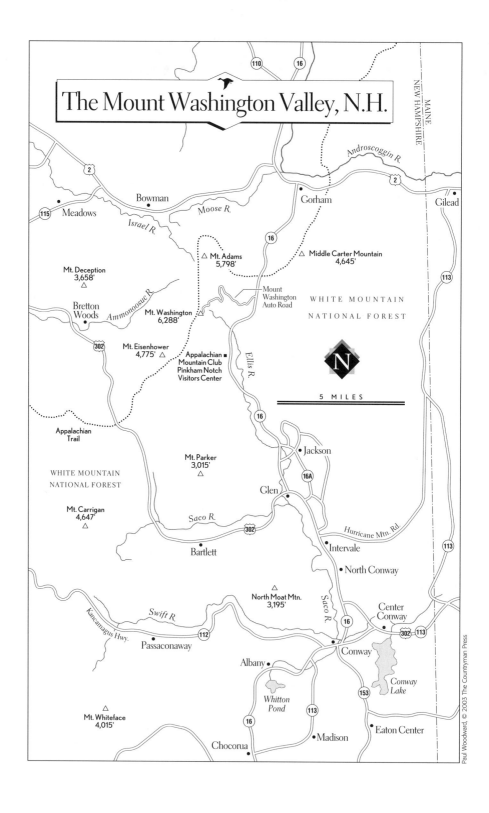

The Mount Washington Valley, N.H.

The White Mountain National Forest—which encompasses these peaks and forests—started with a 7,000-acre tract of land purchased by the federal government in 1911. Today the area includes more than 800,000 gorgeous acres and is a major draw for the public.

Abel Crawford and his family—for whom Crawford Notch on Route 302 is named—are credited with being among the first hoteliers in the region. Crawford built boardinghouses and taverns to respond to those who wanted a mountain holiday. Not that they necessarily wanted to rough it. The first visitors were fairly well-to-do folks from eastern cities who expected to have all the comforts of home. Therefore, many of the earliest places to stay were grand hotels with luxurious appointments. There was even one—the Tip Top House—at the very summit of Mount Washington, reached by the famous cog railway.

By 1936, when Black Mountain was first used for downhill skiing in the village of Jackson, the allure of the mountains in the snow season began to be seated. Nearby Cranmore Mountain in North Conway brought Austrian ski instructor Hannes Schneider to America, and the sport's popularity exploded. Now five downhill ski areas and as many cross-country ski centers provide lots of variety.

Even snow bunnies will find this rugged outdoor area appealing. What, after all, is more pleasurable than curling up with a book by a fireplace when the snow or wind is blowing just outside the window? How can you resist the hearty and delicious meals served in style in several area restaurants and dining rooms? And what's better than snuggling under a down quilt, possibly in front of your own in-room fireplace, as you drift off to sleep at night?

The locus of this weekend trip is the area north of commercial North Conway. It includes the wonderful mountain villages of Intervale, Jackson, Glen, and Bartlett, as well as Pinkham Notch (with the main lodge for the Appalachian Mountain Club) and the Mount Washington Auto Road. It extends west through Crawford Notch to Bretton Woods—location of the famous Mount Washington Hotel and the Bretton Woods Mountain Resort with downhill and cross-country skiing. There's plenty to do, or not to do, for a weekend. What's certain is that you will find winter here in all its glory, and folks who know exactly what to do with it.

Getting There

By car: From New York City, take Route 95 to Route 91 north through Hartford, Springfield, and on into Vermont. Take the exit for Route 302 (through Littleton and Bethlehem and eventually east to Route 16). This takes you through Crawford Notch and avoids commercial, congested North Conway. Via this route you can reach all of the areas mentioned. Some drivers like to take the gorgeous Kancamagus Highway (Route 112) through the mountains from Route 91 to Route 16 in Conway. Be advised that this route is frequently closed due to snow in winter; check road reports ahead of time.

From Boston, take Interstate 93 north. You can then take Routes 104 and 25 northeast around the top of Lake Winnipesaukee to Route 16 north through Conway and North Conway and into the village area to the north.

By bus: Concord Trailways (1-800-639-3317; www.concordtrailways.com) serves Conway, Jackson, and Pinkham Notch—as well as other White Mountain towns—from Logan International Airport in Boston.

By plane: From Boston's Logan International Airport, it's about a 2- to 2½-hour drive into the mountain areas. Manchester (New Hampshire) International Airport is about 1½ hours away. Both are served by many major carriers.

For more information: Contact the **Jackson Area Chamber of Commerce** (603-383-9356; 1-800-866-3334; fax 603-383-0931; www.jacksonnh.com), Box 304, Jackson, NH 03846. This chamber of commerce—with a small office in Jackson—covers the Intervale, Glen, Bartlett, and Jackson areas. The staff is friendly and will help you find reservations if you need them. When in town, pick up (free) *The (Mountain) Ear*—a weekly news and lifestyle journal for the Mount Washington Valley area.

SEEING AND DOING

Downhill Skiing

♦ **Attitash/Bear Peak** (603-374-2368; fax 603-374-1960; www.attitash.com), Route 302, P.O. Box 308, Bartlett, NH 03812. This ski area spreads out wide along Route 302. You can park in the lot across the street or pay $10 for "premier parking" closer to the base lodge. The vertical drop is 1,750 feet from Attitash and 1,450 feet from Bear Peak. There are 12 lifts, including 2 high-speed quad chairlifts. Snowmaking covers 98 percent of the mountain. There are 70 trails and glades rated 20 percent beginner; 47 percent intermediate; and 33 percent advanced. Thirty acres of glades allow for "tree skiing" on Bear Peak. For lodging reservations, call 1-800-223-SNOW. On weekends, adults pay $53; teens $44; seniors $36; kids $32.

♦ **Black Mountain** (603-383-4490; fax 603-383-8088; www.blackmt.com), Five Mile Circuit Road, P.O. Box B, Jackson, NH 03846. "Since 1935" says the literature for Black Mountain. For sure, it's one of the oldest ski areas in the state. Bill Whitney made a tow with shovel handles to get things started. Today it's known as a fun family area where it's rare to have a lift line. Black advertises the economy of skiing there: $32 for an adult on the weekend, compared to $40–50 elsewhere. Kids (up through age 18) pay $20. Seniors 65 and over pay $20. There are 40 trails and four lifts. The mountain is one-third beginner, one-third intermediate, and one-third expert. The vertical drop is 1,100 feet. With primarily a southern exposure, it's a pleasant mountain to ski—with country views.

♦ **Bretton Woods Mountain Resort** (603-278-3320; www.brettonwoods.com), Route 302, Bretton Woods, NH 03575. Calling itself "New Hampshire's Largest Ski Area," Bretton Woods faces the historic Mount Washington Hotel across the road. They are operated jointly. The ski area opened West Mountain in 1999 and planned another expansion over Mount Stickney in 2003. Currently it has 76 glades and trails, eight lifts including two high-speed quads, and snowmaking on 95 percent of the trails. The vertical drop is 1,500 feet. With 200 inches of snow annually, on average, condi-

Skiers at Wildcat have an unparalleled view of the Presidential Range.

tions are usually good. Twilight and night skiing are offered on Friday and Saturday. Snowboarding is allowed on all trails, and there's a small snowboarding park in the center of the area. The toughest trails to ski? Probably the second half of Minahan's Ridge, Over the Falls, and Sierra's Crest with a 65 percent grade. Adults and seniors pay $53 on weekends/holidays, teens $43, juniors $33.

♦ **Wildcat Mountain** (603-466-3326; 1-800-255-6439; www.skiwildcat.com), Route 16, Pinkham Notch, P.O. Box R, Jackson, NH 03846. With a 2,112-foot vertical drop and direct views of Mount Washington and the Presidential Range, Wildcat is a mountain for serious skiers. It's apt to be cold and windy (it was closed on a windy day when we visited), but fans of "The Cat" are intrepid and loyal. The Wildcat Gondola was the first lift of its type to be erected in the United States, opening in 1957. The first trail—opened as a ski racing trial area—was designed in 1933 by Charley Proctor, the all-around ski champion of Canada in 1927. Wildcat has a long history. The Polecat Trail, 2¾ miles long, is the longest ski trail in New Hampshire .It winds all the way down from the summit and gives even fairly new skiers a fabulous ride. Wildcat boasts the fastest detachable quad chair in New Hampshire. Because Wildcat faces north, it holds the snow and is apt to be open well into April each year. Adults $52; teens and seniors $42; juniors $25.

♦ **Mount Cranmore** (603-356-5543; 1-800-SUN-N-SKI; www.cranmore.com) in North Conway is another venerable downhill ski area. It has 34 trails. For information, contact Cranmore Mountain Resort, P.O. Box 1640, 1 Skimobile Road, North Conway, NH 03860.

♦ **Tuckerman Ravine.** Skiing "Tuck" is for excellent skiers who are in good shape. In order to ski the steep headwall of this bowl carved into the side of Mount

Washington, you must hike up—with all your gear—from the base lodge of the Appalachian Mountain Club in Pinkham Notch. The distance is a little more than 2 miles. Most people do this in spring when the snow has disappeared from the alpine ski areas and they want to have one more run. However, on a February visit to the AMC we ran into skiers who had skied Tuckerman that very day. Granted, the temperatures had gone up into the 40s. But—in February?

Cross-Country Skiing

♦ **Bear Notch Ski Touring Center** (603-374-2277), Route 302, Bartlett. The Garland family offers more than 60 km of groomed trails in a scenic, wooded environment. Brothers Doug and John Garland began cutting trails in 1994 on land where the family had previously only rented out summer cabins. The half circle of cabins remains, but the Nordic ski center also has become very popular. Snowshoers in particular love a trail along Albany Brook where only snowshoeing is permitted. There's a warming station out on the trails, and it's "serve yourself" for soup and snacks, with a donation box for payment. Well-behaved dogs are welcome on the trails. Ski and snowshoe rentals are offered, and the headquarters barn has a warming area and basic food. A weekend day pass is $12 for adults.

♦ **Bretton Woods Cross Country Center** (603-278-3320; 1-800-258-0330; www. brettonwoods.com), Route 302, Bretton Woods. Located adjacent to the Mount Washington Hotel, this Nordic ski center offers 100 km of tracked and skate-groomed trails. They are considered among the best in the area. The trails can be used by traditional and skate skiers and by snowshoers. Rentals are available.

♦ **Great Glen Trails** (603-466-2333; www.mt-washington.com), Route 16, Pinkham Notch, Gorham, is located across from the auto road to Mount Washington. It has 25 miles of Nordic trails, plus snowshoeing and tubing. The main building for the center burned in 2001, but a new one—combined with the Mount Washington Auto Road Stage Office—was to open in late 2002. There's a rental shop and a ski school.

♦ **Jackson Ski-Touring Foundation** (603-383-9355; 1-800-XC-SNOWS), P.O. Box 216, Jackson, NH 03846. With 154 km of trails, JSTF has the most extensive cross-country ski trail system in the East. There are 66 trails maintained specifically for cross-country skiing. Nearly 100 km of trails are groomed and double-tracked. The trails wind around the picturesque village of Jackson. The system was designed in 1972, and Thom Perkins has been director of the nonprofit organization that oversees the trails for many years. The attractive modern headquarters building—where you buy your passes, rent equipment, sign up for lessons, or warm yourself in front of a fire late in the day—is located next to the golf course of the Wentworth Resort. Here's where trails start. The 6½ km Ellis River Trail is scenic and not too difficult; there's a cantina on the trail where you can pick up a snack. Many of Jackson's inns are directly on the system, as are a few restaurants and pubs. Most of the trails also can be used by snowshoers. There's a repair shop, too; a friend had her old wooden skis pine-tarred overnight while we were there. Open December to late March. Adult weekend day pass, $14.

◆ **Mount Washington Valley Ski Touring & Snowshoe Center** (603-356-9920; www.crosscountryskinh.com), located in the Ragged Mountain Equipment shop, Routes 16/302, Intervale. The 60 km of trails operated by this organization lace through North Conway, Kearsarge, and Intervale and can be accessed easily from inns in Intervale. Equipment rental and ski lessons are offered. An adult weekend day pass is $9.

Snowshoeing

Snowshoeing is permitted on trails at **Bear Notch Ski Touring Center, Bretton Woods Cross Country Center, Great Glen Trails, Jackson Ski-Touring Foundation, Mount Washington Valley Ski Touring and Snow Shoe Center,** and at **Nestlenook Farm** in **Jackson.** Many of these operators offer guided snowshoe treks. Some of the major winter hiking trails in the White Mountain National Forest also are excellent for snowshoeing. Another very good place to snowshoe is **Bear Notch Road,** which connects Route 302 to the Kancamagus Highway. It's closed to vehicular traffic in winter. You can snowshoe along this road for as long as you want. **Rob Brook Road** (Forest Road 35) off Bear Notch Road is also a place to snowshoe. Some inn proprietors will let you snowshoe on their own property. If they don't have a good area to do this, they will know where to direct you.

Snowmobiling

The village of Jackson does not allow snowmobiling. It's probably just as well, what with all the cross-country skiers. Those who want to try the sport can head west on Route 302 to **L'il Man Snowmobile Rentals** in Bartlett. The operators give lessons on an open field next door and then have several trails that extend into White Mountain National Trail. A 2-hour rental on a single snowmobile is $90; double, $110. Call (603) 374-9257 for information. Or for guided tours with the White Mountain Adventure Team, call (888) 440-6441.

Snowmobiles may also be rented at **Northern Extremes Snowmobiling, Inc.** (603-356-4718), Route 16, North Conway. Guided tours are offered.

Sleigh Rides/Skating

◆ **Nestlenook Farm** (603-383-0845; www.nestlenook.com) in Jackson is like a Victorian stage set—and it draws lots of people for horse-drawn sleigh rides or ice skating on Emerald Lake. The sleigh rides are bell-jingling junkets behind Belgian draft horses through the trees and around the grounds of this romantic spot. There's even a luxurious bed & breakfast inn where you can spend the night (see *Where to Stay*). The ice skaters' pond is a graceful, long curving length of ice where you can skate under a picturesque bridge and to a small island with a bonfire. Skate and snowshoe rentals are available. There are also trails for snowshoeing on the property.

A winter sightseeing tour climbs Mount Washington

Snow Coach up Mount Washington

Described as an "ultimate winter experience," this may be the ride to beat them all. Vans that take tourists to the top of Mount Washington in summer are converted with a special four-track wheel system so they can climb the auto road to just above tree line. The 12-passenger vans stop at their destination, let you out for a brief tour in a white and snowy world, and then—if you have the nerve—let you snowshoe or cross-country ski back down the auto road. Or you can simply remain in the comfort of the van and ride back down (most people do this). The Snow Coach is boarded at the **Great Glen Outdoor Center,** Route 16, Pinkham Notch. Tours take 1½ hours round-trip. Adults $35. For information, (603) 466-2333 or www.greatglen-trails.com

Scenic Drives

This is a beautiful part of New England, and many drives are spectacular. These include the Kancamagus Highway (Route 112) if it's open, Route 302 through Crawford Notch, Route 16 north through Pinkham Notch, and the loop road around Jackson Village. West Side Road—which allows you to skirt the busy center of town in North Conway where there always seem to be traffic jams—is also a pretty route.

Covered Bridges

The little red "honeymoon bridge" through which you enter the village of Jackson from Route 16 is particularly picturesque when viewed against a winter landscape. Built in 1876, the Paddleford truss bridge was repaired and widened in 1939. Bartlett's covered bridge, also a Paddleford truss style, was built in the mid-1800s and can be seen just off Route 302 west from Glen. It has been closed to traffic since 1939, and now houses a gift shop open in summer only.

Indoor Activities

♦ **Hartmann Model Railroad Museum** (603-356-9922; 603-356-9933), Town Hall Road, Intervale, NH 03845. Some guys never get over playing with trains, and Roger Hartmann, who grew up in Switzerland, is one of them. His collection of more than 2,000 model locomotives and 10,000 freight cars and passenger coaches—most in landscape settings—are on display in this large museum. Roger and his wife, Nelly, traveled extensively before settling on New Hampshire as a home for Roger's extensive train collection. Although he never worked for the railroads, both grandfathers did back in Switzerland, and he grew up enthralled by trains. Altogether there are 15 layouts in various gauges, European and American. There are also a good-sized souvenir shop and a small café. Open daily, 9 or 10 to 5. Adults $6, seniors $5, children $4.

♦ **Conway Scenic Railroad** (603-356-5251; 1-800-232-5251; www.trainsnh.com), North Conway. Would you like a ride on a real train? In December the Conway Scenic Railroad operates two special trains—the "Santa Claus Express" and "Polar Express." The latter, a re-creation of the Chris Van Allsburg story of a mystical journey to the North Pole, is so popular that a ticket lottery is held. For information on it, call (603) 447-3100. During the summer the railroad operates all sorts of interesting itineraries, including a 5-hour round-trip to Crawford Notch. There are also lunch and dinner excursions.

♦ **Mount Washington Observatory, Weather Discovery Center** (603-356-2137; 1-800-706-0432; www.mountwashington.org), 2436 White Mountain Highway (Routes 16/302), North Conway, NH 03860. Serious weather buffs (more than 4,000 of them worldwide) are members of the private, nonprofit organization that runs the weather observatory on the top of Mount Washington. This museum is primarily devoted to the way wind shapes our world—after all, the highest recorded wind *ever* was on the top of the famous mount. In The Wind Room, you can experience (mostly through audio) how it felt to be there during that world-record wind in 1939. There are many hands-on exhibits—fun for children (aged 8 and over) and adults. In summer visitors can also view exhibits in a small museum at the summit. The ultimate winter experience, however, may be an overnight trip to the summit. It's possible (1) if you are a member of the Mount Washington Observatory organization (single $40, family $65) and (2) if you shell out $350 for the single overnight. This includes a ride to the summit in a snow tractor, overnight accommodations, meals while there, and the opportunity to work alongside the meteorologists and weather observers who chart the intense weather every hour on the hour year-round. "It's one of the toughest tickets in New Hampshire to get," says a spokesman. The 15-or-so winter trips—taking 10 persons apiece—are sold out every year. The discovery museum is open daily (except closed for one or two midweek days in winter) 10–5. Adults $2, children $1.

Shopping

North Conway is known for its outlet shopping. We think the strips of outlet malls have all but ruined what used to be a charming mountain village, but if you want bargains, you may find them here. Outlets include J. Crew, Reed & Barton, April Cornell, Black & Decker, Nike, Reebok, Brookstone, and The Gap. In Jackson **Flossie's General Store** is a place to poke around. There are several excellent sporting goods stores, including the headquarters store for **Eastern Mountain Sports** in North Conway and **Joe Jones Ski & Sports** in Intervale. **Jack Frost** in Jackson has ski equipment and clothing.

Special Events

Three weekends in late November and early December are designated **Traditionally Yours** weekends in Jackson and the surrounding towns. Inns are decked out for the holidays, Santa Claus visits, and tree lightings and carol sings are scheduled. There are art gallery sales and shows and more. For information, contact the Jackson Chamber of Commerce at (603) 383-9356.

On a January or February weekend, Jackson is host to a New Hampshire state-sanctioned **snow sculpture competition.** Winners go on to compete at the national level. Visitors get to see the snow sculptures being created and then judged.

WHERE TO STAY

Options are plentiful and range from the grande dame of resort hotels, the Mount Washington in Bretton Woods, to luxurious hotels and B&Bs, to simple motels and places for skiers. The villages north of North Conway are quieter and more pictur-esque than North Conway itself, so that's where we focus.

IN BRETTON WOODS

♦ **The Mount Washington Hotel** (603-278-1000; 1-800-258-0330; fax 603-278-8828), Route 302, Bretton Woods, NH 03575. Opened in 1902, this majestic red-roofed hotel almost appears to be a fantasy as you drive along the interesting mountain route, 302. It's set into a flat area, with a backdrop of snowcapped peaks including Mount Washington. It was built by Joseph Stickney, Pennsylvania Railroad tycoon and native of Concord, New Hampshire. In 1944 the hotel was the site of the famed Bretton Woods International Monetary Conference, held toward the end of World War II in an attempt to stabilize international economies in the wake of the war. In the late 1990s its consortium of owners—four local families—decided to open the hotel for the winter as well as summer. The amenities are potentially terrific. There's the expansive Bretton Woods alpine ski area just across the street; an excellent network of groomed cross-country trails on its golf course and into wooded areas nearby; an indoor pool; dining rooms, shops and—expected soon—a spa and new Nordic Ski Center. The massive lobby has two huge wood-burning fireplaces with sofas and chairs grouped nearby. The hotel has 200 guest rooms on the second, third, and fourth floors. They have high ceilings, and many have wonderful views of the mountains. Rooms have one queen bed, a king, or two queen beds. Corner Vista rooms are extra large with good views. The deluxe rooms with a separate sitting room in front of a fireplace and a kitchen area are especially large and have a sleeper sofa in addition to king or queen bed. Room fireplaces were not functional when we visited, but the hotel was talking about making them so. Most bathrooms have a tub-shower combination and are on the small side. Room 314 has a queen canopy bed that once belonged to Joseph Stickney's wife—who married a European prince after Stickney's death and was known as Princess Caroline. This room also has a double Jacuzzi-style tub. Rooms have wall-to-wall carpeting, TV in an armoire, lounge chairs, and plenty of space. The pool is on the hotel's lower level, where you also find **Stickney's** (for light lunch and dinner), the Bretton Woods post office, clothing shops, and game rooms. **The Cave** is an after-dinner entertainment area with stone walls. Men must wear jackets to dine in the main dining room. Also on the property is the Bretton Arms Country Inn, a Victorian-style B&B with 34 guest rooms. Doubles at the Mount Washington Hotel, including breakfast and four-course dinner or buffet, $135–295. Suites are priced $425–629, and family suites go up to $829. The Bretton Arms rooms range from $109–125 weekends, with breakfast.

IN HART'S LOCATION

♦ **The Notchland Inn** (603-374-6131; fax 603-374-6168; reservations 1-800-866-6131; www.Notchland.com), Route 302, Hart's Location, NH 03812. Here's a great winter destination. Seven fireplaced rooms and four suites in the main granite inn plus two more suites in the School House out back come equipped with wood-burning fireplaces. That makes staying here in winter particularly romantic. Two newer suites under the eaves in the main house are especially cozy. Evans has a queen bed under a skylit roof, a double Jacuzzi-style tub, and a double-faced fireplace that can be seen from the bed, from a separate sitting area, and even from the tub-for-two. Carter has a queen bed, a large deck, and a whirlpool tub in the bathroom. In the suite known as Kinsman, there is a king bed and a soaking tub with reading lights! A full breakfast is served to inn guests in an attractive wing that was once part of Abel Crawford's tavern. You step down into this bright windowed space—with fireplace at one end—and order from a menu offering pancakes, French toast, eggs, breakfast meats, and cereals. The Gustav Stickley room with games and magazines is a great gathering place. Dinner at 7 PM is prix fixe at $30 for guests ($35 or $40 to the public), and you might be tempted to enjoy lobster consomme, mussels with lemongrass and coconut broth, fillet of beef with Stilton demiglaze, and molten chocolate cake. The **dining room** is also open to the public by reservation Tuesday through Sunday. Doubles, with breakfast, $180–260; suites, $240–290.

IN BARTLETT

♦ **The Bartlett Inn** (603-374-2353; 1-800-292-2353; fax 603-374-2574; www.bartlett. inn.com), Room 302, P.O. Box 327, Bartlett, NH 03812. This place is a find. The big red inn with white trim and large parking area out front, plus 10 little red cottages in a line to the right, is enjoyed especially by skiers, hikers, and families. Innkeeper Mark Dindorf runs a big friendly place where guests are apt to gather in an oversized and casual living room for conversation, games, or watching TV. The six rooms in the main inn are clean and comfortable but not fussy. One is a small space with single bed; other rooms have double beds or doubles and singles. All share two full baths with stall showers. An inn room on the first floor has a brick fireplace and half bath. Four of the cottages are efficiencies with fireplace; all cottages have TV. There is a hot tub outdoors. A full breakfast is served to all guests in a comfortable dining room with several individual tables. Homemade muffins, fruit, juice, and a main dish such as French crêpes with berry sauce are served. You can cross-country ski right from the house on trails run by Bear Notch X-C Ski Center nearby. Well-behaved pets are allowed in cottages. Inn rooms with shared baths are $85–118, double; cottages are $95–144, double. Single rates are also available.

♦ **The Villager Motel** (603-374-2742; reservations 1-800-334-6988; fax 603-374-1965; www.villagermotel.com), Route 302, P.O. Box 427, Bartlett, NH 03812. Vinny and Sharon Zerveskes run an impeccably maintained complex with motel rooms, efficiencies, private cottages, and an efficiency apartment with fireplace. Altogether there are 37 different units, three of them freestanding chalets. All have a full tub-shower combination bathroom and large TV. The Riverside Chalet beside the Saco River is ideal for a family, with a queen-bedded bedroom on the main floor and a loft with queen bed and two twins up above. There's a living room with fireplace and complete kitchen. Many motel units are quite spacious with two queen beds; a few are smaller and have just one queen bed. Motel rooms have refrigerators. Doubles, $74–169.

IN GLEN

♦ **The Bernerhof** (603-383-9132; 1-800-548-8007; fax 603-383-0809; www.bernerhof-inn.com), Route 302, Glen, NH 03838. Long known for its dining, the Bernerhof also has attractive guest rooms on its second and third floors. Altogether there are nine guest rooms and two suites, all with private bath. Sharon and Ted Wroblewski have been in charge here for more than 20 years; guest chefs run the dining room. Quilts on beds—mostly kings and queens—and braided or hooked rugs give a country feeling. Third-floor rooms are reached by a rather steep staircase and have their own game room/parlor to enjoy. Rooms 8 and 9 are especially spacious, and the latter has a large whirlpool tub. A couple of rooms also have Franklin stoves or fireplace. On the fourth morning of a stay, a champagne breakfast in bed is offered.

Otherwise a full breakfast is enjoyed in the space occupied by the first-floor restaurant, The Rare Bear, which has a great reputation in the valley (see *Where to Eat*). A Taste of the Mountains Cooking School—held in December and in May—offers guests a weekend of cooking and dining along with accommodations at the inn (approximately $500 per person). The inn has an especially atmospheric Black Bear Pub with carved oak paneling and fireplace and a chess set made with salt and pepper shakers. It's a great place to hang out. Doubles, $125–175.

♦ **The Red Apple Inn** (603-383-9680; 1-800-826-3591), Room 302, Glen, NH 03838. This really is a very handsomely appointed motel next door to The Bernerhof, and also owned by it. Fourteen rooms and two suites have two double beds or a double and a queen. The two suites have gas fireplaces. There's a large fireplaced breakfast room where a continental-plus breakfast is set out; it includes hot oatmeal in winter. Doubles, $99–129.

♦ **Storybook Resort Inn** (603-383-6800; 1-800-528-1234), intersection of Routes 16 and 302, Glen, NH 03838. Jan and Charless Filip are the second-generation owners of this hillside complex that is especially favored by families. Although most are motel-style units, there are also seven rooms in the main inn building. There's an indoor pool and Jacuzzi-style tub for winter-weary bones. Altogether there are 78 units, ranging in style. Most have a queen-sized bed; several have two doubles; and there are a few kings. All have hair dryer and TV, and more than half also have refrigerator. A couple of family rooms have four beds: two doubles and two singles. An adjacent restaurant, Prince Place, is well regarded (see *Where to Eat*). It's open for breakfast and dinner in winter. Rates for up to four persons in a room, $99–145.

IN INTERVALE

Intervale is a separate loop off busy Route 16. It has a comfortable "out-of-the-mainstream" feeling once you're there.

♦ **The New England Inn and Resort** (603-356-5541; 1-800-826-3466; www.newenglandinn.com), Route 16A, P.O. Box 100, Intervale, NH 03845. Chris and Chet Hooper and their son, Dale, oversee this well-run complex with luxurious accommodations in a recently added log lodge building. There are also three individual log cabins. The cottages, built in 2001, have gas fireplace, Bose radio, refrigerator, and large TV. Some have a Jacuzzi-style tub for two. The Lodge, with its special moose antler chandelier in the common foyer, offers 12 comfortably appointed rooms and suites in all. Eagle's Nest is a "loft" room with a king bed in the upstairs loft area and double shower and Jacuzzi-style tub on the first floor. A sofa faces the fireplace. One "standard" room has a handsome stone fireplace with king bed and access to a small porch out back. Beaver Dam, a typical cottage, is one large room with fireplaced sitting area with sofa, a double Jacuzzi tub, high ceiling, and king-sized bed.

Appointments are all in keeping with the mountain theme—linens with wildlife motifs, Adirondack-style furniture, exposed pine beams. The rooms in the main white inn building are smaller and more traditional. They might have a canopy bed, a tub-shower combination in the bathroom, and a reading chair. Ten duplex cabins—all with fireplace—are popular with families. Altogether there are 42 accommodations. A full breakfast, served in the main inn, is included. Doubles, in the inn, $75–115; cabins, $125–148; Lodge rooms, $150–235; log cabins with Jacuzzi, $190. Dinner can be added at $26 per person. Package plans are available.

♦ **Old Field House** (603-356-5478; 1-800-444-9245; fax 603-356-7688; www.oldfield-house.com), P.O. Box 1, Route 16A, Intervale, NH 03845. Here is a comfortable place to stay. A large barn-style red building offers 19 rooms and two suites. Out back, in the town houses known as The Farm, are several more suites. Rooms—with two double beds, or a single king or queen—have dark wood beams, floral spreads, and wall-to-wall carpeting. The suites, with king or queen bed, all have a sitting area, fireplace, kitchen or kitchenette, dining area, and large Jacuzzi-style tub. Most fireplaces are wood burning; a few are gas. Breakfast is served in a sunny greenhouse-style room and includes breads, fruit, and cereals. Nordic ski trails of the Mount Washington Valley Ski Touring Association can be accessed in Intervale. Doubles, $60–125; suites, $160–195. Suites at The Farm range $135–195 for two people.

♦ **The Forest** (603-356-9772; 1-800-448-3534; fax 603-356-5652; www.forest-inn.com), P.O. Box 37, Route 16A, Intervale, NH 03845. This white inn with green mansard roof has been catering to guests since 1890. Lisa and Bill Guppy bring both warmth and fastidious attention to their innkeeping duties. They offer eight rooms in the main inn, three with gas fireplace. In addition, there are two back-to-back fire-placed rooms—one with a wood-burning fireplace—in a stone cottage to the side of the inn. Yet another separate cottage with one room is out back. It has a gas fireplace. All rooms have a queen-sized bed and private bath, although one bath is across the hall. All are charmingly and neatly decorated in country Victorian style, with quilts on the beds and floral wallpapers. A Victorian-style parlor has a fireplace. There is a woodstove on the porch that Bill occasionally lights and where hors d'oeuvres are sometimes set. Guests are served in a pretty burgundy-and-white dining room with light wood Windsor-style chairs grouped around separate tables. Bill is the breakfast cook; blueberry pancakes and cinnamon French toast are among his specialties. There are hiking and groomed cross-country trails nearby, and guests can snowshoe in back of the inn on its own acreage. Doubles, $80–125 for a standard room; $80–140 for fireplaced room; $95–160 for cottage rooms. Closed in April.

IN JACKSON

Jackson is the premier village in the region. A hilly place, it has been catering to guests since the mid–19th century and continues the innkeeping tradition.

♦ **The Inn at Thorn Hill** (603-383-4242; 1-800)-289-8990; www.innatthornhill.com), Thorn Hill Road, Box A, Jackson Village, NH 03846. Innkeepers Ibby and Jim Cooper run one of the most delightful inns in New England. "We cater to romance and the adult world," says Ibby. Sadly, a fire damaged the inn in late 2002 but reconstruction was underway. Estimated reopening is in fall of 2003. The plan was to retain a luxurious Victorian ambience at this, one of Jackson's most attractive hostelries. Doubles ranged from $200–450.

♦ **The Wentworth** (603-383-9700; 1-800-637-4265; www.thewentworth.com), center of Jackson Village, NH 03846. Swiss-born hotelier Fritz Koeppel runs a full-service resort hotel in the center of the village. One side of the property is bordered by the scenic Jackson Falls of the Wildcat River; on the other, the resort is framed by the 18-hole Wentworth golf course, which becomes a major portion of the Jackson Ski-Touring Foundation trails in winter. Built in 1869, the large sand-colored clapboard building with striped awnings has turrets and porches and the look of a settled resident of town. Since its restoration in 1983—and constant upgrading—it is an elegant place to stay. Altogether there are 52 rooms—somewhat fewer in winter until all of the six former summer hotel outbuildings are slowly winterized and brought on line. Four large "cottages"—each with several rooms—and the main inn are currently open in cold weather. King-sized beds—sleigh style or four-poster—are found in the cottages; queen beds are in the main inn's guest rooms. Room number 409 in the recently completed Arden building has a hot tub in its turret and is a suite. The Thornycroft Room, reached off the porch of the main inn, is an elegant space with king canopy bed and Jacuzzi-style tub in the bathroom. Gas fireplaces are found in both bathroom and bedroom. Rooms upstairs in the main inn are plainer, with queen beds in light wood and perhaps a clawfoot tub in the bathroom. The huge main lobby has several appealing sitting areas; in the morning, coffee is set out with china cups and saucers. A special cross-country ski package is offered. Doubles, MAP, including a five-course candlelight dinner and country breakfast, $175–335.

♦ **Carter Notch Inn** (603-383-9630; 1-800-794-9434; www.carternotchinn.com), Carter Notch Inn, P.O. Box 269, Jackson, NH 03846. Jim and Lynda Dunwell, innkeepers in Jackson back in the 1970s, left for several years and entered the retail business. In 1995 the opportunity to fix up the house that had been the original owners' residence for the Eagle Mountain House next door lured them back into innkeeping. The green-shuttered, white pillared house has been impeccably restored. There are now eight guest rooms, including four with gas fireplace and two with double Jacuzzi-style tub. All have TV. The "treetop" suites toward the back of the house are especially spacious and elegant, and an outdoor hot tub draws guests even in frigid weather. Guests can access trails to the Jackson Ski-Touring Foundation cross-country trails directly from the property; these can also be used for snowshoeing. Jim and Lynda are cheerfully informative and can steer you to good hiking, including the trek to Lowe's Bald Spot in Pinkham Notch and Mount Willard off Route 302. They recommend the book *Snowshoe Hikes in the White Mountains* by Steven Smith (and will lend it to you while you're there). Full breakfasts are served in the morning and are inclined to be hearty—fruit-stuffed French toast the morning I stopped. Doubles, $69–199.

♦ **The Inn at Jackson** (603-383-4321; 1-800-289-8600; www.innatjackson.com), Main Street and Thorn Hill Road, P.O. Box 807, Jackson, NH 03846. The ski rack on the big wide front porch and the mammoth pile of fireplace-sized wood logs mean this inn is serious about winter business. A wood-burning fire in the breakfast room adds an extra touch as you feast on vegetable omelets, French toast stuffed with raspberries and cream cheese, or piping-hot oatmeal. Craig

Higgins, formerly with the Wildcat Tavern and a native of North Conway, is the chief cook and bottle washer as the inn manager. The big red house was designed by the architect Stanford White in 1902 and has one of the widest front halls imaginable. But the feeling is comfortable and casual, with one common room filled with sofas that look as if they've been well used, along with fireplace and chess set. All 14 guest rooms have private bath; seven have a fireplace, three of them wood burning. Beds are king or queen sized. In the afternoon, tea is available in the pub that also doubles as the breakfast room, with individual tables. Doubles, $99–199.

♦ **Eagle Mountain House** (603-383-9111; 1-800-966-5779; www.eaglemt.com), Carter Notch Road, Jackson, NH 03846. This sprawling white inn with mammoth front porch—280 feet in length—is located across the road from its own nine-hole golf course and, beyond that, the picturesque Wildcat River that rushes through the center of Jackson. It's a beautiful setting, and in winter the golf course becomes a place to try cross-country skis or even—on a small slope—alpine skis. (One mom had her kids out doing just that when last we stopped.) Families enjoy the Eagle Mountain House. Rooms tend to be comfortably large and prices, affordable. There are also two-room suites. Ours had a good-sized queen-bedded room, a sitting room with sofas and TV, and a bathroom between the two. The inn is now a condo association, with all rooms individually owned. But it's run as a hotel, and it's hard to tell the difference when you stay here. A cheery wood-burning fireplace in the lobby is a comfortable place to sit. In addition to 93 guest rooms with recently upgraded private baths, there is a game room with billiards and pinball machines, a 10-person hot tub, and a small exercise area. The main dining room is large and overlooks the porch; it's especially fun to watch out the windows when snow is falling. Accommodations are offered EP, B&B, and MAP; a special "Escape" package includes 2 nights, two breakfasts, and one dinner in the large main dining room. Lighter fare is available in a small and cozy tavern off the lobby. Doubles, EP, $69–159; doubles, B&B, $99–170.

♦ **Nestlenook Farm** (603-472-5207; 603-383-9101; www.luxurymountaingetaways. com/NestlenookFarm/index.html), Route 16, Jackson, NH 03846. This elaborate pink Victorian B&B is part of a complete resort. You almost don't have to leave the property if you don't want to. You can ice skate on Emerald Lake, take an Austrian sleigh ride, snowshoe through the woods, or pull up a chair in front of a warm parlor fireplace. The B&B has seven rooms and suites with several common rooms for guests' use. These include a lower-level TV and game room (no TVs in individual rooms), a parlor where wine and cheese is served in the afternoon, a library-style room for lounging, and a breakfast room where full country breakfasts are served. The individual accommodations are all named for local artists, and their works are on the walls. For example, the Myke Morton Room is named for a currently active Jackson artist who has her own gallery in town. Located in the original part of the inn, it has hand-hewn beamed ceiling, queen bed with high carved headboard, and semiprivate access to a side porch. The third-floor C. C. Murdoch Suite accommodates up to four and has three rooms and views from three sides. All rooms and suites have a two-person whirlpool tub. Doubles, with breakfast, $175–340.

♦ **The Crowes' Nest** (603-383-8913; 1-800-511-8383; fax 603-383-8241; www. crowesnest.net), Thorn Mountain Road, Jackson, NH 03846. The location of this B&B, high on a hill overlooking the village of Jackson, is one of its prime features. From here you can actually walk to a couple of good restaurants and to the Jackson Ski-Touring center to take off on their cross-country trails. Seven rooms—five in a remodeled barn/carriage house and two in the main house—are available. Get one in the barn (known as The Lodge) if you can. These are larger, with more amenities in general. The two premier guest rooms are Peter's Room (my favorite), a large space with king bed, fireplace, Jacuzzi-style tub, and balcony, and Eddie's Room with queen bed, fireplace, Jacuzzi tub, and sliders to a private balcony. The Lodge has a small common room with gas stove. All guests take breakfast in the main house—on the enclosed front porch with wrought-iron furniture and glass tables and nice views of the village, or in the dining room adjacent. The common TV is also in this porch area. Christine Crowe, innkeeper, sometimes surprises guests with a special item at breakfast like the butter-sautéed hot orange slices we had one morning. Her husband, Myles, is an avid cross-country skier who gives helpful advice when asked. Furnishings are eclectic, a mix of Asian pieces and art picked up on the Crowes' world travels with Myles's accountant job plus antiques and country pieces. Doubles, $79–199.

♦ **Wildcat Inn & Tavern** (603-383-4245; www.wildcatinnandtavern.com), Route 16A, Jackson, NH 03846. Known primarily for its kitchen (meals are served in the main dining room as well as the convivial tavern—see *Where to Eat*), the Wildcat Inn also has 13 cozy guest accommodations on the second floor, plus a two-bedroom cottage out back known as The Igloo. The rooms are decorated in simple Colonial fashion with quilts on beds and antique bureaus and such; they are very cheerful and welcoming. Most rooms have a queen or double bed and private bath; suites have a bedroom plus living room with pullout sofa and private bath. A couple of rooms share a bath. The Igloo has two bedrooms, one and a half baths, a living room, and a kitchenette and is ideal for a family or friends traveling together. Rooms have TV, VCR, and phone. Rates include a full country breakfast. Doubles with private bath, $129; with shared bath, $109; suites, $149; the Igloo cottage, $350.

♦ **The Snowflake Inn** (603-383-8259), Route 16A, Jackson, NH 03846. Sue and Garry Methot, who owned properties at Hampton Beach, New Hampshire, made the move to Jackson in 2001. This new inn, scheduled to open in late 2002, was to have 18 suites and two oversized rooms all with double Jacuzzi-style tub, gas fireplace, and two-person shower. Located on the site of the former Jack Frost clothing and ski shop, the new inn has a very central location on the flat area in the middle of the village with trails from the Jackson cross-country ski system just outside the door. A large wraparound porch and a gazebo on the back of the building are places from which guests can watch village activity, including skiers as they shoosh by. A massive Great Hall with 10-foot wood-burning fireplace was to be the site of a buffet breakfast each morning. An indoor spa has a 19-foot waterfall. The Jack Frost Shop and two other boutiques will be relocated to the building itself. Doubles, $150–300.

♦ **Windy Hill Bed & Breakfast** (603-383-8917; 1-877-728-8927; www.windyhillbandb. com), Black Mountain Road, P.O. Box 462, Jackson, NH 03846. If you want to be off by yourself at what feels like the top of the world, this could be the spot for you. This well-named farm sits on a bare hilltop close by cross-country ski trails and just a short hop from Black Mountain for downhill skiing. Anne Peterson, who is also active in the local historical society, offers three rooms with private bath in an informal setting in her own home. One room has a queen bed, one a double, and one a king or two twins. There is no TV in the house at all, but there are games and puzzles and a resident dog. "The people who stay here are usually between 25 and 45 and don't want to be on a traveled road," says Anne. "We are low-key." She's happy to have guests visit the seven cows in her barn and even help feed them. Breakfast is serious: Caramelized French toast and pear sundae French toast (with ice cream) are two of her specialties. Doubles, $75–95.

IN PINKHAM NOTCH

♦ **Appalachian Mountain Club** (603-466-2727; www.outdoors.org), Route 16, Box 298, Gorham, NH 03581. The Joe Dodge Lodge at the AMC Visitor Center is chosen by hikers, skiers, and outdoorspeople. It's also great for families, because accommodations are generally affordable. The lodge has bunk rooms with four bunks or private rooms, all with large shared bathrooms. The rooms are simple with knotty-pine walls, curtains at the windows, and reading lights over the beds. Linens are provided. The visitors center next door has information and maps for hiking in the White Mountains, and the AMC offers many guided hikes and lessons in skills like ice climbing. The area is very close to the Great Glen cross-country area and to the Wildcat downhill ski area. Per-person rates, lodging only, in a bunkroom run $33–35 for adults, $22–24 for children. Bunk with breakfast and supper, $46–50 for adults, $32–34 for children. Double room, $66–70 (without meals); quad room (three or more beds) $84–93. You can purchase meals separately at the visitors center; just make sure you have reservations for dinner, as it sometimes fills.

WHERE TO EAT

Meals can be hot and hearty—perfect for après-ski appetites—or more elegant if you want to dress up just a tad. Note that casual attire is acceptable just about everywhere.

IN BARTLETT

♦ **Big Bear's Place** (603-374-6950), Main Street (Route 302), Bartlett. Barry Williams is the chef-owner of this very popular and casual eating spot. Two dining rooms—one a knotty-pine bar area with bentwood chairs at the tables and baseball caps hanging from the ceiling; the other a front room with a few antiques and early tools to set the mood—get crowded with regulars as well as visitors. This is a good place to bring kids; the menu has burgers, hot dogs, sides of fries, and homemade desserts to keep them happy. The two most popular items at dinner are the chicken and broccoli sautéed with tomatoes, basil, garlic, and cheeses and tossed with penne pasta ($10.95), and the homemade chicken potpie ($5.95). For vegetarians there is a spinach potpie—the spinach is layered with cheeses and almonds. Under the "Bear Beginnings" are overstuffed "Couch Potatoes" filled with veggies and cheese or chili and cheese; nachos in three sizes (Baby Bear, Mama Bear, and Big Bear); and mussels steamed in white wine, garlic, and tomato sauce and sprinkled with cheese. Soups are listed as "Porridge" and include clam chowder, lobster bisque, and the "soup du bear." Entrées include London broil, baked stuffed haddock, barbecued chicken and ribs, and several stir-fries ($8–14). A grilled prime rib sandwich on Texas toast, or portobello mushroom with roasted red peppers and Havarti cheese, is found on the sandwich menu. There's a good selection of imported beers. Cross-country skiers sometimes stop for lunch on weekends, since the Bear Notch trails pass right by. Dinner daily 4–9; lunch on Saturday and Sunday only.

IN GLEN

♦ **The Rare Bear at the Bernerhof** (603-383-4414), Route 302, Glen. Everybody raves about the food being served at the dining room in the Bernerhof. Theresa Stearns is the chef-owner; her husband, Scott, does host duties at this, one of the finer dining spots in the mountains. White cloths set the tone in the two brightly painted dining rooms—yellow in front and tomato-colored walls to the rear. There's a fireplace in the center. Starters ($7–9) include such possibilities as butternut squash and sage risotto, grilled shrimp served on crispy goat cheese polenta, or cheese fondue for two (the latter, $19). Salads might be roasted beet with candied kumquats, goat cheese, and herbs; wild mushroom salad with sherry truffle vinaigrette; or mixed greens with apples, walnuts, Gorgonzola, and a herbed balsamic vinaigrette ($6–7). Main courses ($15–26) might be oven-roasted salmon with a lobster brown butter citrus sauce and sweet potato puree; pepper-crusted venison with a red onion marmalade and Yukon Gold mashed potatoes; or braised lamb shank with creamy risotto and rosemary sauce. The salads and appetizers can be ordered in the atmospheric **Black Bear Pub** at the Bernerhof. Here burgers, a chicken BLT, and a BBQ beef wrap are among the sandwiches, all served with homemade coleslaw. Entrées include grilled bratwurst served over spiced red cabbage; Wiener schnitzel with spaetzle and red cabbage; and grilled steak with caramelized onions and steak fries ($11–15). Open nightly except Sunday for dinner. Reservations are important at The Rare Bear, especially on weekends.

♦ **Prince Place at the Storybook Inn** (603-383-9484), Routes 16 and 302, Glen. Mark Prince, who was formerly a chef at the Bernerhof, opened his own spot in 2001 in this restaurant space tucked toward the back of the Storybook Motor Inn complex. It's a little hard to find, but business was building steadily as the word got out that Mark was here. His wife, Korie, assists as hostess in the dining room. There is also a pleasant fireplaced pub (where no children are permitted). Dinner is served at wood tables with pink place mats. The most popular entrée is the Wiener schnitzel offered two ways—German-style with pork cutlets, or Swiss-style with veal. Other entrées ($13–18) include beef tenderloin Prince (topped with a potato Roquefort crust and served with Marsala sauce); shrimp scampi served with angel-hair pasta and garlic toast; and baked salmon with a lobster lemon cream sauce. Appetizers include salmon and rice cakes; smoky tomato soup; and fried calamari served with a spicy marinara sauce. The chicken Caesar salad has jerk chicken in it; there's also a tomato and fresh mozzarella salad in-season. Sandwiches are available and include a char-grilled burger or a pistachio chicken sandwich. Kids have a choice of hamburger, cheeseburger, grilled cheese, and macaroni and cheese ($5–6).

The desserts are actually listed first on the menu as a warning to save room. They include gingerbread with vanilla ice cream and butterscotch sauce, crème brûlée, an espresso Kahlua brownie sundae, and something called Chocolate Madness (chocolate mousse with chocolate sauce and cookies on the side). Open nightly except Tuesday in summer; sometimes the restaurant is closed Monday in winter, as well.

♦ **The Red Parka Pub** (603-383-4344), Route 302, Glen. Located near the junction of Routes 302 and 16, the Red Parka Pub has proved enormously successful over 30 years. Locals love it, skiers flock to it, and travelers return time and again. By the way, the name comes from the ski parkas that were worn by ski patrollers in the old days—red parkas with yellow crosses on the back for easy identification. A young, spirited crew staffs the place, whose menu is in the form of a newspaper. An incredible array of beers is offered, including local Tuckermans and Pig's Ear, and the bar is always jammed with drinkers and popcorn eaters. The salad bar is famous and adds just $1.95 to the price of the entrée (or is $6.50 alone if that's enough for you). Bands play from 8:30 PM on Friday and Saturday and sometimes Thursday. For appetizers, try fried popcorn shrimp with honey mustard; nachos; mushroom caps crammed with seafood stuffing; and beer-battered onion rings ($5–7). The Pub-Pub Platter at $14.95 is a sampling of ribs, Buffalo wings, popcorn shrimp, and jack cheese sticks for the whole table to share. Clam chowder and French onion soup are among the regulars. Entrées ($11–20) include beef, seafood, pasta, chicken. Aged sirloin steaks are offered in beginner, intermediate, and expert sizes; a 16-ounce or 10-ounce prime rib is available; and you can also get scallop pie, baked stuffed shrimp, broccoli and chicken Alfredo, and chicken teriyaki. Up for a sandwich? Try the Sir Loin Burger (half a pound) served with lettuce and tomato on a bulky roll; Cajun chicken; or a prime rib sandwich. For dessert, how about mud pie? Oh, forget the diet! Open nightly for dinner 4–10.

IN INTERVALE

♦ **The New England Inn** (603-356-5541), Intervale Loop, Intervale. A large formal dining room and the jumping **Tuckerman's Tavern** for the après-ski crowd are found at this popular inn. Dinner is served nightly in the main dining room, and it's an ambitious menu. Start with clam chowder or a soup of the day or possibly a shrimp cocktail or baked stuffed clams. One of the most popular entrées ($15–21) is the Shaker cranberry pot roast. Other possibilities include a wild mushroom sauté served with angel-hair pasta, rack of lamb, veal Marsala, and steak Diane. A house salad, inn-baked breads, potato or rice, and seasonal vegetables accompany all entrées. At **Tuckerman's** you can stick to nachos, teriyaki skewers, BBQ ribs, and other bar fare or have dinner—New York strip steak, a shepherd's pie, lasagna, and fish-and-chips. The dining room is open from 5:30 nightly; Tuckerman's opens at 3:30 Friday and Saturday, 4 other days.

IN JACKSON

♦ **The Inn at Thorn Hill** (603-383-4242), Thorn Hill Road. This has been one of the most romantic spaces for dining in the area. Wallpaper is deep red with a fleur-de-lis design; tablecloths are pink damask; and high-backed tapestry-upholstered chairs are used for seating. A wood-burning fireplace adds to the experience. The adjacent bar is small but atmospheric with window seats and small tables. The dining room has won the Best of the Award of Excellence from *Wine Spectator*. The menu entrées are presented with a suggested wine accompaniment. Following a fire in late 2002, reconstruction was in progress, with expansion of the dining room planned. Reopening was scheduled for fall of 2003.

Appetizers here ($7–10) were things like roast shiitake mushroom and spinach cannelloni served with a spiced cheddar flatbread crisp; pastrami-spiced duck breast with a red pepper and Gorgonzola samosa; or crabcakes with bacon and sautéed red onions, accompanied by a saffron ale cream sauce and carrot-lemon slaw. Entrées ($22–26) could be roast chicken breast with a wild rice and bacon custard served with a caramelized onion and rosemary sauce; roast pork tenderloin with a mushroom, mustard, and thyme sauce, served with braised red cabbage, cheddar cheese mashed potatoes, and spiced pecans; or sautéed shrimp with roasted butternut squash risotto and wilted spinach. Desserts have been as creative as the rest, changing regularly. One favorite has been Grand Marnier parfait with blackberries. Dinner nightly from 6. Reservations are a good idea.

♦ **The Wentworth** (603-383-9700). The dining room at the Wentworth Resort is a soft, elegant space. Plum-upholstered chairs and pink tablecloths set the mood. There is a fireplace as well. Starters ($7–9) could be wild mushroom strudel with scallion oil and citrus syrup; an "untraditional shepherd's pie" with layers of pheasant sausage, roasted shallots, and potato; or confit of duck over linguine with caramelized onions and dried figs. Roasted tomato bisque is on the menu with a soup of the day. The Caesar salad has sourdough croutons and a creamy anchovy dressing; you can also get salads of field greens or chicory. Entrées ($18–27) might be grilled tenderloin of beef with mashed potato and grilled asparagus; herb-roasted Cornish hen with potato risotto and marinated pepper salad; or pan-seared orange roughy served with lentils and baby arugula. Dinner is served nightly, and reservations are requested.

♦ **Thompson House Eatery (T.H.E.)** (603-383-9341), Routes 16A and 16. This delightful spot is extremely popular with locals as well as tourists. The old red farmhouse in which the restaurant is located dates from the early 1800s. There are three separate dining areas plus an outdoor terrace in summer. Calico tablecloths in deep blue and pink are overset with burgundy place mats and topped with vases of fresh flowers. One space as you enter has a wood-burning stove at one end and a few especially cozy tables. Longtime chef-owner Larry Baima is always trying new things and the cuisine has an original, sophisticated bent. As you enter, check the many specials listed on the blackboard. In the evening the house salad arrives with what seems like a mini salad bar of toppings in a muffin tin: raisins, sunflower seeds, walnuts, poppy seeds. Appetizers could be crabcakes, or shrimp scampi-style with minced vegetables, served on pasta ($7.50). Lighter fare includes Lorenzo's Loaf (a meat loaf made with spinach, mushrooms, onions, and herbs and served with gravy and potato) and Larry's Bird, a marinated chicken breast grilled and served atop a bed of greens with "garden goodies" as a garnish ($9). Among the entrées ($14–18) you might try pork tenderloin Piccata with fresh lemon, capers, and artichoke hearts, or Tofu for Drew, fresh veggies and tofu sautéed with roasted garlic, red pepper, and tomato pesto and served on pasta. At lunchtime try a curried chicken salad sandwich or one with turkey, ham, roast beef, melted Swiss, and Russian dressing. Salads include Currier & Ives—fresh chicken, toasted almonds, and raisins in a light curry dressing atop fresh greens ($5–8). There's a full bar and a bar menu of munchies. Lunch daily 11:30–4, dinner 5:30–10.

♦ **Wildcat Inn & Tavern** (603-383-4245), village center. Marty Sweeney, innkeeper with his wife, Pam, oversees the kitchen at this restaurant. It's consistently rated tops in the area. Combining country charm and coziness with sophisticated dining at rational prices, it can hardly be beat. The Wildcat's blue-gray building is located in the heart of Jackson Village. Three dining rooms offer an interesting mix of furnishings with creative placement of tables, homespun cloths and napkins, and soft candlelight in the evening. The more casual tavern just across the entryway—with its two huge wood-burning fireplaces and laid-back atmosphere—is the epitome of what's expected in winter in mountain country. Sit here for a few minutes with a glass of wine or a brew and you'll take the chill off your bones—and fast. The menu for the main dining room is augmented by specials. Typical starters ($8–9.50) would be shrimp wrapped in double-smoked bacon and baked with a sweet-and-sour sauce, or Mediterranean artichoke hearts in balsamic vinaigrette, baked au gratin. The Cassius salad is rosemary-grilled lamb tossed with mixed lettuces, Vermont goat cheese, roasted red peppers, grilled potatoes, toasted walnuts, and artichoke hearts ($10.95) and is a meal in itself. Entrées ($17–26) could be oven-roasted turkey tenderloin served with a peach and fresh basil cream sauce and sprinkled with roasted pecans; Lobster Lorenzo—fresh lobster meat sautéed with button mushrooms and simmered in white wine, cream, and Parmesan cheese sauce and served over fettuccine; or oven-roasted pheasant breast, sliced and served with a Chambord raspberry sauce.

In the tavern, start with southwestern nachos or a classic shrimp cocktail. Consider a Tavern burger (half a pound of char-grilled ground beef on a toasted roll served with a garden salad); a Greek spinach pie (served with a Greek salad, and an excellent choice for us one evening); or venison stew. Prices in the tavern hover around the $8 mark. An especially large number of beers—both draft and in bottles—is available. Sycamore Lane was the house wine.

The main dining room is open for dinner nightly from 6; lunch is served weekends only in winter. The tavern opens for supper 4–9 nightly.

♦ **The Red Fox Pub** (603-383-6659), village center. This is a popular, casual place in Jackson. A huge TV in the bar; a small fireplaced room with Windsor chairs and floral cloths on the tables; and a huge main dining room on a lower level with beamed supports and lattice dividers make this a place where just about everybody can feel comfortable. The all-day menu is expansive and includes appetizers like chicken quesadilla, potato skins filled with diced teriyaki sirloin and creamy spinach, and Parmesan dip served with tortilla chips ($7–9). A Buffalo chicken salad is served with blue cheese dressing. Pasta specialties include spaghetti and meatballs and lobster ravioli ($11–15). Bourbon-glazed sirloin steak and herb-crusted sirloin are two of the pub's signature items ($13 each). Other entrées include chicken Marsala, barbecued baby back ribs served with fries, and baked scallops. You can get burgers and sandwiches. On Sunday a buffet of eat-as-much-as-you-can breakfast items is available 7:30–12:15 at $5.95 per person and is popular. Open from 11:30 to 9 or 10 nightly, except Sunday for breakfast/brunch.

♦ **Chefs' Palate Restaurant** at Whitney's Inn (603-383-8916), Route 16A, Jackson. Chefs Christian Boucher and Richard Nickerson took over the restaurant at Whitney's in early 2002, and people were raving almost immediately. The comfortable, mostly green dining room had been operated under several different managements, but this looked especially promising. Mussels Provençal (mussels with andouille sausage tossed with a marinara sauce); baked artichoke with cilantro, pesto, and melted cheddar; and onion soup au gratin, with two cheeses, were possible appetizers ($5–8). Entrées ($17–21) included grilled swordfish served with sautéed tomatoes and fennel butter; roast duckling with a raspberry orange Grand Marnier sauce; and chicken sautéed with mushrooms, spinach, prosciutto ham, and penne pasta in a light Parmesan cream sauce. Entrées are served with a house salad, a vegetable, home-baked bread, and a choice of rice or potato. Open for dinner nightly.

♦ **The Shannon Door Pub** (603-383-4211), just off Route 16 north of Jackson Village, is a good place for entertainment after 8 PM. Pizzas are popular, but there are also nightly specials like pot roast and roast turkey.

IN PINKHAM NOTCH

♦ **The Appalachian Mountain Club** (603-466-2727), Route 16, Gorham. The big cathedral-ceilinged dining room in the visitors center at the AMC is the place to have dinner when you're in the mood to rub elbows with those who have skied Tuckerman Ravine that day, or when you yourself have accomplished the feat. For $15 ($13.50 for AMC members) you get a hearty dinner, good discussion, and—on Saturday evening—a free lecture after dinner on such topics as avalanches or hypothermia. The food is always good. There is basically one set menu, but it's posted or available ahead of time in case it's something you just can't eat. You sit at long wood tables on benches. Home-baked bread and butter are on the table when you sit down. Water and coffee are available; you may bring your own wine or beer. We had bowls of clam chowder, green salad, delicious baby carrots and pearl onions, pot roast, oven-baked potatoes, and apple crumb pie when we last ate here. Kids are welcome. It's a nice convivial atmosphere, and you can't get such a filling meal at this price anywhere else we know. But—you must have a reservation for dinner. So call ahead.

22 Vermont's Northeast Kingdom

The Northeast Kingdom of Vermont—so dubbed by one of Vermont's U.S. senators more than 50 years ago—is a vast area encompassing the northeast corner of the state. It reaches north from the town of Wells River on the Connecticut River to the Canadian border. To the east it bumps up against New Hampshire; its western border zigzags to capture Jay Peak, one of the most challenging alpine ski areas in New England, as well as towns of Craftsbury and Hardwick.

The Northeast Kingdom is comprised of three Vermont counties: Essex, Orleans, and Caledonia. It is the state's largest region, filled with high mountains and pristine lakes, home to dairy farms, forests, hiking trails, and picturesque towns. In winter it's a playground for alpine and cross-country skiing, snowboarding, snowshoeing, horse-drawn sleigh rides, snowmobiling, ice skating, sledding, and even dogsledding. There's simply a lot to do here.

For the purposes of a weekend visit, we concentrate on the southern part of the region, primarily Caledonia County. This section is anchored by the kingdom's largest community, St. Johnsbury. St. J, as the locals say, is a Victorian town, much of it built and bequeathed by the philanthropic Fairbanks family. Fairbanks was the manufacturer of the first platform weighing scale; there is still a plant in town. Two Fairbanks brothers built museums that are gems to visit today: the Fairbanks Museum and Planetarium and the St. Johnsbury Athenaeum.

The town has a wealth of beautiful homes, some truly unique shops, and some good restaurants. You'll also find a maple museum, a bookstore run by the American Society of Dowsers, and a fine private high school, St. Johnsbury Academy.

Just 10 miles north of St. J, Lyndonville boasts more Victorian mansions along with a pretty town green and active downtown. Lyndon Institute is its revered private high school. Lyndonville—and the larger town of Lyndon—was once a thriving railroad depot. There are five covered bridges in this New England town.

East of Lyndonville is East Burke, home of Burke Mountain. Burke is an alpine ski area with a 2,000-foot vertical drop that is enjoyed by novices and experts alike. Burke Mountain Academy—which owns the mountain—was the first ski academy in the country, a preparatory school where an elite group of skier-students train and study. The academy has sent more than 40 alumni on to participate in the Olympics in downhill skiing.

The landscape in this part of Vermont is gorgeous in winter, when snow softens the contours of the ground and tall, dark green pine trees offer stunning contrast. The restored monumental red barns at Mountain View Farm in East Burke, built in 1890, are shown to advantage in snow. So are other farms in the area. East Burke is home to some fine country inns and B&Bs.

The picturesque towns of Greensboro, Peacham, and Danville—southwest of Lyndon—are worthy stops on a weekend trip to the Northeast Kingdom. Danville welcomes loads of snowmobilers who cut through the countryside around it on a great network of trails. Greensboro has a lodge and cross-country ski center that is one of the largest and best in New England. Peacham is so picture-perfect that several moving pictures have been shot there.

This part of the world may be less commercial than other tourist destinations, but it's hardly unsophisticated. In winter, it is special.

Getting There

By car: Interstate 91 runs through the kingdom from south to north—and connects with other roads, such as I-93 to Boston. Boston is about 3½ hours away; Hartford, 4 hours; New York City, 6 hours.
By air: Major airports serving the region include Burlington, Vermont (2 hours away); Manchester, New Hampshire (3 hours); and Boston (3½ hours). A municipal airport, **Caledonia County Airport,** is located in Lyndonville (802-626-3353).
By bus: Greyhound and Vermont Transit Lines combine to bring service to the kingdom on a daily basis from several other New England areas. There are links directly to airports in Boston; Manchester, New Hampshire; and Albany, New York. For information on Vermont Transit, call (802) 864-6811.

For More Information

Contact the **Northeast Kingdom Chamber of Commerce** (802-748-3678; 1-800-639-6379; www.travelthekingdom.com), 357 Western Avenue, Suite 2, St. Johnsbury, VT 05819. The **Lyndon Area Chamber of Commerce,** P.O. Box 886, Lyndonville, VT 05851, can be reached at (802) 626-9696.

Pick up the daily *Caledonian-Record* for current events while visiting.

Winter Sports and Outdoor Activities

Vermont was made for winter. The hardy residents of the Northeast Kingdom don't retire inside at the sight of the first snowflake. As one innkeeper says, "I like a little snow every day or two—just to keep everything clean and white." Residents have learned how much fun it is to play in the snow and the cold and invite their visitors to do the same.

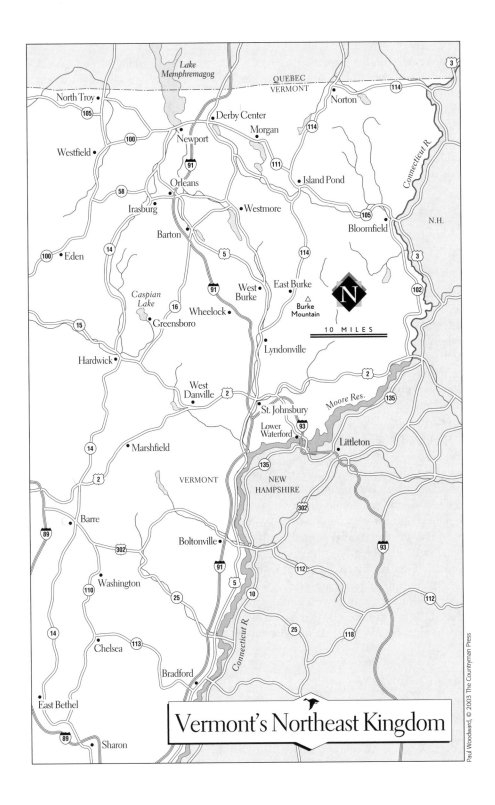

Vermont's Northeast Kingdom

Downhill Skiing

♦ **Burke Mountain** (802-626-3322; snow phone 802-626-1390; lodging 802-748-6137; www.skiburke.com), off Route 114, East Burke, VT 05832. Burke Mountain is currently owned by Burke Mountain Academy, which uses its trails to train alpine skiers. BMA was founded in 1970 and picked up the mountain at auction in 2001. Burke is a dream for beginners and new skiers, who have plenty of easy runs from the Base Lodge. More advanced skiers take the quad chair from Mid-Burke, a second lodge halfway up the mountain. Lift lines are rare. **Snowboarding** is popular here, too. All equipment can be rented, and lessons are offered. A Learn-to-Ski package is $49. Day care operates weekends and during holiday weeks for kids from 6 months to 12 years in age. Weekend/holiday rates are adults $39, seniors and teens $29, children $25.

Cross-Country Skiing

♦ **Burke Cross Country Ski Area** (802-626-8338; 802-467-8861; burkexc@kingcon. com), The Mountain Road, RR1, Box 62A, East Burke, VT 05832. With 85 km of trails—all tracked and groomed—this is one of the most expansive Nordic ski areas in the state. Owners Cherrie and Geoff Boone also operate a small snack bar and ski shop with a good selection of rental equipment. A separate dome-shaped building is used for waxing and picnics. Snowshoes are welcome on the trails. Trail fees: adults $12; juniors or seniors $8. Under 7 and over 70 ski free. A combined trail fee, rental, and lesson is $30 for adults, $23 for juniors/seniors. Open, late December into early April, daily 9–4:30.

♦ **Highland Lodge** (802-533-2647; www.highlandlodge.com), Caspian Lake, Greensboro, VT 05841. More than 50 km of groomed cross-country trails are attached to this cozy mid-19th-century inn. The 16-mile great loop is especially loved. The place is popular with both day skiers who often lunch in the inn's excellent dining room, and those who settle in for a weekend or longer. Trails include glades through balsam forests as well as challenging hilly terrain. The inn sometimes offers a special package with 2 days' skiing, a full breakfast and dinner, and gratuities included for the price of a night's lodging. The red shed out back is a complete cross-country ski center with daily instruction, a ski shop for rentals and repairs, and maps to pick up. Snowshoes and sleds are also supplied in the shop. Trails here connect with those of the Craftsbury Center, 6 km distant. Trail fees: adults $11, children $7 (from 1 PM, $8 and $5). Kids under 8 and over 70 ski free. Seniors 60 and older ski for $8 a day, $5 a half day.

Snowshoeing

Snowshoes are being used more and more—Geoff Boone of the Burke Cross Country Ski Center says there's a 50 percent increase in the sport annually. This part of Vermont is perfect for snowshoes. Many using snowshoes don't want to trek in deep snow—even though that's what snowshoes were originally designed for.

Skiers at Burke Mountain

Here, cross-country trails and snowmobile trails are generally open to snowshoers. This makes for a walk in the woods on a packed surface, somewhat easier than breaking trail. Snowshoes can be rented at cross-country ski areas. Trail fees are the same for both sports.

♦ **Kingdom Trails.** These cross-country/snowshoe trails can be accessed from East Burke Sports in the village of East Burke, from the Inn at Mountain View Farm on Darling Hill Road, East Burke, or from The Wildflower Inn, also on Darling Hill Road in East Burke. The trails are for anyone's use. Deposit a $3 fee and take a trail map. The trails are not patrolled, and skiing is permitted only in daylight.

Horse-Drawn Sleigh Rides

What's more fun than snuggling under heavy blankets and being driven by horses through the frosty air? **Sugar Ridge Campground** (802-684-2550) in Danville has horse-drawn sleigh rides on weekends noon–4 or by appointment. **LaPlant's Sugar House** (802-467-3900) in Sutton offers horse-drawn sleigh rides by appointment only. **Bruce Brink SleighRides** (802-684-1163) in Danville require a reservation.

Snowmobiling

This is snowmobile country. The kingdom claims to be the best area in New England for snowmobiling, and residents frequently see dark shapes whizzing across the distant hills and pastureland. The Vermont Association of Snow Travelers (VAST) has organized a large network of numbered trails—more than 3,500 miles of trails in the entire Northeast Kingdom—that are used by snowmobilers. Rent snowmobiles at **All Around Rental Equipment** (802-748-7841) in St. Johnsbury or from **Kingdom Cat Corp** (802-723-9702) in Island Pond. Rentals are in the range of $200 a day, $400 per weekend. A 1-hour rental from All-Around is $75. Reserve in advance.

Dogsledding

♦ **Hardscrabble Mountain Sled Dog Tours** (802-626-9895), Sheffield. You can sample dogsledding with a 20-minute basic beginners' tour for $25 a couple, or $12.50 an individual. Keith Ballek is the musher, driving the six dogs while beginners ride in the sled. For a more in-depth experience, he offers a "Musher's Package" whereby you get to drive the dogs if you feel up to it toward the end of the tour. This takes about 2½ hours and costs $90 per couple, $55 for an individual.

Ice Skating

The only indoor rink in the area is the **Fenton Chester Ice Arena** (802-626-9361) in Lyndon Center. Skate rental is $2. Adults pay $3 and kids, $2, for a 2-hour skate time. Usually public skating is available from 12:30 to 2:30 PM on Sunday, but call to confirm. Skating is also available outdoors on ponds or outdoor rinks, weather permitting.

Sight-Seeing

You may prefer to view winter from inside a car or museum. The Northeast Kingdom can provide plenty of indoor pleasures.

Museums

♦ **Fairbanks Museum and Planetarium** (802-748-2372; www.fairbanksmuseum. org), 1302 Main Street, St. Johnsbury. A huge stuffed Kodiak bear and a polar bear stand side by side to welcome visitors to this incredible museum. More than 100 years old, it has a natural history collection that is remarkable. The red sandstone building and collection were given to the town in 1891 by Franklin Fairbanks, nephew of the man who invented the platform scale. The interior is interesting for an oak barrel vault ceiling, and lots more oak and cherry—giving it a warm, inviting feeling. Exhibits are in vintage glass cases and include 3,200 birds from all over the world. Other stuffed animals are presented in dioramas showing habitat and activities. Downstairs in the museum is the New England Weather Center, which serves commercial radio stations and Vermont Public Radio. Open Monday through Saturday 9–5, Sunday 1–5. Planetarium shows on Saturday and Sunday at 1:30 PM. Admission: adults $5, seniors $4, children 5–17 $3; a family admission with no more than three adults and any number of children is $12. The planetarium show costs $3 per person.

The Fairbanks Museum & Planetarium in St. Johnsbury

♦ **St. Johnsbury Athenaeum** (802-748-8291; www.stjathenaeum. org), 30 Main Street, St. Johnsbury. Horace Fairbanks, brother of Franklin—of the Fairbanks Museum and Planetarium—was a great benefactor to the town of St. Johnsbury. His major gift was the athenaeum. Located in a lovely mansard-roofed brick building in the center of St. J, the athenaeum is notable for the fine woodwork in the interior and for its collection of art, which is in an art gallery at the rear of the building. The most notable painting is Albert Bierstadt's large *Domes of Yosemite*, which dominates the space. This is a closed collection, all of the works having been donated by Horace Fairbanks. It's a charming place. Open weekdays 10–5:30, Monday and Wednesday until 8 PM, Saturday 9:30–4. Free. Donations accepted for the art gallery area.

♦ **Maple Grove Farms of Vermont** (802-748-5141), 1052 Portland Street, St. Johnsbury. Maple sugar candy is made from molds at this business dating back to 1904. A museum is open May to October. The gift shop is open year-round but only weekdays from January through mid-May.

♦ **Dog Mountain Art Gallery of Stephen Huneck,** Spaulding Road, off Route 2, St. Johnsbury. The creator of whimsical dog and cat sculpture, furniture, and art (mostly dogs) lives and works at this mountainside complex. The art gallery and dog chapel are generally open 11–4 June through October. In winter you can still drive up and see the exterior of the buildings, including the amazing dog stained-glass windows in the little chapel. Huneck is a renowned artist with several galleries around the country, including Woodstock, Vermont; Martha's Vineyard, and Nantucket.

Classical Music

The **Northeast Kingdom Classical Series** operates from late fall through early spring. Performances are in various churches and auditoriums in the area. For information on dates and programs, call (802) 748-8012 or (802) 626-9204.

Dowsing

♦ **The American Society of Dowsers** (802-684-3417), P.O. Box 24, Danville. This group, which uses sticks and pendulums to find water as well as for other prognostications, operates a bookstore on Railroad Street in downtown St. Johnsbury. Here you can buy all sorts of New Age materials, books, and back issues of *The American Dowser* quarterly publication. There are also pendulums and dowsing sticks (plastic now instead of wood). You can pick up a catalog listing many items offered for sale. The group has its annual convention in the Lyndon area in summer.

Covered Bridges

All five covered bridges of Caledonia County are within the town of **Lyndon.** You can drive through **Miller's Run Bridge,** constructed in 1800 and most recently restored in 1995. It's found on Route 122 in Lyndon Center.

Scenic Drives

Darling Hill Road in East Burke offers fantastic views as it passes mansions and country inns. Route 2 to Danville and then Route 16 to Greensboro are pretty roads with farms and open fields. The Access Road to Burke Mountain is pretty. The road to Peacham from Danville is a lovely road that twists and turns. But just about anywhere you drive is great.

Shopping

St. J is the best place for shopping. On **Railroad Street** find **Caplan's Army Store** with serious vests, wool socks, hats with earflaps, Woolrich items, parkas, long johns—everything to keep a person warm in winter. **Moose River Lake & Lodge** at 370 Railroad Street is one of our favorites with Adirondack-style furniture, Pendleton blankets, April Cornell clothes for women, tasteful home decor items, antlers, and a good wine and microbrew selection.

Northern Lights Bookshop and Café has a good range of books and a terrific café (see *Where to Eat*). Also on Railroad Street, the **Artisans Guild** has a shop carrying the work of local crafters and artists. **Uniquity** has handcrafted gifts and furniture. On **Eastern Avenue** are more shops, including **Sunshine Boutique** for jewelry, giftware, and unusual women's clothing, and **Through the Woods,** known for fine gifts and home decor items. You can pick up maple candy and gifts at the gift shop of **Maple Grove Farms** on Route 2—only open weekdays in winter.

In **Greensboro** the **Willey's Store** is one of the best general stores in the state, with everything from groceries to housewares, hardware, and clothing. **The Miller's Thumb**—just across the street from the general store—is in a former gristmill. It has two levels filled with Italian pottery, clothing for women, candles, cosmetics, and other tasteful gift items. A special opening in the first floor allows you to look down at the rushing stream below the building. The **Caspian Hot Glass Studio** a short way west of the center has hand-blown glass items by Jacob

Barron and Lucas Lonegren, including Christmas ornaments, glasses, pitchers, decorative plates, and bowls.

Danville is home to **Farr's Antiques,** a barn full of antiques and collectibles on three levels. You could spend hours there. The **Cabot Creamery** in **Cabot** is a famous producer of cheddar cheese. Factory tours are offered Monday through Saturday—except during January, when the visitors center is closed. The **Rowell Sugarhouse**—where you can see equipment used to produce maple syrup—is one of several sugarhouses in the region. This one is located on Route 15 in Walden, between West Danville and Hardwick. Although it claims to be open daily year-round, it was closed the January Sunday we drove by. The phone number is (802) 563-2756.

In **Lyndonville, Green Mountain Books & Prints** is a treasure trove of new and used books. **Route 5 Collectibles** is a multidealer shop with antiques and consignment items.

Bailey's & Burke Country Store in **East Burke** has artwork, craft items, fudge, clothing, all well organized on a main floor and a mezzanine level above. **East Burke Sports** has ski and sporting equipment.

WHERE TO STAY

IN THE BURKE MOUNTAIN AREA

♦ **The Wildflower Inn** (802-626-8310; 1-800-627-8310; fax 802-626-3039; www.wildflowerinn.com), 2059 Darling Hill Road, Lyndonville, VT 05851. The Wildflower Inn was once a working farm, now turned into a family-friendly inn with loads of activities for kids and parents. Owner-innkeepers Jim and Mary O'Reilly have been in charge since 1985; their sure hand has resulted in a noted establishment with many returning guests. Altogether 21 rooms and suites, all with private bath, are offered in four buildings. The rooms have many different configurations; some are large with queen bed and bunks for parents and children. There is an efficiency suite with fully equipped kitchen, two bedrooms, and even a washer-dryer. All rooms have wall-to-wall carpeting, and many have their own balcony. Some allow you to lie in bed and gaze out at snow-covered Burke Mountain. A full breakfast is served here with teddy-bear-shaped pancakes for kids. On the 570-acre property is a network of cross-country ski and snowshoe trails. There's easy access to the VAST snowmobile trails. There is also an outdoor skating rink with skates available and a splendid sledding hill. Horse-drawn sleigh rides are arranged by the inn when weather permits. Sometimes packages include passes to Burke Mountain for downhill skiing. A barn with animals and a kids' activity barn are on the premises. On selected Saturday nights, kids can be fed separately from adults and enjoy an evening in the activity barn. A full country breakfast and afternoon snack are included in the rates. A **restaurant** on the premises allows you to stay in for dinner if you want. Closed in April and November. Doubles, $140–250.

♦ **The Old Cutter Inn** (802-626-5152; 1-800-295-1943; www.pbpub.com/cutter.htm), 143 Pinkham Inn, East Burke, VT 05832-9707. A Swiss couple, Fritz and Marti

Walther, have run this deep red mountainside inn—just about 5 minutes from Burke Mountain—since the late 1970s. It's spotless and comfortable and has a highly acclaimed dining room, where Fritz is chef (see *Where to Eat*). The four rooms in the main inn are simply furnished and may have two double beds, a queen and a twin, or something similar. These rooms share baths. Five rooms in the Carriage House across the parking lot have private bath. Also in the Carriage House is a two-level apartment suite with two bedrooms, private bath, fireplaced living room, and kitchen. Rooms are offered EP at $62–76 per night or MAP with breakfast and dinner included. A 2-day MAP package is $118–128 per person. The apartment suite rents for $165 per day, EP. The inn is closed in April and November.

♦ **Inn at Mountain View Farm** (802-626-9924; 1-800-572-4509; www.innmtnview.com), Darling Hill Road, Box 355, East Burke, VT 05832. This exceptional hilltop site was chosen by local man Elmer A. Darling, owner of an elegant New York hotel, for the farm that would supply the hotel's meat and dairy products. It was built in 1883 and is notable for its monumental red barns, which tower over the rest of the complex. The creamery is a brick building where most of the inn's rooms and its well-rated restaurant (see *Where to Eat*) are located. The steam engine for operating the creamery is still in place in the breakfast room. Nine rooms are offered in the inn—all individually and tastefully decorated and with private bath. Many rooms are done in tones of green and red and are cheery and warm. Next door, in the yellow Farmhouse, are five luxury suites with queen bed, sitting area, and whirlpool tub or fireplace. A common room in this building is unusual for the green interior shutters on the windows. Cross-country ski and snowshoe trails are easily accessed from the property, and the views are grand. Doubles, with breakfast and afternoon tea, $145–245.

♦ **The Village Inn of East Burke** (802-626-3161; www.villageinnofeastburke.com), Route 114, Box 186, East Burke, VT 05832. Innkeepers Lorraine and George Willy have been renovating and upgrading their well-located farmhouse for many years now. The result is a neat, homey establishment with six spacious guest rooms, all with private bath, ideal for families and skiers. And the price is right. The guest living room is divided into two comfortable areas, one with games and books, and the other with fireplace. Both have long sofas and comfortable chairs. Three guest rooms are on the first floor, and three upstairs. All have a bath with tub-shower. The Hay Loft Room is especially large, with a queen bed on the main level, twin beds in a loft, and a bathroom with clawfoot tub. A full breakfast is served in a pristine kitchen area, where guests are also encouraged to make their own dinners. Well-behaved dogs are permitted. The Willys keep hives and have their own canning business so honey and canned vegetables are available for sale. Doubles, $75.

IN LYNDON/LYNDONVILLE

♦ **Branch Brook Bed & Breakfast** (802-626-8316; 1-800-572-7712), off South Wheelock Road, Box 143, Lyndon, VT 05849. Ann and Ted Tolman rescued a derelict 1830s farmhouse and converted it into a charming B&B. Main-floor common rooms include a parlor with long windows to the floor; a comfortable breakfast room where you can have your own table or join others; and a little TV room with a vintage wood-burning stove. Upstairs are five gracious guest rooms, two of them queen-bedded rooms with private bath. One has a four-poster and one, a canopy bed. Our corner room was spacious and comfortable with a down quilt on the bed to keep us warm in January. Two rooms—one with twin beds—share a bath, and one room has been carved out under the eaves. Ann loves her AGA cookstove and turns out breakfasts to order from an expansive menu listed on a blackboard in the dining room—everything from light-as-air buttermilk pancakes to orange scones with orange butter to poached eggs on toast. She has a background in food service and nutrition, and it shows. Doubles, $65–85.

♦ **Darling Manor Bed & Breakfast** (802-626-5583; 1-800-387-5210; fax 802-626-7229; www.darlingmanor.com), 745 Center Street, P.O. Box 166, Lyndonville, VT 05851. Guests at this large yellow Dutch Colonial Revival home enjoy the attention of Texas-accented innkeeper Nancy Clarke, whose mother was born in this region of Vermont. Nancy (and her husband and daughter) came north from Texas when he retired. They share the large home and offer three rooms to guests. Interior wood-work in the house is amazing and mostly original. All guest rooms—located on the second and third floors of the house—have TV. Two rooms on the second floor are joined by a bathroom, used by parties traveling together. The Cherub Room has a king-sized bed, and the Queen Anne Room offers a queen bed and a fireplace filled with pillared candles. There is a hall bath that can be given to one of these rooms to make private baths for each. Up a rather steep flight of stairs on the third floor is the Texas Hill Country Room, with twin beds and a bathroom with clawfoot tub and handheld shower. Nancy serves a full breakfast at a large table in the dining room. She also sets out coffee and snacks on a table in the second-floor hall. Doubles, $85–95 for shared bath; $110 with private bath.

♦ **Colonnade Inn** (802-626-9316; fax 802-626-1023), Route 5, Lyndonville, VT 05851. Located just off exit 23 from I-91, this two-level, 40-room motel offers rooms with two doubles or one queen bed. TVs with HBO are advertised. Children under 12 stay free with parents. Complimentary coffee and doughnuts are served in the lobby in the morning. Doubles, $45–60.

IN THE ST. JOHNSBURY AREA

♦ **Rabbit Hill Inn** (802-748-5168; 1-800-76-BUNNY; fax 802-748-8342; www.rabbit-hillinn.com), P.O. Box 55, Lower Waterford, VT 05848. One of the most exquisite inns in New England is located just 7 miles southeast of St. J. Leslie and Brian Mulcahy, innkeepers, describe themselves and their inn as "hopelessly romantic." It's the kind of place to go for a celebration or a special needed getaway. And although the innkeepers have put together wonderful ideas for spending a day in the Northeast Kingdom—from a "Taster's Tour" to a detailed plan for exploring St. Johnsbury—Brian says, "We also mandate a nap." The white pillared main inn and the Tavern building next door offer 19 tasteful, luxurious guest rooms, most with a working fireplace. The Mulcahys classify their rooms as "Luxury" (the largest rooms, with sitting/reading areas by the fireplace); "Fireplace" (good-sized rooms with elegant furnishings and a fireplace, of course); and "Classic" (four smaller rooms without fireplaces). Every room has a floppy-eared stuffed rabbit perched

The Rabbit Hill Inn

somewhere to welcome guests. Rabbit Hill Inn is viewed as a "destination proper-ty," and winter guests have 8 km of cross-country ski trails out back, as well as sleds and toboggans to use. A massage therapist can provide a massage in your room. On Saturdays in winter, longtime chef Russell Stannard prepares a special hot lunch by the fireside—usually a stew or pasta dish—that guests are welcome to enjoy. A full country breakfast is served in the handsome dining room (which is also open to the public for dinner; see *Where to Eat*). In addition, a charming little tavern with chess and other games is a place to while away a few hours or have a late-day drink. Public rooms are comfortable with several sitting areas. Closed the first 2 weeks of November and first 2 weeks of April. Doubles, $260–375.

♦ **The Albro Nichols House** (802-751-8434), 53 Boynton Avenue, St. Johnsbury, VT 05819. This white house with lavender shutters is right in the heart of town, and guests can walk to the athenaeum or the Fairbanks Museum. Margaret Ryan, a retired private school English and theater instructor, offers three rooms to guests. One is a double-bedded room with private bath on the main floor. Upstairs, two rooms—one with twin beds and one with double bed—share a bath. Margaret serves a full breakfast with juice, fresh fruit, a hot dish, and homemade muffins. Double with private bath, $80; with shared bath, $60.

♦ **Fairbanks Inn** (802-748-5666), 32 Western Avenue, (Route 2 East), St. Johnsbury, VT 05812. This 46-room motel is well located just on the outskirts of town. Rooms are large and furnished with two doubles or a king-sized bed. There are also an effi-ciency suite and a large two-room suite with Jacuzzi. All rooms have TV, wall-to-wall carpeting, and balcony—some with wonderful views of the mountains. A pool is available in summer. A continental breakfast—with coffee, juice, and muffins—is complimentary and served in the attractive lobby in the morning. Doubles, $70. Sometimes good packages with Burke Mountain are offered to skiers.

♦ **Comfort Inn** (802-748-1500; 1-800-228-5150), 703 Route 5 South (at Exit 20 off I-91), St. Johnsbury, VT 05819. This chain motel has 107 rooms, an indoor pool, sauna and whirlpool, fitness room, and video arcade. Rooms have two queens or a king-sized bed, TV, phone, and private bath. An expanded complimentary continental breakfast served in a special breakfast room includes items like fresh fruit, juices, cereals, waffles, and French toast. Doubles, $90–129. A special lower snowmobilers' rate is usually offered in winter.

IN DANVILLE

♦ **Hamilton House** (802-684-9800; 1-866-684-9800; www.thehamiltonhouse .com), on the village green, Danville, VT 05828. Five guest rooms with Victorian women's names—such as Abigail, Beatrice, and Dorothy—have been beautifully decorated by innkeepers Nancy Hogue and her mother, Shirley LaPorte. The mother-daughter team opened the inn in 2001. The building, dating from 1884, was home to the old Caledonia National Bank; the bank vault is now in the living room. This large front room has seating by the fireplace, a library corner, and a spot to watch TV. It opens into the dining area, where guests have a full country breakfast provided by Shirley. Baked French toast with a pecan caramel sauce is a specialty. All guest rooms are on the second floor. Two large front corner rooms—Dorothy, with two double beds, and and Elizabeth, with a king bed—have working fireplace. Elizabeth, decorated with red floral wallpaper and red-and-green-plaid draperies, is especially cozy. Like the other rooms, it has refinished wide-plank wood floors. All rooms have private bath, although one is in the hall. Doubles, $109 and $129.

IN GREENSBORO

♦ **Highland Lodge** (802-533-2647; fax 802-533-7494; www.highlandlodge.com), Caspian Lake, Greensboro, VT 05841. David Smith, whose parents originally owned the lodge, began to cut cross-country trails through the property in the 1950s. Half a century later David and his wife, Wilhelmina, operate one of the most authentic ski-tour inns in Vermont. The inn and cottage complex offer 11 simple guest rooms and 11 cottages (only 4 of which are open in winter). Books seem to be everywhere in the two large public rooms on the main floor of the inn, inviting you to select one and sit by the wood-burning fireplace. Local art is displayed on the walls. Guest rooms in the main inn are country cozy with maple furniture, white George Washington spreads, blankets folded at the foot of the beds, and calico-flowered wallpaper. The private bathrooms are serviceable, if not particularly large, with tub-shower combinations. Usually you'll find a queen and a single bed in the room, although a few have one queen bed. Cottages have two bedrooms, living room with gas fireplace, and kitchen. Winter guests are often devoted to Nordic skiing and can access 55 km of groomed trails directly from the inn. The lodge is on a hillside in one of Vermont's prettiest towns; in summer Caspian Lake draws the crowds. Rates are MAP, $96–128 per person, double occupancy in the main inn. Those in cottages pay $128 per person, per day.

WHERE TO EAT

IN THE BURKE MOUNTAIN AREA

♦ **River Garden Café** (802-626-3514), Route 114, East Burke. David Thomas and Bobby Baker, two New Yorkers with a sense of style, opened this restaurant in 1991—and it deserves the rave reviews it gets. The small gray house with green trim has a cozy bar in front as you enter, and two dining rooms. One is the enclosed windowed porch to the rear that overlooks the garden in summer and a yard usually covered with snow at this time of year. Little white lights twinkle on the ceiling; calico-style tablecloths dress the tables. Lunch starters can be a warm artichoke dip with grilled French bread or smoked salmon ($7–7.50). The soup of the day was tomato with roasted corn when we stopped. Salads might be Jamaican jerk chicken salad—chicken tossed with black beans, rice, greens, and a tangy lime dressing—or cold poached salmon served on lettuce with house-made dill cucumber yogurt dressing. You can get a veggie burger, pizza, steak sandwich, or chili made with black beans. In the evening, entrées ($15–20) could be chicken Marsala; roast stuffed pork tenderloin with dried prune and wild mushroom stuffing; or baked rainbow trout. Open for lunch and dinner Wednesday through Saturday, brunch and dinner Sunday. Closed Monday and Tuesday in winter; closed Monday only in summer.

♦ **The Old Cutter Inn** (802-626-5152), 143 Pinkham Road, just off the Burke Mountain Access Road, East Burke. Everyone wants to be near the fireplace in the main dining room at this very popular spot. But only four tables have a view of the fireplace, and so we had to settle for a table around the corner and a little removed. The food is the star here, anyway, with Swiss owner-chef Fritz Walther providing excellent fare including some Swiss/German specialties. One of us had the famous Rahmschnitzel—veal medallions sautéed in butter with shallots, white wine, and finished with mushrooms in a light cream sauce. The other had rainbow trout amandine. Both were very good. Entrées come with a tossed salad and choice of dressings, vegetables (broccoli hollandaise and carrots for us), and a choice of potato or starch. Roesti potatoes are always on the menu but at extra cost. A tray of celery, radishes, and carrots with a creamy cheddar dip started the meal in an old-style but appreciated way. Appetizers include French onion soup, smoked rainbow trout, and mushroom pâté. Other entrées can be roast duckling à l'orange; fresh omelet with choice of fillings; tournedos of beef; and chateaubriand for two. Beef Wellington and rack of lamb (both for two, and ordered 24 hours in advance) are offered. An affordable wine list—including carafes and half carafes of house wines—is available. A pub dining room has lighter fare. Open nightly except Wednesday for dinner.

♦ **Inn at Mountain View Farm** (802-626-9924), Darling Hill Road, East Burke. The small and very attractive dining room at this hilltop inn is considered excellent. There's a warm feeling in the room, with burgundy and white the color scheme. A big old black stove adds to the charm. Appetizers could be sautéed calamari over garlic, or spinach or shrimp bruschetta served over Tuscan toast ($5–6). The inn's signature salad includes Cabot cheddar with green apples and toasted pistachio nuts served with mesclun greens and pistachio vinaigrette. Entrées include honey-glazed salmon with butternut risotto; fire-roasted chicken with penne pasta; grilled pork tenderloin over grilled radicchio with balsamic reduction; and grilled filet mignon with truffle mashed potatoes. Entrées are priced $16–22. Open Thursday through Sunday evening 5–9. Reservations are a good idea.

♦ **The Pub Outback** (802-626-1188), behind Bailey's & Burke Country Store, East Burke. This informal eatery is a place to go when a burger or nachos or something as simple as meat loaf is on your mind. "The Starting Gate" lists chicken digits (chicken fingers deep-fried and served with honey mustard or barbecue sauce); fried mozzarella with ranch dressing or marinara sauce; deep-fried mushrooms; and nachos with chili or guacamole ($5–6). The club salad is turkey, ham, bacon, and mozzarella cheese on crisp greens, and you can also get chicken salad or Caesar salad. Nine different varieties of burgers (including Mexican, Texas, and Montreal—the last with French Canadian spices and blue cheese dressing) are offered at $7–9. Meat loaf, broiled haddock, rib-eye steak, and teriyaki chicken are other possibilities. Open Monday through Thursday 4–9, Friday through Sunday noon to 9 or 10.

IN LYNDONVILLE

♦ **Miss Lyndonville Diner** (802-626-9890), Route 5, Lyndonville. You want a club sandwich? A plate of spaghetti or meat loaf dinner for under $7? A banana split? This is the place to come. Two clean and attractive dining rooms with light wood booths and aqua touches are open for coffee at 5:30 AM, breakfast from 6 AM (and served all day), and lunch and dinner items until 8 at night (or 9 on Saturday). The food isn't exactly fit for a gourmet, but it's filling and affordable.

IN ST. JOHNSBURY

♦ **Cucina di Gerardo** (802-748-6772), 1216 Railroad Street, St. Johnsbury. This atmospheric little Italian restaurant has been going strong for several years. Three intimate dining feel like they're in Italy, with large charcoal drawings of Italian sites on the walls. Everything is prepared here, including the bread. The menu offers lunch or dinner portions of items such as chicken Marsala, veal limone (with veal medallions sautéed with broccoli and artichoke hearts and served with pasta or Caesar salad), eggplant parmigiana or Marsala, or spaghetti Bolognese. The place has a heavenly, garlicky scent. When cioppino is on the menu, it's a favorite. Pizza and calzones are also available. Reservations are suggested, especially on weekends. Open for lunch Monday through Saturday 11:30–2:30; for dinner Monday through Saturday 4–9, Sunday noon–9.

♦ **Surf & Sirloin** (802-748-5412), 264 Portland Street (Route 2 East), St. Johnsbury. Chef-owner Mark Grenier and his wife, Sandra, are the stalwarts behind this popular little restaurant, located in a yellow-gold house on a street corner. Parking is in a large parking lot across the street, the size of which is a clue to the popularity of this place. Three meals a day are offered. At lunchtime, the lobster roll ($7.95) is especially prized. Other offerings on the daylong menu are burritos and nachos; sandwiches such as French dip or sirloin burger; a spinach salad plate; and entrées ($11–16) like pork chops, sirloin tips, prime rib, and shish kabob. All dinners are served with soup, salad, vegetable, and choice of potato or rice. Open 6 AM–9 PM daily.

♦ **Northern Lights Book Shop & Café** (802-748-4457), 378 Railroad Street, St. Johnsbury. This is the best little café in a terrific independent bookstore in the heart of the shopping district. Wood booths along one wall in one room and more tables out by the counter draw a mixed crowd of young and older folk. You can get breakfast items all day, including scones, blueberry sour cream coffee cake, breakfast sandwiches, and omelets. For lunch, good soups (vegetable Creole the day we ate here), three-bean chili, and great sandwiches (grilled cheddar on homemade whole wheat bread, a turkey burger with cheese and Canadian bacon, and homemade hummus among the possibilities) are offered. A bistro menu is served on Thursday and Friday evenings 5:30–8:30—how about tenderloin of beef with creamy bourbon horseradish sauce at $16.95? Desserts are—well—sweet. They include Aunt Rose's Famous Cheesecake and Awesome Chocolate Cake. Open daily from 8 AM Monday through Friday and from 9 AM Saturday and Sunday. The store is open late on Thursday and Friday nights.

♦ **Rabbit Hill Inn** (802-748-5168), Lower Waterford. Rabbit Hill Inn is open to the public by reservation for prix fixe $45 five-course meals. Chef Russell Stannard, who has been at the inn for a dozen years—and who has starred at the James Beard House in New York City—comes up with inventive and delicious cuisine. A typical winter menu offered appetizers including pheasant confit with poached fruits in a hazelnut tuille basket with pomegranate molasses; grilled lobster-pumpkin ravioli; and seared beef roulade. The Rabbit Hill Caesar salad was offered along with two other choices: seasonal mixed greens or a green bean and radicchio salad. After a fruit sorbet in champagne you could indulge in braised chicken breast with cider-sage maple jus with parsnips and carrots; poached vegetable risotto with baby artichokes and red beets; or grilled venison with cranberry juniper orange glaze. Dessert could be Grand Marnier chocolate cheese torte, chocolate hazelnut Charlotte, or raspberry and white chocolate mousse terrine with a mango puree. Open nightly for dinner. The inn is closed the first 2 weeks of April and November.

IN GREENSBORO

♦ **Highland Lodge** (802-533-2647), Greensboro. The dining rooms at Highland Lodge are country casual with pink tablecloths topped by blue woven place mats. The walls are knotty pine halfway up. Local artists' work is displayed—and for sale—around the two rooms. We were seated in the sunny wing with windows on

Highland Lodge and cross-country ski center in Greensboro

three sides on a cold January Sunday when brunch was being served. One of us had salmon with roasted vegetables served as a salad; the other had the excellent carrot parsnip soup and a BLT on homemade whole wheat toast. The inn is open to the public daily for breakfast and dinner, and Thursday through Sunday for lunch or brunch also. The Vermont Country Breakfast ($5.75) is pancakes served with ham and slices of Cabot cheddar, made in nearby Cabot. Lunch can be a Caesar salad topped with anchovies; a sirloin burger with lettuce, tomato, and onion; or the classic Reuben. Desserts include the famous Ishkabibble, a homemade brownie topped with vanilla ice cream and homemade hot fudge sauce. Dinners might begin with Billi Bi, a French mussel soup, or a crostini trio. Entrées ($15–20) could be roast loin of pork with apples and onions, pan-seared salmon with sauerkraut, white wine, and vegetables, or a sirloin steak. All are served with salad, roasted red potatoes, and a vegetable of the day. A caramel pot de crème could end the meal. Breakfast is served 8–10, lunch noon–2, dinner 6–8 with reservations.

Index